Remaindered *Life*

NEFERTI X. M. TADIAR

Remaindered *Life*

Duke University Press *Durham and London* 2022

© 2022 Duke University Press All rights reserved
Printed and bound by CPI Group (UK) Ltd, Croydon, CR0 4YY
Designed by Courtney Leigh Richardson and typeset in
Warnock Pro by Westchester Publishing Services

Library of Congress Cataloging-in-Publication Data
Names: Tadiar, Neferti Xina M. (Neferti Xina Maca), [date] author.
Title: Remaindered life / Neferti X. M. Tadiar.
Description: Durham : Duke University Press, 2022. |
Includes bibliographical references and index.
Identifiers: LCCN 2021040322 (print) | LCCN 2021040323
(ebook) | ISBN 9781478015147 (hardcover) | ISBN 9781478017769
(paperback) | ISBN 9781478022381 (ebook)
Subjects: LCSH: Capitalism—Social aspects. | Globalization—
Social aspects. | Feminist theory—Political aspects. |
Marginality, Social. | Imperialism—Economic aspects. |
Decolonization. | BISAC: POLITICAL SCIENCE / Globalization |
SOCIAL SCIENCE / Feminism & Feminist Theory
Classification: LCC HB501.T3225 2022 (print) |
LCC HB501 (ebook) | DDC 330.12/2—dc23/eng/20220112
LC record available at https://lccn.loc.gov/2021040322
LC ebook record available at https://lccn.loc.gov/2021040323

Cover art: Lyra Garcellano, *After Amorsolo's Planting Rice
(1924)*, 2019. Oil on canvas. 36⅛ × 48 in. © Lyra Garcellano.

CONTENTS

Preface: What This Book Is About • ix
Acknowledgments • xix

PART I. IN A TIME OF WAR

1 • THE WAR TO BE HUMAN: VALUE • 3
The No Longer—The War to Be Human—Figures of Inhumanity—Discourses of Dehumanization—Political Emancipation and the Rule of Law as Assault on Social Reproduction—Living in a Time of War—To Remain Human, to Finally Become So—After Man, after Freedom

2 • A GLOBAL ENTERPRISE: WASTE • 23
A Global Story—The War to be Human Is a Global Enterprise (of Punishment)—Waste Is the Product and Productive Strategy of Capitalist War—Waste Is the Object of the New Imperialism—Late Imperialism Is the War for the Expanded Reproduction of Capital over All Life—Original and Abiding: Nonhuman Milieus of Capitalist Accumulation—Land—Ground Rules of Dispossession—Modern Codes of Value: Land, Labor, Life

3 • BECOMING-HUMAN IN A TIME OF WAR: REMAINDER • 49
The Life-Form of Value—In Servitude to the Commodity Form—Neither Simply Cheap Inputs, nor Extra-economic Costs, but Live and Living Forces—Other Modes of Living: Serving a Way of Life—Living and Dying for the Life of Capital—"Still Unconquered Remnants": Unreckoned Forces of Sociality—Remaindered Life

INTERREGNUM • 73
Times of War—A Time of War . . . in Reverse

PART II. LIFE-TIMES

4 • OF LABOR AND FATE PLAYING • 87
New Political Economy of Life—Surplus and Disposability—Fate Playing and the Surplus of Social Reproduction—Primitive Survivals

5 • OF DISPOSABILITY • 109
Discrepant Times of Neoliberalism—Cleavages and Thresholds—Land, People, Time

6 • OF SURVIVAL • 123
People as Rubble: Temporalities of Spectacular Destruction—International Aesthetics, Transnational Politics—People as Coin: Temporalities of Stagnant Liquidity—Uneven Times

PART III. GLOBOPOLIS

7 • CITY EVERYWHERE • 141
City Everywhere—Uber-urbanization: Connection as Content, Content as Connection—Total Mediatic Dominion—Fractal Enterprise: City Emulants—Metropolitan Platform, Global-National Franchise—Turning Bases of War into Bases of (Capital) Life—Eddies: Servers and Servants, Servility and Servitude—Vital Infrastructure—Liquidity, Mobility—Subaltern Fuel: Infinite Life-Times of Waste—Congestion and Bypass—Subaltern Driver: Vital Platforms

EXCURSUS • 173
Servitude—Sinister Design, the Splitting of Life-Times—Submerged Lineages, Subaltern Forces—Media, Milieu, Machines—A "Free" Pathway out of Absolute Expendability—Vitality—Mortality

PART IV. DEAD EXCHANGES

8 • POWERS OF DEFENDING FREEDOM • 199
Constraints of Freedom—Fields of Dead Exchanges—Imperial Codes in the Making of Global Infrastructure—Imperial Shift: After Normative

Culture, after Economy—Ratios of Life and Death—Calculus of Words: The Waning of Content, the Withering of Subjects—Time of Persistence, Powers of Sustaining Life

9 • POWERS OF EXPENDING LIFE • 229
Just War—Insurgent Shadow Urbanism of the Provinces—Derivative Enterprises—Populism, Platform Totalitarianism—Objects of Punishment—Power Signs: Bodies, Money, Help—Zones of War Are Times of Living—Kin, Clans, Dividuals

10 • LIVE BORROWINGS, LIVING CONNECTIONS • 257
Waste as Art—Art as Counterattack—Live Media, Live Exchange—Irreverent Borrowings, Serious Play, Irredeemable Flourish—Many Pasts Continue, Many Presents Lie in Wait

THRESHOLDS • 279
At the Farthest Distance from a Life Worth Living—Numbers—Liminalities, Shifting and Holding—Multifarious Forms of Life—Mixed Passages

PART V. BY THE WAYSIDES

11 • BYPASS AND SPLENDOR • 301
Bypass—Striving—Strife—Splendor—Nightmare Landscapes, Ambient Dreams—In the Weeds—The Time of Expectation

12 • AND THEN SOME • 329
The End and All—Not Consumed in the Moment of Action, Not Subsumed by Politics—And Then Some

Notes • 335
Bibliography • 387
Index • 411

PREFACE. *What This Book Is About*

Remaindered Life is an extended meditation on disposability and survival in the world we live in today. It presents an analytical and political tale—a theoretical fiction—about our global present. It casts this moment as the aftermath and perdurance of decolonization, those processes and practices of quotidian as well as formal, organized social struggles among the colonized to live nevertheless and otherwise—beyond the constricted fates that Western European-American colonialism's transfiguration into a dominant global mode of life continues to impose. Even as it is now perched on a precipice, seemingly stilled by a global pandemic, this moment we suffer and strive to live through continues to be an era of relentless war waged by the assumed and would-be inheritors of colonialism's bequest—valued life—to retain, regain, or arrogate the rights to its enjoyments. It is an era of relentless expropriation of life, seeing not only to the upholding of valued life as a universal social ideal but also to its manufacture as the central object-medium of contemporary capitalist production, the MacGuffin, the lure-fetish, the commodity capital, of strategies of accumulation and aggrandizement, whose real end and present yield is more than enough riches and powers to command and consume all of earth and its futures.

In this telling, forms of living and survival among the dispossessed are certainly the conditions of possibility of these riches and powers, the "life" resources placed at their disposal. But they are more than this, more than life stolen, destroyed, consumed, expended. Creatively persistent and adaptive practices of sociality, which for so many peoples are the means and forms of their living, often indissociable from the very meaning and aim of their own personal "lives," are—as much as the nonhuman natural world—*engines* of life-making and life organization that are made to serve as machines of production for capital, which capital neither creates nor pays for yet utilizes and depends upon for its own exponential growth and gain. But in acting beyond the role designated for them within this imperial relation—that is, beyond their role as the enabling milieu of proper human agency and achievement—the descendants and kin of "the damned of the earth" are turned into the instigators of punitive, disciplining wars against them.

Decolonization, our constant and historical struggle to live against and beyond the bounds set by an imperial, racial capitalist order, is thus made into the casus belli of relentless campaigns and programs of ruthless, insidious violence. Aimed at reproducing disposable captive life as material, instrument, collateral, and currency for the securitized production of valued life, these campaigns and programs—inflicting diminishment, pain, injury, and death—comprise what I refer to in this book as "the war to be human," a revanchist war and global enterprise that reinstalls the tenets of colonial sex-gender and race orders as codes for the organization and continuous parsing of life-times between value and waste in what appears to be a new global political economy of life.

Remaindered Life thus retells the story of the global capitalist present that is often told as the story of capitalist restructuring in response to workers' struggles in the Global North, with the resulting innovations of capitalist exploitation and value production spreading to the Global South. It recasts the global present as instead the aftermath and continuing effects of unfinished movements of decolonization against an extant imperial relation of dispossession that serves up enabling milieus for the labor-capital relation. Even as it might be relegated to no more than a supplementary fix in moments of capital crisis (a political-economic solution to systemic crisis), imperialism is in fact no less than a systemic dispossessive relation to the living and the life-making capacities of the colonized that operates in the debased service of the reproduction of capital in all its forms. Pressed to the limits posed by imperial dispossession at the "outer" edges of formal, proper capitalism (and therefore also within the interstitial peripheries of the most advanced capitalist social formations), the decolonizing struggles of the colonized—our striving and our strife—draw on and generate unconquered forces and resources of living, becoming in turn the object of new and continuing wars to subdue and subsume them under the global, racial capitalist order. Here in places where circumscribed and proscribed social being shores up the channels of capitalist flows, the inventive, adaptive practices of living by people of no account have propelled global forms of innovation, growth, and development that they are not meant to share—that, on the contrary, will see to their repeated privation and expiation. Here we find, for example, the elaboration of dynamic forms of life-time trading, value-extractive "happenings," variable service commodities: highly liquid forms of petty enterprise and livelihood on the part of people with little to no property, making means of life (money, food, help) out of means of life (bodies, time, sociality), informal and illicit economic practices that will come to figure more centrally in postindustrial capitalist modes of production, particularly in the capitalization of mediatic connectivity and the monetized expenditure of people's life-times, two features of the contemporary global order of derivative finance and permanent, counterinsurgent war.

This book is therefore also a theoretical account of imperialism as a specific relation of reproduction of contemporary global capital and an argument for the tremendous role played by the social reproduction of surplus life, which imperialism secures, in the accumulation of stratospheric global wealth and power. It is also an account of the immeasurable role of this living that is precisely the power and capacity, the predicament and effort, the pain and joy, of life making and "becoming-human"—the status, condition, and work of disposable life that is the very basis of "global life."

In this book, I try to provide a conceptual vocabulary and a panorama of figures for rethinking the dynamics of contemporary global capitalism in these terms, most centrally, in terms of a notion of "life-times" that would encompass a broader range of social reproduction beyond the recognized value-producing "life as labor" of the socialized workers of post-Fordism, and that would include the social reproduction of disposable populations who are marked by global structures of racism and heterosexism for fates of diminished and minimized life. Beyond a critique of the state of disposability that particular social groups—identified by race, gender, sexuality, nationality, and religion—are structurally made to occupy, this is a theoretical account of the overlooked value-productivity *and* superfluous remainder of the life-making capacities of those who live such disposable life-times in their survival and livelihood. It is an account of life-times of disposability not merely as hidden labor but as an array of forces and resources of living that remain in most accounts of contemporary globality theoretically and politically diminished, if not altogether dismissed.

The analytical and political tale I tell is a feminist story long understood and told by the colonized, especially those harnessed by means of punishing exactions for sex-gendered reproductive labors put to the furtherance of capital life, who are at the same time left to see to the social reproduction and care of their own shared life of other belonging. It is a tale of indictment and lament, a record of the living we endure and abet, suffer and invent, in a time of war, even as we know quite well that *how* we live is not exhausted by the world we make and make possible nor by the interbraided political and economic antagonisms (between forces of the *already human* and forces of the *becoming-human*, between valued and disposable life) that I argue shape and constrict the everyday decisions and conditions comprising our lives. In this way, it is a tale told not *about* but rather *from* the side of remaindered life, the activity and sociality of living that is not exhausted in the expenditure of the life-times of others—leftover practices and forms of living that remain superfluous to the production of valued, and even of disposable life.

Remaindered life is not therefore simply an object to be found, identified, exemplified. What we are able to discern as remaindered life is as much the effect and expression of a mode of attention and method of interpretation as it is the by-product and excess of theoretical and material subsumption—life that escapes valorization. This is a heuristic that emerges out of contemporary political, artistic, and scholarly efforts to explore experiences that elude the codes of political and economic value that structure representation more generally. In the wake of successions of perceived political failures of socialist, Third World, nationalist, racial, and sexual liberation movements from the 1950s to the 1970s, and of urban democracy movements from the 1980s to the 2000s, diasporic and postcolonial filmmakers and writers as well as visual artists have grappled with the legacies of these failures and the unfinished or continuing histories of social struggle that permeate present, everyday life in ways yet to be reckoned with. They have endeavored in various ways to revise these continuing pasts in their intimate renderings of their own presents and the ambient and direct pressures limiting and shaping people's life efforts and desires (including the pressures of the global market that they, as artists, must also navigate and reflect upon). In the face of gross and insidious forces draining as well as demolishing people's lives in the aftermath of the freedom struggles of an earlier era, what remains—as inordinate excess, as untimely persistence, as unrecognizable potential—becomes an unrelenting question.

Remaindered life is thus also posed as an aesthetic problem and intellectual preoccupation of Global South artists attuned to the paradoxes of living in the contemporary world for those who must bear the burdens of its unresolved because inadmissible pasts. Such paradoxes are characteristic of a fully globalized world, which elaborates and intensifies old and new forms of unsettlement, prohibition, and dispossession at the same time that it beckons and welcomes an unprecedented level of participation and incorporation of those whom an earlier order had deemed not yet fully human. This book sees remaindered life as a political heuristic and aesthetic challenge that has arisen out of this very moment when the politics of a prior moment of decolonization confronts its insurmountable impasse. In my own analytical register, remaindered life approximates and emulates the practices of living it seeks to render, remember, and redraw into another way of viewing and making the world (into all the ways we might remake the world).

How to Read This Book

Remaindered Life comprises five extended parts, each dwelling on a major theme or situation and foregrounding a set of conceptual figures and interpretive codes for understanding the phenomena of disposability and surplus life-making in particular contemporary sociohistorical contexts. Each part can be read independently of the others, as an exploration of one aspect of a larger global situation. Together, the five parts are intended to provide a layered picture of connections across the particular phenomena and social groups they cite or describe—human smugglers on the US-Mexico border, refugee detention centers in Australia, slum dwellers in Metro Manila, urban migrant workers in China, former US military bases converted into microcities (which I call city emulants) and special economic zones in the Philippines, "third country nationals" working on offshored US military bases in West Asia, overseas Filipino contract workers in the domestic and seafaring industries, the US prison and punishment industry, Duterte's "war on drugs," extrajudicial killings in the Philippines, and feminicide in Ciudad Juárez, Mexico. These connections are also to be thought as suggesting submerged political lineages shared across given social groups and formations, some of which I attempt to trace but most of which are yet to be uncovered, grasped, or further understood as part of the making and living of our worlds. These too might be considered traces of remaindered life.

Part I, "In a Time of War" (chapters 1–3), is a panoramic exposition of the political antagonism between "the war to be human" and "becoming-human in a time of war" shaping our global situation. Drawing on select examples from diverse yet connected social contexts in the United States and the Philippines, from the late twentieth century to the present, I describe the way this revanchist war of punishment in the aftermath of decolonization is made into a global enterprise, incorporating reproduction into global value-production through a strategy of the active wasting of life. I describe the imperial conscription of the modes of living and survival of wasted life as enabling milieus for the productive life of capital, arguing for the role of unreckoned forces of sociality among the becoming-human as unaccounted machines of production in a new political economy of life. And I argue for the importance of both the subsumption of reproduction and the reproduction that exceeds this subsumption for understanding our present moment. As an excess of reproductive activity beyond the necessary reproduction of disposable life, remaindered life is broached as a place and view from which we might reimagine and remake the world.

Part I draws out the broadest outlines of the relations and tendencies defining what I understand to be our global situation. It thus serves as an overview of many of the conceptual themes and analytical propositions animating the other parts, acting as a kind of theoretical overture for the rest of the book. But as such it can be read either before or after the other parts, which dwell longer and more closely on concrete contexts for understanding the relations and tendencies it identifies.

Part II, "Life-Times" (chapters 4–6), focuses on the notion of *life-times* as a way of understanding the vital role of redundant or excess populations ("idled," "abandoned," and "warehoused" in late liberal societies, targeted for injury and elimination in policing wars or for "rescue" in humanitarian campaigns), in the order of global capitalism today. Beginning with a critique of the notion of "life as labor" in the new political economy of life, it argues for a distinction between life-times of value and life-times of waste as crucial to understanding another side of capitalist production, which centers not so much the productive activity of life but its expenditure. It proposes how we might attend to other life-times that remain unabsorbed by such a theoretical and material subsumption of social reproduction within global capitalism by way of exploring fate-playing practices among Filipino and Filipina overseas workers and slum dwellers.

This part goes on to argue for a related distinction between different forms of money (money as capital vs. money as exchange) for understanding another side of the changes in rationality and subjectivity that are attributed to and defined by the project of neoliberalism. In contrast to the entrepreneurial or investor model of the self through which neoliberal subjects in the Global North are enjoined to imagine themselves (as capital subjects), surplus populations in the Global South are treated as a pool of disposable life-times that can serve as liquid reserves (soft currency) for speculative maneuvers of the state. The latter are produced as such through the state's instrumental use and control of land. I then turn to the structuring of life-times of disposability and the life-times of survival of surplus peoples as they are rendered in films responsive to the specific neoliberal contexts of China and the Philippines (Jia Zhang-ke, Brillante Mendoza) as a way of understanding remaindered ways of living, beneath the threshold of subjects centered in Global North critiques of neoliberalism.

Part III, "Globopolis" (chapter 7), explores the defining tendencies of urban expansion in an emergent global platform economy. Largely attending to urbanist developments in Metro Manila (but also attentive to connected developments in other globalist metropolises), I describe the projects of construction of channels and platforms to host the value-productive life activity and movements of globopolitical urban life, a fractal enterprise whose animating program involves the mediatization of human capacities in technologized forms of servitude. Such mediatized capacities can be understood as comprising a kind of vital infrastructure, demonstrating in the contemporary moment the role of servitude or *serviceable life* as life-time–saving and life-time–producing machines of production in capitalist industries organized around activity and connection rather than around the manufacture of goods. I highlight the figurative codes of city everywhere, exemplified in the incorporation of the logic of war into the metropolitanist enterprise, not only in urban platforms' provision of capitalist freedoms (liberated movement, total access) as exemptions from servitude and punishment but also through the active production and use of the liquidity of disenfranchised people's lives to lubricate, accommodate, and enhance valued life. In this chapter, I discuss the distinction and relation between vital infrastructure and vital platforms, organized and organizing programs of livelihood and life-making through which humans function as media for other humans. By understanding the vitality of human practices of living in terms of infrastructure and platforms, I seek to underscore the other kinds of human life (ghostly only to the already human) animating the machines and machinic "base" of global metropolitan life.

Part IV, "Dead Exchanges" (chapters 8–10), foregrounds two related powers that the war to be human claims. Chapter 8 dwells on the powers of defending freedom by depicting the varying fields of exchange through which freedom and democracy operate as code-scripts in the making of the global infrastructure of capital. I use the case of Philippine democracy-making from its founding in US colonialism to its deployment in the Cold War and post–Cold War periods to demonstrate the role of these code-scripts in the making and maintenance of US security architecture, particularly in the Asia-Pacific and West Asia. I then turn to a shift in governmentality and political economy, a separating off and raising to another (derivative or more highly abstracted) level of exchange, whereby these code-scripts operate not simply as ideological signs but as skeuomorphs (image-metaphors) serving as sign-command functions in an integrated sovereign capitalist platform system. It is under this "new" global dispensation of state power and capitalist accumulation that the antiliberal, authoritarian regime of the Philippine president Rodrigo Duterte can be understood as continuous with the liberalism it opposes. In chapter 9, I discuss this higher, financialized political order under which Duterte's war on drugs exemplifies the logic of and aspirations to powers of expending life, a derivative enterprise that creates and trades on the absolute expendability of the lives of the urban poor. Understanding the rise of Duterte as the emergence of an insurgent urbanist national political platform, I demonstrate the intertwining of disposability and survival through the relationship between the political-police machine undertaking extrajudicial killings as a derivative enterprise and the kin networks of the poor that they prey upon. Finally (chapter 10), I discuss the struggle of a coalition of artists (RESBAK) to resist this authoritarian command and impunity in the wasting of lives, and the live politics of their word- and image-making against the fatal signifying practices of the Duterte regime and against the centrality of waste in the entwined valorizing capitalist enterprises of global art and war.

Part V, "By the Waysides" (chapters 11–12), dwells on the perceptual and sensorial forms that a few artists offer for attending to the excess of survival over disposability. I try to delineate a method of reading that follows one effort to represent and elude the violence of capitalist value-making exemplified in the work of a particular artist, Lyra Garcellano. In the work of Garcellano as well as that of a few Global South filmmakers (Apichatpong Weerasethakul, Tsai Ming-liang) I see examples of a mode of attention and practice of time attuned to, and indeed, yielding to remaindered life—a kind of biding one's own life-times of refuse, a form of idling that makes, rather than kills, time, a remaking of the political landscape of one's expulsion into a place of other belonging. This political-aesthetic heuristic allows us to look more closely at the landscape by the wayside of capital's urbanizing pathways and make out another outcome and horizon for remaindered life. Here in the wasteland is to be found the time of expectation for a thorough change in the global order, for that flourishing of life that we might expect upon capitalism's end.

The three chapters in part I—corresponding to value, waste, remainder—prefigure a structure and a method that are repeated at different scales within the parts and across the book. They trace a movement of thinking that tends, with a little more weight and amplitude as the book progresses, toward the last of those terms. The movement at any point is itself, however, never simply linear (as in a three-step procedure), for each of the terms is a moment that implies the others. This is a movement of thought that I believe is both immanent and excessive to the movements comprising global capital. It exemplifies my own method of following while also departing from the various pathways through which the life-times of people are subsumed in the machinations of capitalist accumulation yet are never quite fully consumed or exhausted, even at that most painful and seemingly final point of death.

Interspersed within the main parts are three detours or eddies. "Interregnum" follows the work of the artist, filmmaker, and activist Kiri Dalena as she strives to make art respond to and help undo the spectacular violence of the ongoing wars of the Philippine state against its own people. "Excursus" reflects on the social conditions and genealogies of contemporary global servitude, its work as vital infrastructure for the global life economy, and its role as a hinge, or gate, between valued life and absolutely expendable life. "Thresholds" dwells on the liminality of the urban poor produced by an urban ideal of life worth living and the role of humanizing stories in maintaining a limit on our perception of the vitality of people's life-making. Each of these interstitial chapters—or "excursions"—is a lingering over the lifetimes of people casually placed at the disposal of power, value, and humanity.

This book does not set out to make a case about our contemporary reality through the presentation of new evidential material but rather intends, by means of synthesis and articulation of much radical decolonizing critique, to provide a way of seeing and interpreting abundant empirical cases and reports across diverse contexts, and to offer a conceptual vocabulary and syntax for understanding them and their connections to one another in order to mount a perspective and narrative of our global moment from the side of the historical experiences of the becoming-human. It is not an explanation of the world but an interpretation of its workings from the side of remaindered life. In this writing, I try to make connections among the political expressions and social experiences and senses of survival of peoples with whom I feel the people I belong to are deeply tied, even if they are not already affectively bonded. It is my attempt to link the historical experiences of the becoming-human in diverse contexts—peoples who are my interlocutors and inspiration, their members my intimates and associates, those who love with me and mine, those who are political kin, relations in colonialism, even as we might find ourselves opponents, rivals, enemies, masters, and servants to one another in a world where that is what peoples are made to be. My effort to provide serviceable connections, through arguments and examples, proper routes of understanding and occasional meanderings, will aid, I hope, in conjuring or presencing immanent and possible relations of another kind. In this tale, Filipinos are a transnational zone of social life that figures in all the categories of life worth living and life worth expending. They are also the in-between, "wild cards" in the political antagonism between the war to be human and the becoming-human in a time of war, whose diasporic and local practices of living form the tissue of this tale and bear the heart of my own story. In this way, they are my case and medium for the remnants of a collective project, a nation and a people both exploded and never one to begin with, creatively persisting and revising our own ways of being human into vital platforms. In us, I also see the media and milieu of another mode of life.

ACKNOWLEDGMENTS

This book was written with the kindness, support, and brilliance of many people. Its inception was a new global war declared in 2001, with many of its central ideas as well as structures of feeling issuing from my efforts since then to understand this long period of unceasing military and police campaigns against peoples in Afghanistan, the Philippines, Iraq, Palestine, the United States, Mexico, and too many other places, even as movements everywhere rose in the names of peoples and lands and lives being depleted and taken outright for powers of a rapaciousness the world is hard-pressed to truly see.

This was not the book I meant to write after finally publishing *Things Fall Away*. World events overpowered whatever writing I had planned to follow that last book, commandeering my writing attention in ways that are manifest in this book before you. I wrote to mark moments of witnessing the vile atrocities of states toward countless peoples considered enemies and threats to the people they defined as their own, as proper to them, as well as the movements that have simmered and erupted, rising against the violence of these states and the capitalist powers they defend and arrogate to themselves. Though some of this writing took the form of talks and teach-ins not included in this book, I thank the people and organizations who invited me to think and feel with them during these years, providing the occasions for my reflections on our global situation, which have made their way into this book. Thank you to members of the Research Cluster for Women of Color in Collaboration and Conflict, Incite! Women of Color against Violence, the Feminisms against War Group of the Institute for Advanced Feminist Research, and the Culture against War Committee, all at the University of California, Santa Cruz. Thank you especially to Anna Tsing, Lisa Rofel, Anjali Arondekar, Maylei Blackwell, Michelle Erai, Nadine Naber, Needra James, Nicole Santos, Terry Valen, Mariko Drew, Janine Lim, and Eden Jequinto for the galvanizing intellectual-political engagement in organizing events against the global war on terror, in particular. Thank you to Sarah Raymundo and Roland Tolentino of CONTEND (Congress of Teachers and Educators for Nationalism and Democracy), and to Sunaina Maira, Magid Shihade, and

Rana Barakat of USACBI (US Academic and Cultural Boycott of Israel), for invitations to dialogue with activists in the Philippines and Palestine. I am also indebted to Robin D. G. Kelley, Bill Mullen, J. Kehaulani Kauanui, Cindy Franklin, David Palumbo-Liu, David Lloyd, Malini Schueller, Charlotte Kates, C. Heike Schotten, and many more in the organizing committee of USACBI for their continuing solidarity and camaraderie.

The earliest versions and parts of chapters of this book were occasioned by invitations to share my work as talks and published essays, invitations extended by Robyn Wiegman, Bettina Aptheker, David Palumbo-Liu, Jane Elliot and Gillian Harkins, Rebecka Thor, Melinda Cooper, AbdouMaliq Simone, Stephanie Misa, Marina Grzinic, Geraldine Pratt, Lisa Duggan, Paula Chakravarty, Aren Aizura, Kelly Chung, Timothy A. Simpson, Thomas S. Davis and Nathan K. Hensley, Jack Turner, Shu-Mei Shih, Denise Ferreira da Silva, Mark Harris, Alyosha Goldstein, Beth Capper and Arlen Austin, Christopher Connery, David Palumbo-Liu, Andy Wang, Ian McKenzie, Anna Stileau, and Aaron Doughty, and Randy Martin. My thanks also go to interlocutors at other places where I shared versions of the work in this book, including Duke University, the University of California–Santa Cruz, the University of Copenhagen, the Jan Van Eyck Academy in Maastricht, the Night School in Vienna, the University of British Columbia, the University of Washington, Seattle, Yale University, the Pratt Institute, New York University, Brown University, Northwestern University, the University of Minnesota, the University of Macau, Humboldt University, the University of the Philippines, the University of California–Irvine, King's College London, and the Max Planck Institute for the Study of Religious and Ethnic Diversity in Göttingen. Thank you to the audiences at these talks for much-appreciated feedback.

I thank Janet Jakobsen, Beck Jordan-Young, Elizabeth Bernstein, Manijeh Moradian, and Marisa Solomon for being wonderful colleagues. I am especially grateful to Janet Jakobsen for her incredible, generous support and sagacious ways that have made Barnard a good place for many and an enabling space for my own work. My appreciation also goes to all my students at Barnard College and Columbia University, with whom I explored many of the themes of this book in seminars, and to Ellen Louis, for some initial research. Thanks to Dorothy Ko, Anupama Rao, Lila Abu-Lughod, Rebecca Karl, Vinay Gidwani, Sam Miller, Macarena Gomez-Barris, Jack Halberstam, Vicente Rafael, Sheila Coronel, Duncan McCargo, Earl Jackson, Chandan Reddy, Gina Apostol, and Steffen Jensen for the animating conversations. The Social Text Collective has been a vibrant intellectual and political community. I thank especially Tavia N'yongo, Anna McCarthy, Jayna Brown, Ed

Cohen, Brian Larkin, David Sartorius, David Eng, Nicole Fleetwood, Alex Pittman, Nikhil Singh, Marie Buck, Allen Feldman, Micki McGee, David Kazanjian, Josie Saldaña, Nick Mirzeoff, and Julie Livingston for their collaborations and participation in important salons over the years. I am indebted to Lyra Garcellano and Kiri Dalena for keeping alive my relations to the politically-committed art world in the Philippines, through their own work as well as the work of others, and to all the inspiring young artists and activists I have come to know through them and through the Alfredo F. Tadiar Library in the last few years.

Deep affection and gratitude go to my dear friends Anjali Arondekar, Lucy Burns, Angela Davis, Gina Dent, and Saidiya Hartman for knowing, guiding, and accompanying me through the larger journey. Thank you, my dears, for the vibrant intellectual sustenance and political spirit, for the care, and for sharing life's joys and pains, which lie behind all that we write and do in the world.

Warm appreciation to my editor, Courtney Berger, for the encouragement and crucial guidance. I am greatly indebted to Gerry Pratt and AbdouMaliq Simone for their brilliant insight, critical feedback, and helpful suggestions. All remaining faults are mine.

My father, Alfredo F. Tadiar, died suddenly at the end of 2015, in the middle of everything, shaking so much that made me who I was and could be in the world, and what I hoped for in myself as well as for the larger world, including the nonhuman nature he loved dearly. I try to channel his vitality in these pages. The love of my mother, Florence, my siblings, Aisha, Carlo, Thea, Alfredo, and Gino, and their spouses and children, Mae, Evelyn, Ric, Gino, Annika, Storm, Tiger, Seren, and Arianna, have sustained me.

Jon and Luna have endured every political rant I have let loose over breakfast, lunch, and dinner. They have made room for and softened the expression of my rage and lament. Luna has opened new vistas of understanding for me with her tremendous intellectual and artistic gifts and powers of feeling. Jon has nursed me through all my sorrows, talked with me about everything under the sun, including all my ideas, big and small, and shared all my hopes and delights. This little, tender corner of full, unconditional support is what made the writing of this book finally possible.

PART I. IN A TIME OF WAR

1

THE WAR TO BE HUMAN
Value

The No Longer

A significantly audible critique orients itself toward the end of man, the end of the West and its seeming closing era of the human. Yet beneath much of that critique is a barely concealed fear that what has fallen apart is the presumed political community of a world civilization whose only significant others are now internal to it—those who *no longer* feel part of the centuries-long project of universal human freedom and equality and who now bitterly, vengefully, and even vaingloriously reject its democratic ideals. In Europe and in the United States, the electorally trounced explain the defeat of democracy as the consequence of galloping losses—losses of social wealth, political enfranchisement, cultural participation. *They*, the others who have seized the political stage in vociferous, contemptuous repudiation of liberalism, are testaments to the predictably dire effects of a political economy that strips people of all that had been supposedly theirs but is *no longer*, testaments to the alienation of their very humanity (defined as their capacity to participate in the production of symbols to make the world they inhabit) to such an extent that the fight for human rights and welfare, especially of the barely human, can only appear as sheer mockery, if not the machinations of either the global victors to get more spoils or the undeserving to stealthily come up from underneath to usurp their once rightful place.[1]

Democracy's internal others live in this tense of the no longer, even if in actual experience they may have never had, nor ever have been, what is now said to be no more. Or so say the purveyors of this view, which sees the world of the twenty-first century in the trail of a sudden and accelerating (though for us, long and protracted) decline. The world of the no longer is the time of the already human experiencing the ravages of their own war. If not decline, still the measure of the no longer is always from when and where man prevailed. The reference is always the society from whence man, however now pluralized as *human*, emerged—the historical constant that makes for pronouncements of now, and the distance from then.

What is proclaimed new—the instantiation of some singular now, whether it is a new form of subjectivity or a new form of organizing the society within which it operates—is always a declaration of the no longer, a world "as we know it" that has ceased or is ceasing to exist.[2] In that way, the no longer is memorialized, and made eternal, as an always and ever existent past, the very past at a distance from which a new way of being human or posthuman can now be found to obtain.

The already human make melancholia for themselves and for others, for they are source and referent for a universal ideal that they will inevitably fail to achieve (the would-bes, the have-beens), because to achieve it they must deny it to others (the never-weres, the never-will-bes).[3]

The War to Be Human

We live in a time when every day brings ample evidence of the disposability of human life. It is a casual use of the word—*human*—for the very disposability of this life, its condition as destined waste, would seem to put into question its designation as human, bequeathed to us as the term for the defining conditions of ideal, valued, and invaluable existence.

In the age of permanent war, the question of what it means and what it takes to be human appears to be at once urgent and all too late. With the waning of the Western civilizational belief in a higher purpose for humankind and the rapid decline of man as a universal conceit, the claim that we live in a posthuman age rings with the certain, almost foretold, air of truth. The dominant worldly pursuits of this time are limitless and infinite, processes without ends. Even the notion of progress seems strangely antiquated.

It seems therefore anachronistic to inquire into what might once have been called the human condition. And yet, the question of what it means to be or to become human remains pressing, to the extent that at no other time in history have more and more people been pushed to the very edge, if not completely beyond the bounds, of global humanity.

In the middle of the last century, as philosophers grappled with the meaning and future of humanity in the aftermath of the terrible atrocities of World War II, Aimé Césaire charged Europe with the brutal, dehumanizing crimes of colonization perpetrated in the spirit of its own formal humanism. Of "the crowning barbarism that sums up all the daily barbarisms," that in its appearance as Nazism jolted awake the humanistic, Christian bourgeois people of the "Western" world, Césaire pronounced, "before they were its victims, they were its accomplices." Held responsible for "the highest heap of corpses in history," Western civilization stood indicted for its crimes before another human community comprised of the very peoples whose systematic torture and destruction under colonialism and slavery proved the genocidal end and spirit at the heart of man.[4]

A decade later, Jean-Paul Sartre tolled the death knell of colonial Europe and decried the "fresh moment of violence" with which Europe answered the decolonization of the third world as the desperate attempt of man to hang on to the exclusive privileges of its racist humanity.[5] In this realization pressed on Sartre by the raging struggles of "the wretched of the earth," powerfully portrayed by Frantz Fanon, neocolonial war was nothing less than a war for the West to remain human in the face of the monstrous barbarism that the third world revealed to be but the West's own. Decolonization posed the question of what it might mean to become human in the wake of the destruction of colonial, racist humanism, a half-forgotten question for which our own present has yet to provide an adequate answer.

At the end of the twentieth and beginning of the twenty-first century, neocolonial wars resurfaced with a vengeance, in the name of the civilizing influence of a globalizing neoliberal democracy, while humanism in new guises and in both fractional and fractal forms returned as the ethico-political arbiter of rights and responsibilities, privileges and burdens, value and nonvalue, in a world of unfathomable wealth and unmitigated violence and deprivation. It is in this context that I have described and continue to think about our political moment in terms of a complex, potentially antagonistic relation between *a war to be human* and *becoming-human in a time of war*.[6]

The moment the United States began bombing Afghanistan—in retaliation against the crime against humanity it perceived to be directed against itself and the American way of life—was a pivotal reminder that this world has been embroiled in a political antagonism, which is the culmination of an era half a millennium old, an antagonism whose endgame may very well spell this era's own end or its irrevocable turn. This is a political antagonism between the war to be human and becoming-human in a time of war—the war on the part of the already human to remain so, with all their proxies in tow, and the struggle to live on the part of those who can never be fully "human," the abiding category for valued existence or what the global deems life worth living.[7]

Even as the meaning of being human undergoes revision in the face of contemporary social and technological forces undermining the tenets of bourgeois humanism, still the inheritances of this colonial history continue to determine the subjective and material protocols ensuring *human* as a status of primacy and globopolitical belonging. Such a status confers the rights, powers, and enjoyments by definition denied to or deferred for those at pains to claim it—those I refer to as *the becoming-human*—descendants of "the wretched of the earth" whose damnation to a status of the nonhuman or subhuman in the centuries-long process of establishing colonial humanism set the parameters for a global relation that, as the work of Sylvia Wynter amply and profoundly argues, has all but replaced the Manichaean dichotomies of colonizer and colonized, master and slave, master species and lower species, as the central political antagonism of our present times.[8]

This centuries-long political antagonism finds both predication and support in the contradictory socioeconomic relation between valued and disposable life, which constitutes a crucial structural dynamic of the finance-driven global capitalist economy. What an older scholarship had seen as a site of unproductive, reproductive, hidden, and supplemental work—a "noneconomic" relation that merely supplements the capital-labor relation comprising the central dynamic of accumulation—has become the primary site of value accumulation in the new financialized capitalist economy of life, also understood as post-Fordist, biocapitalist, and cognitive capitalism. But while such hitherto supplemental reproductive life has taken the place of labor as capital's constitutive contradiction (where life is labor), the work of living is parsed continuously through categories of value and waste, categories that operate through complex local and universal systems for calculating social worth (sex-gender, race, ethnicity/nationality, sexuality, religion). It is this latter relation (valued vs. disposable life) that underwrites contemporary financial capital as an everyday rule of living and survival and not just as an egregious crisis-inducing exception to an otherwise humane order. Although it is a relation immanently antagonistic, which finds its most prominent political expression in war, it is also widely accepted as simply a phenomenal expression of the laws of natural selection.

The interaction and braiding of the two antagonistic relations above is thus indispensable as a conceptual frame for illuminating the dynamics of power and capitalist accumulation that shape the unprecedented scale of inequalities characterizing our contemporary world. Together, these two relational principles, which govern contemporary survival and aspiration, provide a way for us to understand the conflicts of global social life beyond the geopolitical and territorialized subjects (with their national, racial, gendered, and sexual identities) that animated the narratives of a prior era of imperialism. As relational tendencies, they provide directional impetus at multiple levels of practice, within the "same" individuals as much as the "same" social groups, serving to divide and integrate at shrinking as well as at expanding scales of being.

The war to be human and to live a life worth living is waged against a life of waste and absolute expendability, which is the very condition and consequence of this war. A life worth expending is the perpetual threat and catastrophe to which others are condemned, the object cause of a deep horror that everyone is compelled to flee, the fate of nothingness coded as black and as disappearance or absence—paradigmatic forms of negation and dispossession of social value, the abundant evidence of which is challenged by the most vigorous political movements in the United States today (prison abolition; Black Lives Matter; No Dakota Access Pipeline; No Ban, No Wall) with vigorous protest and resistance. Meanwhile, elsewhere in the non-Western, formerly colonial world, spectacular and barely visible forms of extermination and depletion of life have been carried out with stunning regularity, producing a mass exodus of unprotected people from the Global South that, with the escalated threat that they have come to pose to the Global North's way of life, has attained the status of a full-blown global refugee crisis. Here, too, vigorous political movements (Stop the Killings, Ni Una Más, Land for the Landless, Justice for _____) rage against the forces of impunity taking, violating, and expending the life of the disenfranchised.

Such political antagonism between forces of the already or would-be human and the becoming-human animates and shapes contemporary global wars. It not only provides impetus and form to the most prominent of these military combats (the continuing global war against terrorism) but also, for its representative subjects, a repertoire of actions and feelings, behaviors and strategies, projects and campaigns (humanitarianism, postracism, posthumanism) that derive from the continuously revised historical playbooks of

Western European colonialism and US imperialism. The "just wars" carried out by Spanish and Portuguese colonizers against indigenous communities in the New World, Africa, and Asia from the early modern period on; the wars of captivity and disciplinary powers of freedom waged on behalf of transatlantic slavery and white Christian abolitionism against African peoples and their descendants during the same period; the United States' "savage wars" against Native peoples in North America and the Pacific in the age of imperial "manifest destiny"; Cold War neocolonialism and wars of counterinsurgency across the continents in "the American century"—such are some of the most important archives of operative moves for the contemporary wars of the already human to remain so, civilizing moves both violent and sentimental, used with a vengeance as well as taken to heart by those who seek to join them or take their place.

The war to *be* human consists of, most spectacularly, the political-military project and the atrocities exemplified by the global war against terrorism, launched and waged by the United States and its subsidiary militaries throughout the world from the turn of the twenty-first century to the present. The violence of this imperial project to secure and further aggrandize the privileges and powers enjoyed by, as well as bequeathed by, the already human within a capitalist order is amply documented. It ranges over the global landscape in wars against immigrants and refugees as well as against demonized, despised domestic populations, wars of protection against the always imminent threats these people pose to the new vulnerable—the no longer strong, who yet by right are entitled to security and care.

In the Philippines, the global war on terror was formally launched under Gloria Macapagal Arroyo's presidency (2001–10). In this period, more than a thousand activists, human rights workers, and community leaders were killed by paramilitary units directly linked to the government under a state of emergency legitimated and financially and militarily aided by, as well as legally-juridically modeled on, the domestic and foreign policies of the regime of US president George W. Bush. Closely conforming to the shift from the strategy of low-intensity conflict—that of covert counterinsurgency operations conducted through counterintelligence practices in the United States during the civil rights movement and through proxy wars in Latin America, Africa, and Southeast Asia during the Cold War—to the strategy of open and preemptive aggression in the imperial operations of global security in this renewed moment, the Philippine state's political-military campaign, Oplan Bantay Laya (Operation Freedom Watch), which directed the extrajudicial executions, was part of a concerted effort to extinguish all radical challenges to a global order about to prevail.

But the war to be human suffuses this order beyond the spectacular counterinsurgent campaigns to defend it. Indeed, it shapes the very claims made on behalf of those suffering its dehumanizing effects.

Figures of Inhumanity

A poem by Alexander Remollino, in a collection of writings protesting such political killings under Arroyo's regime, depicts the democratic order (supposedly restored after the fall of a long dictatorship) as an economy of ranked forms of life, in which the slain are "those who live so that they will again become human, they who are made to live as animals by those who rule by means of arrogated wealth and stolen power."[9] Remollino's poem portrays these political killings as a purposeful act of diminishing an entire social body, with every killing resulting in some part taking leave of each and every one of us, a diminishment inflicted to make us surrender to a groveling, doglike existence and release our small hold (*bitaw*) on becoming human (*pagpapakatao*). Steeped in the figurative conventions of five decades of armed revolutionary struggle, the poem's depiction of radical social struggle as a form of dedicated living so that all may become human is undoubtedly also shaped by the prominent emergence of a discourse on human rights on the scene of global affairs at the end of the Cold War.

The question of the liminal human status of certain strata of people has also been raised in other contexts, notably in the context of the burgeoning "warm-body export" industry of overseas domestic labor. In the 1990s, the Filipina artist Imelda Cajipe-Endaya made a series of sculptural installations depicting the figure of the overseas domestic worker as, in one representative work, a humanoid assemblage of household cleaning implements, personal belongings, and bodily appendages and, in another work, as an installation of travel cases, personal effects, and furnishings of an absent transient—that is, as an artificial human, a technological apparatus, equipment for living. Responding to the increasing reports of the violent treatment and physical, sexual, and psychological abuse of overseas Filipina workers, feminists like Cajipe-Endaya called attention to the plight of these women by foregrounding the inhuman or dehumanized forms of life that they are made to inhabit and even embody. From the side of her employment, the ideal migrant domestic worker images the archetypal robot, capable of offering emotional as well as menial help to humans without expectation of human feeling in return. Migrant women workers not uncommonly suffer various forms of physical abuse, sexual violation, and unmitigated exploitation at the hands of their employers—treatment fitting with their status as maid machines or domestic technologies. That status in part defines the dehumanizing conditions in which overseas Filipinas, among other migrant women workers, had been found, stirring nationalist and transnational outrage and lament over their plight and critical reflection on the human costs of the nation's participation as labor provider in the new global service economy.

Since the 1990s, numerous feminist scholars and artists have commented on and depicted the conditions of inhumanity imposed on and experienced by migrant female workers. As Aihwa Ong observes, "The underpaid, starved, and battered foreign maid, while not the statistical norm, has become the image of the new inhumanity in the Asian metropolis."[10] For Ong, the ethical exclusion of foreign maids from the moral economies of their host societies, and therefore the suspension of moral obligations to them, creates the conditions for their subhuman treatment. This hierarchic othering is not simply the product of national-ideological defense strategies against the putatively corrupting influence of morally suspect, because economically devalued, migrant populations, as is evident in almost all advanced capitalist nations. It is also the consequence of what Ong calls the neoliberal norms of "technopreneurial citizenship," norms that are increasingly prevalent in those new industrial nations in which foreign maids are employed to help reproduce the intellectual-managerial classes serving the demands of global capital.[11]

Elsewhere, other geographical and bodily sites of the realization of this new gendered inhumanity gain prominence. In Ciudad Juárez, on the border between Mexico and the United States, the horrific murders and forced disappearances of hundreds of women—almost all poor *maquiladora* workers—in the last decade of the twentieth century gave rise to the Mexican maquiladora worker as a gendered figure of disposable humanity, whose expendability and nonvalue are variously accounted for as the consequence of the gendered and racialized logics of capitalist expropriation and of the equally gendered and racialized logics of an emerging necropolitical order of power.[12] For Melissa Wright, the disposable woman is a global figure of feminized labor whose destined worthlessness and diminishing capacity to produce value embody the wasting end of "the dehumanizing process behind forming variable capital."[13] For Rosa Linda Fregoso, the "new category of the persecuted, disposable subject, the racially profiled mestiza or indigenous poor woman," is created by a necropolitical order in which multiple forms of sovereignty converge and operate through the suspension of human rights that the denationalization at the border enables.[14]

Discourses of Dehumanization

In response to the dehumanizing conditions that migrant women workers face (in foreign countries as well as in the borderlands), many activists have advocated for the guarantee of their human rights and humanitarian treatment. Such political claims on behalf of women unmoored by processes of globalization as well as by war invariably invoke but also problematize humanity as a category of valuable life from which a growing global majority of people are systematically excluded. It is this violence—which is inflicted on, in order to construct, the expendable lives of poor migrant women—that indexes and defines the condition of their exclusion from humanity. Violence and suffering become the constitutive traits of dehumanization, while humanity becomes equated with freedom from violence.[15] It would seem that today "humanity" has become primarily a category of the protected, a status that accrues to full-fledged subjects under the universal law of state sovereignty. Sold off by their own nation-states as commodified national natural resources, migrant women lose the universal guarantee of their humanity and are left exposed to the practices of violence that others engage in both to exercise their own claims to sovereign power and to ensure their own protected human belonging.

A more complicated story could surely be told about the genealogy and meaning of the humanisms invoked by activists in these postcolonial contexts. Certainly that story and others should be told to uncover what will be and has been betrayed in the transcoding of experiences of ordained pain and perdition into claims of human inclusion. For as these social struggles assume a transnational cast and international audience, their political claims increasingly tend toward advocating for the ethico-political recognition of this population (along with other "unprotected" groups, such as refugees and undocumented migrants) under a global regime of human belonging. The war to be human is in this way waged in soft or benevolent ways, through liberal projects of redressing the dehumanizing "excesses" or "abuses" of states and other subjects engaged in forms of spectacular violence, subsuming the political claims of these struggles within the very logic of humanization whose consequences they were fighting against.

There is no lack of valuable critiques of the discourse and practice of human rights and humanitarianism, pointing to the limits and dangers that the latter's implicit secular liberal humanism poses for diverse and radical social struggles and claims.[16] Departing from the critique of human rights discourse in particular, my own concern is with how the increasingly prevalent deployment of a broader logic of political emancipation—deployed to address conditions of disposable life as a matter of expulsion from a juridical (i.e., state-defined and protected, legal) humanity—occludes and abets by naturalizing the violence of other dominant forms of humanization in the realm of everyday material social life.

We can see this most clearly in, for example, Catharine MacKinnon's project to make women human and, relatedly, in the deployment of "gender" as a technology of humanization in various economic and political projects to redress gendered forms of inequality, disenfranchisement, suffering, and oppression. MacKinnon's effort, in her book *Are Women Human?*, is to rethink international human rights and humanitarian laws in order to redefine "human" in a way that includes women.[17] I bring up MacKinnon here to highlight the political limits of a particular emancipatory approach to the problem of dehumanization, and perhaps even of the ready critiques of such an approach in the name of "substantive" (rather than merely formal, legal) justice.[18]

MacKinnon's strategic construction of "women" as a people, that is, as a unit of humanity that can gain legal recognition and enfranchisement as a polity, is in response to their inhabiting what Hannah Arendt had famously theorized as a condition of "statelessness," which, as a consequence of the merging of the question of human rights with the question of national sovereignty—that is, of the "identification of the rights of man with the rights of peoples in the European nation-state system"—became equivalent to one's expulsion from humanity.[19] As we have seen, other feminists have identified this condition of "statelessness" and "rightlessness" with the denationalized status of female migrants, and while many would disagree with MacKinnon's invocation of state power to redress women's expulsion from legal humanity, the prevailing NGO use of a language of sovereignty, freedom, and rights to challenge the rule of exception under which new categories of inhumanity obtain ironically results in similar ends.

Not surprisingly, MacKinnon suggests that violence against women can and perhaps should be opposed through the intervention of transnational military forces justified by international state power. Moreover, her presumption of "women" as a people subjected to transnational "gender oppression" or gender-based violence affirms, if not promotes, a condition of permanent (gender) war, one that requires the formation of a transnational state and its monopoly of local forms of "patriarchal" violence to keep the peace and ensure the protection of women in their newfound status as recognized citizens of global humanity.[20] What is misguided about MacKinnon's project to humanize women is therefore not simply her overestimation of the liberatory potential of the law or her inattention to the limited efficacy of the law in transforming the material conditions of women's lives.[21] It is that the emancipation of women into the political category of the human serves only to naturalize and expand the authority and rule of Western liberal secular law, an expansion supported in the post–Cold War period by "democratizing" wars for economic restructuring and regime change. It makes the case and stages a new arena for carrying out the war to be human.

Political Emancipation and the Rule of Law as Assault on Social Reproduction

Early in his work, Karl Marx had argued that political emancipation serves only to restore and preserve the social relationships of civil society (i.e., capitalist relations) on which the secular political state is founded.[22] As the site of the alienation of human freedom and the sole guarantor of the rights of man, the secular political state actively *presupposes* and implements a conception of the human confined to what Marx called "egotistic man," or the private bourgeois individual upheld by the Declaration of the Rights of Man and of the Citizen (1793). In the contemporary moment, Talal Asad has argued that the norm of the human as sovereign, self-owning subject, which the Universal Declaration of Human Rights (1948) circumscribed within "the rule of law" politically enforced by imperial states, has converged with the norms of neoliberalism insofar as the political and economic regulation of "desirable conduct" in the world is made through the realpolitik use of cost-benefit market analysis.[23] Beyond its own "humanizing" effects and trajectory, political emancipation upholds and naturalizes the practices of "humanization" already operating in the realm of "civil society"—or, put another way, it normalizes the violence of everyday protocols for being human that are embedded in the practices of what Karl Marx and Friedrich Engels would theorize more broadly as "a definite *mode of life*."[24]

Today, that mode of life is a global one, an order in which *life* itself has become central to production, and *human*, a code of valorization—a measure and instrument of economic calculus and political enfranchisement. As we will see, everyday humanization is a crucial process in making the abstract category of life a capitalist social form, making human life a value-constitutive activity and its living itself a form of labor. The emancipation of the dehumanized, that is, their ethico-political recognition and inclusion within the protected status of humanity, furthers, even as it obfuscates, the expansion of this capitalist mode of life with its intrinsic colonial logic for parsing existence along the lines of ordinal humanist values now figuring algorithmically in the everyday social organization of productive life.

Constrained by polar oppositions between exclusion and inclusion, rights and rightlessness, security and threat, freedom and unfreedom, human and inhuman, political emancipation evacuates this very organization of concrete material life as a site of political potential, serving to disempower and depoliticize other practices of making social life. These other practices of lifemaking consist of tangential, fugitive, and recalcitrant creative social capacities that, despite being continuously diminished, impeded, and made illegible by dominant ways of being human, are invented and exercised by those slipping beyond the bounds of valued humanity in their very effort of living, in their making of forms of viable, enjoyable life. It is these practices of lifemaking that I think of and introduce here as *remaindered life*—modalities of living that exceed the necessary reproduction of the becoming-human as a resource of disposable life for capital.

Although I present remaindered life as the core of this book's tale, we can glean life remaindered only in relation to life deemed necessary and life upheld, as well as to life denigrated and life expunged—that is, in relation to life valued and life wasted. What is remaindered is the leftover of a theoretical and practical operation now everywhere performed, that is, the subroutine absorption (or subsumption) of all "life" into global capital. To find the remainder, then, we must follow this subsumption of life through the categories of value and waste to see how dominant protocols for being human and the war to be human are intertwined with the protocols for making life into labor and for wasting life as enterprise.

To the extent that capital requires an ever-increasing surplus of disposable life-times as the means of a global life-and-death economy, it must in fact destroy the independent thriving of the becoming-human in order to transform their life-making capacities into a disposable, even expendable, resource. On this view, the disempowerment and depoliticization of the social reproduction of disposability can be understood as being crucial to this aim. Liberal projects of political emancipation do not only accomplish this disempowerment and depoliticization of the ordinary social survival of the dehumanized whose "rightlessness" they seek to amend. They also strengthen the social institutions through which this continuing violence of imperial dispossession is exercised.

Through such projects of political emancipation, the reach of the "rule of law" broadens over the world, and a specifically US culture of legality—what Roxanne Dunbar-Ortiz notes as a "cult of the covenant," a cultish adherence to the law as the enshrinement of the values and rights proper to an exceptional free humanity and as the instrument of righteous action, its rule expressing and enacting the will, vision, and agency of the sovereign power of a chosen people—becomes increasingly globalized.[25] As demonstrated by the massive social and human destruction resulting from the interlocking of immigration and crime control in the United States since the 1990s, the mechanisms of policing bolstered and socialized by this US culture of legality only facilitate what many scholars and activists recognize as a broad-scale assault on entire communities' and peoples' capacities for social reproduction.[26]

Mary Pat Brady convincingly argues that a grid of intelligibility organized around a newly invigorated emphasis on legality has succeeded in contextualizing the "slow-motion massacre" at the US-Mexico border—of more than 3,000 people in the ten years after 1994, when Clinton's border-policing measure, Operation Gatekeeper, began (the San Diego activist group Border Angels estimates that number to be 10,000 total as of 2018)—as a "kind of passive capital punishment for an immigrant's willingness to skirt entry regulations."[27] The common sense of illegality as an ontological status places such death and dying beyond the bounds of human sentiment or response. Prison abolitionist intellectuals and activists observe the same ontological, "commonsense" understanding of the status of criminality, made the binary opposite of legality, as a key component of the shift in prison goals from rehabilitation to *incapacitation*.[28]

It is not only that *"the rule called law* in effect usurps the entire universe of moral discourse," as Talal Asad asserts. It is also that this broader culture of legality, as a lived imagination of the law as actual or potential means and measure of a moral justice, facilitates the large-scale assault on the capacities for social reproduction of entire communities and peoples considered outside of the bounds of the law, or worse, transgressing it (as in the notion of "crimes against humanity").[29] The assault is carried out as part of the civic policing work of states, by military, paramilitary, government, and civilian agents, through preemptive war, counterinsurgency, terror, and the everyday disciplining and punishment of labor and nonlabor, as well as through more mundane international trade agreements and national domestic policies supporting systemic economic exploitation and social divestment and dispossession.

The law itself is exercised as a form of war. *Lawfare* is the contemporary way of referring to the exercise of legal proceedings as an act of direct violence.

If, as Sherwin de Vera suggests, the capacity to express grievance, complaint, and dissent is a vital part of people's survival, the use of the law to silence voices of criticism and protest against intensifying militarist violence and resource extraction is no less than an assault on life.[30] In a manner not unlike what Darius Rejali describes as the disciplinary work of torture in shaping the graded civic and human order of citizenship in modern democracies, the assault on the social reproduction of certain collectivities' capacities to subsist and survive tangentially to capitalist ways of life keeps vast populations in a permanent condition of the not-yet-human.[31] This assault on particular communities' social reproduction takes place by "surplussing" people and their resources through relentless war and deadly policing, including terrorizing communities with interventionist public welfare campaigns that disrupt their own reproduction and determination of their own futures—such as in US practices of child-taking from Black, Native, immigrant, and refugee communities and other communities of color, movingly described by Laura Briggs—practices imagined by the already human as righteous actions taken for the greater human good.[32] This broad assault on the becoming-human depends on mobilizing techniques of social devaluation (racism, sexism, homophobia, transphobia) intrinsic to moral projects undertaken under the rule of law, making legal disenfranchisement a key process in the production of disposable life.

Living in a Time of War

While the social reproduction of the becoming-human is under constant assault, global industries of domestic and service work have arisen to employ their specifically gendered social reproductive capacities for the everyday reproduction of the shareholders of humanity—the would-be true citizens of an emergent globopolis. That is to say, war dispossesses communities of their independent life and commandeers their reproductive capacities for the maintenance of the lives and properties of global civil society. This domestication of an entire array of diverse reproductive powers in the globalization of "women's work" is a case, then, of producing certain subordinated forms of humanity as the route out of social ruin and into viable existence.

The Filipina poet Joi Barrios suggests this in her poem "Ang Pagiging Babae Ay Pamumuhay Sa Panahon ng Digma" (To be a woman is to live in a time of war) when she describes the being or becoming (*pagiging*) of woman as a living (*pamumuhay*)—that is, a form of work, of surviving and making a living—under conditions of great violence. She suggests that this social identity of being or becoming is both living and a form of livelihood under duress, where fear is a constant companion, in the home as well as in the streets, where the future is staked on the men in one's life, where "the cruelty of war / does not only lie in the rolling of heads / the drawing of the sword / but in the little-by-little finishing off / of food on the table."[33] To be a woman, then, is a form of survival, a way to live with and against the ever-present threat and reality of assault, violation, pain, and wounding.

Today, in heeding this insight, we might also recognize that *becoming-human is a living in a time of war*. The recourse to claims of illness and injury on the part of undocumented immigrants to gain legal residency in France, and its attendant rights of economic subsistence, through humanitarian exception (medical claims to protected belonging through "a very specific, limited" category of biopolitical humanity, as Miriam Ticktin shows) might be considered an example of becoming-human wielded as a living in the contemporary global context.[34] Political emancipation through recognition under the rule of law is a humanizing process, creating kinds of subordinate living that will be accorded some protection as serviceable life. Becoming-human is a form of work meriting humanitarian protection, a concessionary status guaranteeing a modicum of human "rights" to those who cannot accede to the status of the fully human. This, too, is the accomplishment of war.

For Barrios, who was writing during the counterinsurgent war of authoritarian modernization and, later, a "democratization" waged by the Philippine state against its own people, to be a woman was not only a form of lifework, a living with fear and cruelty, but also a never-ending struggle to live and be free ("walang katapusang pakikibaka / para mabuhay at maging malaya"). What, for the becoming-woman, or for the becoming-human, might it mean to live and be free beyond a time of war? What kind of living? What kind of freedom?

For those who protest women's dehumanization as the consequence of the deprivation of rights concomitant with a condition of statelessness, freedom is always on the side of an already-achieved humanity. It should come as no surprise to hear in these protests against dehumanization echoes of Hannah Arendt's liberal critique of the dehumanizing effect of statelessness. That liberal critique, with its call for inclusion in humanity, is predicated on a notion of a specifically human life (*bios*) that is enabled only by a transcendence of and liberation from a life enslaved by the endless and fruitless labors of necessity, a "natural" life (*zoē*) associated not only with the merely reproductive work of the domestic household (*oikos*) but also with the condition of slaves and the not-yet-human life of primitive peoples who, lamentably, remained in a state of nature.[35] Arendt's critique of dehumanization was in defense of a specifically *human* freedom attained through accomplishments that would endure beyond "the darkness of pain and necessity" that is the relentless toil of "life itself."[36] Arendt's critique of dehumanization thus exemplifies a commitment to a politics predicated on an equation between humanity and freedom drawn in opposition to the denigrated sphere of the unfree, meaningless, merely reproductive labor of making life, without "durable" immortal culture. It is not an accident that the transnationalization of this politics of emancipation coincides with the broad assault on and disciplining of forms of social reproduction that threaten to exceed the parameters of a dominant mode of producing human life. For in fact, the emancipatory politics of expanding freedoms is the means of continuing and softening a war waged by a privileged global polity so that it might remain human.

To Remain Human, to Finally Become So

The more recent wave of populist rejections of US imperialism (interventionist foreign policy) and US-global liberal multiculturalism (social justice, human rights, and "political correctness") does not, however, represent a turn against the war to be human waged by bourgeois liberals but rather represents the revanchism and insurgence of rival claims to its historic and future entitlements and privileges.

In the last half of the twentieth century, decolonizing peoples won more and more freedoms from colonizing metropolitan states, albeit at the cost of unfathomable pain and generations of loss. A majority of colonies in Asia and Africa achieved the formal independent status of postcolonial nation-states, even as many others in those continents and elsewhere have continued to fight liberationist struggles well into the present. Meanwhile, the violence and suffering inflicted on these third world countries, which served as pawns and spoils of the Cold War contest over global dominion, could no longer be contained in those territories of colonial enclosure. The costs and consequences of ceaseless imperial wars against the "darker nations" increasingly rebounded to the very metropolitan nations where anticolonial, Black, third world, feminist, and sexual liberationist movements had also already won more and more freedoms from their own majoritarian states and social orders, creating the conditions for unprecedented transnational alliances and solidarities among what would later become known as the Global South.[37]

However, the virulent means and logic of counterinsurgency—in postcolonial social and economic projects of authoritarian modernization and development, as well as in low-intensity military and paramilitary proxy warfare—also created the means and conditions for the thriving of subsidiary entrepreneurial actors in the illicit, informal shadow economies that liberal, democratic states relied on to sustain their imperial projects and domestic capitalist freedoms.[38] These subsidiary entrepreneurial actors, who now claim the state powers whose legalities they bought and sold as much as skirted, are rivals in the war to be human. Not to remain human, but to finally become so.

Nowhere is this rival claim better demonstrated than in the Philippines under Rodrigo Duterte, where the organized criminal activities of police and politicians, and a general flouting of the law, find open state sanction and support. Here, as I will discuss at length in chapter 9, we see the ascendance of entrepreneurial agents and networks that had thrived on the zonal edges of legal and formal capitalist enterprises and political order under the modernizing, developmentalist state during the Cold War and under the democratizing, globalist state in the brief post–Cold War moment. Repudiating reclaimed US pretentions of humanitarian concern and moral world leadership under Obama as extant colonialism, the Duterte state has nonetheless adopted the war on terror as its own moral, territorial project, purportedly shorn of its imperial character but not of its political effectivity.

The Philippine war on drugs, the centerpiece of this state's moral project and its potency, is the war to be human on the part of those who, by certain measures, have never been fully human—a political-policing campaign that borrows from and extends and revises the playbook of imperial, moralistic military wars (the British opium wars, the US war on drugs), which historically served to extend imperial powers' capitalizing control over illegal trade and criminal economies that they themselves had abetted, if not initiated. For those who support it, the war on drugs is a just war, a war waged by the yet to be human against the inhuman elements impeding the full redemption of what has long been due—the attainment of the valued life of the already human, with all its secured rights and privileges of capitalist freedom.

After Man, after Freedom

Freedom as right, as achievement, is a casus belli, a case and cause for war. Those who are authorized by it and defend it (as right to speech, right to offense, right to self-expression, as way of life), who speak on its behalf, on the grounds of its inheritance, wage the war to be human. In the world built by man, freedom equals war.

Against the freedom of man are those among the belligerently also-human who seek to roll back centuries of Western rule, or to hasten its demise, to

FIGURE 1.1. "Is this the life we really want?" Photograph by author.

restore a lost imperial order of protection and governance with the establishment of a state of their own kind. Despite the turn against liberalism, they, too, are waging a war in terms that mirror their enemies', those of their rivals in global dominion. Like the Duterte state, which holds out the promise of care and protection to its constituency, these rival powers of sovereignty hold out other words, in place of *freedom* and *democracy*, to call on the becoming-human to fight back, to finally regain what they have lost or what should rightfully be theirs. Yet they, too, offer freedom as a franchise of war, and valued life as redemption.

What might it mean to live when such living drives the global economy, to fight for freedom when freedom is a franchise? These are the questions raised by the becoming-human in our struggle against this war to be human, everywhere waged as violent answer to the question posed by decolonization: What might it mean to become human in the wake of colonialism? Becoming-human is this continuing struggle, neither an ideal nor a model of a political project, nor yet a polity, but, rather, multiple strategies of survival and thriving against the disposability of one's own life, including the shared being of one's belonging. This struggle thus poses a different question, beyond the question of the human that founds its own disposability.[39]

Far from simply portraying the dehumanizing conditions of violence facing migrants, peasants, and other disenfranchised laboring classes as the realization of a political state of exception, figurations of the not quite human in the works of Filipino poets and artists should be read as depictions of an impossible form of everyday being and living in the world, experiences of an ordinary violence of negated being, which is the condition of survival of people deemed superfluous, the waste product of global capitalism, the very refuse of a prevailing order of the human as valued life. Such depictions of the not quite human cannot but also be the expression of a grievous, yet potentially radical, question: *What kind of life?*

2

A GLOBAL ENTERPRISE
Waste

A Global Story

For several decades a story has been told about the rapid changes the world was undergoing. That story has a protagonist (or antagonist) whose name is *globalization*, with a usurper sidekick called *neoliberalism.* However complex the story is in its clamorous telling, with its two main actors fractioned and multiplied, what it does not often admit was that this is also a story of the unraveling and rebraiding of the social fabric and political and economic relations of global capital in a broad retaliatory response to decolonization. In this other telling, the story of globalization is principally a story of the long aftermath and afterlife of decolonization, and it must therefore include pasts that persist in the present in the form of predation and brutality, not only on the part of the colonizers but also on the part of the colonized.[1]

This other story thus bears longer narrative threads than the story of globalization and neoliberalism, which finds its beginnings in the pivotal actions of capital in the late twentieth century—in key economic decisions or the policies of international banks and the US state (the end of the Bretton Woods system and the Keynesian economy, the rise of the Chicago school and the "Washington consensus"). This other story calls up pasts that might appear to be long gone or to emerge as anachronisms in an entirely changed global situation but that, in fact, shape the very contours of this present. Here, primitive accumulation, the logic of punishment (as just war and as slavery), and imperialism all figure centrally in postindustrial modes of capitalist production, not simply as some kind of regressive behavior on the part of those pushed to the margins by these latest modes, but rather as intrinsic structural components of contemporary modes of accumulation. In this chapter, I discuss how war, punishment, and waste—integral features of primitive accumulation in the colonial era—operate today, in the expanded reproduction of global capital over all of life, which is the aim and function of the new imperialism.

The War to Be Human Is a Global Enterprise (of Punishment)

People do not hand over their land, resources, children and futures without a fight, and that fight is met with violence. —ROXANNE DUNBAR-ORTIZ, *An Indigenous People's History of the United States*

The overseer's book of penalties replaces the slave-driver's lash. All punishments naturally resolve themselves into fines and deductions from wages. —KARL MARX, *Capital, Vol. I*

War and the administration of war has been for centuries the means of domination of the imperial states of capital. For us, it has been most acutely the means of domination by the dying imperial United States, even as its global hegemony is rapidly on the decline, its economic power increasingly overshadowed by the rise of new state-corporate powers, arguably led by "China." Not unlike its predecessors but even more so, the United States built itself into a modern nation-state and premier global capitalist power through relentless wars of territorial seizure and colonial settlement, human trafficking and enslavement, genocidal displacement, and violent dispossession.[2]

A war of dispossession is the mode of accumulation dominantly understood as the "original" or "primitive" basis of the rise of capital, even as those who struggle to survive in this moment know intimately well that a racist, sexist war of dispossession is the beating heart of contemporary global capitalism. The fight that people put up to resist the theft of their collective life (their land, resources, children, and futures, as Dunbar-Ortiz reminds us) is met with a violence that does not only persist but has also become a systematic part of the latest modes of capitalist accumulation.

Though liberal democracies and their conscientious intellectuals occlude its abiding centrality, the war to be human is a daily enterprise of violent seizure and dispossession—sometimes declared, sometimes not—necessary for the maintenance and expansion of capitalism and its ruling state powers. Beyond its spectacular expressions in the global war on terror, as we saw in the previous chapter, the war to be human is also found to be waged in the most banal of ways—in the innumerable, daily acts of punitive exaction that ultimately yield a world of staggering power and capitalist wealth. The conditions of such everyday dispossession and the assault on their capacities of social reproduction are what countless people have made their life's work to survive. This is in part what it means to live in a time of war.

And yet such lifework has been folded back into the maw of what it had sought to escape. Assigned by liberal democratic states to ensure the private welfare of free citizen life, insurance agencies and the police have today become exemplary institutions of actuarial capitalist enterprise, both high and low. These protection rackets are only two contemporary examples of the accepted forms of ransom on human health and well-being—even on continued being (ransom on pain of disability, confinement, or death)—which for more and more people might cost more than the worth of their own lives. People suffer the ordained incremental losses of life because they are barred from being able to pay the high price of full citizenship and its protections. Of course those without such ensured "ontological security"—those regarded as falling short of full citizenship and, by extension, full humanity—have already been paying the hidden toll that the citizenship of others exacts, serving as the effigies of enemies of the democratic state, incurring the punishment that all protection rackets threaten in return for the refusal of their services.[3]

Punishment is central to the genesis and continuing, expanding reproduction of capitalism. Punishment of idleness followed on dispossession, which in the just wars of Spanish colonialism was itself carried out as punishment (the means and ends of just war). Enslavement as the meting out of punishment continues today, though in distinctly modern forms.[4] As Angela Davis points out, forms of punishment that came to be racialized through the institution of chattel slavery nevertheless persist in disguised forms in the present through the prison system.[5] In the United States, the prison system, including the police who serve as its scouts and brokers, serves as the foremost image-means of "negative affirmation" of the freedoms of capitalist democracy. The prison is "the paradigmatic institution of democracy," Gina Dent argues, not only because it institutes a form of "egalitarian" punishment through its deprivation of that universal good, "liberty" (or "freedom"), in the wages-form of sentence time, as Foucault notes, but also, as Dent and Davis write, because it serves as the constitutive limit border of citizen humanity (who reside in the "free world")—a holding pen where capital punishment, torture, and political disenfranchisement obtain as fair and necessary measures to guard the privileges and rights of that free world.[6]

There are other everyday forms of negation that sustain capitalist democracy, and these are meted out not only by the imperial state founded by white settler colonialism (and emulated by its proxy states) but also by people entitled by dominant social norms and enfranchised by that state. Every day the enfranchised find ways to punish others in small but painful gestures of humiliation and degradation, as well as through the extra daily fines exacted from the immiserated and the censured for access to basic necessities of living—food, water, shelter—the rent they pay for borrowed existence. For the dispossessed, the costs of living are always greater because life and its guarantees are, by definition, the right and prerogative of the enfranchised.

The disciplinary, penal form of daily fines and deductions from wages that Marx had seen as replacing the slave driver's lash become the form through which racialized punishment enters into capitalist production itself. If racialized punishment was fundamentally a counterinsurgent instrument for the reproduction of racialized property relations both under and after slavery,[7] it has become widely practiced in the post-Fordist moment as a direct mode of value extraction in rent-capitalist (extortion) industries as well as in subscription-model service businesses and circulation enterprises (communication, transmission, and transportation). Racialized punishment has also become a mode of production of permanent liquidity in the form of disposable life-times, for derivative financial enterprise.

The punitive mode of value extraction can be seen in the exaction of skyrocketing fines and fees by the US criminal justice system and all the other auxiliary enterprises around policing and security on the proliferating borders of what I will argue is emerging as a global urban archipelago of city-states (see chapter 7). In small US towns and tertiary cities with sizable Black and brown populations, such as in Ferguson, Missouri, mounting municipal court fees for trivial civil infractions (catching a fish out of season, getting drunk in public, driving a car with a tinted window or blue taillights, playing loud music—signs of racialized actors and activity for algorithmic penal attribution) generate millions of dollars of revenue for the state.[8] Such revenues are compounded by more fees for "government services"—public defenders, room and board for jail time (incurred not for the infractions but for the failure to pay the fees), drug and alcohol rehabilitative treatment, probation and parole supervision and monitoring devices—services that were once "free" for its "users" but now come at a charge.⁹

Petty penalties become part of the broader logic of accumulative strategies that rest on both gross and also ever more minute border-making (from security walls and detention prisons to pay-as-you-go spatial and cultural, class and citizenship divisions in utilities, including rights and access to vital means of movement). Petty profits are made through the imposition of petty hardships, through the creation of difficulties or inconveniences within services themselves (interruptions in streaming platforms) or the deprivation of gratuitous or complimentary utilities or goods (a blanket on a frigid airplane, clean water from the tap) as "differences" and gaps that only additional payments will close or fill. The proliferation of value-extractive opportunities through the implosive parsing out of graded services within privatized or subcontracted public service and utility industries, all based on and backed by punishment, can thus be seen as part of a broader economic trend.¹⁰

Beyond such forms of direct value extraction, however, punishment is also a *force of production* of permanently liquid and liquefiable populations. As I argued earlier, the systematic assault on the social reproduction of entire communities creates underclasses of unwanted social groups—the undocumented, the unemployed, the immiserated, the criminalized, the displaced, and the homeless—whose lives and life-times can be placed at the disposal of capitalist enterprises. However, the produced disposability of the lives and life-times of others no longer functions only as newly available, supercheapened labor (as in the global reproductive industry), or even as reserve labor (to further cheapen employed labor)—those surplus populations intrinsic to capitalist dynamics.¹¹ Produced by the capitalization of punishment, disposable life also importantly functions as expendable biogenetic matter (raw material and means of production) for precisely those financialized industries that are profiting from the revaluing of waste.

Waste Is the Product and Productive Strategy of Capitalist War

Waste and the act of wasting have become revalued—as matter and technique that can make revaluation (and therefore the production of value) possible. Many scholars have pointed out the ways that capital has for centuries profited from the disposability of human and nonhuman lives.¹² Waste, as Vinay Gidwani argues, is "the origin and constitutive other of capitalist value." It is both the warrant for and the sentence of capitalist dispossession, defined against the kernel principle and highest ideal of capitalist life, which is the creation of value. What might perhaps distinguish or specify this moment is the multiplying, fractal scales in which the intensive capitalization of the waste and wasting of things, people, space, and time—and their derivatives—is carried out.

In Flint, Michigan, the state abandonment of poor, Black, and people of color populations—including the toxic neglect of infrastructure and the environmental disaster left by industrial capital—serves as the material basis for the financialization of urban public policy.[13] As Laura Pulido shows, the financialization of the devastation left by deindustrialization in the 1980s follows a history of devalued lives of nonwhite peoples subsidizing white capital in Flint: from the Ojibwe people, on whose land white settlement in the early nineteenth century prepared the ground for the development of the automobile industry (General Motors) in the twentieth century, to the racialized and racially divided labor populations that were subject to violent processes of abandonment as General Motors offshored its operations abroad to maintain global competitiveness in the early 1980s. The poisoning of Flint's water supply, which has affected thousands of predominantly Black residents with grave health problems ranging from Legionnaire's disease to lead poisoning, was built on the industrial pollution of the Flint River and on the leaching of lead from decrepit water pipes crumbling from infrastructural neglect. Pulido identifies this toxic infrastructural neglect—the reduction and discontinuation of social investment in infrastructural maintenance—as a deliberate act of violent abandonment premised on the disposability of the lesser citizens who would be affected.

Continuous with the processes of waste making intrinsic to the capitalist production of value (or what Gidwani calls "the waste-value dialectic"), the violence of such abandonment by white capital, white residents, and the white settler colonial state in the course of deindustrialization is further compounded by an added layer of productive investment in a moment of capital crisis.[14] As Pulido shows, the key decisions to continue to use this water supply, that is, to actively poison the surplussed, predominantly poor, Black residents of Flint, were motivated, in the postindustrial moment, by investment capital's conversion of urban public policy into a financial instrument, or, in other words, by the financialization of local government.

From 2011 to 2015, under the Obama administration, the venture capitalist governor of Michigan appointed municipal emergency fiscal managers to address the fiscal crisis produced by capital abandonment and tax cuts in the wake of deindustrialization and by the 2008 recession (in turn resulting from the subprime mortgage housing crisis). The financialization of urban policy meant that the decision to poison Flint's water was the result of a calculation of the human life costs of using Flint River water in terms of (and in exchange for) the fiscal savings this urban policy would produce. In the terms of understanding I present in this book, the future life-times of Flint's Black residents were liquefied ("sold" or "cashed in") to cut the costs of investment capital (creating "savings") and to realize the growth rates promised by emergency fiscal managers to the bondholders from whom loans for urban renewal were secured.[15] In other words, the "waste" (disposable people, contaminated river) that was created in a previous moment of accumulation re-enters another cycle of value extraction as a repurposed resource for finance capital—as a monetizable asset that can figure (as derivative exchange value) in the calculus of the investments of finance capital.

Contemporary developments in the centuries-long capitalist exploitation of the work and life activity of racialized human and nonhuman beings demonstrate many examples of this *investment* in the waste produced by the previous era of accumulation, which by the 1970s had reached crisis limits of profitability. The expanding California prison system, as Ruth Gilmore has argued, was the result of postindustrial surplus capital looking for new investment opportunities and finding it in the state's need to manage its own forcibly idled populations.[16] It comes as almost no surprise that today a similar opportunity has been found in the management of homeless populations. Craig Willse shows, for example, how contemporary social service programs targeting unsheltered populations have emerged to reduce and manage the negative impact and costs of politically abandoned populations, transforming the illness and death that result from racially organized housing insecurity and deprivation into productive economic enterprises in the postindustrial service and knowledge economies.[17]

No doubt such opportunities for profiting on waste could be found in the past, as a rebound strategy for cutting losses or a form of wartime profiteering. But such strategies did not define a generalized mode of accumulation (much as working for money in precapitalist societies cannot be equated with waged work under capitalism). Under modernity, waste was an undesirable by-product of efficient productivity. It served at once as a legitimating rationale of capitalist dispossession and as an object of elimination for the improved production of value. Reducing or eliminating waste was about cutting costs, cutting losses.[18] Only in the present context has waste become directly valorizable—the combined consequence of the limits posed by decolonizing struggles to continuing capitalist profitability and late industrial capital's efforts to recoup its losses through a massive reorganization of its processes of productive exploitation (or theft of surplus value). Crucially enabled by the profound developments in digital mediatic technologies, this reorganization was to effect the subsumption of the lifework of social reproduction and survival of differentiated populations, giving rise to what many have pronounced as a new global political economy based on the value productivity of life as labor (upheld, I would argue, by the generativity of life as waste).

Waste Is the Object of the New Imperialism

Hitherto cast as the bathwater of progress, and therefore a matter of the merely reproductive work of lesser life—"slaves of necessity," helpers, handmaidens, and housewives of capitalist productivity, garbage pickers, scavengers, and salvagers—waste became the object resource for a new round of capital expansion in the late twentieth and early twenty-first century, its gross pursuit shaping the features of the "new imperialism." Rather than a distinctly territorial project, this latest phase of imperialism has been a project to encompass and recolonize its own minimally managed, now increasingly unruly detritus—that is, to reabsorb the very ruin and ruination of past accumulation into present processes of valorization. In this way, the military warfare of states and parastates in the global war on terror has been both paradigmatic and symptomatic of a broader political-economic maneuver to extend the life system of accumulation by cannibalizing its unwanted byproducts. Among those unwanted byproducts for the United States has been the very postcolonial state regimes and paramilitaries that it had sponsored as proxies during the Cold War but that had since also grown and morphed into their own monsters.

Long before the US war on terror began in 2001, it had already become clear that the used and discarded third world pawns of more than half a century of small wars had struck out on their own, cutting deals beyond their constrained political contracts and pursuing ambitions well beyond the petty rewards of modern fiefdom offered them by their global higher ups. The Contras in Nicaragua, the Taliban in Afghanistan, Saddam Hussein, Ferdinand Marcos, Augusto Pinochet, Manuel Noriega, the death squads of dirty wars in South and Central America and the Philippines—these were only some of the proxy players picked and promoted in the decolonized world to do the dirty wars that kept the capitalist world clean and operational. They had of course never been simply pawns, for the job had required skills and capacities already at work in situ. Before embedded journalists, colonial powers had their embedded warlords, "chiefs" and other "big men," titled and conscripted to represent and manage their "tribes" and villages, or whatever divisible social units the former had concocted in the image of their own patriarchal households. Colonizers and capitalists tapped and cultivated, as well as fashioned out of whole cloth, little systems to hook up with theirs.[19]

In their hyperactivity after use and discard, however, the pawns, proxies, and subordinated political systems proved more brazen, unruly, and antagonistic than expected. Buoyed by enormous waves of popular and radical political movements against them and their imperial benefactors, which propelled the initial formal shift in US foreign policy from Cold War counterinsurgent war to post–Cold War "democracy promotion" in the mid-1980s, these subordinate rivals found themselves the target of a reinvigorated US interventionist policy and series of campaigns, from the aggressive "regime change" policy of Bush's global war on terror to the more accommodationist yet lethally surgical doctrine of Obama, to the belligerent, anti-immigrant, anti-Muslim "America first" policy screed of Trump. While there is more incoherence and chaos in the political developments of the last three decades than I present here, particularly set against a changing geopolitical scene with other rising imperial powers and fortunes in an increasingly multipolar world, one can detect in the vicissitudes of US global empire a newly significant, endless, and productive drive toward resolving and exploiting the multiple crises presented by what it regards as global detritus.[20] Imperial security has found the bases of a new "infinite" strategy for its survival and growth: making the very refuse of imperial wars past, present, and future into the raw material and means for the capitalization of permanent war.

In this way, the masters would appear to take after their servants and slaves, the settlers after the natives. Or so the descendants of the master warlords say.[21] Waste, after all, has historically been the designated fate of colonialism's wretched. Treated as natural resources up for grabs in colonial conquest and enterprise, the colonized and enslaved and their descendants have had to live *as* the spoils of capital's rise and rule, while surviving on the cast-offs and leavings of their erstwhile masters. Everywhere in the Global South, people constantly make do to get by; it is they who have fine-tuned the arts of revaluing modernity's waste into the arts of life-making.

Survival is not, however, the monopoly of the virtuous, neither proof of the fittest nor reward for the deserving. Capitalism and its victors are also battling to survive, though survival here—the right to be—can only mean supremacy. Overlords and overseers learn from the strategies of those who refuse to be conquered. This is in fact part of the colonial genealogy that military planners themselves trace for the project of open-ended counterinsurgency—the small wars, low-intensity conflicts, and psy-ops methods used and honed in the third world during the Cold War—now required on a global scale.[22] *Insurgency* is the imperial code for all rebellion of survival of the expendable in the extended moment of capital's global expansion.[23] More than a discursive sign for colonial, sovereign control, it has become a procedural code for identifying opportunities for investment in militarist enterprise.

If the sovereign agents of the war to be human adopt the measures of survival that the becoming-human take, they do so only up to the point and in order that the vital-mortal system upholding their paramountcy can be conserved.[24] This is the context in which all kinds of waste come to be regarded as a resource and means for capital's revitalization—wasted people, wasted lands, wasted life-times—and what was once an auxiliary activity of managing the crisis of the contradictory surplus of capitalist production (the strategy of containment), becomes the central mode of the new imperialism, the process of capital's expanded reproduction.

Everywhere there is strewn waste to be reused, recycled, and redeemed. There are so-called idle or abandoned, useless, degraded, even toxic lands and waters to be reclaimed. In a world awash with the destruction wrought by the production of disposability, of objects that with a single use turn immediately into waste (Styrofoam cups, plastic forks and plates, soda and water bottles), of humans "on demand," their labor made so increasingly "casual" to the point of making the very notion of employment increasingly archaic if not altogether obsolete (a casualty of "just-in-time," single-use services), of fields of cash crops and waters of cash catch, ecological systems siphoned to the point of near absolute depletion, there is so much recycling, repurposing, and rehabilitation to be done. Suddenly, even if long in the making, cleaning up is big business.

In the future, a bank ad announces, there will be no difference between waste and energy. Such a future has in fact already arrived, for the positing of this nondistinction has been the leading bid of present capital, as evident in the symbolic capture of accumulated and promised life-times of entire populations through art and currency markets and the mediatic capture of otherwise idled or idling life-times of supranations of content and service providers through capitalist software-as-business platforms. This nondistinction between waste and energy is precisely the kernel proposition of the financial derivative.

If waste has been found to be productive of value, forming, as Gidwani and Reddy argue, "a new frontier" of primitive accumulation, then the act of wasting has been too.[25] The productive wasting of lives scales up and down. From the wasting of populations in the big wars of colonialism to the wasting of smaller, minoritized subpopulations and subgroups (exemplified, as we will see, by the enterprise of extrajudicial killings in Duterte's war on drugs), capital punishment has become a capital enterprise in its own right, a financialized franchise of state violence. If waste is the object of a new imperialism then war is its means for making more of it, the means of foreclosing or "de-potentializing" future possibilities of life in order to make that life disposable in the present both as waste and as labor to remediate waste.[26]

The role of the territorial state in the productive capitalist wasting of populations is crucial and indispensable. The intensified and active capitalization of state violence has in fact been the predominant way that new "insurgent" state powers have been fighting the threatened obsolescence and demise of the international nation-state system and the end of the long "political enclosure movement" that historically gave rise to it.[27] For the state is seat, scepter, sword, and server of rival players in a great game that has not ceased being played. But while the great game of late nineteenth-century imperialism sought the capture of peoples through territory, now, in the twenty-first century, it seeks to capture the *activity* of life.[28]

To understand this shift, as at once change and continuity, we must reexamine imperialism as the process by which capital expands, a process entailing two kinds of reproduction.

Late Imperialism Is the War for the Expanded Reproduction of Capital over All Life

There are at least two components in the latest imperial movement of capital expansion: one, the war for capitalism's own leavings, fought as much with financial instruments as with military power; two, by means of such war, the stimulation and reorganization of social survival through the massive, continuous destruction of social life.

On the one side, late imperialism consists of the expanded or enlarged *reproduction of capital* based on the pursuit of capitalism's own leavings: places, people, and other "natures" completely spent, or nearly so, from the ravages of industrialization, third world developmentalist projects, and the counterinsurgent wars that opened and maintained ("stabilized") the terrains for both; the "extra" products of social efforts to survive, primarily new generations—children and youth—increasingly made extraneous much more quickly than their own parents (making for the surplus population "explosion" that itself became the object of developmentalist containment strategies); and the outgrowths of such social survival in the form of informal and illicit economies, and the cast-offs of those economies' asset-making and trade. These are the leavings that provide new resources as well as new impetus for big capital, which today prodigiously, intensively ventures on projects of "original accumulation" not as a disavowed systemic condition of formal capitalist exploitation, but as its core strategy and cutting edge.[29]

On the other side, and as a corollary to the first, late imperialism consists of processes that see to the global *reorganization of social reproduction* as a productive basis of capitalist accumulation. Generations of feminists have long insisted on the fundamental importance of the appropriated, unpaid work of women, colonial peoples, and "nature" in the capitalist accumulation of value, carefully tracking not only the historical, structural relation between formal labor exploitation and the "invisible" unpaid labor of captive and indentured social groups identified with a "free" and denigrated nature, but also the late twentieth-century tendency, under a new international division of labor, toward the "feminization" of labor as a continued means of cheapening necessary costs to capital.[30] In the last few decades, new generations of feminists have furthered this work by following contemporary developments in the creation of an "international division of reproductive labor" through the restructuring of the world economy, as well as by tracing ever-deeper historical genealogies for the contemporary capitalization of reproduction.[31]

In the capitalist past as well as the present, the reorganization of reproduction is accomplished through the destructive ends and effects of war. As Silvia Federici writes, "The destruction of life in all its forms is today as important as the productive force of biopower in the shaping of capitalist relations."[32] The destruction of subsistence economies in the Global South through structural adjustment policies; the state disinvestment in the reproduction of the workforce through the dismantling of the welfare state in the Global North; the aggressive corporate and industrial pillaging of forests and mountains, oceans and coral reefs, undomesticated flora and fauna, and their genetic information program and biomaterial capacities in occupied territories and subjugated regions of the world—this is the profitable, decimating work of imperial war provisioning the globopolis with the means of its own social reproduction through the consumption of the accumulated and future life-times and life-making capacities of nearly the entire planet.

Here, expansion over all of life means more than the destructive absorption of these existing independent life forms in the peripheries. It additionally means the creation and spread of new "peripheries" for capital—to serve as sites for outsourced reproductive labor as well as sites of productive investment. If colonized territories and bodies provided the foundational and continuing bases of capital over the longue durée—"free" nature that would be appropriated and converted into commodity, money, capital—the relation that colonialism established between human society and nonhuman or subhuman nature has become internal to capital's growth and expansion in the present.

Original and Abiding: Nonhuman Milieus of Capitalist Accumulation

As the intense competition for capitalist leavings (rather than precapitalist spoils) generates ever-intensifying conditions of crisis and conflict, crisis/conflict control itself becomes an independent province of accumulation for global capital, which not only consumes its own byproducts to survive but capitalizes on that survival strategy in the permanent war of open-ended counterinsurgency.[33] Permanent war produces the very crisis/conflict conditions that serve as the object of the "services" of the military-security-industrial complex. In this way, the military-security-industrial complex is model and means of a more general strategy of late capitalist accumulation.

That general strategy is an intensified expansion over the full range of human and nonhuman life-times, that is, the imperial conquest and subsumption of "surplus" lifeworlds by capital, the founding and continuing techniques for which are those modes of dispossession of colonialism and slavery we understand as "primitive accumulation." For capital, born, bred, and developed in and through conquest, sees no limits to what and how it might gain. As Rosa Luxemburg argued: "In its forms and laws of motion, capitalist production reckons with the whole world as the treasury of productive forces, and has done so since its inception. In its drive to appropriate these productive forces for the purposes of exploitation, capital ransacks the whole planet, procuring means of production from every crevice of the Earth, snatching up or acquiring them from civilizations of all stages and all forms of society."[34] So-called primitive accumulation persists in a fully capitalized global world to address the inherent limits of capital accumulation driving its expansion. As Luxemburg stated, "Capital knows no other solution to the problem [of the limits of accumulation] than violence, which has been a constant method of capital accumulation as a historical process, not merely during its emergence, but also to the present day."[35]

In the early twentieth century, on the brink of imperialist world war, Luxemburg readily understood the extant structural necessity of so-called original or primitive accumulation in capitalism, demonstrating the indispensable role of the violence of modern colonialism in the latter's expanded reproduction or growth. Both historically and in her own present, she argued, capital requires the violent transformation of the noncapitalist means of production and the labor-power of colonized countries—the mineral resources and pastures, forests, and waterways of their lands; their fauna and livestock; native peoples and their social formations—into capital on a massive scale. Luxemburg argued, "From the standpoint of capitalism . . . the violent appropriation of the colonial countries' most important means of production is *a question of life or death* for it."[36]

The "vital necessity" of noncapitalist formations to capital's existence and growth—and the two coincide, for without growth or expanded reproduction, capitalism cannot exist—obtains from its historical genesis to the present day: "Even in its full maturity, capitalism depends in all of its relations on the simultaneous existence of noncapitalist strata and societies. . . . The accumulation process of capital is tied to noncapitalist forms of production in all of its value relations and material relations—i.e., with regard to constant capital, variable capital, and surplus value."[37] Although it might be argued that Luxemburg's theoretical analysis reduces the role of noncapitalist strata to serving as an indispensable *source* of natural resources and labor-power (means to renew constant and variable capital), and as *purchasers* of capitalist surplus product (and therefore as a means of realization of already produced surplus value), her formulation of noncapitalist spheres as forming the *milieu* of capitalist accumulation—and the relation between the two as "a *constant process of metabolism*" without which capital, "*in all its value relations and material relations*," could not exist—bears more far-reaching implications for thinking about the dynamics of value production in the twenty-first century than one might surmise.[38]

Luxemburg's argument that "the movement of capitalist accumulation requires an environment of noncapitalist social formations—that it is in a constant process of metabolism with the latter as it proceeds, and that it can only exist for as long as it finds itself within this milieu"—provides a way of understanding the notion of noncapitalist social formations beyond the imperial humanist understanding of them in the form of given, historical colonial nations.[39] They are "milieus" and "environments" with which capitalism shares a vital metabolism "in all its value relations and material relations." They provide capital "its fertile soil," even as capitalism "lives from their ruin," their "constant and progressive erosion" serving as the very condition of its continued existence.[40] The clear references to the natural environment and earth, as well as to organic metabolic processes, are neither arbitrary nor merely symptomatic of an extant vitalism nor of a piece with physiocratic thought. Rather, they register an apprehension of the whole life systems comprising the social formations colonized and "swallowed up and assimilated" by capital (detailed in her examples of projects of colonization of the "natural economy" and the "peasant economy" in British India, Egypt and South Africa, French Algeria, and the US West and Northwest in the early twentieth century).

As principal ways to understand the structural relation of noncapitalist modes of production to capitalist modes of production—that is, as a source of sustenance and an object of denigration—*milieu*, *environment*, and *soil* signal the broader spheres of lifeworlds that serve as "the treasury of productive forces" for imperial capital. These notions do not only highlight the ways that original accumulation continues today with respect to nonhuman "nature" as noncapitalist strata for capitalist agricultural and extractive industries.[41] That has undoubtedly been the central insight of critiques of contemporary wars as resource wars—whether of oil, water, food, medicinals, or seeds—interventions that also crucially highlight the entwined human and nonhuman relations intrinsic to such "nature."[42] These notions also open up other implications for our understanding of the significance of primitive accumulation in contemporary modes of value transformation.

Milieu highlights a technical, material, social, and political relation (and "metabolism") beyond what is encapsulated by *labor*. Reinterpreted through Gilbert Simondon's concept of the "associated milieu" with respect to the concrete technical object, the "milieu" that noncapitalist social formations provide for capital can be viewed as the medium or ground that autonomous capital processes harness and shape as the indispensable condition of their own operation.[43] Simondon uses the notion of the associated milieu with respect to the concrete technical object or being, which in its definition as bearing "the burden of alienated human reality which is enclosed within it," and in its evolution through progressive scientific and economic developments as an autonomous being capable of putting into play a recurrent causality necessary to it, I understand as a crystallization of capital (its reification of value in process as an independent being). The associated milieu is simultaneously natural and technical, mediating the relation between elements of both, and linked to the regime of elements that constitute the technical being, thereby serving as "that through which the technical object conditions itself in its functioning."[44]

On this view *milieu*, as used by Luxemburg to understand the role of noncapitalist social formations, suggests the abiding force of the imperial relation in positing constitutively discrepant spheres or strata and subordinating them to and in the service of the most advanced technological modes of contemporary capitalist production. As a discrepant sphere harnessed and shaped but not fabricated by the object it sustains, *milieu* suggests a realm of mixed and fused agencies perduring beyond recognizable precapitalist, precolonial human "societies." It highlights the organic and nonorganic material infrastructure and social and technological environments with which *surviving* noncapitalist, or as Anna Tsing dubs it, "pericapitalist," social forms of lifemaking are significantly interlaced.[45]

To understand the implications of these metabolic processes between capital and its noncapitalist/pericapitalist milieus for understanding contemporary value production is hence to see not the foretold disappearance of these noncapitalist lifeworlds (marking the absolute limits of capital, in the political gesture of predicting the latter's imminent end) but rather their dynamic *survival*.[46] Such implications can be drawn out, however, only from the "standpoint" of that milieu—orientations and sensibilities that are to be distinguished from the standpoints of the subjects of labor and capital, the relation between which is held to define centrally and critically the proper dynamics of the capitalist mode of production.[47] That "standpoint" registers the breach between the world that seeks to absorb it and its own lifeworld, as well as the measures undertaken to ensure that breach's closure.

Land

If you in your search for the good life destroy life, we question it.
 Such arrogance to claim ownership over the land, when it is we who are owned by it. How can you own something that will outlive you? —MACLI-ING DULAG, QUOTED BY DOYO, *Macli-ing Dulag*

In the contemporary moment, Native and Indigenous studies scholars have posed some of the most vigorous arguments that primitive accumulation, in the exemplary form of settler colonialism, is not only foundational but ongoing.[48] Lenape scholar-activist Joanne Barker argues that Dutch and British settler practices of predatory lending, violence, and fraud in the early colonial United States established the material grounds—the very economic infrastructure—for the global dominion of Wall Street, the imperial seat of US finance capital.[49] The dispossession of the Lenape, as well as of other Indigenous peoples, of their lands of belonging and inheritance, not only provides, as its outcome, the territorial capital and economic infrastructure for all succeeding moments of accumulation in the United States. The processes of such dispossession—principally through settler-colonial fraud, predation, and corporate-government collusion—also act as the very means to establish the historical, legal grounds on which successive corporate powers and moves are sanctioned.

Analyzing key US Congressional statutes and core juridical decisions between 1790 and 1887, Barker finds that the legal erasure of the independent sovereignty and rights of Indigenous nations and their subjection to US sovereignty (on the basis of the doctrine of discovery), as well as the repeated legal sanction of fraudulent federal, corporate, and private individual acquisition of Indigenous territories in the United States, were concomitant with and crucial to the establishment of corporate rights of personhood, and the entitlement to the protections provided therein.[50] Dispossession sets the rules according to which "corporations" and "tribes" would be constituted as political "bodies" with diametrically distinguished political and economic rights and legal recourse. These are the established rules within which finance capital continues to play, garnering political and economic support even in the face of flagrant, criminal behavior and spectacular ruin, precisely because the rules of play *are* "the corporation," the very system and ground on which all successive plays depend. As K-Sue Park demonstrates, foreclosure in the theft of native lands through the extension of credit on the terms of settler's monetary economy served to establish the narrative and legal apparatus that would naturalize that economy in the course of and as the ground of US history.[51] Forms of government and corporate collusion and fraud in the present, as exemplified by government bailout of the banks ("the corporation") during the financial crisis of 2008 (itself catalyzed by the subprime mortgage housing crisis produced by predatory lending), are thus to be seen as recurrent processes of imperial dispossession operating in the present.[52]

As in the history of Indigenous dispossession in the seventeenth-, eighteenth-, and nineteenth-century United States, such processes of imperialism in the present accomplish not just a new round of dispossession of Indigenous peoples' acquired and remaining minimal assets (cash, debit cards, and even food stamp cards as collateral for predatory payday loans and auto loans). They also, significantly, retroactively resanction past dispossessions in the reestablishment of "the corporation" as a recognized "person" entitled to legal protections and state help.[53] From the standpoint of Indigenous peoples, or from what Barker calls "indigenous territory as an analytic," imperialist dispossession repeatedly accomplishes both the accumulation of assets and the establishment of the legal, territorial, financial, and epistemological order through which such accumulation is naturalized, guaranteed, and further enabled. Such dispossession is predicated on the condition of Indigenous peoples' disappearance and the naturalization of an ontological order in which that disappearance is repeatedly performed.[54] The imperial imperative of Indigenous disappearance is closely tied to the imperative of desocialization and depersonalization productive of social death under slavery and its contemporary afterlife, privations that continue to shape and define the state of global servitude and absolute expendability that people find themselves in today (as we will see in parts III and IV).[55]

While the Lockean rationale for deeming native land to be waste, and therefore deserving of settler colonial appropriation for more value-productive ends, is widely noted, what is particularly crucial to highlight in this critical work is the role played by recognition in both historical and ongoing imperial dispossession.[56] As Barker writes, the very recognition of the *existence* of "the Indian tribe" is constituted by the *logos* of imperialist humanism, reflecting the latter's truth criteria while voiding imperialism's own relevance as a condition for conjuring this existence in the ontological and teleological terms of a proper, civilized humanity. In the context of US settler colonial state legal and social entitlements, recognition is "the negation of Native humanity—grief, loss, pain, passion, joy—and the foreclosure of a Native future. And it is all of these things while promising to recognize Natives as equals, as *righted* to self-determination."[57]

Political recognition in the liberal democratic contexts of North America, as Yellowknives Dene political scientist Glen Coulthard shows, has in fact been the means by which Indigenous political rights and residual Aboriginal rights and titles to remaining lands of the Northwest Territories have been surrendered in exchange for a circumscribed set of rights that reduce land to a material resource. In postcolonial nation-states such as the Philippines, such political recognition has also been an important mode of dispossession of Indigenous land and life since US colonization in the early twentieth century differentially integrated these unconquered communities as minority "tribes" within the modern political structure, which colonial tutelage itself installed.[58] Deeply shaped by US Indian policy, this national integration and subordination is precisely what undergirds the continuing impunity of state sovereign violence in the appropriation of Indigenous lands for the good of the nation. In 1974, ostensibly seeking to give overdue recognition to what the US colonial government had dubbed "non-Christian tribes," the dictator Ferdinand Marcos created the Office of the Presidential Assistant on National Minorities (PANAMIN), which acted as an auxiliary agent for the World Bank–funded state project to build four hydroelectric dams in the Chico River basin in the Cordillera Range of Northern Luzon.[59] Under the authority of martial law, Marcos ordered the National Power Corporation to expropriate these lands, which were the ancestral lands of the Bontoc and Kalinga peoples, invoking statutory rights over the land for the greater (national) good: the provision of electrical energy.

Confronted with intense community resistance, PANAMIN offered salaried positions as well as outright bribes of money and women to coopt Indigenous leaders, while army troops were sent to harass and intimidate villagers with raids, arrests, and incarceration as well as strafing. But neither monetary and sexual bribes nor the threat of violence could move people like Macli-ing Dulag, *pangat* or village leader of the Butbut people among the Kalinga, who, despite being detained and threatened for his pivotal role in organizing a broad, unified collective resistance, continued to call into question the terms of that very good life on behalf of which the rights of the whole superseded the survival of the Kalinga as a people. "If you in your search for the good life destroy life, we question it. We say that those who need electric lights are not thinking of us who are bound to be destroyed. Or will the need for electric power be a reason for our death?"[60] For the Kalinga, the submergence of their lands would spell the destruction not only of their livelihood as farmers but also of their very collective life, which depends on honoring the sacred gift of the land and the continuing presence of their dead who have become part of that earth to which they belong. To an army engineer's demand for land titles, Macli-ing countered: "You ask us if we own the land. And mock us, 'Where is your title?' Such arrogance to claim ownership over the land, when it is we who are owned by it. How can you own something that will outlive you?"[61]

Macli-ing was assassinated in his own home by military forces on April 24, 1980. The outrage and protest generated by his killing finally compelled the Marcos government and the World Bank to abandon the project. And yet, nearly forty years later, as the Duterte government mounts three new China-funded mega-dam projects on the same Chico River as part of a major infrastructural state capitalist project (Duterte's "Build, Build, Build" program), we see the continuing negation of the mode of life that the Kalinga defended, a negation enabled by the political recognition of their rights as a people within the scope of national sovereignty. Through the passage of the Indigenous Peoples' Rights Act in 1997, the "individual and collective rights" of the Kalinga as well as those of other Indigenous cultural communities came to be recognized "within the framework of national unity and development in accordance with the Constitution," which means that claims to those rights are now adjudicated through the National Commission on Indigenous People, a government agency established by the same act and placed under the office of the president.

Through this national political recognition of Indigenous peoples, the titling of lands, which the Kalinga and Macli-ing in particular had contested, continues, this time in the form of the "certificate of ancestral domain title" and the "certificate of ancestral land title," legal documents that ensure Indigenous peoples' individual and collective "rights of possession and ownership" to these lands, which the commission oversees. In the Cordillera as well as in other ancestral homes of Indigenous peoples, difficulties in obtaining these legal titles, as well as loopholes in the laws themselves, have enabled the appropriation of Indigenous lands for government-backed extractive mining, logging, and energy industries.[62]

The story here is a very old one, one that continues to be played over and over again. Today, just as in the past, the law is "the instrument by which the people's land is stolen."[63] Or as the regional peasant alliance Alyansa dagiti Pesante iti Taong Kordilyera asserts, with respect to the government agency implementing the Indigenous Peoples' Rights Act, the law is an instrument "to neutralize, coopt or overpower resistance of indigenous communities" against projects of accumulation that depend on their dispossession.[64] The law does so by translating people's *belonging to the land* into claims of *rights over the land*, forcing a shift in the terms of living. It changes the landscape before their very eyes.

Recoding ancestral land as nature and resource (as a means of subsistence), over which Indigenous people have rights of ownership, the rule of law shifts the ground under their feet, putting the protection of such rights in the manipulative hands of state agencies, dividing and splintering the political community that had united in resistance against the Chico River dam project under Marcos.[65] By the side of the Kalinga, we sense a belittling of "indigenous beliefs," a brushing away of "sentiment" for the material presence of the dead, and the subsumption of both as "indigenous knowledge systems and practices," a cultural good to which they have "intellectual rights," one set of rights among the "universal, indivisible, interdependent and interrelated rights of every human being."[66] This process of humanization under the law demands that the Kalinga recognize the law of the nation, rather than Apo Kabunian (Elder Kabunian, their divine spirit), as bearing the power to confer and protect belonging and the life possibilities that such belonging might imply. It demands the alienation of spirituality and divinity from the land. It strips the land of its divinity and endows it with "a new social soul."[67] In so doing, it makes these other claims superfluous. By proclaiming through the language of rights the value of these possessions, it wastes an entire way of life, while preserving it as a milieu for another mode of life.

In this way, the legal-juridical recognition of Indigenous peoples as subjects, whether "righted" or "rightless" (bearing or yet to bear the symbolic endowments of the human, as the embodiment of, and entitlement to, social value), is at once the ontological negation of radically other modes of life, which they also still live, and their epistemological, material dispossession of the very grounds for living (the means of making and making sense of) that life. As contemporary struggles for "land for the landless" attest, the continuation of this dispossession of land is crucial to capitalist accumulation today, even in its most "advanced" forms of exploitation enabled by digital informational technologies.[68] Land as a matrix of life is made into land as an instrument of capture. The landlessness of communities is certainly what continues to act as a crucial urbanizing force. At the same time, territorial sovereignty (state proprietary rights over territory) continues to serve as an instrument of biopolitical control over captive populations, and as a means of financial leverage in debt-fueled economic growth.

The land and life of the Kalinga continue to be bulldozed to make them into environments for proper urban life and its growth. In October 2020, the Department of Public Works and Highways ordered the demolition of the monument built by the Cordillera People's Alliance to honor and memorialize Macli-ing Dulag and others who fought the Chico Dam Project, seeking to erase even the memories of the fight. And yet, people protest and resist against this latest onslaught, the threat they pose to the state attested to by the continued assassinations of land and environmental defenders, which have resulted in the naming of the Philippines as the most murderous country for environmental defenders.[69] People fight and fight to remember, and in so doing, they guarantee that some things remain. Like the words of Macli-ing Dulag, which we, too, remember and continue to pass on here: "The question is life—our Kalinga life."

Ground Rules of Dispossession

If I've dwelt at length on the role of legal recognition as a dispossessive force in relation to Indigenous land, it is because the law is a language, a system of writing, deployed to overcode the land and life of others, so that they might be subsumed as working parts of a world that can make sense (and use) of them. It demonstrates in particular that more general process that is fundamental to global capitalism, which is the destructive and reconstructive operation of imperial coding.

Where the ground rules (the playing field) are themselves the means of erasure and "disappearance" (the means of conversion into the proper terms of the game), the recognition of those rules and of the proper player-subjects by the rule of law becomes a principal means of overwriting (principally, recoding) the very life systems—other orders of life-making and sense-making—that can thereby serve as the milieus of capitalism. Whether in punctuated moments of political and economic crisis or in the seemingly interminable season of Indigenous and anticolonial struggles, the imperial recoding of other lifeworld views and countertales, which surface, take hold, and threaten to shift or disorder that colonized ground of civilized human life (their effective submergence into *liminality*), is the practice of dispossession that precedes and accompanies every moment in the process of commodification.

Luxemburg did not grasp that this coding operation—a continuous material and symbolic process of inscribing forms of life as non- or less than human in a vital relation to capitalism as *the* human mode of life—is part of the "constant process of metabolism" between capital and its noncapitalist milieu. Yet, in the midst of revolutionary, decolonizing, anti-imperialist, labor and civil rights, environmental, and radical antiracist, feminist liberatory social movements, renewed and pronounced after World War II, Marxist feminists saw in Luxemburg's insights an extant structural relation of dispossession and appropriation that applied to all unfree, nonwaged forms of human and nonhuman labor and life (women, colonies, nature) with respect to capitalist accumulation. Black and third worldist feminists in particular also apprehended the "interlocking" sex-gender and race codes through which this relation of appropriation and dispossession continues to be organized, and the perpetual threat and infliction of violence alongside ideological coercions and compensations through which that relation of "so-called original accumulation" is perpetually secured.[70] More, they grasped that these "heterogeneous" relations (imperial, sexual, racial) "where the rules and regulations governing wage-labor are suspended" were intrinsic to capitalist accumulation.[71]

Many now acknowledge the role of the imperial plunder of the Global South (and of the convenient catch-all of so-called noncapitalist milieus, "women, nature, colonies") in capitalist accumulation.[72] But even among those who pay homage to the "price" these social and natural worlds have paid and continue to pay, few have paid attention to this matter of coding, except as the practice of abstraction (the unifying metrics) in the making of exchange value. And yet the history of colonialism has been nothing if not also the development of coding systems for the organization of capitalist processes in *all* its relations, programming protocols not only for the making and reproduction of "labor" in its relations to capital (relations of production), but also for the making and maintenance of other key components of capital—notably, the raw materials and instruments of labor, or "means of production," including the disposable social formations and modes of living constituting capital's "noncapitalist milieus," not least the "land" claimed for possession by rights of discovery, eminent domain, and legal recognition.

Organizing the meaning and function of land and life for colonial gain, a modern grammar of sex-gender and race in particular came to act as the means for the centuries of capture and compelled reproduction of free "natures," out of which "surplus" the elemental and scaling constituents of commodity, money, and capital would be continuously built, ultimately structuring the ecological, geographical, political, economic, and social lifeworlds that are given to us as countries and regions in the geopolitical world of the present. These were and continue to be codes working in tandem and in contradiction to produce reproductive outcomes conducive to colonial domination and capitalist gain: codes of sex-gender as a mode of making familiar, subordinate, and supplementary; codes for the making of colonial as well as "domestic and dependent" territories—of civilizing, domesticating, and regulating what is wild, savage, "natural" (uncultivated, unsettled), which it also serves to index, as well as of making deviant and freakish, "unnatural" and useless (unreproductive) and therefore unfit for survival; racial codes as a mode of creating absolute social distance, of negating, discounting, and eviscerating the social, and therefore human, value of the captive, enslaved, and domesticated in order to treat them as beasts, chattel, and machines; codes of making objects of property, things with properties, comprehensible and capturable—making empirical and masterable, subject to sovereign control and experiment; as well as codes of figuring chaos and disorder, pure entropy.

In a limiting logic of combinatory, syntactical "messages" (*Nature is a bitch*; *Filipinas are little brown fucking machines fueled by rice*), these sex-gender and race codes of organizing social practice have been crucial in the establishment of colonial, Christian dominion over distant civilizations and lifeworlds; in the propagated reproduction of human and nonhuman species as colonial and capitalist forms of wealth; in the development of monoculture plantation systems as models for capitalist industry (in manufacturing as much as in agribusiness) up to the present-day; and in national as well as transnational biopolitical population management and control.

Modern Codes of Value: Land, Labor, Life

Sex-gender and race codes develop out of and shape the history of global capitalism, at every step of the way. They form the social history of capital, in the originary and abiding form of land as *means* of production (taken through territorial conquest and enclosure, developed through colonial encomiendas and haciendas, mines and plantations, where land was both means of production and source of free labor, and today under the regulatory command of nation-states as territorial-jurisdictional authority over people, land, and life). These codes also inscribe and organize the social history of the commodity, foundationally the human commodity in its early colonial forms (as forced Indigenous and abducted and enslaved African slave labor) and, as Jennifer Morgan importantly demonstrates, through the appropriated reproductive capacities of enslaved black women, the history of commodity capital with speculative potential for "increase."[73] As we will see, sex-gender and race codes figure contemporary forms of the labor commodity (as nominally "free" yet heavily coerced and disciplined forms of wage labor). Beyond their important and extant role in shaping divisions of labor through normative social identities (social norms for reproducing dominant relations of production), sex-gender and race codes also operate as subrules in the organization of capitalist production.[74]

There has been an immense body of important scholarship on the role that social identity categories of gender, sex, and race have played in the valuation and devaluation of different laboring populations, both historically and in the contemporary moment. Whether in the constitution of the proper "white working class" in the United States through ideological and materially motivated racial divisions among diverse laboring populations;[75] or in the import of "coolie" labor in the Americas to replace slave labor in the course and wake of nineteenth-century abolition and emancipation;[76] or in the structuring of waged domestic service by African American women in the US South, Mexican American women in the US Southwest, and Japanese American women in California and Hawai'i in the nineteenth century;[77] or in the stratification of contemporary health care service work, particularly nursing, in the United States, Canada, and elsewhere;[78] or in the "feminization" of industrial labor in Mexican, Chinese, and Southeast Asian factories in the 1980s–2000s,[79] the codes of sex, gender, and race figure prominently in the organization of social groups comprising hierarchized national and transnational divisions of labor.

My own earlier work explored the role of sex-gender and race in the coding of political and economic relations among nation-states within the region of the Asia-Pacific (what I called the "sexual economies" of the new world order) and the effects of such coding—carried out through international trade treaties, national political and developmental policies, and economic strategies—on the gendered, sexualized, and racialized labor conditions of women, men, and children in the Philippines in the late twentieth century.[80] Viewing the operation of these codes at this geopolitical level of exchange relations and practices among nation-states allows us to better see how the very geographical terrain and geopolitical territories of the "world" over which capitalism prevails as a global mode of life are already the product and also the continuing means of development of these coding systems in a longer history of colonialism.

That is to say, these coding systems of sex, gender, and race (and, crucially, age), which operate in spheres of production, are historically developed through proprietary relations to the land, people, and life that colonial powers took as the direct means of their accumulation of value. Thus colonial practices do not merely install prior sex, gender, and race systems of coding and organizing social practice in the colonies, as is most obvious in the later imperial moment of "humanization" (through bourgeois civilizing institutions of mass education, self-government tutelage, public health, judicial reform, banking systems, and so on, for example, in US colonial Philippines). Colonial practices are also crucial in the development of the very sex-gender and racial coding systems that obtain as transferable disciplinary social and cultural logics regulating modern normative social identities, through "basic" bourgeois social institutions such as the heteronormative nuclear family.

Colonial practices, in other words, become part of the codes themselves—the "subrules" subtending not only the extant humanism of liberal democracy, with its juridically regulated representative identities (the ideal and normative, binary expressions of gender and sexuality). These colonial codes also subtend the very field of operations of modern political economy, the geopolitical world of nations, regions, and peoples on which variant modern sociopolitical orders (disciplinary, liberal, fascist, authoritarian) operate.[81]

In the contemporary global political economy of life, where all life is to be subsumed in the production and extraction of capitalist value (however impossible such an aspiration might be), these codes remain central, if not even more salient. As has been highlighted in the scholarship on global domestic, care, and sex work, they figure prominently in the capitalist reorganization of reproduction as a value-productive global industry. They also figure prominently in the production of criminalized and enemy populations as material for the global "security" industry. They provide organizing logics in the unequal distribution of life-detail and life-chances—in the grossly discriminatory, now algorithmic, allocation of the burdens of vitality and mortality that fall to lives of serviceability and lives of absolute expendability.

Sex-gender and race are primary codes shaping the contradictory socioeconomic relation between valued and disposable life, a key structural dynamic of the finance-driven global capitalist economy. They compose the protocols for parsing out not only whole social existences but also divisible "life-times" in terms of value and waste, that is, in terms of their accumulability and disposability. As such, they continue to be salient in a moment when capitalism works at ever smaller, or infrasocial, as well as ever larger, or suprasocial, scales—insofar as what they have made and shaped and continue to make and shape is nothing less than *the life-form of value.*

3

BECOMING-HUMAN IN A TIME OF WAR
Remainder

> No human contact, but relations of domination and submission which turn the colonizing man into a classroom monitor, an army sergeant, a prison guard, a slave driver, and the indigenous man into *an instrument of production*. —AIMÉ CÉSAIRE, *Discourse on Colonialism*

The Life-Form of Value

What, after all, is the human if not the life-form of value? What is essential for capital is exchange value, the abstract, quantifiable character of commodity things that makes for their exchangeability, which is determined by the "socially necessary" labor time required to produce it. The measure of "socially necessary" labor time has historically been productive human labor, that is, the specifically human time spent in the making of recognizable *social* use values, by which is meant use values for other humans—according to what Sylvia Wynter identifies as "the new master code of the bourgeoisie and of its ethnoclass conception of the human."[1] Value, in this sense, already bears the imprints of what a colonial order underwriting capitalism defined as distinctly *human* activity, as opposed to nature, embodied in the being of natives, slaves, and women.² Set apart from the world of commodities (as alienable nature, property, and chattel goods, including slaves) and the colonial capitalist relations of their production, the human embodied in the power and being of the colonial bourgeois master thereby becomes the universal independent measure and store of value. The human expresses the "sublime objectivity" of its "soul of value," mirroring the sovereign power and being of its Christian God.³

While the moral-social category of the human has broadened to differentially include its former others (defined in sociological racial, gendered, and national terms), it has not fundamentally altered its functions as a determinant and expression of value. If the human has ceased to operate, or has at least become attenuated, as a limited, concrete normative social ideal (the subject of bourgeois humanism), it has nevertheless attained the sublimated force of an abstract universal form, operating in the circulatory systems of global social life in the image of its apotheosis, capital. Indeed, as the independent being of *value in motion*, a being *unified and consistent* throughout multifarious transformations of substance in spatially and temporally dispersed processes of production, over which it exercises singular sovereign command, capital is the model and epitome of the sovereign human subject that was once its controlling agent. While a distinctly human life historically defined it, value now becomes the life-in-itself that determines—through its amniotic atmosphere, the global economy—the lives of all. We might say then that the human is now *no more* than the life-form of value.

The life-form of value thus refers to the ways of living and function of individual human lives (the human function) as bearers of a social value that is potentially capitalizable or convertible to other forms of value: the commodity form, the money form, the capital form—the last of which is exemplified by the celebrity life, the mediatic capture of others' life-times of attention, and more generally by the neoliberal subject acting as entrepreneur of their own life.⁴ The capital subject, the incarnation of value in its independent being-in-itself and movement of growth, bears the codes of social valuation through which capital ascended as a dominant social form. It expresses the "character" of colonizers, slave owners, white settlers, bosses, and lords, whose command over lesser life embodies the very command, or power of disposition, over the life-times of others that capital would ultimately subsume and that money mediates.

Though the human function is no longer the Human (the subject of man in the image of God), it bears the Human's historical and genealogical imprints as a form of genetic code. As hierarchical relations of colonialism, sex-gender and race enter into the very constitution of the life-form of value, comprising informatic protocols for comparing and differentiating and parsing out not only whole social existences but also divisible "life-times" or times of living in terms of value and waste, that is, in terms of their accumulability and disposability. While under the contemporary political economy, all life has the capacity to yield value, it is the sex-gender and racial entailments of the human that determine the highest-value life. The generalization of the commodification (and financialization) of human life has in fact resulted not in a flattening of differences but simply in their scalar reconfiguration such that life-times of value, while linked to and associated with the historical forms of being human (self-possessed, propertied, white heteromasculine sovereign subjects), are no longer contained and unified within those units we call sociological individuals ("lives") but are available to and livable by others, at least in discrete moments that may not necessarily add up or accumulate to a life worth living. We thus also see the work of sex-gender and race as the effect and means of differentiation between a distinctly human labor (as source of value) and nonhuman means of production (tools, machinery, and raw material), creating the social differentiation and relation between capitalizable life (life as labor), serviceable life (life as infrastructure), and absolutely expendable life (life as waste).

What is important to remark on here is that the imperial dispossession that continues in the present is therefore not to be viewed simply as a matter of appropriation of existing, past and present, forms of objectified wealth. It is also, as Wynter's work has particularly and importantly emphasized, a matter of *coding*—in the international context, the coding of noncapitalist or nonhuman social worlds in ways that place them and their living capacities in the service of the capitalist mode of production.[5] More precisely, it is in the service of the capital-labor relation, wherever that relation might be found. Constant coding, which carries out the divestiture of those worlds of the means of their sense-making, which is also their means of life, is a necessary means to ensure that the "constant process of metabolism" of original accumulation between capitalism and its noncapitalist milieus continues— to reproduce the "service" those milieus provide (as means of production). It is part of the process of subsumption that Michelle Murphy redefines as "the making of the surround itself, the creation of the atmospheres and assemblages that capitalism conjures for itself and as its own context."[6] If life has been "economized"—parsed out through measures of discrepant worth—it is because "the economy" (now acknowledged as global) has become the very atmosphere in which the life of humans is perceived to be possible at all.

The constant coding and remaking of noncapitalist or not fully human milieus is necessary, for the lay of the land for capital powers ("land" as part of its own enabling environment) has not been set once and for all, can never be fully or finally fixed.[7] Land, as Indigenous peoples have always known, is a complex living matter, a living matrix, made possible and making possible native life and all other life.[8] It is precisely because it is alive, a matrix of life, that land, and the nonhuman natures for which it serves as synecdochic part, can be treated (but only through the violence of relentless war) as a "substitute for machinery," as "a force of production in servitude to the commodity form."[9]

In Servitude to the Commodity Form

In the twenty-first century, the commodity par excellence is life, that is, valued life. We might say then that the noncapitalist milieus of today are diverse other modes of living *in servitude to the life-form of value*. As Eduardo Galeano surmised in his devastating epic chronicle of the centuries of barbaric colonial rule over Latin America, the metabolism between those whose specialization is to gain and those whose specialization is to lose is maintained through an international relation of servitude: "The centuries passed and Latin America perfected its functions. It is no longer the reigning era of wonders where reality vanquishes myth and imagination is humiliated by the trophies of conquest, the lodes of gold and the mountains of silver. But the region continues working as a female servant [sigue trabajando de servienta]."[10]

Galeano understood that this relation of feminine servitude constituted the "open veins" through which the colonizer drained the colonized of its natural wealth (*la riqueza de la tierra*), of generations of human and nonhuman life—millions of native peoples (*indios*) "devoured," poisoned, crushed, and used up as fuel (*el combustible*) in the silver mines of Bolivia and the gold mines of Brazil, massacred from the time of Columbus to the present; in Uruguay, Argentina, Mexico, and Guatemala their lives turned into the precious metals and riches that powered European empire and its fledgling mercantile system; millions of abducted and enslaved Africans, brutally spent to procure the very gold with which they were bought and sold, the unprecedented mass scale of their trade as commodities acting as the force that "multiplied the ships, factories, railroads, and banks" of mercantile capital, which their own labor in sugar, coffee, and other monocultural plantations (especially sugar plantations) produced, proving that, as Sergio Bagú wrote in 1949, slavery in the Americas was "the most potent force for the accumulation of mercantile capital," which in turn became "the foundation stone on which the giant industrial capital of modern times was built."[11] These were the effects of a geopolitical, gendered relation of servitude established in the fifteenth century, which, Galeano understood, continued to the present day.

Writing at the height of anti-imperialist third worldism in 1971, Galeano envisioned this relation as obtaining predominantly between nations and between regions of nations, as well as between national racial and class elites and subalterns, between internal socio-geographical centers and peripheries. Yet in his own detailing of the life-consuming colonial violence that founds global capital well into the present, Galeano is able to foreground a crucial metabolism between life expenditure and the autonomous wealth of capital that today works on a variety of scales less strictly bounded by these historical social forms.

The colonizers turned the subjugated Indigenous peoples and enslaved Africans into coin: "The poor Indian a coin with which one can get whatever one needs, as with gold and silver, and get it better," wrote one mine owner in the sixteenth century. "Slaves were called 'the coins of the Indies' when they were measured, weighed and embarked in Luanda in the Portuguese colony of Angola," exported to be exchanged for clothing, liquor, and firearms.[12] The colonized were circulated and used like other commodity forms, but as currency they were in a specific relationship to capital: of the same substance but on an opposite trajectory, that is, on a trajectory of being spent rather than a trajectory of growth and accumulation. As we will see in chapter 5, this relation between two kinds of money—coin and capital, medium of exchange and means of valorization—operates in the present as disjunctive but deeply connected moments of depreciation and valorization of life-times in the financialized global economy, a relation that also subtends the distinction between the soft currencies of human disposability and the hard currencies of human value.

The life-consuming colonial violence that Galeano painfully chronicles can be understood as the violence of "the willful expenditure of the Other," which Lindon Barrett argues is the occluded origin of value, whereby violences performed on the other are rendered other, disfigured as value-making forces through the establishment of boundaries in order to realize value as the form of a privileged and preeminent being (the white self, or what Denise Ferreira da Silva analyzes as the transparent subject).[13] Barrett's formulation of these processes of (cultural, racialized) valorization in the context of US literary criticism allows us to see the symbolic operations fundamental to the operation of value, operations that issue out of and accompany the material expenditure of degraded and "impeached" life (coded as black) on which capital accumulation depends, from its originating instance under colonial and chattel slavery to its afterlife in the movement of capitalist valorization at all instances.

The other of value discloses a violating force, "an original, violent expenditure," which is occluded in its objectification as a devalued thing—blackness—even as that violence remains a force both *determining* and *unsettling* the dualism to which it gives rise. These dynamics are exemplified in the extrajudicial killings in the Philippine war on drugs, as well as in the continued killing of Black people in the US law-and-order war on crime, as much in the enforced deaths of migrants on the US-Mexico border and in the border zone of the Mediterranean Sea as in the relentless massacres in Gaza and in the global war on terror. These contemporary wars to be human bear the codes of the metabolism established between life expenditure and the autonomous wealth of capital that Galeano traces to the colonization of the New World and its five hundred–year aftermath. In them we see the production of absolutely expendable life in the ever-morphing, amorphous, monstrous figure of criminality and perversity as the casus belli on the part of states and their constituencies seeking to retain or gain the supreme powers of the capital form of value.[14]

What seems crucial to add to this formulation of the complex dialectic between value and its occluded "exorbitant foundation"—as well as to the waste-value dialectic elaborated by Gidwani and Maringanti (with which it is aligned)—is the no less important geopolitical relation of servitude through which this metabolism is maintained and reproduced—the mediating agency between absolutely expendable life and capital value. Servitude is the code not only for a degraded, feminized (domesticated) kind of natural work, but for the wholesale naturalized subordination, degradation, and instrumental use of lesser life (predominantly lands/territories and peoples/races) to meet the needs and wants of greater, human life.[15] Latin American dependency theories, world development or underdevelopment theories, and third worldist critiques of neocolonialism often used notions of indentured servitude to highlight the structural subordination of peripheral nations to core, metropolitan powers. Comprador states and their postcolonial bourgeoisies were rightly seen as bought, through international loans, foreign aid, and a variety of coercive means, into "servicing" the needs of metropolitan capital. But the neocolonial relation was critically depicted in ways that also underscored the emasculation of these nation-states with respect to their former masters, evincing the way the master gender codes of sovereignty and agency continue to be absorbed by those who would critique the neocolonial relation.[16]

The gendered servitude that anticolonial and anti-imperialist movements protested also entailed a gendered difference that obtained between these client crony capitalist states and the life of the nations that they helped to indenture, and ultimately to expend, to "service" the debts. That "life" is offered up in the form of the nation's natural resources—feminized biogeographical properties—that must of their own accord find ways to survive and reproduce (with the "rehabilitating" aid of international development, an early form of "workfare" in its command of work for assistance), in the midst of its own unremitting expenditure. The servitude of postcolonial nations thus provides the model for what they will themselves produce in the contemporary moment: domestic, care, and other reproductive labor that is a form of serviceable life subordinated to the "needs" of productive capital life. Its history arguably extends before capitalism to the colonial practice of the encomienda system, whereby a feudal Christian relation of compulsory service/servitude (*servidumbre*) to God and king was extended as form of *franchise* (*encomendar* is to entrust, commend, and give charge of) awarded to conquerors in the Spanish colonial territories in the New World and in the Philippines, which granted them monopoly over the land, labor, and fruits of native life as rewards for securing and controlling these territories on behalf of the crown. In this view, global servitude is a relation that does not begin with the globalization of reproductive labor but rather culminates in it.[17]

Today the relation of dispossession between disposable living and valuable life also permeates every moment of every day of capitalist time. To understand this relation as "servitude," however, is to perceive that the noncapitalist, "nonhuman" milieus of capitalist exploitation—which serve as forms of "machinery," instruments or means of capitalist production—have also always consisted of forms and forces of survival on the part of those who serve, the plural forms of living they make in a time of war.

Neither Simply Cheap Inputs, nor Extra-economic Costs, but Live and Living Forces

Just as land and soil are not mere sites and sources of the event of plunder that provides appropriated capital (already objectified wealth) for expanded capitalist production, the "milieu" of the nonhuman, noncapitalist environments and lifeways on which capital depends consists not simply of alienable, extractable entities or "property" (with sets of material and symbolic use values, or, intrinsic "properties," as in a substantive notion of labor), nor even simply of unremunerated, hidden "labor," or work. Just as importantly, this "milieu" consists of transpersonal *faculties* and *capacities* (converted into functions and instruments), which play important roles in generating and maintaining the continuing service that the strata of becoming-human provide.

Techniques of contemporary dispossession, including predation, fraud, privatization, financial devaluation, and outright destruction, certainly solve the problem of the overaccumulation of capital from the previous era by releasing valuable assets—land, air, water, labor power, infrastructure—at very low, next-to-nothing costs for a new round of productive use and investment.[18] The "freeing" or extraction of hitherto protected, bounded, common, or withheld assets or resources for capital is, however, only one aspect of the contemporary role of original accumulation.

In his own 1975 analysis of primitive accumulation as "a permanent, and until now an *accelerating* phenomenon" of the free transfer of values, the anthropologist of slavery Claude Meillassoux argues that the only way that value can be extracted *continuously* through original accumulation, is by *preserving* the dominated domestic mode of production.[19] Writing in a moment of global transition when newly independent former colonies were targeted for capitalist integration and underdevelopment, Meillassoux notes the essentially paradoxical process by which "the domestic mode is simultaneously maintained and destroyed—maintained as a means of social organization that produces value from which imperialism benefits, and *destroyed* because it is deprived in the end of its means of reproduction, under the impact of exploitation. Under the circumstances the domestic mode of production both exists and does not exist."[20] Even as he emphasizes the role of *maintaining* noncapitalist social formations within the imperial relation, however, Meillassoux does not account for the inventive agency of domestic communities in preserving (or better, persisting in and renewing) their modes of life and, what's more, in creatively adapting and transforming these *means of social organization* as important means of capital's relentless growth.

That is to say, imperialism's outsize agency in maintaining inherently heterogeneous relations between capitalist exploitation and its noncapitalist milieu (an important corrective to the notion that capitalism is essentially homogenizing) eclipses the role of domestic communities' *survival*—their creative persistence, adaptation, and invention of life-making in the face of their paradoxical destruction and preservation as an auxiliary mode of production to capitalism. As we will see, without the continued life-making of these other strata, primitive accumulation could not continue to be a *permanent* and *accelerating* mode of global capitalism. Only a regard for the social survival of the becoming-human—social arts of *living* in the suffocating thick of permanent catastrophe—will allow us to see subaltern forces of making that have been indispensable to the operation and expansion of this global mode of life, to glimpse what the most powerful and ambitious political-critical claims would foreclose or forget out of fatal indifference and neglect.

Luxemburg understood that colonial expansion is always accompanied by "capital's relentless war on the social and economic interrelations of the Indigenous inhabitants and by violent looting of their means of production and their labor power," and that the means of production and labor-power of these formations are indispensable to capitalism, wrested by it, and annihilated as independent social structures. In a feminist spirit, in contrast to the masculinist glorifying focus on violence, she also perceived that it was the strength of the social bonds of Indigenous inhabitants that imperialists sought to destroy through this relentless war, that these formed "the strongest bulwark both of their societies and of the latter's material basis of existence."[21] But she did not anticipate how these very social bonds, the social organizational means of survival of these very formations meant to be annihilated, would themselves become part of the directly appropriable means of production of capital, subsumed as forms of infrastructure and machinery for contemporary capitalist enterprises. To understand the current moment of capital's expanded reproduction hence means to cognize the importance not only of the survival of these "noncapitalist" social formations, but also, crucially, of the persistence and adaptive dynamism of their own life-making and sense-making activity. It means to apprehend the milieus of capitalist accumulation as *live* formations and forces.

Continuously assaulted in order to be destroyed as polities and economies independent of capitalist command, yet at the same time recurrently "abandoned" to their own imperiled fates, colonized and postcolonial social formations survive through modes of social reproduction—modes of *living*—that exceed the protocols of reproduction under capital command. Only in this way, in their social survival through changing modes of social life-making and organization, which go beyond the delimited boundaries of capitalist reproduction (in excess of the necessary reproduction of labor), can these live formations paradoxically continue to serve as "noncapitalist" milieus of capital growth. As I will argue in more detail in this book, it is precisely owing to this fact, that the modes of social reproduction of the becoming-human come to figure as instruments of production—as precisely a form of *machinery*—subordinated to the commodity form of productive life. Insofar as these machines are also programmers of their own platforms, they are also subaltern *drivers* of global capitalism.

Other Modes of Living: Serving a Way of Life

What makes the destructive forces of open-ended counterinsurgency or permanent small wars profitable then is not only the capitalization of state military-security activities (weapons manufacturing and "security" services, including border policing and prison management), but also the creation of a whole array of other auxiliary services—communicative and cognitive labor, reconstruction industries, and life rescue and recovery operations (private security, intelligence, infrastructure, refugee camps)—developed around war.

Investigative journalists and social activists have compellingly detailed the most recent historical forms of state and corporate collusion in the creation of conditions of profit-making through war as a form of "disaster capitalism."[22] They detail, for example, the operations of private military companies (PMCs), paradigmatic examples of the twenty-first-century "corporation," which, as the managing director of one PMC working in Afghanistan put it, "survives off chaos."[23] PMCs deliver a service that increasingly, they claim, states cannot provide—security, assistance, and ultimately the very running of empires. In offshored sites of what are effectively present-day concentration camps, multinational private security companies such as Serco and G4S are in the business of managing and processing refugees, surplus populations "freed" up through war. Refugees are people whose own accumulated value and capacities for social reproduction are, in one blow or in innumerable attacks, destroyed through war. They consist not merely of those forced to move, floating populations with ever reduced chances of permanent residence. As demonstrated in open prisons of occupation (such as Gaza, Afghanistan, and Iraq), closed prisons of judicial punishment, urban slums and ghettoes, and forsaken periurban and rural zones, refugees also consist of those who are pushed into indefinite territorial and temporal confinement by legal, economic, and social forces of imperial dispossession.

As I argue in the next chapter, we miss too much if we understand these groups of people and their captive lives principally through the category of "labor."[24] Undoubtedly, recent imperial wars have been at the center of a new round of global proletarianization, freeing up new and ever-cheapened pools of wage labor. However, in the case of refugee camps, prisons, detention centers, and other sites of security and border control, "superfluous" populations serve, before their selective processing into migrant labor, as matters requiring attention, response, action: management, transportation, containment, disposal. They compose machinic flows for the pipelines (school to prison; war to camps/slums), bureaucratic and legal channels, and centers for processing and warehousing that they become instrumental in making. They are aggregate matter propelling the innovation of capitalist forms.[25]

Private military companies exemplify the way security and punishment have evolved into capitalist industries, which produce the means and conditions of their own expanded reproduction. Angela Davis points out, "The term *prison industry* can refer precisely to the production of prisoners even as the industry produces profits for increasing numbers of corporations and, by siphoning social wealth away from such institutions as schools and hospitals, childcare and housing, plays a pivotal role in producing the conditions of poverty that create a perceived need for more prisons."[26] What Davis calls attention to is the fact that "production" in this sphere of capital accumulation entails not just the siphoning of public funds (tax money disbursed by the state), but also the active remaking of the social landscape to serve as the enabling milieu of the industry. The disinvestment in social welfare (schools, hospitals, childcare, housing), or the active "wasting" of the institutions supporting marginalized social life, which the prison industry (and more broadly the security industry) commands through the state, provides both the ideological legitimation and motivation ("a perceived need") and, I would underscore, the practical, material environment ("conditions of poverty," but also "criminal" labor markets in the illegal economy in which people make their livelihood) for making the very individual lives that are at the very center of the prison industry. These lives, shaped by a produced environment, become material for "the production of prisoners"—yielding the life-times of sheer waiting/life wasting, units of time whose forced expenditure is at the center of "production" of the security industry).[27]

Proven to be expanding industries, prisons and detention centers are now global businesses locally franchised by imperial states, drawing on local populations both for labor (as police, prison guards, and other prison/detention center employees) and, importantly, for the social refuse (prisoners/detainees), or life-times of waste, they are tasked to designate, store or (ware)house, and process, manage, or productively expend. Further, as these lives come to count as populations, they become part of all manner of numerical calculus placed to political and economic ends. Alfred McCoy has shown, for example, how with the carceral regime's concentration of US prisons in conservative, rural districts, the numbers of permanently politically disenfranchised prison populations, as well as their prison guards, are put into play in the creation of "rotten boroughs" supporting the Republican Party.[28]

While the meting out of violence has undoubtedly become a general mode of value extraction on which many security enterprises are now based, enterprises that have proliferated around the byproducts and casualties of permanent war are not limited to those based on the delivery of forms of punishment. The Asia-Pacific regional security wars of the Cold War, which aimed at containing the threat of communism and making the world safe for capitalism, have in the last decades transmogrified into the "peace and development" strategies of the US government involving "international development and disaster assistance" in regions destroyed and reeling in the aftermath of more than half a century of counterinsurgent wars.[29] Both the World Bank and USAID (US Agency for International Development) have now become "stakeholders" (partners and investors) in multinational projects of "relief, rehabilitation, and development" conducted in sites of "humanitarian crisis" such as Mindanao, in the southern Philippines, a zone of continuing counterinsurgent warfare. Partnering with the US Department of Defense through a 2008 "civilian-military cooperation policy" agreement, which formally laid down "a whole-of-government approach to contemporary national security," USAID shifted its mission from international development assistance as Cold War foreign policy strategy (emerging out of the Marshall Plan) to international aid as financial investment in complete social reconstruction, including projects in agriculture and food security, biodiversity conservation, governance, environmental management, gender equality and women's empowerment, financial technologies and electronic payment ecosystems (mobile money platforms), education, infrastructure (water, sanitation, housing), maternal, child, sexual/reproductive, and community health, and sustainable urbanization.[30]

In these ways, the domestic and global security department of capital operates not simply as a manufacturing industry (as in the weapons industry of the military-industrial complex) but also and moreover as a service industry.[31] Provisioning biopolitical goods and utilities (health, food, water, shelter) to the very populations it has attempted to destroy, the civilian-military–defense-development complex lives off chaos, crisis, and conflict—*selling "life" back to those from whom it had taken it*. In its destructive operations, therefore, permanent war acts at the same time as a form of financial speculation—an investment in "wasting," destruction, and accelerated mortification that, through proliferating enterprises of security, crisis management and rebuilding, will generate more "futures" of surplus value extractable in the present. A vital-mortal business model, this.

These are derivative enterprises of the war to be human, which has found yet more ways to humanize those whom it continually strips of other modes of life-making and sense-making in order to furnish them with the languages, tools, channels, and connections for rebuilding social life (the provisions of capitalist platforms and communicative cultures) in ways that hold out the ideals of life worth living as the eventual goal of indenturing oneself in its service. Expanding beyond arms production to militarized culture production and to security services beyond national defense (ensuring food and medicine provision, guarding intellectual property rights, supply chain flows, currency transfers, vital systems and corporate protection), the derivative enterprises of war certainly rely on a share of already produced capital (extracted and issued through taxation). But they also produce proliferating forms of new value production and value extraction out of what would seem to be secondary and tertiary businesses of "redressing" the continuing damage that capitalism and its necessary wars inflict on the world, reconstructing and rebuilding entire social environments to protect against the historically produced "vulnerabilities" of certain peoples to poverty, conflict, and other forms of humanitarian crisis, and strengthening their resilience against impending and ambient disasters. These are "vital systems" projects, that is, projects to install systems critical to the political and economic order of a capitalist way of life (infrastructural channels and network systems of communication, finance, transportation, food, water, and energy in the ever-improved, sustainable development model of advanced capitalist societies). Rather than the installation of particular social norms (the imperial project of a prior bourgeois humanism), these projects are environmental, infrastructural, and systems changing.[32] And they are enormous sites of investment.

Through its multiplying derivative enterprises, permanent war becomes a province of accumulation in its own right, and not just a supplement or fix for either industrial or postindustrial capitalism, in so far as it is able to generate a new global array of corollary activity in capitalized spheres of life reproduction and assaulted social survival. After all, what makes for the production of absolute surplus value is the intensified *activity* of social reproduction of disposable lives—lives targeted for productive consumption in wars, policing, border patrol, refugee processing and detention, and other industries of life expenditure—as much as in industries of productive labor exploitation (including immaterial, cognitive, communicative, and affective labor).

Hence, the intensified social reproduction of assaulted Global South communities provides the conditions for the absorption of immense strata of life-making capacities in the capitalist socialization of life reproduction of Global North classes, as evidenced by the global capitalization of domestic, sexual, and care work and service work more generally. This war-led production and sourcing of "freed" life-making capacities of "feminized" members of assaulted Global South communities for the reproduction of the lives of enfranchised globopolitical citizens gives added meaning to the idea of empire or imperialism as a way of life.[33] We could say that the war of the expanded reproduction of capital (the war to be human of capital itself) is "the way of life" of the globopolis, which all other life is made into the means of reproducing. Put another way, the war of the expanded reproduction of capital is "life worth living"—what would appear to be the means (war) is an end in itself, the very end that it would appear merely to be a way to achieve (the capitalist way of life).

Living and Dying for the Life of Capital

While it would appear then to be only one particular form and constituent part of global capitalism, capitalized reproduction at the same time encapsulates the general mode of capitalism today. That is to say, the capitalized reproduction of globopolitical "life" in a constant state of threatened, rightful existence (and therefore in an endless condition of just war) is front and center of contemporary capitalist accumulation. Not surprisingly, the expanded reproduction of its own valued, chosen mode of life becomes the central mandate of settler colonial democracy: all other life, devalued and inconsequential, must yield to its own overriding "right to exist."[34] Capitalized reproduction is the core of a system of value production that draws ever more directly on the reproductive activity of sheer human (and nonhuman) survival for its own continued existence (for its own inhuman "survival" as the vital system of the planet).[35]

In this sense, the capitalized reproduction of "life worth living" (and the corollary processes of its technocratic management and "mercantilization"[36]) can be considered as mere means for the continuation of the capitalist mode of life. Life itself appears only as a means to capital life.[37] This has of course always defined the life of capital, which cannot exist except in the movement of "growth" or expanded reproduction, entailing the subsumption of "life worth expending" made through war. But today, rather than only the state "solely dedicated to saving capitalism from itself," it is all the derivative enterprises of permanent war and reproduction, the vital-mortal system of living-dying that nation-states, militaries, banks, cities, networks, people (individual and collective), and all manner and scale of "corporation" (reconceived as platforms) engage in to extract value, that together are saving the life of capital.

Pressed against the limits of profitability of industrial capitalism in the wake of decolonization, capital now pursues its own leavings—its largest leavings in the spheres of reproductive work left outside the "social factory" and in the spheres of survival of communities continuously assaulted by imperial war.

The socialization of reproduction under capital thus appears as a late global capitalist development in an era of permanent crisis. As the unacknowledged correlate of the global distribution of production, the global distribution of reproduction (its socialization) has become the primary growth driver of the migrant labor industry, the global service economy, and the shift of capital investment from manufacturing "production" to biopolitical, cognitive, immaterial "circulation" and "reproduction" as sites of its highest value extraction (where contemporary exploitation is distributed and multiplied over wider and more layered expanses across the entire social field than in its predecessor, industrial production, which of course had relied on geographical and social peripheries of noncapitalized, cheap "inputs"—raw materials and fixed capital that were "free" or cost next to nothing—as unrecognized sources of value).

Rather than naturalizing this "shift" from delimited spaces of production to "limitless" space-times of reproduction (insofar as space-times of reproduction can multiply and aggregate in varying ways beyond the working day, beyond even its expansion in the 24/7 work life, as these are eked out in ever-more-minute ways, and in multiple spaces simultaneously) as the natural evolution of "real subsumption" (the absorption of the entirety of society within capitalist production), we must see it as the product of the unvanquished and insubordinate social survival of those noncapitalist formations subject to formal subsumption in the long centuries of colonialism.

"Still Unconquered Remnants": Unreckoned Forces of Sociality

Even as reproduction becomes capitalized and thus socialized, it continues to rely on another, devalued and diminished sphere of social reproduction, this time among the becoming-human who rely on older social practices and institutions held over from times purportedly past in order to live and thrive.

The survival of those designated for that paradoxical state of being and not-being, of being destroyed and being maintained, to which the colonized were condemned (the paradoxical condition of living on the part of "those who were not meant to survive," as Audre Lorde puts it) depends after all not only on assimilation to capitalist norms but also on the constant renewal, reinvention, and improvisation of "noncapitalist" social lifeways and bonds.[38] Only in this way can the becoming-human continue to be pressed into service as noncapitalist milieus of capitalist accumulation, to serve in this moment of capital's expanded reproduction as the *vital infrastructure* for the value-productive globopolitical human life that capital has made the medium of its own self-valorization and growth.

If the social bonds that propel the colonized's defense of their own integral and independent ways of native life are the target of counterinsurgent war (bonds that are also purposefully destroyed in the processes of natal alienation and social death undergirding enslavement), it is those very noncapitalist social bonds or relations, whether socially transmitted, inherited, or invented, that have also comprised their genealogical descendants' means of reproducing their communities. For as capital increasingly took and depleted what it could recognize as appropriable wealth (labor, tools, land, people, and their alienable techniques of making), what was left to the social formations that it lived on, as if they were its own naturalized enabling environment (as if nature were man's own "inorganic body"[39]), was their own social reproductive "software": their initially inalienable (but perhaps ultimately technically reproducible and anthropologically representable) systems for continuing, remaking, and furthering their shared domestic, familial, or otherwise consociate life.

More than just their "bodies," which are presumed to be all that is left to workers after the capitalist use of their labor-power (similarly stripped by capital in the process of their constitutive alienation and severance from their independent means of subsistence, as "free" labor), what remains for those becoming-human are transindividual modes of social living, which are at the same time forms of knowledge and know-how transmitted across historical and generational times. In contrast to but also alongside the socialization of the reproduction of wage labor through imperial racialized, gendered relations (through which the becoming-human can gain a living as global third world "women" employed in "women's work") the colonially dispossessed continue to engage in modes of sociality that are part and parcel of their own life-making but that are diminished and devalued, destined for obsolescence, or seen as archaic forms in the relentless expansion of the power and value of "free" individual life.

On the one hand, the social reproductive capacities of the becoming-human (often reified and sold as extrahuman, socially intrinsic, culturally particular, and individually possessed capacities for "care") are subsumed as vital infrastructure or living instruments for the capitalized reproduction of this "free" life.[40] On the other hand, their modes of social reproduction also consist of other social practices and logics not recognized as bearing the lineaments of free, human life. These include dividual social logics in extant gift economies, whereby people wield lines of lineage and affiliation as their own "stock" (in Ilokano, *puón*, social lineage; and *puónan*, capital), in which they are both shares and holders of shares (*kabagián*, relatives, "members" of a shared body, *bagí*), in order to subsidize their affordances of exchange value (i.e., income/wages) and to buoy up their individual lives as well as their collective (kin/family) life. These social mediatic kin networks (in the expanded sense embracing "ritual" as well as domestic familial relations, which have never been simply "biological") are their *vital platforms*, which come with their own sets of particular capacities and needs, both expressed in material and immaterial forms that may or may not be used or "satisfied" by the market.

Vital platforms is my tentative, inadequate translation of a means of social reproduction on the part of the becoming-human—Philippine and Filipino/Filipinx peoples principally but neither definitively nor exclusively—that exemplifies *unreckoned forces of sociality* that figure in the growth of global capitalism but are not wholly the product of capitalist socialization. These unreckoned forces of sociality are harnessed by both states and nonstate movements seeking to capture state power in ways that exceed the compromised settlements of political movements within liberal and neoliberal societies, settlements reached through "rights" and "freedoms" that only further the rule of capitalist value and globopolitical citizenship (the polity of the war to be human). In this way, they bear ambivalent political potentials, everywhere now being explored in the transformation of the world, everywhere readily explained as the outgrowth or perverted consequence of capitalism's financialized, technologized (digital) revolutionary development.

To view such means of social reproduction of the becoming-human as vital to the global economy, its forms of governance, and the political struggles within it is to consider that "the development of the productive forces," which inspires many a revolutionary hope, did not proceed by capital alone. As part of the historical process and metabolic system of capitalism's expanded reproduction—which ultimately depends on spheres of life-making that it must both destroy and maintain; "waste" in order to "free" up to recycle and siphon; jettison from proper capitalist forms ("free" subjects) in order to formally subsume as nonhuman milieus (machinery and infrastructure)—the practices and inventions of social reproduction that people structurally targeted for disposability have had to rely on also necessarily impacted, impelled, and shaped capitalist development. These forms of life-making are what Marx referred to as "the partly still unconquered remnants" of past modes of production that continue to course through the structure and relations of bourgeois society, participating in and informing the latest capitalist developments.[41]

We can see this in the case of what Randy Martin has called the social logic of the derivative, a financial logic of creating value out of generated conditions of risk and volatility, speculating on "immaterial" variations based on the disassembling and reassembling of attributes of things (rather than changes of the things themselves), which manifests itself in the social as the infinite contestability and constant, fluctuating valuation of what once appeared to be stable realities.[42] Rather than being the effect or result of the digitalization and financialization of capital, we might consider that this social logic of derivatives has operated in postcolonial contexts as a matter of both survival and rapacity. Under postcolonial conditions, where the ideals and structures of a proper capitalist democracy are impeded if not completely foreclosed by the imperial relation, the logic of derivatives can be found in practices of the pricing of contingencies, of extracting value through the hazarding and fixing of a present, or of producing goods out of symbolic acts of opening and closing channels, practices that are ubiquitous, from the slums to the highest social circles.[43] Where current discussions of derivatives and debts (almost all in the advanced economies of the Global North) locate political possibility in a reconfiguration of current practices and effects of financialization into opposite formulations ("debt that cannot be repaid," unguaranteed debts, progressive dividualism—"molecular everyday practices that reverse the concept of debt"), we might see an abundance of evidence in the postcolonies that practices of debt, derivatives, and dividualism have long operated in the survival of local cultures, and in their takeover or reverse subsumption of the apparatuses of their colonizers. Such practices account for the perverse and failed, "damaged" forms of the state, governance, and sociality identified in postcolonial nations and subject to the disciplinary regimes of international political oversight even as these very practices now return to the metropolitan nations from which they were outlawed for decades.

What so many commentators on capitalism mistakenly reiterate, even when they are arguing for the creative force of labor, is a history of capital confined to all the developments that capital itself introduces—a reiteration of capital's own understanding of itself—without considering other, longer antecedents for the present, which have been operating in creatively persistent ways through the time of capital. Even those who frame the longer history capitalism within the more encompassing rubric of colonialism attribute all modern phenomena to the originary and founding violences of colonialism. They have become metaphysicians of the contemporary world whose only means of the negation of the present is its absolute totalization and completion (as a condition of its final overturning).[44]

In contrast, many Black, feminist, postcolonial, and queer scholars have called into question the dominant temporalities of global histories of the present.⁴⁵ They encourage our consideration of the plural times (and spaces) of making that course through the ontologies of a global present. Cedric Robinson, for one, calls for the amplification of world history and the deepening of time, finding not only a longer history for modern racism beyond what Western radicals are able to apprehend, confined as they are to the epistemological boundaries maintained by "the political economic code emergent from capitalist society," but also, smuggled in the cargoes of enslaved persons, the hidden transmissions of other terms of humanity, bearing elements of pasts that created a ground in the making of another lineage of living and invention, the Black radical tradition.⁴⁶ Such lineages attest to the presence of other temporalities of living from past modes of production that survive in and as the modes of social reproduction of the becoming-human.

Remaindered Life

It is from this devalued side of social reproduction, the life-making practices of those designated for lives in varying degrees of proximity to a social state of valuelessness, that we might glimpse the immense though not inexhaustible plethora of acts, capacities, associations, and aspirations in practice and sensibilities whose expressive figurations, in the liminal cultural-lingual social formations within which they are exercised, remain minoritarian terms of living, elements of an immanent, transformative political world that is in the making and yet to be realized as such.

I take inspiration from the unrelenting critique made by Black, anti-imperial, and Indigenous feminist movements of the continuing, if mutating, indissoluble bond between the free and the unfree, of surplus value and superfluous being, of the human and the less-than-human, and of the constrictive political imaginations that uphold that bond as the constitutive relation of a seemingly eternal global capitalist mode of life. That critique urges a reimagination of human living and planetary possibility; it urges, as well, projects of building new institutions and ways of life rather than the rehabilitation of old ones or the restitution of losses, such as the losses of rights and past entitlements and glories, incurred under them. To embark on these projects requires the cultivation of our available cultural literacies for expanding our political vocabulary for the forms and temporalities of life that people and their intimacies with other life both hold on to and generate in the process of survival against the willed destinies of their disappearance, in their thriving beyond the conditions of some putative sheer, disposable existence to which they are constantly reduced.

Against the premises and prescriptions of the counterinsurgent philosophical and practical defense of the human that permeates transnational politics, Angela Davis has viewed the question of freedom from precisely the side of the delimited yet always potentially insurgent conditions of assaulted and remaindered life. In an early essay, Davis counters Jean-Paul Sartre's existentialist notion of freedom with an understanding of "the fundamental condition of freedom, that is, the slave's experience of living, human reality."[47] Freedom is the abolition of the master-slave relationship and the negation of the slave's concrete condition, which this relationship defines. At the same time, however, it is this "living, human reality" that is the site of a potential insurgency and, as her later interventions clarify, the condition and object of radical social transformation that such insurgency makes possible.

Davis's argument, in another early essay, that "the slave-master's sexual domination of the black woman contained an unveiled element of counterinsurgency" underscores this far-reaching political viewpoint. The specific subjugated conditions of the black woman's life under slavery, which shapes the experience of the "unnatural" character of her lot (conditions that Davis, in other essays, also characterizes as "the almost total prohibition of endemic social life within the community of slaves," the denial of motherhood and other norms of a natural human life, and the "surrogate" status they occupied with respect to such human norms), are the very conditions that enable her to play "a pivotal role in nurturing the thrust towards freedom."[48] It is the enslaved black woman's *experience* of living and making life under conditions of prohibition and exclusion from "human" life (*including* the denial of endemic social life and its own norms of "natural" human life) that enables the vital part she plays in "nurturing" insurgent potential. Rape was, on this view, a form of terrorism directed toward the destruction of the black woman's potentiality for insurgency as well as that of her community, a potentiality that was "directly nurtured by the social organization which the slaves themselves improvised."[49] We might say that rape was a counterinsurgent assault on the slave communities' independent, creative, and freeing capacities for producing and improvising social and domestic life, beyond the instrumental use of their individual and collective being for the human values begotten by capitalism and slavery.

It is difficult to overemphasize the importance of this critical viewpoint for our present moment, when all life appears to have been subsumed into the biopolitical and necropolitical logics shaping the resource wars of late imperial capitalism. The place of foreclosed humanity is also the place of improvised, experimental, as well as persisting and surviving social life-making and organization—in my understanding, the place of different human becoming, which threatens the order of a proper (and propertied), enfranchised humanity. For Davis, such forms of denied human personhood and surplussed humanity are not confined to slavery. She views this status as obtaining in the postemancipation context of reinvented slavery in the convict lease system and in the context of Black domestic life deemed superfluous and unprofitable under apartheid in South Africa, as well as in contemporary contexts of the systemically neglected and abused health and reproductive capacities of poor women of color; in ideological and physical offensives against single motherhood and against queer, gay, lesbian, and transgender configurations of domestic life, safety, and well-being; and in the expansion of prisons as an institution for disappearing and incapacitating "the detritus of society."

In all these contexts, the position of *remaindered*—neither simply oppressed nor exploited, neither disposable nor wasted—life is a situation bearing possibilities for the radical remaking of "human" social relations. In this way, it is also a site of the necessary reconceptualization of certain naturalized politico-theoretical norms, whether those of worker, woman, or citizen, and of a critical revisioning of the strategies of political movements based on the claim of reappropriation of rightful property (whether understood as labor, sexuality, or rights).

I find both theoretical-political solidarity and inspiration in this consistent stance in Davis's work, which is profoundly abolitionist with respect to the human-destroying, socially ruinous practices and institutions of contemporary global life and unwaveringly focused on the reimagination and remaking of social life as the very condition and meaning of abolition. It urges projects of building new institutions and ways of life rather than the rehabilitation of old ones and bears an understanding of freedom that does not transcend the work of living in the here and now nor forsake a yet-unrealized future for human flourishing. In my view, to embark on this radical project requires the cultivation of our available cultural literacies for expanding our political vocabulary for the forms of life that people generate in the process of survival against the willed destinies of our disappearance and in our thriving beyond the conditions of some putatively disposable existence to which so many of our peoples are constantly reduced.

Modes of social reproduction that are part of the inventions of survival include extant, for lack of a better word, "cultural" modes mobilized and operating in the life-making of social groups of the historically and presently becoming-human. These are other subaltern forms and modalities of life-making that are let to live by indifference or purposive negligence, not eliminated through disciplinary or other forms of normative prescription under capitalism in part because they are the very means by which such groups are kept disposable, insofar as they are at once what help them survive yet paradoxically what code and produce them as devalued life. These are after all forms and practices of social cooperation and imagination, including transpersonal cognitive, affective, aesthetic, and communicative capacities, that are subjected to all forms of racist and sexist phobic forms of disciplinary punishment, diminishment, and cultural enclosure or ghettoization, segregated and jettisoned from the capitalizable properties—skills, capacities, and styles—of life worth living. Such forms of social life are to be gleaned in the low-down habits, uncouth gestures, trashy looks, chaotic conduct, and noisy presence of its member-parts. They are therefore themselves devaluing of the very lives they make possible, insofar as they are markers and makers of life of lesser worth. And yet, embedded in the poiesis and practices of living of these communities are ways of organizing personhood, shared being, and enjoyment that are not entirely overwritten or disciplined by proper forms of human being, ways of making life (and *doing* sociality) for which a flourishing of Black, Indigenous, people of color, feminist, queer and trans writing, art, and culture in our contemporary moment has offered up an abundance of expressive and analytical forms.

To attend to these remaindered forms of life-making and unreckoned forces of sociality, I have sought to understand the role of social reproduction within global capitalism today through the concept of "life-time," which draws on but also expands the concept of "labor time" beyond its masculine, industrial parameters to include racialized and gendered forms of living (domestic reproductive work certainly but also other forms of activity subject to noneconomic expropriation).[50] It is a concept for reckoning with the diverse, unrecognized life-making capacities that people exercise in the creation of value and for the work that living requires, for the being that is a living for people besieged in a time of war. Just as women produce themselves as forms of normative femininity to meet the requirements of the industries that exploit their gendered creative capacities (whether as light manufacturing workers, department store ladies, nurses, maids, or sex workers), people engage in a whole range of socially organized subjective, bodily, cognitive, psychic, and affective practices in the very production of their own lives and beings as particular kinds of labor and in the production of their material conditions, including their social relations, which are the very conditions of capitalist exploitation. The notion of "life-times" refers to these social and cultural capacities and practices, and to the heterogeneous temporalities within which these concretely operate from the standpoint of people's lifeworlds, rather than those activities contained within the homogeneous temporality of abstract labor from the standpoint of capital. In this way, "life-times" is also a concept for foregrounding the texture and qualities of experience and times of living otherwise absorbed within value and waste, and the significance of those textures and qualities for the struggle that living demands.

Remaindered life-times, however, refers to the uses, experience, actions, and effects of reproductive life-times made and lived that are *not* absorbed into the processes of production and maintenance of the life-form of value nor into the processes of generating value from waste. Remaindered life is not disposable life but is the superfluous effect and performances of life-times made and lived by such disposable life in its social reproduction—the excess of life-making (or "survival") that does not merely produce disposable life for capitalist serviceability or expenditure. These are life-times of waste that are not productively consumed in the new political economy of life—that is, neither serviceable life in the production of "life worth living" nor "life worth expending" as mere means of production of valued life (where value does not come from the expiation of expendable life but rather from the mobilizations and activity, the circulation and production that that expiation occasions). But neither is remaindered life to be understood as surplus life, where *surplus* designates an accumulable excess—an embodied or encapsulated measure of extra life-making, a resource that can be channeled to alternative ends (such as the reappropriation of that extra "sociality" as value for ourselves). There is no guarantee that what was remaindered will not find itself valorized at another moment, just as today the "merely reproductive lives" of many have become directly capitalized. Remaindered life is rather a vanishing horizon, one not of potentiality but of actual living without value.

My focus on remaindered life stems from a recognition of capitalism's vitalism—from an understanding that for capital, the object and source of all value is *vitality*, animated and animating capacities that capital associates with the forms of organic life it captures and absorbs (what makes for the specificity of the commodity: labor), even if, in much understanding of captive life itself, those very vital capacities could not exist or make sense without the inanimate world or the dead (which are also animate in their own ways). Under a global capitalism that has become organized around vitality itself as a "product" (the potentially infinite forms of living of humans requiring all forms of cultivated and gathered auxiliary living, and the exploitative cannibalization of the by-products of this mode of production, such as absolutely expendable life), political economy is itself vitalist in its understanding of production. Rather than "immaterial" goods or services, which undoubtedly are the immediate products of this vitalist political economy, it is vitality that is the object of valorization of twenty-first-century capital.

"Vitality" as labor power (in contrast to labor as activity) has of course been understood as that over which the worker sells the "right of disposition."[51] Put differently, what the worker sells is the divestiture of that vitality as "value-positing activity." The "vitality" that does not come fully under the disposition of capital is the set of capacities of social reproduction that maintains the worker, as "a presupposed perennial subject," beyond that provided for by the wage—that is, the "life" that belongs to the worker and those with whom it is shared and cooperatively made.[52] In this way, in my own understanding, vitality is not encompassed by living labor, conceived as the creative capacities of humans. It also happens or obtains in encounters, in interactions with others (ourselves and our others, as well as our other selves). It is not a positive object but a simultaneous happening making (in Filipino, *pangyayari*) that is also a capacity for bringing such happening making about, which is inextricably a part of the "life" that capital sets out to capture and reproduce for its own aims. Vitality then refers also to the vibrations of ephemeral existences that compose the substances and durations that we call "lives," and yet it is not contained by them. My focus on remaindered life is thus a regard for this vitality that surpasses capitalism's own vitalism.

More personally, my attention to remaindered life, as an analytical imperative and political hermeneutic, a mode of regard rather than a particular object (though the attention will yield phenomena to consider), also stems from the peculiar and common social world with which I am intimately and irrevocably connected, a world among many other worlds out of which global servants, service workers, caregivers, drivers, call center agents, seamen, entertainers, daughters, and sisters—helpers—emerge to attend to the reproduction of capital life, becoming serviceable life at the cost of also reproducing the expendable life out of which they are temporarily redeemed. This is a world of ignominious survival, but it is also a world of living with gratuitous splendor.

INTERREGNUM

Times of War

For ten years before her first solo exhibition, *Found Figures*, in 2007, Philippine artist Kiri Dalena was a political documentary filmmaker and member of Southern Tagalog Exposure (ST Exposure), an independent media collective committed to representing the social struggles of disenfranchised and minority communities in the Philippines, as well as the struggles of political resistance and liberatory movements in the Southern Tagalog region. Portraying internal refugees from militarized zones and documenting disappearances and extrajudicial killings of leaders of unions, peasant organizations, and human rights organizations, Dalena and her fellow ST Exposure members directly experienced the very conditions of violence that they were tracking when, on April 21, 2003, the human rights and activist leaders of the fact-finding mission they were documenting (Eden Marcellano and Eddie Gumanoy), as well as one of their own crew members (King Catoy), were abducted by the military. The military soldiers were operating under the sanction of Oplan Bantay Laya (Operation Plan Freedom Watch), a program of counterinsurgent war renewed by President Gloria Macapagal Arroyo, modeled on the strategies of the US global war on terror, and funded by the Bush administration. Although Dalena's colleague King was finally released (after being interrogated and having their equipment confiscated), Eden and Eddie were summarily executed, their bodies dumped in shallow graves.

ST Exposure continued to document these human rights violations and the ever-present threat of state-sanctioned death, which not only defined the conditions of the subjects of their films but also of their own filmmaking practice. I offer this brief summary of Dalena's experience as a member of the ST Exposure collective in order to provide a way of understanding the themes and modalities of her work as an artist, as well as the dangers incurred in oppositional representations and performances of political community.

In her work titled *The Present Disorder Is the Order of the Future* (2010), Dalena projects onto a bare floor, strewn with bodily fragments in cast marble, outtakes of two of her documentaries: one of a violent dispersion of informal land settlers, and the other of the 2009 Maguindanao Massacre, the abduction and brutal slaying of fifty-eight people, including thirty-four journalists, connected with an electoral candidacy challenging the ruling political dynasty in a province in the southern Philippines.[1] Originally derived from two life-size figures curled up with arms protecting their heads from police truncheons, which were cast in unfired clay for an exhibit two years earlier, *Barricade, Book of Slogans, Erased Slogans and Isolation Room* (2008), and which had begun to disintegrate during the exhibit, the bodily fragments were first translated into wood by woodcarvers from Dalena's hometown for another show, *Found Figures in Stones Translated by Pakil Carvers* (2009), and then cast from wood into marble for this exhibit. Scattered on the moving landscape made by video images of roads, highways, and grassy areas shot en route to sites of forced disappearances and evacuations, human rights violations, and political killings, the bodily fragments stand absolutely still as human ruins, broken stumps, in a devastated human environment, leftovers of political movements targeted for disappearance by the state. Those political movements are referenced in the twenty-four found slogans sourced from archival photo-documentations of past protests, now engraved on marble funerary slabs lining the wall on one side like a mausoleum, each ephemeral utterance of dissent serving as the name of, as well as a call to, a life entombed and memorialized.

In this work, Dalena invokes social practices of radical bereavement that have propelled and shaped political uprising and movements in the Philippines for more than a century. Such radical bereavement figures centrally in

FIGURE INTERREGNUM.1. Installation detail from Kiri Lluch Dalena, *The Present Disorder Is the Order of the Future*, 2010. MO_Space Gallery, Metro Manila. Courtesy of the artist.

FIGURE INTERREGNUM.2. Installation detail from Kiri Lluch Dalena, *The Present Disorder Is the Order of the Future*, 2010. MO_Space Gallery, Metro Manila. Courtesy of the artist.

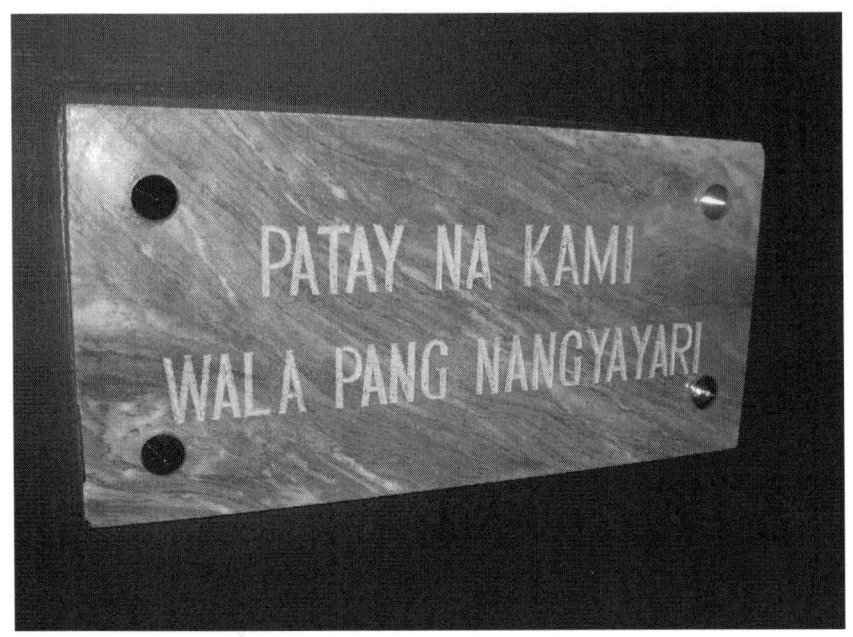

FIGURE INTERREGNUM.3. *We Are Already Dead, Yet Nothing Is Happening*, marble funerary slab. Installation detail from Kiri Lluch Dalena, *The Present Disorder Is the Order of the Future*, 2010. MO_Space Gallery, Metro Manila. Courtesy of Trickie Lopa @Manila Art Blogger.

FIGURE INTERREGNUM.4. Marble funerary slabs. Installation detail from Kiri Lluch Dalena, *The Present Disorder Is the Order of the Future*, 2010. MO_Space Gallery, Metro Manila. Courtesy of the artist.

the modalities of social experience articulated in the poetry of Elynia Mabanglo, which, in the context of overseas migrant labor, imagines a political communion out of the sharing of suffering and the exhilaration of collective passage beyond existential human life. It is also evident in revolutionary poetry, in the experience of sentient communion with the dead in the time of divine sorrow, a time beyond human measure when the law of merely human sovereignty is suspended. In these contexts, radical bereavement becomes a grievous expiation—a breach in the order of merely human life, in which the remains of one life can fertilize the life movements of others, a moment when the barriers between the living and the dead, between separate but linked forms of existence, become permeable, and social, personal debts to the dead are exacted, forgiven, or fulfilled.

In Dalena's work, the life lost and grieved is not "life itself," mere bodily life, the "bare life" on behalf of which humanist sovereignty is claimed, but rather the social lives of historical dissent and struggle. In gathering and mourning the words of past movements, she foregrounds a "life" that is inextricable from language and hence from a social intellect, a *sensus communis*, consisting of modes of thinking, acting, and feeling that can move beyond the enclosures of the time and space of nationalist histories. The lives of social dissent eerily speak from their destined graves, continuing to create presence with the very markers of absence—presences of grief, humor, outrage, command, mockery, defiance, threat—modes of address that themselves remain utterly present, each slogan a testament to a particular moment of social effort, will, and aspiration, past and yet present, seemingly dead yet still calling us to action, staging mourners as readers (and readers as mourners) who might receive and resurrect these words and a collective life that might also become theirs.

At the same time, bodily fragments, which cannot be pieced together to form an individualized self, appear to be unmemorializable. They appear as the material remainders of a continuous process of "salvaging" (in the Philippines, the term for extrajudicial executions) and, in the face of human wastemaking, traces of the duration of a grievous search for justice. Such material duration, embodied in these recycled and transformed bodily fragments (in clay, wood, marble), suggests the time of abidance, accompaniment, and gathering, when the stumps and stones of lifetimes spent in struggle call for some kind of remembrance and restitution in the living that is left behind.

If this is what Dalena's work makes sensible, I think it also raises, however, the possibility that these words (though not the lives beneath the words) might indeed be dead, that they cannot adequately deal with the remainders

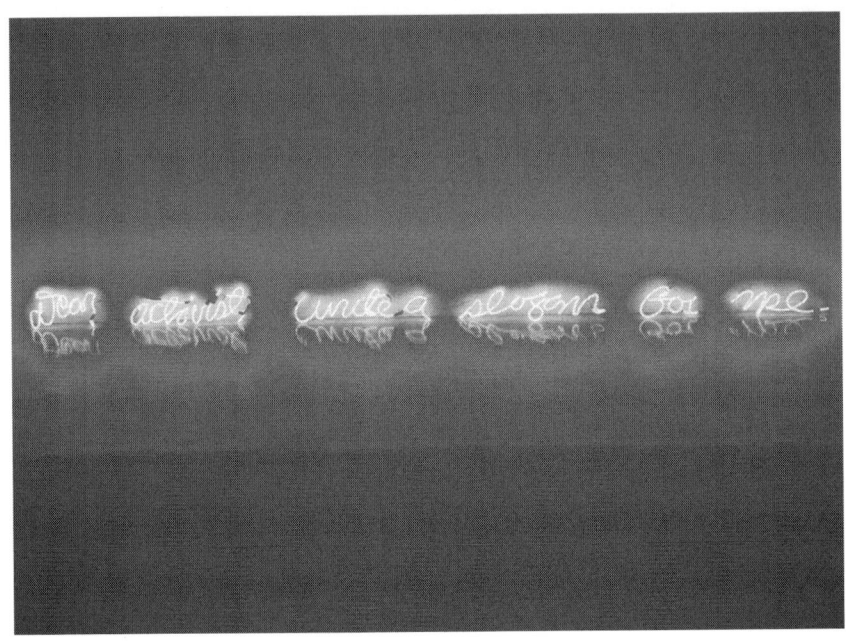

FIGURE INTERREGNUM.5. Kiri Lluch Dalena, *Dear Activist, Write a Slogan for Me*, 2010, installation. Ateneo Art Gallery, Metro Manila. Courtesy of Trickie Lopa @Manila Art Blogger.

of contemporary projects of humanization—projects that entail not only the dispossession of human life but also the dispossession of other cultural resources and literacies of people's striving. There is in fact in this work a difference registered between such ordinary striving and the organized struggles that heed, articulate, and act on the insurgent potential of everyday life, a perceptible breach between the words of protest memorialized and the traces of remaindered lives that can appear only as rubble on the moving political landscape. In this way, perhaps, Dalena's work points to the grave need, certainly in the Philippine context but also elsewhere, for different modalities and media of political imagination and constitution. It poses anew the problem of the relation between subaltern forms of striving, or the illegible "life-times" of historically and/or culturally remaindered political acts of freedom, and the political-artistic symbolic acts that summon and articulate those life-times for the struggles of the present, as poignantly staged in another work titled *Dear Activist, Write a Slogan for Me* (2010).

Dalena's installation of an epistolary request made into a fallen neon sign, sitting on the floor against the wall, plays on Filipino artist Nilo Ilarde's own appropriation of the title of German artist Martin Kippenberger's 1981 exhibition, *Dear Painter, Paint for Me*, a series of paintings executed by a Berlin billboard painter, whom Kippenberger had hired, and based on photographic images supplied by the latter. While Kippenberger's mode of producing "his" work highlighted the close links between commercial work or commodities and art, Ilarde's literal reproduction of Kippenberger's title as the subject of his own artwork (in the form of a white-painted wooden board with paint scratched off to form the letters of the titular request), which included the display of hundreds of used-up paint tubes collected from fellow artists, foregrounds the material labor, the practical and social enterprise, and the process of evacuation of that materiality (or abstraction) that together constitute "art." (Ilarde's show was titled, *Painting as Something and the Opposite of Something* [2020].) Dalena's revision of the Kippenberger/Ilarde title into a plea for activism that is rendered in commercial neon lights can thus be read as extending this transnational political-artistic reflection on commodification and labor and the politics of representation (as abstraction) and valorization that suffuse the art world, to a reflection on and staging of the unrepresented political claims of lives subtending the global world of commerce and art.

Dalena's revised quotation of the male painters (substituting activist for painter, slogan for painting) is a repetition with a difference that voices another difference that will not cohere into an identity or subjectivity, insofar as it is staged as an ambivalent (bright and commanding but fallen and diminished) presencing of the absent or the "disappeared." It plays on and plays down, repurposing and downsizing, the forms it borrows, an unfaithful replication of a gesture in a changed context that summons another social universe nevertheless intimately connected to the one from which it derives. Insofar as artworks are claims within an attention economy—commentaries on and participations in the attraction and extraction, the aggregation and accumulation of surplus life-times—this materialized communicative gesture is a beckoning by an unknown, elsewhere victim seeking political representation, seeking adequate speech, seeking the gift or help of words, addressed to one (the "activist") who may or may not be found in the world of art.

Like the found slogans on funeral slabs, this enunciation does not turn the defeated into "a constituency, a repressed historical entity, which every reading is obliged to bring into visibility."[2] Rather it represents only itself, a form of supplicatory speech that appears as a leftover artifact from an urban world of commercialized and commercializing attention.

The title of the exhibition in which this work appears, *Watch History Repeat Itself* (2010), is itself a slogan borrowed from activists in the past, one among those memorialized by Dalena, engraved in marble in the earlier work. As the speed of turnover in attention forestalls memory, these borrowings from the past, infused with the urgency of the present, are a way of holding on to the life of resistance that the dead leave behind. They are like the bodily fragments resculpted in enduring stone on a floor now serving as the screen of a moving landscape in the search for these very remains, flickering with light and shadow as if the ground were moving under our feet. Holding on, these remainders stay the forces of disappearance, stilling the time of war in a space hallowed by grief.

A Time of War . . . in Reverse

On the morning of November 23, 2009, in the southern Philippine province of Maguindanao, fifty-eight people were gunned down by over a hundred armed men; the bodies and all their effects, including their vehicles, were dumped and hastily buried in three mass graves by the same backhoes that had just dug the open pits of earth. The victims were part of a convoy of supporters of the gubernatorial candidate Esmael Mangudadatu, led by his wife, Genylyn, two sisters, Eden and Farinah, and other relatives, mostly female, and thirty-two journalists who were accompanying them on their trip to the capital to file Mangudadatu's certificate of candidacy. On their way, they were accosted by the mercenaries of the incumbent, Andal Ampatuan—a battalion of hired killers led by Ampatuan's son and namesake, whose own candidacy and the continuation of whose family's political dynasty were being challenged.

Carried out in broad daylight with a particular brutality that was heinous even by the standards of the electoral violence characteristic of Philippine politics, the mass killing was dubbed the Maguindanao massacre in a demand for justice that, only ten years later and after many witnesses were killed, was finally met with a court pronouncement of a guilty murder verdict for the two Ampatuan brothers and twenty-six others, including other clansmen and henchmen in their employ, while fifty-five others who had been charged, many members of the local police, were acquitted and freed.

Requiem for M (2010, dir. Kiri Dalena) is a video prayer for the dead of the Maguindanao massacre, as well as for the masses of people, including journalists, murdered daily and with impunity, in the Philippines, but globally as well. The seven-minute video is composed of footage of the funerals for many of the journalists, which were held a few days after the killing, as well as of the victims' relatives' and colleagues' visit to the massacre site two months later. Dalena had joined the mourners originally intending to make a journalistic reportage of the event. As she was editing the footage, however, she came to understand that even as she and other mourners all wanted justice in the form of punishment of the perpetrators, "in the end what we really wanted was for these things to not have happened."[3]

To not have happened. That is the prayer that plays the documentary footage in reverse, that makes *Requiem for M* the reverse of documentary and news—"this impossible desire to change what transpired, or change history by turning back time, making them not take that path."

We start off on that path, climbing the dirt path leading to the mound where the bodies were exhumed. A woman is screaming in grievous rage:

> Tama na! Ang dami nilang pinatay! Ang dami na, tama na iyon! Tama na yung maraming tao na nasaktan, ang mga pamilya na naiwan ng mga biktima! Alam ba nila kung ano ang nararamdaman namin ngayon?! Ilang beses kaming pinapatay!

> Enough already! They have killed so many! So many already, enough already! Enough already of the many people hurt, the families left by the victims! Do they know how we feel?! How many times we are being killed!

Ilang beses kaming pinapatay! How many times we are being killed! We see from out of the mass grave, the silhouettes of people peering down. We look at lit candles placed in the depressions and hollows in the earth imprinted by exhumed bodies, newspapers that had covered them, cigarette butts and debris strewn on the grounds of the victims' executions. These are the acts of mourning, the search for the remains of life expunged. But we do not look at the bodies, spectacular images of which abound in the news, the dead killed over and over again in representation, converted into signs for a story to be told.

Instead, we witness the mourners, the living who bear these losses. In *Requiem for M* the details of empirical fact that make for a verifiable truth are no longer to be found. The massacre is no longer the event that is at the center of the news, nor the object of investigation and verification on which justice will either founder or be found. Such events and their apparatuses of production—the very writing of life and death into spectacle, into history—figure prominently in an order of politics based on the command of appearances and, by extension, disappearance. Was the massacre not in fact a flagrant attempt to violently disappear not one or two but fifty-eight persons in one blow as if to bury the very fact of them as a collective act, to rub out their existence as a would-be event that could interrupt the Ampatuans' unbroken storyline of

Interregnum • 81

FIGURE INTERREGNUM.6. Video still from *Requiem for M* (2010), directed by Kiri Lluch Dalena.

power? In a world where the representational power of value is also its command (where the state is the embodiment and instrument of that command), the brutal murder replays the act of preemptive deletion and disappearance of other life on which a dominant field of political representation depends.

The video reverses this path—this course of history in which the events of power comprise an orderly succession, a forward march of representation. Dalena plays back in time the rites of the funerals: a grieving woman crumpled on the floor rises back to her feet, a hearse drives in reverse, tombstones recede as people walk backwards away from the cemetery, white balloons come down to earth, returning to the grasp of those who released them, flowers and dirt thrown on the graves rise back to their enclosing fists.

Against the relentless march of the time of cinema, the image of the consumption of time, *Requiem for M* reverses course. If the spectacular time of cinema is a consumable disguise of the time of production ("time-as-commodity ... is irreversible time made abstract" that we consume through capitalist cinema), Dalena rewinds that same unfolding spectacle, the time of war in which expendable life becomes money and power.[4] Only the woman's grievous tirade sounds out in nonreversed time. All the other gestures and movements shown rewinding the course of their lived action are no longer within the time of accumulation, the nonreversible, abstract time that links the cinematic image to the money-image, the time of what Fernando Solanos and Octavio Getino called "surplus value cinema."[5]

M thus stands in for all that is lost, for whom this requiem is performed. It stands in for what publicly bears only this proper name, *Maguindanao massacre*, as the collective name of the lives of "so many" taken in exchange for the graven image. "Kailan nating gugustuhin na matapos ang ganitong pangyayari?! Gusto nilang manatili sa power. Manatili sila na kumuha ng pera! [When will we want for these kinds of events to end?! They want to stay in power, to continue to be the ones who get money!]," the woman screams. "Pera lang ang lahat na ito! Ng power. Pera lang lahat ang katapat nito. Pera! [All this is only about money! About power! Money is all that is on the other side of this. Money!]"

"Money, that fucking money" is the counterpart (*ang katapat*) she accuses—what is the equivalent of and in proportion to (not the root, but what is commensurate with) all of this death and hurt. Money as *katapat*: the exchange value and coefficient of all these killings.

What is left over after the murders—the grief and rage of the mourners of the dead, the effects of the effect (of capitalist predation)—becomes the beginning. What comes after becomes the before, the prelude to this requiem in time, not a turning back or wishful denial of history but an unraveling of that time that has already happened. No longer documentary or critical account, the requiem is an experiential procession away from the event, from its inexorable internment of the living.

It is easy to think that war is the preserve of these far-flung, war-torn places, on the outskirts of the most advanced capitalist spaces. Yet war suffuses the very way we live and experience this time.

If the spectacle is "a negation of life that has invented a visual form for itself," the reversal of cinematic time becomes the practice of undoing this negation. Against the foreclosure accomplished by the utopian image ("placeless, rootless images"; "images containing no disruptive signs, images from nowhere"), the requiem becomes a careful following of this unraveling of a determinate end.[6] It becomes a process of unfolding and opening time. In this way, a requiem can be a practice of enacting the remaindered time of living.

PART II. LIFE-TIMES

4

OF LABOR AND FATE PLAYING

Digno es hacer de tu vida un acto de sabotaje. —SANTIAGO LÓPEZ PETIT, "¿Y si dejáramos de ser cuidadanos?"

In 2011, occupation protests emerged in Europe and in the United States as the principal progressive political response to the continuing debacle of financialization that was everywhere known as the global crisis. With debt, foreclosure, and unemployment figuring as key mobilizing concerns, and calls for regulation, stimulus packages, and a return to a "real," productive economy gaining audition in many parts, one is led to wonder, can "labor" still serve as a conceptual pivot of political action, a critical lens to hone our visions of "other worlds" beyond the world of permanent crisis and growing immiseration in which we now live?

One could certainly think so. After all, as a theoretical category, "labor" has been an indispensable component of the radical critique of capitalism, within the order of which the transactions of the financial world continue to be both possible and, it would seem, ultimately rational. That is to say, labor compels an examination of the financial economy as part and parcel of the order of capitalism, the modes of exploitation and logic of immiseration that preceded the era of autonomous financial markets and their global fallout. And yet, the popular focus on the failure of current governments to safeguard the interests and welfare of the people they purport to represent, the willed incapacity of states to check the unbridled power of finance and the devastating consequences of its mode of accumulation, and the absolute inadequacy, even irreparable breakdown, of existing political systems of representational democracy—all this may have the inadvertent effect of hiding this fact in plain sight. Our attention is instead continuously steered in the direction of political intervention, state reform, policy-making, and legislation as the main answers to the continuing economic crisis.

To be sure, there has been some significant work on the financial industry as a new form of capitalist value production—on the ways that "financialization" is at once continuous and discontinuous with older forms of value production (paradigmatically represented by Fordist manufacturing industries). Although critical popular representations of the financial crisis such as the documentary *Inside Job* (2016, dir. Charles Ferguson) tend to portray the activities of the financial world as nonproductive—or as making and distributing "fictive" products innovated by Apple, Google, and other IT industries, as opposed to "real" products or to the "real" tangible structures built by engineers before their absorption by the financial world—others, for example, Christian Marazzi, argue that the distinction between the sector of manufacturing industries ("where they 'make things'") and the sector of nonmaterial activities is a sterile one.[1] In supporting wishful efforts to restore the "real economy" through reindustrialization, such a distinction both obscures the nature and functioning of that "real economy" and threatens to hurt the creative, innovative, nonmaterial activities developed over the last years. Marazzi writes, "Financialization is not an unproductive/parasitic deviation of growing quotas of surplus-value and collective saving, but rather the form of capital accumulation symmetrical with new processes of value production."[2]

Those new processes of value production are no longer confined to the sphere of industrial production (the factory) but in fact extend to the spheres of circulation and reproduction where goods and services are exchanged and consumed, and where forms of life are enjoyed and regenerated. With the declining rate of profit and the subsequent crisis of Fordist industries in the 1960s and 1970s, processes of extracting value were extended to the sphere of circulation by techniques of putting consumers to work in the production of what they consumed (e.g., software programs, performances, services, and dreams). For example, through technologies of "crowdsourcing," Web 2.0 companies extract surplus value from the "free labor" of masses of users, harnessing and valorizing the common actions, emotions, desires, and forms of sociality innovated and performed by the latter. In this new mode of accumulation, constant capital is constituted by "a totality of non-material organizing systems that suck surplus-value by pursuing citizens in every moment of their lives, with the result that the working day, the time of living-labor, is excessively extended and intensified."[3]

What makes financial processes of value extraction symmetrical to these new processes of value production is precisely the extension of such processes beyond factory production and into the sphere of circulation and reproduction, "i.e., in the sphere of *bios*, of life."[4] Indeed, for Marazzi, to analyze financialization from a productive point of view is to see it as the other side of the externalization of processes of valorization typical of biocapitalism, by which he refers to the capitalist subsumption of nonmaterial forms of social cooperation, immaterial cognitive and affective labor, and individual and collective imagination located within society.

New Political Economy of Life

Biocapitalism, cognitive capitalism, immaterial labor—these are some of the terms that have become increasingly used in left academic circuits to conceptualize a shift in capitalism from a mode of accumulation described as Fordist to one described as post-Fordist, within which forms of activity that were once situated (theoretically and practically) outside the formal spaces of the capitalist expropriation of value (and instead within the reproduction of both social and biological life), have now become productive forces—in other words, productive of appropriable surplus value.[5] Practices of knowledge-making, intellectual work, communication, social cooperation, imagination, care, affect, performance, and aesthetic and cognitive acts, as well as biological reproduction and the life sciences—such activities that hitherto took place in the sphere of life outside of labor proper have, on this view, become integrated into capitalist processes of accumulation such that labor ceases to be a special, separate practice distinct from other human activities. As Paolo Virno puts it: under post-Fordism, "there is not a clean, well-defined threshold separating labor time from non-labor time."[6] Instead, such a distinction between "labor" and "non-labor" might better be conceived as a distinction between remunerated life and nonremunerated life, which in any case is a categorical distinction that is "arbitrary, changeable and subject to political decision-making."[7] Within this new mode of accumulation, the time of labor is indistinguishable from the time of living; there is no longer any difference between labor and life.

These ideas on the contemporary eradication of the distinction between production and reproduction, between labor and life, are encapsulated in Antonio Negri's reworking of Marx's notion of the "real subsumption" of society within capital, a development that is now widely argued to have superseded the earlier phase of capitalism when capital formally subsumed or absorbed production processes that were generated independently of the capitalist logic.[8] Today, as this argument goes, the entire range of activities and creative capacities comprising the life of society has come under the control of capital. The valorization process obtaining in the factory has come to be generalized to society as a whole (making it a "social factory") such that social cooperation has now become a principal source of capitalist productivity.

If all life has become labor (if the organization of labor has become anchored in the *bios*), the political potential that used to be envisaged in the figure of labor (the proletariat) has now become deposited in the creative, intellectual, cognitive-linguistic, communicative, emotional, and cooperative faculties—the "general intellect" or immaterial social life and intelligence— of the new figure of the productive subject (the multitude). As Negri writes, "When we speak of real subsumption under capital (that is to say, how capitalism is actually developing), we mean the mercantilization of life, the disappearance of use value and the colonization of forms of life by capital, but we also mean the construction of resistance inside the new horizon."[9] For Negri, "a desire for life" always traverses the fabric of capitalist relations, signifying the emergence of resistance to biopower.[10] If "it is life itself which is being exploited," that is, if capital has been extended into every relationship of life, resistance can come only from the surplus generated out of productive life.[11] Against the totalitarian power of capitalist biopower emerges biopolitical resistance. "When capital invests the entirety of life, life itself is revealed as resistance."[12]

There is much in this post-Marxist analysis of contemporary capitalism that I find useful and persuasive, particularly for thinking about the new processes of valorization exemplified by the financial industry and other capital-intensive industries of "immaterial" production. At the same time, I find that the limits of its conceptual framework pose serious challenges to its aspiration to serve as a theory and politics of global revolution. Those limits, which also pose serious impediments to a broader and more concrete antiracist, anticolonial, feminist, and queer consideration of the political potential of "living labor," can be understood in terms mainly of the consequence of this framework: that is, its *theoretical subsumption* of plural categories of life-making, sense-making praxis operating in and as part of global capitalism, within the hegemonic analytical problematic of post-Fordist, postindustrial "immaterial" production and within its provincial genealogy in the modern Western world.

While Negri critiques various theories of totalitarianism for their exclusion of all resistance, arguing that "the so-called absolute totality of their power is a mystifying idea that is long overdue for critical examination," he does not recognize that the idea of the absolute totality of the power of capital to colonize all human life and all social relations is equally mystifying. Indeed, the notion that resistance issues out of some abstract "desire for life" (regardless of what "life" it might be) also seems reductive and ontologically absolutist, even romanticizing.[13] Within this perspective, "life" has become no more than the figure for the totalized abstraction of the labor-subject in confrontation with capital, which is now understood to be fully commensurate with biopower writ global.[14] Such a conception is indifferent to the qualitative gradations and divisions of "life" that obtain as crucial aspects of contemporary processes of value extraction. For though "life" has indeed become productive for capital, it is important to emphasize that not all life is valorized or valorizable, that the extraction of value from "life" takes place through more than one modality, and that "life" in the complex dynamics of capitalist processes assumes radically contradictory forms.

One might compare, for example, the investable and profitable lives of "life entrepreneurs" in various fields as well as high-value "creative workers" in Web 2.0 industries with the unvalorizable lives of "unskilled" women workers in global manufacturing factories in Mexico and China.[15] Beyond the certainly significant quantitative differences in remuneration between these two kinds of "life," there are crucial qualitative differences between their definitive characteristics and functions within the biopolitical economy of capital. In contrast to the *life as interest-bearing capital* of the former—that is, "life" with accumulable value transmissible across generations (through the augmented cultural and educational capital of their progeny as well as through inheritable material wealth)—the "life" of the Mexican maquiladora worker, as Melissa Wright shows, is of diminishing value, operating on a trajectory of consumption and eventual wastage.[16] Embodying "a living form of human waste," the figure of the disposable Mexican woman (generalized beyond the maquiladora worker) represents "life" that tends toward being used up—spent—its intrinsic value declining irreversibly over time.[17] In contradistinction to male workers, who are generally funneled into positions of "skilled" (and often supervisory, managerial) work and, as such, whose value appreciates over time, female workers bear a value that dissipates over time—they personify "waste in the making," a negative accumulation of waste within their persons that will logically end in their predestined "corporate death" and potentially their early, likely violent, physical demise.[18] "Life" in this case is neither investable nor accumulable (at least not directly in this form) but rather subject to a process of exponential decay, a process in which waste rather than value accumulates.

The "wasting process" that Wright makes evident in the case of the figure of the "disposable woman"—a process crucially attendant to the acceleration of capitalist turnover cycles—is part and parcel of a broader immiserative logic that is often overlooked in the new political economy of life. Concomitant with the new productivity of "life" (i.e., its real subsumption within capital) is also the tendency of "life" toward disposability, toward absolute redundancy and superfluity. As Aaron Benanav argues, the expansion of capital cannot take place without creating human superfluity.[19] The expanded reproduction of capital depends on the movement of labor in and out of lines to offset falling profitability, through the "setting free" of workers compelled to find employment in expanding markets. Although this pool of newly released, discounted (at fire sale prices) labor is reabsorbed by capital as an industrial reserve for the regulation of the labor market, it tends to outgrow this function and to become "a consolidated surplus population, absolutely redundant to the needs of capital," a tendency that Marx identified as the general law of capital accumulation.[20] In fact, Benanav argues, for Marx, the proletariat referred not to the industrial working class, as is widely assumed, but rather to "a working class in transition, a working class tending to become a class excluded from work."[21]

Surplus and Disposability

La division internacional del trabajo consiste en que unos países se especializan en ganar y otros en perder. —EDUARDO GALEANO, *Las venas abiertas*

While the transformation of labor-saving technological innovations into consumer product innovations and, crucially, I would add, the twentieth-century imperial expansion in the third world together appear to have staved off this tendency toward absolute immiseration in what would later be called the Global North—by enabling the absorption of both capital and labor in new and expanded markets (raising the material standards of living for the majority populations of industrialized nations as well as for the emergent middle classes of postcolonial nations)—the limits of this dynamic have since been reached. And the catastrophe that is a massive global surplus population barely, if at all, eking out a living can no longer be masked by the reprieve offered by financial-

Table 4.1
Global Life-Times

Life-Times of Value	*Life-Times of Waste*
• **Life worth living:** life with the capacity to yield value as living labor (value-productive life)	• **Life worth expending:** life with the capacity to yield value as disposable existence
• Life as interest-bearing capital, i.e., life with accumulable value transmissible across generations	• Life that tends toward being spent, its intrinsic value declining irreversibly over time
• Life subject to a process of growth and expansion, a process of development and realization	• Life subject to a process of exponential decay, a process in which waste rather than value accumulates

ized debt. As Benanav writes, "For a huge chunk of the world's population it has become impossible to deny the abundant evidence of the catastrophe. It exists now only to be managed: segregated into prisons, marginalized in ghettos and camps, disciplined by the police, and annihilated by war."[22]

The fate of this growing surplus population destined for "management" is the other side of the "mercantilization of life" that would yield biopolitical resistance, or, the "affirmative and positive" expression of the immeasurable surplus of the "living labor" of life subsumed within capital.[23] Here the absolute mercantilization or commodification of "life" (as distinct from its capitalization) manifests itself in global industries of war, security (global antiterrorism, including US military operations in West Asia, Africa, and the Asia-Pacific and in the Israeli occupation of Palestine; border management and the detention of illegals" in the United States and Europe), bioeconomics (organ trade, commercial surrogacy, and pharmaceuticals), and protection (e.g., medical and political asylum granted through varieties of state humanitarianism), as well as local, informal "occult economies" and syndicated commercial trade in life and death (drug and human trafficking, kidnap-for-ransom).

What this other side of the capitalist subsumption of "life" exemplifies and entails is not simply life as object of consumption (equivalent to labor as commodity), in which life is spent and exhausted, but indeed *life as waste*—disposable material whose management has become an entire "province of accumulation," spawning proliferating industries of militarization, security, policing, and control.[24] Within these industries, race, religion, nationality, gender, and sexuality operate as social technologies of biopolitical decision over life worth, critical markers for distinctions not only between rates of remunerable life (high value vs. low value, skilled vs. unskilled labor) but also between *life worth living*, that is, life with the capacity to yield value as living labor, and *life worth expending*, that is, life with the capacity to yield value as disposable existence.

To think about life as "living labor" without sustained consideration of this latter aspect of mercantilized "life" or, for that matter, of the distinctions among modalities of life exploitation in biocapitalism and the "differences" that mark and regulate such distinctions, is to privilege the figure of the post-Fordist socialized worker directly producing social life for capital. It is, in this way, to participate in the theoretical subsumption of all other subjectivities of "living labor" within the socially unmarked figure of the productive biopolitical subject of post-Marxist thought.

This new figure of labor can be viewed as having been implicitly conceived (and contained) within the globalized terms of citizenship as described by Santiago López Petit: "The citizen is someone who owns their life, or more exactly, someone who knows how to manage their life and make it profitable."[25] López argues that the citizen as a regulative ideal is a fundamental piece of the new social contract and mode of subjection actualized by what he calls, in contrast to the notion of democracy, "the democratic" (*lo democrático*), an order of reality that establishes the division between the thinkable and the unthinkable, demarcating "for those who call themselves free" not only what one can but also what one *should* think, do and live.[26] "The social contract is transformed into a *personal contract* . . . 'life in exchange for absolute employability.' In the global epoch one can only live, and to live is to have a life, if that life that one has is the support of a new mode of being: the most absolute employability."[27] The citizen upholds life as property, as investment, indeed, as a form of being capital. "'To have a life' means to invest money, effort and time, in managing one's own life."[28]

Despite the fact that López's injunctions tend to presume an absolutely closed, total reality—uninterrupted, much less perforated or traversed by other older, persistent, and newly innovated realities beyond that of the political order of "the democratic"—he points to a mode of being that, in its failure to accede to the life imperatives of the citizen-entrepreneur, suggests other zones of human existence and living labor that lie just beyond the theoretical scope of the new political economy of life. López writes, "Ultimately, a social failure is not an authentic citizen, but a second-class citizen. Not to speak of an undocumented immigrant who can only be a stigmatized shadow at our service."[29] The allusion to second-class citizenship and the figure of the undocumented immigrant ("a stigmatized shadow") highlights the life conditions of those whose access to the privileges of citizenship and authorized settlement are made extremely tenuous if not altogether barred or foreclosed. The life conditions of, for example, growing surplus populations of "illegal" immigrants, "guest" workers, refugees, undocumented nationals, and internally displaced persons (the number of the latter alone rising from around 17 million in 1998 to approximately 27.5 million in 2010)[30] bring into relief the theoretico-political limits of the economic conceptualization of the new biopolitical subject of labor for whom life is labor, the productive force or *potentia* of capital as well as a form of capital itself.

In contrast to the life of the enfranchised citizen, whose property rights to valorizable life are guaranteed by the state, surplus populations of "illegal" immigrants attest to the precarious condition of life as diminishing value and accumulating waste that I spoke of earlier—life that is to be managed *en masse* by state as well as privatized parastate apparatuses. It is not that these lives do not yield value. One has only to note the profit earnings of the growing global industry of privatized detention and security services, such as those suggested by the increase of the contract awarded by the Australian government to Serco, one of the three publicly traded companies that are now the major players in "the international business of locking up and transporting unwanted foreigners," from $370 million in 2009 to $756 million in 2011, with the quadrupling of the number of detention sites to 24 and an in increase in the number of detainees from 1,000 to 6,700.[31] With a $10 billion portfolio, Serco recorded a 35 percent profit increase last year. What is the price of surplussed life? Nine-year-old Naomi Leong, who was born in a Serco detention center, and her mother, Virginia Leong, a Malaysian citizen who was accused of trying to use a false passport, were detained for three years at a cost of about $380,000. There are many other and more harrowing numbers one might offer in this regard, but the point is that the global "detention-industrial complex" is a business that profits from the management and warehousing of lives that function not so much as labor (though prison labor is of course part of the prison-industrial complex) but rather as social waste. Here, value accrues from the sheer expenditure of life-times, that is, from the work of carrying out, maintaining, controlling, and overseeing the "safe" corralling or sequestration, and often the final removal, of these unremunerable lives for periods of varying duration, the time of detention, of sheer waiting, or, life wasting.

It is clear that in this context the life of each detainee is simply a unit measure of capitalist temporality, in this case, a form of currency of trade (with the state as market), a means for carrying out processes of value extraction that do not issue from the labor of those lives expended. Here, the life-times of expendability of the incarcerated and detained are both yield and measure, part of the total financial calculus of capitalist accounts. Life sentences are guaranteed expendable life-times, while shorter term sentences promise rapid turnover—biotemporal assets (life liabilities) that are tradeable and investable on secondary capital markets, even as their brutal management is the "service" provided by one of the largest global industries. As with other industries in the business of managing surplus populations, it is through economies of scale and the diversification and multiplication of services built around these forced expenditures of life (as raw material and means of production) that the security industry is able to make the loose and petty change—of the disposable existence of what Randy Martin calls "at-risk" populations (the obverse of the figure of "risk-taking" speculative investors)—add up to enormous amounts of capitalist wealth.

We can see the dynamics of extracting value from disposable life in other contexts of border security for democracy through an economic rendering of "life-times," a concept I have proposed to help think about the overlooked productivity of the social practices of life-making that seem to lie outside contemporary modes of exploitation of life as living labor.[32] The concept of life-times derives from the conditions of migrant domestic work in which the appropriation of "feminized" labor is inextricable from the appropriation of the worker's whole bodily being, that is, conditions in which the distinction between labor time and life time is dissolved—not, however, as in the general case of post-Fordist labor but rather in the specific (gendered, racialized) context of live-in migrant domestic servants at the beck and call, or the unlimited disposal, of their employers (whose disposition over servants is not restricted in time). In this context migrant domestic workers are to be viewed, however, not simply in their capacity as reproductive labor but also very importantly as savers and producers of valorized and valorizable "surplus life-time" for their host employers and their socialities (including the cultivation of the growing life-times of their host's children and the extension of the lifetimes of their aging population). Host employers, in turn, are able to invest this purchased "surplus life-time," which is already subsidized by the low-wage reproductive labor of the service and agribusiness industries, in that very productive life into which they are conscripted as "entrepreneurs of themselves, being for themselves their own capital, being for themselves their own producers," as Foucault understood the effective social norms of US American neoliberalism.[33] As auxiliary to the laboring subject, whose productive life-times are stolen and invested as capital, for whom time is money, the domestic woman servant *is* her life-times: her time, her body, her being, and her living the medium and source of life-times of use values for consumption in the production of the exchangeable life-times of others.[34]

Life-times foregrounds such differences in the social uses, practices, understanding, valorization, and inhabitation of the times of life and their relations in a global economy in which the "production time" of capital has encompassed all of life. As I discussed in chapter 3, it is a concept for rendering the discrepant yet intertwined temporal dynamics of life practices from the side of life subjected to capitalist appropriation of value as well as from the side of life destined for disposable superfluity, and, most crucially, from the side of disposable life's own excess—or, remaindered life.

On the US-Mexico border, smugglers of undocumented Mexican migrants have found increased profit margins under homeland security because more intense border vigilance and the effective death penalty clause introduced through militarized security measures has raised the costs of mobility for migrants.[35] One way to think about the economy of life-times at work here is to understand the smugglers as time savers, in this case, life-time savers. The fee they command is viewed in exchange for the difference in earnings the migrants would make in the United States and what they would make in Mexico or elsewhere (an amount that is often near zero)—a great difference, that is, in the value of their life-times. For migrants then, this perilous undertaking is a gamble—or what in the context of Filipina migration is understood as a form of fate playing (*pakikipagsapalaran*)—for which they lay down the ante: the fee they pay beforehand and their bodily life. The handling fee is also a form of insurance against the odds of getting caught (or killed), the premiums for which become higher as the risks of getting caught increase and the punishments of capture intensify. Even as the value of individual lives diminishes (paradoxically, the greater the investment in security, the more devalued each life is), the valorizable potential of their clustered lives augments (in a manner analogous to subprime mortgages). Nevertheless, ostensibly, the fee is to save the migrants' life-times (i.e., to save them from the actual and potential loss of life-times, and to guarantee future life-times or savings of life-times), the exchange value of which, when converted to formal labor time, and taking into account the valorization rates of a higher social currency (residency and citizenship, for example, bringing immeasurable amounts of social and cultural capital, whose transmissibility along proper familial lines is supported by the state and its legal and other ideological apparatuses), greatly increases across the border, at least hypothetically and with higher probability.

Human smugglers can be considered virtual cronies or illicit concessionaires of the state, like fixers who attach themselves to state bureaucracies in order to offer the service of time-saving "cuts" in the system for a fee. What appears to be an "expensive waste of time" devoted to fending off migration is actually a source of profits for all the illicit subsidiary businesses built to circumvent those very state efforts (themselves value extractive, paid for with taxes). Fixing is an informal mode of value extraction geared toward those whose small and petty times are continuously exacted in their effort to secure their papers and maintain legal, documented life (which in liberal democracies is equivalent to the very right to live, as Edwidge Danticat shows tragically in her family memoir, *Brother, I Am Dying*), or simply in the effort to maneuver through the labyrinthine machinery of governance, which like the military operates as a "province of accumulation" through activities consuming and depleting life. For many pushed to the very edges of citizen-life, or those who live at the limit-border of sovereign political belonging, life can consist of interminable times of waiting—or rather, life is consumed by waiting as both the expenditure of one's life and its conversion into waste.

In contrast then to the greater productivity of the life-times of enfranchised citizen-life entrepreneurs (subjects of immaterial labor who spend less time reproducing their individual lives than they spend directly producing valorizable social life), the life-times of those marked for absolutely minimum life (social groups, populations, and even regions whose social reproduction is either under fatal attack—as Silvia Federici writes, targeted for "near-zero-reproduction" or elimination—or in a condition of pernicious, deliberate neglect, what Ruth Gilmore calls "organized abandonment") are increasingly devoted to the work of merely reproducing their lives.[36] This often requires first exchanging work for time with which they can pay to earn enough wages to live another day, as exemplified in the case of mostly migrant New York taxi drivers who must work until the eleventh hour to break even (to cover the operating expenses they are charged for) and who earn their actual wages only during the twelfth hour despite working a full twelve-hour shift.[37] In other words, whether or not migrant workers have monetary debts (or, euphemistically, financial credit), they are always already in *life arrears.*

Beyond merely advancing their work to capitalists, a portion of which they are paid for at the end of the day (with the money produced out of their own past labor), as Marx represented industrial labor, today many low-wage migrant workers enter the workplace (whether in a home or a taxi) having to pay backward with work for life-times already spent. Like most migrant domestic workers who have gone into debt as a precondition of obtaining overseas work (or whose families have gone into debt with their own lives as collateral), their time has been mortgaged, so they must first work to pay off that mortgaged time, which "buys" them more time to work so they can live the next day, a portion of which will already have been mortgaged. Put differently, they pay with work for life advanced to them (life they *owe* rather than *own*)—a form of rent on the delimited parcel of existence they can afford to inhabit within the deterritorialized networked city-state of global humanity, the *globopolis*.

As I am trying to suggest in this economic rendering of quotidian negotiations of life among those with no guaranteed right to it, the life-times of undocumented immigrants, guest-workers, refugees, and displaced persons do not exactly function as "life as labor" in the sense of the value-productive life activities and faculties comprising the general intellect. Indeed, it is crucial to point out the ways in which the forms and practices of their social cooperation and imagination, the cognitive, affective, aesthetic, and communicative capacities they exercise, far from producing general social wealth, are largely ghettoized and permitted extremely limited and ever-contracting space in the general intellect of "democratic" societies, that space of "unitary or homogeneous socialization" said to characterize post-Fordism.[38] Subjected to racist forms of cultural, political, and economic as well as physical sequestration and sexual harassment, the life-making praxis and poiesis of those on the border of full citizenship are themselves devaluing insofar as they are tacitly understood to produce life of already diminished value. And to the extent that the "particular intellect" of surplus people diminishes their access to and participation in enfranchised, politically and economically valued social life, such practices and capacities can only be life impeding.

The enclosure of the privileges and rights of globopolitical humanity through policing, security, and war has become a business in its own right. State and private apparatuses regulate and control entries and exits to and from the civic fold, processing papers and documents required for authorized movement and residency, proper registration and handling of birth and death, management of health and illness, education, work, and all matters within the ever-expanding jurisdiction of the law and its enforcement. Auxiliary petty enterprises proliferate around these legal and police checkpoints in the quotidian affairs of unwanted people, whose life-times are exacted in nickel-and-dime fashion at every turn until the very mortal end.

Fate Playing and the Surplus of Social Reproduction

Rather than times of life as hidden productive labor, the life-times of surplus people can be seen, from one side, to operate as a form of devalued trading currency—petty coinage for their own day-to-day transactions for subsistence and temporary reprieve from eviction, deportation or detention; legal tender to pay for the infractions, civil and criminal, that one will almost inevitably incur; collateral and loan to obtain out-of-reach goods and prospects, including the simple prospect of formal, waged employment. From another side, beneath the abstract temporal calculus of capitalism, that is, beneath the level of the field of exchange on which the abstract value of life-times is determined and negotiated, these life-times consist of diverse bodily, perceptual, affective, and imaginative capacities and practices of life-making under conditions of unauthorized, foreclosed, and prohibited being, as well as the heterogeneous temporalities within which such life-making can and does occur. In this other aspect, the life-times of disposability refers to the forms of inhabitation and actualization of time within which disposable "life" is made, lived, played, and played out, not simply in contrast to or even resistance against its expenditure as capitalist waste or its function as a form of excess liquidity or cheap cash, but as a supplementary condition and refracted consequence of both.

It is from this side, for example, that we can see the dimension of fate playing in the perilous acts of illegal immigration on the US-Mexico border, which I briefly mentioned earlier. Here, and in the Philippine social contexts of remaindered life from which I draw the notion of fate playing (from Filipina workers' reference to overseas work as *pakikipagsapalaran*, or adventure; *kapalaran*, fate; and *pagsapalaran*, to cast one's lot, or to hazard/venture fate), the life-times of people serve as ante and bet for the chance possibility of another fate in exchange, or a windfall of better fortune.[39] What, after all, is fate playing but a cosmic gamble for those for whom life can be parceled out, bought, sold, traded, stolen, or given away, a wasted end, a deepening debt and liability, a seemingly perpetual state of indenture, servitude, and endless waiting—in short, a *fate* determined by forces far beyond one's grasp and control, yet never completely fixed or immutable, and instead always in a dynamic state of play. This is a context in which human sovereignty and self-ownership (or possessive individualism) have never completely prevailed over other practices of selfhood, power, and agency. In the context of Filipina migration, "changing-land" (*pangingibang-lupa*) is a fate-playing action, a recasting of the die with one's bodily self as legal tender for the ante of a collective as well as individual wager; a hazarding of one's present fate (*palad*) to create an opening for the immanent possibility—the unforeseeable yet inducible potential—of a radical change in fortune and destiny.[40]

The life-times of Filipina women embarking on these overseas adventures of fate playing are continuously incorporated into the times of Christlike sacrificial suffering in the narratives and practices of the Philippine state, which seeks the fruits of this suffering in foreign exchange remittances that keep the national economy afloat ($20.1 billion in 2011);[41] the times of commodified and excluded identities in narratives of gender- and race-based human rights claims; and the times of generalized post-Fordist servility in narratives of global labor—political and economic times of capital and citizenship with which they appear concordant. Despite this incorporation, such life-times exceed the terms, the meanings, the forms, and the consequences of Filipina women's dominant function as (re)productive labor and disposable life. Fate playing instantiates a realm of action in which life is porous, sharable across persons, transmissible across distances of space and time, renewable, and multipliable, even as it remains finite and subject to constriction, division, depletion, closure, or an untimely or untoward end. It is within such a realm of action and meaning that the "living" of life destined for capitalist expenditure, exchange, or both is enabled but also differently guided, bearing plural and yet unaccountable social and political effects.

Attending to these other life-times allows us to see and consider entire areas and practices—in a word, *forms*—of life that remain unabsorbed residues of capital's real subsumption of life, even as these life-times are formally subsumed through industries of reproductive labor, security, biopolitical population management, and war. It shows up in what I view as a temporal and cognitive gap that persists in the real subsumption of social relations by capital, yet remains unacknowledged by current theories of labor. That gap is concealed by what Brett Neilson has critiqued as the developmentalism of the Operaismo narrative of the epochal transition from formal to real subsumption.[42] Following postcolonial critiques of Marxism, Neilson argues that the notion of an accomplished movement from formal to real subsumption enforces a normative development, which "obscures the possibility of examining the plural histories that capital encounters, incorporates and overwhelms in its process of globalization."[43]

As it happens, like primitive or original accumulation, with which it overlaps and corresponds, formal subsumption is not a past or "original" stage of capitalist accumulation entirely superseded by later, more advanced stages (overtaken by real subsumption). Formal subsumption continues to play a role in the capitalist management of the very forms of life it jettisons and destroys as a necessary component of its logic of accumulation. Such disposable life, as we have seen, is not fully excluded from capitalism but rather only formally subsumed as a kind of raw material for entire industries based on waste (including the financial industry), the raw material of human life whose reproduction is no longer the concern of biopower but rather is a matter left to "nature."⁴⁴ (No wonder that the squalid, sprawling forest camps where illegal immigrants seek refuge, for example in the northern city of Calais, or in the woods of Andalusia, Spain, are referred to as "the jungle."⁴⁵)

The wholesale jettisoning or forsaking of, if not the outright assault on, the reproduction of superfluous humans, precisely as a consequence of the immiserating logic of capital and as a means of maintaining the condition of "bare life" to which they have been reduced as a free and seemingly infinite natural resource for newly opened or expanded, diversified lines of industry, suggests another form of surplus that is no longer simply on the side of the (re)production of life as labor (where Negri locates the specific excess that is the emergence of singularities, "the pure expression of non-reducible difference," comprising the constituent power immanent to labor).⁴⁶ Rather than that excess "at the productive level of the relations, affects, language, and communication that exalt the new cooperative nature of labor," this surplus is on the side of the assaulted or abandoned social reproduction of disposable life.⁴⁷ While the former takes as its point of departure the capital relation (as that which is to be reproduced), the latter takes as its point of departure precisely what I see as the imperial relation, that extant mode of dispossession, which Marx shows is a necessary and intrinsic component of the reproduction of the capital relation—the securing of this capital relation by preventing workers from "running away" through the annihilation of their means of subsistence.⁴⁸

Although we are no longer simply talking of "workers" in the sense that Marx understood, the crucial importance of the destruction of the independent production of life ("the necessaries of life") in the reproduction of the capital relation is indubitable. That destruction is evident in the besiegement of the social reproductive capacities of particular populations and social groups, which guarantees against the threat that this abandoned, disposable life might live beyond the expected time of its demise by finding a sustainable and independent way of making life. The fact that the social reproduction of superfluous humans is targeted for elimination means that their practices of life-making are in some sense already "surplus." It means, more importantly, that these practices will necessarily bear dimensions of flight from the fate of disposability, dimensions we will be unable to recognize without an understanding what I call remaindered life-times.

The notion of remaindered life-times refers to modes and practices of "living" or life-making that are made superfluous in the process of the production of biopolitical life, including the waste of life and wasted life. But rather than disposable *lives*, that is, whole individuals and social groups (units of human life) deemed disposable, remaindered *life-times* refers to what is not expended in the expenditure of disposable life (in varying measures of organic bodily being and time) as the unacknowledged basis of the new forms of expropriating value. It is the left-over and excess of social reproductive work of *living* not only on the part of disposable peoples but also in the forms of social life-making that persist beyond and despite capitalist subsumption—not directly absorbable by capitalist industries, not completely assimilable within forms of productive life, or, and this is increasingly (though not yet) the same thing, failing to fulfill the protocols of subjectivity and sociality under the political order of democratic life. These forms and moments of life-making (and sense-making) are remaindered life-times also in the sense that they exceed the theoretical accounts of labor and of politics, which see disposable life only as the symptomatic consequence of the logic of capitalist accumulation or of sovereignty, and in this way make the remaindered life-times of social survival among the dispossessed ever more liminal.

Fate playing is an example of the surplus of social reproductive activity that I regard as remaindered life-times, bearing precisely those dimensions of flight that capital seeks to prevent. I see the action of fate playing not only in the context of Filipina migration but also in the context of illicit and informal practices of the urban excess or *lumpenproletariat*. Elsewhere I have called these practices the "speculative adventurism" of such figures of petty graft and corruption as the ubiquitous fixer, who engages in practices of making "cuts" in the system as sites for the extraction of value, generating contingency and mutability in institutions assumed to be solid in order to create opportunities for making something out of nothing.[49] As a form of gambling, fate playing is also perhaps most evident in that ₱40 billion business of *jueteng*, the illegal numbers game that preys on the urban poor by mopping up their petty cash with the hopes of changed fortune.

Like the other famous form of gambling in Southeast Asia, the cockfight, jueteng is, however, also a ritual of social life-making; unlike the "deep play" of cockfighting, however, it is the ritual of the lowest, most negligible, and despised social strata.[50] On the one hand, it is described as a form of social welfare or community charity, in that it helps the *kubradors*, "the ant army of collectors" made up of indigents and the idle underemployed who trawl the neighborhoods for the petty cash of small bets from which they take their wages (or "cut").[51] On the other hand, it is described as part and parcel of "culture" as a mode of collective life. This "culture" is gleaned in the concept of *diskarte*, the ability to find and seize small openings, an ability that is predicated on the trust and goodwill in which the kubrador traffics as a mediator of community life.

Diskarte is also expressed in the countless negotiations revolving around jueteng, transactions that are built on trust and goodwill. A bettor places his bet as part of a social ritual that revolves around the fate of the latest winner, the latest community gossip, intrigues in government, and the interpretation of *anuncios* or supernatural premonitions of a winning combination. This ritual reaffirms the bettor-kubrador relationship. Jueteng does not involve receipts, the implication being that it revolves on a bond of trust stronger than any piece of paper.[52]

Consisting solely of "countless informal negotiations," without the apparatuses of written contracts or formal management systems, jueteng builds as well as profits from the intricate details of people's lives interwoven with the mysteries of the forces of fortune and fate expressed in complex relations between symbols, images, and numbers. Diskarte might in fact be viewed as the practice of derivatives in everyday life.

I bring up the case of jueteng not as an example of radical political potential or resistance, for it is clearly a mode of exploitation that is not only compatible with capitalism but might in fact be taken as a perverse mirror image of the workings of finance capital. As a form of poverty taxation through gambling, rife with graft and corruption, embedded in structures of political patronage reaching to the highest office (that of ousted Philippine president Joseph Estrada), it is precisely the embodiment of the very failure of the Philippine nation to live up to the normative ideals of a liberal democracy. Rather, I bring up jueteng for those dimensions of its practice that escape representations of it as either a perversion (literally, a corruption) of economic behavior proper to postcolonial liberal democracies—namely, developmentalist free-market capitalism—or the very exemplification of finance capitalism today as a form of "casino capitalism."

In the game of jueteng can be glimpsed a lifeworld replete with propitious meaning and ambient power or potential. The capture, accumulation, and preservation as well as the privation of that power both determines and is reflected in social relations of obligation and patronage that are never completely fixed or static but instead always dynamic and relative, open to fluctuation and subject to infinite negotiation and calibration across the social spectrum. The infinite negotiations mediated by the kubrador (as broker of social life) are thus practices of transacting a form of power or potential that exceeds the notion of the (value-productive) potential of labor-power, even as the overall result of such practices might appear as yet another form of capitalist exploitation or even financial capitalist rent. They are also rites of social life-making that produce divisible, decomposable subjectivities and a tributary, kin-based and kin-modeled political order (often understood as "patron-clientelism") that exceed the imperatives of "lo democrático" as the political order of global finance capital even as they might be understood as being compatible with and indeed embedded in the latter's mode of accumulation (e.g., as "crony capitalism," "rent capitalism," and so on).

Two things are remaindered by a theoretical and political genealogy of present-day global capitalism that eschews (even as it attempts to subsume) the historical experiences and struggles of colonial and postcolonial peoples as well as minoritized social groups. The first is the role of such experiences and struggles in creating the very conditions for the emergence of new biopolitical forms of control and value extraction as well as of new forms of resistance and insurgency. The second are the forms and ontologies of life-making practice—in a word, life-times—that are tangential to and in excess of the (re)production of capital insofar as they are the means of fugitive life and flight on the part of those lives and lifeworlds historically devalued and deemed to be disposable resources for the use of others. As tangential, denigrated practices of freedom and power, remaindered life-times can consist of practices of dissolution and corrosion as well as practices of generating contingency and instability, rather than simply practices that conserve the stable sameness of given relations and identities. These dimensions of fate-playing practice can be found in the urban slum contexts of jueteng as well as in the contexts of overseas Filipina and Filipino migrant workers, whose own fate-playing actions corrode, as well as support, the socialities of their naturalized belonging, while constantly generating new spaces of unpredictability and portals of escape as a condition of life in their host societies.[53]

Primitive Survivals

Fate playing can be traced to older practices—of roaming and flight, of debt-bondage and running away, of cosmic gambles and mediumship—which have permeated that land-mottled oceanic social space of insular Southeast Asia throughout the region's long, discontinuous history under tributary modes of production.[54] From precolonial to colonial and postcolonial times, power and wealth have been the object and means, the instrument and consequence, of relations of obligation. Kin, dependents, followers, and bondsmen and bondswomen have all been constituents of power and wealth, which they at once realize and express.[55] While it was in older, precolonial contexts of abundant, variegated, and fertile land, low human density, impermanent dwellings, and few material possessions that control over people rather than territory evolved as the general rule of power in this part (along with other parts) of the world, social bonding as a primary form of organizing human life is a customary practice that continues to shape and inform subaltern and dominant social and political formations in the present.[56]

By social bonding I mean those broad culturally normative practices of creating lines of fealty and obligation, exemplified by the kin-based, bilateral descent mode of social organization characteristic of Philippine and other similar societies, and their tributary (vertical) relations to emergent and established precolonial and colonial states.[57] Such social bonding entails the practical commitment of people and their capacities as appendages, assets, instruments, and media of exchange (or currency) at the disposition of the social beings to whom they are personally bound. This is a mode of production and reproduction of "primitive" societies (or, domestic communities) that is carried over through colonial and postcolonial times insofar as the imperial relation of dispossession provides for the relative autonomy of these communities with respect to the colonial and postcolonial state and its ideological apparatuses.[58]

For people bound by kinship (by ritual as well as "natural" filial relations); people forcibly bonded through debt or war (whether "weaker," stateless communities raided by stronger, wealthier societies, or resource-ruined individuals voluntarily or forcibly put into indentured service); or people living in small villages violently resettled and concentrated in colonial towns (through Spanish colonial *reducción* policies), *flight* was the primary form of alleviation or breach of constraining bonds. Flight and disappearance were constant threats to Spanish colonialism as well as to local lords (*amo*), the means of bonded subjects to escape the violence, abuse, and oppressive hardship they were forced and expected to endure. "The unrestrained movement of natives" was a continuous problem for the Spanish colonizers, triggering all manner of policies of control such as in 1843 a decree outlawing unauthorized transfer of residence.[59] In this nonsettler colony, where "unoccupied" land (nonstate spaces) remained abundant, "avoidance migration" was a strategy—shared by Philippine natives (*indios*) and other Southeast Asian, perhaps also other Austronesian, peoples—that continued to plague the colonial state. Only the grafting of the tethering social logics of European tenancy onto indigenous debt-bond and kinship relations could finally produce forms of social bonding that would stabilize the emergent plantation forms of labor (forms of vertical obligation and tribute that, as we will see, persist in social relations today, constituting the political-police machine networks and family corporations that remain grafted onto kinship networks of survival).⁶⁰ Yet precisely insofar as these forms of social bonding, perhaps much more than capitalist ideologies of subjectivity, were the main means of reproducing dominant colonial and postcolonial relations, flight and abandonment have always been recourses of the first order.

Flight was and continues to be modern people's means of contestation and abjuration of the terms and conditions of their obligatory bonds of belonging, whether those bonds are filial, marital, or associative. It is not for nothing that overseas migration is often colloquially referred to as a Philippine divorce. For all the emphasis on migration as "forced," it is also one of the major routes of flight for many—flight both for persons and on behalf of the social beings they are vital parts of and seeking to pull out of a hard place. Changing-land (*pangingibang-lupa*) has become a well-honed strategy in a repertoire of strategies of departure from ordained or fated life paths.⁶¹ Within this repertoire of cosmic openings are gambles of life trading and petty, speculative adventurism, which the most socially and economically strapped continuously entertain and often pursue.

Those who are the most stripped of life resources—mainly land, as the basis of collective life and livelihood, and kinship, as the matrix of social connectivity and "mutual being" (shared life), which is itself a form of movable "ground" (in common cases of nomadic and liquid fates, the only resource that shores up one's life)—are also the most likely to engage in fate-playing actions.⁶² Such actions put into play the infinite contingency and mutability of existential arrangements, which are belied by the seemingly fixed and objective, known "facts of life" and mandated rules of affairs. They conjure the fortuitous against the ordained.

Like jueteng and other informal and illicit livelihood activities of the urban poor, such speculative practices of hazarding the otherwise solid, impassable, and immovable realities of the present have undeniably become incorporated and scaled up into enormously profitable illicit businesses that have come to delimit and define the operations of the state. Undeniably, the life-making practices of the poor and disenfranchised are constantly siphoned into the accumulative schemes of their purported benefactors. Still within these practices are remaindered life-times, times of hazarding what is one's own or part of one's to lose, in both small and large transactions with never fully known yet familiar potentials, positing humans and their capacities as divisible, mediatic parts of shared being that can be put into play, that is, made into the bet, the stake, and the player, in timings of generated chance or change. However dismal the particular results of past attempts for others, or even for oneself, such acts of fate playing assume an always negotiable present and the ever possible unconquered by the merely actual. Such acts are, in many ways, themselves unconquered remnants of modes of life paradoxically destroyed and preserved in the imperial relation. All these small acts—actual performances of seemingly past, even outmoded ways of life—shore up, even as they elude, the pyramid of accumulation platforms for the productivity of life as labor.

What these considerations of life-times of fate playing and their longer histories might suggest therefore are the very limits of our own political imagination, not only in comprehending the fuller expanse of life-times of struggle under global capitalism today, but also in envisioning how the remaindered life-times of disposable life might ultimately come to shape the timeline of global capitalism's duration and end, the "time of expectation" when the sum of our decolonizing efforts will bring about the hoped-for change in planetary life.

5

OF DISPOSABILITY

Discrepant Times of Neoliberalism

A number of scholarly works focused on the political and economic transformations known as globalization have described the perceived shift from liberalism to neoliberalism concomitant with these late twentieth- to early twenty-first-century transformations in terms of a shift in the logic of the constitution of forms of personhood and governmentality from one constructed around rights and property to another constructed around risk and security.[1] Beyond the domains of political and economic practice and rationality, this identified shift in global hegemony is seen to produce and issue out of changed structures of lived subjectivities and feeling and transformed modalities of social experience and imagination. In this and the following chapter, I want to explore in particular the structurings of time in emerging orders of labor and life as a way of understanding certain cultural and philosophical aspects of the project of neoliberalism and the organized divisions and relations among geopolitical populations and their social lifeworlds, which are composed of and presupposed by this new global hegemonic order.

Seen in light of broad changes in a shared regional and global political economy, films from China and the Philippines—in particular, Jia Zhangke's *Still Life* (2006) and *24 City* (2008) and Brillante Mendoza's *Tirador* (2007) and *Lola* (2009)—are important touchstones for my thinking on this subject. As a spectacular commodity, cinema is not only a principal medium of what Guy Debord calls the "time of the spectacle"—"in the narrow sense, as the time appropriate to the consumption of images, and in the broadest sense, as the image of the consumption of time"—it is also a principal and perhaps paradigmatic medium of the processes of idealization and abstraction that comprise the independent being of value on which financialization, or, let's say, the time of speculation, depends.[2] That said, I do not see these films as simply instances of capitalist media, though they are undoubtedly that, and it is in this aspect that they can be seen as exemplary sites for understanding the transformations wrought by and comprising neoliberal financialization. I see them also as aesthetic forms, experiments in sensorial perception related to located and bounded forms of being and ways of life that may be subsumed by capital but are neither reducible to nor fully exhausted by capitalist forms. It is in this latter aspect that these films in particular, which seek to unfold the times of disposable people (in the contexts of economic reforms in China and elite democratic structural adjustment in the Philippines), make sensible ways of being and living, forms of personhood and cooperation, improvisatory and experimental arrangements of social life, that are remaindered within the enlarged production time of capital.

In his series of lectures published as *The Birth of Biopolitics*, Foucault describes American neoliberalism in terms of an extension of classic economic analysis to the undertheorized domain of labor, now to be viewed as an active economic subject through a theory of human capital, and the generalization of the economic form of the market to domains of social phenomena hitherto considered noneconomic. In neoliberalism, instead of being a partner in exchange, *homo economicus* is normatively understood as "an entrepreneur, an entrepreneur of himself . . . being for himself his own capital, being for himself his own producer."[3] All the activities and time spent on the formation of a child as a kind of capital-ability machine—and Foucault gives the example not only of educational activities but also the time parents devote to the child outside of educational activities, including "the simple time" spent feeding them and giving them affection—such activities and time spent (in what an older vocabulary would have identified as the time of "reproduction") constitute practices of investment that is expected to yield future returns. This conception of labor as human capital that can be augmented through the investment of presumably already valued time (and indeed, the conception of the subject of labor or the worker as the entrepreneur of himself, including his "own," his child), is precisely the effect of the generalization of the "enterprise" form throughout the social body. The generalization of the economic form of the market beyond monetary exchanges," Foucault argues, "functions in American neo-liberalism as a principle of intelligibility and a principle of decipherment of social relationships and individual behavior."[4]

Others have similarly commented on the generalization of a market rationality to all spheres of human life as the defining feature of neoliberalism. Following Foucault, Wendy Brown observes in the current US context the rise of a normative political rationality entailing "the production of all human and institutional action as rational entrepreneurial action, conducted according to a calculus of utility, benefit, or satisfaction against a microeconomic grid of scarcity, supply and demand, and moral value-neutrality."[5] Randy Martin, expanding a similar analysis beyond Brown's argument, argues that as financial reason overtakes a systems-based moral and political economy, the figure of the investor elbows out the consumer-citizen as the new normative focus of government policy. Leverage takes precedence over ownership and fixed benefits, and risk becomes somatized as a way of being, made into a subjectivity shaped by the specific logic of finance, less an entrepreneur than an arbitrageur, preying on fluctuations of price and making wagers on uncertainties made into potential risk opportunities for profitable returns.[6]

If financial reason has moved into the person, becoming a practical form of life, the time frame of its philosophy, whereby the future is already seen as the present, shapes and defines the new temporal protocols and conditions of lived life. On this view, Jane Guyer's analysis of a temporal shift in US public culture, marked by a double movement of the evacuation of the near past and the near future in the discourses of macroeconomics and evangelical Christianity, corresponds to Martin's analysis of the time frame of experience of the investor self, who has "already been dispossessed of a secure past, present, and future."[7] For this self, the new financial plan for living requires a daily investment, assessment, and management of one's contributions "to occupy the kind of time and space once readily conferred on personhood." The temporality of defined benefits, wherein the futurity of the Protestant ethic promised a final settling of one's life accounts, is now overtaken by that of defined contributions, wherein one's mettle has to be proven one day at a time, and everyday becomes Judgment Day.

Cleavages and Thresholds

But what is the social distribution of this order? Which individuals inhabit and qualify for the investor model of subjectivity and its structure of temporal experience? For Martin, there is a racialized cleavage within society between the risk-takers or risk-capable and "those unable to live by risk, [who] are considered 'at risk.'"[8] Such a cleavage is not a problem for neoliberalism, Maurizio Lazzarato argues, insofar as it is precisely the conditions of inequality and insecurity—as "normalities"—that need to be ensured and calibrated for the operation of competition and enterprise as organizing principles of society. What neoliberalism worries about, rather, are the conditions preventing the individual, or I would say potential players (as defined on a variety of scales), from playing the game of competition. Hence, it seeks to establish an acceptable equilibrium between these normalities by defining "a threshold, a vital minimum, above which the individual can become an 'enterprise' and below which he/she falls out of the game and needs punctual rather than systematic state assistance."[9]

Such a threshold draws a line between the subjects and nonsubjects of a neoliberal regime of governmentality and political rationality. It would be difficult to map this distinction onto the older division between capital and labor insofar as it is precisely the subjectification of labor (in part prepared by the compromise between liberalism and labor, or the particular form of liberalism in the United States, as "the antidote to socialism," enabled by US economic expansion beyond its borders in the first half of the twentieth century[10]) that serves as the basis for labor's conversion into "human capital." It is nevertheless a distinction that remains indissociable from the social logics of capital accumulation. One of many thresholds that create and maintain the plural liminalities constitutive of global capitalist life, the threshold for valorizable entrepreneurial subjectivity does not only mark a division between levels and dynamics of operation of neoliberalism's normative ideals and processes (e.g., between its effects on morally elevated, risk-capable individuals and those on morally denigrated, racialized, gendered, and sexualized "at-risk" groups—between life worth living and life worth expending[11]); it also serves as a threshold of theoretical intelligibility and attention that implicates political-intellectual critique in the reinscription of the very institutions and processes that it might seek to radically transform.

There are several points of argument related to this threshold that I need to work through in order to provide a global framework for thinking about remaindered life-times and, in this way, to consider other sites of making and political possibility subsumed within but also tangential to the global order of neoliberalism and its protocols for everyday life.

The first point is that if we see the distinction between "at-risk" populations and "risk-capable" subjects as a distinction between money for exchange and money for credit (i.e., money as capital), we are able to understand the differences between forms of personhood and lived experience that obtain under neoliberal norms not simply as spatially distributed social differences (given racialized, gendered, and sexualized forms of identity or geopolitical areas and populations) in a static framework of contradiction, but rather as moments or aspects of a global dynamic of processes of accumulation set in motion, in which practices of life-making play diverse, conflicting roles as ever-diminishing resources and ever-displaced limits in the production of value.

It is within the circuit of money advanced as credit that we witness the temporality of finance, or the time of speculation, that shapes the form and experience of the neoliberal *homo economicus*. As Melinda Cooper shows, M–C–M′ is the movement of money as capital "where time no longer mediates the exchange of use-values, but enters, as it were, into 'private relations' with itself."[12] The practice of speculation, as an investment of capital, involves an anticipatory time of realization of value in excess of the present value for which it is exchanged. "In return of value to value, capital speculates on its own future realization as something in excess of itself."[13] It is precisely in its capacity to continue exceeding itself, unhampered by the limits of the organic life of labor, or what used to be called the time of labor's reproduction, that the seeming "limitlessness" of capital's movement (and the endlessness of its wars of security) lies. As Cooper writes, the speculative animation of value establishes "an inversion of powers between past and future, production and profit, in which the after-life of a life that has not yet been lived, the purely speculative existence of a future profit, realizes and gives birth to the past of production," a case of male parthenogenesis or self-birthing (of son conceiving the father).[14]

The contraction of past and future, the evaporation of chronology or successive and cumulative time in the infinite extension of present action, the colonization of the future as a means of present realization—such temporal features of life under neoliberalism are, in my understanding, an accounting of the subjective experience of a subject inhabiting money as capital. Or put differently, it is at the level of the operation of money as capital (and the transformation of citizen-subjects into human capital) that much discussion of neoliberal political rationality, including Foucault's, takes place. Such an analysis of neoliberalism becomes thereby confined to the terms of the most "advanced" form of capitalism (postindustrial financialization), eliding an entire arena of

Of Disposability • 113

production processes mistakenly presumed to have been superseded in the purported transformation of the regime of accumulation "from managerial/industrial capitalism to shareholding/postindustrial capitalism."[15] I am speaking, in part, of precisely that circuit of money as payment or exchange, which dead ends in consumption, as another sphere of lived subjectivities and "living labor" that, while laying beneath the threshold of neoliberal intelligibility, nevertheless plays an indispensable role in the broader *global* economy over which and through which finance capital has gained sovereign power.

Beyond the moment of simple reproduction, within which the "free" work of slaves, colonial peoples, and women served to augment the surplus labor-time expropriated from labor through formal processes of capitalist exchange, I am also speaking of the arena of not only this kind of hidden *labor time* in the reproduction of the worker but also forms of disposable and remaindered *life-times*, the times of social reproduction that aid and lie outside contemporary modes of exploitation of life as labor. Such life-times consist of a diverse array of acts, capacities, associations, aspirations in practice, experiential modes, and sensibilities that people engage in, draw on, and invent in their everyday struggles to make and remake social life under conditions of their own superfluity or disposability.

If the distinction between economic forms allows us to recognize that it is money as capital rather than simply "the market" or "enterprise" that serves as the key principle of subjectivation under neoliberalism, then it is important to recognize, and this is my second point, that such subjects include states as well as corporations and emergent sectors of elite classes in developing countries, and not merely individuals. The distinction thereby helps us to understand the differences and relations between the effects of neoliberalist structures and institutions at the level of subjects in both the Global North and the Global South and their permutations at the level of social reproduction of survival, by which I mean devalued informal and naturalized practices of maintaining minimal "organic" or subsistence life, on which global reproductive labor depends. Such capitalized reproductive labor is not simply equivalent to particular sectors of the economy such as domestic and service workers or peasant farmers who produce and subsidize the services and goods that maintain the minimal life or necessary consumption of human capital. This is rather a whole array of nonsubjectified labor, or disposable life-times, that arguably produces both the personal "free time" or valued and value-productive "surplus time" used for investment in human capital, which includes the saved time for the consumption of the image and the savings that become a fiscal resource for defined contributions and investments in the financial market.

The distinction also allows us to take stock of modalities of being, as particular activities of living that come to be expended and disposed, as the very medium of financialization. Such disposable life-times, I would venture, constitute precisely the displaced middle term of M–C–M′, the commodity of "life" that is merely the medium for the speculative genesis of value.[16] As we saw earlier, this formulation applies precisely to the valorizing movement of the neoliberal subject, as an entrepreneur of the self as capital-ability (the investor in and capitalist of one's own accumulable life as commodity capital), for whom life-times of waste can be offshored, relegated to others.[17]

While analyses of neoliberalism tend to focus on the remaking of subjects under its new protocols of life, swathes of other life are merely viewed as the expended, surplussed populations figured as forms of bare life, at-risk populations, warehoused and disposable people, urban excess (in the planet of slums), out of which new political subjects and potentials for resistance already convertible to the ruling political currencies of the day are to be gleaned. It is of less interest to dwell on modes of life lived and practices of living that are remaindered in the process of the production of biopolitical life, that is, on the extra living in the waste of life and wasted life, or what is *not* consumed in the consumption of life forces as the basis of the expropriation of value.

Lastly, even as these times of remaindered life have been the focus of attention of a range of contemporary Philippine and Chinese cinemas, which have made their way into the global cultural marketplace of international cinema, we cannot understand the political import of this aesthetic attention, particularly the significance of their respective modalities of temporalization in relation to the project of neoliberalism, without a grasp of the latter's global and regional dynamics, including the arenas of peripheral social life that US- and EU-focused critiques of neoliberalism as global hegemonic rationality tend to occlude, or at best ignore. A view of these peripheral arenas brings into focus the connections among land, people, and time comprising the less-considered dynamics of neoliberalism.

Land, People, Time

Given the terms of biopower in the contemporary centers of global capitalism (preoccupied with the institutions of governmentality over all social life subsumed by capital, with social death marking that threshold below which certain forms of human life fall out of the game), it is no surprise to find that, as Cooper writes, "what thereby disappears almost from Foucault's field of vision is the question of land appropriation itself, in its relation both to the productivity of 'life'—in all its guises, economic, sexual, biological—and the problematic of security."[18] The question of land appropriation signals those processes of dispossession and direct appropriation necessary for the expanded reproduction of capital, processes of "primitive accumulation" that depend on the territorial international order of sovereign nation-states established through European imperialism.

Usefully drawing on Carl Schmitt's genealogy of international law, *The Nomos of the Earth*, to address the missing geopolitical dimension in Foucault's understanding of classical liberalism as the animating ethos of biopower, Cooper argues that the liberal doctrine of freedom (and its polemics against the sovereign power of the state) is inconceivable and inoperable without the "forcibly open horizon of free space" of the colonial world serving as both the geographical context of liberalism's utopia of incessant economic growth and an actual territorial zone of exception for the constitutive displacement of sovereign Europe's domestic conflicts.[19] In the same manner, understood as an extreme extension of classical liberal economics, the neoliberal politics of the "Washington consensus" must be seen as predicated on the "free spaces" of liberalized unilateral trade and deregulated national financial markets secured in the developing world through structural adjustment policies from the mid-1980s on. Just as the New World constituted a zone for the exoneration of interstate and internal friction in the European states by exporting conflicts elsewhere, the postcolonial developing world has enabled the exoneration of the US domestic economic crisis of the early 1970s (a crisis generated by decolonization movements at home and globally) by serving as the zone of expanding financial risk for speculative capital. As Cooper argues, "the 'free space' represented by the New World in the era of European imperialism has here been overwritten—not superseded—by the zones of 'free speculative movement' forcibly opened up by the so-called Washington consensus."[20]

While in the previous imperialist era the zone of exception deployed by sovereign European states (as a constitutive condition of classical liberalism) was geographical in nature, in the contemporary global era, the "open horizon" for risk-taking economic freedom bears a characteristically temporal dimension. Value-productive risks are located in "the virtual time zone of speculative maneuvers" and in place of a geographical state-of-exception, "an ever-present state-of-emergency" is deployed by sovereign state powers as an instrument for guaranteeing the fundamental economic insecurity of the "free space" of deregulated flows.[21] That is to say, neoliberalism's market and financial freedoms continue to depend on the geopolitical territorial order consolidated through imperialism to both establish and police those zones of open horizon for untrammeled speculative movement, zones that are not merely geographical but also temporal.

The question of land appropriation cannot, however, be confined to the era of classical liberalism; it in fact persists as a crucial though overlooked condition of the global project of neoliberalism. As the process of "primitive accumulation" that must recur for the expanded reproduction of capital beyond the limits reached in a prior cycle (inducing "crisis"), the severance of people from their means of subsistence and their transformation into "free" and "unattached" wage-laborers has as its basis "the expropriation of the agricultural producer, of the peasant, from the soil."[22] Land appropriation not only undergirds the "boom" cycles of economic growth in Asia through the transformation of land into capital (providing new sites of financial investment in commercial and residential real estate, public works construction, and so on), a process most evident in the infrastructural boom in the Philippines (on which I elaborate in chapter 7). As the case of China spectacularly demonstrates, the conversion of rural land into capital through privatization and marketization or industrialization also creates a newly "freed" proletariat for the export-oriented manufacturing and agricultural industries in newly industrializing countries, which, in turn, fuel debt-financed consumption in the postindustrial North.[23] Prior to 1978, three quarters of the population in China was rural and mostly engaged in local agricultural production. By the early 1990s, nearly 120 million of these rural workers were employed in off-farm, township, and village enterprises.[24]

Beyond these familiar "real economy" implications of "primitive accumulation," the question of land highlights a crucial phenomenal shift and condition of neoliberalist financialization: the important role of the violent "surplusing" of populations by their governments and other ruling national (economic) agents in the postcolonial and postsocialist Global South as part and parcel of the latter's respective bids (as neoliberal investor-subjects) to play the global market. That is to say, in order for national developing states and economic elites to become viable players in the financialized global market, they must have *at their disposal* a population that can be made redundant to any particular lines of industry as dictated by the sudden vicissitudes of capital flows and that will ultimately shoulder the costs of fallout of any and all speculative maneuvers. Such surplus populations of sovereign states (i.e., as "citizens"—really, nationals—subject to the regulations and controls of particular nation-states but effectively reduced to the status of nonsubjects, dispossessed of their rights to national commons and claims to their sovereign state) thus serve as securitized assets for the risk-taking ventures of proper investor subjects.

Of Disposability • 117

In other words, these investor subjects do not require the dispossessing processes of "primitive accumulation" solely for the creation of a new waged labor force or, for that matter, a labor reserve army. They require processes of dispossession to create and maintain a captive population of "surplussed" people as monetized aggregates of disposable life.

Monetized, surplus human life can serve not only as flexible labor, readily available and eliminable as capital moves from one site (or one line) to another, in effect enabling the speed of capital circulation and minimizing losses to capital in downturns, crashes, and crises; this disposable life can also serve as *risk-absorbing collateral*, particularly for state and state-allied enterprises, which can offer it bundled as wholesale life commodities promising future life-times of surplus labor and money (in the form of taxes)—value—that can be *advanced*, that is, cashed in *now* (through "cuts" in the national budget, social services, etc., as well as through currency devaluation, to service bad debts—as exemplified in the bank bailouts in the aftermath of the US subprime mortgage crisis and in the austerity programs installed in Europe to address the debt crisis).[25]

In this context, land continues to serve as an important means of production from which rural populations are continually dispossessed even as it remains a "flexible" and supplementary means of subsistence for those newly "freed" and increasingly surplussed people. Indeed, against the widely shared notion of the increasing if not complete obsolescence of the peasant as a historical category, Silvia Federici argues that agricultural work continues to be of great importance in today's political economy, not only because of its size as a productive sector (employing about 2 billion people globally) and evidenced by the World Bank's recent prioritization of agrarian reform in its restructuring programs, but also because subsistence agriculture in particular underwrites the social reproduction of "the millions who would otherwise have no means to purchase food on the market."[26] In other words, land signals not only the overlooked processes of "primitive accumulation" within global neoliberalism but also, as I have discussed, the overlooked processes of social reproduction of disposable (rather than directly productive) life. As the work of Indigenous scholars has long been demonstrating, land continues to be an absolutely vital issue for the survival and future of communities destined for disappearance.[27] In the Philippines, land continues to be the single most important issue for the survival of rural communities, with peasant women's movements at the forefront of the struggle for land as the basis of rural subsistence.[28] It is precisely this survival that is being remade and repurposed in the creation of disposable populations of rural migrants and the urban poor.

As both the consequence and medium of finance-led modes of value production, disposable populations are produced and maintained precisely through the instrumental use and control of land (as capital and as sovereign territory). Surplus people are maintained as surplus through processes that alternately and simultaneously "free" them from the land and tether them to it. In China, Federici points out, a process of "re-peasantization" is occurring alongside the processes of proletarianization and urbanization, as rural migrant workers in the coastal cities are forced by downturns in economic growth to return to the countryside and to constantly move between rural and urban work sites. Deprived of equal access to employment, health care, and education rights by the exclusionary policies of the household registration system (*hukou*), which maintains distinctions between permanent and temporary workers as established by urban or rural residence, migrant rural workers are subject to a process of "unfinished proletarianization" that leaves them in a condition of permanent transience and dislocation.[29] As Pun Ngai, Chris Chan and Jenny Chan write: "China's economy needs the labour of the rural population but does not need the city-based survival of that population once market demand for rural-to-market urban migrants' labour power shifts in either location or industry. This newly forming working class is permitted to form no permanent roots and legal identity in the city."[30]

In many ways replicating domestically what obtains globally for Philippine and other national "guest" or migrant contract workers who are excluded from citizenship in the host countries where they work, the ambiguous identity and floating condition of Chinese rural migrant workers (the new *dagong* class) depend on the territorial segregation of the place of their social reproduction, as a means of radically discounting the costs of this labor force and their exclusion from rights to social goods.[31] Since rural communities long exercised the extended planning of life activities, "the reproduction of labor of the next generation is left to rural villages, which bear the cost of industrial development in urban areas, even though the ability of rural communities to meet reproduction costs is often highly constrained."[32] In effect, through the crucial role of the state, which oversees the differential zoning of living wages (i.e., rates of exchange of labor reproduction) through sovereign control over territory, rural communities in China and the Philippines subsidize the costs of social reproduction of a floating, surplus population whose disposability and absolute "liquidity" is precisely what is necessary to ensure the freedom of movement of capital.

Moreover, the very disposability of these territorialized national populations allows them to serve as securitized assets for the speculative maneuvers of neoliberal state and state-allied economic subjects—the condition of possibility of the latter's participation in the global financial market. That is to say, in monetized aggregate form, surplus national populations effectively constitute the forced open horizon of the neoliberal free market. They constitute the virtual time zone of financial speculation within which new opportunities of value extraction, as well as the risks of these maneuvers, are located. If financial speculation finds opportunities for value extraction in the virtual zone of *time*—after all, what are commodity-futures and "securities" (risk bundles) if not temporal commodities—then surplus populations are nothing but *an entire global zone of disposable life-times for speculative maneuvers*. These disposable life-times are what are necessary to absorb the risks on which financial speculation depends (i.e., on which investors wager) and to guarantee the triple-A-rated time value of prime mortgages and capital loans that proper neoliberal subjects require to fund and augment the value productivity of their life enterprises.

Insofar as speculation bets on price differentials over time, time appears to be productive of value. Such value-productive time is, however, inextricable from the abstraction and expenditure of human life. For neoliberal subjects, life is indistinguishable from labor, and therefore the time of labor is the value-productive time of life. However, while, for the neoliberal subject as entrepreneur of their own life (as capital), one's own time is value productive, for the investor it is *the time of others, the time of nonsubjects* (their promised labor time as embodied in the debts they take out or that are taken out on their behalf by their representative state), that can be bet on or expended now for the extraction of value. The time of others is, importantly, graded to the extent that the worth of life-times varies considerably—life-time being the time of life-making or time of social reproduction, which, with the devaluation of national currency and corresponding devaluation of the people that such currency represents, can be radically debased as a result of state economic policies (competitive currency devaluation, liberalization of protectionist tariffs, regulations), policing (repression of labor struggles, of alternative economies), and war (creation of displaced persons as surplus people through the destruction of communities and their means of subsistence, the making of uninhabitable conflict-ridden zones, forced migration, and so on).

By means of the economic sovereign nation-state system, which determines the global exchange value of different populations, people are forced to increasingly subsidize (by shouldering) the costs of their reproduction (increasingly becoming unpaid labor) and to provide (through taxes) the surplus value directly appropriated through state "emergency" austerity measures and stimulus packages. The relative value of people's life-times must thus be viewed in similar terms as the varying potentials (or purchasing power) of money as a medium of exchange, or the different rates of exchange of monetary currencies, which rest on the unequal political and economic relations comprising the international system of sovereign territorial states.

On this view, the life-times of surplus people can usefully be seen as a form of "soft currency," a medium of exchange that, unlike "hard currency," cannot hold its value and may in fact depreciate rapidly, attesting to the importance of national sovereignty in the determination of money's potential.[33] As "soft currency," that is, as medium of exchange rather than as measure or holder of value, the life-times of surplus people at the disposal of a state and its crony economic elites can thus function as monetized assets used to leverage the latter's position in playing the global financial markets. Such disposable life-times constitute the liquid reserves that the state risks in its bid for foreign investments.

In effect, the disposable life-times that surplus populations represent are precisely the quantified abstract future that is "colonized" (or mortgaged) in the speculative maneuvers of transnational and national elites, with the crucial agency of the state apparatus. From the side of disposability, *the life of surplus people is the future begetting the present*, generating the surplus value now accumulated as finance capital, which appears to be begetting value out of itself. Put another way, the seemingly limitless resource that is the future (as part of the seemingly limitlessness of life itself) is in actuality the lives of people whose own futures are offered up as exchange values extractable in the present.

The condition of permanent transience of this human surplus, which issues from its absolute liquidity, thus presents a structure (or set of structures) of temporal experience that is in striking contrast to the "short-term" temporal framework of finance, most identified with neoliberalism, within which investor subjects seek to make the most out of the present by mortgaging and foreclosing on the future.[34] How do recent films that attempt to render cinematically the life of rural migrants, "floating populations," and slum dwellers in China and the Philippines offer us insight into this "time of war"—the temporal structures of lived experience and life-making for people caught in these zones of disposability? What do we make of these films' own forms of attention to the remaindered life of surplus populations?

6

OF SURVIVAL

People as Rubble: Temporalities of Spectacular Destruction

One of the most striking emblems of the entwinement of land appropriation and human surplussing within global neoliberalism is Jia Zhangke's cinematic image of the Three Gorges Dam in *Still Life* (2006), a public works project on the Yangtze requiring the flooding and complete submerging of the ancient town of Fengjie and the relocation of more than a million and half people, together with the planned destruction of their homes and villages.

Much if not all the commentary and scholarship on Jia has viewed this film, and the work of Jia more generally, as portraying the dramatic changes undergone by China in the era of neoliberal reform through an attention to the everyday lives of people who have been swept up by such changes and yet who are excluded from the promises of integration into the global market.[1] In marked contrast to Fifth Generation filmmakers' modernist depictions of mythologized pasts and "timeless" landscapes (an aesthetics that was itself a repudiation of the previous socialist-realist tradition and of the tenets of Maoist China more generally), Zhang Xudong argues, Jia and his fellow

Sixth Generation filmmakers "staged allegorical fragments of a broken, disoriented reality," their sights trained on the ruins of a social landscape left in the wake of the turbulent transformations of Deng Xiaoping's market reform era.[2] In this context, Jia's films can be viewed, Zhang argues, as an attempt to cognitively map the brute yet barely visible or audible reality glossed over by the metaphysical image of China proffered by his predecessors. Seeking to document this subaltern reality, Jia focuses on the social fabric of the county-level city (*xiancheng*), not only as the setting of familiar scenes of demolition and construction characteristic of China's grand transformation, but also as the ongoing *event* of social disaster wrought by this transformation: "an aching reminder of the failures and compromises of socialist industrialization, of the post-socialist reforms, and even of the sweep of market forces."[3] The focus on the xiancheng—and its revelation of "the silent violence borne by a helpless population" as they find their entire worlds, communities, and norms of life subject to disappearance and extinction—shapes the recurrent theme of vanishing that marks Jia's films and the aesthetic practices through which this theme is formally realized.[4] *Still Life*, the English translation of the film's original title, *Sanxia haoren* (The good people of the Three Gorges), not only reflects Jia's own literary interpretation of this film in terms of a neglected reality, a silent, everyday existence that preserves deep traces of time and therefore the durable secret of life; it also provides a concept for understanding the aesthetics of Jia's filmmaking more generally as "at once a poetics of vanishing and a documentary of rescue."[5]

The aesthetics of this cinematic attention to the vanishing, the immobile, and the silent offers a particular temporal structure for grasping the lifetimes of disposability as embodied in the lives of all the workers portrayed in the film, whom Jia describes as "more or less unemployed . . . more or less homeless, perpetually moving from one place to another with a sense of permanently being in exile."[6] Counterposed to the accelerated tempo of state capitalist futurism and its spectacular promulgation and effectuation of rapid, inexorable, and omnigeneous change, Jia's films tend toward the visual arrest and narrative suspension of that world-historical time of economic reforms as the backdrop of a more lingering, amplifying attention to precisely that form of simultaneous stillness and restlessness that is the everyday time of the perpetually displaced, the human ruins left in the wake of capitalism's "creative destruction." The dialectical image of these contradictory and yet also mirroring temporalities is precisely the content of a "present" that Jia seeks to dwell on against the vanishing effects and foreshortened universal temporality of the global market.

While in Jia's "historical" film *Platform* (2000) the irreversible time of history, the time of political events and economic transformations, appears only in narrative ellipses between scenes, to be gleaned in the small changes on the material surfaces of everyday life (clothing, style, popular music, and so on), in *Still Life*, historical time appears frozen in the monumental infrastructural projects of the state, exemplified above all by the Three Gorges Dam and the magnificent suspension bridge that spans it—a built environment cast in the seemingly suprahuman state and perennial temporality of nature and yet whose rapid and sudden emergence (through massive demolitions and large-scale construction) is experienced as surreal instantaneity. Such instantaneity is dramatized in one magical moment when, with a flip of the switch, the spectacularly lit bridge suddenly appears from out of the evening darkness, wondrously conjured by a state bureaucrat to impress his guests; but it is also depicted as an unremarkable part of the new scenery in the images of entire buildings collapsing in the background.[7]

Against the backdrop of this arrested time of history, imaged as the banalized spectacular time of things, Jia's camera lingers on and dilates—through slow, steady pans and exceptionally long takes—the foregrounded time of the nonevent, the sheer passage and duration of living in "real-time" on the part of those whose homes have already been or are about to be demolished, workers clearing the rubble of buildings they are tearing down, their own lives overnight turned into rubble to make way for the monuments of capital. *Still Life* provides many cinematic images of these opposed and yet mutually dependent times: the time of capital and the irreducible times of living destined toward waste. The near sublime monumentality of scale and profundity of consequence of China's transformations are, for example, encapsulated in the time-image of the enormous lake that has taken the place of the ancient town of Fengjie, whose center now lies at the bottom of this seemingly placid, magnificent expanse of water signaling both the historic realization of a long-standing dream of modern progress and its catastrophic effect. In search of his long-lost wife, whose last residential address turns out to be somewhere in the middle of this lake, the migrant laborer Han Sanming, one of the two protagonists of the film, gazes at the liquid expanse before him with the same slow, steady, almost motionless, lingering attention that is a hallmark of Jia's cinema. Sanming's searching gaze is the cinematic gaze of rescue of a vanishing past, which is also present and future life. His seemingly empty expression registers time passing without visible reaction and yet in this way also registers unknown depths (of time, of experience, of life) beneath this seemingly empty recording of time as the unrepresented human costs of postsocialist reform, the ignored

Of Survival • 125

contents of capital's seemingly infinite resources of value extraction—entire life-times of lived and felt relations, borne disappointments, and worked-up aspirations, pasts never to be memorialized and imagined futures never to be realized—traced on the surfaces of a naturescape ("land") that is the unconscious of capitalist freedoms.

Jason McGrath argues that the structuring of time characteristic of Jia's cinematic attention (slow and steady pans, exceptionally long takes, extremely long shot compositions, and a relatively immobile camera)—a protracted temporality also evident in the "narrative distension" observed by Chris Berry in Jia's earlier films—presents "a radical vision of postsocialist realist time countering any master narrative of teleological progress . . . the time of the reform era's 'losers' rather than the more oft-represented 'winners.'"[8] Understood as a form of realism, the temporal structure conveyed by this form of cinematic attention is posited as both the means of uncovering the "bleak urban reality" of excess populations (the human rubble of global neoliberalism) and the very temporal structure of "perpetual motion" lived by such populations. It could in fact be said that Jia finds in this distension of time passing—this protracted lived time beneath and beyond the time of historically significant actions and events (the time of narrative plots)—a form adequate to the ontological condition of these populations in their status as liquid assets of the state (i.e., nothing but directly expendable life-times): in short, sheer duration becomes the objective correlative for disposable life.[9]

Still Life conveys the paradoxical condition of permanent transience of "floating populations," whose life-times are a form of excess with little to zero value except in large-scale aggregate form. On the one hand, the distension of time not only rescues a historical past and once official present suddenly being evacuated but also represents a zone of human existence that I would underscore is a central feature of global neoliberalism—the zone, that is, of absolutely redundant life, with its status as sheer surplus time, the time of life as expenditure (comprising the virtual time zone of financial value "production"). The cinematic realization of a prolonged present, its dilation into a quasi-spatial condition, brings into perception this zone of disposable life-times as a devastated social landscape whose surfaces Jia attempts to read for the decoded vitality beneath its stilled existence.

Against the volatility and frenetic pace of financial capital's radical presentism, Jia posits a temporal calm, an expanded and tranquil temporal passage (the present progressive tense) in which past and future are immanent or at least can be broached. Curiously, however, this dilation of presence by which the sheer disposability of human life is countered creates a sense of eternality that is reminiscent of natural landscape portraiture in classical scroll painting, which Jia cites as a model for the cinematography.[10] This sense is especially keen in the slowly panning close-up shots of the faces and physiques of migrant workers on the river boat in the opening sequence of the film, as well as in the similarly slow-panning medium shots of the bodies of Sanming's coworkers eating together with their shirts off. Here a certain timelessness has entered into the images of humans in *Still Life*, resembling what in the context of modern literature Kojin Karatani has identified as people as landscapes, realism's representation of "ordinary people" as a reality from which modern subjects have been alienated.[11] In this way the sensation of eternity with which the landscape of disposable human life is imbued—a testament to their survival and an assertion of prevailing against disappearance that is nevertheless also "racializing" in its substantification of time and extension in space—can be viewed as the echo of the temporal structure of the "pseudo-nature" and "pseudo-cyclical time" of the spectacle, arrested in the landscape of capitalist built form.[12]

On the other hand, the distension of time is a means of the reversal of the abstraction, homogenization, and equivalence to which people's life-times are subjected (as monetized aggregates). In this way, the extension of the present is not the process of an infinite accumulation of abstract, equivalent units of time from the past and the future, such as it is in the evacuation of past and future (the past time of dead labor as well as the future time of disposable life) in favor of extractable value in the present for neoliberal investor subjects. Instead, it is a mode of sustained perception that allows the slow revelation or unfolding of the singular qualities of living time, of authentically or actually lived times of life borne on the nonevents of gestures and the absence or sparing presence of words.

In a scene when Sanming presents two bottles of liquor to his brother-in-law as an offering in his bid for information on the whereabouts of his wife, the gesture of his bowed head and outstretched hands is held for what seems an interminable time, without the brother-in-law ever being shown to accept the gift. In this held gesture, cinematic movement at a standstill, the very suspension of a time filled with unfulfilled expectation becomes itself the full content of the image. Here all the singular contents and trajectories of lives really lived, as they leave their indelible traces on the bodies, comportment, gesture, and speech of these nonprofessional actors—the unabstractable passage of personal and shared, anonymous, everyday experience, the nitty-gritty details, matter, and texture of life-times made, maintained, spent, extended, and continued, which compose the lives of nonsubjects[13]—are allowed the time to surface. In such distensions there is time and attention enough to suggest "entire regions and territories of experience," layers of time, of life, of times of living (of the singular being within the mass, which Hortense Spillers calls the "one," "the small integrity of the now that accumulates the tense of the presents as proofs of the past, and as experience that would warrant, might earn, the future") excised from the official account of reforms' gains.[14] As Jia acknowledges, "To me, human beings are always what matters most. When I find myself in front of those people, I am always very moved. I am content simply to observe them, face to face, directly. So it seems right, respectful, to put into the film those moments when nothing appears to be happening. I think there are very profound things involved in those moments."[15]

International Aesthetics, Transnational Politics

McGrath notes that Jia's long-take aesthetic can not only be traced to the inspiring work of Hou Hsiao-Hsien and Tsai Ming-liang, auteurs of the new Taiwanese cinema, which he held in high estimation, and the new documentary movement in China. It can also be traced to the favored aesthetic forms of international art cinema and the film festival circuit, particularly elements of neo-Bazinian realism and the influential notion of the Deleuzian time-image, which helped to make art cinema an "aesthetic and theoretical antipode to entertainment cinema." This international framing of Jia's cinema is important insofar as it points less to a national than to a transnational cinematic language whose particular regional efflorescence in East and Southeast Asian alternative film highlights a broader aesthetic-political project being undertaken in relation to contemporary global conditions. In fact, McGrath's description of the aesthetic imperative of André Bazin's "cinema of time" or "cinema of duration" touches on the salient concern: "The priority is to organize time not according to dramatic needs but rather in accordance with 'life time'—the experience of time as simply duration in a life that is more fully of quotidian movement, inactivity and boredom than spectacular events even in an era of dramatic historical change."[16]

It is entirely persuasive to argue that the popularization of this temporal structuring of the cinematic image in accordance with "life time" in international art circuits bespeaks an aesthetic-political movement against the growing global power of the spectacle, a broad critique of the reifying process of image-production of Hollywood, certainly, and perhaps also of "the cinematic mode of production" more generally.[17] It might even be viewed as part of a broader social movement to put into conceptual and affective language and expressive form that dimension of lived life that increasingly, as it has been overwritten by global capitalist history and negated by the pseudo-events proffered by the spectacular images of film and media, finds itself bereft of any means of perception and communication.[18] It seems to me vitally important, however, not to lose sight of the peculiar variations and contrasts of aesthetic practice within this transnational guild across the different social contexts of filmic production that it brings together. For such nuances help clarify not only the specific socio-historical situations of particular disposable populations and the moments within the global capitalist dynamic that they inhabit, but also the politics of these cinematic instantiations of the life-times of such peoples.

On this view, it becomes instructive to consider Jia's cinematic practices alongside those of Brillante Mendoza, as sensory, attentional experiments shaped and delimited by the social contexts of human disposability that they attempt to render as well as by the histories of their own social conditions of production. Though both Jia and Mendoza attend to the human life remaindered by the spectacular productions and media of capital, it is Jia who in a more focused way brings into cinematic representation the surplussed condition of such life through the perceptual structure of excess time, providing a filmic critique of neoliberalism's materialized time of spectacle through its dialectical image of the life-times of disposability in the form of surplus time. By representing the event of the making of a displaced floating population in *Still Life* and *24 City* as a protracted duration of "life time," Jia provides a filmic genre critically opposed to neoliberalism's own materialized time of the spectacle.

For Mendoza, whose social contexts and conditions for thinking about human disposability are the result of a much longer, directly impactful history of globalizing capital—indeed, a history of neoliberalism that can be argued to have started not in the 1990s, as in the case of China, but in fact in the early 1960s, with the deregulation of the Philippine national economy, including the unpegging of the peso from the dollar ("currency decontrol"), which resulted in a devastating economic crisis and the wholesale devaluation of Philippine labor—the "event" of human disposability has been a slow, long-drawn-out process that now appears to be an enduring condition.[19] Since the economic crisis of the 1960s, which ushered in a new political and economic era for Philippine national life characterized by the adoption and pursuit of strategies of export-oriented industrialization under the technocrat-guided authoritarian government of Ferdinand Marcos, a rural population displaced and dispossessed by debt-fueled agricultural "development" and industrialization has steadily grown, migrating to cities (mainly the greater metropolitan area of Manila) and to other countries in search of work.[20] Promoted and institutionalized by the Marcos government in 1974, the labor export industry overseen by the state began to channel an increasingly significant portion of this latent surplus population abroad, such that today no less than 10 percent of the national population has found temporary work abroad.[21] It is in effect the remittances from this overseas labor force—engaged in largely precarious social reproductive work for their host societies (as producers of valorizable life-times for metropolitan biopolitical subjects, and as buffers and supplements for neoliberalist state withdrawal from social reproduction)—and, importantly, the forced taxation of such remittances by the state that sustains the conditions for a constantly self-renewing "stagnant surplus population" in the Philippines.[22]

While neoliberalism in advanced capitalist economies might seek to liberate individual entrepreneurial freedoms (for the post-Fordist worker by making "life" directly value productive), the provision of the "temporal surplus value" required for the exercise of such productive freedoms depends on the fostering and maintenance of transnational familial and para-kinship networks as the means by which migrant workers subsidize the devalued conditions of their own social reproduction at home (their own cheapened "life-times"). As they cycle in and out of these global labor-commodity chains, they not only act as producers of valorizable life-times for others, but also effectively serve as the channel and media through which such accumulable time values are extracted and transferred from these pools of disposable life-times, the ever-devaluing times of social reproduction of stagnant surplus populations, to metropolitan biopolitical subjects.[23]

Two things are important to note in this brief political economic history. The first is the slower temporality of "neoliberal" transformations in the Philippines, which can be said to have been steadily taking place over the last sixty years, as opposed to the speed with which these have taken place in China over less than three decades. This is not merely a comparative relation. On the one hand, China's closure since 1949 and throughout the Cold War helped to shape the rise of a capitalist regional economy in the Asia-Pacific, including the ascendance of Japan and the newly industrializing countries (South Korea, Taiwan, Hong Kong, and Singapore), which served as the Philippines' sources of foreign capital investment as well as destinations for its labor export. The sequestration of China, among other features of the Cold War, including political and military strategies of "security" to safeguard foreign investments, enabled the gradual and steady dispossession and displacement of people that results in surplus populations. On the other hand, communist China also served as an exemplar of political-cultural strategies and ideals for the radical movement that grew out of the very same conditions of crisis in the 1960s that heralded the beginning of the Philippines' "neoliberal" transformation, influencing directly and indirectly the development of a literary and cinematic language (socialist realism) for "the masses," immiseration, and urban slum life that Mendoza and his collaborators are at once steeped in and compelled to resignify.[24] Today it is also the case that China's aggressive entry into and rapid rise within the global capitalist economy—becoming the "workshop of the world," with 29 percent of the world's workforce—has accelerated and exacerbated the immiseration of Philippine working populations through the driving down of wages and benefits on a global scale.[25]

The second thing is the way the relatively gradual, though fitful, process of making surplus populations through the eruption and "resolution" of political and economic crises since the early 1960s has effectively created the conditions of chronic stagnation for expanding urban zones of social life, to which the designation "slums" is often applied. As perhaps one of the most important means of crisis resolution or management, the channeling of a ratio of this floating population abroad through the mechanisms of the labor export industry during this relatively extended period of "neoliberal" transformation sustains the enduring existence of that stagnant surplus population left behind, a population that would appear to be permanently excluded from formal employment (absolutely redundant and no longer "floating," in the sense of endlessly cycling in and out of the formal labor force) and entirely devoted to the informal, reproductive work of subsisting without the possibility of attaining the exchange value of labor power. Although there is in fact much contradictory liquid movement and discordant struggle within these urban zones of social life, the appearance of an "enduring" condition of human superfluousness, which that threshold for neoliberal subjectivity creates, means that this superfluity is neither perceived as an event (of expulsion or disappearance) nor understood as an immanent fate. Rather, it is simply a mode of life.

In this historical context, it is not altogether surprising to find the marked differences between Mendoza's own experiments with the transnational aesthetic of neorealism and those of Jia. These differences are particularly evident in the former's cinematic structuring of experiential time.

People as Coin: Temporalities of Stagnant Liquidity

The opening sequences of three of Mendoza's films—*Tirador* (Slingshot; 2007), *Serbis* (Service; 2008), and *Lola* (Grandmother; 2009)—display the characteristic temporal structures of Mendoza's work as they introduce the geographical

Of Survival • 131

setting of each film through a protracted series of alternately long and short takes of a movement through space, closely tracked by a mobile, hand-held camera. In *Tirador*, the movement is of the light of police flashlights burrowing through the dark alleyways of a slum neighborhood, picking out in passing inspection random details of ramshackle structures, catching out human figures in the middle of evening activities, and, as voices warn everyone of an imminent raid, effectively pushing people out of the way, scattering them into the darkness of their homes. In *Serbis*, after an initial scene of "looking" at a girl dressing and primping before a mirror, the movement is of a woman going up and down the many maze-like staircases of a dilapidated movie theater, going in and out of rooms, in and out of the shadows of unlit hallways, checking in with other characters who live and work in the theater, their own smaller movements also tracked with a scoping camera motion similar to that of the first scene. And in *Lola*, the movement is of an old woman accompanied by her young grandson, buying a candle, stopping in a church to say a prayer, effortlessly making her way through rubbish-strewn, run-down, harsh, concrete urban spaces to reach a blighted, empty site below the side of a bridge where she struggles, against a strong wind, to light and set down the candle between two pieces of concrete rubble, before making her way back up to and across the bridge.

There is in all of these opening sequences, but perhaps most acutely in *Lola*, a sense of the passage of "real-time" that is not the sense of sheer duration or time passing effected by the more common long take. Rather, the sense of "real-time" is the result of an inordinately protracted, almost dogged, attention to an extremely banal, even chore-like set of actions strung along the barest of narrative threads, which tends continuously to induce but also disappoint anticipations of development. Composed of a series of long and short takes, a palpably mobile camera jerkily following the movement closely from behind or from the front, a tracking motion punctuated with static medium and distance shots, like short pauses in a walk to take a breath or the view, or to recover one's balance or bearings, these sequences convey a rhythm of effort and busyness and low-intensity worry instead of one of placidity and boredom. In them there is simultaneously a lot and nothing going on, a form of running here and there yet going nowhere in the end or in particular, full of activity with next to nothing happening, actions without event. Replete with sensorial—visual and acoustic—input and movement, these are noisy and *dense* images, images *full* of the scattered leavings of time lived out, of life-times expended. This is the rhythm of ignominious struggle on the part of the permanently "idled" and unemployed—composed of uneven, laborious, and frenetic yet tedious times spent swimming in place in the stagnant pool of human refuse.

The time of ignominious struggle is a thematic as much as a formal feature of Mendoza's films. Indeed, the cinematic image he offers in *Tirador* of the activities and goings-on of squatters, slum dwellers, petty thieves and swindlers, street vendors, drug addicts, and dealers are all about visually and aurally communicating the texture, tenor, and timbre of the quotidian struggle of makeshift life-making, of living as getting by, of stealing and swindling and getting caught or getting away, of small-time hustling and wheeling and dealing, of conning and getting conned, of bearing routine harassment, arrests, and beatings at the hands of the police, of getting into and out of deadly scuffles, of eking out a living while money and life keep running out in equal measure. These are trying, exacting times punctuated with times of levity and enjoyment—the small-time pleasures and tortures of living on empty, experienced like the small change gained and lost in the daily racket to survive.

This is hardly a metaphor: making a living is making the small change with which to buy more time of life. In this case, life is the first and last term in the circuit C–M–C, with small change as the medium of coin with which to exchange life for life, the circuit of exchange with ever-diminishing returns that dead-ends without accumulable value. Nowhere, perhaps, is this better represented cinematically than in the film *Lola* (the screenplay for which was written by Linda Casimiro, inspired by a story reported in the news), a film about two grandmothers seeking redress, one struggling to find the money to bury her murdered grandson, the other struggling to find the money to free her arrested grandson as the alleged murderer.

As we follow each grandmother picking through her scant sources of livelihood for extra money, beseeching neighbors, kin, and benefactors for small donations and loans, and pawning every petty asset and meager pension and savings they have managed to put away, advancing their own future life-times and the future life-times of others to settle the debts that their respective grandsons' death and life have incurred, we feel the toll of seeking justice in a social context of daily injustice and hardship, where the acts and forces of offense and injury on human life abound. In following along, we bear the anxious tedium, seeming futility, and onerous effort comprising *the times of life lived as petty cash*. I want to suggest that the structure and object of attention in this film to some degree coincide: it is precisely the time of eking out a living, literally extending life for another day, the time of making (or redeeming) lives of ever-diminishing value, times in which what is expended is life exchanged for money, not to gain but simply to extend (to "redeem," in a nonmoral sense) life that is always on the verge of being completely exhausted.

The narrative of the painstaking, humiliating, exacting, and unyielding efforts to collect enough small change to bury one life and resuscitate another—passages of arduous travel, geographical and social, efforts indissociable from living itself, so that we do not in fact retain any moral distinction between the grandmother of the still living and the grandmother of the already dead (two potential lives, futures, pulled out of circulation)—is also the form of cinematic attention. Here, rather than suspension and distension, we experience the time of waiting as sluggish expenditure; rather than duration, endurance.

And like the grandmothers who eventually find what we might call some form of social justice in the reconciliatory meeting of their lives, and in the exchange of their accounts of their entire lifetimes as survivors (with money exchanged as the means of settlement between one life lost and one life saved), we experience through such passage not so much hope (as the yield of longevity) as the unbelievable reprieve that the achievement of life simply continuing brings.

Though the grandmothers first confront each other in the chambers of a judge, the pathways to the moment of "justice" they eventually find exist outside and on the periphery of the formal halls of state justice (and the prisons, through which the informal economies of survival are policed and contained and the inequalities of economic exchange reinforced) as the pathways of renewing and remaking social lives. When they finally sit down together for the settlement, it is in a noisy food court, and what they exchange, besides the kerchief-bundled cash unceremoniously passed across the table, are stories of the aches and pains of aging and of their own survival (including outliving their husbands, the "stubbornness" of whom, one grandmother quips, is also a cause of premature death). There is nothing utopic in this imagination of "justice." On the contrary, the settlement reached is nothing more than a continuation of what takes place in the everyday life of disposable people: the exchange of life for life. It is thus a notion of justice inseparable from the gendered work of life-making in a time of war.

For Jia, disposable lives entail indefinite duration as the temporal structure of their unfolding, their life-times assuming spatial form in the course of this temporal dilation as surfaces of a rescued humanscape, the effect of slowing down the velocity of their wholesale expenditure as liquid assets (the velocity of their planned disappearance, as labor-commodities, from the sphere of circulation).[26] In his films, there is an attempt to restore time proper to disposable populations and to make, out of such time, subjects of history—that is, an attempt to articulate the superfluousness of their life-times as a time of political reflection and critique. The aesthetic distance and contemplative stance of his gaze, as precisely the mode of critique, contrasts with Mendoza's aesthetic of immersion and complicity in the times of constant negotiation and movement within stagnation. In Mendoza's films, no subject of history can emerge.

If we view these films not as mere cultural symptoms of the material conditions out of which they emerge (unless by symptoms we mean spectacular commodities), but rather as themselves forms of production immersed in the very practices of production of value out of surplus life-times now characteristic of global financial capital, it is possible to argue that Mendoza's cinematic exercise of *abidance* with the life-times of disposability of stagnant populations offers a mode of political mediation (rather than subjectivation) that potentially enables transformation from within those life-times rather than from without. In contrast to Jia, who uses the contemplative language of the spectacle to valorize the life that spectacular capital negates and liquidates, Mendoza exploits the attention economy in which the spectator is called to labor in and through the image-commodity (as "prosumer," as "playborer") in such a way as to enjoin him or her in a labor-practice that hews intimately to the times of informal life-making of the urban excess. Here those life-times are specifically and significantly figured by the widowed aged women who head their households, whose personal "desires," as it were, or concerns we are never given narratively to understand. These aged women are the image-means and nontranscendent ideal of the labor of redeeming life through its expenditure. While undoubtedly harnessing attention for value production in the circuits of international art films, the cinematic experiment is hence also a pedagogical exercise, a form of training that makes us sensorially participant in the practice of producing the very time to be expended.

Mendoza's fine naturalist eye generates this form of cinematic attention, mimicking that ability to make use of the tiniest openings, which I discussed earlier, called *diskarte* (from the Spanish *descartar*, to discard), that "resourcefulness" in making the smallest difference into an occasion for marginal gain honed as a strategy of survival among the urban poor. Undoubtedly, the petty and loose change of disposable life can be put to productive and profitable ends, both politically and economically. Mendoza's later works more explicitly demonstrate the way this naturalist view of the social worlds of the slums, a faithful portrait of the iniquitous conditions of people's survival, might well leave us with a moral injunction to intervene from without.[27] Such an injunction is evidenced by Mendoza's own support for the presidency of Duterte. Here yet again a time of judgment might erupt to "save"—to redeem, in a moral sense—these life-times of stagnation. Even as women are left to pick up the pieces of shattered lives in order to make life anew, exemplifying what it means

Of Survival • 135

to live in a time of war, the sheer endlessness of life-times of racketeering can become the impossibility of gaining or attaining a proper life, with all its sex-gendered codes for what it means for the labor of life to add up to something.

And yet, like those very compromised practices it closely tracks and approximates, the film's mode of attention depends on the resources, the trust, and goodwill of others. While *Lola* is formally the work of Mendoza, it is also the work of the writer, Linda Casimiro, who based the screenplay on a TV news story about two similarly opposed grandmothers. It is also the work of the two veteran actors, Anita Linda and Rustica Carpio, who brought not only their immense professional skills but also improvised on their own aging lives to script their own gestures, actions, and lines. In the care work of Casimiro, Linda, and Carpio, tending to lives glimpsed, felt, fleshed out, and inhabited, we see those resources, those living forces on which a cinematic practice—a practice of making time out of small differences within the time of spectacle—depends. It is these living forces subsumed within the film that crucially sway Mendoza's practice of cinematic abidance in the direction of the gendered life-making that *Lola* represents.

Made to experience cinematic time as a palpable, almost physical, effort of passage (through the visually and aurally dense and restless image), we are enjoined to engage in a gendered and aged practice of abidance that goes beyond the life-times of "eking out" a living. This is a practice of following, of sorting through the loose and petty change of one's own living and the living of neighbors, friends, and kin, suturing the fraying strands of cooperation that keep one alive as one moves through the debris of social waste that is one's dwelling, to salvage not any abstract form of worth but rather simply a person who is one's bond, one's care. To the extent that what these single, old women redeem is life already expended or being expended, futures spent, these are remaindered life-times—times of life-making in excess of the times of reproduction of disposable existence. For us, we find that our own engagement in this practicum of attending as accompaniment, of making time, produces a time of living that is also ours, life-times that are not fully subsumed by apparatuses of capture or consumption or waste, but instead remain at our disposal as perhaps a resource to remake the rules of *just life*.

Uneven Times

Chandan Reddy writes compellingly of the difference between global neoliberalism's relation to the nation-state in the Global North and in the Global South.[28] While in the Global South the national citizen is split off from the state through the impediments to welfare structures posed by neoliberal economic policies, in the Global North the relation between citizen and state is only further consolidated. This consolidation consists of the reorganization of the redistributive functions of the historical welfare state such that they align with the social reproduction and growth of capital whose bearer is the US citizen, in the name of the security of whom the same redistributive functions are revoked from the racialized, poor, and noncitizen population.

Building on Reddy's critical disaggregation of global neoliberalism through an insistence on these indispensable, geopolitical and spatially-distributed social differences, I attend to further discrepancies, here, of time—the uneven times of neoliberalism as it has been deployed as an explicit ideology or implicit socio-cultural logic, a form of political rationality, and a periodizing concept. Critiques of neoliberalism attentive to its uneven social stratifications see such stratifications in terms of subjective ideals normed by race, gender, sexuality, and class and, further, see these categories of difference as the means by which contemporary contradictions between state and capital, nation and state, are "resolved" and put to use and toward ends that only exacerbate the inequalities of our times.

My turn to temporality in processes of accumulation, dispossession, and survival is an attempt to think about this unevenness at a level beneath the threshold of the visibility of subjects, while acknowledging the real effects that the protocols of subjectivity under a regime of a financialized economy have on the conditions of life of precisely those nonsubjects who can only be apprehended in the recognizable social dresses of "bare life." I do not, however, turn to "actually lived" life, but instead to experiments in the very modalities of attention through which such life is abstracted and monetized in and as image-commodities and image-capital under contemporary modes of value extraction (cinema as one means of speculation)—what is, after all, financial capital if not past, present, and future life-times imaged and circulated as value (where the "content" and even the form of such life-times is secondary)? I turn to these experiments to see the way that various temporalities are invoked on the one hand as "ethnographic" realist attention to the life-times of survival on the part of disposable populations, and on the other hand as attempts to instantiate particular life-times as political means of re-mediating social relations. In both cases, these experiments provide other forms of intelligibility beyond the normative subjective ideals of citizens and the racialized, gendered, sexualized, and classed social formations that serve as those subjective ideals' constitutive others.

To attend to the uneven times of the global project of neoliberalism is to interrupt the coherence and homogeneity of the epoch that is assumed to be our shared global present (whether that global present is explained through a diffusionist or conjunctural account of neoliberalism, or through a historically synchronous account in which different sites are affected by a global logic) and to interrupt the time of the "always already" for the redundant populations of the becoming-human. It is to place the zones of disposable life in the periphery in dynamic relation to old and emerging centers of global capitalism, without relegating these zones or their life-making practices to merely the latter's dire effects. Attending to the uneven times of neoliberal transformations through the life-times of disposability opens up the possibility of other genealogies for understanding those remaindered ways of *living* in the world that move and generate that world in ways we would otherwise be unable to take into political account.

PART III. GLOBOPOLIS

7

CITY EVERYWHERE

Let me take you on a ride through a place that is, here and elsewhere, essayed as our shared impending future. Drivers of growth, profit, and progress decree this place, this future fixed to the present—city everywhere—as the ideal provision and destination of present global itineraries, the world in the works for a mobile urban humanity. I follow the pathways of connectivity laid down by global growth drivers to obtain a simulated moving image of city everywhere's imperatives, highlighting its figurative codes like signposts to show the immanent logic of its operation and evolution, the image of thought of the globopolis. *Uber-urbanization* names this immanent logic, the imaginative and techno-infrastructural value-propelled project behind the global fantasy of city everywhere, whose defining tropes also act as programmatic codes for the enterprise. But spliced within this metropolitanist drive are intermittent detours into leftover spaces, where the pools and eddies of excess life-times—the life-times of the urban excess—collect. Attending to these life-times of disposable populations yields other ways of imagining the "liquidity" on which the global metropolitan archipelago of city everywhere rests, the politics of its making, and the potential of its vital platforms—what we might identify as a subaltern driver of global capital expansion.

All my life I have plied the 270-kilometer route between San Fernando, the provincial capital of La Union, and Manila, the nation's capital. For decades, from my family's hometown in the north, we took the two-lane MacArthur Highway, which was laid down by the US colonial government in 1928 following the established route of the now-defunct Manila Railroad, and which ran through every town along the northwestern coast of Luzon and through the provincial towns across its central plains. After the trains stopped running, it was the only way by land to reach *the city*.

In those years the broad, modern multilane approach to Manila was always dramatic in its contrast with the never-quite-straight and often winding, narrow road that connected town to town with a rhythm of clutter and expanse as our car or bus would alternately crawl through the thickets of town centers—with their familiar array of plaza, municipal hall, market, school, and the traffic of pedestrians, street and market vendors, hawkers, bus touters, commuters, schoolchildren, police, cars, jeepneys, tricycles, horse-drawn carriages, and the stray dogs that milled and moved around them and slowed our travel—and then speed through the suddenly spacious but never empty stretches of country road that opened up between the towns. When I began driving this route myself, I learned how to feel and move with this rhythm, to become part of it and one with it. I learned how to bide and accelerate my speed, not simply to conform to the changes in the density and velocity of traffic and vibrant life spilling within and between towns, but also to make time in the fleeting openings in the opposite lane.

Overtaking on this road was and remains a risky, even reckless business. To go, in quick succession, from the liberated speed of 90 km/h just outside of town to a puttering 20 km/h behind a tractor- or ox-pulled wagon weighed down with a teeming load of cane, then to a breakneck 120 km/h in order to use the rapidly closing gap in oncoming traffic in the opposite lane to overtake the wagon and just as quickly decelerate to 40 km/h to slip back into one's own lane behind a tricycle not too far ahead—this was the task one performed over and over again, each time to shave minutes, perhaps cumulatively up to an hour, off the five or more hours it usually took to get to Manila. Like the work of getting by, getting ahead on these roads was always a matter of timing, often life-and-death timing. With all kinds of vehicles on the road, not to mention people and animals crossing or lingering, unpredictable and unflagged breaks in the road (typhoon-felled trees, broken bridges, collided vehicles), and the maneuvers of speed that such weaving and wending required (this erratic rhythm of bide and accelerate), it was always a feat, though unremarkable, even banal, not to kill or be killed. That was no doubt also part of its thrill. But as is more often the case than not in a place of ever diminishing and disappearing resources, unreliable, often hazardous infrastructure compromised by cut corners and kick-back deals, and irregular, nonformalized, nonstandardized rules, it was also simply part of the protocol of everyday life, and almost all the drivers, whether of private cars or commercial buses, took part in this race to make time.

Today, the route from Manila to San Fernando bypasses almost all the towns. We are on one of the connecting elevated expressways redeveloped and newly built over the last ten years—the NLEX (Northern Luzon Expressway), SCTEX (Subic-Clark Tarlac Expressway), and TPLEX (Tarlac-Pangasinan-La Union Expressway)—which in sections has steadily cut across the rice fields on the outskirts of populated centers, in some places parallel to the MacArthur Highway, and the drive is smooth, steady, with no dips or surges of speed or sudden swerves. No rhythm of bide and accelerate, this is a virtually hands-free, no clutch, autopilot drive. Just that tranquilizing hum of the tires on leveled asphalt. And no people or animals to be seen, much less to be encountered, on the road except a sprinkle here and there at a distance in what has become, for a whole new urban social stratum, scenery.

From this moving perch, which hovers just so slightly above the ground, the cultivated plains of Central Luzon are no longer the rural areas one found at the end of the road from the city or that one could glimpse from the road between provincial towns, a place that took effort to reach. Now these quilted fields of small plots of rice and sugar cane, interspersed with tracts of mango orchards and timberland, are merely the scenic backdrop for one's passage through urban corridors, the continuous highways that President Arroyo proposed in 2006 to connect all the "super regions" of the country.[1]

The Arroyo administration had just decreed the establishment of "super regions" as distinct geographical zones based on economic strengths (agribusiness, manufacture and service industries, tourism, information and communication industries), and proposed the super expressways as the means of more efficient transportation of goods and people between them. Highways would extend development and economic growth to the provinces, to which, Arroyo declared, it was time to return sovereign power, against the rule of "imperial Manila." The means of ever faster circulation, flow, and mobility—cutting travel times, easing transport, reducing that debilitating congestion that plagues overpopulated, overvehicled, globalizing third world metropolises such as Metro Manila—expressways are the metropolitan flyover solution to chronic underdevelopment, the strategy and vision of the metropolitanist dream to be "world class." No longer will the nation's capital have a monopoly on the global goods and services, the high-powered, high-value global living that urban innovation and infrastructure bring. What Manuel V. Pangilinan—the chairman of Metro Pacific Investments Corporation, which owns the subsidiary corporations that build, manage, and operate these expressways—predicts for the fate of the privatized national telephone (now telecommunications) company, which he also heads and aims to merge with social media, is bound to be true for the metropolis: it is going nowhere; it is going everywhere.²

City Everywhere

The NLEX, SCTEX, and TPLEX are the toll expressways that—in spanning across the North Luzon Agribusiness Quadrangle super region and linking it to Metro Manila (a metropolitan area now further expanded into the Metro Luzon Urban Beltway super region)—aim to bring them into being as zones of the global urban economy. Toll expressways are not only conduits of urbanization, the infrastructural means to facilitate the core work—circulation—that more than ever defines the city. They are also channels of communicative exchange within a redefined mega-urban domain—interior corridors of a dispersed but coherent metropolitan life. In a global communicative-biocapitalist economy in which circulation itself has become value productive and the channels of conveyance of material, immaterial, human, and nonhuman content have become the very generative site—the *platforms*—of reconstituted urban life, they *are* the city.³

Expressways connecting the super regions—including the Cyber Corridor, which is set to span the entire nation, traversing all the other super regions (ICT industry as supra-urban corridor)—are globally imagined, financed, and executed. Built to the specifications of US interstate highways, from the English-language lettering in white Caltrans font on green background signage, to the distance-based numbering of interchanges, to the designated food and gas service areas with their convenience stores and US global chain concessions (Starbucks, etc.), these urban channels materialize the body-making feel and groove, the drone-like rhythm and controlled, standardized kinesthetic sensibility (the abstract, GPS-based sense of direction and location, dependent on state-regulated textual and numerical symbols rather than on features of the local environment) shaped and instilled by US highways, the gold standard of privatized transportation over land. As domestic airport ads for high-end condominium developments promise, with their sleek photographic images of simulacra of modern European and US built environments, apartment buildings, single-family residences, and gated communities, they bring a global urban sensibility and lifestyle, "home."

All these trends are variably at work within the postcolonial Global South, in all the capital places constantly striving to be "world class"—Mumbai, Bangkok, Lagos. Even as they bear the imprints of particular places—the legible signs of their "differences" from other places—capital cities of the postcolonial Global South provide a platform for the cinematic experience of cosmopolitan travel that can be found everywhere, anywhere. In this way, they act as a platform for the very image-experience of the consumption of time that defines the time of the spectacle, "the time of a real transformation experienced as illusion," as Debord put it, when provincial subjects can experientially participate in global urban life as they live (or return to) the authentic life of the country.[4] Along with airports, banking systems, microenterprise access, mobile, cellular technologies, the internet, and other communication-transportation projects of global circulation, expressways are the technological-infrastructural means of sublation of the (once rural) provinces into a world-wide "trans-territorial city," or uber-metropolis.[5] They are simultaneously the connection as well as the content defining city anywhere. In them the form of connection and the substance of content aim to be one and the same.

Uber-urbanization: Connection as Content, Content as Connection

At the 2012 annual meeting of shareholders of the largest telecommunications company in the country, Philippine Long Distance Telephone Co. (PLDT), its chairman, Manuel V. Pangilinan laid out a vision in which the growth limits of such a (privatized) public utility company could be superseded by its venturing into the new "frontier" of media space. Traditional telcos (telecommunications), he announced, will become obsolete, and hence "PLDT has a choice of staying as a utility, as a delivery system, as an infrastructure system," such as the Manila Electric Company (Meralco), the nation's largest electric power distributor (for which Pangilinan also acts as chairman)—an option whose future is uncertain.[6] Or, such uncertainty and the nonchoice of depressed profit margins could be leaped over by the utility company evolving into something bigger: a total integrated systems company merging infrastructure and media, where utility delivery systems supplying connection will converge with "creative" companies supplying content.

City Everywhere • 145

As chairman of the board of the nation's major companies of power and water distribution (Meralco, Maynilad), public infrastructure such as expressways (Metro Pacific Tollways) and hospitals (Makati Medical Center), broadcast television and newspapers (TV5, and *Business World*, through the media conglomerate MediaQuest), and cellular communications and mobile financial services (Smart Communications), "MVP," as Pangilinan is widely known in the business and media world, envisions a future when the conglomerate he oversees and represents (and whose ownership is shared transnationally by elite family corporations in the Philippines, Hong Kong, and Indonesia) will have a monopoly on the provision of forms of connection and content comprising national life. As this most valuable and visible player in Philippine business concluded in the speech to his shareholders: "At the end, we will as a group entertain people with our media assets, deliver financial services through Smart Money and Bayad Center, manage energy needs with Meralco, care for their health with our hospitals, facilitate travel on our tollways, and supply clean water with Maynilad, all to make the lives of Filipinos productive, connective, and enjoyable."[7]

Total Mediatic Dominion

This is the investor fantasy of "world class": a total, enveloping mediacosm in which "access" is the keyword, the defining feature of *a keyed world*. Full, "all-inclusive" services, complete communicative-transportational access. Anytime, everytime. What is promised by the channels of this "access" is not just definite qualities of speed and comfort, but the relative measures of efficiency and convenience, buying one ample space, ample time. I say "buying," or perhaps I should say "renting," for these are tollways, after all, whether expressways or the internet, water lines or electrical lines, cable TV channels, or cell phone lines. Tolls—not exorbitant but prohibitive, relative terms of exaction carefully calibrated to the variable rates of affordability of a shifting class-clientele and the market price of their life-times—delineate proper as well as illegal forms of tiered access and, more importantly, determine the duration of that privilege of access or use, or subscription. They are a crucial element in the envisioned mediacosm, a mechanism in new modes of value extraction and social regulation and control, which together serve as the basis of the reorganization of urban life and its *fractal* expansion through growing, deepening networks of mediatic highways and byways in and across shared physical, social, and psychic space.

Such envisioned urban evolution, or *uber-urbanization*, entails continuous and expanding subsumption of life beyond the fixed geography and time metrics of "the city."⁸ As exemplified by the Scaling Innovations in Mobile Money (SIMM) Project, a project sponsored by the US Agency for International Development (USAID) to promote microenterprise access and mobile banking, the objective of expanding mobile money (m-money) services and developing the environment for m-money, is "deep inclusion"—in this case, the "deepening financial inclusion" of "the poor and unbanked."⁹ Like other geopolitical third world populations, Filipinos have been among the leading adopters of cryptocurrencies (e.g., Bitcoin), as the means of transfer of global money among members of their globally far-flung families. This latest USAID "foreign assistance" project, now investing in financial infrastructure rather than in ideological social and community development, can thus be considered a preemptive and counterillicit e-commerce campaign to capture one of the biggest markets in remittances and to secure it within its own proper financial vehicles and pathways. Inclusion then is not to be seen as the opposite of exclusion of the "unbanked" urban surplus populations, but instead a more efficient (intelligent) mode of their discriminatory, securitizing control, which is achieved through the sorting and regulatory effects of the very techno-infrastructural channels on which metropolitan life depends and through which it seeks seemingly unlimited extension.

In this way, the project of city everywhere can be said to be modeling the dominant state-corporate strategy for the restructuring of metropolitan Manila in the aftermath of authoritarian modernization under the two-decade-long Marcos dictatorship. This unified strategy and technology, paradigmatically embodied by the archipelagic network of flyovers or highway overpasses that began to be constructed in the early 1990s, was, as I had argued then, Manila's new metropolitan form, designed both as a strategy for the accommodation of the crisis of contradictions between nationalist aspirations and global capitalist demands, and as a strategy for the diffusion and transcendence of the immanent social antagonisms embedded in the congestion and chaos attributed to the urban excess, which could not be contained by the older, more rigid ramparts of state enclosure and repressive control.¹⁰

Representing and propelling emergent transnational strategies of "liberalized" regulation or deregulation, whereby pathways of "liberated" movement or freeways themselves became the means of regulation and decentralized control, the flyovers materially (pre)figured an archipelagic or polynucleated metropolitan form that has become a global platform in its own right. Built as a technical apparatus to *override* the logic of the IMF- or World Bank–funded modernization development of an earlier era of capitalist accumulation—along with the unregulated, informal activities of the floating surplus population, which was its consequence and its refuse (not only the human waste product of modernization development but also the social refusal on the part of the urban poor to remain waste)—this archipelagic metropolitan form provided the paradigmatic means of converting these pools of human excess into forms of surplus liquidity that have been crucial to new modes of value extraction attendant to the latest, financialized cycle of capitalist accumulation. That is to say, it is precisely the paradigm of the urban archipelago—materialized in the flyover network (and reproduced in urban studies theory)—that serves to make the "seas" of unplanned development and stalled mobility the very "fluid" basis on which it rests as a new, value-making metropolitan platform of social life.

Fractal Enterprise: City Emulants

The globalism of this metropolitan platform converts what would appear to be the model into a component. Urban expansion is, as I mentioned, a fractal enterprise, by which I mean to highlight the repetition of certain figurative patterns at smaller and larger, shrinking and expanding, scales, where the component reproduces the figurative pattern of the whole of which it is a part. Rather than suggesting a mathematical, geometric precision to the processes of global urban expansion—although it is such precision that both financial and urban theory in their modeling and predictive pursuits seek—I conjoin *fractal* with *enterprise* to highlight the conditions and effects of the business model program underlying these figurative patterns, a business model that cuts across diverse industries, from utility infrastructure to social media, as the metropolitanist fantasy of MVP above attests.[11]

The polynucleated pattern of the new metropolis has been created through the reconstruction of the main arteries of Metro Manila into traffic light–free radial highways and beltways connecting the scattered and proliferating "all-inclusive" private commercial, business, and residential land developments that have thoroughly reshaped the metropolitan landscape in the last twenty years. Dispersed across the seventeen independent cities and one municipality composing the metropolis today, these urban land developments consist of mixed-use business, commercial complexes and "high-end living environments" that appear less like rich residential suburbs than permanent urban island resorts, which I would call *city emulants*.

City emulants are condensed-scale, "self-sustained" physical and virtual realizations of an urban ideal built out of global forms and tailored to local needs and tastes. They are "islands," built on privatized reclaimed or seized land (i.e., urban space deemed idle or waste land), on which complete living environments are constructed to host the lifestyles of an ascendant global class. For example, Rockwell Center was built on the site of a former thermal power plant owned by Meralco, the electric power distribution company now among the assets controlled by the investment holdings corporation chaired by Pangilinan. As the prototype of newer properties fashioned with the names of national artists (Joya, Edades, Manansala), Rockwell Center sees itself as a pioneer among the city emulants now expanding throughout Metro Manila: "Unheard of in the 1990s, Rockwell Center was guided by a master plan to create a city within a city. A self-contained and mixed-use development that incorporated the construction of seven high-rise residential towers, an upscale shopping mall, office spaces, an exclusive city club, office spaces and a prestigious graduate business and law school, all built to be geared towards the promise of creating the now indelible Rockwell life and style."[12] Designed as a "city within a city," Rockwell promises a particular brand of metropolitan "life and style," which "harmonizes" spaces of "living, leisure, and business" in a "complete environment."

Like the "integrated township" and cyberpark of Eastwood City, the "lifestyle hub" of the Ayala Center, the "live-work-play nexus" of Alveo, Bonifacio Global City, and the Ortigas Center (a commercial, financial, and residential district combining ever-expanding private land development projects for financial and retail businesses, hotels, and condominiums built around signature malls in Mandaluyong), the "city within a city" of Rockwell is one city emulant among many comprising the megalopolitan archipelago that is now Metro Manila. City emulants are "insular" components that repeat at a smaller scale the model of Manila's metropolitan form (a city of cities), which has itself become a component of a global metropolitan form. Owned almost exclusively by four land development family corporations,[13] whose parent holding corporations also dominate the largest industries in the nation (retail, banking, manufacturing, mining, air and sea transportation, and telecommunications), these geographically scattered cities within cities are connected by a three-dimensional latticework of liberated, six- to twelve-lane beltways and arterial roads that have expanded over the last few decades, now integrated with two rapid transit and light rail train systems, which are in turn integrated with the road-based public transport system of buses, taxis, and jeepneys. Increasingly, through the much-touted "public-private partnership" coordination of government and private enterprise, the train and public transport systems have enabled "mass" access to the shopping malls, movie theaters, and restaurants that are central features of these insular cities. This productive inclusion of a growing local consumerist class in the urban archipelago is managed through infrastructural design, particularly the implementation of total grade separation, that is, the construction of separate transport axes (roads, rails, walkways) at different heights or grades in order to facilitate unimpeded traffic flows within alternately parallel and intertwining, nonintersecting conduits.[14]

To be sure, the objective of streamlining class stratification that such urban engineering serves to carry out—segregating carless, pedestrian populations from private-vehicled and propertied, globally mobile citizens by keeping each stratum within its own respective circulatory pathway—has been enormously difficult to achieve. The disciplinary, regulatory effect of channeling, which has been metropolitan Manila's strategy of political and social foreclosure and preemption since the reinvention of elite democracy as securitocratic neoliberal democracy in the late 1980s, has only thirty years later become tenuously operative, after decades of coercive barricading and heavy policing to discipline the unruly movements and activities of pedestrians, vendors, and motor vehicles, a chronic battle that has left the marks of its wreckage on the physically ravaged built environment of the public transport system—every dented metal barricade, damaged poured concrete divider, dilapidated roadway, broken walkway, missing stairway, and demolished sidewalk (where perhaps a small market might also have been) a testament to a still raging battle of eviction and accommodation, as if these were the ruins of a city under siege. Today, there is no doubt that a system of gated channeling is now in place. The struggles of the urban excess for survival and accommodation continue in old and new forms.

However, rather than the permanently fixed, compartmentalized spaces of the classic garrisoned or walled colonial, apartheid city that it once was, or the segregated spaces of authoritarian modernist order of the Marcos years—the contemporary manifestations of which nevertheless remain programmatically if not figuratively (i.e., representationally) exemplary for the fractal expansion of city everywhere—Metro Manila's current sociospatial organization consists of a more dynamic, distributed, multidimensional, and cross-strata transnational form. In fact, what would appear to be one metropolitan archipelago, consisting of city emulants built on reclaimed urban land over a sea of haphazard, informal development, is in fact multiple archipelagos, interlaced with one another through those grade separations called interchanges, whereby different strata flows can efficiently bypass one another in the very same place. What is discernible here is something other than what is typically critiqued—from the perspective of a liberal ideal of democratic society conceived in terms of an equality of access to "open" public space, culture, or representation—as the bulwark-building tendency of security states organizing "fortress enclaves."[15] Such an inert spatial-territorial imagination, including the modern imperial, landed, settled perspective that the expanding archipelagic paradigm is based on and extends, significantly misses the very fluid, "far from equilibrium" dynamics that city everywhere entails.

The practical need for workers and consumers to comprise the various support systems for city emulants requires mass public transport stations that provide access to them. If city emulants are conceived as places of entertainment and leisure, they are internally split between public consumerist pleasures (shopping, eating) and private high-end "living" (exclusivist residences with rest and recreation as well as business amenities). Since both spheres require service labor, and the malls, restaurants, and emulations of public urban space (plazas, parks, and gardens) are open to a more diverse consumer clientele beyond the owners of adjacent condominiums and residential townhouses or the hotel guests (both of whom are paying for the privileges of residence), the gating of socialities and social fluencies happens less through spatial-territorial segregation than by the differentiating or sorting effects of regulatory pathways, which are virtual ("cultural," "stylistic," as in "life and style" or "lifestyle") as much as physical. Just as social media enable specific social groups to make and keep within their own communicative networks in putatively free, open, and self-regulating cyberspaces, metropolitan archipelagos consist of connective technologies and infrastructural systems that not only service and "include" discrepant social strata but also serve as the very means by which those strata are created and maintained as autonomous social constituencies (neither stable nor fixed, such constituencies are continuously ideologically conscripted as "communities").

The socializing and governing effect of these regulatory pathways and connective techno-infrastructures of the metropolitan archipelago (including mobile cellular technologies as crucial navigational, communicative, and financial support systems of urban life), whereby fluency becomes a form of preemptive security or *foreclosure*, can in fact be understood in terms of the kind of control embodied by the notion of *protocol*, the technical standards and codes governing communicative action in the digital world.[16] What this seeming analogy between social media and interlaced archipelagic "networks" comprising the new metropolis indicates is the fractal enterprise that undergirds both as *platforms*.

Metropolitan Platform, Global-National Franchise

We would be seeing only one dimension of this new metropolitan platform if we were to focus only on the spatioaesthetic attributes (the figurative patterns) that make city emulants "world class." It is equally important to see the model of value extraction that makes this a fractal enterprise, and furthermore, to see the socio-political entailments of this enterprise that make each city emulant within the metropolitan archipelago, and each component city within the national as well as within the global uber-urban archipelago, *franchises*.

By franchise I mean not only the purchased rights to a particular business model but also the special prerogatives of performing public functions and exercising jurisdictional authority granted to particular corporations. There is a colonial genealogy to both senses of franchise, that is, as licensed governance and enterprise. If contemporary commercial franchising might be traced to a medieval European method of crown or state control of territory (whereby the crown granted rights or "freedoms" to exact tithes, labors, and taxes to individuals and corporations, such as the church, in exchange for the obligation to protect and defend these crown lands), one could argue that the global development and expansion of franchising proceeded through New World and East Indies colonialism, exemplified by the *encomienda* system in the Iberian empire and the joint-stock company in the Dutch and British empires (the company-states of both Dutch and British East India Companies, largely understood to be precursors to modern-day corporations).[17] In this colonial history, we see the mutual making and entwinement of models of public governance (and political rights, the other meaning of *franchise*) and private enterprise (and the predication of both on landholding or territorial control). This historical suturing of sovereign power and capitalist freedom in the concept and practice of franchises in the contemporary context (through British and US legal-political institutions structuring international governance of global trade and economic relations and, in the Philippine context, national legislative and judicial acts granting rights to private entities to build, operate, and profit from public utilities and, what's more, permitting the additional delegation of the state's own franchise-granting authority) suggests the defining aspects of the program of allocation of socio-political prerogatives carried out through the fractal enterprise of uber-urbanization.[18]

It comes as no surprise to find these defining aspects—or more precisely, controls—of the new metropolitan platform manifesting the latent, historical meanings of *franchise* as "legal immunity or exemption" and, very importantly, "*exemption from servitude or subjection.*"[19] Through the reproduction of colonial political-legal institutions across nations, these historical meanings become the very measures (metrics and instruments) for the building and operation of metropolitan platforms as components of a global enterprise.

It thus makes significant sense that city emulants have emerged on the model of, as well as on the actual sites of, US military rest and recreation (R&R), aviation, and naval bases. As examples of the latter, Clark Air Base and Subic Naval Base have both been converted into international airport–driven, tax- and duty-free port zones (like the island city-states of Hong Kong and Singapore) for the growth of IT industries, aviation, retail businesses, financial centers, tourist resorts and theme parks, casinos, fitness and leisure activity centers, and so on. Such conversion enables military bases to host directly the productive needs of the global capitalist and managerial classes, which in another era they supported indirectly. Other military facility sites providing rest and recreation and logistical support for the US wars (direct and proxy) waged in Asia and the Middle East in the last five decades, such as Camp John Hay in Baguio and the former Wallace Air Base in San Fernando, La Union, have become high-end resort and vacation home subdivisions and recreational and sports complexes, very much on the model of the officer gentlemen's clubs that are the legacy of imperial armies. Both are important nodal points that are to be annexed to the expanded Northern Luzon expressway system, which leads directly to and from the Metro Manila beltway, EDSA, where the capital city emulants (including Bonifacio Global City, a former US colonial military fort established in 1901) are arrayed.

The state-corporate conversion of US military bases and military facilities into civic, recreational, and business centers and economic free port zones, where "sustainable urban communities" could grow and thrive, was a development project undertaken with the decisive global shift to "democracy promotion" precipitated by popular and radical social struggles against dictatorship in both the third world and the Eastern Bloc.[20] It was in fact during the "restored democracy" presidency of Corazon Aquino (1986–92) that the state legislature finally conceded to the leftist demand for the expulsion of the US bases. In the wake of that radical political success, the Bases Conversion and Development Authority Act of 1992 (Republic Act 7227) was signed into law, creating the Bases Conversion and Development Authority as "a government instrumentality vested with corporate powers"—that is, a state agency made into a holding company—to act as a major force in the development of economic centers through the construction of public infrastructure (tollways, airports, seaports) and real estate projects.

What is paradigmatic here is the way that both the logic and the actual physical bases of operation of a global military-industrial complex have become merged with or enfolded into the very business model of city emulants emerging out of converted military bases. For the latter, economic growth has depended not only on the "freed" assets of idled labor and infrastructure (abandoned with the 1991 withdrawal of US military forces), now placed at the service of foreign manufacturing industries.[21] Economic growth for converted military bases has also relied on capital-intensive speculative land development, which has served among the primary forms of financialization that has, in the last couple of decades, turned the Philippines' long crisis-ridden, languishing economy around. In addition to mobilizing the idled and deeply discounted past and present life-making capacities of the people who built and sustained the bases (reabsorbing labor and land "wasted" by the abandonments of prior colonial and postcolonial moments of appropriation), financial speculation converts the future life-times of surplus national populations into monetized assets, which serve simultaneously as collateral and trading currencies of debt-fueled, metropolitan capital-driven development.

To the extent that both entail the direct and active surplussing of human populations (whether as collateral damage of war or collateral for finance), the modus operandi of bases development is hence not too far from the modus operandi of regional security operations, which these bases had served (and continue) to support. In fact, the rationale of one becomes the rationale of the other. Further, each serves as the other's means. As Rommel Rodriguez observed, with reference to Arroyo's praise of the military general charged with over a thousand extrajudicial executions and forced disappearances under her administration (2001–10), while the superregional highways would certainly facilitate the accelerated circulation of commodities and reduce the commuting time of workers, they would also facilitate the military's "internal cleansing" of any remaining radical resistance to neoliberal capitalist development in hard-to-reach rural areas.[22] In this way, the modus operandi of uber-urbanization is the casus belli of preemptive counterinsurgent security wars, and vice versa. The roads to free port zones are the means of war. The roads of war lead to free port zones.

Turning Bases of War into Bases of (Capital) Life

Like (and as) converted military bases, city emulants not only promise high-end homes as living accommodations but also offer them as investment opportunities, advertising the highest rental yields in the country. These urban islands are therefore developed and sustained by global financial investments, both on the construction side (the transnational capital invested in build-operate-transfer infrastructures such as roads, airports, resorts, condominiums, and business offices) and on the consumer market side (the purchase or rental of life-work accommodations and a service environment for business). It is particularly important to note that the global sustenance of such urban islands, while attributed solely to transnational capital, includes the role of diasporic Filipino workers as investors, an overlooked dimension of global urbanization, to which I will return.[23]

Much of the Philippines' reported "infrastructure binge," "fed by foreign direct investment," which accounts for no small part of the registered growth in GDP, is buoyed by the building and development opportunities in trade, real estate, renting and business activities, transport, storage and communication, and especially services provided by city emulants as new frontier spaces of investment.[24] Thus, city emulants function as autonomous but networked sites for hosting primarily the movements of transnational finance capital (or entrepreneurial applications), rather than local social life, which is now reduced to the means of the former. In this respect, as a host of movement ("value in motion") rather than settlement, the bases of city everywhere can be likened to *colonial entrepôts that have been reinvented as mediatic platforms*, whose value productivity is realized less in the sale of finished products than in the sheer volume and velocity of traffic they occasion and host.[25]

Such urban platforms play key and paradigmatic parts in today's modes of astronomical wealth accumulation, which with increasing magnitude arguably issues out of the extraction of surplus value directly from spheres of circulation (e.g., the exchange of derivatives, currencies, goods, and services) and social reproduction (e.g., the cognitive, communicative, affective, and social cooperative activities of investable "life"), and with decreasing share out of the value of surplus labor extracted within traditional industrial production.[26]

These are big player places that produce growth by hosting the movement not only of investor capital but also of metropolitan subjects, for whom the city emulant becomes one nodal point, one way station, in a mobile, distributed transnational urban life. Unlike the settlement paradigm of the former military bases, what city emulants offer are not permanent residences or territorial rights but rather—like the visa-free, duty-free admission and departure (entry-exit) privileges for US military personnel and equipment as stipulated in the 1999 Visiting Forces Agreement between the Philippines and the United States (and renewed in the latest bilateral agreement)—a subscribed (contracted through purchase or lease) hold on and access to the prerogatives of nonresident "citizens," including freedom from certain legal and financial duties and obligations imposed by local jurisdictional authority on "nationals."[27] As the recently passed Right of Way Act (House Bill 5588) makes plain, with its expansion of acquisitional rights to property for public-private infrastructural projects, including exemptions from local court-issued restraints and local taxes, city emulants, like the converted military bases, can rely on legal provisions that expand the privileges and prerogatives of state-corporate actors. Such provisions effectively guarantee the latter *rights to bypass* national or public accountability and sovereignty. It is the provision of these kinds of "freedom, immunity, privilege" that makes city emulants, and the city-states of postcolonial nations that host them, globopolitical *franchises*.[28]

To the extent that what city emulants aim to host is the securitized "free" movement and activities of capitalizable life, or *life as capital*, life that might serve as a form of accumulable, even investable (interest-bearing) value, the freedoms that it offers include variable exemption or immunity from punishment: punishment that has become a generalized mode for the exaction or extraction of value from expendable life, or *life as waste*, developed by securitocratic, neoliberal states in relation to surplus populations, both their own as well as in other countries where they are at war. Functioning as *servers* for capital clients (providing urban platforms for investments of either finance capital or capitalizable life), postcolonial nations are thus increasingly no more than metropolitan-states of city everywhere, which offer their denizen-subscribers, as the core of their guaranteed package of freedom privileges, exemption from that unremitting toll on living that spells the fate of those consigned to *servitude*.

Eddies: Servers and Servants, Servility and Servitude

If the enterprise of uber-urbanization depends on modes of value extraction that issue out of the servicing of circulation itself, such modes of value extraction do not only depend on the capitalizable value of life as labor for the entrepreneurial and investor subjects that comprise the ascendant global urban class. They also crucially depend on the disposable life-times of a worldwide service/servant stratum whose primary work is to save as well as produce the valuable time of their clients and employers—that is, to serve as the means of facilitating the latter's value-productive movements.

We can see the operations defining this metropolitanist enterprise in the business model exemplified by Uber, the mobile app–based transportation service connecting drivers and passengers. This software-as-a-service

(SAAS) business, which understands itself as a facilitator of transactions between customers and independent providers, rather than an employer of service workers, sees to the efficient allocation of human beings and their possessions through the mediatization of urban employment. Chopping up traditional jobs into discrete tasks, or detailed piece service work, assigned to people at particular, instantly scheduled (just-in-time or "on-demand") times, and setting wages and service prices by "dynamic measurement of supply and demand," what has been called the "uberization" or "uberification" of work as a business model in other spheres means converting people's times of waiting (for employment, in the case of the underemployed and laid-off work force, and their "idled" life-times) into the work of waiting on others.[29]

Aiming for frictionless efficiency through the elimination of the inevitable slack in older (bonded, personal as well as industrial) models of service labor, including full-time, lifetime employment, the built-in features of such on-demand mobile services (ODMS) highlight more than the fact that a burgeoning global service economy undergirds the expansion of communicative capitalist industries driving and shaping uber-urbanization, or the fact that the digital mediatization of service industries often entails technologies to facilitate the direct casualization of labor.[30] Converting what would be understood as "waste" (unemployed people's life-times or the unemployed "free time" of the partially employed—in other words, *times of waste*) into on-demand or on-call work detail (often combined with other, diverse on-demand work detail in a frenzied, multitasking model of "employment"—in other words, *productive times*) aimed at soaking up the liquidity of life-times of the urban excess, such leading mobile app–based service enterprises do something else besides directly contribute to the creation of a growing "precariat" in the Global North.[31] These enterprises seek to effectuate a perfect meshing of two orders of social media: technological and human. That is to say, they seek to fuse and incorporate the disaggregated, "dividuated" human parts of the enterprise as component media within a total, integrated platform—*to program the function of humans as media for other humans*.

While one could point to Taylorism as an immediate precursor of these presuppositions of new media, longer legacies of slavery and colonialism must be seen to inform the dominant protocols codified in the most advanced capitalist media technologies as well as the social landscapes within which these are embedded.[32] Here I want to point out one important lineage, which can be gleaned from the striking continuity between, on the one hand, the function of colonial slaves as the bodily instruments and tools of sovereign masters and, on the other, the contemporary function of nonsubject humans as media for the servicing of the "demands" of full-subject humans, particularly in the way that such demands are to be met through contemporary SAAS enterprises. For Marx, what makes for the continuity between the slave and the free wage worker is their *being-for-another*, that is, the bodily life placed *at the disposal* of "his" owner/employer, with the difference that, as a commodity, the slave "is sold once and for all to his owner," while as the bearer of the commodity, labor power, the free worker "sells himself piecemeal."[33] Crucially, what makes for the continuity is the *alien power of disposition* over one's "vitality" that is characteristic of both, with the distinction between the two resting on the question of the *duration* of such disposition over one's bodily life(-times), and the provision or prohibition of the legal *freedom* to exchange oneself.[34]

The situation of one's whole bodily being, or life-time, placed at the absolute disposal of another abounds today in the context of migrant work, where the exploitation of what is effectively forced labor is enabled by new legal mechanisms for "the social organization of unfreedom" of foreign workers.[35] Live-in migrant domestic workers in particular exemplify the conditions of unfreedom and indistinction between work and bodily life (between labor-time and life-time) that highlight the structural continuities between colonial slavery and capitalist forms of racialized domestic servitude today.[36]

However, rather than the generalization of such conditions in the model of *servility* or "servile labor" that Paolo Virno sees as the new basis or source of surplus value in the universal, post-Fordist mode of exploitation, what we see today is, on the contrary, a global polarization of social conditions in the capitalization of reproduction. Within capital's subsumption of all life as productive force—or, life put to work—a distinction holds, that is, a distinction between life-times of *servility* and life-times of *servitude* that comes to be embodied in socially differentiated lives.

Disenfranchisement, or, the systematic denial of those protected freedoms guaranteed to citizen-subjects as well as to immigrant residents of the globopolis, draws this distinction, defining the conditions of nonsubject servitude to which migrant (nonimmigrant) workers are consigned.[37] In fact, it is state-protected, violence-backed practices of socio-cultural alienation from dominant human polities that shape what I find important to note here, which is the role of migrant domestic workers as *machines* for other humans' valuable life-production—that is, their paradigmatic role as producers of the valorizable life-times (life as labor) of others. At the beck and call of their employers for an indefinite range of tasks, such live-in migrant domestic workers act as all-around household appliances, whose design or designated purpose is to "save" their employers' valuable life-times. As Marx writes, what is char-

FIGURE 7.1. "We do chores. You live life." Photograph by author.

acteristic about machinery employed in production is "the *saving* of necessary labour and the creating of *surplus labour*."[38] Like convenience foods and food services, "servitude" provides, besides immeasurable social subjective and affective values of well-being, comfort, and self-esteem, "savings" in that nonmaterial use value of time. Instead of being "wasted" on the chores of life-maintenance, the "extra" time saved—or, put differently, the surplus life-times produced—can then be absorbed into the higher value and valorizable life-times of employers.

Serving as the means of others' social reproduction apart from their own (which takes place in their "home" countries, from which they are "exported"), "guest" domestic workers must be viewed in their aspect as household machines, the source and means of life-times *for* that life-as-labor that is the basis of post-Fordist modes of value extraction from spheres of circulation and reproduction.[39] Viewed this way, that is, as instrument and means of labor-as-life, migrant reproductive workers in general (including low-level service workers in the care, food, delivery/courier, and transportation industries) can be seen to function, within individual homes as well as within the broader "social factory" of their host societies, as a kind of *vital infrastructure*.

Vital Infrastructure

AbdouMaliq Simone has in fact proposed this important notion of "people as infrastructure" to encapsulate when, where, and how people's very "selves, situations, and bodies" serve as mediums of conveyance and articulation, as "conduits, routes, circuits, and pathways through which things reach, pass through, and affect each other."[40] In the former colonial cities of the Global South, such as Kinshasa, which substantially lack more formal, ready-made, and technical forms of infrastructure for people's use, the value of an individual existence does not lie in the elaboration of a "meaningful" (or, I would add, "valuable") life but instead in "an individual's ability to be 'hooked in' to different daily scenarios, dramas, networks, and affiliations that provide a constant set of alternatives for how to put bread on the table or how to become a person that can be taken seriously."[41] As a correlate of their increasing expendability, people bring together the particularities of their social relations (of family, kin, ethnicity, affiliation), their location and connections, personal character and style, to make themselves the "intersections" wherein the opportunities and transactions for eking out some kind of living (though never enough for a valuable life) might happen. In other words, as global finance unbundles infrastructural projects from their territorial sites and interlinks them across cities everywhere, the local urban poor are forced to create (out of their own extensive selves and repertoire of coordinated actions with others) the very systems of provision and networks of connection, access, and movement that they require and depend on as infrastructural supports of their own urban life.

Similarly, Julia Elyachar has argued for understanding the locomotory bodily practices and communicative gestures of poor residents in Cairo as unrecognized forms of urban infrastructure.[42] These social-semiotic, embodied practices, she argues, are not only important for reproducing the social relations of the city, and hence the bases of formation of political action and identity, but they also provide economically valuable outcomes. Dialogic actions and gestures are a form of "semiotic commons," a collective resource like a public good, whose otherwise unrestricted availability for use in the reproduction of communities has been steadily undermined and diminished by those very same kinds of forces of urbanization that I've described as the drivers of *city everywhere*: here, speculative investments on the part of Islamic companies, the army, and the state, as well as remittances from migrant workers in the Gulf, which "fed the rise of a bubble in real estate markets that reshaped the look and feel of Cairo." Noting the severe "toll" that structural adjustment policies, environmental destruction, public infrastructural neglect, gentrification, and forced evictions have taken on such collective resources of embodied practice, she reads the resulting diminishment of the semiotic commons as a form of "*divestment*—albeit unplanned—in an important if unrecognized form of urban infrastructure."[43]

Both Simone and Elyachar highlight the fact that life in cities in the former "developing" world has long depended on an innumerable array of "live" or vital forms of infrastructure, which are centrally comprised of *distributed, coordinated, rhythmic* human capacities and social routines that have to be continually generated, repeatedly performed, endlessly negotiated and modified (in a word, *improvised*) and occasionally, often periodically, revamped. It is this high level of dynamism, provisionality, and processual "productivity" that make such forms of infrastructure "live." While the specificities of different local and national histories of this informal, "organic" development might vary, a shared global history of colonial relations of power subtends the conditions of postcolonial capitalism now shared across these urban contexts, conditions out of which forms of vital infrastructure emerged, serving not only as "a coherent platform for social transaction and livelihood" that has kept a perennially sinking urban excess population afloat or above water, but also as crucial supports of urban life in general.[44] That is to say, while they are means of reproducing the lives of disposable people, vital infrastructures are also the means for facilitating the circulation and movement comprising proper (i.e., valued) urban life.

Whether locomotory and communicative bodily practices that can lubricate movement and buffer collision in seemingly chaotic, impossibly dense traffic on the streets, or makeshift, transient social networks through which illicit goods are marketed and transported, or services rendered, the provisional, facilitative channels created out of social collaboration and routine are the means of survival of a sector of urban humanity whose numbers have been rapidly multiplying in tandem with the aggressive growth of the urbanizing forces of their dispossession. As the forces of financial urbanization erode and diminish these life-making collaborations of the poor through the privatizing "enclosure" of urban spaces and utilities, these same forces also ultimately effectuate the swelling of the ranks of the immiserated and expendable and, in this way, paradoxically contribute to the growth of the very flexible, improvisatory practices and activities of livelihood comprising people as infrastructure. What Elyachar thus sees as "divestment" in a kind of vital infrastructure must also be seen, on another level, as a mode of increasing its characteristic *liquidity*.

Liquidity, Mobility

Liquidity designates the measure of convertibility of assets into other assets, with cash epitomizing the most liquid of assets, as well as the high volume (and velocity) of trading activity that exchanges in liquid assets give rise to. It thus aptly describes the qualitative state of the infinite number of small, everyday deals and transactions of goods, services, connections, bodies, and acts, with which surplus populations make the petty change that buys them another day of life (chapters 4–6). We might say it describes their very state of *being cash*, which means their immediate convertibility into any number of things and actions in order to serve as so many kinds of relays, intersections, components, and channels for the value-producing movements of others.

The liquidity of the livelihood activities of the urban poor depends precisely on their fungible, distributed bodily, rhythmic capacities to absorb the friction, shock, bumps, and drag that delay and detain the value-producing circulation of uber-urban life or that create interference for the lifestyles of *mobility*. It consists of their inventive human accommodations of and compensations for the chronic lack and failure of more formal, solid forms of public infrastructure in Global South cities, which make for the sluggishness of circulation. Like the street vendors who wade and weave through traffic, taking advantage of the pauses and slow-downs of vehicular flow, saving time for their customers in the provision of goods that would otherwise require other trips and expenditures of time, the urban poor find their living in these gaps and breaks in service and flow.

The urban poor live off crucial life services they offer to each other, services and utilities that the enfranchised of the city are entitled to and enjoy. Clean water, waste disposal, electricity and gas, affordable food, living space. None of these utilities or needs are easily accessible or affordable for the poor, so they must provide it for themselves and each other. They collect garbage, collect and sort recyclable junk (newspapers, bottles, scrap iron, plastic containers), collect the food scraps for the pigs, carry water from public faucets, build and repair their houses, maybe build to add space to rent out, or build a food stand or pushcarts to sell banana cue (barbecued bananas) or to collect trash or junk. Men, women, and children are vendors of uncooked vegetables, fruits, rice, fish, and meat. They are vendors of packaged food as well as prepared food, which they make and cook on road carts or sidewalk stands, or carry in baskets on the road in search of buyers. They can be petty retail sellers of dry and wet goods, which they buy in bigger markets and commercial stores, making a small percentage of gain on each and every item. Illicit substances and informal services are also among the needs of their community, and others, which they see to or provide.[45]

But everyone must both specialize and diversify.[46] People's social survival depends on them finding flexible niches where they can, in ways that depend on the social identities they are both compelled to inhabit and able to craft, and in dynamic, coordinating response to each other's changing needs. An eleven-year-old daughter will take the place of her mother at a food stall, while going to school in the mornings. A young tomboy might do the "male" work of collecting junk and pig food, as well as the "female" work of being the dealer/seller of tickets for petty lottery or numbers games. A young boy might run errands for a small junkyard business and collect pig food at other times. A *bakla* offspring will take on women's work as a maid or laundry-woman and on the side deal in the petty drug trade to take on their father's role as main provider for their mother and sisters. People work for a living that is shared, pooled, and apportioned, coordinated within a network of family, friends, province mates, and associates. Work is both divided and multiplied by these relations of mutual obligation. Livelihood is a proliferating series of sidelines, rackets, gambles, and gigs.

Such modes of living contrived by people in urban straits become a cheap resource that proper urban residents can draw upon to facilitate their own comfort, access, and enjoyment. Taking refuge in metropolitan spaces that would otherwise not have them (refugees from the war to be human waged "back home" in the rural provinces), they make their living by filling the openings for service they find or make. The urban poor might serve as other people's shopping carts, carrying the heavy shopping bags of their contractual employer through the crowded market as she picks and chooses and buys, waiting on her until she is finished and gets in her car, where the goods, and the bidding, are transferred to her driver. Or they might "watch your car" while it is parked, doing other things for other people besides, showing up when it is time to collect. They might walk between the cars stopped at traffic lights, selling cigarettes, peanuts, candies, bottled water, or cleaning cloths made of discarded snippets of fabric sewn together. In a previous time on these same streets, young girls and boys would sell small garlands of flowers, *sampaguita* (jasmine), and *ilang-ilang*, which jeepney and taxi drivers as well as other drivers would hang from their rear view mirrors, to scent the vehicle's interiors. Like the cleaning cloths, the garlands were made at home, which is also always a workshop, a mini-factory floor, a warehouse, a store front.

These petty mercantile enterprises of miniscule gains are mixed with livelihood from renting spaces, vehicles, and tools, including bodies and bodily capacities they might have at their disposition. Some might rent themselves or others out for sex work, criminal work, dangerous work. Lending oneself out in a multitude of ways does not only multiply one's sources of miniscule income; it also crucially develops and grows one's social networks, and therefore the very means of one's livelihood opportunities. Diversifying one's tasks means multiplying one's acquaintances and affiliations, building a social safety net for times of emergency or crisis, a distributed means of financial help and social support.

Undoubtedly, the petty livelihood enterprises of street vendors, watch-your-car boys, delivery and errand boys, shopping "carriers" in dense markets, cleaners, laundrywomen, scavengers, garbage collectors—as much as domestic workers—have long formed part of the informal urban built environment for both themselves and for the capital citizens of cities of the Global South. It is, however, the liquidity of their living and "live" transactions—their creative capacities to manipulate, exchange, and convert all available (social, communicative, economic) currencies, including playing themselves as coin—that enables the wholesale incorporation of the ever devalued life-times of the urban excess into and as auxiliary components of metropolitan platforms.

Ultimately, the liquidity of surplus people's disposable life-times has in fact been the enabling condition of the expansion of city everywhere, not only as the stuff and means of proto-ODMS for proper denizens but also, when "mopped up," as monetized assets for financial maneuvers and ventures. As the "independent" producers of this seemingly infinite self-producing resource of excess life-times, disposable (serviceable as well as absolutely expendable) populations thus act as a subaltern "driver" of global capitalist expansion.

Subaltern Fuel: Infinite Life-Times of Waste

Already very much a feature of urban subsistence economies in slums before globalization (certainly in postcolonial "developing" economies after World War II, as well as in racialized inner cities in the "developed" world), the highly improvisatory, flexible, elastic, and contingent activities comprising this liquidity had in fact been the subject of much academic study of "informal economies" during the 1970s and 1980s. One could argue that such attention to the life-times of the urban excess (as times of waste) prefigured, if not impelled, its "discovery" as a new resource for global capital, as the limits of industrial production had been reached.

The modes of value extraction exemplified in information and communication technology enterprises as well as in the conditions of transnationally organized reproduction, which support them, depend on this very "discovery," or capitalized "deep inclusion," of the experimental, risk-taking, shifting, multitasking modes of living developed out of urban conditions in the Global South—what in the slums could be seen as the petty financialization of everyday life, where the poor act as informal bankers, borrowers, investors, speculators, hawkers, pawners, and fixers in daily microenterprises to survive, wielding their bodily times as a soft currency (whether in the form of "savings" contained in domestic appliances or assets, pawned to neighbors in emergencies, or in the immediate coin of living labor-time) in order to extend life, which is always on the verge of being spent.[47]

The casting of all this "wasted" liquidity as a potential resource is evidenced in the Peruvian economist Hernando de Soto Polar's hundreds of initiatives and proposals, from the late 1980s to mid-1990s, to capitalize on the poor's "paperless assets," that is, to turn what would otherwise be "dead" capital into fuel for growth by legalizing the poor as property owners and entrepreneurs. His efforts were recognized by Philippine president Joseph Estrada (1998–2001)—whose own wealth (and subsequent downfall) depended on *jueteng*, the national illegal numbers game preying on the gambling of the urban poor—and his successor, Gloria Macapagal Arroyo, both of whom called on de Soto to advise the Philippine government on economic policy, each highly cognizant of the extractive potential of the urban excess, a global potential value estimated in 2001 to be $9 trillion.[48]

The absolute liquidity of those jettisoned or *disenfranchised* by the franchises of the emerging urban globopolis, is, however, to be distinguished from the mobility of the most privileged denizens of city everywhere, that is, those with full globopolitical citizenship. The latter achieve existential solidity, their paid-for prerogatives and subscriptions guaranteed over their own lifetimes and transmissible across at least one generation, even as experientially their life conditions are characterized by speed, ease, and facility. The former bear existentially liquid fates—highly unstable, impermanent, movable, transferable, and convertible states of being—while experientially their conditions are marked by sluggishness and stagnation, a slow sinking and disintegration.

These are the experiential and existential dynamics of contemporary modes of accumulation undergirding city everywhere, which depend on the consumption and expenditure of the disposable life-times of those relegated to the urban peripheries as the direct means of enhanced accommodation of the valued lives of a "lyfted" metropolitan humanity. No longer simply the rural provinces, and extending beyond paradigmatic slums, these peripheries refer instead to the proliferating coastlines of city everywhere, which become the space for life made unnecessary, spaces of indefinite detention where expendability and punishment are fated to converge. City everywhere is after all not a fixed, geographical place, but rather a form of protected and privileged dwelling, fluency, and mobility predicated on the expenditure of the resources of survival of those who must remain in its temporal outskirts, including, crucially, patience and the ability to bide and make time.

In those temporal outskirts, life's vicissitudes are always a question of "timing"; time is not only the key commodity and medium of exchange but also the central category of experience. In his ethnography of "Looban," the pseudonym of a Manila slum area in the early 1970s, F. Landa Jocano observes the way activities are ordered and coordinated and social identities are framed in terms of time.[49] People speak of neighbors according to how long they have resided in the area, distinguishing between residents and outsiders, between close neighbors (*kapitbahay*) and new arrivals (*mga bagong lipat*), between acquaintances (*kalila*) and intimates (*kapalagayang-loob*), apportioning trust and credit in the reciprocal exchanges of food, service, and other necessities according to residential duration. And they explain the occurrence of events, including murder, less in terms of causal situations or human agents than in terms of time: "Na sa tiempo lang iyan [That's just a matter of time]." Or "na tiempohan lang [It was just a matter of timing; timing did it]."[50]

In these spaces of the urban excess—the refuse of modernization and its synchronous global urban development—the time of its castaways pools.[51] Here are the eddies where infinite life-times of waste collect, life-times for the disenfranchised to bide, make, make available to others, put to beneficial or gainful use (*pakinabangan*). Sometimes those infinite life-times become a menacing specter of despair—what those who are rendered completely unserviceable (i.e., unredeemable through servitude) dread and suffer as interminable present time. As Steffen Jensen keenly observes, in Bagong Silang, a slum relocation site established in the 1970s and today a *barangay* (village) with the greatest population density in Metro Manila, young men face the ever-looming threat of confinement in a deranging infinity of time, an asphyxiating state of perpetual coming to nothing, which they call *buryong*.[52] A term that has migrated from the prison world through which many male slum dwellers cycle in and out, *buryong* expresses in personified form that endless, aimless time of waiting, which haunts these young people facing absolute redundancy with the threat of maddening perdurance as their life sentence.

Whether the work of waiting on others—servicing, making time for others—or the work of simply waiting—killing time, doing time—it is a waiting without end, an infinite dilation of time that floats the archipelagic grounds upon which citizens of the emerging globopolis enjoy their mobility.

When we pull out of the close-up on any specific city, as I do here with the composite picture of city everywhere, drawn from both actual projects and abstract tendencies in global cities in the North and South, we see all along the borderlines of city everywhere the standstill waters of economic stagnation, of sinking life value, where money, time, and life are all running out in equal measure. Indeed, the creation of metropolitan archipelagos of city-state islands everywhere only serves to create more and more of these seas, which are spaces of no social standing, perilous spaces to which migrant refugees flee, taking flight from the ravages of life-expenditure at home only to find themselves afloat or drowned in a place of emptiness where the non-citizens who have lost their human standing are jettisoned as life-time castaways. In the ocean, as one aspiring Senegalese migrant says to his friends in Mati Diop's striking 2009 documentary, *Atlantiques*, there are no borders; but, as his friend—who has survived an unspeakable trauma in his own migratory attempt to traverse the high seas—counters, there is also nothing to hold on to.[53]

Congestion and Bypass

"The whole development of wealth rests on the creation of disposable time."[54] If this verity, uncovered by the critical insight of another era, has become the evident program for accumulation now animating metropolitan platforms, such a program is nevertheless continuously stymied by the staggering density of matter and flows, the surplus of surplus life-times, that it has created the conditions for producing but that it does not by itself generate or fully control.

When we pull back into a close-up view of life in Metro Manila, we see this staggering density and congestion, the massive effect of social contradictions lived daily, experienced and manifested in a vehicular traffic situation that locals and visitors alike suffer and loudly decry as "the worst on earth."[55] On the ground, we see the constant stymieing of metropolitan dreams of the free and easy movement—the liberated flows—of capital life. In place of uber-urbanization's ideals of just-in-time, anytime, every time, unimpeded velocities of productive circulation, a surfeit of conflicting aims and modes of social existence, of daily battles for a parcel of an ever-diminishing ground of life, creates this nearly impassable congestion that forces the idling of everyone's time. All this time wasted on the road to productive ends, continuously undercutting the well-being and value potential of rich and poor alike, though at entirely different scales. How is this not the widespread effect of the very bases of urban platforms as unending war? With travel times within the metropolis quadrupling, even quintupling (where a distance of three miles might require a trip of an hour and a half), only the creative, liquid capacities of the humans who serve as the media of other humans can make up for this exponential space-time expansion experienced in urban, not just rural, life that effects the massive devaluation of people's life-times.[56]

Mar, a personal and family driver in Manila, shaves down, minute by minute, the overwhelming drag that such congestion creates for his employers. He puts at their disposal his own prodigious skills in weaving in and out of the tightest spaces, within the smallest margins, his uncanny abilities of "timing," of biding and accelerating, manipulating and making time, on the road, through constantly inventive, often dangerous and illegal, maneuvers, including making openings and even entirely new lanes where there are none, competing but also coordinating with all the other drivers, each doing the same, all getting away with what they can, in order to get by, in a place where the risks are life and death, and the reward is simply time—the total sum of these private solutions multiplying the impasses they are individually able to evade.

Mar is one of about a million and a half private drivers in Metro Manila.[57] Each driver's work is multiplied by all the other private and commercial drivers that drive the 2.7 million vehicles passing through the metropolis every day, as well as by all the other private service workers with whom he coordinates and collaborates to ease the lives of their employers, in a place that would not be able to run otherwise. Whatever movements can take place can happen only because of the vital infrastructure that they all, in aggregate and in coordination, provide.

Every day a driver calculates, predicts, takes risks—chooses wagers and acts on them. He makes judgment calls, not just in the driving (risking illegal and dangerous moves at every turn and on the spur) but also in carrying out all the big and little tasks that drivers are tasked with, as couriers, proxies, personal shoppers, along with all the other helpers—a thousand little negotiations to facilitate the channeling of flows, without which metropolitan life would not run at all. The less his employers can be bothered, the more he has to decide, to figure out, and make work on his own in an ever-changing environment, fraught with unpredictable contingencies and irregularities, which require what is required of an entire population of servants—infinite patience and unlimited adaptability.

These are the highly adaptable capacities of people who serve as vital infrastructure.[58] A driver's abilities to slice through a thicket of flying as well as puttering vehicles, each weaving a trajectory of its own, across roadways that change from nine lanes to one, with barely any warning or graduated approach, are no less impressive than the skills of a surgeon. To shave the time is to cut within inches of other cars, to cut in the lines of waiting to get on the overpasses, to cut off other cars, to weave and slice through them, overtake, get ahead, get ahead, get ahead, then wait, wait, wait, for that opening, that little bit of slack in another driver's mission to get ahead and make time, that moment of distraction or release of attention, the margin of another's error, which is all the opening one might find in the sludge. To bide and accelerate. To create a path where there is none, in a sludge of moving metal and people, requires more than timing and precision. It requires the ability to see in all directions, to sense vectors of movement from all directions—pedestrians crossing from behind, motorcycles squeezing through along both sides, things thrown or falling from above, overtaking vehicles coming headlong. It requires *a constant hazarding of lives.*

And yet, while these liquid capacities are at the disposal of his employers, every day yielding savings of time and facilitating the connections that the latter's lives require, they are not exhausted by the immeasurable service they provide. Just as overseas migrant workers are both "life support" for their employers and *life extension* (sustaining but also drawing on the life sources) of the disposable populations from which they emerge as global labor, and to which they remain vitally and fatally attached, Mar is the means of living (connecting, communicating) not only for his employers but also for his own dispersed but connected family and kin, the extended, open, and flexible transnational social network of which he is a vital component.[59] That is, he is not only a part of the vital infrastructure upholding city everywhere; he is also a key player and component of a mediatic network of socially coordinated capacities that serves as a *vital platform* for his own personal life-ventures.[60]

Subaltern Driver: Vital Platforms

The difference I draw here between infrastructure and platforms is not so much a technical distinction (between kinds of objects) as much as a theoretico-political distinction (between aspects/moments and states). Vital infrastructure allows us to see when and how people's mediatic capacities become a part of the built environment in the way the means of circulation (roads, communicative media, currencies, mobile banking) enables the movement and possibility of exchange. In this aspect, their mediatic capacities serve to maintain and reproduce the conditions of capitalist accumulation. Vital platforms allow us to see when and how people's mediatic capacities become themselves machines of production in the way branded network systems of connective, coordinating activity (social media and other content-sharing networking platforms, software-as-a-service systems, creative digital apps, operating and logistics systems, information/mapping engines, mobile communicative apps, programmable currencies) draw on and generate immaterial social use values that serve as the basis of value productive and accumulable exchange. In this aspect, people's mediatic capacities act as constituent elements and nodes of a distributed, coordinated means of their own social reproduction, which serves at the same time as a machine of production of exchangeable values.

As a form of organized servitude, vital infrastructure consists of capitalist-coordinated aggregates of human means, or instruments, undertaking what built physical environments, technical systems, and technological infrastructure cannot fully undertake (book scanners, copy machine operators, content moderators, trolls), or facilitating connections and interfaces between capitalist machines as effectively their replaceable components (couriers, runners, and cursors *for* machines, acting on behalf of employers but also as transmission agents enabling capital machines to communicate with each other). If migrant workers, low-waged service workers, humans meshed with machines (as domestic and other time-saving appliances), are placed in the service of the social reproduction of valorizable life, that is, as the means of *productive* social reproduction, they comprise in aggregate form capitalist means of production of capital life, which capital does not itself pay for. In this way, just as individual servants provide "savings" of life-times for their enfranchised employers, their sum total as vital infrastructure provides capital it's "savings" in constant capital (what it would expend on its machinery), "savings" that are in fact the product of a systematic "free"—that is, stolen—transfer of values produced elsewhere.[61]

As differentiated parts of vital platforms, which they themselves organize and constitute as the collective means and object of their own social reproduction, that is, as the means of production of shared life, members of kin-social networks participate in the processes of valorization of their own distributed transpersonal capacities, substances, and effects. It is in this latter aspect that overseas migrant workers can be viewed as agents of their own liquid life-times, processing "foreign exchange" transactions between discrepantly valued life-currencies (their families', their own, their employers), according to flexible exchange rates that their own significant remittances (as the Philippine economy's second most important source of foreign exchange earnings) affect. The complaint that they are sometimes used by their own local relatives as ATMs and the fact of their entrepreneurial and speculative investments back "home" demonstrate their role as both currency and bank, investor and asset. Played by themselves and their kin as the ante in fate-playing gambles of metropolitan migration, offered up as collateral for debt-fueled life-ventures, and depended on as "securities" for present dividends and future gains by the people to whom they belong, migrant workers also embark on microcapitalist, microsocial enterprises, investing their own monetary savings and mobilizing their own network-extended capacities in risk-laden speculative projects for remaking their own shared presents and otherwise fated futures.

Like the expendable communities from which they are redeemed and which they support (as the means of reproduction of their own lives), migrant workers and other global servants at home and abroad thus act at once as manipulators of liquidity and as liquid assets themselves, that is, as the "vanishing mediators" of a plethora of value-producing exchanges. It comes then as no wonder that as a global aggregate, their "liquidity" acts precisely as a means of capital valorization and accumulation that is disappeared from the accounts. The powerful role of strata of disposable *peoples* as a "driver" of global urbanization—their role as *generators* and as channels of capital flows—is critically as well as hegemonically bypassed, subalternized through global servitude, even as creative strategies of bypass are some of the key forms of disposable peoples' social survival and thriving.[62]

All the capital pumped into city everywhere cannot fully or quickly enough absorb, recycle, or channel back into its own high-value platforms the surplus liquidity that it has "freed." More and ever-evolving strategies for survival, which respect none or little of the formal or legal protocols of urban life—including, but not limited to, all those life-activities criminalized and made into the basis of life-expending security industries—make for a surplus of the surplus that can take on an assaultive character with respect to metropolitanist projects and their desires. As the elevated grounds of uber-urban life push up and out of the increasing surfeit of disposable life-times that buoy them up, people look for all the ways they might trade in their ever-depreciating life-times—betting or lending them on perilous sidelines, sudden transactions, precarious gigs, and reckless predatory rackets—all for the possibility of upgrading to higher-value life-times, or simply for the chance of staying afloat and living at all. Meanwhile, the biding and accelerating rhythms and beats of this improvisational life-making mount to a riotous, cacophonous pitch, the vectors of quick runs and narrow escapes ever at cross-purposes, creating impasse after impasse and overall drag, often to a point that can stop a great many dead in their tracks. In this sense, the inundation and sludge experienced as the unbearable, unlivable congestion of Metro Manila, and increasingly of so many of the component cities linked to the nation's capital, should also be understood as the presence of conditions for actual and potential antagonism everywhere.

EXCURSUS

Serviceability and Expendability in the Globopolis

Servitude

In the early 1990s in the Philippines, the airing of the problems of overseas Filipina domestic workers had reached a particularly intense pitch on the national scene. Harrowing reports of the physical and mental violence inflicted by employers on these workers—psychological and physical torture, mutilation, sexual assault, rape, starvation, confinement, and murder—brought the Philippine state and the nation into a moral, political, and economic crisis, precipitating a whole set of national legal reforms and international agreements that finally resulted in the reformation of the Philippine state into one of the most successful "labor-brokerage states" in the world.[1] Today, the Philippine state oversees the annual deployment of around 2.3 million workers as overseas or migrant labor in some two hundred countries and territories, including sea-based commercial fleets, around the globe. These workers join a total of between 12 and 15 percent of the total Philippine population (of 106 million) now overseas, whose annual remittances (in 2019 reaching $33.5 billion) were until 2018 the third largest in the world, following only India and China.[2]

While the tendencies leading to this crisis were already beginning to be evident then, ever since Philippine labor export began in the 1970s under Marcos,[3] in the 1990s it was the ubiquitous figure and sometime reality of slavery, gleaned from the conditions of overseas domestic workers in particular—this charge of modern-day slavery representing a notable precursor to current global abolitionist (antitrafficking, or "free the slave") campaigns—that shaped the way the problem of overseas domestic labor has come to be understood and addressed. On the one hand, my own account takes seriously the problematic that connects the conditions of servitude and slavery, and sees these connections as systemic and historical. On the other hand, as in the civilizing project of US colonialism in the Philippines at the turn of the twentieth century (as well as in its analogue in British India), "slavery" has been the object of negation of numerous protectionist humanist campaigns, which together have served to uphold the "freedoms" of global capitalism and have helped to install the provision of reproductive work as the cornerstone of the Philippines' role in the global economy.[4] That is to say, protectionist humanist campaigns have led to the transformation of the Philippines (not just the state but a whole array of participating institutions, including universities) as a global provider of the means for the direct social reproduction of other societies.

While there is no gainsaying the importance of the legal protections and labor rights won by activists and NGOs from the Philippine state (which passed the Migrant Workers Act and Overseas Filipinos Act of 1995, the Magna Carta of overseas Filipino workers, offering legal assistance and protection of their individual rights and welfare), the reconfiguration of what were effectively and discursively the labor commodities of a warm-body export national economy into worker-subjects and "migrant citizens"—the process of "humanizing" them (against the racializing acts of violence that inscribe them as less- or other-than-human, as mere commodities)—has been part and parcel of the Philippines' political and economic transformation as a major global manufacturer, provider, and broker of reproductive workers worldwide.[5]

The consequences of this national transformation—effected through the refiguration of its "warm-body" products for export into martyrs and heroes; hardworking, self-sacrificing skilled workers; family-oriented, faithful citizens (their interpellation as well as marketing as exemplary, valuable and value-making subjects)[6]—are multiple: the enormous cash remittances of overseas Filipino workers have kept the Philippine economy afloat (as 10 percent of the GDP), thereby legitimating the labor brokering strategy and authority of the Philippine state; the remittances have staved off crises of unemployment and unrest, and sustained by subsidizing the very conditions of social reproduction of low-cost migrant labor. Moreover, these remittances, as well as workers' transnational needs for communication and transport (cash, goods, people), have catalyzed the proliferation of business and development enterprises, which aim to take a sizable share of this new, burgeoning market.

Migrant workers are in fact investors in the booming real estate industry in all the urbanizing sites both in and beyond Metro Manila, their affective investments in their homes translated into property development gains.[7] While they strive to support their own present households, which produced them and to which they are bound to return, as Geraldine Pratt, Caleb Johnson, and Vanessa Banta argue, they are also investors in the collective futures of their families through the education of their children, who are themselves likely to become upgraded skilled labor slated for a new round of overseas migration.[8] In this way, migrant workers are not only engaged in the social reproduction of their host societies, at little or no cost to the host nation's social capital. Through their (financial, material, affective) remittances, they are also tasked with the social reproduction of the otherwise expendable populations and postcolonial states that serve as the condition of their own reproduction.

Much of the scholarship on global reproductive labor and overseas migrant Philippine workers—the majority of whom are women employed in domestic and care work, though a large percentage are men employed as low-level seafarers in the global shipping industry (where Filipino contract workers comprise a quarter of the world's seafaring labor force of 1.6 million)—adheres to this economic approach: to global domestic, care, and service work as labor; and to migrant workers as laboring subjects. I neither deny nor diminish the critical importance of viewing global reproductive work as labor. It is quite obviously the case that reproductive work has been capitalized globally.

However, insofar as the global capitalization of domestic and care work in particular (global industries within which migrant Philippine workers have found a significant niche) is of a piece with the capitalization of reproduction more generally, the category of labor tends to obscure or oversimply the organization of important differences in the kinds of reproductive life activity subsumed by capital and their designated roles and relations within a fully globalized mode of production. In fact, as we saw in previous chapters, it is the organized separation of different spheres of social reproduction (between metropolitan and postcolonial nations, between majoritarian citizens and racial or tribal "minorities," between legal, permanent residents and illegal,

Table Excursus.1
Global Servility, Global Servitude

Servile Labor, or Servility	*Servitude*
• Life as value-making labor	• Life as disposable time
• "Unremunerated life" within broader "production time" in the "social factory"	• Humans as media for other humans, as time-saving machines
• Globopolitical citizenship	• Noncitizen or secondary citizen, tentative residence
• Productive consumers of time	• Resources and producers of time

transient populations, between urban residents and rural dwellers, etc.) that maintains the great discrepancies in the rates of "life-times," which serve as the very basis of the global economy.

As I have been arguing, in a new global political economy wherein all life bears the potential to serve as a direct means and source for the extraction of capitalist value, "life" (as reproductive activity) is invidiously parsed into different modes and moments in the production of value. It thus seems politically essential to grasp and hold on to a distinction between the servile life characteristic of the exploitation of the communicative performances and social, cognitive, and affective labor of post-Fordist workers, and the servant or serviceable life characteristic of contemporary domestic, care, and service work conscripted for the social reproduction of valued life.[9] Between the post-Fordist experience of universal servile labor, which alludes to the disappearance of a clear distinction not only between life and work, but also between performance and production; between the product and the act of producing, on the one hand, and the experience of global servitude, on the other, lies a refurbished racialized and racializing divide.[10]

Sinister Design, the Splitting of Life-Times

The line separating service strata and the valued life they serve is undulating. It snakes through all spaces, public and private; street, home, car, office, mall, hospital, restaurant, parking lot, park; never losing its formidable, tensile strength. As transparent and impassable as glass, as unyielding and inviolable as steel, the line is expressed and exerted as a matter of aesthetics—protocols of bodily form, dress, comportment, architectural and interior design, food, sound, smell—that would separate the server from the served, accompanying both in all their intimate movements through and across urban spaces, keeping them at the farthest distance from each other even in the spaces of their closest proximity, like the thin wall or short distance between a dining area and a tiny kitchen in a small Hong Kong apartment, or like the grade separation instituted for the transport system, keeping cross-cutting channels flowing yet apart, or like a very thin, prophylactic membrane of a glove preventing the contaminating threat of touch.[11]

The aesthetics of this grade separation of the lives and life-movements of the fully enfranchised from those of their "helpers" is less a matter of any particular form (though glass and steel crystallize and emblem the sleekness and smoothness of unimpeded circulation that the upper echelons so desire to embody and inhabit, to wear as the very polish of their being) than the high–production value cleanness of legible, articulable design, the clarity of defined, reproducible style, which would make all other sensorial arrangements of haphazard living nothing but disturbance, garbage, noise. Or it might simply be the aesthetics of bodily appearance and bearing on the part of a ruling, majoritarian population distinguished from what they sense and code as the degraded and degrading bodily differences and habits of its contemptible guest workers as well as of its own homegrown idled, worthless folk.

The line would appear to be as rigid and quasi-ontological as that political boundary of "race," a boundary that some might call a form of global apartheid (and undoubtedly it is a line drawing on and revising the sex-gender and race lines established under colonialism and chattel slavery between the human and the non- or subhuman, expressible in the line between clean, contained, disciplined human bodies, and unruly, dank, penetrable, and permeable monstrous flesh).[12] And yet this particular line is also one that all are enjoined to imagine they could permanently leap over, rather than simply cross or fudge. To leap over this line, which marks the threshold between life worth living and life worth expending, requires a leap of fortune or a leap across states of being (from the unfinished, semiprocessed, permanently transitional state of the becoming-human to the achieved, completed state of the already human). Few leading expendable lives can make this leap with the whole of their lives in tow—that is, to make that entire upgrade of existence. Those with the greatest chances of such a leap are the ones who have attained a minimum of enfranchisement in their roles as legally, formally employed workers, in the service of capital life. But even among them, often the best that one can do is to split their lives between two states of being across a spatial or temporal divide.

For migrant workers, that divide might be a transnational one—in the host country, one might live a life worth expending, all one's life-times placed in the service of others, used up and exhausted, while in the home country, one might temporarily enjoy the affordances of a life worth living otherwise beyond one's reach: alongside an abundance of consumerist pleasures, leisure, unfettered sociality and social standing, settlement, and belonging. The differences in living standards obtain as the immediate effect of differences in the rate of exchange between the monetary currency of one place and that of the other (global rates of life-times), even as such differences (of living and of currency) are in turn predicated on a longer, deeper set of violently enforced differences sedimented in the political and economic structure and geopolitical order of relations of nation-states. A life of barely minimal wage in the United States, Italy, Singapore, Japan, Hong Kong, Saudi Arabia, Qatar, or on a merchant ship moving across the oceans—cleaning up children, kitchens, toilets, galleys, bedpans, the sick and elderly—might translate into a life of global middle-class comfort and privileges "back home." If the price of one's serviceable life-times in the host country is the cost of its continuous expenditure, its remuneration (one's monetary compensation) can nevertheless be traded for greater value life-times, to be spent in worthwhile pleasures or investments (on the higher education of children, the building of a house, the buying of land, the starting of a small business) that might consolidate seemingly squandered, or inordinately exacted, life-times of effort elsewhere in the accumulated form of a solid, citizen life of value here "at home."

The spatial splitting of one's life across continents and nations is also often recapitulated in its splitting across days, weeks, months. As Sumayya Kassamali shows, migrant workers in Lebanon (Filipinos, Ethiopians, Sri Lankans) divide their lives between the unremitting time of work during the week, where work is experienced as "empty of content but always happening," experienced not as itself a kind of time but as "the condition of possibility for time to be inhabited and acquire any sense of meaning"; a time of rest on Sundays, experienced as a time of frenetic activity, when events for and by migrants take place, the only day when they have time to do any and all things for themselves; and "a time of accomplishment, of meaningful action and its completion," measured in years away from home, the place of anticipated reckoning upon return, even if such return might be no more than a long-held aspiration.[13]

We see these complex reckonings with and negotiations of time in *Sunday Beauty Queen* (2016, dir. Villarama), a documentary on overseas Filipinx domestic workers in Hong Kong who devote their one day of rest, in a week of round-the-clock routines and demands, to beauty contests—as organizers, contestants, supporters, and viewer-participants. The domestic workers themselves remark on the stark differences between *times of drudgery*—unending life-times of giving and giving up of oneself to the point of nearly having nothing left, where all that is endured within awaits redemption at another time, another place, for one's own as much as for one's self—and *times of flourishing*—brief life-times of personal self-realization and thriving, where one's invention and expressivity can be outwardly performed on and as an individual representative (nation, region, province) of recognizable social value.

As I have written elsewhere, the activities of social enjoyment of overseas migrant workers in spaces outside the proper homes that are their workplaces (participating in beauty contests, sharing of food and stories, watching porn) might appear, from the perspective of a productive life and in contrast to their work as producers of time for others, as a sheer unproductive consumption of time, a waste of time.[14] And yet in the vanishing time of their own reproduction, "time in which labor-power 'belongs' to itself," the idle practices of social enjoyment can also be viewed as a time of recovery and restoration, a time for the restoration of life-times lost in the production of time for others.[15] While these times of waste can be viewed to thereby support the reproduction of waged reproductive labor, within such times of reproduction can also be gleaned times exceeding sustenance, times "freeing" experience from the emancipated subjectivities of labor, times of flourishing and elaboration that cannot be subsumed in the life-times of disposability reproduced.

Like the majority of people who cannot fully outsource the time-costs of their unproductive reproduction, migrant workers parse out their life-times between waste and value, only perhaps in a more dramatic way than others insofar as the place of their work and the place of their social reproduction or "living" are at a visible distance from each other. Even as capitalism today is blurring the distinction between work and life, in what is effectively, for many, the real subsumption of individual lives as labor and, for the rest, the formal subsumption of social life-making as the raw material and machinery of labor and production, that distinction continues to play out for all on many different, relative scales—from populations and bodies, to sets and styles of activity and moments and durations of living, as the distinction between life-times of productive, accumulable value and life-times of waste.

Submerged Lineages, Subaltern Forces

How might we account for this racialized divide in the sinister design of global life? There are important historical accounts of the continuities between gendered forms of slavery and contemporary forms of domestic servitude, which allow us to understand the historical and political lineages that remain submerged or leaped over in accounts of the generalized exploitation of life as labor. My own early attempt understood the connections between these conditions of servitude and slavery as resting on the intersection of gender and racial systems of differentiation with the logic of commodity fetishism, that is to say, the racializing objectification of national, class, and gendered social relations of dispossession realized through acts of violence inflicted on the bodies of domestic workers. Regular acts of violence inscribed migrant domestic workers as less and other than human, things without subjectivity, in a historical moment when humanity was itself being redefined through globalization. As labor-commodities in a burgeoning warm-body export national economy, migrant domestic workers were territorialized bodily resources (alongside other raw and semiprocessed natural resources) of a developing or third world nation-state whose own aspiring heteromasculinist sovereignty depended on its management of its national body. As commodities, they embodied the economic as well as racial, sexual "difference" between their "cost" (deemed cheap by dint of natural abundance) and their employers' "worth" (deemed dear by feat of human skill and achievement), a difference that translated into directly appropriable surplus value. I understood the continuities between contemporary servitude and slavery thus to lay in intertwined sex-gendered and racial logics intrinsic to the very structural tendencies of capitalism in a new moment of global expansion, where the "feminization" of labor was also crucially a racializing process—an ungendering into a state of being-for-others that was also a being-in-pain.[16]

Contemporary servitude's genealogical link to slavery is affirmed by this endemic use of racial violence (of punitive, criminalizing, and rights-denying laws as well as of physical and psychic acts of injuring) in the creation of a standing population pool of those charged with what Arendt denigrated as mere "labors of necessity"—labors of merely reproductive life that natives and slaves by nature performed (as opposed to the culture-producing work of a civilized, free humanity).[17] These are undoubtedly practical manifestations of deep codes of European colonialism and slavery operating within the protocols of the global economy of racial capitalism.[18]

The social conditions of global servitude are, however, more than the structural outcome of capitalism's disavowed yet continuing colonial history—more, that is, than the systemic operations of racial capitalism. For us to see what more there is (subaltern forces at work, superfluous forces in play), we must consider its buried historical and political lineages. I have in mind two ways to think about these lineages of servitude in a global context: the first is genealogically, through anti-Eurocentric global histories of colonialism and capitalism, and the second is synchronically, through a dynamic picture of transnational social networks of disposable and expendable populations from former and present colonies.

Genealogically, what is important to note is colonialism's alienation and objectification of local forms of social dependency, obligations, and power (power as enablement and enhancement of capacities rather than as colonial or capitalist command or proprietorial sovereign agency), transforming them into forms of colonial bonded labor that in a modernizing moment is to be freed while also remaining territorially, racially fixed or attached to the postcolonial nation-state.[19] These genealogies are important for thinking about the making of both reproductive and productive labor today, as well as for grasping their overlooked capacities and activity, which help produce global life in ways beyond their role as labor.

Eurocentric accounts obfuscate the logic, strength, creative persistence, and elasticity of non-Western domestic community life-making, practices of social reproduction that remain significant to global capitalism. Moreover, such accounts' conversions of native life into the terms of comprehension of Western, bourgeois property relations, even in the critique of the same (most evidently in affirmative accounts of other people's subjective "agency" against the dehumanizing and masculinist narratives of capitalism), actively and indirectly take part in the violent transformation of native life into postcolonial societies that are the behest of capitalist freedoms.[20] (Freedoms that serve as ideals and rights, which Western democracies had already achieved and the postcolonial world was struggling to gain.)

Critiquing such accounts, Indrani Chatterjee shows how, in the colonial South Asian and Southeast Asian contexts of what is now Burma, Bangladesh, and northern India, British imperial censorship of local terms for "slavery" and the translation of such native practices and relations of coercive domestic obligation into the terms of Christian morality and bourgeois exchange economies (e.g., establishing equivalence between food sharing and freedom, proximity and intimacy, social bonds and monetary debt, etc.) were part and parcel of the transformations wrought by the imperatives of settlement, forced labor and taxation, commercialization of agricultural production, the proliferation of markets, and increased monetization of local economies mandated by the colonial order.[21] These transformations both exacerbated and changed local practices of slavery and naturalized obligation, destroying even as they were instrumentalizing such practices in the name of Christian-based, capitalist freedoms.[22]

Elsewhere, Chatterjee draws out the epistemic continuities between colonial Christian abolitionist campaigns—whose triumph in defining slavery on the model of Euro-American colonial Atlantic slavery according to a Christian theology of humanity served to lay down the social basis of capitalist development in the postcolony—and contemporary global antitrafficking campaigns.[23] There is much excellent feminist critique of the imperialist and racist, carceral logics of these contemporary "abolitionist" campaigns, logics that I understand to be intrinsic to the war to be human, which such humanitarian campaigns can be seen to wage.[24] What I find notable in Chatterjee's historical critique is her foregrounding of the productive effects of the latter in the proletarianization of the slaves they free. Such an emancipation not only forcibly implements a Protestant regime of work; it also nullifies local forms of making and negotiating social relationships of cooperation and support and, what's more, criminalizes the very people that this "freeing" action had served to dispossess and deracinate.

It is striking that, in this account of the historical accomplishment of liberal freedoms, Chatterjee mentions human smugglers as an example of such people, deracinated by being practically defined (through new terms of imperial domesticity) further and further away from the domestic households that once supported their lives, who are now criminalized. To see either them or the migrants they smuggle as primarily individual or collective subjects, whether of labor or of crime, only builds on and furthers this deracination, participating in defining these people away from those domestic households that were and often still are their means of life—relations of their social reproduction that even now continue to operate, even if in attenuated and precarious forms—and thereby proffering the same dominant globalizing view, which disappears the lattices of transpersonal relational activity and sociality (comprising their "agency") that capital freely disposes of to its own gain.[25]

This brings me to the second way of thinking about overlooked lineages of servitude in a global context: that is, synchronically, across the geographically dispersed sites of life-making activity among disposable populations, tracing lines of connection (rather than descent) across the different "sectors" in which they make their living.

As I suggested earlier (in chapter 4) human smugglers are, like domestic workers, drivers, and errand boys and girls, life-time savers. They are, besides an alternative mechanism of transportation and channel of movement for reproductive labor-commodities, alternative machines of *foreign exchange*, facilitating (at enormous fees) the transactions between discrepantly valued life-time currencies that illegal migrants (their clients who are often compatriots) try to make.[26] In other words, along with other informal fixers, recruiters, and brokers operating in the cracks and interstices within legal, bureaucratic systems (openings that they often make themselves), human smugglers too are engaged in a form of service work, though also brutally preying on the disenfranchised for whom they act as illicit infrastructure within a shadow economy of circulation. They are contraband Uber drivers, working as independent providers. "Traffickers" are shadow couriers and drivers, charging hostage price fees, using illegal channels, charging exorbitant protection tolls, but, as Jeremy Harding observes, they exist in a mirror relation to the border police who seek to capture them, like pirates in relation to the colonial states that they helped to constitute. If border police are agents of the state of citizens, "traffickers" are agents of a parastate apparatus, offering alternative services and "protection" to noncitizens at the price of an exorbitant toll.

As we will see in the following chapter, these forms of direct predation among the disenfranchised participate crucially in the growth of capital. Beyond their moral reprehensibility (often the exclusive focus of accounts that spare legitimate, highly mediated, and protected forms of predation, such as the global service economy and its beneficiaries, from the same moral outrage), these agents of parastate criminal industries are processing exchanges of life-times, highly liquid and precarious transactions of spatiotemporal fates and bodily goods, which are undertaken by the disenfranchised in their own social reproduction under conditions of assault. Like the global circulation economy it shadows, the illicit trafficking economy crucially depends on these exchanges of life-times, which are their "goods." Like migrant workers, smugglers are life-time savers for others, facilitating conversions of life-currencies across the geopolitical, territorial divides that significantly determine their rates, with the crucial difference that smugglers risk their ventures on lives that are not their own, or lives in which they have no share.

My point in highlighting these similarities and direct connections (and conflicts) between migrant workers and smugglers through an economy of discrepant "life-times," which they participate in "processing," is to get to another way of understanding the role of servitude in contemporary global capitalism beyond its construction as invisible or unaccounted-for, unremunerated labor, and beyond therefore its redemptive potential as a free political subject, a citizen, if you will, of a globopolitical humanity.[27]

An attention to the historical lineages of contemporary servitude enables us to understand how the legacies of colonialism and slavery continue to inform the dominant (racial, sex-gender) protocols codified in the most advanced capitalist media technologies (as means of value extraction), as well as the social landscapes within which these are embedded. Moreover, it also allows us to glimpse forms of agency that the becoming-human have developed and depend upon for their survival, in the systemic interfaces that they are compelled to inhabit (living in social formations both preserved and destroyed by capital in order to serve as its milieus). In this way, we might also differently consider the "agency" of these service strata as forms of media.

Media, Milieu, Machines

As means of production in the capitalized circulation of valued life, the human media of global servitude cost capital something. But their cheaply priced, relatively high value is produced at the expense of their own nations, a value they incrementally transfer to the life they (re)produce (in the children of their employers, as new life as labor; and in the quantity and quality of surplus life-times of labor they produce or save for their employers and "beneficiaries"). On the model of imperialism and colonial slavery, an appropriation of already created surplus value (embodied in guest workers) takes place in the spending down of their life-times in service of the present and future life-times of value of others. But unlike earlier times, the natal and social alienation of global servants is temporally and spatially bracketed, insofar as they remain vitally connected to the nation and social life that produced them and that they spend entire lifetimes to maintain.

As we've seen, when viewed within the broader "social factory" of global capital, service workers serving as the instrument of labor-as-life compose part of capital's means of production.[28] In many cases, working as content moderators, screeners, scanners, and provocateurs (trolls), they also function as auxiliary machinic components (not just as productive users) of capitalist platforms. But they are also part of the means of life of their own kin and kind, and in this aspect act as the means of production of the very depreciated noncapitalist or nonhuman *milieus* that capital relies on for the cheap, abundant resources it has at its disposal.

This view of global servitude as consisting of mobile and shifting strata of disposable means of reproduction, not only of their "host" societies but also of the very expendable populations and postcolonial nations that serve as the condition of their own reproduction, is not, however, simply an argument about the role of servitude in the reproduction of class relations (capitalist reproduction). It is, rather, an argument about viewing reproduction as a discontinuous, variegated site and process of world-making, which bears unseen agencies as well as unforeseeable effects. Even as reproduction has long served as the site and strategy of capital accumulation, the social reproduction of disposable life (the life of disposable reproductive labor), especially, precisely because it is deemed to be of little, next-to-nothing value, is the site of other practices of life-making beyond the ideals and protocols of human subjects.

To see servitude or reproductive work as the *means* or instrument of labor (as *machine*) rather than as the *subject* of labor, allows us to see other possibilities in their mediatory "agency." We see, for example, the way migrant workers, as well as the expendable populations from which they are temporarily "redeemed" as servants, are, as I've suggested throughout, both manipulators of cash (as speculators, investors, and bankers) and cash themselves, that is, a form of "soft currency" that they speculate on, invest in, and gamble—money that can be exchanged but cannot store value. Just as the life-times of entire populations are made into monetized assets for financialized enterprises, global servants (whether internal urban or overseas migrant workers) and their dispersed networks deploy their own distributed selves, capacities, and channels as collective liquid assets for survival, relying on a social calculus that is made to converge with, but is also in excess of, those financial logics too easily summed up by the word *neoliberalism*. The other side of this "liquidity" that the disenfranchised at once create and bank on is a "vitality" that capital lives off but neither fully commands nor controls.

Overseas workers are in fact constantly solicited by state as well as private corporations to start businesses and invest in, donate to, and plow their resources into the nation through the channels that the public-private partnerships of state and capital provide (e.g. Balinkbayan, an online portal encouraging diasporic entrepreneurship, investment, philanthropy, and technology and skills transfer).[29] But driven by shared rather than individual survival, their vital transactions involve calculations that spill well beyond the latter's financial ledgers and terms of account.

As "live," vital media, global servants rely on a social calculus that is not easily apprehensible in narratives of them as laboring subjects or as neoliberal entrepreneurs. These forms of social calculus consist, for example, of dividing and distributing, differentiating and allocating, but also integrating and coordinating, persons and their substances and faculties, practices and theories of social action that we miss if we adhere to uninterrogated property assumptions behind the oppositions between individual and society, persons and things, humans and nonhumans (or nature), subjects and objects, technology and culture—as well as a trenchant habit of conflating the gender logics of capitalism with gendered social identities, which continue to structure our thinking about social activity, particularly the activity of the social reproduction of non-Western communities, as Marilyn Strathern argues.[30] It is these forms of coordinated capacities that enable their networks to function not only as vital infrastructure but also as vital platforms.

The vital platforms of Filipino kin-based social networks are not only "support systems" that allow them to adapt and survive in the host country.[31] These networks are also soft tissue of shared being—life-giving and life-making matrices of mutual being, which anthropologists identify as forms of kinship.[32] The platforms of migrants' own social reproduction are elastic, flexible, dynamic skeins of intersubjective relations with constraints and possibilities that are to some extent preformatted through domestic kinship protocols. But they are also dynamic and changing, even transferable, as a result of being stretched across continental and transnational contexts and within systems over which communities have little control, and enlivened and transformed in interface with capitalist platforms. In Hong Kong, Taiwan, and other places with a long-standing presence of overseas Philippine domestic workers, Filipinx migrants work to maintain the families they leave behind, but they also make new families and kinship relations with and among each other—through nonnormative, queer socialities, women take on all the social roles of kinship, which provide the codes for the vital relations of their mutual existence: fathers, mothers, lovers, husbands, wives, siblings, and their affiliative relations.[33] These affiliative relations are not limited to kin-based forms but also based on shared times, on times of accompaniment that structure long-lasting kinlike, desirous, and affective attachments of shared life.

As performing kinship systems, which are pragmatic distributional, allocational social logics, the vital platforms these workers create and maintain consist of coordinated channels of information, goods, funds, persons, and actions—organized recruitment systems, credit systems—social mediatic systems for the self-replenishing and self-renewal of their overseas families and communities, transnational households, and extended families "back home." Such is their importance that employment and state agencies themselves rely on and tap them as reliable mechanisms of their capitalist industries and as systems of welfare provision, which thereby subsidizes the costs of "production" of this stratum of servitude as a permanent, if continually depleted and replenished, resource.[34]

The social reproduction of serviceable life must thus be seen as consisting of modes of life-making sociality developed as the means of perdurance and thriving under colonial and postcolonial conditions of dispossession and depletion that has undergirded the urbanizing expansion of capital and its new forms of valorization. More than the associated milieus of capital, they are social engines that have served as a subaltern driver of the global economy, vital to the capitalization of reproduction and circulation in the new political economy of life.

A "Free" Pathway out of Absolute Expendability

Feminists have long argued that the assignation of *cheap* to feminized, third world labor, along with its relegation to dirty, degraded, menial chore-like work, whether in the household or in the factory, was a deliberate, active process of devaluation, requiring the violence of states, militaries, and police to quell strikes, demands for better treatment, labor conditions, and pay, as well as other forms of resistance.[35] The notion of the "feminization" of labor suggests that these deliberate, organized processes are gendered and gendering beyond "women's work." These are gendered and gendering processes of violence that are in fact intrinsic to capitalist production, the heterosexist codes of which shape capitalist practices of labor recruitment, organization, and management, as well as the constitution of the very category of labor.[36]

Practices of obtaining free labor are not simply some vestige of the past, or egregious "returns" to practices long outlawed under capitalist democracy, as is implied in the widespread use of the words "modern slavery" and "human trafficking" to refer to such practices, which casts them at a moral remove from the legal, formal, and thereby seemingly good practices of proper labor.[37] Rather, even as they appear to lie outside of its formal spaces of exploitation, these are practices of dispossession that have been an indispensable part of the metabolism of capitalist accumulation since its genesis. Social codes continue to operate not merely to justify ever-renewed and revised forms of appropriating free labor, but also, importantly, to organize them. Among the key social codes legitimating and organizing these forms of appropriation is the code of servitude.

In the global maritime industry, Roderick Galam argues, servitude is a "technology" that shipping labor recruiters or manning agencies use to exact unpaid labor from thousands of young Filipino men aspiring to employment as seafarers.[38] Called "utility men," these young men work essentially as free "helpers" for recruitment agencies, doing clerical and janitorial work as well as errand and courier work for the agency, while also performing domestic cleaning and laundry duties and child care for agency owners' families and serving as personal drivers and additional labor in the owners' other businesses. They may do this free work for up to two years in exchange for a future job. The expectation that utility men work for free and incur whatever financial costs or debts are necessary in order for them to do this work, is based on the notion that such service rendered and its future promise "saves [them] from wasting away in unemployment."[39] This voluntary servitude, called "utility manning," is a path of promise, the promise of a way out of a place of permanent stuckness, a place of ordained deterioration and loss of value (of "wasting"), often by virtue of serving as offshored resource zones for the global metropolitan economy—a place that for so many migrants and would-be migrants is "home." "Home" is the place of one's birth, early life, and continuing social reproduction—the place one is forced to flee and compelled to return to, for a better life, or for life to continue at all.

Hence, like so many others seeking a better life that can be found only outside this paradoxical "home," utility men are made to advance their lesser, next-to-nothing life-times for the possibility of remunerated, worthwhile work elsewhere, in the nations and homes, and cruise and cargo ships, of others. Like utility men, other new workers from lower-value social places of "origin" (an economic as well as geographic designation, such as postcolonial provincial rural, agricultural, or Indigenous communities and areas) offer their life-times up to be freely spent by labor brokers as payment to secure a form of "employment," which they are deemed to be, by virtue of their "origins," lucky to gain. In the scores of nail salons all over New York City, for example, new manicurists often have to pay between $100 and $200 just to get the *opportunity* to work for no wages, only tips. Largely recent migrants from Asia, they may work essentially for free for up to three months before finally receiving an hourly pittance that can sometimes be a quarter of the hourly minimum wage ($8.75), while also being made to work overtime without additional compensation.[40] In this way, they are kept continuously in life and work arrears. Decried as illegal forms of wage theft and other forms of labor code violations in journalistic exposés, these practices of extracting free labor are nevertheless tacitly supported by the clients of these services to the extent that these workers and the work to which they are relegated are devalued as unskilled, unnecessary, or superfluous, and degraded. In fact, it is the extraction of free labor that makes for this devaluation—a deskilling of people for and by menial service. Reduced to "help," their life-times are purchased and spent as forms of *gratuity*.

For workers, such "voluntary" free service time (not necessarily "labor-time" insofar as it might consist largely of waiting, of being on hand) is, in effect, a conversion fee—for exchanging the volatile, devalued soft currency of their local life-times for the stable, higher-value hard currency of global employment. Global employment most often entails work in the lowest levels of global service industries, industries devoted to the reproduction of capital life (domestic work, health and elderly care, food industries, and the logistics of global capital circulation, such as the shipping and transport industry, and lower-ranked communicative and cognitive work of business process outsourcing, such as customer service).[41] However, it is remunerated in the hard currencies of metropolitan powers. Workers from the Global South unsurprisingly usually suffer a loss of social status for the opportunity of global employment—teachers become maids, elite university graduates become call center agents, doctors become nurses or medical technicians, nurses become orderlies—because the exchange-value of their "deskilled" labor-power in hard currencies will translate or convert into higher-value subsistence-power in the places of their social reproduction—the home to which they will return and where their families (the social being of which they are a vital member-part) remain.

Philippine workers are highly conscious of currency exchange-rates among potential host countries and their own. It is in fact one of the "top reasons" that certain employment destinations are chosen over others, though some destinations, such as the United Arab Emirates, might be way stations en route to even higher-value, more stable currency-nations, where universal value resides, such as a US dollar–denominated nation.[42] No matter that one's wages might fall well below the wages of citizen-workers in high-value nations, as long as the remuneration of one's global employment (whether as migrant worker or as employee of a global industry at home) translates into more life-times of social reproduction (greater subsistence for oneself and one's kin). The great differences in national currencies of life-times (the value of labor-power based on the cost of reproduction) is what makes voluntary servitude a worthwhile investment. Advancing life for work (indenturing oneself with advance payments of cash or service time) makes sense only from a place of sinking life, a place of "wasting away."

Even as servitude is held out as redemption from a lifetime of waste, it is itself a means of "wasting" the life-times of those it "saves." Far from the skills-building training expected in forms of apprenticeship and internship, with which it might be ideologically associated (e.g., "on-the-job-training"), utility manning, for example, entails only the arbitrary prolongation of men's time of servitude (extending the time of waiting for a job) or its sudden termination without reward (that is, without adding up to employment). Such practices of "wasting" people's time are inflicted as forms of punishment for whatever their superiors consider punishable offenses, a punitive measure with a pedagogical, disciplining bent. As Galam insightfully argues, along with practices of making utility men stand at attention (disallowing sitting) and making them control their emotions, keep quiet, and swallow their pride, practices of "wasting" their service time by extending it or by discounting its cumulative value altogether at will are principally a means of "preparing utility men for subservience," "manufacturing docility," and more generally instilling the "proper dispositions" of a seafarer at the lowest rung of the industry.[43] More than this disciplining function, the careless expenditure of people's life-times is a means of their further devaluation. It is not because people are of lesser value that their time is wasted but, rather, that the wasting of people's time is a way of decreasing their value (the value of their life-times). To waste people's time is to make that time itself mere waste. To make those people the bearers of such waste (worth nothing) is to make them *akin* to waste themselves (worth next to nothing).

Servitude is a master code for gendered and gendering violence, the quotidian violence of making/having someone lesser at the disposition of a superior, who might also be of a kind. Not surprisingly, the qualities that utility manning "servitude" inculcates—namely, a readiness to serve, an attentiveness to the needs of another; being "made to function as a device or tool to make others' lives easier," made to "become like a piece of furniture"; a habituated inclination to keep one's thoughts and feelings to oneself, to take another's abuse, to suffer being "treated like toys (*laruan*)"; and a pliant, accommodating, and enduring "nature"—such qualities are precisely what feminizes or more accurately emasculates and infantilizes the Southeast Asian men to whom these qualities of servility are ascribed.[44]

Though it is not often explicitly noted, the gendering of qualities of servility and subservience as "feminine" and "effeminate" importantly take place in precisely the Western European–centric international arena where migrant workers more generally are to be employed, and therefore within the gendered terms of which they are destined to be understood, even when these gendered norms are invoked as part of a putative "national culture."[45] In other contexts, often domestic and sexual labor contexts in other parts of Asia, such expected servility and subservience may have the racializing effects of "ungendering," which Hortense Spillers describes as part and consequence of the American grammar founded on slavery.[46] Migrant Filipino workers often face this racializing "ungendering" in their depiction by employers as "dogs," "tools," or "slaves."[47]

Although these sex-gender and racial codes of subordination are dynamic and changing across space and time, they are at once overdetermined by the colonial history of such codes (hegemonic modern sex-gender and race systems emerge out of their roles in the organization of colonialism in its varied forms) and undergirded by subaltern histories of social survival (and their consequently illegible codes). Youth, for example, naturalizes as well as mitigates the subservience required. In Galam's account, the gendered suffering of utility men's servitude is narrated as an important rite of temporal passage into male adulthood. It becomes a liminal state—a transitional and intermediate moment that leads to an ideal outcome and status, which is the form of proper adulthood of full employment that would allow the expected performance of one's obligations to parents, siblings, and other intergenerational kin and social affiliative relations.

While the proper adulthood of full employment, which utility men are seen as aspiring to, might be interpreted in public as well as academic discourse as "masculine" (as is the notion of "breadwinner" with which adult masculine employment is equated), it is in fact the case that, within the domestic communities where their performances are also judged, the fulfillment of obligations to family is the role of all genders of kin members. Thus although the figure of the overseas Filipino worker has been heroized by the Philippine state through heteronormatively gendered figures (caring domestic workers, brave sea men), the "sacrifice" for which they are similarly hailed accords with the "reason" that all would-be and actual overseas or sea-based Filipino workers themselves offer for their pursuit of global employment: that is, to help their families. If the hardship they must suffer as the unpaid, abused, or exploited "helpers" of others is inordinate, it might nevertheless be offset or compensated for by the fact that it is undertaken to "help" the members of their own shared social body (*kabagián*—relatives, literally, of the same body, or fellow body).

Within Philippine communities, servitude has historically been naturalized as a temporary measure, as *liminal* (in the anthropological sense) precisely in its bracketing as a temporal, qualitative state (consisting of rites of practice pertaining to a period in one's life). Whether the duties of a child to do the bidding of adults; the domestic service that young, unmarried women enter into for other families before they have a family of their own; the period of indentured work of someone who "pawns" themselves for a monetary sum or a favor or gift in kind; or the free work enslaved war captives were forced to do until they redeemed themselves by payment or assimilation, the compulsory tributary work that servitude organizes was conventionally a temporally-bracketed practice of subordination. Some of those practices are still audible in the words for servant in the Ilokano language: *adípen* (slave/servant), *babaonén* (messenger or errand person; literally, one who does the bidding [*baon*] or obeys the

FIGURE EXCURSUS.1. "Wanted All Around Boy or Girl." Photograph by author.

command of another), *katúlong* (helper), or *ubing* (child) are all understood as relational roles in defined social contexts that begin and end.[48]

However, implicit in contemporary as well as historical usage are local status hierarchies among different family or clan groups, as well as class stratifications within the same communities, which have naturalized domestic servitude in particular as a permanent institution within families. Even as people cycle through this liminal state, the permanence of the institution makes for the possibility of one being a servant for the duration of one's entire life, and of one's children becoming the servants of one's employer and their children. While such relations endure, the institution is increasingly offshored, as the disenfranchised increasingly take on this liminal status elsewhere to better their lives at home, and as more industrialized domestic services are provided and made accessible to the local middle class (laundromats, fast and prepared food, delivery services, agency-provided caregivers). The institution of servitude has in this way been urbanized. Not only industrialized (depersonalized) but also parceled out across industries, its tasks "Taylorized" across the urban social factory, with the just-in-time and on-demand labor of a legion of contractual human capacities.

Today, servitude acts as a generalized social protocol in the imperial appropriation of value. Beyond the units of social identity that we are accustomed to recognize, modern sexuality, gender, and race are codes for subordinating particular lesser life-times to the better life-times they serve—they provide ways of discriminating not just among persons but also among kinds of activity, kinds of sociality, kinds of times of living.[49] As codes, they are the protocol for determining *which* life-times are worth expending for the valuable life-times of certain social strata—at once for the reproduction and for the further valorization and accumulation of those valuable life-times.

For those who enter these relations of servitude in the global arena, servitude continues to be temporally (and geographically) bracketed. Their life-times of subservience (suffering subordinated, serviceable being) take place in the space and time of franchise, yielding greater shared subsistence and higher status at home, which one can enjoy periodically in person with carefully timed and saved up visits, or in real time virtually, through ubiquitous cell phones and social media and through transmissions of money, gifts, images, looks, gestures, and words.

As the means of reproduction of capital life, global servitude is a structural, temporal moment in the productive circulation of value. It is a hinge or conductor between life-times that are absolutely consumable (raw material life) and life-times that are accumulable (capital life). It is the machinery or

Excursus • 193

instrument for converting the vitality of social survival into serviceable life-times, life-times with some measure of value that can be passed on or transferred to the capital life they reproduce. Serviceable life is after all *produced*. It is the product of the work of social reproduction of life or life-making that is not to be reproduced by capital; it is, in other words, the product of the *vitality* of disposable life. The disposable life that produces the serviceable labor on offer in the global market is, instead of being slated for reproduction, either simply expended by other industries, or left to "waste away."

Even as the serviceable life of migrant workers might be provided an equivalent for the reproduction of their individual life capacity, that equivalent is made possible only by their reproduction taking place elsewhere with the vital help of others to whom they belong (and who belong to them), and this belonging constitutes the very condition of their individual lives. These unaccounted vital forces are comprised of the transpersonal practices of life-making among kin, defined as "a network of mutualities of being." These are vital forces in the cooperation and sharing of the work of social reproduction beyond what the remuneration of serviceable labor (wages) can ever provide.

In fact, the price of globalized service labor is made affordable by the discounting of the value of the communities to which they belong and the larger territorialized populations to which their fates are affixed (a devaluation reflected in and implemented through devalued currency rates and lowered "qualities of life" conditions—food, health, and safety). Ultimately, it is the struggle for social survival on the part of absolutely expendable populations that subsidizes the costs of capital, in their unaccounted part in the production of vital infrastructure for valorizable human life and in their part as national assets to be liquefied for immediate, present gains. This holding on and living on of peoples dispossessed of land, labor, and life, as well as the nonhuman animals and "natures" they work with and live on, comprises the greater share of stolen vitality that now appears as the stratospheric wealth of global capital, wealth as unfathomable as it is unrealizable without the gobbling up of all of earthly life.

Vitality

What is the vitality that subsidizes capital? That ultimately capital cannot "live" without?

The vitality of vital infrastructure consists of the life-times of others put directly in the service of valorizable life, to enhance or facilitate the latter's productive reproduction—the capitalized or socialized reproduction of productive, valued life. Such vitality is passed on to productive life, which makes use of the life-times produced and saved by drivers, housemaids, janitors, and servants, all of whom are additionally charged with extending and preserving the life-times of the cars, appliances, houses, and buildings—the physical, technological infrastructures—of that productive life in circulation. This vitality is transmitted not only as saved, abstract life-times for capitalizable life but also as immeasurable qualities of calm, equanimity, and magnanimity, the lift and lightness of unburdened time and mind, the confidence of ever-available, reliable support and assistance, which will further translate into other "finer" cultural qualities and works (including writing, such as this) of the higher value life-times they produce.

The vitality of vital platforms consists of the particular generative relational activity of affection, succor, and support that acts as the means and end of the reproductive production of shared life—the (assaulted, impeded, abandoned) social reproduction of expendable life. Vital platforms are, after all, extensive filiative and affiliative modes of sociality that serve not only as the means of life of its members but also the very form of this intersubjective, mutual existence in which they participate as intrinsic parts. Such vitality is both potential/source and actual product/object of wealth, embodied in the profound capacities, faculties, and inventions of this shared life, including the ever-adapting, dynamic, or "live" systems of coordination and cooperation of its component parts (persons and their individual and transindividual abilities and goods), which comprise its generative, organizational power. It is, however, a vitality (the vitality of sociality) that is siphoned as capitalist value not only through the forms of servitude and disposability it produces and offers up in exchange for capitalist means of life, but also as freely available subsidiary platforms of transactional activities harnessed to the biggest industries of capitalist production.

Mortality

It remains to be remarked that the serviceability of life is completely intertwined with absolutely expendable life, vitality with mortality. Philippine workers replaced expulsed Palestinian labor after the second intifada and now compose the largest ethnic group of caregivers in Israel. As in other colonizing nations, serviceable populations sourced elsewhere, whether imported or used in offshore sites, serve to sustain the expendability of the populations they replace (whose jobs they might be accused of taking, whose dispossession they can be the means of exacerbating). But serviceable life is also intertwined with absolutely expendable life to the extent that the latter is the former's origin, condition, and eventual destination. It is in fact most often the case that serviceable life is a temporary role for members of a household or a community facing expendability, its serviceable members fielded abroad as the means of a temporary reprieve—a form of redemption—from a life sentence of unremitting collective, sometimes capital, punishment.

People flee from these zones of everyday war, often only to face other punishment, their flight arrested, and the arrest itself—the punitive suspension of their life trajectories—made into the means of extracting life. Punishment surrounds. It is the technique for yielding value from life worth expending, which assaults the disenfranchised at every turn. In the United States, migrant children separated from their parents and jailed in holding pens and camps are made to pay for their punishment by being forced to clean and maintain the facilities in which they are held—made into the servants which they are already assumed to be.[50] In this way the time of waiting, or waste, extracted from them through detention can be repurposed into servitude, into servicing the very carceral enterprise of their own capture and warehousing. Servitude becomes the condition of temporary deliverance from capital's ceaseless assault on people's social survival. But as the condition and medium of capital's own expanded reproduction, life conscripted for servitude is also the means of reproduction of its own expendability, even if, as its part in vital platforms proves, it is never only that.[51]

If serviceable life is thus a hinge, a lever, or a hold, mediating between the productive life that it supports and the absolutely expendable life that it sustains and extends, how its vital platforms are mobilized is a pressing political matter. The heroization of hardworking serviceable life as deserving human life (not just the actual votes and support of migrant workers for Philippine president Duterte) has in fact prepared the ground for the absolute expendability of the, so far, thirty thousand lives of the extrajudicially killed in the ongoing war on drugs, and the connections of this order of battle to illicit shadow economies of violence. Here we see the widely-supported killings as the process of "dehumanization" that is the other side of an aggressive political campaign to secure the long-awaited, long-flouted rights and privileges of humanity for a deserving nation. To that count, of those actively wasted, must be added the thousands more of activists and defenders of life and land in the countryside, thousands more executed in intensified counterterrorist wars. All these lives, the raw material and necessary "costs" for the financialized enterprises of rampant security wars.

PART IV. DEAD EXCHANGES

8

POWERS OF DEFENDING FREEDOM

In the last years before the ascendance of a post-truth, anti-Enlightenment, antiliberal US regime, there was a lot of talk of "academic freedom." In the proclamations and debates ensuing among scholars, university presidents, and public officials and advocates in the wake of the 2013 American Studies Association resolution endorsing the boycott of Israeli academic institutions, "academic freedom" was what was held to be violated and upheld, threatened and defended, ignored and defeated.[1] According to those opposed to it, the boycott violated the principles of free speech and academic freedom, as well as the free exchange of ideas, that are the bedrock of education, scholarship, and ultimately democracy. Supporters of the boycott and critics of opposition to it on the basis of academic freedom pointed out that such "defenses" of freedom willfully ignored, and by doing so condoned, the absence of effective or substantive academic freedom of Palestinian academics and students, as well as the lack of basic freedoms of Palestinians more generally, in both the occupied territories and within Israel.[2]

There have been many serious and acute reflections on the conflicting notions of freedom at work in those debates, as well as on the questions and conditions that liberal notions of academic freedom deflect attention from or foreclose.[3] Though closely aligned to this latter critical approach to the issue of freedom in the global Palestinian solidarity movement—an approach that I see as akin to or at least congruent with Marx's critique of political emancipation and part of contemporary critiques of "rights-based" struggles for political recognition and inclusion, which I myself have drawn on to critique global humanitarianism—my reflections here on the constraints of freedom are guided by a slightly different perspective: one that is historical and cross-regional in its purview, and centrally shaped by a concern for how we might understand and struggle against imperialism today.

Constraints of Freedom

Certainly, it is important to argue that the defense of already existing, legitimate freedoms, as precepts codified and protected by the laws of an unjust order, is a defense of that order and its defining structures of inequality and injustice, including unrecognized, racialized forms of unfreedom. As the Black radical tradition has movingly argued and shown over and over again, today these forms of unfreedom, which underwrite the formal, abstract freedoms of US democracy, are largely borne by the descendants of the enslaved and the colonized. The sense of freedom's imperilment or its privation begs the question of what "freedom" is at issue that it requires protection or guarantee, even extension (in time and space), and, further, what such freedom depends on or entails to be realized. As Angela Davis poses: "Democratic rights and liberties are defined in relation to what is denied to people in prison. So we might ask, what kind of democracy do we currently inhabit?"[4]

Davis's point, which is echoed by an entire body of critical resistance and prison abolition work, is that systemic forms of unfreedom, such as those carried over from the historical institution of slavery and reinstalled within the prison system, serve as key ideological supports and practical mechanisms for the state bestowal and "protection" of the prescribed rights and liberties of US citizens.[5] The racialized deprivation (*disenfranchisement*) of those same rights and liberties by means of the institutions of the prison and police secures the meaning and substance of the freedoms defining US "democracy" and the "American way of life." As Saidiya Hartman writes of an earlier moment, when the formal rights of freedom were extended to the formerly enslaved only for that freedom to be encumbered by economic and extra-economic forces of indenture, peonage, white discipline, terror, policing, and constraint, "the illusory universality of citizenship once again was consolidated by the mechanisms of racial subjection that it formally abjured."[6] Insofar as the stipulations of abstract equality continue to be predicated on racial subjection, she argues, "emancipatory discourses of rights, liberty, and equality instigate, transmit, and effect forms of racial domination." Certainly these extant contradictions of liberalism, which grow ever more belligerent in the face of challenges to it, can be seen in the racism of its institutions, blatantly evidenced in the suprasubjection of Black, Latinx, and Native people to the judicial and extrajudicial violence of its penal provisions, practices, and laws.[7]

As central tenets undergirding the expansion of the already bloated US prison system and the globalization of its privatized maximum security models, freedom and equality continue to this day to serve as political ideals of both soft and hard wars of imperial humanization undertaken in the name of emancipation—for example, a global imperial feminist movement bent on spreading its normative, resistant subject of freedom to those it wishes to save, through various humanitarian and nongovernmental projects, as well as military campaigns of regime change in nations and cultures deemed "unfree."[8] It is no accident that such a feminism bears the same carceral logic of the liberal democracy it wishes to expand.[9] For as Black, postcolonial, and third world feminists have allowed us to understand, the extension of these liberal freedoms of the already human to those deemed not fully human entails furthering the forms of punitive violence on which these freedoms intrinsically depend.[10]

In the international arena, the upholding of democracy and freedom (as already realized accomplishments to protect and expand) constitutes one of the most important lynchpins of the US-Israel regional militarist project of security in the Middle East or West Asia. (It's worth remembering that Operation Enduring Freedom was the official name of the US war against terrorism launched in Afghanistan and in Iraq.) *Freedom* and *democracy* have also been the rallying cries of the transnational political ideological and military campaign against insurgent struggles beyond this region, just as they were in the Asia-Pacific during and even long before the Cold War: notably, in the US imperial conquest of the Philippines (along with Puerto Rico, Hawaiʻi, Samoa, and Guam) while Filipinos were waging their final, winning battles of anticolonial revolution against Spain at the turn of the twentieth century, and in the US war against Vietnam in the middle of the latter's own anticolonial, communist revolution in the second half of the same century. This longer history allows us to view the post–Cold War "shift" of US foreign policy to "democracy promotion" and "democratization" as the continuation

Powers of Defending Freedom • 201

and refurbishing of older security, proxy wars in Southeast and Central Asia as well as in Latin America, which had intended but largely failed to crush the "insurgencies" of what could be considered a global antiimperialist and decolonizing movement.[11]

From the late 1970s to the early 1990s, these older, counterinsurgent Cold War security wars faced outright defeat (in Vietnam and Nicaragua), the transformative rise of "people power" insurrections against US-supported dictatorial regimes (Philippines), and prodemocracy movements in other Cold War "nondemocracies" (in China and the Eastern Bloc), spurring the late twentieth-century shift in US foreign policy. At the same time, as we will see, decades of Cold War counterinsurgent warfare also produced the conditions for the proliferation and empowerment of transnational, violence-based, illicit enterprises (drug trafficking, gun-running, piracy, smuggling, labor trafficking) and the emergence of "illiberal" regimes with deep links to this transnational shadow economy. Yet, despite these uncontainable and threatening consequences of an earlier era of "freedom and democracy" security wars, *freedom* and *democracy* once again returned as organizing ideals for new imperial state and military projects, which took these consequences and the very proxy forces of violence they abetted to their own ends, as the casus belli of a new era of unremitting "global" wars.

In light of the permanent wars that the tenets of freedom and democracy serve to organize, how are we to understand these scholarly and public exchanges over freedom? What is the status and role of the field of discursive exchange (the arena of "debate") in which notions of "freedom" figure, with respect to the logics, institutions, and infrastructures of empire?

Fields of Dead Exchanges

Freedom and equality are not only compromised by the narrow scope of claims to political rights with respect to the bourgeois state. Freedom and equality are also the idealized expressions of the productive, real basis of capitalist exchange. As Marx observes, it is the relations of equivalence established through the exchange of commodities that both stipulate and prove the equality and freedom of the subjects of exchange. "Equality and freedom are thus not only respected in exchange based on exchange values but, also, the exchange of exchange values is the productive, real basis of all *equality* and *freedom*. As pure ideas they are merely the idealized expressions of this basis; as developed in juridical, political, social relations, they are merely this basis to a higher power."[12] For Marx, this field of exchange on which equality and freedom evidently operate in everyday, ordinary transactions in fact maintains and occludes the depoliticized arena of practice within which real inequality and unfreedom are produced. While for Marx this depoliticized arena is the arena of production where the exploitation of wage labor takes place, it is importantly also the arena of reproduction where life is made and taken; both are arenas in which the depoliticized hierarchical "differences" of sex-gender, race, class, and so on, are "presupposed" and "allowed to act in their own fashion."[13] As ideological notions wielded and elaborated within the institutions of the law, in the public sphere, and in the social life of individualized subjects, equality and freedom form part of the superstructure reproducing the material basis of capitalist life.

Following this familiar critique of liberalism for a moment, we might say that the field of discursive exchange on which debates about freedom and democracy take place around the question of Israel (as subject) similarly serves an ideologically occluding as well as reproductive function with respect to those violent processes and structures of elimination and dispossession directed toward Palestinians that are fundamental to the logics of settler colonialism and racism (logics through which capitalist accumulation historically and currently depends). On this view, such debates might be compared to how one *New York Times* editorial describes the way that diplomatic talks toward a two-state solution for Israel-Palestine function: that is, as a *camouflage* for de facto land expropriation through annexation and settlement. In camouflaging these de facto processes, the peace process industry, "with its legions of consultants, pundits, academics and journalists," and Washington's efforts to protect peace talks thus also served to enable "the very process of de facto annexation that were destroying prospects for the full autonomy and realization of legitimate rights of the Palestinian people that were the official purpose of the negotiations."[14] We could say that, like these "negotiations to nowhere," talks about given freedoms, and efforts to abide by or protect them—as the substance of rights or the stipulated condition of social and individual contracts—are *dead exchanges* in which any potential for real change is already dead in the water.

There is, however, another aspect to these exchanges of and over freedom. Marx asserts that equality and freedom are, as "pure ideas," idealized expressions of de facto economic processes of capital accumulation, namely, "the exchange of exchange values." However, "as developed in juridical, political, social relations, they are merely this basis to a higher power"—that is to say, they *are* this basis, they *are* economic processes, but operating exponentially, that is, at multiple, expanding levels above it. Beyond acting as formal and abstract ideals, equality and freedom are, in this reading, also *practical mechanisms* for the ordering of behaviors into forms proper to capitalist life. Just as Marx once argued that the dispossessive violence of primitive accumulation was "itself an economic power," these expressive ideals, as code-scripts of juridical, political, social apparatuses, act as forces directing and implementing "the exchange of exchange values," that is, as forces of capitalist exchange.[15]

Hence, the recognition and granting of juridical rights guaranteed by nation-states and their legal apparatuses serve not only to "hide" the structural racial, sex-gender inequalities that contradict the illusions of democracy whose material basis they constitute. The granting of these narrow juridical rights claims can also buttress and propagate proprietorial and territorial conceptions of the subject, individual as well as collective, on whose behalf those claims are made—institutionalized conceptions that we could argue install, within the subject, a relation of colonial possession and enslavement of others as the very psychic structure of self-possession. In doing so, they make antiblackness, racism, heterosexism, homophobia, transphobia—the systemic forms of social devaluation, subordination, and punishment that are internal to capitalist life and its regulatory state apparatuses and social institutions (the ideologies of their operation and reproduction)—into "experiences" shaping the "cultural" attributes and dispositions of the free, sovereign subject, if not its very intrinsic nature. Moreover, they make *inadmissible* (even imperceptible) in the courts and public spheres of judgment and their apparatuses of redress the broader milieus intrinsic to those subjects' being and action.[16] They repeat the social alienation on which the proprietorial subject is founded. As an instrument of proscription of these broader milieus of being and action as salient agents (plaintiff, defendant, witness, accessory, accomplice), legal adjudication can indeed become the means for further deracinating the becoming-human from the matrices of their making, and in this way can play an important part in the processes of their dispossessive (mis)recognition and collective disenfranchisement (as we already saw with respect to land and Indigenous people). The performative action of the law, particularly in its punitive function, is such that it executes this very "freedom" for which it stands—in Chandan Reddy's words, a "freedom *with* violence"—implemented "in the name of securitizing civil society for its entitled subject, the citizen as capitalist."[17]

This freedom is, on the one hand, for the legally enfranchised, the exemption from and transcendence of the punishment of racial, sex-gendered subjection (which, as we have seen, is to be borne by expendable life). On the other hand, for the disenfranchised, this freedoms spells the deracination and dispossession of "individuals" from their means of life, that is, from the matrices of transpersonal, even transspecies being—socialities of human and nonhuman life—which thereby become illegible in the claims for particular, discrete and integral *lives*. These socialities of life-making among the dispossessed surpass, even bypass, the organized conditions of domination and exploitation, milieus of toxicity, disease, mutilation, incapacitation, and death—entire environments—with which they are programmatically conflated as well as forced to inhabit.[18] Yet, juridical, political, and social rulings along these codifying lines (in compliance with the freedoms they uphold) overwrite these social matrices of living as simply the background of their proper subjects. They help to disappear the dispossessions they enable.

Finally, the deployment of the code-scripts of freedom and equality to demand rightful, punitive responses of the state, even to demand reforms of its policing-prison systems, shores up the very criminal punishment system that ensures the production of disposable, unfree life within the nation-state.[19] Further, it directly impels the making, organizing, and expanding of punishment as a global political and economic enterprise.[20]

Understood through these far-reaching critiques of the practical work of the law (that is, beyond its representational function), Marx's mathematical metaphor for what has come to be understood as the base-superstructure model (or analytic) for understanding capitalist societies can be suggestive beyond the context and perhaps conceptual reach of Marx's own argument. Against the more static, topographical model shaping much of political critique of the constraints of liberal freedom, and beyond the bounds of the nation-state within which much of this political critique is confined, the metaphor of exponents, with its suggestion of repeated multiplication of the base and amplification through scaling, allows us to think of the function of these exchanges over freedom in more dynamic and variable ways, that is, within a less fixed spatiotemporal framework, and on much larger (as well as much smaller) scales than the human subjects (whether individual or social) scale of civil, democratic discourse and debate.

Imperial Codes in the Making of Global Infrastructure

Things in fact begin to take on other dimensions when we move beyond the field of national and international bourgeois liberal democratic civil society exchanges and look at imperialism as a project of dynamic expansion rather than a seemingly static condition or state of affairs, as the notion of "empire" might imply, and as a multiscalar project that today has reached "higher powers."

Although today Israel is represented as a bastion of democracy in a region purportedly culturally hostile to freedom, with a "special relationship" to its partner and benefactor the United States, it was not so long ago that the Philippines was represented in exactly the same terms. From well before and certainly during the Cold War, the Philippines was upheld as a showcase of democracy, colonized in its name, reshaped with its institutions and norms, and put into service as a pivotal neocolonial military platform from which the United States could shape the politics and economics of the region that would eventually see the rise of newly-industrializing economies and the Asia-Pacific as a rival center of global capitalism in the post–Cold War period. Freedom and democracy were not simply *ideological screens* for business as usual, but rather central symbolic *organizing protocols* for the project of capitalist expansion in the region, that is, for the imperial "annexation" of new associated milieus for capital. It is in this sense, that is, as regulatory, programmatic rules of behavior, that we can understand "freedom" and "democracy" as *codes* of the dominant international Free World fantasy-production operating through the political and economic policies of participating nation-states such as the Philippines.[21]

The *work* that Philippine democracy-making both accomplished and required (or "exacted," as Edward Said wrote about Zionism with respect to its Palestinian victims) throughout the twentieth century can in fact be told as the history of US imperial capitalist infrastructure building in the Asia-Pacific region.[22] Compelled by the insurgent, revolutionary demands of both its own new citizens and its targeted colonial subjects, soon to be made into new "nationals"—on the one hand, what Robin D. G. Kelley calls the "freedom dreams" of Black people in America rising up against the intensified wave of mob violence and lynchings in the aftermath of the abolition of slavery, and on the other hand, the revolutionary movement of Filipinos successfully fighting to free themselves from the colonial rule of Spain—the early twentieth-century US overseas empire refashioned the naked brutality of its near genocidal conquest with the lofty political ideals of liberty and freedom.[23]

More than mere rhetoric, the ideals of self-government, fundamental individual human rights and liberties, and democratic citizenship practically guided and infused its colonial, tutelary rule, acting as the very means of colonization and cooptation of an emerging, revolutionary nation. In fact, it was through the installation of all the apparatuses of US-style liberal democracy, including its form of government, electoral system, laws and legal system, police, central banking, public mass educational system, and modern infrastructures of public transportation, communication, and health—colonial "experiments" through which the United States developed and refined, and against which it distinguished, its own—that the grounds for a "mixed" economy of metropolitan and elite-dominated free enterprise built on a peasant agricultural base would be fully established.²⁴ Such were the conditions of granting freedom and independence to the colony that it had subjugated, the means by which the United States accomplished the subsumption of the Philippines as a key "pericapitalist" milieu—an economic as well as political-military platform—for global capital.

The human and other costs and consequences of this under-told historical accomplishment can be gleaned from the postcolonial authoritarian development of Philippines as a sexual economy servicing mili-tourism and export-oriented manufacturing industries from the 1960s to the 1980s and, subsequently, beginning in the early 1990s, its conversion into one of the biggest export labor economies fueling the global reproductive domestic, care work, and service industries today, not only in Western Europe and the new industrial nations of East Asia, but also in other places including, importantly, Israel and Palestine, and other countries of West Asia (notably Saudi Arabia, United Arab Emirates, Jordan, Lebanon, and Libya)—the leading regional destination of Philippine overseas workers.²⁵

In addition to its prominence in the global reproductive labor economy, the Philippines is the second largest single source (after China, which only recently displaced it as top producer) of seafarers in the global shipping industry, providing a quarter of the entire labor force in an industry that transports 90 percent, by weight, of all global trade.²⁶ Since the late twentieth century, the Philippines has also become the world's largest destination for business process outsourcing (BPO), with the majority of its clients comprising US companies, and today it serves as the leading call center country globally.²⁷ It is in this capacity—as a major producer and provider of deterritorialized, serviceable, ancillary humans as disposable service labor in industries of global reproduction and circulation (of capital)—that we see the importance of the Philippines' historical transformation for today's new global economy.

In its "special relationship" with its democratizing benefactor, the United States, the Philippines went from serving during the Cold War as a central, semipermanent US military base for developing, establishing, and maintaining regional security—a role that depended on low-intensity counterinsurgency operations, which devastated entire swathes of rural life, "freeing" newly dispossessed labor and land resources for an expanding transnational urban economy—to serving during the post–Cold War period as an authorized temporary station for "visiting" or mobile US military forces on patrolling and invasive missions in and beyond the region in the unending global war against terrorism.

The Philippines has certainly long functioned as a "special" provider of labor, land, and other natural resources to its foremost neocolonial patron, as well as to a growing array of multinational capitalist buyers. But it has just as long territorially functioned as a pivotal military platform for maintaining hegemonic political and economic relations within the Asia-Pacific region (after World War II, as a US platform for fighting security wars in Southeast Asia to curb communism, including "processing" the people displaced by its own wars in refugee camps; and after the Cold War, for projecting "presence" in the region to curb the imperial reach of China as well as the reach of political Islam in Indonesia, Malaysia, and the Southern Philippines).[28] Such a geopolitical location, and the history of continued political access to it, has also enabled the Philippine nation-state, in the post–Cold War shift in imperial policy, to function as a pivotal military platform for launching US "global" coalitional military campaigns in the farthest reaches of West Asia, including the subcontracted enterprises of privatized "reconstruction" that accompany the destructive projects of war, for which it additionally provides migrant contract labor. For example, enlisting in the "coalition of the willing" in the global-US war on terror, the Philippines functioned as logistical and maintenance support for the global-US invasion and occupation of Iraq, supplying the largest number of foreign contract workers to service U.S. military coalition camps and to labor for private corporations charged with "rebuilding" the destroyed nation.[29] Philippine contract workers were additionally brought in to build the detention facilities of the US military base in Guantánamo Bay, Cuba, a base that they also currently maintain.[30]

In fact, Philippine contract workers are part of the "offshore captive labor force" (referred to in military argot as third country nationals, or TCNs), which Darryl Li argues, plays a central role in "contemporary US security architecture."[31] Working as adjuncts to the US military in countries where the latter is at war, TCNs find themselves, like other migrant and foreign subcontracted workers, in a legal interstitial zone of little to no protection (subject to governmental power but not due its protection) and thus of heightened vulnerability to direct violence and egregious exploitation and abuse. Yet precisely in this liminal state, they perform a significant function for the military enterprise that they service. In addition to the deeply discounted reproductive, service labor they provide as vital infrastructure for the global

US military-security industry, migrant military contract workers (like the Muslim extraterritorial prisoners of war who are neither local nor American, and who are also called TCNs) also play a nonlaboring role. Invisibly circulating "between different nodes in a global network of sites under US control and influence," like the prisoners they help to make and maintain, Philippine migrant military labor and other TCNs operate to incur and disappear the life costs of US military exploits.[32] As Li astutely observes, military migrant workers constitute "an offshore military labor force that allows the United States to keep politically sensitive troop numbers low while also reducing dependence on local populations with suspect loyalties"—that is, they function as extraterritorial proxy forces that can be expended with little cost and next to no obligation—their fatalities a matter of neither care nor responsibility, constituting neither sacrifice nor risk—to the US nation.[33]

As "the first democratic nation in Asia" and as "America's oldest ally in Asia," accomplishments that, at the moment when it was enlisted to join the global war on terror, George W. Bush both paid tribute to and claimed US credit for, the Philippines was "naturally" made for this role of servicing US military needs. While historically it did so with its territorial hosting of US military bases and offshore personnel and operations, today it continues to do so in extraterritorial fashion. Just as they serve as vital support for capital life in the globopolis—the life of globopolitical citizens as well as the life of circulating capital—overseas Philippine contract workers serve as vital support for the fatal, violent policing and war machines of imperial governance. In all these ways, as semisovereign territory to host US military and capital flows (as we saw earlier, a *server* for capitalist platforms) and as a producer and provider of ancillary human strata in the maintenance of its life-and-death enterprises, the Philippines has served as an important component of the global infrastructure of US empire.

What the far-reaching role of the Philippines—in its "special relationship" to the United States, which I have briefly rendered above—should highlight is how the field of exchange among subjects, on which the terms of freedom and democracy operate as ideological-practical codes for organizing political, military, and economic practice (we might understand them as global *command functions*), has long operated in and through the international system of nation-states. Moreover, this discursive field of exchange continues to operate today, though in new and refurbished ways. As we saw in the project of city everywhere (see chapter 7), freedom as a scaling protocol of capital life organizes the form of enfranchisement built into the protected freeports and zones comprising the global metropolitan archipelago. Like city everywhere, the logic of the (Operation Enduring) "freedom" war enterprise (destruction and reconstruction) applies in conflict zones everywhere and at varying scales, including, as we will see in chapter 9, in the southern Philippines, where long-standing conflicts over land and more recent conflicts over territorial monopolies over violence (between transnational state and parastate forces) have occasioned and legitimated decades of direct US and multinational investment in sometimes indistinguishable military and humanitarian life-and-death projects.

The example the Philippines provides should additionally remind us that imperialism is not a dyadic relation between two states, peoples, or nations, but rather practical imaginary relations among many states, not only within the same region (e.g., the Asia-Pacific or West Asia) but also, importantly, across regions. It is the system of these multilateral, transversal unequal relations (cooperative as well as competitive) among states that oversees the management and coordination of social relations of production on a regional and global scale. That is to say, imperialism's recruitment of the cooperation of multiple states (in multinational economic projects through trade and currency agreements as much as in transnational policing/military governance projects, such as the "US security architecture" or the "security archipelago" of South American and Arab states, as Paul Amar shows[34]) is the process and condition of expansion of its social bases. By the expansion of the social bases of imperialism, I mean the subsumption of people, their forms of social cooperation and social reproduction, within the structures of production and reproduction of this global mode of life. All these relations of cooperation between and among states, and between and among peoples, whether "hardened" or "solidified" in information, security, financial, communication, and transport systems, such as military and civic airports, flight paths, shipping routes, satellite, web, and cellular technologies, or maintained as "soft" or vital systems of migrant contract work in domestic, care, and agricultural industries or in offshored auxiliary military and business functions (as well as outsourced life services), can be understood as comprising the milieus of global capital built through the protocols of political and economic freedom and democracy.[35]

So while it would seem that the example I offer here of the Philippines' "democratic" role in the Asia-Pacific during the Cold War suggests a simple (analogical) comparison with that of Israel in the Middle East during the post–Cold War period—certainly there is a comparison suggested here between the Philippines' ideological and military role in Cold War security in the Asia-Pacific and Israel's similar role in post–Cold War security in West Asia—I intend rather for the example to foreground direct connections across these regional areas and projects. These are connections in which developmentalist democracy-making in one region (the Asia-Pacific) enables and supports liberalizing democracy-promotion in another region (West Asia): through flows of military-security personnel, apparatuses, and operations (the history of US counterinsurgency wars from Vietnam to Iraq), capital (between China-financed, debt-driven growth in the United States and "creative destruction" through wars in Afghanistan and Iraq), and labor (waves of Filipinx and other foreign immigrant labor to replace or supplement Arab labor in Israel, Lebanon, Jordan, and the Gulf States).[36]

These inter-Asia connections, within and across the Asia-Pacific and West Asia and their respective imperial democratization projects, are undoubtedly long-standing. Democracy security wars before and during the Cold War established the precedent and foundation for democracy security wars in the post–Cold War period. In the early 1960s, with state concern over the possibility of a pan-Islamic movement reaching the Southern Philippines, a top Philippine military officer was sent on an intelligence training course in Israel under sponsorship of the Joint US Military Assistance Group, bringing back with him new communications technology for counterinsurgent surveillance.[37] More recently, under the partnership of Presidents Benjamin Netanyahu and Rodrigo Duterte, the Israeli Defense Forces has begun training the Armed Forces of the Philippines in counterterrorism techniques, while the Philippines has purchased missile systems, radars, and drones from Israel, bypassing the United States altogether.[38]

These "deadly exchange" programs surely attest to the expanding global military-security industry engaged in profitable, counterinsurgent and terrorist wars to be human. They are structural means for the "exchange of exchange values" installed through the code-scripts of freedom and equality, which are written out in bilateral and multilateral agreements, treaties, and exchange programs. But the cross-regional and intraregional connections that make for the global infrastructure of capital life, which such dead exchanges enable, are ongoing and multifarious. They include important connections between different forms of disposability, whereby the conditions and consequences of the assault on the social reproductive capacities of certain populations (e.g., Iraqi, or Palestinian) might be offset and supplemented with the labor resources of another population whose own social reproduction is under different assault (e.g., Filipinos)—predominantly, though not only, to the final end of imperial reproduction and expansion. It is no accident that among the many bilateral agreements signed by Netanyahu and Duterte during the latter's historic state visit to Israel in 2018 were memoranda of agreements for reducing brokerage fees for the 28,000 Filipinx caregivers in Israel and for encouraging mutual investment.[39] This too is a field and product of deadly exchange.

The international field of exchange for the adjudication of freedom and democracy should thus be viewed as the plane of action where processes of subjectification and social identification with respect to nations operate—whether the public sphere of "the international community" or the political sphere of institutional apparatuses of states. It is where we would readily locate the disciplinary, normative work of race, gender, and sexuality in shaping the distribution of life-devaluation across particular given ethnonational social groups and racialized populations. That is to say, as norms of subjectification, such categories of identity work at the level of both domestic and international relations to configure and regulate the global social relations of production through which various peoples emerge and encounter each other as immigrant or foreign workers, illegals, and criminals, the unemployed and permanently idled, refugees, and internally displaced persons, or as fellow citizens—so many social categories subtended by organizing ontological codes of the human. The organization and coordination of these relations among states and among the social groups, peoples, and populations over whom states have jurisdiction mobilize these normative codes of *free, sovereign subjects* as regulative mechanisms of "the global economy" and its constituent forms of governance. Today, some of the most powerful subjects bear the names of corporations, banks, and entire financial sectors (e.g., Wall Street), the vicissitudes of their daily fortunes told with gripping, personifying detail, like the lives of kings.

Finally, it is on this field of subjects, whether domestically or internationally configured—that is, whether the "free world" of citizens defined against the world of the prison in the domestic arena of US democracy, or the "free world" of nations defined against communist or Islamic states in the global arena—that political claims continue to be made on behalf of specific "peoples" and bridges of solidarity or coalitions built across. It is the field on which both warfare and lawfare campaigns take place, to defend, renegotiate, and resolidify the freedom contracts upholding the dominant nations, institutions, and peoples of the globopolitical free world. It also the field on which political counterclaims of the becoming-human are made—claims of antiimperialist nationalisms, of radical Islamic transnationalisms—often on behalf of the same organizing terms of humanity whose freedoms they might contest, yet, as we will see in the case of the Philippines' recent political transformation, with unanticipated, contradictory, sometimes uncontrollable, proliferating effects.

Imperial Shift: After Normative Culture, after Economy

But here I would like to raise the question of the role and status of this field of exchange with respect to imperialism in today's global context, particularly in light of notable shifts in the dispensation of state power (i.e., the exercise of its monopoly on violence) and in the calculuses of capitalist value extraction. Two aligned and overlapping features come to mind: (1) a shift in governmentality, and (2) a shift in political economy.

The first is what has been widely understood as the shift in political rationality or governmentality from one constructed around rights and property to one constructed around risk and security, which many identify with neoliberalism (discussed in chapter 5). Contributing to scholarly work on this shift, Eva Cherniavsky argues that neoliberal governance entails the abdication of the disciplinary project of the state in relation to the nation and hence the erosion of "normative culture as such," which had been tasked with the production and reproduction of rights-bearing citizens. She notes that rather than the field of legal recognition through which democratic rights have been claimed and obtained for particular social identities in relation of formal equivalence to the abstract norm (and measure) of *citizen-subject* (according to logics of disciplinary societies), neoliberal "societies of control" entail what she calls *serial culture*, operating on a "field of virtual sociality," a social environment that is ideologically saturated with a fictive reality and minutely regulated, "regulated not because [neocitizens'] positions are prescribed, but rather because their movements and affiliations are tracked (as so much social data), archived, mined, risk assessed, and so (variably) policed, overlooked, or supported."[40]

Militarily, the shift in political rationality can be gleaned in the shift from imperial states' use of counterinsurgent strategies of low-intensity conflict (in proxy wars) to their tactical uses of high-intensity preemptive targeted strikes (paradigmatically exemplified by drone warfare in the international arena as well as police and vigilante "patrol" execution killings in the domestic arena). The shift is encapsulated by the transformation of the US permanent bases in the Philippines by the 1999 visiting forces agreement, which stipulated "access" to distributed sovereign capacities (territories, forces of violence, and labor) rather than ownership and settlement—a model of enterprise now characteristic of the platforms of city everywhere (chapter 7).

The visiting forces agreement was one of ninety similar agreements worldwide, signaling the strategic shift in US defense policy from fixed bases to a more diffuse and agile global response stance, predicated on a dispersed network of floating "lily pads" from where "sudden strikes against rogue actors anywhere in five continents" could be launched.[41] The shift in defense strategy is supported by the restructuring of the US military since 2001 through extensive privatization, particularly the significant offshoring of its logistical and security functions to TCNs, as Li shows.[42] These changes signal the autonomization of military logistics, not as the means of waging war as event but rather as the means of everyday governance. Incorporating administrative mechanisms for governing emergencies, this new military logic of "vital systems security" is organized around the same principle of indeterminacy and risk around which financial capital has structured its modes of value extraction.[43] While in their broadest outlines democratization wars (wars against terrorism) continue much of the same work as the wars of democracy (wars against communism) of an earlier era—they demonstrate a much closer integration or synthesis between governance and enterprise than ever before.

The second feature of today's imperialism, closely related to the first, is what I have attempted to lay out in previous chapters as the new political economy of life, which war—both in the exercise of direct, coercive, and punitive violence and in the practice of humanitarian and humanizing rehabilitation—is a primary instrument for bringing about. As the process of the expanded reproduction of capital over all of "life," through the overcoming of spatial and temporal limits posed by an earlier era of exploitation (formally based on a model of industrial labor-time), imperialism effects, through war, calibrated punishment, and discriminatory assaults on social reproduction, qualitative gradations and divisions of "life," and distinctions among "times of life," or life-times, on which different modalities of expropriation of value are based. This is not simply a top-down process exercised by a unified agency from above, insofar as the very code-scripts that imperial war deploys and executes through powerful states, corporations, and institutions also serve as a general social calculus for people's everyday parsing and parceling out of their own as well as other's life-times into value and waste.

While this distinction obtains in the form of distinct *lives*—that is, in the wholesale distinction between lives worth living and lives worth expending—the distinction also traverses the sociological categories of individuals and groups, obtaining in *kinds of times* lived, differentiated by activities, modalities, and spaces of varying worth, appraised through codes of race, sex-gender, nationality, religion, and so on. As we saw in the excursus, servitude or serviceability consists of a range of life-times subordinated to the production of lives worth living, for which purpose they are redeemed temporarily or permanently from life worth expending. As the case of military contract workers shows, serviceable life-times are also put toward the production of absolutely expendable life. What is important to note, however, is that the divisibility, factorability, and aggregability of *life-times* is what allows the multiplication and scaling of levels of value extraction beyond the famous limits of labor-time embodied in the working day. Indeed, it is as parceled and aggregated *life-times* that entire populations—rendered absolutely expendable by the social calculus of white supremacist, antiblack, settler colonial, heterosexist, ethnic and religious racisms—have become the matter and medium of proliferating profitable enterprises of punishment and control.

The paradigm for this logic of the new political economy can be found, as I discussed in earlier chapters, in the sheer expenditure of life-times (rather than whole lives and whole bodies, which are nevertheless used and destroyed in this expenditure) of warehoused and indefinitely detained populations, around which national security industries of policing and war build their expanding mortal enterprises (gruesomely exemplified in the open prison of Gaza). It can also be seen, in the contexts of foreign investment–dependent nation-states, where the disposable life-times of surplus populations represent the quantified abstract future that is colonized, mortgaged, and brokered by states on behalf of transnational elites and ethnonational constituencies precisely through their sovereign control of national territories, to which the disenfranchised both at home and abroad are tethered as captive populations.[44]

The financial calculus to which the aggregate life-times of absolutely expendable life are subject points to the ascendance of the social logics of the derivative in the moment Randy Martin calls "after economy."[45] Martin's claim is that the logic of derivatives—which is no longer the logic of the commodity as a bounded thing but is instead a logic of disassembling and bundling of attributes of both old and new materialities (commodities, identities, ideas, weather, DNA)—is calling into question the fantasy undergirding both liberal democracies and leftist critique, that is, the fantasy of an autonomous domain of reality called the economy that would be behind or beneath a more immediately legible politics of representation or recognition. It suggests that the financialization of life through the logic of derivatives undermines "the social imaginary of individual selves and collective masses," which had been based on the autonomous thing-in-itself status of the commodity form.

The logic through which growing security enterprises build themselves on the sheer expenditure of people's life-times (grafting multiplying layers of service industries contingent upon the actual or threatened enforced expenditure of the life-times of criminalized populations) is not, however, merely the outgrowth of finance capital's search for investment opportunities—that is, its expansion through capture of the aggregate futures of captive populations (guaranteed by longer and repeated forms of sentencing).[46] The development of derivatives as a mode and instrument of value extraction contingent upon the distributive divisibility or disaggregation of integral things with and as properties (houses, human lives) is not only the logical extension of their abstraction as exchange values.[47] Nor is it simply the effect of a monetizing view that comes to encompass all of life. Rather, as Martin himself argues, this is also the logic of "money after decolonization"—that is, the social logic of the derivative is the very consequence of decolonizing movements transgressing and unmaking the naturalized ruling ontology, with its "imposed unities and alignments of persons and places," of a prior political economy.[48]

In my own thinking, the financial logic of derivatives is part and parcel of the rebounding of racial capital in the aftermath of decolonization, certainly by feeding on the ruin and detritus it created but also by preying on the capacities of those laid to waste for continuing to live against their organized devastation. Preserved and destroyed to serve as the open secret cache of capital, the milieus of such life rendered free for the taking consist of modes of survival that both formal and informal forces of enterprise prey upon, copy, and scale. These modes of survival were of necessity never predicated on ownership or property, relying on notions of life and vital power that remained unbound by the forms of their capture and subsumption within bourgeois societies.

Crystallized in the persona of the arbitrageur, for whom "leverage takes precedence over ownership," volatility and risk over stability and equilibrium, the logic of derivatives can be glimpsed prefigured in those improvisatory practices of livelihood among the systematically disenfranchised, such as the petty financial and entrepreneurial practices of the urban poor who use and sometimes generate the very conditions of uncertainty, contingency, and blockage that they live in as the conditions of their own value-extractive bets, cuts, and other acts of timing (as we saw in chapter 7). It is these same practices of life-making that become subsumed by the capitalist logic of derivatives at an altogether different and staggering scale.

Ratios of Life and Death

In the wake of these imperial shifts in governmentality and political economy, two different but tightly intertwined fields of symbolic and material exchange, or planes of communicative action and interchange, manifest themselves, and it is on these analytically distinct planes that "politics" obtain globally: on the one hand, *democracy*, the field of subjects and legitimate *peoples*; and on the other hand, *demographics*, the field of nonsubjects and disposable *populations*. While there is no doubt that the first plane continues to bear relevance for the organization of imperial relations (serving as the ground rules of conduct of citizens and nation-states), it is also undermined as an autonomous and privileged domain of power by the politicization and economization of both life and death in the current moment of imperial expansion. Increasingly, the ambit of democratic politics is narrowing, even as it is predicated on this other plane of demographics, which is steadily expanding.

If life as interest-bearing capital is the modality through which neoliberal subjects are made into life-entrepreneurs and investor-subjects, it is for such lives that the democratic political-representational claims and actions of globopolitical "neocitizens," "netizen"-subjects, humanitarians, and so forth, continue to take place and make sense. Life as waste, on the other hand, is the modality in which the lives of disposable populations are dissolved into liquid life-times, which can be used by various kinds of capital as numerical units of capitalist temporality, measurable in terms of duration/endurance as well as of potentials/futures, to be expended as labor-times or sentencing times, calculated for investment and remittances, and packaged, priced, and traded on derivative markets. Such lives certainly provide the biomasses that are at once the consumers for and the raw, metabolic material consumed by food, health, and pharmaceutical industries.[49] But these biomasses also figure, on another level, as risk factors, consuming capacities, earning potentials, life and death and illness expectancies, actuarial projections and numerical sums that can enter a financial calculus no longer tethered to the stable commodity of yesteryears. Here it is not so much a matter of populations as polities or peoples as it is a matter of populations as aggregate and disaggregated biogenetic materialities convertible to quantitative sums and micro- or molecular units of "life" expressible as digital values.[50] Hence, in another register, disposable life becomes converted to, as Jonathan Beller puts it, "a standing reserve of information," bits of data processed through the algorithms of speculation and warfare.[51]

Such a demographic/algorithmic logic is nowhere clearer than in Israeli military parlance and strategy. Consider for example the Israeli deterrence strategy known as "cutting the grass," where Palestinians in Gaza are figured as "the grasses of hatred" that must be periodically mowed down, "a task that must be performed regularly and has no end."[52] Representing the Israeli military invasion of Gaza in 2008, which resulted in the deaths of over 1,400 Palestinians, as "necessary maintenance operations," the figurative military code of "cutting the grass" demonstrates that "relations" between Israeli military forces and Palestinian lives do not concern subjects or peoples (obeying an order organized by principles of gendered, racial, or sexual norms of independent social identity). What these "relations" concern are rather conflicting or opposing "forces": machinic or technical operations and natural phenomena. From the Israeli side, war thus becomes an experiment to find and maintain "optimal balances" of materialities ("maximum land, minimum Arabs"), with the effect of normalizing the violence of settler colonialism.[53]

Rather than any mandates of human freedom, or human or civil rights, the established protocol for regulating such "relations" thus follows a logic of calculations involving optimal balances of security and threat, in which human life and death are not so much objects as they are variables of measure. Such calculations are grotesquely evident in the research presentation to the Israeli Ministry of Defense for the purposes of formulating policies for the embargo of the Gaza Strip beginning in 2007, titled "Food Consumption in the Gaza Strip: Red Lines."[54] This research set up parameters for the calculation of what it called "the minimum subsistence basket," that is, a formulation of "nutrition that is sufficient for subsistence without the development of malnutrition," which would guide the limits for the entry of goods into Gaza during the embargo-siege. "Minimum subsistence" indicates the way Gaza Palestinian *lives* are conceptualized as a single quantitative unit of measure—subsistence, or "a basic fabric of life," set as a sum consisting of grams and tons of food consumption and caloric and nutritional values required daily on average according to age, gender, and ethnicity/race (Arab vs. Israeli), against the needs of "the security situation in the Gaza strip" and with an eye toward preventing "a humanitarian crisis" in the same.[55]

While humanitarianism comes to act as a counterforce of exemption from violence, proportionality becomes the guiding principle for dispensing pain, injury, and death. As Eyal Weizman shows, Israeli military strategists increasingly rely on a principle of proportionality, which "approximates an algorithmic logic of computation" of death ratios in its calculation of risks of collateral damage against effective destruction of militant organizations or situations.[56] In this context, proportionality is a moderating principle employed to constrain the use of force according to "a 'proper relation' between 'unavoidable means' and 'necessary ends,'" that is, a balance "between military objectives and anticipated damage to civilian life and property," maintained through calibrated measures of violence.[57] The principle of proportionality is also clearly exemplified in the IDF "policy of injuries," or what Jasbir Puar calls "sanctioned maiming," which is a strategy of keeping Palestinian "casualties" low—that is, to keep the injured out of the "dry statistics of tragedy," evading "the optic of collateral damage," which depends on the whole number of countable deaths.[58] Debilitation in this case is a strategy of number, part of an algorithm put to economic as well as ideological ends.

This demographic/algorithmic logic, ascendant in imperial governance today, is guided by concerns of what Stephen Collier and Andrew Lakoff call "vital systems security," where what is to be protected is not the life of any specific population except insofar as that population is identified with what is effectively "life itself"—that is, the very "vital systems" (interlinked utility systems critical to economic and social life, such as transportation, electricity, and water) whose operations make it possible for (valued) life to exist at all.[59] The perceived "vulnerability" to threat of these socio-economic operating systems has led to the significant expansion of security complexes as political technologies of emergency: that is, as forms of governance designed to protect against and preemptively contain the effects of anticipated catastrophe.

If we follow the logic of vital systems security, we can readily see a continuity between, on the one hand, the targeted destruction of other people's homes, exemplified in the demolitions of Palestinian houses in Israel/Palestine and of squatter homes in urban centers everywhere, and on the other hand, the protected building of homes and infrastructures for valued life (settler residences, urban real estate development and gentrification projects), as well as the service projects to protect that life (the building of prisons, checkpoints, walls, and detention centers as well as the provision of security services, including intelligence reports, risk analyses, cash processing technologies, etc.). In fact, these are two sides of a vital-mortal system that operates through punishment and its exemption, freedom. As we've already seen, punitive measures of violence exercised through security wars have become integral to capitalist enterprise. Permanent security wars are also policing measures, and the forms of racist collective punishment that they deploy against the populations they target also come to figure in algorithmic ways for value extraction.[60]

Calculus of Words: The Waning of Content, the Withering of Subjects

Although we are all well acquainted with the way algorithms are at work in the value production of Web 2.0 industries, and specifically of social media platforms, we may underestimate the way that the discourses of debate and arguments of contestation and persuasion through which we conduct our politics are themselves becoming mere fodder for algorithmic operations. We might consider, for example, the way news and social media language is used as data in new kinds of algorithm-based data-tracking projects to predict war, insurgency, genocide, and political violence, where words and phrases that signify tension, such as *crisis, clash, combat*, and so on, are used to create a mathematical model to predict when war is likely to break out between nations a year in advance and, within nations, six years in advance.[61] In such projects, words and phrases are no longer parts of larger semantic assemblages with ideological effects but are instead indices used to map and predict crisis, violence, emotions, actions, and their attributes.

The Global Database of Events, Language, and Tone (GDELT) Project based at Georgetown University, for example, seeks "to create a real-time computable record of global society that can be visualized, analyzed, modeled, examined, and even forecasted."[62] Providing some of the most sophisticated tools for visually rendering the enormous data sets created from "the billions upon billions of words of new information published each day," the project codifies and "extracts" from these words the physical activities comprising "events" happening all over the world, as well as the persons, organizations, locations, emotions, and "themes" (categories such as cost of living, refugees, drones, borders, food security, democracy, and free speech) that purportedly "underlie" these events and their interconnections. With people ("who's involved") and their emotions ("how they're feeling about [what's happening]") included in the second dataset figuring as the "base" of physical events, we are very far away indeed from the model of the economy underlying our juridical, political, and social relations.

There are no sovereign subjects in this scenario, a scenario that takes place on the plane of action of demographics/algorithmics. Like the "grasses of hatred," events are "outbreaks" of quasi-natural, most often catastrophic or at least turbulent physical phenomena. Certainly words are also constituted as events themselves, as often reported by the media as so-called real, physical events. But they are reported as signs or memes of crowd movement (either mass mobilizations or affective movement), much in the way the stock market watches for signs indicating changes in the moods affecting the value of shares—that is, as information that, it is posited, will ultimately be reflected in asset prices. In this scenario, which is paradigmatic of not simply commoditization but more specifically the *financialization* of life on earth in general, there is a continuity between word and things posited by a logic of derivatives that overrides the force of rational debate.[63]

This last example, should perhaps lead us back to Marx for another meaning attendant on *dead exchanges*. If these discursive exchanges are, as Marx's formulation would have it, "the exchange of exchange-values" at a higher power—words and phrases (the semantic bits and pieces that rational civil society exchanges) as the exchange values of speculative informatics (the financialization of ideas and arguments about freedom as exemplary of the exponential function of the abstraction of value)—then "dead exchanges" could be thought of in the sense of "dead labor," that is, as the objectification of living labor in the instruments and means of production and circulation of a higher order of capitalism.

Freedom certainly continues to operate as an ideological code mobilized not only for imperial military campaigns but also for ICT- and cyberdevelopment projects, which both diffuse and extend the Israeli settler colonialism through digital-technological means, as Helga Tawil-Souri and Miriyam Aouragh argue.[64] In these forms of "digital occupation" and "cybercolonialism," *freedom* functions as a code for building and securing the logistical systems that bring war and capital together.[65] At the same time, however, talk of freedom is itself among the many forms of content fueling these new capitalist enterprises, where all social exchanges provide the impetus and material for a value extraction that issues out of the sheer activity of circulation of statements, thoughts, and sentiments among socially valued beings (as part of their interest-bearing lives). *Freedom* is thus a skeuomorph, a metaphorical image of an older technology that works as a sign-command function on the front end of integrated systems of power, including capitalist platforms. As the facilitative means of reproducing the "civil" life of already "free" social subjects, civil debates about free speech and other "freedoms" guaranteed by imperial democracies are semiotic gestures that also function as socio-symbolic components of infrastructures for the politically and economically enfranchised. Through constant iteration, they create the "hard" channels of any meaningful and legitimate exchange, and thereby attempt to foreclose the threat of other modes of life seeking to fully emerge.

As we see in the United States today, the most clamorous political claims to these "freedoms" are made by white supremacists, fascists, Zionists, racists, imperialists, and patriots. Their liberties to speak, act, and express their entitlements as well as ressentiment and hate against those they believe have stripped those entitlements from them (making them "no longer")—all these liberties of the already human are defended, even heralded, as much by the state as the capitalist platforms they fuel and uphold with their vitriol. In this way, the exchanges over freedom are also the immaterial matter and means of new high-financed forms of capitalist enterprise. The liberties they finally espouse are freedoms for the making of competitive environments of extreme cutthroat survival.

These new imperial strategies, which have raised freedom exchanges to a "higher power," are the result of the dominant systemic efforts on the part of the rulers of the world to recoup the power and profitability that decolonization movements all over the world had radically undermined. The very capitalist expansion of the global business of counterinsurgency through security industries of policing and war at the end of the twentieth century attests to the threat that such movements posed to global elites (whose own wealth and rule has depended on the monopoly on violence held by their protective states). At the same time, the virulence of such industries based on the war to be human has spawned grave effects. Unremitting wars in the peripheries of a globopolis buoyed by them have given rise to more and more people dispossessed of land and livelihood, refugees fleeing to urban shores, offering themselves as serviceable life to reproduce others' lives elsewhere or to expend the lives of even their own, all for survival. The wars have also generated transnational shadow political economies trading on the same disposable life, in bids by local warlords to play the great game in their own ways and to their own gain.

When we turn to the context of the Philippines, we see a massive rejection of and indifference to this talk of "freedom," a flouting of liberal democracy and its preoccupation with "rights." Rather than "freedom" figuring centrally in political claims, we hear denunciations of the corruption and collusion of liberal elites, of their reasonableness and politeness, their well-behaved manners and regulations, as merely the screens of insatiable greed, indifference, and unfairness. And yet the rejection of "freedom" and the liberalism of elites on the part of the becoming-human can also be an embrace of the violence that promises a "life worth living." Instead of radical change, we see a transformation of demographic politics through another field of "dead exchanges," in which extrajudicial killings undertaken by the Philippine police state under Duterte's war on drugs operates on the logic of derivatives, with dead bodies or spent life as its underlying assets. That the Duterte regime, which is founded on and proudly espouses an antiliberal ethos, should be in a new, historic partnership with the Netanyahu regime, which maintains the ethos of liberal democracy (in a purportedly antiliberal, unfree world) comes as no surprise. Both use the global master's tools to build masters' houses for the valued life they define as their own.

Time of Persistence, Powers of Sustaining Life

In the meantime, within the so-called bastion of democracy, those expelled from their homes to make way for the urban settlement of the newly colonially enfranchised persist in their political claim and everyday struggle, as Magid Shihade writes, "to live in dignity, to be able to move freely, and to go about their lives as usual, working, creating and re-creating, and dreaming."[66]

Sitting in a small living room in January 2012, listening to Maryam Al-Gawi recount her family's violent eviction from their home across the street in the Sheikh Jarrah neighborhood in East Jerusalem, I notice behind her, just above the red roses on the coffee table between us, a security monitor sitting on a lace-covered side table. It is an odd fixture in this domestic interior furnished with patterned upholstered chairs and a framed embroidered picture of a tranquil lakeside house in an idyllic woodland setting. The monitor's screen is divided into four smaller screens, two of which are turned on, one showing a security cam view of the street and the other of the concrete pathway leading from the street to this house at the back of the lot. Seeming to rise from the monitor's screen view of the street are the first three letters of a word written on the wall: FRE. I wonder if perhaps the word is *freedom*, but I doubt it and do not really know.

Maryam is talking to us, a voluntary group of five U.S.-based academics who have been invited to Palestine to hear its people's claims.[67] She is describing how at 4:45 in the morning of August 2, 2009, a group of Israeli police forces, masked and dressed in commando gear, fully armed, set a bomb off in front of her door. Having gone to answer the loud pounding that woke her up, she was thrown across the room by the blast together with the door, and all the windows were shattered. Dragged out of the house barely dressed in her nightclothes, she ran to gather the twelve children living in the house at the time, including her own six children, who were being thrown out of the second-story window. Her twenty-four-year-old son was thrown down and detained, and her nine-year-old son, shocked and terrified, frantically ran back into the house to seek refuge in a place that was no longer his home. Within an hour, the police had cleared the house of the thirty-seven members of the extended Al-Gawi family (not counting the baby born on the day of their eviction) as well as the house of the Hanoun family, their neighbors. Trucks were brought in to take away their furniture and belongings and then dump them at the UN Worker's Relief Agency (UNWRA), as if it were the latter's property or problem. As soon as the soldiers emptied the houses, more trucks entered the neighborhood to bring settlers to take the place of these recently evicted people, who were left on the street to witness the scene of their own dispossession and displacement.

It was a scene reminiscent of many other scenes, past and present, in this violently contested colonized land. It is a common and even ordinary scene that at once epitomizes and repeats an original injustice that continues to remain unrecognized as such by that self-appointed guardian and arbiter of humanity, the international community. More than sixty years after this historical atrocity—what Palestinians remember as al-Nakba, "the catastrophe," the mass expulsion and dispossession of Palestinians from their ancestral lands in the aftermath of the 1948 war, which founded the State of Israel—the scene is repeated countless times throughout the lands within the shifting borders of the nation of Israel. This relentlessly repeated enactment of Palestinian dispossession is the very instrument for shifting the outer and interior borders of this expansionist colonial nation-state as it encompasses ever-greater stretches of land under its sovereigntist power. Conducted with impunity and met with international apathy, the dire situation of constant evictions, house demolitions, and land confiscation that leave Palestinians homeless has been made banal to all but themselves and those others who, through their own historical experiences, feel their plight as the recognizable condition of a colonized, disposable people deemed barely human.

There is no other reason to explain the dearth and inaudibility of international outcry against the routine and relentless way that Palestinian life is destroyed. In the name of a gated "democracy" that must be preserved at all costs, Palestinians are seen at best as merely the casualties of a permanent global war of security waged by the allied sovereign states of the Western world, including its latest and most avid and exemplary member, Israel. At worst, they are the very defining instance of that "democracy's" declared enemy: Arab/Muslim terrorism. "Democracy" is the alibi and rallying cry of the already human, whose ranks Israel has joined with a vengeance, defending its conceded place in the roster of sovereign states of globopolitical humanity with the violent zeal and anxiety of a coerced convert now serving as exemplar and rampart of the imperial civilization that was once the executioner of its own people.[68]

Hailed as "the embodiment of Western values and democracy, surrounded by backward and savage people bent on its destruction an ever-present external threat to the Jewish state," Israel garners support not only from those who are gripped by the myth of eternal ethno-religious strife propagated by Zionism, including a Christian Fundamentalist world with which Zionists have found themselves in an "unholy alliance."[69] As the bastion of Western "democracy" in a region believed endemically hostile to such modern ideals, Israel finds support from those who feel their own status of privileged humanity steadily eroded by the very consequences of imperialist civilization (what Césaire identified as its own deep-seated barbarism) and threatened by the refusal of the wretched peoples of the earth to be reduced to the status of the less-than-human. Such support for Israel, above all and crucially from the United States, is what one man from among those evicted from Sheikh Jarrah tells us, "fills us with shame."[70]

Against such seemingly endless recurring violation and in defiance of all pernicious will and might to have them disappear is the power of Palestinian persistence. Recounting their forced "evacuation" from their homes, Maryam and her neighbors, Maher Hanoun and Nabil Al-Kurd, tell us that their families came from a group of five hundred Palestinians (originally refugees from 1948) who were subsequently relocated in this neighborhood in East Jerusalem in 1956 by means of an agreement made between the UNWRA and the Jordanian government. With the Israeli annexation of East Jerusalem after the 1967 war, the land in Sheikh Jarrah came under Israeli authority, enabling the disputable Israeli Jewish claims of prior ownership that undergird these evictions.[71]

Maryam relates how the tent they put up to live in by their occupied house was taken down seventeen times by the municipality in the six months they lived on the street. Seventeen times the municipality evicted them from the tent, confiscated all kinds of belongings, from the portable gas tank they used for cooking to the rocks and strings that kept the tent in place, and then exacted fines from them for being on the street. Seventeen times they set up their tent again. The harassment continued with repeated arrests and detention of the young men in the family. Discriminatory apartheid Israeli law allows for this arbitrary detention of Palestinians without charge or trial. The ever-imminent threat of arrest and incarceration permanently defines their collective and individual lives. Maryam, Maher, and Nabil recall how the Israeli police were soon arresting everybody, exacting fines with each arrest and threatening imprisonment. When I am sitting with them, hearing their stories, it has been more than two years since the eviction of the Al-Gawi, Al-Kurd, and Hanoun families, but they refuse to leave, to give up their rights to their homes, to be made refugees yet again.

But the little children bear deep and open wounds from the night of their militarized eviction and the persistent, daily violence against their families since then. Maryam's youngest child has separation anxiety and cannot sleep at night without her mother beside her. Three months don't go by without Maher Hanoun's four-year-old daughter having to go to the hospital for anxiety attacks. The settlers had made sure she saw them burn her bed with her

Powers of Defending Freedom • 225

dolls in it, a seemingly petty, gratuitous, and yet profoundly injurious act of cruelty intended to destroy all feeling of freedom, safety, and carefree happiness that accompanies and defines children's play. It seems to have been successful. Today she keeps waking up in the middle of the night screaming about her toys. For whom is it a triumph to shatter the sense of at-homeness-in-the-world of a two-year-old child? "Settler trauma," Maher says, is the diagnosis. An infliction of pain meant to irreparably sear that sense of belonging essential to a collective future.

Seeking some semblance of normal life for the children, Maryam and her family have rented an apartment elsewhere. But every single day Maryam takes out her chair and sits under a tent outside her house to make a physical claim to her house and to this land just outside it, the rights to which she says she will never give up. She says she was born into a refugee status, and she refuses to have done to her what was done to her parents' generation. Maher and Nabil, whose family was the first in Sheikh Jarrah to be shut out of their home by court order, tell us that the settlers continuously harass Maryam, calling her dog and pig, yelling at her that she is going to die, that they will kill her. Every day the settlers occupying their houses (who do not remain the same people but in fact are changed periodically) harass them with acts of belligerent personal confrontation and physical and verbal attacks, including throwing excrement on them and setting dogs to tyrannize and defile their domestic spaces (the presence of dogs prohibits the practice of prayer in these spaces, according to the tenets of Islam). All these are clearly tactics in a deliberate campaign of daily harassment to coerce all of them, particularly Nabil's octogenarian mother who still manages to live in this house behind her son's occupied home, to leave the neighborhood and ultimately to abandon these lands claimed for and as Israel.

Beneath the thresholds of political meaning and concern drawn by the global codes of freedom undergirding Israel's own war to be human, Palestinians engage in daily persistent practices of living as a powerful political act and claim. Against the relentless physical and verbal assaults of settlers in East Jerusalem—the words and images as well as the objects violently lobbed against them to prevent the very possibility of continuing life, the tarps and tents that the Al-Gawi, Al-Kurd, and Hanoun families put up as tenuous defenses—are small yet vital political acts of survival. Like the tarps and wire mesh put up by Palestinian vendors over their stores and pathways in the Hebron market to prevent the similarly relentless projectiles of rocks and excrement launched by settlers, these are acts and accoutrements for staying on the land, for holding on to and continuing the living of generations, for living in defiance of the willed disappearance of one's people.

Here, on the intimate plane of everyday survival, where the calculus of financialized military enterprise and governance manifests itself in what Nadera Shalhoub-Kervokian calls "the physics of power," which Palestinians contend with daily and on the ground—a calculus inflicted on Palestinians by means of demolished homes, checkpoints, confiscated land, denied transportation services and building permits, discriminatory legal exclusions, and the prohibition of memory—are to be found a plethora of small acts of undaunted living.[72] If that physics consists of "strategies of protecting and ensuring the survival of a certain power" by impeding the past, present, and future of the Palestinian people, here other powers obtain—powers for sustaining life.[73] Here, against the ever-divisible calculus of demographic/algorithmic logics, with their ratios of life and death, proportionalities of means and ends in the calibration of violence, and derivative gains to be made of signs as events, we find an altogether other temporal and spatial scale and sense coursing through the life-making practices of people in a time of war.

At the site of the Kufr Qasem massacre, where Israeli Border Police soldiers killed forty-nine Arab villagers, Mahmoud Darwish writes, "Here they sleep. The sunset grows larger and changes into forests of dry trees. There is no hour to commemorate their death, no occasion, and no appointment. The stones themselves are time, and the expanse of the pale sunset is time."[74] When Darwish and others try to mourn the killed villagers at the site of their massacre, their killers prevent them from offering condolences. Yet Darwish writes that they, the Palestinian people, know how to commemorate and avenge their dead—"by holding on to the soil of the homeland with their nails and teeth."[75] He continues, "We realized that stones are made of time, and we sat down on them to sing to the homeland."[76] No hour, no occasion, no appointment to memorialize. Holding on, the commemoration and avenging of the dead by the surviving as well as the very form of this survival rest on the kind of place and time that stones and skies are made of. A time of persistence as the time of struggle to live free and a place where, as Nada Elia puts it, "justice is indivisible."[77]

9

POWERS OF EXPENDING LIFE

By now we have heard plenty about the murderous toll of Philippine president Rodrigo Duterte's war on drugs. Its horrors have been folded into that ever-ready placeholder for the atrocities that abound in the world, always seemingly suffered by and inflicted on people of the same kind, those descendants of the wretched of the earth who continue to be mired in tragedies of their own making. Such spectacles and the distance they secure are part of the continued great vanishing act of an emergent global humanity (among whom we must count ourselves) for whom these grotesque, barbaric wars to become human through the wanton expenditure of life could never resemble that civilized war continuously waged on their behalf, a war for the already human to remain so, as well as for others to join their ranks and to pursue "lives worth living."

Just War

The war for lives worth living is always waged and experienced as a just war. I invoke the idea of "just war" from the early Spanish colonial religious efforts to subjugate the mountain peoples of the Cordillera in the Philippines in the sixteenth century. At a meeting of theologians convened in the lowlands of the northern Philippines to determine whether it was morally justifiable to wage war against the Igorots, the Spanish colonizers concluded that, according to the definition of just war provided by Saint Augustine, it certainly was: "A just war is wont to be described as one that avenges wrongs, when a nation or state has to be punished, for refusing to make amends for the wrongs inflicted by its subjects, or to restore what it has seized unjustly."[1] W. H. Scott writes, "The list of wrongs inflicted by Igorots on Spanish subjects was satisfactorily impressive." They were bandits and murderers who killed for revenge, robbery, intimidation, or extortion; they prevented other natives from becoming Christians and gave refuge to convicts, lawbreakers, and delinquents. The worst of their offenses was their *prevention of innocent passage* to Spanish vassals from one place to another, "this crime alone render[ing] the Igorots sufficiently culpable for punitive invasion."[2]

Far from being anachronistic, Saint Augustine's writing on the subject in late antiquity has come to serve as the foundation of a tradition of just war theory that has seen a remarkable flowering of both scholarly and policy work from the end of World War II to the present, unequaled since the late seventeenth century.[3] Moreover, it has undergirded all the international interventions of liberal, democratic Western states since then, including most recently the US war on drugs, international humanitarian interventions, and global counterterrorist wars. Just war theory in fact continuously rehabilitates, by application, the ideological and legal rationale for colonial violence, providing a moral calculus that enables assessment of just cause and just ends, according to principles of proportionality of aim and of violent means gauged through the measure of "the general good."[4]

The moral calculus that inspirits the idea of a just war infuses and permeates not only the wide support of Philippine president Duterte and his war on drugs but also the very world that the regime of Duterte is widely presumed to oppose (sometimes characterized as global liberalism or even neoliberalism). Central to this moral calculus is the practice and idea of punishment, so pronounced in Saint Augustine's Christian formulation and in its implementation in the context of Spanish colonialism but also so pertinent to our contemporary moment as the means of racializing devaluation through violence, processes of value appropriation and power making that figure in everyday liberal democratic governance as well as in conservative, right-wing direct assaults on criminalized populations both within and outside of the borders of postindustrial Western nations. So it is with Duterte's war on drugs.

The picture that first drew international attention to the unabated extrajudicial killings carried out in Duterte's war on drugs since his election in May 2016 was a photograph of a woman, Jennelyn Olaires, cradling her partner, Michael Siaron, who lies slumped in her arms. Siaron, a tricycle driver, had been shot and killed by masked gunmen on a motorcycle, left on the street with a piece of cardboard by his side, scrawled with the words, "Drug Pusher. Do Not Emulate." Taken by the photojournalist Raffy Lerma, the photograph made the front page of the *Philippine Daily Inquirer* on July 24, 2016, with the headline in bold: "Church: Thou Shalt Not Kill." Dubbed "La Pietà" for its resemblance to Michelangelo's sculpture of the Virgin Mary holding Jesus Christ, the photograph went viral and was reproduced and recaptioned in Western media, even as Duterte decried the photograph for being melodramatic and his supporters accused it of being "fake news." Numerous photo essays on the drug war followed, featuring in major international newspapers and garnering many awards for their vivid photo coverage, as the murders were carried out in the open and the bodies strewn daily in the putative zones of war: the streets of poor urban neighborhoods, inside houses in the slum areas, alleyways, sidewalks, train tracks, and intersections of major thoroughfares—everywhere in the city, it would seem, but in the neighborhoods of the affluent.[5] All the bodies of the dead in plain sight.

How are we to think about this war that largely targets petty drug users and sellers, clearly signaling that it is a war against the urban poor, a standing or pending death sentence for those whose lives are already expendable?[6] The war on drugs has been central to Duterte's promise to rid the country of its ills—its rampant corruption, criminality, insurgency, poverty, and elite rule. Since its launch in July 2016, the violent antidrug campaign has resulted in nearly 30,000 murders (EJKs, or extrajudicial killings), including 6,600 suspected drug users and dealers admittedly killed by the Philippine National Police and another 22,983 considered "homicides under investigation," most likely at the hands of mercenaries.[7] A bloody order of extrajudicial capital punishment has taken hold, executioners enjoy impunity, and there is no end in sight to the murders.

Extrajudicial killings are, as anyone might know, far from new. Under the dictator Ferdinand Marcos (1965–96), tens of thousands were tortured and arrested, and thousands were disappeared and killed. Ousted by popular and military rebellion, the dictator was replaced by Corazon Aquino (1986–92), whose declared "total war" against left and right terrorism in defense of a restored democracy left thousands more dead as well as more than a million displaced.[8] Under Aquino's defense secretary, Fidel Ramos, who would succeed her as president (1992–98), martial law methods and policies that Ramos had himself crafted as Marcos's former internal security chief were extended, expanding the police as an independent force, creating civilian militias, and proliferating the number of extrajudicial killings.[9] Under Gloria Macapagal-Arroyo (2001–10), over a thousand extrajudicial executions and forced disappearances of leftist political activists, human rights advocates and workers, local journalists, community leaders, and clergy were carried out in the name of the "war on terror," under the counterinsurgent military campaign, "Oplan Bantay Laya" (Operation Plan Freedom Watch), which relied on a secret "order of battle list" that is now seen as the predecessor of Duterte's very public "drug watch list" (or "kill list"). None of the perpetrators of these past state-sponsored killings have ever been brought to justice, and indeed the Marcoses (wife, son, and daughter) have slowly returned to national political power. In spite of public outrage, Marcos was given all the formal rites and honors of burial in the Cemetery of Heroes (Libingan ng mga Bayani).

In Duterte's postdemocratic order can be seen not simply echoes but replays of Marcos's authoritarian rule and the culmination of decades of counterinsurgent warfare, begging questions of the evolution of the Philippine state (as well as the evolution of the police as an autonomous and highly politicized state institution) in the course and aftermath of so-called democratization and globalization. To view this domestic evolution within a transnational context is certainly to recognize the new rules of state that have prevailed since the global war on terror launched by the United States and its allies in 2001, a war in which Mindanao, in the southern Philippines, was declared the "second front," after Afghanistan.[10] On top of its role as general manager of capitalist social relations, insurance agency for capital, and protection agency for territorialized life, the state has taken on a new role as uber-arbitrageur of captive life.

This new role and the new rules of state, which accompany the shift in imperial governmentality, have developed out of having to deal with the pernicious consequences of US military counterinsurgency policies of an earlier era, which, in arming local civilian militias and deputizing parastate elements through shadow economies or illicit commerce, set the stage for the decentralization of the state's monopoly on violence and the extensive expansion of the role of what Alfred McCoy calls "the covert netherworld" in formal political affairs.[11] McCoy details the way this covert netherworld formed during the Cold War and its aftermath through the increasing reliance of modern states on covert methods, giving rise to a clandestine social milieu composed of secret services and criminal syndicates and an illicit economic nexus that sustained its nonstate actors. That clandestine social milieu, which had been growing alongside and symbiotically with the global security complex in the interstitial and peripheral zones of the emerging city-state/free port archipelago, now figures centrally in national government and in its domestic and transnational affairs.

To situate Duterte within this transnational context is therefore also, importantly, to understand the driving forces of the form of urbanism that has emerged since the 1990s, an urbanism evolving out of the Philippine transition from the Cold War authoritarian modernist capital urbanization of Marcos to the post–Cold War, democratic global metropolitanism of Marcos's successors.

Insurgent Shadow Urbanism of the Provinces

For twenty-one years, Duterte served as mayor of Davao city in Mindanao. Dubbed "The Punisher" by *Time* magazine for the "Davao Death Squads" he organized to clean up the city and bring business-friendly peace and order and security to its citizens, he is credited for making Davao, purportedly, the safest city in the Philippines or even in Southeast Asia, and among Asia's fastest growing cities. The city is notable for its imposition of a curfew on minors, the prohibition of the sale and consumption of alcohol after 1 a.m., and the prohibition of smoking in public and work establishments. Touted by crowdsourcing sites as having one of the lowest crime rates in the world, Davao was paradoxically also known as the "murder capital" of the Philippines, reported to have the highest murder rate and the second highest incidence of rape in the country. During Duterte's successive terms as mayor, human rights organizations documented 1,400 killings of petty criminals, street children, and drug users (mostly youth), attested to by witnesses as the work of the death squads organized and authorized by Duterte himself.

As Philippine president, Duterte now seeks to "nationalize" his accomplishments as mayor—to scale up his own brand of provincial urbanism against the imperial metropolitanism of Manila, the national capital, and to gain ascendancy and control over city everywhere, that globalizing urbanization project of constructing metropolitan platforms for the value-productive movements of connectivity (rather than settlement) of globopolitical life (see chapter 7). The securitization of liberalized or "free" movements of transnational financial capital and capitalizable life (the freedom of exchange), which such platforms host, entails the active wasting of other lives through policing and war, the costs for which are offset by the disposable life-times that these brutal wars make available as infrastructure for capitalized reproduction as well as raw material for industries of life-expenditure. Under Duterte, Davao city had in fact been developing its own metropolitan platform along these lines, promising worthwhile life (its motto, under Duterte's daughter, who succeeded him as mayor is, "Davao, Life Is Here"), but with even more intense securitocratic and securitization features.

Davao is the main urban economic hub in Mindanao, whose Muslim and Indigenous peoples were finally subjugated, after three centuries of Spanish colonial war, only with the triumph of US colonialism in the early twentieth century and the extension of the latter's settler colonial models of land seizure, homesteading, and forced education to the colonized Christian Filipino populations in the north. In fact, US colonialism reprised its own settler colonial model by expanding US corporate investments in the region (logging, rubber, and fruit plantations) and propelling local as well as foreign migration and settlement into Mindanao, including Japanese abaca plantation companies, whose personnel and their families made up 60 percent of new migrants in Davao by 1930.[12] That it was a frontier of US settler colonialism, viewed as resource and means for imperial political and economic gain, is evidenced by the telling historical detail that in 1939, the US president's advisory committee on political refugees conducted an exploratory study of Mindanao's potential as a long-term place of settlement for European Jewish refugees fleeing Nazi Europe, a plan for a new "Palestine" that was cut short with the outbreak of World War II and made moot with the postwar creation of the state of Israel.[13]

As land seized by settler colonial capital, Mindanao has been the site of a great and continuing dispossession of Muslim and Indigenous communities who have long inhabited it. It has also served as an instrument to absorb and contain the prior colonial and capitalist land dispossessions of peasant and rural communities from the north.[14] Mindanao has thus been a place of deep and longstanding struggle against foreign and national imperialist projects, the site of Muslim secessionist and insurgent movements, and the site of relentless Cold War and post–Cold War counterinsurgent warfare. As Francisco Lara Jr. has shown, it is out of these conditions of unceasing warfare, buoyed by the growth of the transnational drug trade in the 1980s and the influx of massive amounts of local and foreign aid in the 1990s, that a shadow economy of illicit and violence-based enterprises under the control of dominant political clans, with their paramilitary groups, has expanded.

This history helps us understand the importance of Davao city as a key player in the "peace and development paradigm" of counterinsurgency directed toward Mindanao since the 1990s and sponsored by the USAID, the

World Bank, and the UN Development Programme, as well as by the multinational capital investments that poured into the region as the means and consequence of its role as a laboratory for counterinsurgency under the auspices of US military training and assistance.[15] This history and its legacy of militarization also helps us understand the rise of Duterte as a strongman or outlaw figure able to create business-friendly conditions of public order through "tough" negotiations with conflicting paramilitary actors and factions of war, and the deployment of a fatal policing machine built out of recruits from these same wars.[16]

In these provincial zones of war, on the outskirts of global and national capital cities, far from metropolitan liberal democracies, we see the rise of a model of urbanism predicated on the intimate, direct relations between violence and value. That model can be gleaned from the twenty-first-century integration of antiterrorism operations with making Mindanao an open market for multinational trade and investments (in the prospecting for crude oil, coolants for nuclear reactors, and petroleum and natural gas substitutes, as well as in projects of rehabilitation, rebuilding, and economic development through agribusiness, microbusiness, and infrastructural assistance and loans).[17] It is a model in which the personified state brokers the relationship between free enterprise and punishment in undisguised, blunt fashion for a citizenry willing to forego its own liberal rights to achieve the modicum of privileges and enjoyments of securitized urban life. Rather than making distinctions, however, between licit and illicit economies, the "insurgent" state of Duterte integrates both in its calculus of "growth," insofar as its emergence as a strong power of its own (rather than a mere instrument and source of power for local political clan leaders) depends on the very violence-based, illicit economies and protection services of local parastate networks that it accommodates (and now dominates) as uber-political patron and benefactor. It is these features that make it a shadow version of the very global urbanism of metropolitan neoliberalism that it purportedly rebels against.

The enabling conditions of this shadow urbanism have left their mark not only on the composition of the Davao death squads (made up of former military and paramilitary vigilantes as well as former rebels) but also on the signature modes of killing these death squads brought to the war on drugs in the urban slums.[18] Here we see the policing units of death squads in the provinces as the model and source of personnel for the extrajudicial killings that have now come to be routine operations in the capital, their "style" of summary executions now simply a detail of the modus operandi of urban policing as disciplinary punishment.

The rituals of killings are well known. Video images and even CCTV recordings of the body disposals are innumerable and viewable online. "Oplan Tokhang" (the "Knock and Plead" police operation), the ostensible campaign to dissuade drug users from their habit but in reality simply a prelude to execution, is now the subject of innumerable video shorts. Reports of the murders are abundant, numbingly the same in the kinds of facts they record: gunned down, point blank, by the police or masked men "riding tandem" on a motorcycle, head wrapped in brown packing tape, a poster board with variations on the message: drug addict/pusher; do not emulate. While these flagrant "signatures" left on the dead of the drug war have faded, as the murders have drawn widespread condemnation and global symbolic sanction, the killings continue unabated as the central piece of Duterte's state terror.

Duterte's state terror is undoubtedly the performative production of legible sovereign power in the political currency of international state-making. It draws on the playbook of its erstwhile US colonial benefactors, whose "wars on . . ." campaigns—targeting drugs, crime, poverty, terror, and illegal immigration, from Nixon to Reagan, from Clinton to Trump—have seen the enormous growth of its own war machines capitalizing on the deadly policing and warehousing of its own criminalized Black and brown populations. But the history that brought this regime to power is also much longer and broader, more layered and mediated, than this direct unilateral technology transfer would suggest.[19] In more recent history, McCoy shows, for example, that the transcontinental expansion of Nixon's declared war on drugs in the early 1970s and over the following decades stimulated drug trafficking on five continents, buoyed by the synergistic stimulus of narcotics suppression and covert counterinsurgency operations during the Cold War.[20] This same conjuncture composed of intricate, clandestine alliances between US counterinsurgency and illicit commerce, local parastate elements (warlords, smugglers, vigilantes, and former rebels), and national militaries, from Latin America to Southeast and West Asia, has helped to create the conditions for Mindanao, out of which Duterte arose.

As I have tried to emphasize, the logic and consequences of past and present colonial just wars have pervaded a global system of intersovereign state relations, providing an international lexicon of state action (e.g., as the guarantor of domestic law and order) and credible threats to states' human polities that would warrant the punitive action of just war.[21] Moreover, colonial wars have created the protocols (including the evaluative measures) and material conditions of such action as well as the enormous, proliferating apparatuses of security and their systemic interaction across multiple states, which now compose the global "security architecture" protecting the vital systems of capital life. As we've seen, this global security infrastructure has itself become a site of numerous auxiliary capitalist industries beyond weapons manufacturing and beyond prison manufacture and maintenance, including illicit predatory capitalist enterprises that have grafted themselves onto it (smuggling, kidnap for ransom, mercenary operations, etc.)—all based on the productive management and expenditure of the disposable life created through various kinds of war.

It is against this background that we can understand the systemic character of the Duterte state. State terror in this current instantiation acts as the spectacular display and exercise of that direct, active power of expending life, which guarantees the preemptive securitization of the urbanized Philippine nation-state and the life it promises its citizens. In scaling up the shadow urbanism developed out of the zones of war into a global platform, it also boosts the expansion of the so-called "shadow" or illicit, informal enterprises under the franchising power of national government. These enterprises include, first and foremost, the political-police machine led by Duterte, which has made extrajudicial capital punishment a financial instrument authorized by the state.

Derivative Enterprises

Under the Duterte regime, killing has become a lucrative, deregulated, derivative enterprise. As an Amnesty International report has publicly made known, and as the investigative journalist Sheila Coronel details, police are well-compensated for each killing, garnering varying rates of remuneration, from ₱8,000 to ₱20,000 for small-time drug offenders, not to mention what they are able to gain from the theft of victims' cash and personal belongings (cell phones, jewelry) and the bonuses they receive from their civilian superiors, which can amount to several hundreds of thousands of pesos.[22] Duterte has openly promised rewards for the killing of more "valuable" suspects on the watch list, from ₱50,000 for a Barangay council man to ₱5 million pesos for a drug lord. It is for this reason that, Coronel incisively notes, in the drug war police are no longer simply acting on behalf of their political patrons (in relations of debt-obligation), but through the leveraging of state connections and access to state violence, they are acting as "entrepreneurs looking for maximum gain."[23]

The profits from the drug war are not limited to the act of murder. Extortion of drug suspects during arrests, the ransom of abducted suspects and their relatives (kept hostage in secret jails hidden behind false walls within precincts and other buildings), and even commissions for funeral parlors, which in turn demand ransom from the relatives of victims for the release of the bodies of their loved ones—these are some of the many ways that actual and threatened murder become opportunities for financial gain. With the multiplication of possibilities of cash rewards, kickbacks, rents, protection money, promotion, and profitable connections along the vertical chains of power as well their horizontal relations of graft, this police enterprise demonstrates the congruence of the political-police machine and financial capitalism—in particular the congruence between police operations and derivatives, the instruments and logic of pricing attributes of an underlying referent or asset that is set to experience variability over time. As the underlying assets of dead and potentially dead bodies attest, this is a variability that is both virtual and very real.

The killings are part of a derivative economy in both senses: derivative as ramification and outgrowth or byproduct (taking the leavings, the cast-offs of others), which has long figured as part of the everyday survival strategies of surplus populations; and derivative as financial contract (pricing contingency, volatility, and variability predicated on an underlying asset that is secondary in importance, or immaterial). Here, as everywhere, derivatives testify to the limits reached by a prior mode of accumulation that, in maximizing productivity, also undermines the basis of profitability, cheapening life-times and the surplus value extracted from them—and in response, accelerates value extraction through the absolute minimization of circulation time, to capitalize on the vicissitudes of time and to profit off of the "borrowings" of colonized futures.

As we saw with regard to the algorithmic/demographic logics of war and finance (see chapter 8), the derivative economy depends on this foreclosure of the future—on the trading of foreclosed futures. It is no accident that the anticipation of failure and dead ends has always already been present for the urban excess—redundant populations who must live by inventing forms of value extraction out of the fits and starts, the sluggishness of circulation, forms of symbolic and virtual "fixing" so rampant in the third world that in the Philippines it requires its own glossary of codewords (or "corruptionary").[24] Surrounded by impassable blocks to embarking on pathways of proper urban life (formal employment, licit and legal livelihood), pressed against the limits of this surround, they have long traded on derivative qualities and immaterial "things" (services and events, shortcuts and loopholes), on practices of timing and contingency, on happenings and accelerations, on creating and removing drag, on making full stops.

FIGURE 9.1. Miko Aguilar, *Santoterte*, June 2016, San Diego, California, digital collage. Courtesy of the artist.

This very modality of value extraction and the proliferation of dead-end lives is also what allows the police to subcontract disposable assets (hitmen) and what provides the supply of targets, or underlying zero-value assets (drug addicts who are themselves the figures of no future), for the derivative enterprise of murder. Mercenary gangs are drawn from different slum neighborhoods in the same pools of urban excess. Drug users and pushers are also tapped as killers for hire, yet are also likely to be killed in turn. The round robin serves. But people pay forward with the whole of their wasted lives, and there is no second round.

Executions are thus preemptive acts, a cashing in on the promised lifetimes of captive populations, promissory futures of discounted life for investment capital. While financial securitization undermines prior fundamental values, state securitization aspires to refound it.[25] In this way, like the threat of US military violence, on which the strength of the dollar is predicated, the "power sign" of Duterte (bearing cult value)—the command function of money-as-capital that he performs, suggested by his figuration in the place of God and state in a bill of currency in Miko Aguilar's portrait, *Santoterte* (see figure 9.1)—is underwriting the fundamental value of the

Powers of Expending Life • 239

life-times that the Philippine state has long been selling/offering to global markets.[26]

The costs of these powers of expending life underwrite the greater total aggregate value of the political-economic platform that they found. Hence the leap in foreign direct investments (an 11 percent jump to $1 billion in the first months of 2017, six months after his election), attributable to Duterte's move to become "friends to all and enemy to no one," which has opened other foreign markets (such as China and Russia).[27]

That Duterte has continuously allocated a lion's share of the annual national budget for infrastructure (his "Build, Build, Build" master plan to construct more roads, bridges, railways, trains, and airports to further develop the expanding metropolis received ₱1.18 trillion in 2021)[28] merely proves that the distributed, and scaling, form of protected and privileged dwelling and fluency of movement of city everywhere, that platform of globopolitical humanity who are guaranteed "freedom" from punishment and servitude, rests on the expenditure of the disposable life-times and lives of others.[29] The state expends the excess of the nation's captive populations in order to offer the valued portion of that same population as "captive markets" and "captive centers" for the multinational businesses whose offshored operations it aims to attract and secure.

In a similar way, Duterte also represents for his constituency the redemption of the value (moral and economic) of Filipino *life*, revising the meaning of the rallying antidictatorship slogan of the mid-1980s, with its gendered Christian morality play, "the Filipino is worth dying for."

But whose life? Which Filipino life?

Populism, Platform Totalitarianism

Many have commented on the widespread "populist" appeal of Duterte's tough-on-crime persona, his appeal to upper and middle classes as well as to marginalized sectors and regions, such as Overseas Filipino Workers (OFWs) and Mindanao, even the very same slum dwellers whose husbands and wives, fathers and mothers, sons and daughters, brothers and sisters—*asawa, magulang, anak, kapatid*—became fodder for the war on drugs. Many have historicized the emergence of Duterte and his regime, but few historicize the "people" that are the object of his populism. While I do not aim to do that here, it seems important to consider that the same conditions that have given rise to Duterte as a political formation have also shaped the polis that has emerged as its constituency.

Many critical commentaries view his supporters as so many stable sociological subjects with ideological needs and desires that Duterte, as a symbolic, representational persona and rhetorical force, is able to attract, even satisfy. My own view is that to understand this political formation as simply or primarily a form of reactionary nationalism or even fascism (viewed as an ideological, representational relation between leader and followers) is to miss the multiple levels of dynamic processes that are crucial to its emergence, including those intertwined transnational modes of value extraction and life-making that I have discussed as driving global urbanization: the mediatic valorization of circulation and reproduction, and the financialization of securitized forms of life expenditure, which the humanist, subject-centric plane of democratic politics tends to subsume and eclipse. We have to consider then that the conditions of global servitude and global security wars, which have greatly shaped Philippine life since the so-called restoration of democracy more than thirty years ago, have also reconfigured the polis and its role in relation to the state.

Almost a generation and a half of direct, immediate, and intimate relations that ordinary Filipinos have had with the globopolis, through their transnational social kin networks with a growing diaspora providing reproductive care and infrastructural maintenance all over the world, has in many ways urbanized the Philippine population, freeing or loosening people's attachments to local networks of patronage while tethering them to the nation-state, which continues to decide and define their fates.[30] At the same time, unceasing assaults on people's capacities to make life for themselves, the endlessness of wars, the daily experience of the expendability and deprivation of life, and the wanton violence committed through small- and large-scale predations, have propelled flight and aspiration for another life that these same forces also make impossible to achieve. The rejection of the demeaning of life encapsulated by servitude, the promise of protection so little afforded to people by the state to whom they belong and whose charge it is to provide, the frustration of pursuits of life worth living everywhere heralded by the urban worlds they service, the exhaustion and menace of living in a time of constant war and social assault, the anger and pain of suffering the loss of what and who you hold dear, everything taken away by those who always get away with it—all these affective currents run through, animate, and electrify the polis constituted of Duterte's supporters. Rather than an identifiable voting bloc or a unified people represented by a symbolic leader with whom they identify, that polis consists of multiple, diverse, and distributed social components of a global urbanist platform.

The fact that social media was and continues to be one of the most vibrant sites of operation of Duterte's supporters is not simply the result of the migration of civic, public spheres into new media. Social media are capitalist platforms that the vital platforms of people's social-kin networks have used and grafted onto as the constitutive means of their own continued operation and extension, but they have also been the means for the pluralization of those very platforms beyond their domestic, familial forms. Thus, support for Duterte, as subscription to and active participation in a national political platform, has cut through and divided families, classes, social identities, and older communities in an unprecedented way. But just as we might see in the constitution of this new polis an insurgent global urbanism that is comparable to, because connected to (but also sharply distinct from), revanchist, right-wing political formations elsewhere, we also see in this political platform the scaling of family and clan political networks to the fit of the transnational nation, as suggested by references to Duterte by his supporters as *Poón* (literally, the trunk of a tree), a word for leader and capital, but one that in older contexts also refers to family lineage.[31]

Critical artists, such as Magpies Press, have understood this formation in their satirical renderings of Duterte as *Tatay Digong* (Daddy Digong), as family or clan patriarch whose provision of formidable, courageous protection and empathetic care (emblematically conveyed by Duterte's slogan "Tapang at Malasakit"—"Brave and Empathetic") is understood to apply to all loyal kin, regardless of their infractions of the rules of licit life or deviations from modern sex-gender norms and religious morality, and across diverse ethnic, regional, and religious communities.[32] What galvanizes the diverse affective currents coursing through this platform—its pact and promise, which Duterte might be said to act as the figurative, practical instrument for realizing—is precisely the redemption of that collective life of national, clan belonging, for which its familial members will claim the proper name, *Filipino*.

As suggested by Miko Aguilar's collage of armed Catholic cherubim and World War II pinup poster girls symbolically buttressing Duterte as money form and sovereign (see figure 9.1), a long history of violent colonial promises, however, seeps into the imagination and realization of such redemptive power.

Tagapagligtas Ako (I am the redeemer) is the title of a sculptural piece by Jason Dy (see figure 9.2), featuring a plaster cast figure of the Santo Niño (Baby Jesus) swaddled in the same packaging tape used to wrap the heads of killed suspects in the drug war. We glimpse in this protest artist image, mocking Duterte's God-like pretension, the retributive powers invoked in

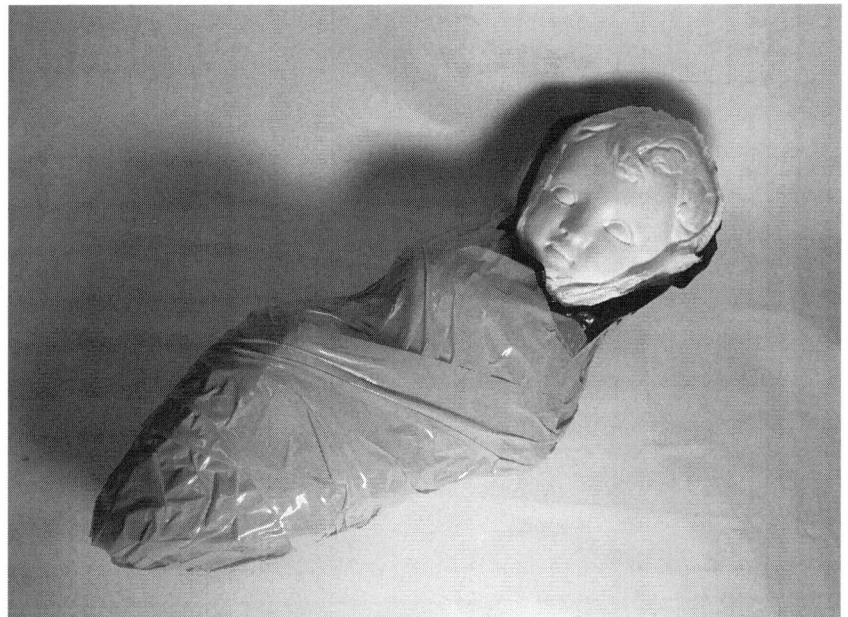

FIGURE 9.2. Jason Dy, *Tagapagligtas Ako* (I am the redeemer), 2016, plaster cast, tissue paper, black plastic bag, and packaging tape. Collection of Binggoy Panlilio De Ocampo. Metro Manila. Courtesy of the artist.

the insurgent state's reconquest of the nation. As this work and Aguilar's *Santoterte* highlight, in Duterte lies the convergence of money, father, and god as the figurehead and legal tender of an aggressive platform of vengeful redemption. In a global context of platform totalitarianism, that bid for valued life necessarily bears colonial and racial capital's moral and economic injunction of punishment. No wonder that we hear echoed in Duterte's speech, thrilling to his supporters, the tones and address of conquest's foundational injunction of just war.[33]

Objects of Punishment

Punishment as a mode of extraction has grown and flourished through the opportunities presented by policing and militarism for securing some of the largest allocations of capital to the Philippines since the closure of the US bases in 1992. The threat and exertion of violence has become a rampant, decentralized means of exacting "rent" (through informal and illicit connections to the formal state apparatus), including kidnap for ransom, kickbacks, and extortion, as well as a symbolic financial instrument capable of inflating the price of survival and of living (even of burying one's dead)—the product of the decentralization and devolution of violence in the franchising and subcontracting of counterinsurgent warfare. As we saw in the urbanist economy, this punitive mode is now in the process of being generalized in contemporary modes of production (through rents, or the exaction of tolls on the qualities of life to sell quality of life services), from software as business industries (digital apps operating on subscription models) to airlines and airports and other communication and transport industries developing out of circulation rather than traditional manufacture, and in this way very much emulating smuggling, fixing, and other corrupt and improper forms of capitalist accumulation beyond wage labor.

I have argued throughout, however, that this punitive mode has long operated as a standing practice of racialization that is intrinsic to capitalism. As organizing codes of discernment and discrimination of conduct and status, race and sex are inextricable in the work of devaluation, not necessarily or solely of given social identities but as means of violence that serve to inscribe through physical and psychic force what is disposable, free for the taking, worthless, and yet a gift and slave of nature, as the negative defining boundary for what is valorizable labor, consciousness, culture, and creative intellect (which distinguishes the architect from the bee)—that is, what are distinctly human qualities that define value-making life. Many Black, antiracist, feminist, and Indigenous studies scholars have highlighted the ways in which violence in everyday wars of punishment produces its objects (or targets), whether the category of social being called "women" as subordinated bearers of natural, human reproductive power (in the centuries-long war to capture and control "life" as consciously disavowed source of capitalist value); the savage Indian/*indio* who must be killed or thoroughly remade to rescue the human; or that of the Black slave as natural commodity, as nonhuman or animal resource and instrument of capital accumulation. The legacy of such racial and sexual wars of punishment is carried on in the continuing transmission of such violence not only through disciplining social norms, but also through the humanizing, value-conferring apparatuses of the state, the legal system, education, the banking system, the culture industry (film, music, arts), and so on. What we witness in this context of deregulated, decentralized financialized killings is a similar, as well as derivative, making of a contemporary object of just war—the figure of the drug user or addict who embodies absolutely expendable life, a racializing project that is crucially connected to, and indeed supported and subsidized by while being counterposed to, that other racializing project of feminized reproductive labor that is global servitude or serviceable life (see "Excursus").

The fact that this particular fraction of the urban poor (differentiated as worthless beings—zombies—already dead or dying) has not achieved a positive social identity on the basis of historical struggle perhaps makes it difficult for a politics centered on representable identities to cohere. Indeed it has been nearly impossible for the victims to represent themselves in ways that might easily conform to proper political subjects of grievance as well as grief, except perhaps in that trope of value, which is the human. It might in fact make it counterintuitive to think about these killings as processes of racialization, if we predominantly understand that racialization always produces and posits distinct and identifiable collectivities. To the degree that the victims are inseparable from their killers, many of whom are drawn from the same urban slum populations, neither can they be thought of as "enemies of the state" in the way that the communists, or the Muslim separatists, are understood—in other words, as "terrorists." However, it is precisely this nonpolitical status that undergirded the just cause of Iberian colonialism—"*ni rey ni roque*" (having neither king nor castle) is the phrase that encapsulates the perspective of sovereignty, which racializes natives as savages who cannot be accorded the same rights as peoples, and therefore all of whose "wrongs" can only be crimes.[34] By means of punitive violence, native persistence in living an unrecognizable, independent life is redefined as inherent culpability.[35]

Today that status of sheer culpability is embodied by the figure of the poor drug user. Dispossessed of political patronage and social belonging (without state or parastate protection or guaranteed welfare afforded by kin connection)—embodying complete disenfranchisement by the state and expulsion from humanity defined by kin-based social community—the immiserated drug user, sometimes homeless and ascriptively kinless, is proclaimed the cause for the impunity of violence that in fact produces it. For in fact, the significant object of this war on drugs and its use of power signs (money, violence, bodies) as its primary weapons is precisely the production of this absolutely expendable life that is necessary to uphold life as value. Such is the aim of punishment under the new political economy of life. The deracinating violence of wars that forced many to flee the countryside and seek refuge in urban slums now severs them from the communities they might have retained or created. It is this brutally enforced social alienation or even social death—the relentless destruction of people's deep social ties, the makingkinless which the war on drugs accomplishes even as it points to drugs as the agent—that expels its victims from humanity, the category of valued life.[36]

And yet just moments before their preemptive total liquidation, the people rendered absolutely expendable by forces of violence were tricycle and taxi drivers, runners and couriers, messengers and porters, conductors and vendors, garbage collectors, and all-around utility persons, the very readily available, serviceable life facilitating the value-making movements of people and goods (including drugs) in the city. As drivers and bodily vehicles or utilities for the life-movements of both the upwardly mobile and the poor, whose liquidity and serviceable disposability urban life depends on, they were vital components of the infrastructures of capital circulation and mobility. "The truth is," Nanay Jemy writes of her killed husband who was a tricycle driver, "he was only doing [drugs] because he would work for twenty-four hours conveying passengers."[37]

Gideon Lasco shows that many of the so-called drug users in the underclass take methamphetamine (*shabu*) as "skills and performance enhancers" (*pampagilas*), as boosters and inducers of necessary affects and moods (confidence, calm, enthusiasm, diligence) as well as of physical capacities (alertness, wakefulness, energy).[38] Drugs serve for many users as crucial supports in informal livelihoods that require their engagement in and performance of largely illegal, irregular, risky, stressful, illicit, and life-expending activities, bodily services placed at the disposition of others and often straddling the borders of the moral, acceptable, and normative. We might say that drugs enable the work of expending their own lives for a living—they are helpers for the help, lubricating agents that enable the liquidity of the poor. It is not so strange to learn from the killers themselves that drugs also enable them to completely expend the lives of others for the killers' own living.[39]

Ironically, the life of value, toward which all such expenditures ultimately tend, is the capitalizable life of a globopolitical humanity that was and continues to be the aspiration of many of the very same people being killed, even as it is not for them but rather for the enfranchised that such a life is promised and understood to be deserved. It is in fact a political identification with the racism of the deserving (those who deserve, by dint of work or inheritance, fate or past suffering) over the undeserving, that fuels these forms of authoritarian populism surfacing everywhere. In the drug war, the undeserving are those who have "wasted" their lives, who are also the embodiments of an unjust or unfair (illicit) enjoyment, just as the drug trade is the site of illicit wealth. And yet what is fair and just carries with it the globally shared expectation of things and people costing less, of having less value, of approaching next to nothing. The expectation that life, having already cost us so much, should not, by virtue of these wasted lives that threaten to waste others, cost us more.

A further irony of the war against addicts, who are the ostensible object of this war, is that they emblematize precisely the freedom or liberation from the moral-economic order that drives, constrains, and strangles peoples' lives—the impossible yet addictive desiring production of capitalism, with its utopian promise of complete emancipation from a contemptible, denigrated human and nonhuman "nature" it rapaciously feeds on yet whose reproduction it assaults and destroys.[40] In my own thinking, addicts represent liberation from this impossible freedom held out as an addictive ideal that only tethers people to the kind of life they are compelled to live and work for. Addicts represent, then, freedom from the promise of freedom whose true "accomplishment" can only finally be death, not as inevitable future or part of the living, but as elimination and absolute expenditure of existence. But for this reason, they must be expunged, turned into the very harbingers and mirrors of death itself (figured as *salot*—pestilence, rot).[41] Killing the addict thus restores the primacy of the "life" against which such addiction defines itself, indeed, rejects or defies. The fact that the single-word that the police use to justify almost every acknowledged killing is *nanlaban* (they fought) signals that any resistance to this "life" is a crime worthy of capital punishment.

Power Signs: Bodies, Money, Help

However, rather than the notion of absolutely expendable life as a form of "bare life" placed outside the law, as its symbolically, constitutive, foundational moment, these "disqualified forms of life" serve more practical functions, incorporated into economies of power signs beyond political representational values.

The fatal signifying practices of the drug war machine point to the ways that dead bodies are no longer only signs of covert counterinsurgent terror displayed on the margins and outskirts of representational democracy. Under Marcos, forced disappearances and extrajudicial assassinations were, like squatter demolitions and displacements, part of clean-up campaigns that attempted to rid the presence and representational evidence of contradictions. Such was the strategy of authoritarian modernism. Meanwhile, in the countryside, in the Cold War counterinsurgent war against the communists, military and paramilitary units were, under the guidance of the psy-ops campaigns and training of the CIA, already using dead, mutilated, and dismembered bodies as terroristic signs inflicted on rural communities as well as on the radical activists and guerillas those communities might attempt to harbor or protect.[42] In the era of covert violence under modernist development, the hiding of contradictory violence in urban areas was supplemented by the display of sovereign power in rural sites of guerilla warfare—a dual representation regime.

Under the postauthoritarian, antiliberal regime in a financialized political economy of life, the use of bodies as the medium of threatening messages ("Drug addict. Do not emulate.")—or as the journalist Patricia Evangelista has called it, "murder as meme"—points to the fact that dead bodies are no longer only covert signs of terror in spaces of minimal to nonrepresentation (in a "democracy" where the liberal media exercises an important ideological role in "exposing" what the state attempts to hide). Dead bodies are now also forms of content-provision for the communicative capitalist media (spectacular and generative of viral circulation), with which political platforms have interfaced—disposable media of morbid derivative enterprises, material signs for communicative capitalism (shared by Duterte critics as well as supporters) and its fields of democratic and demographic politics. If they were not enlivened by socialities who claim them as their own (as the loss of *our* lives) these dead bodies would indeed be, not only in this case but also more generally, merely the metabolic vehicles—or as Jonathan Beller argues, the mediatic substrates—of computational capitalism and the conditions of its new political economy of life.

The body—dead, stilled, without the possibility of or potential for transformation, variation, improvisation, and disaggregation—is used as a messaging device, a placard in the war of signs of political claims. Like money as capital credit, dead bodies figure as what Mario Lazzarato calls "power signs": "instead of representing something they anticipate it, create it, and mold it."[43] What we see in the operation of political-police machines is precisely the deployment and functioning of power signs, in the form of money and dead bodies (capitalist credit and fatal command—twin signs of sovereign power). Money and dead bodies act directly to create and break alliances, connections, obligations, and indebtedness, that is, to make and transform relations. In the political-police machine, patronage and taxes/tributes are also contracts and rents/kickbacks—these are signifying and asignifying flows that connect and run through social networks across the entire gamut of sociological class divisions.

Far from a politics of representation, which nevertheless acts as part of the formal system that is the complex overlay and provision of participation in a globally governed and juridically regulated world (where the "law" as a formal system, for example, becomes one of the power signs wielded by and over the police, mostly over the general citizenry, even as it is rejected by Duterte, in the context of international judgment), here, recognition and distribution of material allocations are always operating in tandem with and internal to one another. The culture of "help" (*tulong*) that saturates so-called patronage politics and the so-called moral politics of the poor consists of practices of recognition and conferral of recognition of authority and power, as well as a material allocation of or claim on assets—labor or money, services or goods, resource capacities, proxy "agency" or "being."[44]

Thus, it would be quite mistaken to view the figure of Duterte in simply symbolic, ideological terms. We in fact risk bolstering those liberal dead exchanges that have contributed to his rise if we do not consider the generative and regulatory modes of life and livelihood that are completely entwined in his emergence and rule—that is, the intertwined logics and socialities of survival and predation as forms of living that have developed out of the open zones of war.

Zones of War Are Times of Living

The operation of money, bodies, and help as power signs in the war on drugs extends to words and images deployed in social media, a major site of operations of the war of the Duterte platform. The organized deployment of social media was not only key to the decentralized presidential campaign but also to the civic counterpart of the war on drugs launched by self-proclaimed Duterte "cyber warriors": a virulent communicative campaign of verbal, textual, and image harassment, abuse, and attack directed at critics and launched on Facebook, which they called Oplan Cyber Tokhang (after the police campaign, Oplan Tokhang).[45] While the Duterte cyber warriors saw their own communicative vigilantism in term of "attacks" and "special ops," with the aim of eliminating targeted social media accounts accused of spreading "false information" against the government (the rubbing out of users, which they dubbed "extrajudicial reporting"), other supporters saw themselves in the figure of the Davao Death Squads, embracing and playing on the latter's initials to call themselves "Die-hard Duterte Supporters" or "Digong Duterte Supporters." Although much of the "weaponizing" of the internet in this context was the result of systematically organized and financed disinformation campaigns through bots, influencers, "click armies," and paid fake accounts for trolling, these campaigns also galvanized innumerable individual netizen supporters as distributed independent operators and agents of a shared political platform.[46] Here words and images are veritable "weapons"—less representational means than asignifying practices that create and maintain the social relations of righteous, retributive causes that constitute the authoritarian platform while drawing on other socialities that they try to break and destroy.

This authoritarian political platform found an ideal interface with the capitalist platform Facebook, which had a few years earlier seized on the "social media–loving and—hungry" country with poor internet infrastructure as a site for an aggressive experimental marketing campaign that would result in 69 million people—or two-thirds of the population (effectively all the country's internet users)—being on Facebook.[47] The partnership between the Duterte platform and the megaplatform of Facebook emblematizes the merging of governance and enterprise in a form of platform totalitarianism aimed at total domination and subsumption of the life-times of entire populations (and, in the ambition of capitalist megaplatforms, ultimately the total global population) as "free labor," data, social machinery, fuel.[48] Needless to say, such platform totalitarianism is ultimately securitized through violent repression, exemplified in the government's shutdown of a major broadcast media network, its continuous murderous attacks on journalists and leftist activists, and the recently passed antiterror law that promises ever-greater suppression of the growing criticism, protests, and expressions of dissent on all media.

That capitalist social media has been both the object and the means of this totalitarian warfare rests on the importance of the social vitality that animates and makes such platforms. Social media is after all one of the most vibrant sites of operation of vital platforms, the social organizing systems of kin networks that act as subaltern self-maintaining machines of production, subsidizing this last phase of capital's imperial expansion. Social media in fact capitalizes on the imperative for open and constant connectivity as part of the mode of reproduction of socialities dispersed by the deterritorializing effects of capitalism. It is therefore not simply fortuitous that the Philippines should find itself the "social media capital of the world," providing not only a captive market for these capitalist platforms but also legions of content moderators, trolls, and click farms—"live, paid social media operatives"—to global companies, politicians, and governments.[49] What the industry espies as "the raw energy of young and aggressive social media shape-shifters" to be harnessed might also be understood as capacities immanent in and honed through the capitalist subsumption of the dividual logics of vital platforms.

As I have described, vital platforms are dynamic human-mediatic technologies and institutions of social survival composed of kin and affiliative connections that act as active mediatic conduits of transmission, transaction, augmentation, depletion, conversion, and redemption of values in multiple currencies. Consisting of people deploying themselves, their bodies, their faculties, and their connections as creative media and objects of sociality-making exchange, these living platforms act as collective means of life, interlacing the gift economy of domestic communities with commodity exchanges of the capitalist economy. Hence, the vital platforms of kin communities are organizational forms that the political-police machine has long emulated and preyed on. After all, political machines and clans have long mixed up and fused ritual kinship practices with modes of tributary "help," practically subsumed under rent or crony capitalism. It is not surprising that these vital platforms have also been actively mobilized and grafted on as organizational systems supporting the war on drugs and its derivative enterprises of punitive value extraction. The political-police machine, which is central to Duterte's governance (the Philippine state platform), feeds on the risk-taking ventures of informal living on the part of the small-time social and kin networks of the poor.

Like the capitalist platforms of purportedly free, democratic exchange, which it ostensibly contests, the political platform of the illiberal Duterte regime relies on dynamic, nonfree modes and agents of life-making on the part of the disenfranchised. Police rely on these petty vital platforms of the poor as additional sources of revenue in the war on drugs (in subsidiary schemes of extortion, kidnap, or jail for ransom), even as they themselves are beneficiaries of value allocations (cuts, kickbacks, promotions) embedded in the vertical chain of command and the patronage of the state. In the drug trade and in *jueteng*, the petty gambling enterprise I discuss earlier, as well as in the police machine with which such illegal industries are carefully braided, the petty platforms of the poor are sources of liquid value, even as the individual components of such platforms are ultimately, completely expendable, their life-times of survival (embodied or objectified) intended to be finally used up or fully exhausted. But the aggregate value mopped up by these apparatuses of capture does not lie only in the expendable life-times of individual bodies or lives, but also in the generative engines of distribution and coordination of capacities, actions, performances, and events that are their kinship socialities, on which they vitally depend for their social reproduction.

The police thus benefit from two intersecting networks of "help" to summon flows of obligation—the vertical patron-client pyramid (with suppliers or sellers of money, drugs, power, or vote enterprises) and the horizontal or laterally extensive networks of subsistence of the poor communities involved in them. As documented by investigative reports, the police prey on people's filiative and affiliative communities, holding a member hostage in order to force their kin to generate revenue from their own connections and capacities, actual and promised, to pay for their lives.[50] Forced to source and hand over whatever resources of help that can be converted into money, and thereby producing, seemingly out of nothing, amounts of money that they would never have held in their own lifetimes, the families thus function for the police as a distributed mechanism for cashing in on multiple life-times beyond even the entireties of their own. What the police prey on, then, are not people as individuals but rather people as dividual components of social being.[51]

That it is living socialities that are the resource-objects of predation explains how the extraction can continue even after death. "Our children already died and they still want to rob us," Maria Isabelita, the mother of sixteen-year-old Sonny Espinosa, cried as she and others pleaded for the "authorized" funeral parlor to release the executed bodies of their kin. Blocking the mortician vehicles bearing the bodies, Jenny, the sister of fifteen-year-old Jonel Segovia, screamed, "You cannot take them and make us pay a fortune. We have no money to give you. Give us our dead!"[52] Where care for the dead remains part of life for the living, murdered bodies become the means for yet further extraction. Kristina, twenty-six-year-old mother of five, could claim the body of her murdered partner only upon signing a document attesting to her debt to the morgue.[53] Unable to afford the burial fees, she begged for donations for a month before the body's stench drew the local parish's attention and help in allowing her partner to be interred. The deaths of loved ones are made into debts for their surviving kin, who are in turn made into agents of value extraction. Mothers, grandmothers, sons, and daughters incur losses they are forced to pay for with their own lives and the lives of others, their own survival freely drawn on as resource for others in the aftermath of their own destruction.

Kin, Clans, Dividuals

"Kinship is a decisive marker and maker of value, not in terms of genealogical rules or norms of behavior, but because certain basic productive resources express and legitimate social relations and the cosmological antecedents in spite of all the exigencies that create loss."[54]

When her youngest son, Juancho, a garbage truck driver and scavenger, was killed by the police in a buy-bust operation, eighty-five-year-old Trining said, "It was like I died as well."[55] Kin, Sahlins writes, are "people who live each other's lives and die each other's deaths."[56] Accused of being a *kunsintador* (enabler, consenter, one who condones bad acts) of drug use, Trining is blamed by the police for her own son's death. With Juancho's wife, Lea, still in prison after being arrested months earlier as his substitute when the police could not find him, Trining became sole parent to their seven children. But what was initially felt as a burden—compounded by the eldest sixteen-year-old daughter's refusing to eat, for months, as a traumatized response to her father's death—became a lifeline. "My grandchildren are the only reason I wake up in the morning," she said. "Without them I have no more reason to live."[57]

Kinship networks have played complicated roles in postcolonial survival. In insular Southeast Asia, and perhaps in the broader Austronesian world, they persist as domestic communities, forms of precapitalist sociality organized as extended families and affiliative or ritual kin that, in serving as persistent modes of collective subsistence, paradoxically subsidize and maintain the periphery as a site of appropriation for capital. But kinship networks have also figured prominently within capitalist institutions, not least state apparatuses, and have even operated directly as capitalist corporations, including conglomerates of enterprise run by clans. Though kinship has long operated within industrial and postindustrial capitalist societies, its strength as an extant open logic of social organization (beyond the heteronormative, nuclear family) is structurally supported in the contexts of social strata that have historically served as noncapitalist milieus of capitalist accumulation (that is, modern colonized formations).[58] Hence it has been integral to the subsidiary forms of capitalism associated with the Global South, or what is known as predatory and crony capitalism.

For the police, as well as for other state apparatuses, these forms of kinship overlap and converge, even as the state form of political relations, sometimes known as "patronage politics," subsumes and overcodes the more ordinary cognatic forms of domestic kinship (comprising open, extended families, including their "ritual" relations) within its more vertical system of allocating power and privilege. Political clans and dynasties exemplify the fusing of modern state forms with traditional domestic (cognatic) kinship, becoming ways for kin networks to get access to powerful, legitimating forces.

Forces of sociality are not only the means of a domestic community's social reproduction but also the means of production and distribution of wealth, resources, and power. When directly connected to the state apparatus, or to ruling elites with political connections, the police are able to tap and manipulate their connections and, importantly, to leverage their authorized access to violence, in exchange for money, goods, privileges, and even greater or more valuable connections. Like the urban poor, with whom they are in proximate relations, and whose social, class worlds they are often intimately connected to or emerging from, the police moonlight as informal "fixers," extracting rent, ransom, convenience, and exoneration fees, as well as "gifts" or gratuities, through a manipulation of rules, regulations, and punishments of a bureaucratic system of civil and criminal justice. Police corruption depends on this simultaneous "playing" of the legal codes of modern social order and the social codes and tissue of older domestic communities.[59] They are, like urban poor "fixers" and other informal forms of livelihood, "petty adventurers" exacting value from conditions of instability that they themselves participate in generating through their selective manipulation and transgression of rules and connections.[60]

In contrast to the police, however, as the poor get poorer and poorer, more and more disenfranchised, their own social connections to powerful and wealthy families and clans become weaker and more tenuous, those relations replaced by "thinner" political relations established by monetary gifts and small favors. Certainly this describes the urban poor's relations to their political patrons, those who buy their electoral votes with public services, programs, and outright bribes. It also describes their relations to the police, the connections to whom mirror their connections to more powerful patrons. Ultimately, however, the poor's lack of "deeper" and more comprehensive social relations of mutual being with their benefactors, or with social networks of greater power, leave the disenfranchised without the protection of *authorized* belonging, making for their conditions of heightened exposure and vulnerability to absolute expendability.

In this way, the police in the drug wars and financial traders of derivatives are alike: the underlying "assets" they deal with are increasingly matters of indifference that can serve as pure means of value extraction, which are without value themselves—not simply that they are things, but that they are things without attachments, referents without social meaningfulness (*bagay*, or thing, also means "pertaining to" and "fitting," implying that things are never in-themselves but always of-other-things), enabling them to function as abstract signs and the vehicles of abstract signs. Money and violence as value-bearing signs are traded on the derealized lives that are these other signs (bodies without subjectivity, without connection to the transpersonal, mutual being of kin).

Like the matter of derivatives, those targeted for killing are priced (and ultimately derided) for the variability and contingency of their state. What more dramatic encapsulation of such contingency as that between life and death, the variability of being alive or dead? The arbitrary variability of their states can be imposed as precisely the consequence of the weakness or absence of their connectivity to power (not so much their complete atomization, since the urban poor continue to have vital social connectivities of their own). This "abstraction," in other words, is accomplished through their absolute desocialization, where "social" is at once defined by hegemonic parameters of political and class power and predicated on the fundamental rule of sociality of kinship, which *adiks* (addicts) are widely believed no longer to honor, such that even the urban poor share the sentiment that "drugs" put their users and purveyors completely out of reach of the basic bonds and obligations of domestic community (that "they would rape their own grandmother" is the rationale/proof of their expulsion from humanity). This imaginary removal from a shared social world is what enables their function not only as goods for material and monetary exchange—"exchanges in which human-life is price-tagged," as Jensen and Hapal put it—but also as simply the medium of other orders of exchange.

Put differently, desocialization, or the production of addicts in particular as the scourge of all sociality, is what permits others to dispose of them in ways that people have long offered up and deployed themselves, that is, as kinds of currency, but with the crucial difference that here they are without the social attachments that backed up the social significance and substance (or "value") of their lives. In this case, addicts are produced as tokens with no intrinsic social use-value, except for an attributive capacity and variability that allows them to function as underlying assets of others' financial speculation and return. This is in fact the crucial difference between their role as media of transaction for the families to whom they belong (for whom they are constitutive, agential parts) and their treatment as socially dead coin for others' gain. This latter treatment is encapsulated by the practice of *palit-ulo* (literally, "head exchange"), whereby a family member, friend, or acquaintance is kidnapped in place of another, to flush out or extort an exchange of persons or cash (where the price of one's own life is the life of another, or its monetary equivalent). For the police, each and every one of these slum dwellers exist only as "pure," abstract specie of capitalist exchange.

This nationwide desocialization of a sector of the nation has been the accomplishment and aim of a generalized, decentralized counterinsurgent war shifting its sights from a contained, rural threat (communist guerillas, Muslim rebels) to a criminalized, urban population. Through its installation in everyday practice and feeling, such counterinsurgent war and its retributive justice has facilitated the transformation of the local social order from an older postcolonial order of routine tributary violence (predictable everyday police abuse and exploitation, which is fundamentally negotiable because always personal)[61] to a global capitalist order of violence and punitive value extraction that is algorithmic, expanding exponentially through the franchising of state violence, scaling fractally, not unlike the expansion of city everywhere, of which it is an indispensable condition.

Like the powers of defending freedom, the powers of expending life are exercised to reclaim a global form of life deemed human. But as the cases of Israel and the Philippines demonstrate, the life of value promised by these sovereign territorial states is secured and paid for by means of an unending war of multiplying dead exchanges.

How then to defend or militate against "life worth expending" without redeeming it through servitude or conscription to a global, capitalist "life worth living" with all that such valued life depends on? Along with money and violence, words and images are not only among the contents and actions (the currencies) fueling these subaltern capitalist platforms but also among the power signs (gifts, help, tributes) *making* them (creating the pathways of these organizing systems of both life-making and life-taking).

In the context of the fatal signifying and asignifying practices of platform totalitarianism, we are confronted with questions about the political import of the words and images we circulate among ourselves. As Dalena's "Dear Artist" poignantly demonstrates (and—as I hear it in another, related urban context of systemic, inflicted Black death—in Kendrick Lamar's "Sing about Me, I'm Dying of Thirst"), these are questions asked by and to artists themselves, posed in the voices of the slain and the suffering, beseeching artists for slogans and songs, voices we might hear addressing us all.[62]

10

LIVE BORROWINGS, LIVING CONNECTIONS

A tremendous amount of public, scholarly, and artistic attention has turned to waste. Whether in the form of mountains of garbage accumulating in toxic sinkholes, or in the form of people deemed the human refuse of the social orders from which they are expelled and from which they will continue to be excluded, "waste" has become the object of much critique and concern, serving to crystallize the violence endemic to the creation and accumulation of modern, capitalist value.

For some, the wasted lives of others—those appearing on the shores of the Global North, trying to climb its fortress walls and cross its desert and ocean moats, placed in camps in indefinite detention—are merely the outcasts of modernity. The production of "human waste," as Zygmunt Bauman writes, is "an inevitable outcome of modernization and an inseparable accompaniment of modernity," that is, the untoward side effect of order building and economic progress, for which colonization and imperialism provided the territories for dumping and containing, making the disposal of human waste produced in the so-called modernized and still modernizing parts of the globe "the deepest meaning of colonization and imperialist conquests."[1]

Now, the sociologist argues, with the planetary dominion of such "modernity," these untoward effects "have come home to roost."

Besides occluding the obvious fact, or meaning, if you will, that there would have been no modernization of Europe without the prior violent wasting of humans and lifeworlds in the colonies, the critical sociologist repeats and reproduces an all-too-familiar stance of the West envisioning the rest of the world as no more than the consequence of an original agency identified as exclusively and deplorably its own. The critical view toward such wasted lives as a lamentable tragedy of the West's own doing—the tragedy of imperial ruination—provides impetus for another familiar response, which is the reassumption of that original agency to resolve the problem it had the power to create, or, worse, the contemplation of the sublime image of imperial power that can lead to one's safe restoration as an ethical human subject.[2] More than a will to action, this is a sensibility of the already human toward their wretched others, who provoke in the cosmopolitan inheritors of the earth that mix of pity and disgust, compassion and contempt, nostalgia and resentment, indignation and regret, which the very colonial idea of human waste provokes. After all, human waste can only be the abjected part of a humanity that some assume themselves to have already attained, whether as a natural condition or an achieved status, like freedom. It only remains for the already human to bring the outcasts back into the fold of protected, rightful belonging.

Waste as Art

In the humanitarian turn of the arts, something of this sensibility appears to obtain. It is perhaps no wonder that museums and other institutional purveyors of valuable culture should participate in this form of redress and redemption. In an exhibit entitled "Solution or Utopia: Design for Refugees" held at the Stedelijk museum in Amsterdam in 2017, for example, artists and designers were called upon "to improve the temporary situation of refugees" and "to devise practical, real-life solutions" to the problem of "60 million people fleeing war, or displaced for some other reasons."[3] The exhibition, which included submissions to the 2016 Refugee Challenge competition sponsored by the UNHCR (UN Refugee Agency) and IKEA, features a biodegradable sheet that turns into a tent and can be worn as a raincoat; a baby carrier that converts into a hammock and children's outerwear; flags and totes made from the life jackets worn by refugees and discarded on the beaches of Greece; refugee-specific visual aids, directional signage, and emojis; and improved, environmentally sustainable, and humane disaster shelters and temporary housing, including a "pee power" urinal that converts urine into electrical energy to illuminate refugee camps, making it safe, for women especially, to walk at night and saving host governments and citizens financial costs.[4]

While there is no gainsaying the brilliance of many of these designs, it is also impossible not to see how art and design are conscripted to ameliorate catastrophe, to make refugees at home in the very condition of homelessness and forced nomadism that they find themselves in, to revalue and incorporate the excluded, indeed, to make the disposable life of others the occasion, the impetus, and the material for creative endeavor and innovation. In these artistic projects turned to humanitarian ends, we see a sensibility shared and expressed by contemporary capital, a feeling sense of the potential value of refuse, a disposition toward the excluded, inassimilable, and excremental as the aim, means, and object of a redemptive, creative agency, one that can fulfill in the present a vision of the future in which "there will be no difference between waste and energy."[5]

The nondistinction between waste and energy pronounced by one of the world's leading international banks confirms the reconfigured centrality of expenditure to the mode of life of global capital. What Baudrillard had argued as the logic of the sign, in contradistinction to that of capital, and Bataille had argued as a general economy in opposition to the restricted economy of capitalist production, that is, a logic and economy of *expenditure* of surplus (counterposed to a logic and economy of production and accumulation), has in fact been the disavowed colonial and imperial mode of so-called original accumulation that has until the present continuously buttressed the capitalist processes of value production. As Baudrillard writes, "In the economic order, it is the mastery of *accumulation*, of the appropriation of surplus value, which is essential. In the order of signs (of culture), it is the mastery of *expenditure* that is decisive, that is, a mastery of the transubstantiation of economic exchange value into sign exchange value based on a monopoly of the code."[6] Although Baudrillard argues that this political economy of the sign, as a logic of expenditure, proceeds in the opposite direction of political economy, the logic of accumulation, "this immense transmutation of all values (labor, knowledge, social relations, culture, nature) into economic exchange value,"[7] could we not argue that expenditure has, in the contemporary confrontation with the limits of global accumulation, become internal to—been made a moment or aspect in—the expanded political economy of life? We could argue furthermore that this system of sign production has become a process of productive consumption, which realizes in expenditure the values of speculative enterprises: that is, the promised life-times of others.

Today, forms of life expenditure are at the visible forefront of a permanent capitalist war economy, which cannibalizes and profiteers off of the forms of social detritus and debility it actively produces (fueling derivative enterprises dedicated to managing, securing, eliminating, warehousing, processing, and even partially recuperating, lives that are to be spent down). Through financialization (predatory international loans and investments procured and paid for with currency devaluations, casualization of labor, and the like) entire disposable populations' past and future life-times are aggregated and monetized, cashed in, liquefied.

In this global context in which not only wasted lives but the active practice of wasting lives has become a new energy source for global capital, when life worth living means "spending it well"; when the valorization of metropolitanist communicative, social, and cultural activities—which form the highest value-accruing capitalist industries of circulation (social media and software-as-business platforms, currency markets, and global art)—depends on the expendability and expenditure of the life-times of populations of the dispossessed, the spent life of others that makes for the splendid living well of some; and where stratospheric currency and stock values can finally only ever be realized through their spending down (the liquidation or promised allocation) of the infinite life-times of others, past, present, and future (in produced goods, live service, future generational life), how do we attend to disposable life without converting it into merely the matter and means of value-productive activity and enterprise?

Art as Counterattack

This low-production protest graphic art portraying the dead bodies of the killed as background matter to spell the name and power of their expending (figure 10.1; EJK is the common way to refer extrajudicial killings) was part of a collection of zines published by RESBAK (Respond and Break the Silence against the Killings), a broad alliance of artists, media practitioners, and cultural workers formed in political response and resistance against Philippine president Rodrigo Duterte's war on drugs. Since the beginning of this war, RESBAK has produced an outpouring of work, performances, events, workshops, and demonstrations with the stated objectives of advancing public awareness of the extrajudicial killings and of giving voice to the frontline victims of the state in its war on drugs—those they identify as that sector of the poor who do not have anyone to take their side (*walang makilingan*). Hence, RESBAK, which is Filipino slang for collective retaliation, or "counterattack"

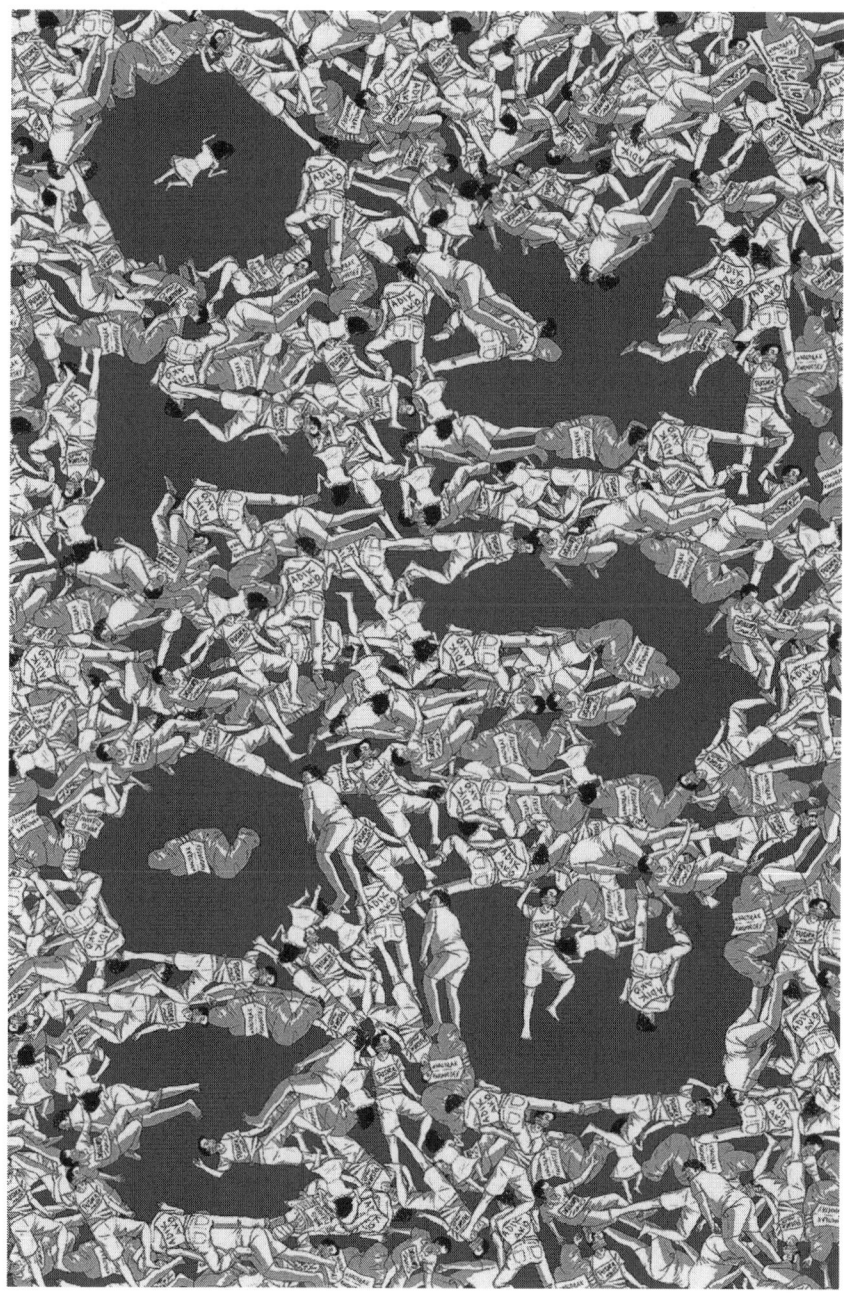

FIGURE 10.1. Andoyman Komikero, *No to EJK*, August 18, 2018, digital artwork, Philippines. Courtesy of the artist.

(from the English, *wrest back*), is a form of "getting back" by the people who have your back. In many ways, it makes good on the rationalizing accusation by the police that victims "fought back" (*nanlaban*) by making this "crime" (of fighting back) an act of collective resistance.

The images of Andoyman Komikero register the apprehension of the scale of the death toll, which RESBAK was carefully recording, alongside a group of journalistic photographers called the Nightcrawlers who, according to Ezra Acayan, a member of the group, have committed themselves to photographing each and every killing as part of a continuing collective plea for public sympathy and as part of a documentary archiving of evidence of the murders and the murderers' impunity for the possibility of future justice.[8] The preoccupation with numbers undoubtedly speaks to the alarming scale and acceleration of a phenomenon that is not unknown in a country that has seen tens of thousands of cases of extrajudicial killings, disappearances, torture, rape, and other forms of punishment carried out by the counterinsurgent Philippine state over the course of almost fifty years, since the dictatorship of Ferdinand Marcos.

Graphic images of bodily suffering and hardship, spectacles of human disposability embodied in the dead and dying of the Global South, have been ubiquitous in the global media. Undoubtedly, such images reflect the realities of a global order of open-ended counterinsurgent civil war. But this very fidelity to such realities, the adherence to the very protocols of what Gayatri Spivak long ago called attention to as "the staging of the world in representation" that overdetermines its factual givenness (the givenness of visual media's worldly referents), has also proven to be a near insurmountable limit of much photographic media reportage, or at the very least, its reception.[9]

In their appeal to the prior humanity of their viewers—a humanity whose gaze out at the rest of the world has been aesthetically shaped by the high production value, glossy global cinema of spectacle, and the infinite pulverization and titration of value-adding attention by social media feeds—images of the violence of human disposability can reprise the violence of the enumerability of the always already violated and violent less-than-human, embodying the brutality they suffer, which is presumed to be endogenous to them, this "cyclical and death-dealing numeration of the condemned," which Katherine McKittrick calls the mathematics of black life.[10]

The mathematics of black and blackened life bears multiple, exponential uses in a capitalist war economy of signs. As these cartoons of the dead of the drug wars illustrate, dead bodies have become the media of messages—in the case of the drug war, of fatal messages, the very matter on which sovereign nationalism is erected and stakes its glory. The continuing piling up of the bodies, despite the extensive coverage, testifies to the limits of graphic, realist documentation of the murdered bodies to rouse and sustain the humane sentiments expected to disturb the just war. That war after all speaks to a humanity that defines itself against these expendable bodies. Moreover, in an era when waste becomes the object and site of revaluation of new (up)cycles of valorization, dead bodies are also always a matter and means of signifying and asignifying exchanges in derivative enterprises of communicative capitalism.

It is in this context—in which a political economy of death is upheld by a political economy of signs through which the expenditure of life is made productive—that many of the oppositional images and artworks created by RESBAK artists "borrow" signs from the material imagery and general aesthetic order of the war on drugs, repeating and reversing them or spinning them in other directions. Many of the protest works reference, for example, the cardboard signs killers used to leave either on or beside the dead bodies of victims, a characteristic feature of the killings during the first years of the operations. The hand scrawled messages, which were always variation on a theme— "Drug addict. Do not emulate."—were part of the "signature style" of the killers, which included wrapping the head of the murdered body in brown packing tape, a "style" that has also become the subject of numerous works of art.

Jason Dy's sculptural piece *Tagapagligtas Ako* (I am the redeemer) (which I discuss in chapter 9), cites this signature style by wrapping a plaster cast figure of the Santo Niño (baby Jesus) in the same kind of brown packing tape used to silence, suffocate, and obliterate the human countenance of the killed. Dy's switching out of the head and face of the condemned with the body of baby Christ, which converts the death-dealing weapon into a life-protective cloth, is an unholy mixing of the message of this medium of murderous power with the message and figure of divine redemption, evoking the feeling of sacrilege and abomination among the devout. The play on the signs of the murders constitutes an aggressive, retaliatory gesture, a mockery of the mock redemption promised. Like many protest works recasting and playing on Raffy Lerma's photograph "Pietà," which went viral and induced Duterte and numerous supporters to denounce the photograph as "melodramatic," "staged," and "fake," Dy's work exemplifies numerous attempts to resacralize those who precisely cannot be sacrificed, calling for a revaluation of the values that underwrite the war.

In the popular imaginary of those who support the war on drugs, addicts are figured as *salot* (scourge, or pestilence)—what would destroy life and thus must itself be destroyed—the object of a racializing project that is supported and subsidized by, but also counterposed to, that other racializing project of feminized reproductive labor that is global servitude. Against the Christlike sacrifice of ordinary Filipinos servicing the nation with their overseas labor, which had long been heroicized by the labor-exporting state for its state-saving remittances, *adiks* came to figure a disgusting blight of useless, worthless, criminal slum trash laying to waste all that had been hard-earned and well-deserved, a plague of the living dead destroying the nation with the disease of their own pronounced social death. That the same materials used to "sign" the killings—cardboard and packing tape—are materials identified with the *balikbayan* boxes full of goods that overseas Filipino workers periodically send home as gestures of their love and care (like their remittances, proving their worth to the nation) indexes the material-semiotic connection and opposition between the worthlessness of one and the serviceability of the other.

The "style" of the killings is thus a reflection and exercise of an aesthetic judgment on *salot* as an object of just hatred and fear that anchors the sensus communis of an avenging nation, a "style" that is rhetorically exemplified by the widely-enjoyed vulgar, smutty, and aggressively foul character of Duterte's speech and humor, which is experienced as the inverse of the inaccessible, misleading, and hypocritical polite speech of elite democracy, identified with the oligarchic liberalism installed after the fall of Marcos. An aesthetic of graphic, vulgar speech and representation permeates the social mediascape of the Duterte platform, where dead bodies and cardboard signs, things and words, are equally message and medium, vehicles of value-productive circulation, where derealized lives are memes, word-images, circulating affective structures and performative gestures that drive political fascism and capitalist platforms in tandem. As satirized in Mikael Rabara's political parable "Doon Po Sa Amin" (Over where we live), which tells the tale of a place where people addicted to the type font Comic Sans are slain, the killings issue out of an aesthetic (as much as out of social, political, and economic command) which stokes disgust and revulsion at the object of filth and takes pleasure in its riddance.[11] In contrast to employment, which has come to embody sacrifice through the figuration of the heroes and martyrs of the nation working overseas, young men hanging out on street corners (or *tambay*, from "standby") are the image of the permanently unemployed, figured no longer as idle "reserves" (waiting, ready to be disposed, on standby) but rather as corrupting detritus, "lazy and given to wicked habits" (*tamad pero mabisyo*)—the designation *salot*, the very proof of being so: "they are pestilence because they look like and appear as pestilence" (*siya ay salot*

FIGURE 10.2. Juan Luna, *Spolarium*, 1884, oil on canvas; National Museum of Fine Arts, Manila. Awarded a gold medal in the *Exposición Nacional de Bellas Artes* in 1884, the work has long been viewed as an allegorical critique of Spanish colonialism, and part of the reformist Propaganda Movement preceding the nationalist revolutionary movement against Spain in 1896.

dahil mukha at asta siyang salot).[12] Like names on the watch list of drug addicts, the distinction between sign and being, act, judgment, and execution has collapsed. It is this political-aesthetic order that resistance art struggles with great difficulty to oppose and reverse through a recasting of signs.

Against these dead exchanges, RESBAK artists endeavor to rework the materials, signs, and images of the state-sponsored and state-upholding visual and aural order. They are drawing on different times, reconnecting to past struggles through a replaying and recasting of images from those times, extending the timeline of social grief and broadening as well as redrawing the social body of that grief.

Images by Bam Doctor (figure 10.3) and Patricia Ramos (figure 10.4), for example, recast, respectively, torture and murder under Marcos and extrajudicial killings under Duterte in the form of Juan Luna's late nineteenth-century anticolonial painting *Spolarium* (figure 10.2), literalizing the scene of dead gladiators that Luna used as an allegorical depiction of the brutality of colonial Spanish rule. Other artists replay images from the Marcos era, switching out the faces of Marcos and Duterte, juxtaposing them, or merging them to make uncanny resemblances, morphed forms.[13]

Live Borrowings, Living Connections • 265

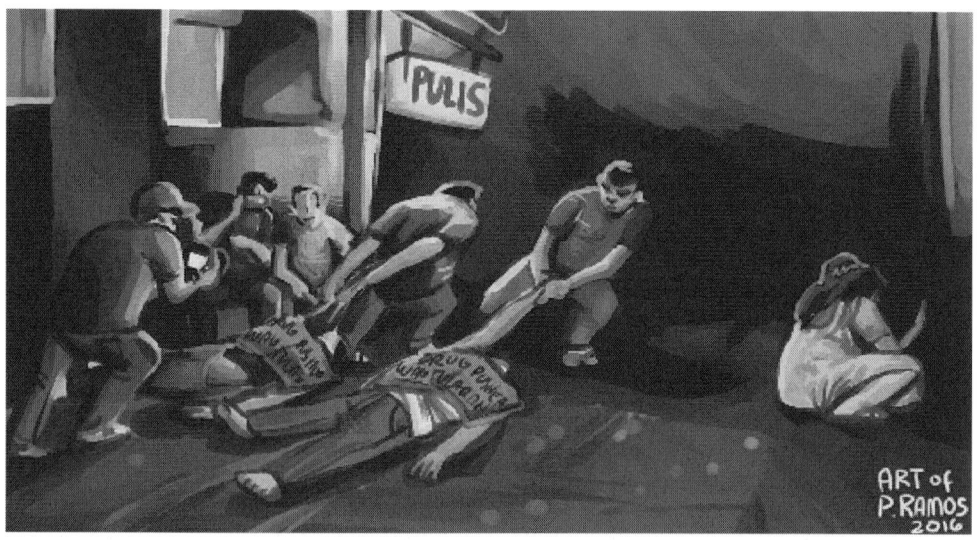

FIGURE 10.3. Bam Doctor, *Tortyur Rum*, November 14, 2018, digital artwork. Courtesy of the artist.

FIGURE 10.4. Patricia Ramos, *Spolarium*, July 19, 2016, digital artwork. Courtesy of the artist.

FIGURE 10.5. RESBAK Collective, "Stop the Killings." A traveling public intervention displaying a fabric banner with words composed of mosaic tile. Pictured at the Plaza Simón Bolivar in November 2017, led by Kiri Dalena, as part of *Tiempos Migratorios* (Migratory times), VIII Bienal ASAB, SALASAB, Bogotá, Colombia. Photo courtesy of Yu-Wen Wu.

The artists are trading on derivative means to oppositional aims. Challenging themselves to work with the materials and on the very media platforms on which dominant forces were staging their retributive power, they "fought back" with old and new popular forms.[14] From a Christmas song videoke (video karaoke) circulated on Facebook—in which survivors in slum communities as well as diasporic Filipinos hold cardboard placards written with politically resistant lyrics to be collectively sung, each shot flickering with light and movement and held to the rhythm of a rewritten popular song—to a banner with the words STOP THE KILLINGS, their letters composed of eight thousand mourning pins (symbolizing the number of deaths at the time of its making), passed on from gathering to gathering across different parts of the world, with other people enlisted to literally stand behind it in solidarity, artists are engaging in live borrowings. While the words in the videoke are prompts for a collective, political carol, with members of targeted communities "signifying" the sentiments to be sung, their living bodies, sitting or standing in their homes and neighborhood, serving as the standard bearers of another "messaging," the words on the traveling STOP THE KILLINGS banner serve not only to convey a semantic message, but also function as an enunciative physical object whose own conveyance across contexts through the social and political networks of RESBAK artists is itself the process of extending those networks of solidarity and dissent. From Manila to Bogotá, Washington, DC, to Berlin, the banner traveled with and through artists and allies, occasioning the temporary organization of audiences and strangers, physically requiring people to stand behind and support the unfurling of a message in plazas and streets elsewhere. With every group performance of the upheld words photographed and shared on social media, humans offered themselves as the media of communicative acts geared toward the constitution of a different translocal and transnational political platform.

If words and images are the means for making and remaking the socialities that are "social networks"—that is, if they are part of vital platforms, the very means of social reproduction and the survival of disposable life—the political import of the configuration of words and images, of signifying and performative gestures, lies in great part in these kinds of social making that they are moments and means of. In this context replete with speech acts as political claims, representational statements, and expressive demands, the evacuation, by RESBAK's founding artist Kiri Dalena, of the placards of historical photographs of past protests and demonstrations do not only call for new words, new slogans (see figure 10.6).

Dalena's photographs also show people standing with nothing but poster paper as barriers, protection, and screens—as if self-guarded but defenseless against police and cameras and spectators, "speechless" yet demanding, "wanting" participatory inscription, like unfinished memes. We might compare them to the kerchiefs with which survivors wrapped their own heads, on which expressive faces were drawn to mask their own to protect themselves and their families as they joined protest rallies against the government.

Photographed by Raffy Lerma and others, the kerchiefs at once reiterate and depart from photographs of the wrapped heads of those killed, smiley faces drawn on them by their murderers. In striking contrast to the latter, the kerchiefs worn by survivors present sad faces and tearful eyes—expressive slogans donned by live persons circulating among the crowds marching and protesting on the streets. As in Dalena's emptied photographs, the living are the bearers of signs awaiting action or response. The survivors are live media of messages of their own persistence and resistance against being the mere substrates of the state's writing, speaking their grief in minimalist strokes, with their fullest expression yet to be realized.

FIGURE 10.6. Kiri Lluch Dalena, *Erased Slogans*, 2016, digitally altered archival photographs. 1355 Mabini, Metro Manila. Courtesy of the artist.

FIGURE 10.7. Raffy Lerma, *Masks (The Ones Left Behind)*, 2018, photograph. Among a crowd of thousands, relatives of victims of extrajudicial killings (whose faces are covered to conceal their identities) listen as names of those killed under President Rodrigo Duterte's administration are enumerated during a protest held simultaneous to his annual third State of the Nation Address on July 24, 2018, on Commonwealth Avenue, Quezon City, Philippines. In his address, Duterte declared that the war on drugs would not stop and would be as chilling and relentless as the day it began.

Live Media, Live Exchange

Talk of weaponizing language, images, and performative utterances obscures how representations have also long served as things and forms of action, where signs are also gifts of live exchange, as in the case of so-called ritual speech, which serves as much to constitute social relations as to impart meaning. Artists and photographers themselves have been lending themselves as the means of such sociality, dividual parts of emergent vital platforms of another kind. With the crucial cooperative help of the urban poor activist organization KADAMAY (Kalipunan ng Damayang Mahihirap; National Alliance for Filipino Urban Poor), RESBAK artists have sought not simply to represent the suffering of urban poor communities but to commune and collaborate with them in the creation and performance of expressive forms with practical aims. Ea Torrado and the Daloy Dance Company, for example, worked with survivors in movement workshops and performances, engaging them in the bodily working through of their grief, in the bodily telling of their stories, which also became acts of healing and, through this shared grieving, the suturing of a community of survival.

Moved by the suffering of grieving families of the killed and called on by them to "help," many of the Nightcrawler photographers have departed from the documentary realist aims of photographs of the dead, attending hundreds of funerals, listening to the stories of their families, becoming their friends, their witnesses, and their advocates. They train their lenses on the living—the parents, grandparents, siblings, and children of the killed—sharing their stories and the images of their pain and strife, the places and details of their aspirations. Many have become activists, answering the plea staged by Dalena's work, not by writing new slogans but rather by amplifying the cries and demands of people with whom they have forged relations. The images as well as the words they offer with them, the stories they tell of their own experiences and the experiences of the suffering, and the photographs of mass actions and protests on behalf of these communities they are making their own—which photographers like Raffy Lerma and Ezra Acayan share from their own personal or collective accounts on social media—these words and images become gestures of *pakikidalamhati*, social practices of sharing and participating in grieving, through which their own networks are reshaped and extended.

The creative works of RESBAK and its growing network of collaborating partners shift our attention away from the redemption of old values or the production of new values. As this alliance reaches out to other groups, other people, who themselves are parts of other groups, in multiple cultural collaborations, in the organizing of collective events and activities, the words and images they produce together serve as gifts, offerings, and help in a different social economy intended to sustain them all. Working and making an expanding network of social networks create the possibility of making and doing more. As Faye Cura, of the feminist collective Gantala Press, one of RESBAK's collaborative partners, writes in the context of another project that sought to defend and listen to the most subaltern social strata (in response to Duterte's military siege against Marawi and imposition of martial law): "We could do this if we claimed and strengthened our own spaces of movement. As individuals, it's easy to contribute financial help to fellow citizens who have been victimized. But we were already a group that was friends with other groups and with other individuals, each of whom also had their own group. That being the case: there was still more that we could do."[15]

Describing the series of activities and events made possible by this network of networks, "movements" that fueled activist organization programs for food and psychosocial services for the evacuees, including the clearing of spaces in evacuation centers for the practice of Islamic faith, Cura articulates a feminist ethos and practice of embracing and strengthening the very spaces and means of people's survival, including that deterritorial space of distributed movement and action consisting of vital, life-making connectivity, which domestic communities continue to depend on as the matrices of their social reproduction. It is these newly interlaced matrices of people lending themselves and their own networks of social belonging that make for the possibilities of making and doing more.

Put toward remaking social life with communities, which the nation consigns to disposability, these creative works call attention to the social milieus that art emerges out of and reproduces within the global order of capitalist production and consumption.[16] Rather than reproducing dominant social milieus of art for its own sake (that is, to reproduce the art world as a value-productive industry), the activist artwork of RESBAK mobilizes and extends and recreates existing socialities of dissent and sustenance.[17] Here, words and images serve as gifts and help in the making of another social economy in which those who struggle the most to survive, "those hard up and without anyone to lean on" (*mga mahirap at walang makilingan*), can fully belong. In this collective project, art returns to its role as mode of expressivity for collective life, healing and sustaining and animating transpersonal spirit and feeling, affirming and building, reaching for another community.

FIGURE 10.8. Video still from *Tokhanginamo Unabes!* (2017), directed by Sigrid Andrea Bernardo. Courtesy of RESBAK.

Irreverent Borrowings, Serious Play, Irredeemable Flourish

Those who struggle do not struggle on the edge of life, but in the midst of it. Struggle is life and vice versa. One does not struggle in order to live "later on." The struggle requires organization—the organization of life is equivalent to the organization of struggle. And in life, as in the struggle, there is everything, including enjoyment. —JULIO GARCIA ESPINOSA, "For an Imperfect Cinema"

In the effort to both adopt and speak to the aesthetics of a broad, entertainment-saturated, beauty pageant–watching nation of Facebook users, RESBAK produced a comedic infotainment video, *Tokhanginamo Unabes!* (2017, dir. Sigrid Andrea Bernard), to circulate on the very capitalist platform on which the war on drugs was simultaneously being waged, as a way of disseminating important information for communities affected by Oplan Tokhang, the "Knock and Plead" drug war operation of the police. The video stages a small version of the popular genre of the *bakla* beauty pageant, here "Miss Unabes"—a play on "Miss Universe"; and swardspeak, or queer Filipino slang, for (girl)friend—in one of the slum neighborhoods targeted by the drug war, with *bakla* members of the same community acting as beauty contestants.

On the catwalk, beauty contestants each carry cardboard placards, like the ones used in the killings, with the names of the countries announced—Kenya, Haiti, Malaysia, and "Pinas" (slang for Philippines)—representing not just the proper names of nations they purportedly represent but also partial or whole Filipino words as declarations of "messages" about the killings. For example, the candidate from Kenya plays on the word *kanya* (his/hers/theirs) to declare that the rights of victims are not anyone else's (not yours, not ours) but their own; the candidate from Haiti plays on its imperfect homophone, *eighty*, to declare that the number of killings has reached nearly eight thousand, and to proclaim against those responsible, "I hait [hate] you"; the candidate from Malaysia plays on the word *malay* (aware/conscious) to caution the lack of, and insist on the need for, greater awareness; and the candidate from "Pinas" plays on the word *pinaslang* (slayed) to denounce how many family members, beloved, and siblings have been killed.

Although it is impossible to adequately reproduce and convey the funny, cheesy wordplay and rhyming performances of each candidate's "speech" in English translation—which reduces the multilingual play to monolingual utterances—I want to note the effect of their everyday humor in disarming the words and images of the drug war, here the fatal "identifying" function of the cardboard placards and the "meaning" of such killings for the nation (*Pinas*; *pinaslang*). The play continues in the parodic "interview" of "Pinas" who, in a complete turnaround from her initial performance of the stereotype of the Filipina beauty contestant—made dumb and ridiculous by having to make sense in English (a long-standing inside joke that plays on the gap between cosmopolitan ideals and local realities, between veneer and vernacular)—suddenly switches languages and demeanor to become a clear, confident spokesperson conveying important information on the rights and resources of people targeted by Tokhang, even as that message continues to be conveyed through the frivolous gestures of hyperfemininity.

Irreverent borrowings based on the sensual rather than semiotic properties of signs are the means by which other messages are smuggled and communicated within conventional forms, other social acts performed. The name of the video itself, *Tokhanginamo Unabes!*, is the conjugation of the coined word for the deadly operation, *tokhang* (knock-plead), in the form of the widely used curse, *putang ina mo* (fuck you; your mother's a whore), which came to be associated with Duterte's foul speech as president. *Tokhanginamo* might thus be understood as *fuck your knock-plead*, or *your knock-plead is a whore*, or *knock-plead, your mother* (your mama!). Combined with *bes*, or (girl)friend, with which the beauty pageant is also dubbed (*Miss Universe* becoming *Miss Unabes*, signaling a unity or solidarity, rather than a competition, of girlfriends), it is a form of retaliatory speech (a verbal form of *resbak*) as inside joke, a collective-solidifying, emboldening jest.

In this serious play, variation, and transmutation of forms, with their abundant smuggled and stolen meaning effects exceeding the important practical information finally conveyed, we might glean an aesthetics of remaindered life. Not simply an oppositional aesthetics of the slums, set against the aesthetics of metropolitan urbanism bearing down on the life it would expend, but a glorious, hilarious surfing of signs and an indulgent, sensuous, substitutive, and perverse play of bodies, words, and things as artifices with infinite mutational capacities. Counterposed to the stilled, abstracted bodies and identities and straightforward speech—fixed by the value logic of the spectacular killings and the territorial capture and subsequent holding of globopolitical life, transubstantiating expendable life into capitalist wealth—these are transmutational, shape- and sense-shifting practices with no calculated end. Like the play time of children and others, which Cindi Katz sees as intrinsic time, "time lived as 'disposable,' but not at all a 'waste of time' as it is so often constructed," these are practices that are "generative and full of possibilities."[18] While no doubt a generalized notion of "creative play" (as labor) has itself become valorized in contemporary capitalist platforms, these are practices of play that derive their pleasures from invoking and eluding codes of being, practices of flourish that create thriving and enjoyment on the tangents and cusps of enclosure, which make them difficult to program into more serviceable protocols for life-times of value.

After all, these transmutational, shape- and sense-shifting practices and capacities are also the mode and excess of everyday living on the part of those who are themselves considered without a serious stake in or hold on humanity—passing through, never arriving, forever becoming. They are parts of the experience and experiment of habitual "release from the confines and constraints of proper speech" for *bakla* or queer/queen and trans communities and the open communities who embrace their belonging, all creating social survival on the live borrowings, puns, and play on cast-offs, copies, derivatives, and remnants of ideal and proper or normative forms and languages of social life, which Martin Manalansan, Lucy Burns, and Sarita See consider part of the performative cultures of Filipinx communities making life and resistance in the interstices and margins of a colonial, sexual order.[19] These are forms and spaces of life-times sustained by and delighting in mercurial mutation, the play of living in transit, moving between dominant and subordinated, multiple codes, performing an extravagant virtuosity, which reverberates with the modes of living of the becoming-human.

Here is one fleeting glimpse of remaindered life, here the unexpected gratuitous abundance, or splendor, that might unfold in the everyday arts of survival. Splendor is in the play of nation's names, the flourish of wordplay, the pleasures of the surface play of signs, of bodies as signs, within the practical communication of rights—surplus gestures, surplus meaning, words and images in excess of their signifying and asignifying political intents, enjoyed by the communities themselves.[20] These are also life-times of expenditure, times of waste, but unredeemed, not simply placed to more productive ends—times of waste that are also times of re-creation, openings, cheap thrills, and boundless relation. This is an aesthetics of splendor, not unlike the petty rapture glimpsed and honored by the playwright Floy Quintos in his homage to the low, unrighteous life elevated by the "Pietà" photograph circulating in search of the dead's redemption:

> the righteous will never know
> the highs of love among the dazed,
> or the soaring rush of joy that frees the damned.
> They who have lived all their lives in righteousness
> will never know
> what you and i have known.
> Ah yes, the wrong we have known, *bebe ko*.[21]

Many Pasts Continue, Many Presents Lie in Wait

Thinkers in advanced capitalist nations like the United States tend to stress invention and innovation as the mode and space of resistance and transformation. They are enamored with the idea of constitutive performances, forms of making out of material nothings, as if blank states were transgressive against the baggage and bonds of history and order, and norms and conventions the enemies of that elusive ideal of freedom.

The bravado of masculinist, liberal sovereignty coursing through quasi-radical, emancipatory veins only makes things worse. It pretends it owes no one or nothing the grounds on which it stands, the flesh on its bones, the glimmer in its eyes, the sweat on its brow, the figment of its imagination. Always, the agent or place of promise must be an in-itself, first and foremost, and never fundamentally a being-for-others, or being-in-others. That is reserved for natives and savages, those who continue to stand at the opposite end of the human, on the other side of the spectrum of value and culture. If one thinks that this might have characterized the past of humanism and not the present (*its* present), they ignore the tenacity of colonial axioms in capitalist inventiveness and innovation as well as in many political radicalisms. For it is a colonial axiom that the past is overcome or superseded by the present, that, precisely in the image of settler ideals of cleared, uncultivated land, what continues through time is only the essence or spirit of matter in some value form, which sovereign agency itself introduces, as the fruit of its own, proper seed.

Yet many pasts continue, not least in the resistance that is happening constantly in the world, the forms of organized and unorganized everyday resistance without which there would be even less survival. These are pasts of unfinished decolonizing struggles, which bequeath to generations the methods and memories of communal aspiration and life-making. It is these immaterial inheritances that are also important to the present: the pasts present in continuing living. Not only the new political economy of life, with its permanent war and derivative economies, that now obtains as the latest development of global capital. Nor only the relentless foundational programs of dispossession and tortuous assault and murder that continue to animate the present. But also the ways of living, passed on and adapted, that have made and shaped such developments—the lives of liquidity and their malleable social assets (their platforms); the modes of living that are both invention and convention of assaulted social life, that have also become an important feature of capital's and capitalist survival; the splendor of *retasos* (remnants) and useless nothings (of tossing around imaginary footballs in proscribed games,[22] of playing for unreal, of small highs and elaborate send-ups) that are, only for a little while, part of the ephemeral commons which have not yet been subsumed by capital, only unknowingly remaindered, left to a newly discardable nature (in the face of an unruly nature foraged, grasped, and valorized—where "roughness," "wild variability," and "disequilibrium" in financial and urbanist imaginations are the fetish objects of a new calculus, replacing the romanticized savages of past idylls and utopias with the newly discernible geometric patterns of nonhuman natures: cellular automata, turbulence, edge-of-chaos models of complexity and emergence).[23]

Often what is forgotten is the sadness. The sadness of being shorn of being for others to whom one belongs, shorn of their being for one in return. In the course of rallying forces to fight for another world or this one, to go to battle for a future one foresees or knows, we look past the sadness, even make light of it. The sadness might be nodded to in passing, as further proof of suffering and pain, as reason for restoration or change, as argument for action. And yet still it weighs.

We feel that sadness in Nanay Mameng (Carmen Deunida), the eighty-year-old urban political and women's rights activist who is the focus of Adjani Arumpac's 2013 documentary of the same name. As we follow Nanay

Mameng's inspiring life and spirit, protesting and fighting against structural injustices for more than forty-two years, through thirteen presidencies, undaunted by not having witnessed any radical change ("nothing has happened"), we sense the sadness lining the tale of struggle and hope, of rebounding and fighting against hurt and disappointment. It is a sadness that sits at home, a place where her husband used to beat her, stoking a fury that has not left, even after his death. Memories of the hurt and near-death pain she experienced have never left, accompanying her thoughts of others being hurt and killed. It is a sadness she expresses for never having experienced the love proclaimed and promised to her—a love of which she is reminded by the sight of old couples walking hand in hand—a love that has never been hers.

Life-times of sadness gather, pooling in places of succor on which the rest of us depend. At the bottom of one's heart, at the bottom of our oceans. In a single life, sadness ebbs and flows with every passing day and month and year, as the seasons of fortune and misfortune turn while one searches for signs of their design, the rules that might govern what in profound grief one can only see as chance, or the hidden timing of one's sentencing or possible reprieve.

For some, sadness is a force against which one must contend. "Sadness really defeated me," Luis, an overseas Filipino worker in Saudi Arabia recalled of his first time in Saudi Arabia, a place where he learned the saying of workers, "Welcome to this prison without bars."[24] Sadness defeats. It can overwhelm your hours and days, cast a pall over everything you see. In sadness that defeats there is great loneliness. For if you were accompanied on this passage, a little of that sadness might lift off, its weight shared by your fellow pallbearers.

A sadness that defeats. It is not the feeling of a loss shared. Nor is it the feeling of a loss spread over the world, one's loss enveloping all, disappearing into the loss that now engulfs oneself. Rather, it is a weight that pulls on you from beneath, or from the hollow that hides, that draws on the reserves you keep trying to replenish to get through the hours, the days, the weeks, the years. Sometimes the passage doesn't end. It continues underneath the daily tread, exerting that pull that is greater than the grounding pull of gravity. Although she feels healthy and, while walking in outdoor rallies, experiences none of her many physical ailments, when she is at home, Nanay Mameng says, she feels weak, sometimes feels unable even to stand up. It is a place in which she doesn't want to stay. Her home is on the streets, with her fellow activists, a place in the world she fights for as if it were her very own life.

Sadness can also be a place in which we find each other. A sadness shared can be a net of lifelines people make together, which can remake the milieus of sundered lives.

If I began part IV with a watershed moment in the US academic and cultural boycott movement against Israel, it is because this movement of solidarity with the Palestinian people is a "somewhere" that many of us feel called to join and actively help make as part of the possibility of our own lives, which we see as so deeply bound to the lives of others.[25] Political movements such as this one are also those somewheres that, Simone argues, improvised lives want and require as a place of continuing and hoped for collective life, a place where those lives can be held. The somewhere that a political movement builds as its own vital ground of possibility is a living social scape that, like the somewheres that Simone writes of, hold us "just enough to enable a mutual witnessing" and perhaps even more to enable a mutual care and imaginations of shared flourishing.[26]

As just these vital somewheres holding and upholding actual and hoped for collective life, the networks emerging out of and driving these movements are also made of words and images, as well as actions and expressions, occasions and moments—gifts—that pass among the colonized. These are live exchanges, communicative acts and gestures of sharing experience that liven other imaginable, feeling connections of the becoming-human to each other beyond who we might be to and for each other in the global fields of dead exchanges.

In *The Time That Remains* (2011), the Palestinian filmmaker Eliah Suleiman allows us to glimpse one imagined connection between his own aging mother, living out the end of a life-time of interdiction under Israeli colonization and domination, and her Filipina caregiver who looks after her and her home, as he renders their strange domestic intimacy in a time of deep suspension. It is a fleeting glimpse, ambiguous and uncertain in its import—an image of immanent relations of care, even love, among the differently dispossessed, one also explored in the Philippine musical *Care Divas* (2012, dir. Maribel Legarda, written by Liza Magtoto), which rescripts the Israeli documentary *Paper Dolls* (2006, dir. Tomer Heymann), which features a group of transgender Filipino elder care givers, in part by imagining a tragic romance between the *bakla* Filipino caregiver and an illegal Palestinian worker.[27]

In these dreaming practices of activists and artists—attempts to remake the social imaginary bases of our "present disorder" and in this way engage in the poiesis of a world of another becoming—we find remaindered modes of living, differently situated, recast, revised, sometimes subordinated and denied, yet also still continuous and alive in people's everyday ways of making life in excess of what is simply required to keep us all going.

THRESHOLDS

On the reticulated shores of city everywhere—the global urbanization project to rebuild cities as total mediacosmic platforms hosting the capitalizable life of globopolitical citizens—sites of a vitality little reckoned with emerge, hold on, disappear. These are places with particular names and histories and geographies, organic and inorganic pressures, though in public discourse and academic writing they are often referred to mainly in the generic as slums, squatter colonies, inner cities, informal settlements, or *looban* ("inner city," literally, interior). The generic terms alone conjure conditions of exceptional privation and peril ("squalor," "crime") that demarcate a boundary between these places and the "common" spaces and general order of the city. This imaginary and material boundary delineates the spaces and modes of habitation that constitute urban life proper and those sites it marks off as on the margins of that proper life. More than a line of demarcation physically segregating some from others, the boundary defines. It surrounds. It deems these marginal sites, which it seeks to contain or eliminate, "uninhabitable"—a designation that makes them available to intervention, "particularly interventions that operate at a distance, that sought to affect things by being removed from them."[1] As such, the boundary is neither fixed nor stable; it operates rather as a shifting threshold, which like the notion of standard of living depends on variable criteria for measuring and ensuring a valuable, a properly human, way of life. This threshold serves as a measure and a means of an ideal of existence, a course and tool of action for the beginning or end (of state of being) that it designates, a marker and a maker of seemingly absolute difference or distance from (while at the point of greatest proximity to) a life worth living.

At the Farthest Distance from a Life Worth Living

Fires erupt often in Metropolitan Manila. Sometimes a whole neighborhood of shanties will burn down to the ground. Or a fire will race through a district of the very poor, consuming all that is flammable in its path, leaving only charred cement blocks and galvanized iron structures standing, the furnished interiors and personal effects they had housed now no more than burned out hollows and embers. Almost always they will say the problem was electrical—faulty wiring, illegal connections. Almost always everyone suspects arson. In most such cases, fire becomes pretext for and prelude to demolition. Carried out by a small battalion of hired guns, iron mallets, and shovels, urban demolitions of squatter settlements are as frequent and persistent as the fires that precede them but more thorough and deliberate in their destruction.

Fire becomes an inherent propensity. It points to the immanent condition of these places, which finds evidence in the aftermath of its uncontrolled eruption—reason and proof that these places are uninhabitable. In the first six months of 2018 alone, there were 2,200 fires in Metro Manila, the majority of them erupting in slum areas, neighborhoods said to be "sprawling, unregulated tinderboxes."[2] Combustible. Poor materials are combustible materials—fuel. The very poor live in houses made of discarded pieces of cheap, thin plywood, cardboard, and plastic tarp, when and where they cannot source or afford cheap cement or scrap metal, even as others manage to build sturdier structures right alongside them. Their houses are tightly packed, the wall of one serving on the other side as the wall of another, the banks of narrow walkways between them used as areas for idling, washing, selling, eating, excretion. Privation creates density, not austerity. Dense quarters, dense encounters. People in the slums are described as being like matchsticks—easily ignitable.[3] Given to spontaneous combustion, while also at the same time festering with all manner of chronic disease (of deviant and illicit behavior as much as bodily illness), the people and the place become mirrors of each other, interchangeable in their reflection of an entire "way of life" of its own—a culture and ecology—paradoxically untenable and persistent.⁴

This paradox of being untenable and persistent, a condition of disaster, which is both imminent and chronic (waiting to happen, long happening) suggests that the slum is not simply or only a real place (multiple, diverse, heterogeneous, peculiar social universes of their own), but also the designation of the point at which urban life, in all its variegated, heterogeneous forms, comes to be seen as no longer viable. Fire is the event, the outcome of a threshold crossed between potentiality and actuality. The threshold marks a break in a continuum, the point at which what might only be guessed at or inferred becomes palpable, evident, *real*—reaching the level of shared perceptibility. Fire is the opposite of durability, continuity, structure, organization; it is entropy, the opposite of organicity, of life itself. It destroys what life would build, what would and could host life. It thus figures the very condition of unlivability, which is always immanent in, while also being placed at the greatest distance from, a life of value.

As a prelude to urban demolition, as the means of effectively pronouncing a place unfit for human life and making it so, fire foregrounds the expendability of the social and other life it consumes as fuel. The use of arson to clear slums is well-known.⁵ Known as "hot demolition," it would sometimes take the form of a kerosene-drenched live rat or cat set on fire and let loose in an area of squatters, igniting all that it touched with its body in flames as it ran, setting off a fire strong and rapid enough to raze a slew of homes while burning to its own death.⁶ While this particular tactic used by landowners is no longer in much use (replaced by planted resident arsonists), it gruesomely illustrates how arson is a punitive sentence against life deemed urban refuse.

The destruction that "hot demolition" achieves is the fate to which expendable, consumable life is condemned, a form of capital punishment from which life worth living is promised to be exempt. Not just a globally touted ideal (a social value), life worth living is, after all, the "product" of global enterprise, the predicate of global, urban capitalist "production" and subject of globopolitical protection. A form of commodity capital that also functions as a political right. While mass evictions and urban demolitions have been carried out in the national capital since the early 1960s as part of the state's project of authoritarian modernization (under Ferdinand Marcos), since the 1990s, when the postdictatorship government of Fidel Ramos began aggressively "globalizing" the economy, mass evictions and urban demolitions have been carried out with greater frequency and on a greater scale by the state in partnership with corporate capital to clear and enclose these lands for the expanded reproduction or growth of capital life. In 1993–1994, 80 demolitions were recorded as having displaced around 80,000 people.[7] By 2008, 31,171 families (or around 155,000 people) had been evicted from their homes.[8] From 2011 to the middle of 2017, a recorded 2,045 demolitions demolished the homes of 65,704 families, displacing an approximated 328,520 people (1:5).[9]

Numbers

The numbers of people, families, and households forced into homelessness through demolitions are many and fluctuating, varying across different measures (how many in a family, what constitutes a household). But overall they provide a picture of increasing displacement and dispossession of those with no "right to the city."[10] At best they render the accelerating devastation wrought by new urbanization projects, which mandate the removal and relocation of informal settler communities living in proclaimed danger zones or zones targeted for business real estate development. Maps and graphs attempt to show the dramatic progression of this contemporary urban enclosure movement, a violent war of dispossession and land reclamation that forges the ground for Metro Manila to realize the fantasy of city everywhere.[11]

Graphs, maps, and numbers are criticized for making general and abstract, purely analytical, the otherwise concrete lives of humans. They are charged with making those lives *unreal*. Undoubtedly, these are the very representational tools wielded by urban planners, economists, and battalions of technocrats, not to mention financial advisors, traders, fund managers, international lending institutions (banks) and international organizations overseeing the global monetary system (such as the IMF) and global financial stability more generally, tools that have in fact made people into populations, aggregate statistics that can figure as information for dominant actors who are not them, while derealizing peoples' own roles and capacities as subjects in the world. It would seem, from this critique of abstraction, that these representational means only exacerbate the liminal humanity to which displaced, dispossessed, and disenfranchised Global South populations—figured as an unwanted excess that poses a criminal threat or inordinate liability to nations as well as cities—are already consigned. Such abstractions would appear only to place them further beyond the threshold of human feeling and regard.

And yet the hard opposition between numbers and human experience, maps and the real world, is sorely inadequate, repeating the upholding of human values as the object of war to protect. Even as this war is waged by algorithms and demographics, by the cold facts of data and metadata, the humanities, with its warmth and depth of feeling, have long been part of the soft war of humanization that accompanies the conquest.[12] They, too, become a measure and a proof of life worth defending, protecting, honoring—techniques for rendering, reading, and feeling the sentient being of others as lives of value, on a par with those already human. In this way, like numbers, the affects and sentiments of human stories can also draw the bounds of life-enabling regard.

As suggested in Bryan Costa's poem, "Isang Libo, Isang Buwan" (A thousand a month),[13] which searches for this seemingly small figure's significance ("What value or use does this have for the nation?"), numbers are nevertheless also parts and forms of people's daily life experience: one's monthly rent, the money owed to the store, the cost of electricity or water, the school's tuition fee, the increase in a mother's pension, and so on. Although "a thousand a month" is revealed to be the rate of sanctioned murders carried out by the police under President Duterte's war on drugs, the poem's rummaging for this number's meaning in everyday concerns demonstrates that there is also a mathematics of survival in the midst of a hanging death sentence for the urban poor, an everyday social calculus in which numbers, as practical and propitious signs, do play a crucial part.

Numbers as well as sentiments, quantities as well as qualities, are the terms with which we understand the world and manage our lives. They can tell hidden as well as explicit stories. They can paint portraits and landscapes. A number, too, can be felt ("In truth / a thousand a month is very scary"). While numbers are precision instruments of control, seemingly unlike the raging fires let loose through "hot demolition," numbers, stories, and fires can all be employed to enhance as well as destroy life. What matters here are the rules animating them, how they are arrived at, and what they effect—the thresholds they maintain or create.

Liminalities, Shifting and Holding

A threshold is a *limen*, the limit point beyond which a phenomenon ceases to be perceptible or sensible. A threshold is also a magnitude or intensity that must be surpassed for a certain reaction—a material transformation or sensation—to occur.[14] There are many thresholds that prevail in city everywhere. Some are never crossed; some are crossed every day. Some thresholds lead to other thresholds, each one depending on the effect of the previous one having been traversed. For the slum dwellers, squatters, and other bearers of tenuous life, subject to willed (state and structural), environmental devastation (including flooding), one threshold has been crossed while another remains, shifting yet continuing to hold.

During the postauthoritarian period of the 1990s, the flyover or overpass strategy of urban development promised to resolve the contradictory, bulimic relation of the metropolitan government to its own feminized body of informal, illicit labor.[15] As the unchecked pace of demolitions would suggest, that strategy has reached a limit. While this flyover network strategy for liberalizing capital life flows continues to obtain, and in fact has been scaled up nationally and globally to create a global urban archipelago, the current Philippine state has resolved its "gender trouble" (its contradictory binary gender identifications with global capital and global labor) and now no longer abides by its alternately purging and indulging approach to the slums and the informal life of the urban excess.[16] Instead, it now engages in a project of unmitigated annihilation of those sites of informal settlement and their communities, in projects of reclaiming public land for the installation of entire urban systems or environments (or, *city emulants*) as capitalist platforms.[17]

For these informal settlement communities, some of them established during World War II by war survivors fleeing the decimation of their homes, a threshold has definitely been crossed.[18] That this is so is harrowingly expressed in the unfathomable devastation of social life accomplished by tens of thousands of murders and by the countless acts of violence that accompany them (extortion, kidnapping for ransom, theft) carried out under the cover of the war on drugs. The killings devastate entire families, often targeting more than one member for assassination while targeting others for other forms of auxiliary violence. Carried out in unpredictable and uncontrollable ways and on an unprecedented scale, instigated by rumors and telltale information about suspected drug users and dealers, the killings have also further torn asunder the already fragile and frayed social fabric and everyday informal economy of these communities to a point of possibly permanent disrepair and irreparable destitution.[19]

Even as these communities have been forced to suffer beyond a certain threshold of pain and violence, they remain below the threshold of national, civic concern and sympathy. In an ocean of publicly available photographs, videos, articles, social media postings, only two particular visual representations induced moments of national uproar, breaking through the bounds of widespread civic acceptance. The first was Lerma's famous "Pietà" photograph (discussed earlier) of a murdered tricycle driver, Michael Siaron, cradled in the arms of his partner, Jennilyn Olares; the second, a CCTV recording of Kian De Los Santos, a seventeen-year-old male high school student, being dragged to his execution by two plainclothes policemen. Despite these moments of uproar, Duterte's popularity remains at a record high, with a trust and approval ratings pegged at 85 percent.[20] In the context of a country that has had a century-long tradition of mass demonstrations of radical bereavement, spurred by similar sacrificial images of slain Filipino victims, the failure of these two particular moments, as well as of the mounting war on drugs–related deaths in slum areas more generally, to *move* the nation, if not to protest then at least to withdraw support for the Duterte regime and the war on drugs, would suggest that for the nation at large, a certain other threshold of human sentiment and care has *not* been reached.

Put differently: for the Philippine nation, despite the mounting demolitions and mounting death toll afflicting these communities, despite the increasing magnitude and intensity of suffering that they sustain, these communities continue to remain liminal, that is, beyond the point where their plight and suffering might be perceived, made sensible to others as a pain that might be shared.

But what constitutes this liminality? It would seem to many, including to the victims of this ongoing spectacular and everyday war, that it is their humanity that is liminal. Indeed, family and friends of the murdered repeatedly express the violence inflicted on the victims in precisely these terms—*it is as if they were animals*, they cry in protest, *as if they were not human*. "My son just turned sixteen, and they killed him like a chicken, as if he were an animal," Maria Isabelita said when her son and six other people were killed by masked gunmen when they opened fire at two shanties in Bagong Silang in search of a drug suspect.[21] She and other relatives of the murdered were pleading with the employees of the police-accredited funeral parlor, where the bodies of their loved ones were being held hostage for exorbitant fees, to release their dead.

Ideological boundaries are continuously drawn around the victims of the drug war, drug users and dealers (*adiks* and *pushers*) are figured as *salot* (rot, pestilence), zombies so crazed they would rape their own grandmothers, deadbeats already dead and dying who proffer nothing but destruction, figurations that place them outside the bounds not only of the nation but also of all that is regarded as human. As the secretary of justice countered, against the accusation that the drug war constituted crimes against humanity, "I already said that is not true. The criminals, drug lords, drug pushers, they are not humanity."[22]

A dominant response to the sheer instrumentality with which such lives are reduced is to bring them to the level of perceptibility as humans, by uncovering and representing their suffering, desires, emotions, and subjective lives, to tell their stories in human terms—and in this way, to restore or recognize the humanity of those who would be granted none. I do not disparage such work by journalists, scholars, writers, and filmmakers, which I draw on for my own understanding of the way such lives are made and expended. However,

I want to shift our attention to home in on something else that these zones of disposable lives generate, namely, a kind of vitality that is not quite or simply "human," nor for that matter the unequivocal negation of the necrocapitalist logic that defines their fate.

Multifarious Forms of Life

With their sociological (and anthropological) protagonists—individuals and the collectives they purportedly represent or exemplify, that is, specific ethnolinguistic groups whose "cultures" pertain to them, even as they might be comparatively related to those of others—"human" stories can eclipse the multifarious vitality subsumed in the object-category called "life," as a condition or attribute of all individual organic being, and principally, universal human being. In the new global political economy, such "life" can be enhanced, improved, made more efficient, made more valuable, productively spent—in a word, capitalized—as well as protected, guaranteed, specified, and regulated—in a word, politically recognized and enfranchised, to the diminishment and at the expense of other forms of life, as the continuing histories of imperial, bourgeois humanisms amply show. While they appear to counter the dehumanizing abstraction created by numbers and other instruments of analytical thought, to represent the deaths as "unjust," to make them grievable and elicit sympathy for the slain, "human" stories may also inadvertently buttress the very portals through which some life can pass into valued being, while others not. In this way, they make even more liminal what I see as equally vital, inextricable aspects of those lives that they seek to redeem by "humanizing" them.

Part of what such "human" stories eclipse is the forms of shared, transpersonal, and morphing being, as well as the partibility, elasticity, convertibility, and fluidity of personhood, their substances and faculties, which are characteristic of the most ordinary lives of those who serve as the means of reproduction of valorizable life. As I have argued, migrant domestic, care, and low-level service workers in host countries as well as in urban excess populations in their own countries function as human machines and media for other humans. In the temporary, repeated, on-demand lending of their bodies, capacities, social relations, and coordinated practices and routines to the ever-changing and moving needs and demands of employers and patrons, they function as "all-around" domestic instruments and utilities for the reproductive and productive life activities and enterprises of others.

On a larger, aggregated scale, they serve as part of a built environment, like roads and vehicles, facilitating the movement and circulation of the life-forms of value, embodied in individual lives of mobility, around whose value-productive movements city everywhere and the global political economy of life organizes itself. As I discussed earlier, this vital infrastructure acts as what Gilbert Simondon called the "associated milieu"—the produced condition of existence and viability—of that technical object of global urban circulation, which is human capital life.[23] As "that through which the technical object conditions itself in its functioning," vital infrastructure can be considered the coordinated ensemble of conditions that valuable and valorizable life (the lives of globopolitical citizens bearing human capital) requires to reproduce itself. If, as Rosa Luxemburg argued, the noncapitalist social formations of imperial colonies served as necessary milieus for the expanded reproduction of capital accumulation, life-system environments with which capitalism is in "a constant process of metabolism" and without which it could not continue to exist, then it becomes clear that such noncapitalist social formations have in the course of the postcolonial history of capital adapted and transformed the live forces of their own life-making and survival into providing, in the contemporary moment, an associated milieu for capital life that is less territorialized, more globally distributed, and more fluid in character than in the past.[24] With the late capitalization of movement and life activity and mediation over "product" or "property" in the mode of platform capitalism (as described in chapter 7), what obtains for these associated milieus of late capital production is necessarily constant flux, rapid turnover, disaggregating movement.[25]

"Human" stories may eclipse a large-scale picture of these lives of liquidity continuously drawn upon to lubricate, fuel, and maintain the infrastructural channels of high-value life flows, which make for the content and connectivity of metropolitan platforms, including those of the shadow economy (parastate, violence-based, illicit, organized criminal enterprises), which have proliferated and grown in the wake of decades of Cold War counterinsurgency wars. Humanizing stories also tend to eclipse the intimate, ordinary experiential dimensions of the liquidity of these serviceable lives, which enables them to play disposable mediatic and machinic parts (or, means of production and means of labor) of both life-producing and life-expending enterprises. By liquidity I mean the ready convertibility, malleability, and variability of people's bodily being, capacities, relations, spaces, and times, which can be made into the means of any ends. The way people can lend themselves, become the hands, feet, a partial (or whole) body for someone else, at the disposition of others, in the domestic, sex, and care industries, as well as for each other in the most ordinary efforts of collaborative survival in the slums. In these spaces of seemingly infinite informal transactions (actions of transference and conversion), through which the urban poor might make a living, people can take each other's places, pass on duties, tasks, faculties, presences; become another's body, substituting for one, or several, or serving as a channel to another, a means of transmission of licit and illicit substances, favors, debts, and actions, not only across geographical distances but also across time, where currencies of exchanges are multiple, even potentially infinite, though ultimately dominated and limited by the money-form of value.

These are in many ways familiar modes of personhood and social being in postcolonial lifeworlds, bearing ways of living and understanding (sense-making practices of life-making) which feminist anthropologists of Melanesia, South Asia, and Southeast Asia describe as characteristic of extant gift economies or cultures. These anthropological accounts describe, for example, how a singular person comes into being as a derivative of plural relations, or how they might behave and be imagined as dividuals, composite beings that are divisible or partible, for particular circumstances, social actions, and events.[26] In the Philippine context, such accounts describe a social world in which persons are potentially changeable in every interaction with others; where, far from homeostatic conditions, instead conditions of ambiguity, tension, and uncertainty characterize all exchanges and their sequels, and persons become, as it were, their own mediatory objects in a place accustomed to the convertibility and substitutability between persons and things; where forms of social, personal being, which a Western bourgeois property-oriented analytical view might want to call "identity," "is largely conducted through the making and remaking of potentially transformative relationships with others . . . [particularly] asymmetric relationships with human and supernatural superiors, who moreover remain resolutely plural."[27]

The resonance of such analytical descriptions with descriptions of the posthuman effects of a digital informational and mediatic world seems to me to be neither accidental nor insignificant.[28] It foregrounds the broader social conditions and entailments of the experiential and practical liquidity of the lives of that worldwide service/servant stratum serving as vital infrastructure. Those social conditions and entailments include most crucially what I have argued are vital platforms, forces of sociality that are also organizing systems, subaltern forces and means of a global metropolitanist platform economy. Even as kinship studies might emphasize systems of "social relations" between and among individuals as members of collectives, they also suggest transpersonal capacities and transspecies, transexistential transmissions of matter and mind, protocols of sense-making that organize "relations" between the living and the dead, spirits and bodies of mutual being scattered and distanced across space and time.[29]

The fluidity, partibility, convertibility, and coordination of persons and capacities in these networks is a vitality that can be missed in the focus on the urban poor as particular kinds of subjects, whether as workers or citizens, men or women, rural refugees, squatters and slum dwellers, in contradistinction to other sectoral subjects such as overseas workers. If we look closely and more broadly at the life trajectories and social scapes of communities of the disenfranchised, the picture we get is not of stable social groups like "overseas Filipino workers" or "slum dwellers" but rather of people flowing through urban channels, transnationally as well as nationally, cycling in and out of sites of temporary work and temporary residence, a constant cycling through jobs, homes, and identities for those placed in conditions of permanent unsettlement and tenuous existence.

In countries in Asia, including West Asia, where opportunities and incentives for overseas workers to permanently reside are near zero, the flows are periodic, recurrent, constant. Memorie Morco worked at a gas station in Palau, before working as a nanny in Morocco for six years and then, since 2017, working in the United Arab Emirates, caring for another's child.[30] In the Philippines, labor policies effectively support these itinerant flows by increasing contractualization of labor, not only depriving workers of long struggled for and gained benefits during so-called five-month "probationary" periods but also legitimating their firing or "nonrenewal" after "probation." Ate Rose worked while she was a minor as a canteen "helper" for two months, then on and off in a garment factory for three or six months at a time, as an overseas domestic worker in Brunei for two years, finally returning to the Philippines as a factory worker in different companies as each one closed down.[31] Amira, a Tausug woman who is sister and wife to imprisoned insurgents, migrated to Manila from Mindanao at the peak of the war between the Moro National Liberation Front and the Marcos government, worked as an overseas domestic worker in Saudi Arabia, and now lives in Maharlika, a Muslim majority settlement village in Manila, where she heads a household of other Muslim women who also worked or intend to work in the Gulf for varying periods of time.[32] When they are not themselves the ones moving and sojourning, overseas workers and their relatives are conduits and host sites for one another's itinerant movements.

Families are fractured and remade, as members of kin and consociates flow in and out of places, seeking refuge and reproduction for themselves in places of violence and hostility everywhere, in lands fought over, seized, or surrendered, exchanged for a penance or a ransom, or sequestered and enclosed. These life trajectories demonstrate the continuous transmogrification of what would appear to be bounded social identities in place—the liquidity of minoritized populations forced to live nomadic, probationary lives, which reproduces at a larger scale the liquidity of individuals living what AbdouMaliq Simone and others characterize as the ever-improvisatory lives of informality.[33]

Slum dwellers do not experience eviction and demolition once but many times. They too cycle in and out of these urban sites, the lives they build—home, neighborhood, livelihood—periodically wholly destroyed, only to be built again upon their return. As Elisea Adem notes, the past and present of life for the urban excess rests on the problem of landlessness. After all, it is dispossession and disenfranchisement that has brought them to this place, which is a social condition before it is a geographical place—a form of perpetual unsettlement that becomes a way of life. For the Carlos family who migrated to Manila from Zambales after losing their land, life became "a continuous thirty-year search for a home." Sixteen times they had to move, six of those times as the consequence of evictions, in "oscillating movements towards and away from the *riles* [railway]."[34] To be a squatter, Elisea Adem writes, "can invariably mean being a wanderer in the wilderness of urban living."

What these oscillating movements evince is that, despite being brutally set adrift, slum dwellers constantly rebound and rebuild. They fight back and resist.[35] *Tumbalik*, they call it, this practice of springing back—the conjoined actions of knocking down (*tumba*) and returning *(balik)*, which Kaloy M. Cunanan views as part of the urban poor's *diskarte*, or spatial practicality.[36] They do so by deploying themselves as any resource or capacity whatsoever, finding flexible niches where they can, in ways that depend on the social roles they are both compelled to inhabit and able to craft, and in dynamic, elastic coordinating response to each other's changing needs. With the railway upgrading project, the *riles* squatter area has been demolished, yet their lives continue, in ever more difficult circumstances yet in ever persistent ways.

Sites may disappear without the vitality that they host disappearing. The willed disappearance of communities is an act of dispossession that does not eliminate the disposable life-times continuously drawn upon to create ever more staggering accumulations of capital, but on the contrary only makes more of them. For war multiplies disposable life-times, creating through destruction the very disposability of that vitality which, as capitalist enterprise, it requires. But like other "natural resources," this vitality is not infinite; rather it is diminished and ever more ravaged by such creative destruction—by what is essentially the enforced liquidation of the lives of the disenfranchised. It is this liquidity that has enabled global capitalism's spectacular rise from the ashes of economic crises in the 1970s, precipitated by worldwide decolonization struggles since the second half of the twentieth century. And as the example of

Duterte's war on drugs demonstrates, it is this same liquidity that pretending insurgent regimes attempt to corner in their own warring bids to take larger dividend shares, if not usurp the majority power, of globopolitical sovereignty.

The continuous flows of fungible people and the continuous exchange of their convertible capacities fuel and support global industries in the new political economy of life, as component apparatuses (machines) as well as content-matter (raw material) of these industries of circulation (transport, communication, service, social media). It comes almost as no surprise that the Philippines has become central to global social media, with two thirds of its population (roughly 69 million people) on Facebook, and a global hub for content moderators and internet troll farms.[37] But these global capitalist flows are importantly sustained by other transnational flows and forms of circulation—that of sustenance and subsistence (goods, money, affect, connectivity), which some have identified as "care," and which I would understand as a broader array of life-making practices comprising the social reproduction of communities of the becoming-human. What Geraldine Pratt and Valerie Francisco-Menchavez see as the social reproductive labor required to maintain the transnational families of migrant workers, and which Francisco-Menchavez calls "multi-directional care," I also understand in terms of the practices and organizing logic of vital platforms.[38]

Generated and programmed by "the non-noble technics" of domestic kinship protocols, part of "a technical subconsciousness" of communitarian life, vital platforms are platforms of social reproduction, which are grafted to as well as intertwined and interfaced with capitalist platforms (social media, the integrated mediacosms of urban systems, state apparatuses, including the political-police platform, which preys upon them as revenue-generating mechanisms).[39] As the means of life and the life itself of affiliative and kin networks (that is, as the means *and* the very object of reproduction of *shared life*), whose members are both components and users, the sociality of vital platforms sustains both serviceable life and the absolutely expendable life from which such serviceable life is drawn, in what would appear to be a temporary reprieve from the capital punishment that is the latter's standing sentence.

The reconfiguration of what were effectively the labor commodities of a warm-body export national economy, into worker-subjects and "migrant citizens"—this process of "humanizing" and heroizing overseas Filipino workers as part and parcel of the Philippine's political and economic transformation as a major global provider of reproductive and service workers worldwide—belies the fact that what are often represented as separate social groups (OFWs and slum dwellers, workers and war refugees, and, among the urban poor, the police and the policed, the killers and the killed) are more intimately related, sometimes of the "same," or deeply intertwined, social networks. Biographic stories as well as "social" feature narratives cannot adequately represent these transnational sinews of connective social tissue (neither unified nor homogeneous, but on the contrary, variable, mixed, and dynamic) that sustain and make possible what would appear to be discrete, integral, numerable "lives."

Mixed Passages

Heart de Chavez was killed on January 10, 2017, by the Philippine National Police, just one of the 22,983 deaths thus far that the Philippine National Police classify as "homicides under investigation." Three days earlier, she had been picked up, placed in what the police called "a hold" (rather than an arrest), and then released—though only after Heart's mother, Elena, pawned her entire life pension for ₱7,000 ($130) to pay for the bail that the police extorted from her in exchange for her child's life; a small sum compared to the ₱50,000 ($1,000) they had demanded, yet still amounting to the entirety of Elena's life savings. The outlines of the narrative of Heart's murder are familiar, as Patricia Evangelista, the journalist covering these war on drugs killings, observes: "a threat, a false arrest, police extortion, and a brutal execution."[40] Heart was dragged out of the shanty home that she shared with her mother and sister, Arianne, in San Jose Village, Navotas City, by at least seven armed men who barged into the house and held the family at gunpoint, as one of them grabbed Heart by her long hair and pounded her head on the table while another grabbed her by the front of her skinny black sweater to drag her away, Heart screaming. "Ma . . . Help me." When the men left, Arianne, clutching her five-month-old baby, and Elena ran out looking for Heart, only to find her dead body on the floor of an empty house, a bullet in her cheek and another in the back of her head.

The police report of Heart's murder lists the victim as Alvin Ronald de Chavez, alias Ron-Ron, single and jobless. "The alias, as far as details go," Evangelista writes, "may have been the first inaccuracy embedded in the short spot report filed at the Navotas City Police Station. . . . Alvin Ronald became Heart de Chavez more than a decade before they were dragged screaming down Quintos Street." The police misidentification of Heart is part of a series of blatant lies that they and their paid witnesses proffer about the killing, a symbolic violence which continues and compounds the violence of Heart's cold-blooded abuse and murder, even after they are already dead. This act of violence is further inflicted in Heart's burial. The funeral director insisted that

Heart be buried as a man, invoking the Catholic Church's wrath should the family's wishes be respected, which was to bury Heart in the floral purple dress that Arianne brought back from Dubai, along with false eyelashes, red lipstick, and the big round curls, which Heart loved. Though Arianne fought back, the family finally gave in, and Heart was buried in a long sleeved shirt, black trousers, her long hair clipped back to give the proper appearance of a man.

The lead picture for Evangelista's article (taken by the Nightcrawler photographer Carlo Gabuco), an overhead shot of the open casket, with Heart dressed as a man lying inside, visible in the open half of the coffin, and a tarp printed with her picture as a woman draped on the outside, over the closed, bottom part, movingly evokes the pain of this violence inflicted by the police, the Church, and the heteronormative social order they uphold and implement. In its rendering of the impossible contradiction and conflict of claims over Heart's identity, it also crystallizes the subject and tenor of Evangelista's portrait, that is, of the harrowing injustice to which the urban poor are relentlessly subjected—the impunity and sheer power of dominant forces to override the wishes, desires, agency, and subjectivities of people regarded as lesser humans, whose fates are theirs to decide—this sheer power to define, and materialize the disposability of, their lives. All of this is true, and the pain and suffering they speak is keen.

Within this narrative, however, there are other details Evangelista attends to besides those that expose the lies, and besides the antagonism emerging or lying in wait in the irreconcilability of conflicting reality claims. Details such as the fact that Heart's father was a former seaman, that Heart worked as a maid for an overseas worker, that Arianne was in Dubai (presumably as an overseas worker herself), that when their father died the responsibility for the family fell to Heart, who began dealing drugs as the debts and financial burden of a mother and two single-mother sisters, with four children between them, mounted—such details not only point to the indistinction and intertwining of the categories of slum dwellers and overseas workers, and the social liquidity I discussed earlier. These details also point to the connective social tissue in which Heart's life is embedded—the vital platforms that are the condition and burden of shared survival, which the vertical political-police network both models itself on and preys upon, in derivative enterprises of value extortion directed at shared, social, rather than individual, life-being (their vital platforms as the objects and mechanisms of these deadly, extractive enterprises).

In the video accompanying the article, Arianne says, "My sibling was sentenced immediately. She was sentenced before even appearing in court. They killed her like an animal. As if she were just a bird, that even if it weren't sick, just died like that, as if nothing. And them so pleased with themselves that they were able to get money from this. They'll go up in the ranks. They'll feed their families with what they earned from this."[41] In Arianne's comments, we hear an expression of what it means to be *not* human, to be a bird, flying free without intrinsic attachments, without precisely that recourse and obligation of familial bonds or bonds of mutual being, which others not only continue to enjoy but also feed and grow. The sentence is swift, without personal negotiation, like a bird that is struck down with a fatal illness, "as if nothing," as if without kin and connection, without "help," that code word for the gift—money, favor, prerogative—in a culture economy of "help," all manner of acts and things that help to produce people's lives and their relations of obligation and debt, affiliation and alliance, on which those lives are staked.

If I have seized on these details, it is because they evoke what humanizing stories might make liminal in their constrictive focus on the lives of autonomous beings, the subject-effects of a specific order of signs. What they make liminal is the forms of vitality that I have attempted to render in terms of the transmutability, permeability, and conductivity of persons, and more, the forms of transition, transmission, transaction, movement—in a word, passage—for which they might act as mediatic conduits. This is a vitality not of the lives of individuals comprising a group, but rather the vitality of vital platforms, the vitality of precisely the forms of transmogrifying passage that their human components make possible for each other, the vitality of the nonnoble technics of technologically uncoded forces of sociality operating as subaltern forces of production.

Viewing this frozen shot, representative of a world insistent on thorough knowability, dependent on the reifying signs of stable, fixed or fixable, proper being, we might miss such forms of mixed, inconsistent, and dynamic passage, passages that are routes of departure and return, itineraries of living, and rites of experience and becoming, of continuity and discontinuity, where Heart, in local language, was and continues to be for her mother *anak* (child), ungendered offspring, whose ungendered pronoun before and after "'becoming' Heart" is *siya* (translated in the English article and sometimes here as "she," in a reparative move to honor what would be denied); where self-transformation, that process of becoming beautiful as a process of the making and remaking of selves, of adopting multiple names (where Heart for their friends is also Barbie—"Barbie is alive," Heart exults, after being released), of claiming *biyuti* as self, disposition, life, and power, which Martin Manalansan demonstrates is part of the repertoire of everyday *bakla* and Filipinx queer and trans* survival, is not the work of one but also of others; where becoming woman is a living, a feat of social survival, a struggle to live (a joy to be alive!), in a time of war.[42] A dress from Dubai, a plea ("Mama, help me"), and plural names give scant suggestion of those forms of sociality through which persons—and in particular persons for whom transition is a way and exuberance of living—are produced and performed, shared life movements in which a person's life, desires, and becoming, as well as their end, are deeply and messily enmeshed.

There is another detail, the detail that is both the deed and consolation of Heart's mother, Elena. In the coffin, "Every item of clothing Heart wears is cut for a woman, from the stylish slacks all the way to Arriane's blouse, whose shiny black buttons fastened up to Heart's chin." Against the body stilled, the boundedness and consistency of social being seemingly fixed by inflicted premature death, these are details, gestures, and things of womanly care aimed at preparing Heart's body for another passing—sending them along this existential passage accompanied by familiar accessories of their becoming in life, in the expectation of unknown returns in death. Through the transmissions that the cut of a pair of trousers, the buttons of a blouse, enable, another related transition is made. This is the vitality that I suggest emerges, holds on, disappears—but here we see, it is a vitality that also persists not beyond but rather in the midst of death, indeed, in the abiding passages between the living and the dead.

Perduring across life and death, such vitality can be seen as the converse of the fires of "hot demolition," modern fires of destruction set to completely lay waste to and eliminate urban excess, to signal and bring about unlivability or imminent death for lesser life in order to host life worth living. As instruments of the state, fires of urban destruction are present-day forms of colonizing scorched-earth military campaigns, part of an arsenal for political and economic enclosure and dispossession. Fires make places of living into wastelands and tinderboxes to be cleared, dead ground on which to build things of value like condominiums, offices, and malls, transforming lands of survival into just so much real estate and making the lives they destroy nothing but fuel. It is its deployment as the means of a modern "pyropolitics" in pursuit of the enhancement of valued (human) life above all that has given fire its modern resonance as destruction, breakdown, and death (understood in capitalism, as John Berger writes, as elimination),[43] the opposite of order, of organicity, of life itself.

And yet in other, older understandings, fire is so much more than a destructive force. It is also the enabling elemental medium and mediator of human and planetary living, a technique and process of transformation vital to the changing worlds of collaborative existence, which modern regimes willfully forget to our present and future ecological detriment.[44] In a similar way, the vitality I write of here is not a property of "life itself" nor a property of the laboring subject, as Marx surmised, even as he described the vitality divested from the worker as "the living, form-giving fire . . . the transitoriness of things, their temporality, as their formation by living time."[45] It is rather the activity and power of formation and transformation, happening and making happen, in the "living time" of collaborative relations, a vitality that is also to be found in the mixed passages between the living and the dead, in transformations and transitions across states of impossible being through which the cooperative shared living of the dispossessed continues, a vitality on which life worth living under the aegis of global capital ultimately depends.

Passages and transitions foreground these forms of life-making and events of liveliness across ordained units and proper forms of life. Despite a tyrannical order of reified normative states obtained through decimating punishment, people's transmissive and transmutational capacities for making things happen and transform in their ordinary striving are what enable them to tend to each other's pains and desires. These are mediatic capacities put toward rebuilding and renewing collective life where it is brutally condemned. Rather than disorder or entropy (which is itself a measure relative to a narrow set of variables, exemplified in the order of proper global urban life), what we see is a plethora of life-making activity, plural forms of social survival and care under conditions of anthropogenic, capitalist duress.

This vitality confronts us with the threshold of understanding that makes it liminal. Thresholds are not, after all, simply given; they are established over and over again, instruments of practical measure and estimation within a particular order, which place bounds on what we might see be able to see, what may or may not be salient or become so, and what we could ignore, disdain, or esteem. In this context it is the threshold of capitalist life worth living that makes it impossible to see the mediatic function of humans as something more than simply the denigrating consequence of colonialism and capitalism (serving as the instruments of others). It prevents us from recognizing this form of being human (as means, component, and conduit, vitally attached to others) that is not conflated with its opposite—all that is less than or not human (object, animal, slave). And yet, a cultural economy of help and helpers, which does not obey these ontological divisions—that is, an ordinary subaltern mode of life which mobilizes extant and remnant practices of convertibility of selves and things, made possible by the porousness and mutability of personhood and sociality (households, kinship, genealogy), and by the exchangeability and changeability of fates—comprises the forms of activity, cooperation, and exchange within which people move, informing and shaping the life-making practices of the serviceable and expendable.

If vital platforms are the forces of social reproduction of colonized domestic communities that survive the ceaseless assaults against them, then they are also forms of centuries-long historical passage, the kind of passages still being made by their descendants under a global capitalism that would not and could not exist if not for the vitality of their modes of survival. Embodied in these capacities, faculties, and inventions of shared life, this is the vitality of people's life-making socialities, the generative matrices of their survival and thriving under colonial and postcolonial conditions of dispossession and depletion, and undergirding the urbanist expansion of capital and our present globopolitical mode of life. Vital platforms are built out of such vitalities and their connections, traversing human and nonhuman spheres insofar as the parts and components are not integral individual humans, but dividual attributes and appendages, partible or divisible, transmutable persons and beings, composed and connected by secularized logics that once also (and sometimes still) included animated objects, animals, spirits, and the dead.

In *Señorita extravida* (2001, dir. Lourdes Portillo), an investigative documentary film which probes the hundreds of murders of women taking place in Ciudad Juárez, Mexico, since the end of the twentieth century, the mother of one of the murdered women, María Sagrário González Flores, recalls the day her daughter was killed. "I knew something was wrong," she says. She recounts that on the day Sagrario disappeared, one of the pair of small yellow parakeets that were her daughter's pets, the one named Clint, was found dead. She reached out to take the other parakeet, the one named Luis, the one that would not let anyone but her daughter hold it. "I started to take him out, and I was no longer afraid that he would bite me, and I took him out. And I asked him about Sagrario. So, I said to him, Luis, do you know where she is, where is Sagrario, where is Mari, and he shook his head yes. As if he understood, the parakeet kept shaking his head this way, saying yes. Take account that the parakeet left on Tuesday, on Tuesday it departed from here, and on Wednesday they found my daughter. They found her on Wednesday. . . . And it really struck me that the parakeets, yes, they knew."

"The parakeets knew," Sagrario's mother says. In this other, related context of unsolved, rampant murders, which the work of feminists has crucially tied to the hundreds of maquiladoras, or global factories, located in this special economic zone and globalizing metropolis on the border of the United States and Mexico, where the expendable life of poor women is put toward urban, industrial growth, state sovereignty, and masculinist power and impunity, the families of victims with little to no recourse in the institutions of valued life reach out to other channels of help.[46] Sagrario's mother appeals to her daughter's parakeets for a knowledge she can find nowhere. The parakeets partake in the fate of the human who cared for them. One dies, as if its fate were vitally, symbiotically connected to the life taken. The other speaks, where no other can, as if it shared in a communicative, interactive, knowing, and sympathetic world not bound by place or species. These "as ifs" point to the logics of social compossibility and cooperative coexistence that continue to shape the social survival of those jettisoned from the protected being of the human.

In the collusion of forces of state-sanctioned impunity and the forces of capitalist humanity, those condemned to pay the price of their wars seek answers elsewhere, with the help of nonhuman others. In the photographs taken by Ezra Acayan of the funerals of the drug war victims in the Philippines, we see little, yellow chicks feeding on morsels of food on the glass windows of the open caskets. Even as they fight and call for justice in this world, the families of the killed—the fathers and mothers, children and siblings, grandparents they leave behind—put them there in the hopes that the pecking of the chicks on the glass will be the pecking on the consciousness of the killers, calling for a justice through other channels and by other means than what can be found in the present order. As in Dalena's reversal of the time of spectacle (see "Interregnum"), such practices—spiritual habits held over from previous times—attest to openings other than to futures colonized by preemptive speculative ventures of finance and security.

Those channels and means suggest another realm of temporality within which people move and live and aspire, other than the temporality of expendable and accumulable life-times. We might understand this temporality in terms of potential simultaneity of plural times (the instantaneity of conductivity and connectivity across discrete space-times, across existences), not to be thought of as the simple effect of digital technologies but rather the effect of the modality of people's experiences, which rest on the expectation of an openness of time strangely intimated by that experience of imminence and chronicity—waiting to happen, long happening. This openness—this unbounded horizon of living and expectation—which exists in the passages of transmission across the living, the human and the nonhuman, and the dead, beyond the life spaces and life-times of individuals and their social, regulatory, and identificatory groupings, beyond the designated means and ends and forms of valued life, and which makes fate-playing and social survival possible, is remaindered life.

PART V. BY THE WAYSIDES

11

BYPASS AND SPLENDOR

If Benjamin said that history had hitherto been written from the standpoint of the victor, and needed to be written from that of the vanquished, we might add that knowledge must indeed present the fatally rectilinear succession of victory and defeat, but should also address itself to those things which were not embraced by this dynamic, which fell by the wayside—what might be called the waste products and blind spots that have escaped the dialectic. —THEODOR ADORNO, *Minima Moralia*

I want to understand the philosophy of a growing flower in the middle of a swamp. —LAV DIAZ, "The Decade of Living Dangerously"

Bypass

A woman's voice on a black video screen asks, "When you imagine the home you wish for, does it imagine you back?" A moving shot of a distant horizon fades from black into view, as she continues, "If you were to walk across the horizon, would you be able to find what you are looking for?" The silhouette of the distant horizon becomes fields of grass and farmland quickly moving against a fixed sky, shot from a passenger's window of a vehicle speeding

FIGURE 11.1. Lyra Garcellano, *Borders II*, 2014, oil on canvas, 60 × 84 in, 36 × 48 in, 18 × 24 in, 9 × 12 in; and *Sweep*, 2014, moving image, 2:38 minutes, video. Finale Art Gallery, Metro Manila. Courtesy of the artist.

by, while the woman wonders out loud where you might find "the space that actually welcomes you, as though you belong there."[1] And whether such a place even exists.

We are looking out the window of a vehicle, watching this bucolic scenery rapidly going by, blurring in acceleration, as we are enjoined to reflect:

> Where is the location where you would feel that the mountain has moved to accept you?
> Where the land feels like home under your feet?
> And where it seems to say, "Hey, this is the place where you can become."
> This is the place where you can attempt "to be."
> This is the place where your strange brown face can actually live.[2]

But the landscape continues to whiz by, now turning into hedges and then stone walls, sometimes filling the screen, as the woman tells us what the

FIGURE 11.2. Lyra Garcellano, *Borders I*, 2014, oil on canvas, 9 × 12 in, 18 × 24 in, 36 × 48 in, 60 × 84 in. Finale Art Gallery, Metro Manila. Courtesy of the artist.

place itself seems to say, neither as whisper nor threat but simply as declaration: "You belong elsewhere. Somewhere. But definitely not here."

Philippine artist Lyra Garcellano's 2014 installation *Sweep* mounts this short video meditation on the experience of expulsion from belonging and love, the prohibition of self and life possibility, between two quadriptychs of paintings in expanding, evenly scaled sizes, each doubling the size of the one before. On canvas, the rural scenes in the video—taken on the artist's travels in France and Bacolod, Philippines—are stilled, rendered in oil in that genre of nineteenth-century European painting, the pure landscape. Here, the pure landscapes are somewhat morbid and forbidding; their shapes droop in macabre fashion, unyielding, ominous, opaque, in drab monochromatic black and white, tinged and smeared with hues of red and blue and yellow. Closely aligned in progressively augmented sizes, with their horizons touching, the paintings physically construct the borders they affectively enact. Opaque and translucent, rag-like forms are scattered over the landscape as if on the surface of the lens or screen of one's sight. Like the fleeting reflection of the hand-held camera caught every now and then in the video, the rags of color evoke the subjective place of viewing even as these same shreds also appear simply to be a part of the land and sky, lifted from them, daubing the clouds and trees.

To mindfully (one might say "critically") describe what one perceives is to bring into objective being and form the interpretation that makes for the sense of one's perception. Description is the performance of one's interpretation, which can be understood as a form of analysis. For Adorno, the interpretation of music through performance was necessarily an analytical act, even in the elementary process of reading notation. As a practice of intimate knowledge and close study ("to reveal as clearly as possible the *problem* of each particular work . . . to become aware of a work as a *force field* [*Kraftfeld*]"), analysis is not, however, only the prerequisite of performance.[3] Adorno suggests that the analytical process must precede and might even converge with the compositional process.

Like Garcellano's speaking in the declarative voice of the borders, the rags of diaphanous and muddy paint—draped over the landscape or hovering in the sky among clouds and other natural forms that they ambiguously evoke, blend in with, and set themselves apart from—these tattered and nebulous forms bring into expressive being the artist's intimate experience of borders. They inscribe onto the landscape the latter's effect on and meaning for the subject who can see and feel her own repulsed absence in the world that would deny her belonging. Video and paintings thus compose something like a critical performance of a reality the subject seeks to displace.

In a similar vein, our own analysis ("a form in its own right . . . one of those media through which the very work unfolds . . .") might read Garcellano's artwork as a form of striving as well as a form of strife.[4] By this I mean that the work is a communicative practice that aims to be meaningful and relevant even as it might also want to dislodge or depart from the terms of perception that would make for its very meaning and relevance. Adorno suggests that this apparent paradox is a characteristic tendency of modern music, as of all works of modern art. For Adorno all modern art, and, even more broadly and pointedly, modern "culture," depends on the conditions of capitalist production that it seeks to distinguish itself from, if not explicitly oppose.[5] The paradox of assimilation and rebellion is intrinsic to "culture" in a reified world dominated by commodification. It is the enactment of the program of capital's confrontation of its own limits, and the political response to such limits—the expression of constitutive contradiction and social antagonism.

In the age of cognitive or communicative capitalism, however, "culture" has spilled beyond its autonomous sphere as either purified vocation or specialized industry, expanding throughout the social realm and permeating all social, economic, and political life. More than a dimension of all these spheres, "culture" names the creative, cognitive, symbolic, and affective activity that in many ways defines the leading paradigm of capitalist accumulation today. In a sense, it constitutes the "forces of production" of contemporary global capital, in its most "advanced" stage. Where communication and cultural production are value-productive activities comprising some of the fastest growing capitalist industries(most evident in capitalist media platforms), with arguably the highest profit margins today, *striving* in the context of contemporary global art must be understood as the living labor of the artist as a cultural producer.

Striving

In this global view, *Sweep* can be interpreted as staging the peculiar form of alienation characteristic of finance-dominated global capital: the experience of being bypassed, always close to the circuits of value but kept at once *on the move and at a standstill*, as the world passes one by. Here the experience of bypass is to be thought of less as *loss* of one's own self, than as its *interdiction*.[6] Not so much loss of life, as its being kept at bay. Bypass is the experience of not getting somewhere—anywhere—even as one is running (operating, trading, fleeing) all the time, as if one were running in place, for life.

Such an experience is the effect and condition of the fractal expansion of modes of value-extraction that issue out of the servicing of circulation itself, and not just from the processes of manufacture (where circulation was merely a necessary means and cost for realizing value). As circulation becomes value-productive in its own right, and hence the paramount activity of valued social life, servicing that value-productive activity increasingly becomes the core work of global cities, defining and upholding these metropolitan spaces as emergent autonomous economies and polities, if not formally independent states. To be bypassed is to be placed always just beyond the boundaries of these channels of valorizing movement, to be forced to tread water to simply stay afloat.

While the expanding landscape paintings of *Borders I* and *II* are large, objective, and public, the video is small like a personal device, and one puts on headphones to overhear this interior monologue of one of the itinerant "could-have-beens" and "should-have-beens" who litter the same path she finds herself on as she imagines walking across a landscape that, she says, is unfinished like history. That voice reveals that, in this evolving landscape, it isn't *what* that is bypassed but *whom*. That it is the one kept on the move but *stilled*, like refugees placed in what Eric Tang describes as a permanent state of never arriving, who sees boundaries and walls suddenly appear.[7] That for the likes of her, maybe of you, the "could-bes" and "would-bes" are foreclosed social possibilities nevertheless held out as compulsory ideals. It is this small personal video that provides the key for subjectifying the walls, or borders, of a seemingly vast and spacious yet prohibitive and forbidding land and sky.

The stark contrast between the seeming mobility and dynamic visuality of the video image, on the one hand, and the seeming stillness and fixity of the painting, on the other, stages the contradiction of a fully globalized economy underlying Garcellano's own conditions as an artist (the subject of her other diverse forms of work, which probe the driving aspirations, protocols, and barriers within global art circuits and institutions).[8] The contradiction that *Sweep* stages is between forces beckoning an unprecedented level of inclusion of the once marginalized periphery and forces impelling an equally unprecedented level of abandonment and expulsion of entire swaths of the same. It is the contradiction between the divergent fates of the existentially soluble and the existentially solid—fates attending those who embody the social conditions of, respectively, liquidity and mobility, which I discuss earlier as composing the dynamics of contemporary modes of accumulation, the tendencies undergirding the global fantasy project of uber-urbanization, which I call *city everywhere*.

City everywhere is also the space of art everywhere. As the project of capitalist culture, such art is by definition a project of value making, which also depends on and expends the life-times of others as the realization of its value as a form of hard currency, able to maintain and even increase the value it stores. It is instance and site of the contradictory tendencies that its own global metropolitanism requires.

Strife

Sweep provides a crystallization of these global tendencies but from the side of the untenable being and belonging of "the unfixed" and "the dispossessed." It is this aspect of the work that constitutes its *strife*. From the side of strife, the paintings are the socioscapes of city everywhere as "land, sky, and mountain" that can "spit you out, leaving you dead cold," the forces of exclusion and expulsion that are the condition and consequence of this new round of accumulation, as the crisis of refugees and the displaced, deported, and detained everywhere would attest. They are also landscapes of forced disappearances, the rise of extrajudicial punishment as the other arm of the securitizing state, the merged public-private "company" that serves as the nation-state franchise of global capital.

We see these other figures of displacement in Garcellano's earlier 2008 painting series *Short Stories*, where white silhouettes of poor children, playing, fleeing, huddling, are starkly placed against the muddy, broody, and heavy-colored landscapes of sinister emptiness. White silhouettes are the painting equivalent

FIGURE 11.3. Lyra Garcellano, *Children of the Depths*, 2008, oil on canvas, 48 × 72 in. Richard Koh Fine Art, Kuala Lumpur, Malaysia. Courtesy of the artist.

of forced disappearances, political killings rendered as a form of derealizing and expunging of active life, with the outlines of children serving as traces of the rubbing out of the simple right "to be," to live out life. They directly refer to the flagrant use of extrajudicial capital punishment by the Philippine state (then under Gloria Macapagal Arroyo) against community activists and the disenfranchised communities they work for and with, struggling for an alternative collective future.[9] In guaranteeing the preemptive securitization of the metropolitanist nation-state as a global platform for capitalist ventures, extrajudicial capital punishment has become a fundamental part of an emergent mode of governmentality as well as a rampant financial enterprise (see chapter 9).

In the transnational space of *Sweep*, the detail of a homeless "brown face," mentioned once in passing, speaks to the racism that subtends this new governmentality and its role in the reordering of global capitalism as a political economy of life-times. It speaks to what is fundamental to the experience of bypass, beyond a notion of unmarked capitalist alienation: that is, a global racism that is old and new, an old racism that harks back to W. E. B. Du Bois's problem of the color line, recalls Aimé Césaire's indictment of colonial humanism,

FIGURE 11.4. Lyra Garcellano, *Peinture 1*, 2013, oil on canvas, 60 × 48 in. Finale Art Gallery, Metro Manila. Courtesy of the artist.

and echoes Arendt's depiction of the fate of surplus peoples—stateless people expelled from humanity—in the march up to World War II, formulations that underscore the direct state forces of war propelling the expulsion of refugees and immigrants today.[10] At the same time, this fleeting reference to an identified face is attributed to the utterance of the land, the mountain, the sky, underscoring the seemingly natural forces of racism's agency in the making of permanent unsettlement. This new racism, in tandem with an older racism, is the racism of an automated calculus for producing disposable life-times:

financial-cultural algorithmic programs operating in the uber-urban world, including the global art world, which, by means of the relentless, exponential super-inflation of the value of its currencies necessarily facilitates the spending down of the ever-cheapened, ever-discounted life-times of others (for that value's realization). This new algorithmic racism operates at every possible scale, no longer only at the scale of the Western European, Anglo-American human subject, which served as the norm of all social life and now subtends the new political economy as the measure of value of all life. It is a posthuman racism that, all the same, relies on the all-too-human forced disappearances of clean-up campaigns (decades of counterinsurgency and counterterrorism operations, now refurbished as urban policing) as part of its operation. It is also the racism of the temporary redemption of the absolutely expendable from such punishment, into the second-class citizenship of global servitude.

That almost negligible detail of the brown face stands, therefore, as the sign of a host of attributes that determine calibrated measures of nonbelonging. A smudge on the glass window or screen, it alludes to the devaluation, abjection, and expulsion concomitant with the liberalization of the sociocultural norms and protocols (the order of cultural values) that regulate and thereby enclose the channels of metropolitan belonging. It signals the human refuse that is to be jettisoned and bypassed as a matter of such enclosure and the "unfinished" histories that have made them so. In this way and as part of its strife, it points to the extant though revised colonial racism that animates contemporary value production, not least of all the order of cultural value production that is metropolitan life and global art.

Splendor

Within the very communicative labor of striving and strife that constitutes this art's meaning, however, a surplus is produced. As with Adorno's referenced "fatally rectilinear succession of victory and defeat," the contradiction presented in the work does not exhaust the generative forces of even the wasted, that is, the life destined toward waste. So Garcellano's critique, in its active disenchantment with the world, its mournful rendering of dispossession and displacement in terms of the rejection of love, nevertheless also tenders a surplus of imaginative gestures in the sensuous paintings of these worlds, lining the walls of an interior scape with aimless shapes of uncertain provenance, offering succor in experience, memory, and yearning.

In the documentary film *Tungkung Langit* (2013), the artist Kiri Dalena views the joy of children playing on the ruins and carcasses of rapacious forces

FIGURE 11.5. Lyra Garcellano, *Sleepwalk*, 2009, oil on canvas, 72 × 53.75 in. Finale Art Gallery, Metro Manila. Courtesy of the artist.

of destruction (enormous trees felled by logging companies in Mindanao, in the aftermath of a devastating typhoon that they survived but with the loss of both parents). One can find in the bleak landscapes of Garcellano's work a strange, similar surfeit in the midst of dearth and depotentiating limbo, which the Thai filmmaker Apichatpong Weerasethakul, in a recent film, also renders as some kind of "splendor."

In Weerasethakul's film *Cemetery of Splendor* (2015), the dead end is a rural home town, Khon Kaen (the Thai title of the film), a world of sensuous syndromes, of overlapping subjectivities and simultaneous pasts and presents subsisting in spaces of neglect, which are perceivable only in the heightened sensorial state of one with a sleeping sickness (as if in a coma) or by those contaminated by such wakeful dreaming in their caring attention to the ill. In this wakeful dreaming—both affliction and respite from the nightmarish somnambulant existence proffered by states and corporate industries—several worlds might inhere or take place in the same abandoned park, and thoughts, sensations, and desires might be bodily transmitted and shared through humans as mediums for each other, in ways that make not debasement but love. If the places explored by Garcellano and Weerasethakul are places of bypass—from the point of view of a mobile global humanity at home in the world they would make entirely theirs, what can only be seen as dead ends—they are also places of spillover, things spreading beyond their bounds, overflowing or unwinding, wandering and unraveling.

We can sense the splendor of Garcellano's landscapes if we juxtapose them with her painting *Sleepwalk* (2009) from the series *Old Pain*, sensuous but depthless portraits of clothed human figures in ambiguous positions of inertia or languor, where she lingers on the indistinct borders between resting and wasting away, paralysis and escape, sleep and death, repose and defeat—also ambiguous meditations on the extrajudicial killings under Arroyo and "our creeping desensitization" to them.[11] In these works and later revisions, submission is not simply resignation but also an immersion in and blending with one's surroundings—floors, beds, walls, furniture, all offering themselves up as surfaces on which to place and harmonize a bodily form, with its shape and dress, hair and appendages—exploring the place of forms as an alternate landscape that collapses depth and surface, exteriority and interiority, instantaneity and eternity. Even blanched bodies, which suggest the derealization of life and the draining of vitality, offer hues, shape, and texture to the mulch.

In these set pieces of reprieve and rest or exhaustion, mise-en-scène for plaint and hope, the ever-increasing acceleration and ceaseless instantaneity that define the temporality of value-producing circulation is stilled with the

FIGURE 11.6. Lyra Garcellano, *Belle Epoque*, 2012, oil on canvas, 60 × 84 in. Finale Art Gallery, Metro Manila. Courtesy of the artist.

flatness of filled surface, one that suggests planes of overlapping memory images, like the decor and design of diaphanous bits of wallpaper and upholstery laminated over and alongside one another, layering untold life-times. The eye is drawn to the arrangement and rearrangement—the superfluous play—of things and bodies, the sensuous patterns of accommodations, infinite accommodations over time that leave their remnants like the tattered banners of plural, ambient dreams (see figures 11.4 and 11.6).

What Garcellano's work explores, and in doing so might be likened to Weerasethakul's own meditation on the leftover people and spaces of by-passed towns, is the unexpected issue—rather, by-product—of tending to one's own wounds by way of tending to the wounds of others or, better, of simply tending this wound that is one's self as well as another, this wound that is the you-we of her address. With little regard to promised worlds, or at least with a fullness of leftover life-times, Garcellano's work explores a life-making activity restored to itself. Hence, in it we see the sense of nontime or timelessness that feels like fullness rather than emptiness.

We might say these works present a genre of time akin but also in contradistinction to Manila slum-dwelling young men's experience of *buryong*, a kind of boredom or insanity, which Stefen Jensen has analyzed as the temporality of masculine redundancy (see my discussion of this in chapter 7). *Buryong*, Jensen argues, is the objectification of "the threat of confinement in a present tense being perpetuated into the future."[12] Jensen reads this personification of the empty time of endless waiting—this embodied figure of an infinite present—as representing "the fear that present-day predicaments will be perpetuated into a future temporal and spatial wasteland."[13] Such fear I see as the real apprehension of the evacuation of the future life-times of disposable populations for the present capital life of globopolitical humanity.

Buryong, the stifling experience of the worthless, useless, meaningless time of disposable life, is the other side of *diskarte*, slang (from the Spanish *descartar*, to discard) for "the ability to make something out of the tiniest possibility," a kind of creative resourcefulness in places of scarce and diminishing resources.[14] *Diskarte* is an art form and a form of getting by and surviving, the profane art of making life out of scraps, fissures, and shifts of space and time, the habit of Philippine artists of borrowing and taking derivative forms from the worlds that determine global values, the art of making life as a matter of timing, of biding and making time, which, as we've seen in previous chapters, has been key to the social reproduction of the urban excess of the Global South. In Garcellano's work we sense the proximity of both these relations to time—the sprawling of an endless present and its further unspooling into bits and pieces of flourish; the monumental stillness of stalled life and the lively, small embellishments of improvised life making.

As the highest-value-producing department or sphere of production of capitalism today, "culture" is not simply the arts and the culture industry but the very production of capitalized social life. Hence cultural activity for globopolitical humanity is geared toward an aesthetic of instantaneous, smooth, and continuous circulation (the aim and ideal of social media apps where networking and marketing have become indistinct), subscribed, uninterrupted access, and ceaseless and seamless fluency of communication and movement. This is an aesthetic attuned to the temporal as well as sensorial and affective qualities of life-times of value.

It is against such a political aesthetic that the work of artists and filmmakers attentive to *remaindered life* offer glimpses of other social life and the unexpected, gratuitous abundance or splendor of remaindered life-times that might unfold in the everyday arts of survival. In this work, such as the films of Abderrahmane Sissako, Apichatpong Weerasethakul, Eliah Suleiman, Lav

Diaz, Jia Zhangke, and Tsai Ming-liang, which demonstrate remaindered life as an aesthetic problem as well as a political hold on attention emerging out of the Global South, it is forgotten pasts and neglected presents, all manner of unaccounted times, that call out to us from the wayside of a foretold future.[15]

Garcellano and Dalena exemplify this attention to remaindered life in their respective restagings of the disappeared. Dalena's disappeared include the forgotten slogans and actions of past political movements, which she restages as live enunciations and memorial claims (as collected proverbs and as individual gravestones). Both artists present the murdered and disappeared as incomplete landscapes, erased images, whose missing pieces are asking to be filled in, their sense(s) to be unraveled and therefore still to be made—live imaginations that compel the continuing and never finished work implied by an anachronistic notion of "culture" as cultivation.[16] It is, as Garcellano says in *Sweep*, as if they are inviting us to partake in this endeavor: *"Let us imagine a home that can imagine us back."*

There are no roads without the places they pass through, without the waysides they create to define the perimeter and parameters of their protocol of movement, what allows them to channel what they aim to convey.[17] Works of literature, art, and even urban infrastructure are always in medias res to the degree that they are never objects in themselves, as origins or effects.[18] They are always already in the course of sense-making projects and efforts to institute, follow, implement, alter, corrupt, or corrode the codes that organize certain forms of life. To what and how we connect these worldly artifacts (other artifacts, perhaps) is a matter of interpretation, itself to be viewed as a sense-making effort on par with its objects. That is to say, our own "critical" analysis is also a world-making effort, in its capacity to mediate, to relate (to bring into relation, to heighten the palpability of relations that might be overlooked, actively forgotten or denied because of indifference to or lack of the necessary cultural languages), to generate or contribute to the generation of another material imagination (other modes of perception and feeling, other sensibilities) than that which now governs the value-productive mode of life we are compelled to make a living in. These forms and the contents we contribute (in our own role as content providers) are our political bids, what we put out and what we put in as our part in the cultivation of a world that is different from, though also immanent in, the world that now rules us.

My own bid entails an attention to the surplus that *Sweep*, in its communicative labor to render the experience of bypass, creates impromptu: what I suggest is some kind of splendor. That surplus can be viewed among "the waste products and blind spots" that Adorno acknowledged as escaping—

indeed, outwitting—the historical dynamic. The seemingly outmoded (but not obsolete) sensuous care with which the landscapes are painted (in the old-fashioned art of oil painting), rendering at once longing and the emotional marking (the scarring, sullying effect) of that longing's betrayal—this now artisanal artistic labor produces something more and other than the meaning that the work might bear for global consumption. It produces the occasion and ground for the revaluing expenditure of otherwise lost or wasted life-times, indeed, for the biding and making of another kind of time. This is a form of *idling*, not a state or condition but an activity, like an engine running slowly in place, that dilates further, with every brushstroke filling out a pattern, a decorative motif, a figure of sensorial feeling. In this way, the seemingly infinite time of waiting that stretches out indefinitely before one who cannot find a place of belonging (a place, that is, of social meaning, relevance, or purpose) becomes a plethora of immanent life-times of possibility.

While the video might encapsulate the "meaning" of this installation in the familiar form of a subject, with a legible political claim, it is in the paintings where that subject is both recalled and undone, in tatters, so to speak. It is in the superfluous (for Adorno, "puerile"; for us, childlike, playful[19]), aimless, imaginative gestures of these paintings across the different series of Garcellano's work that we glimpse a rendering of the temporal character of what is eclipsed by the installation's "meaning": that is, the life-times of persistent "being" that make the world that would not have them. These are life-times of making time, of filling (not just killing) time, made sensible and rendered back in the constitution of the land, mountain, sky—life-times of waste restored as a feature of the built environment, what now passes for "nature." In this idling (idyll-ing), wasting and thriving, suffering and dreaming have become one and the same, like the splendor of making life in the midst of life's remains.

Nightmare Landscapes, Ambient Dreams

The painterly landscapes of Garcellano's border experiences can be linked to Jia Zhangke's dystopic, placid cinematic image of the Yangtze River—soon to flood the town of Fengjie to realize the Three Gorges hydroelectric dam project long desired by the Chinese state—in *Still Life* (2006); to Jia's scenes of barren mountain ranges and valleys, in *Platform* (2000), across which trains run, at once heralding ambivalent change in the era of China's incipient reform from 1979 to the 1990s and leaving the very people desiring and impelling such change behind; and to the empty, urban high-rise buildingscapes of Taipei that serve as backdrop and ulterior cause of the homelessness of the poor, engulfed by sheets of relentless rain, in Tsai Ming-liang's *Stray Dogs* (2013)—all landscapes that inscribe the emerging archipelagic geography of city everywhere, the polity and space-time (the chronotope of dwelling) of the citizen-subjects of the future-now, as experienced from the side of its castaways.

Such landscapes evoke an imaginative geography that alters the meaning and form of land from what these might have been in another era. From the view of capital life, land is just so much real estate—ground of value-productive activity and, as such, bearing its own exchange value, alienable as a commodity, and abstractable and divisible as an underlying asset for derivative finance, the real and virtual base of multiple life-times extracted, sold, and traded or collateralized. But from the experience of peripheral life, such land has become an animate force (inimical, arduous, portentous), a live power shaping and intertwined with human hardships and demise in mysterious and even sublime ways. It is witness to the repulsion, devastation, exhaustion, and depletion of lesser life, which it itself inflicts as this quasi-independent force of dispossession and extraction. No wonder that, in the imaginary of Global South filmmakers seeking what remains of "life" beyond the image of "surplus value cinema,"[20] beyond the global life synchronized by spectacle, experience should itself be environmental in form and feeling. Inscribing the violence it would seem to perpetrate, land becomes at once the scribe and the scroll of a writing that would appear to be happening on its own, legible in the actions of all but "owned" by none.

As scroll, land (and water) is the place of performance and recording of disposable life-times expended in the building of entire environments of value. Here on the terrain of global ambition and desire—whether depleted fields and barren mountains, shrinking rivers and rising oceans, or skylines of sheer, vertical pillars of monumental wealth urging each other higher, all linked together by the intricate latticework of flight paths, freeways, railways, and subscription channels—are etched life-times of disposability spent: life-times of infinite waiting to no end, for those whose futures have already been foreclosed, cashed in, or loaned out with no expectation of return (those who pay, with their own promised life-times or the promised life-times of their kin, for the chance to work, which is a chance to survive). Landscapes register the different temporalities of people's disposability, whether the temporalities of their spectacular destruction or the temporalities of their noxious stagnation—the slow, nearly imperceptible running out of life and time, or their sudden, complete wasting; the constant drain of one's life-times outpacing their refilling, or the total spill; the stillness and turbulence of running in place, never getting anywhere; the sputter of brutal termination, the imposed, irrevocable end.

As scribe, land delineates the range of values across which all life is spread. It draws the lines between proper and improper residence, marks the borders between the cultivar and the weed, encloses and protects the habitable against the uninhabitable—dividing viable and unviable existence and being. No doubt, in its capacities to circumscribe and sanction, grade and degrade, appraise and depreciate the forms of life found and founded within the scope of its ever-expanding terrain, global capital land would appear to be merely the projection of the actions of real, human agents—a reification of the social relations of domination, exploitation, and expropriation that humans alone set in motion. Certainly one might read the looming agency of empty landscapes and the vast built environs comprised of factories, offices, storage facilities, highways, sea lanes, cellular towers, optical fiber cables, digital subscriber lines (DSL), electromagnetic and radio waves, as the embodiment of so much past, dead labor.[21]

Yet only a stubborn insistence on human sovereignty would miss the way that land, as a major instance and condition of a broader lifeworld, which we call the environment, is no mere instrument of another—as surface, screen, and scroll. Land also serves as accomplice and actor in an order of life, which is also an order of battle, in which its own forces have been conscripted.

On the US-Mexico border, as Jason de Leon painstakingly and unflinchingly testifies, the harsh, smoldering, and desolate terrain of the Sonoran Desert has been enlisted as a major ally of the US Border Patrol.[22] This strip of desert between the Baboquivari and Tumacácori mountain ranges, just south of Tucson, Arizona, which has been the lifeworld of the Indigenous Tohono O'odham ("Desert People") for millennia, has become deployed by the federal US government as an especially effective agent of violence and hostility that can better stop the flow of unwanted populations into the United States from the south. As de Leon argues, the Prevention through Deterrence US border policy implemented in 1994 was predicated on enlisting the "hostile" and treacherous desert environment as the new "victimizer" of border transgressors (in place of Border Patrol agents shooting and arresting people after they crossed the border), drawing on the agency of animals and other nonhuman "nature" to inflict the grave harm that would impede and deter attempted passage into the United States.

Many Global South artists and filmmakers, including those I mention here, make palpable this very experience of land as an animate force, an actor or actant. It is the experience of the surrounds, the mediating atmosphere and environment, which not only shape and spell the fates of so many—becoming forces that people importune with their own petty gambling and fate-playing. Atmosphere and environment are also what the actions of people comprise—not the sum aggregate of their disjointed, random, atomistic actions, but rather the synthetic absorption of their cooperative systems of social reproduction into a higher order of value production, for which these lower strata are to serve only as enabling milieu.

Yet atmosphere and environment—ambient spaces, circumjacent times—are tapped by many artists seeking sensibility and succor from their intimate surroundings, the place times of their making that they share with others as modes of attention. Both Garcellano and Dalena use the video shot from a moving vehicle to mark out a search for what cannot be found (belonging for one, remains of abducted life for the other). The looking out into what is ostensibly scenery becomes a recording of that time (not lost but persisting), which I have elsewhere called the time of castaways, the temporal structure of violent displacement and upheaval, the indefinite suspension of any sense of time moving forward.[23]

In Adjani Arumpac's *War Is a Tender Thing*, a documentary exploration of the overlap and breach between the two sides of the filmmaker's family in Mindanao, Muslim and Christian—the poor Ilokano settlers on her mother's side fleeing poverty and now landless in the north; and the besieged Muslim people on her father's side, struggling to survive the seized settlements of their lands and continuous military onslaughts—Arumpac turns her cinematic eye to the land and the expressive hands and faces of the women in her family, places of tenderness and war. Lingering on these bodyscapes and landscapes becomes a time of longing and expectation, a time in which we can see, in the very spaces of devastation and unforgiving desolation, traces and signs, things and happenings, of another world of splendor, where several worlds might inhere, filled with plural, ambient dreams.

In the Weeds

Around the middle of the five-hour drive between Metro Manila and my hometown, San Fernando, La Union, there is a stretch of the new highway that runs through the lands of Pampanga and Tarlac. Along this stretch, you can see parts of these lands still blanketed by *lahar*—mudflows of volcanic ash and pyroclastic debris mixed with rainwater—from the June 1991 eruption of Mount Pinatubo. The event, consisting of a series of eruptions taking place over three days, was the second largest in the twentieth century, its global impact evidenced by the volcano's injection of 20 million tons of sulfur dioxide into the stratosphere, creating a gas cloud whose dispersal caused global temperatures to drop by 1°F (0.5°C) for a couple of years after.²⁴ Flows of *lahar*, brought about by rains and wind from a typhoon during the days of the final eruption on June 15, killed over seven hundred people, nearly half from roofs that collapsed on them from the weight of spewed rocks, pebbles, and wet volcanic ash.

Unlike the volcanic eruptions and the earthquakes that accompanied them, *lahar* flows are not discrete, punctual events. The flows occurred then and over the following years, in varying intensities and geographical patterns, induced by monsoon rains mixing with ash and pyroclastic debris sedimented on the slopes of the mountains and in river channels. In the following two years, over 329,000 families, or two million more lives, were affected as periodic concrete-like slurries completely buried 28 *barangays*, or villages (under up to three meters or nearly ten feet of volcanic debris), partially or wholly destroyed livelihoods or households in 364 barangays, and covered almost 1,000 square kilometers (or around 247,105 acres) of agricultural land (largely rice and sugarcane crops) and approximately 180 square kilometers (or 4, 447 acres) of forest lands.²⁵

These are some of the measurements that researchers, scientists, and journalists have offered to help represent the scale of loss and damage sustained by the social worlds impacted by the cataclysmic event. They are hard to translate into the visceral experiences of ordinary people—how big is a thousand square kilometers or a hundred thousand hectares to a farmer who can barely survive tilling one hectare of land? How large is the loss suffered by two million people displaced when the loss of one home is devastating? Still, everyone repeats the prices of rehabilitation and rebuilding, the heavy losses of property and industry, including agricultural crops and livestock, the measurable values of all that was lost, numerical indices that can be found in abundance in all the literature about the Mount Pinatubo eruption. Fewer measures exist for the deaths of uncultivated flora and fauna—uncounted losses of coral reefs and fish, various species of forest and river life. What measures of what loss matter for whom?

The numbers themselves are merely still shots of moving landscapes of continuing aftereffects, like the before and after photographs taken of ash-buried towns and rice fields, which record the consequences of the eruption in familiar visual terms—rooftops of buildings, houses, and churches appearing to peer out of a freshly-poured, monumental slab of concrete. As repeatedly expressed by Cynthia Bautista, Luisa Camagay, Carmen Jimenez, and other members of an all-women, multidisciplinary university faculty research team that documented the destruction up close, however, more difficult if not impossible to represent is the harrowing misery, grief, and desolation of the people who suffered these losses.²⁶ In their collected volume, *In the Shadow of the Lingering*

Mount Pinatubo Disaster, the researchers weave the data they collect with stories of the people they knew and met from living among them in the aftermath of the eruption. The stories are vivid chronicles of the overwhelming fear and suffering of individuals and communities, tales of desolation, anxiety, and despair in the face of an overwhelming and continuing disaster, not only the natural events comprising the "act of God" but also the processes at the hands of people's human saviors—the governmental agencies, private contractors, local officials and authorized organizations charged with evacuation, resettlement, rebuilding, and rehabilitation. The tragic losses of homes and livelihoods that people suffered became compounded by yet more losses incurred in the course of organized relief. Tales of bureaucratic corruption and siphoned resources in the rebuilding follow on tales of devastation and rescue.

Of all the people detrimentally affected by the Pinatubo eruptions and lahar flows, none had their collective lives as radically overturned as the aboriginal Aeta communities living on Mount Pinatubo and its immediate environs. "By far, the most heart-rending evacuations were those of Aytas who drew physical and spiritual strength from the volcano."[27] Forced to flee the slopes of the mountain where they lived by hunting, fishing, gathering, and small subsistence farming, around 7,800 Aeta families (around 35,000 people) were placed in evacuation centers where poor sanitation and shelter conditions led to the illnesses and deaths of 157 of their children from disease and exposure.

But the stories neither begin nor end with the volcanic eruption in June 1991. A geologist activist involved in the emergency fieldwork occasioned by Pinatubo's eruption, Kelvin Rodolfo, writes that an earthquake along the Philippine fault a year before on July 16, 1990, which killed 1,600 people, may have triggered the eruption, loosening blocks of the earth's crust, "liquefying" the ground of old, water-soaked river sand on which the coastal city of Dagupan stood, and sinking heavy buildings several feet.[28] Yet, as Rodolfo remembers, media coverage of the earthquake with a "world-class" magnitude of 7.8 and a death toll of 1,600 people vanished with the Iraqi invasion of Kuwait less than two weeks later. As in all the other natural disasters that have beset the peoples and lands of this postcolonial, archipelagic tropical nation—typhoons such as the 2013 supertyphoon Yolanda/Haiyan, earthquakes, floods, and volcanic eruptions, such as Taal in January 2020—the course and effects of Mount Pinatubo's eruption were deeply shaped by human social, economic, and physical geographies (and valuations) laid down years and decades before. Here as well as elsewhere, the patterns of loss, human as well as nonhuman, trace the same patterns of life exaction (and indifference) that the rampant pursuit of profit and power has drawn over the places these forces continue to colonize.

Three decades of sudden, intermittent, and slow movements of *lahar* clogging river channels, causing the flooding of adjoining lowland agricultural plains and densely populated towns, have dramatically changed this landscape and the lives of those who inhabited it. The new highway built over this expanse of land in 2005 is at least several kilometers east of the old highway, the two-lane road running through the towns that my family and I have plied since I was a child in the 1970s and that has also been reclaimed for new urbanizing developments. On one of our last drives on a section of the old highway, my father, before he died a few years ago, pointed out to me in angry and anguished tones the marks of "girdling" on the magnificent acacia trees lining both sides of a stretch of the road in Pampanga, railing against this signature of a rapacity we were all too familiar with. Girdling, he explained, was the cutting of a circular strip of bark round the trunk of the tree in order to kill it. To make way for undoubtedly more lucrative ends, the trees were to be eliminated, and with them the life that had grown underneath their canopy, where people hung out and strolled in the afternoons and roadside vendors sold fruits and other goods. Since the new highway through these provinces was completed, I have not been on that stretch of old road again.

Today, driving to or from my hometown, to or from Metro Manila, I squint my eyes to catch a fleeting glimpse of the once very familiar landscapes on the old route, which now lies near the horizon from the new highway I am on. What lies between this new road and that horizon now are fields of white blooming grasses of *talahib* growing in stretches of fine lahar, like desert sand.

Thirty years after a catastrophic event is a whole generational lifetime. A generational lifetime can spell the difference between one world and another. At the end of the brutal World War II, the final battle between US and Japanese military forces killed between 100,000 and 240,000 Filipino civilians and almost completely demolished Manila, which was reduced to not much more than concrete building shells and rubble by the blitzkrieg bombing campaign of US military forces seeking to minimize their own casualties. Thirty years later, Manila was an emerging modern metropolis, gleaming with monumental promises of urban "beautification" projects, "human settlements" (low-cost housing), and industrialization. A "city of man" was in the making through massive infrastructural development—its road system modernized, international luxury hotels, cosmopolitan art centers, and high-end residential neighborhoods built to host the tourist consumers and capital investors aggressively courted by the national government, and export-processing manufacturing zones constructed—laying down the grounds out of which the program that is now city everywhere would emerge.

Though a whole other world can appear to succeed and entirely supplant its predecessor, traces of the older world persist, and the ways and protocols that shaped it may well continue to shape the world that replaces it. When the volcano erupted, the US military permanently evacuated its two large military bases, Clark Air Base and Subic Bay Naval Base, the renewal of whose colonial leases were at the time being vigorously debated in the Senate. The volcanic eruption destroyed the bases, just after the US forces and their families abandoned them, making the national decision to reject the renewal of the leases all but redundant and moot. Today those former US bases are special economic zones, duty-free industrial, commercial, and residential entrepôts, which have become paradigmatic platforms hosting global, metropolitan life. They have become the sites of many infrastructural development projects comprising Duterte's "Build, Build, Build" program for national economic growth, including new highways and airports that keep them nodes in the orbits of global capital flows. And while no longer housed in these bases, the US military has, through the visiting forces agreement with the Philippine state, remained a powerful presence of extrasovereignty in the country.

While many of the evacuated Aetas eventually returned to their lands, much of the mountain forests of their homes were buried or destroyed by the flows of ash and lahar, and with them the lifeways of hunting, fishing, foraging, and swidden farming, which they had followed for hundreds, perhaps thousands, of years. After years in government resettlement sites where they were taught livelihood skills and adapted to lowland ways of life, many now sell vegetables, work as janitors and other staff in the Clark Freeport and Special Economic Zone, and offer their skills as mountain guides and teachers of jungle survival tactics to a growing number of domestic and foreign tourists, drawn by the breathtaking new natural landscape left by the geological changes. Although the lands had no monetary value for Aeta communities before the volcanic eruption, the 1997 Indigenous Peoples' Rights Act endowed them with legal, communal rights to them. As in the Cordillera Highlands (chapter 2), those rights are now both activated and infringed upon as commercial developers and builders seize and purchase their lands to construct New Clark City, a planned world-class, smart, green, climate-resilient city, for which many of the Aeta are now employed as construction workers and promised future employment as maintenance workers. Yet many continue to fight to remain on their lands, and to recover a way of life that is now more than ever besieged.

FIGURE 11.7. Talahib. Photograph by author.

The story feels as old as the colonialism it rehearses. The story of dispossession and displacement, of capital conquest and subsumption, as well as the story of struggle and survival, which is the story of living in a continuing time of war.

The Time of Expectation

When I gaze upon the landscape of this story from the roads of war that shaped it, I cannot help but be struck by the wide stretches of beautiful grasses of talahib (*Saccharum spontaneum*) with their white feathery blooms adorning the carpet of lahar. To almost everyone the talahib is a nuisance, its rampant flourishing—in what used to be cultivated, agricultural fields where now nothing else can grow—signaling that this is indeed a wasteland. "Useless," I am told, when I remark on their abundance and wonder what people might make of it. Unlike the many kinds of grasses that women weave into baskets, that men weave into roof thatching, that can be harvested as bedding or fodder for stock, or made into other immediate use values, this perennial, polymorphic grass appears to be nothing more than a weed, difficult even to pull out because of the sharp edges of its stalks.

Bypass and Splendor • 323

While there is no lack of bioscientific, entrepreneurial searches to make profitable use of the plant's inherent properties, talahib still remains no more than a placeholder, literally what holds a shifting terrain together, preventing the continuous erosion of the land and the collapse of river banks. Lahar is in contrast more economically valuable, used and promoted as a cement supplement for the road building and construction industry. Talahib is a survivor species, not unlike the matsutake mushroom that Anna Tsing describes as thriving in the ruins of capitalist nature—except that it has not succeeded in becoming a global commodity or even a gift within local cultures.[29] Perhaps it is a superweed.[30] At the very least, it is regarded as a serious weed. And yet, its persistence indicates "an active natural plant succession," that is, an evolutionary transformation of pure grassland into a savannah plant community stage that has happened before, the evidence for which can be seen in the lower parts of Mount Pinatubo.[31] The very name Pinatubo means "made or allowed to grow." Although talahib also maintains soil productivity by fixing nitrogen from the atmosphere and has been found to increase microbial count and the succession of bacterial communities for vegetation recovery,[32] it is merely part of a preliminary stage that is to be overcome, playing a small, helping role in a long process of natural healing, whereby marginal substrates will recover their fertile states and be able to support the growth and flourishing of more plants and animals, a diversity that some might see as ultimately supporting and enhancing human life.

In the foreshortened timescale of capitalism and its politics, talahib grasses bear no use value. Indigenous to South Asia, the byproduct and bioecological trace of oceanic connections of trade as well as colonial agriculture spanning precolonial to colonial times, *Saccharum spontaneum* is a coarse, uncultivated grass that has never been favorable to capital life, deemed an invasive species for causing severe losses in plantation plant productivity (sugarcane, cotton, sorghum, pineapple) and hosting insects and diseases that infest the cultivars. The slow temporality of environmental restoration of plant biomass production and improvement of faunal populations in which it plays a small part, as a fixer and an indicator of better times to come, is made even longer with the continuous, devastating impact of lahar flows, which create unstable and volatile conditions that make recovery uncertain, or at best full of fits and starts.

If I am drawn to this splendiferous grass in a meditation on remaindered life, it is not because I see in it some political moral lesson or a symbol of the resilience that, in the present conversion of some of these lands into industrial parks, capital life is itself held to exemplify.[33] It is rather because talahib, like so many other seemingly inconsequential, useless, even deleterious beings, is a material part of this landscape that is the history and possibility of our transforming lives. It is the trace, consequence, and elemental agent of a history of sweeping devastation and discontinuous survival, of domination over land and life and their wasting, of struggle, defeat, and endurance. But it is also itself an extemporal burst of splendor, neither the cause nor merely the product of sovereign forces of capital will and desire, even as it has invisibly contributed to the very resilience of the noble cane (*Saccharum officinarum*, or sugar factories) whose modern cultivation was central to capital's global powers of accumulation and destruction.[34]

Time and again, passing through these landscapes in the summer, I see not the white plumes of the talahib shimmering like the sea, but the red plumes of fire razing them down, smoke billowing from their depths. The burning of the grass is for many a step in making the land useful once again. Although today much of the clearing prepares the land for agricultural plantations and other capital industries, the use of fire has also long been part of people's living on and with the land. It is characteristic of swidden or rotational agriculture, or what is pejoratively termed slash-and-burn farming, largely understood to be backward practices, unsustainable and harmful to the environment, and therefore needing to be replaced by more modern ecological methods.[35] The uncontrolled use of this cultivation method, without the indigenous knowledge and management that had made it a sustainable practice for hundreds and thousands of years has in fact been seen as the very cause of the establishment of so-called invasive species, such as these grasses. And yet fires are also vital elemental parts of this natural world with and within which people do know how to live, even as that know-how is constantly and paradoxically relied on and destroyed.

There is a legend that the Aeta tell, which evidences a folk memory of Mount Pinatubo's penultimate eruption at least five hundred years ago.[36] The legend, as well as the common Aeta warning to children that their god, Apo Pinatubo Namalyari, will throw down stones if they don't behave, suggests that the Aeta have long lived with the possibility and reality of volcanic eruption. Like other peoples of this archipelago, they have long lived with natural forces beyond their control even as they have also brought natural forces within their spheres of mutual cooperation, such as fire.

Like fire, talahib has no intrinsic meaning or value, even as both have taken on pernicious associations that align them with entropy and unlivability. Yet, also like fire, talahib is not some form of pure nature, removed from history and systems of human making. In fact, fire, talahib, and humans are acting in concert, playing interactive roles in the aftermath of this last volcanic eruption. Against expectations of their detrimental effect on vegetation recovery, the slash-and-burn cultivation practices of the Aeta who have returned to the mountain ridges, together with the growth of talahib and ararong (*Trema orientalis*), have contributed to the restoration of soil fertility and the recovery of the land.[37]

However alienated humans might be from this florescent organic life form that is part of their surrounds, talahib too is part of history, part of that human nature which is separated out from the rest of nature, now called environment (its surrounds). It speaks to me—as do the birds that are part of people's worlds of reference, the yellow parakeets and the chicks in the diverse yet related contexts of continuing wars of expending life—of a broader milieu for thriving than what a human politics would allow.

Writing about the contemporary struggles for self-determination of the Lumad Manobo of Lianga Surigao del Sur, in particular, among the Indigenous communities also targeted by Duterte's revanchist war against terrorism in Mindanao, Sarah Raymundo argues that the difference between Indigenous justice and Christian justice lies in the fact that for the latter, God is external, while for the former God is embedded in a nature that Indigenous peoples are also a part of.[38] The very terms for Indigenous peoples—Katutubo (native, from *tubo*, meaning growth, as in *Pinatubo*, meaning made or allowed to grow) and Lumad (native, of the earth)—speak of this bond between them and the nonhuman nature in which they live, speak of land and people as kin. The talahib grasses beckon us to consider this larger, sacred world within which we might find the justice that we now are at pains to find, a world in which neither waste nor value reside. They beckon us to consider much longer, deeper, and more diverse timelines for our efforts and our aspirations, beyond the pasts, presents, and futures of our present calculus for measuring gain. To imagine a revolutionary openness and abundance of life-times for all.[39]

If, as Raymundo observes, for Indigenous peoples of this land, there is no difference between collective myths and membership in collective, political organized life, for folk beliefs are a matter of how people live, we are urged to heed the stories of our Katutubo and Lumad kin, of our own native ancestors, of our own survival, of all the becoming-human who are living in a time of war, to believe that all that appears disposable can belong, and to live in accordance with this belief. To live as if this were in fact a home that might still imagine us back.

Beyond the thresholds that our histories continue to be bound to and thereby continue to uphold, with their definition of meaningful action and transformation, another time beckons. The time of expectation for the quantum leap, the change of configuration and order of things, can be immediate and very long. But at every interval between now and then, in this time of expectation, we engage in small vibrations of great abundance that appear to bring no change, to never amount to anything, to be of no consequence whatsoever. And yet all the small and medium vibrations we manage to make in and to this system, in unorganized and organized ways, reverberating with each other, as we withdraw in the smallest of ways from this order and amplify in the largest of ways the forms, affects, visions, and practices of other modes of living subsisting in this order of life (and waste) so violently fighting against its own dismantling and disintegration, all these vibrations will matter in bringing this era to an end.

12

AND THEN SOME

The End and All

Everywhere, the end is near. Disaster looms over the globopolis like a foretold dream. Any future is clouded over by billows of noxious conditions, accumulated over centuries of predation and indifference, and fueled by the dreams of infinite potentials waiting to be released. The youth contemplate their own future lives being lived in vain, paths of aspiration and effort that will come to nothing in the end. *Everywhere* is strewn with failure and catastrophe.

It would seem that the world is at the point of exhaustion. The historical experience of peoples and species destined for expenditure and extinction is now the experience of everyone, the fate of all. Yet many of those peoples, our peoples, have in fact survived the peremptory expiration of our fellow members, our kith and kin, and the constant spoliation of the other natures with which our lives were always entwined. They are testimony to the reverse of the generalizing, flattening ends of war. Only their status as the less developed, "developing," "becoming," decrees that such experiences were particular and partial, the precursors of those of everyone. But have we not always also been *all*?

Although our stories are continuously diminished and sidelined in favor of the main act, the world-historical self-tellings of the already human; though our travails are mostly reduced to cautionary tales for the disasters that await everyone; those stories and travails are the secrets and hidden keys for the regeneration and survival of all. For they are not mere emblems of catastrophe. They are also a plethora of other languages, modalities, and grounds of life-making in a time of war.

Not Consumed in the Moment of Action, Not Subsumed by Politics

Remaindered life is not offered as a consolation. It is not a willful affirmation of what we would like to see—subversion, resistance, valiant strength, inextinguishable hope. It is not necessarily an inspiring tale, though it could well be.

What it seems to me that I am trying, and feel a need, to do, is to express the order of the world as a deeply rapacious, indifferent, pernicious, sad, and brutal state of affairs in which all, barring none, are enjoined, coerced, and seduced to participate in or somehow negotiate and maneuver and manipulate. But it is also an order that, in requiring the survival and life activity of those human and nonhuman strata it would consume and destroy, has come to depend on what it despises, on forms of life that remain and become what lies just beyond its control, what must and cannot be fully incorporated in it and therefore always defines its limits and the fraying edges of its command.

There is in these zones of disposable life, of life put at the disposition of valued life, a remainder—life-making not absorbed, superfluous expenditures that yield no material or immaterial social use value. This is not resistance by any existing political measure. Nor is it a potential to be tapped, mobilized, and organized. What that remainder might be is inseparable from a kind of attention ill-disposed to producing value, that is, value that is accumulable somewhere, a surplus that can accrue outside the moment and duration and means—including the human means—of its realizing action. By this I mean what we take as remaindered life is as much the method or mode of our attention, of our tending, of our tenderness, as it is a life-making practice. The mode of this attention—the hermeneutic of remaindered life—is itself a mode of living that we glimpse and feel in ourselves and in others, often in actions and moments when there is nothing more to gain and nothing left to lose, but the very live happening then and there that is its thrill, its grace, its gratuitous opening.

Although remaindered life—this living without value—is not a political program, it comes out of the unfinished political project of decolonization, out of the vital memories, longings, and enjoyments of the becoming-human who continue to seek pathways to escape the order of their fate (a fate of perpetual, because immanently failing, becoming). That fate is, by effect and by design, useful to global capital because it serves up the milieus of dispossession on which capital—its powers of command—depends. But it is a fate that so many hazard, play with, and survive, living nonetheless beyond its bounds, but always in coordinated acts, depending on, entailing, helped by, socialities of shared and mutual being.

Remaindered life reminds us of times of living that long for a place of belonging, which shared and mutual being beyond the dominant ontologies and ecologies of global life might allow, even nourish. These times of living—as unordained gifts, *appoggiaturas* or grace notes adorning mundane movements of practical life, moments of fleeting splendor—are not to be implemented or mandated. They are not to be made into political ideals. But such times of living, which can neither be consumed nor subsumed by a value-making order that transcends them, might help steer our sensibilities toward other modes of life in which the enjoyments of these times—what might be no more than the burst of an opening, the shimmer or vibration of a mutation, a passing trill—would be aplenty.

Though the examples of remaindered life-times I offer might appear trivial, they appear so only in a global mode of life that relentlessly seeks value in every morsel of existence, including what it would cast out as waste. For this reason, these small excesses, which cannot amount to anything, hold a tiny power of elusion, like glints or floaters in our eyes, which can remind us of our own transience and embeddedness in this global mode of life even as our sensation of them might also be proof and instance of the immanence of an excess, openness, and abundance of other life.

And Then Some

While remaindered life is not itself resistance, it lives within resistance, making it possible (it is "the predicate rather than the plan"),[1] even as resistance is what wins us the spaces where such remaindered life might dwell, perhaps thrive, and hopefully move us toward each other in ever more generous worlds of mutual being and shared living.

People fight back. They organize. Their fighting is lifesaving, life-making. Their organizing creates the openings and connections so they are not engulfed.

Without the constant organizing of social and political movements—animated and propelled by an abundance of life remainders, shaped and capacitated by unreckoned forces of sociality of survival—we would not be able to see the world differently. These movements and the eruptive expressions of resistance that they keep alive provide the apparatuses for a broader consciousness of the world from perspectives that otherwise have little traction in the worlds of writing (worlds dedicated to higher pursuits predicated on lower labors of necessity). Sylvia Wynter writes that the Los Angeles revolts, sparked by the brutal beating of Rodney King in 1992, confronted us and enable us to think new thoughts, against the legacy of an education made by "the best and brightest" which plays no insignificant part in reproducing this global order of the already human and its war to remain so.[2]

So it is with the revolts of our present time. Organizing is an important moment and aspect of the broader tectonic shifts we are now experiencing, witnessing, and making in the world. It is in fact what this writing, as well as the writing it is inspired by, see themselves as part of. We owe the movements in the streets, in the mountains and in the fields, in the homes and in the hallways, the critical, fugitive, and remaindered ways of looking at and feeling the world around us that we attempt to extend and further in writing. In this way, writing as well as other art making are also part of these movements that seek to recreate the material, social bases of an entire global mode of life.

If I have placed my own efforts in seeking remaindered life, it is because I want to remember and bear in mind the limits of what we might, at any given moment of struggle, apprehend in our critical consciousness, without which we might overlook and quickly subsume the kinds of know-how of living that make for collective survival in these times of war. Those limits include the imperative to find political value, function and use, in what we find—an instrumentality that might persist in our visions of a better world, in our commitment to political ends located in the future—that inadvertently would leave behind all that might itself be deemed waste or not worth the revolutionary time of our political movements, even as these movements are replete and replenished with what would appear to be in excess of their aims.

What might be remaindered now is what I have tried to show here as another kind of organizing, the organizing practice and logic of open socialities of survival—the organizing that is life-making, often left to others—us—cooking, cleaning, growing, repairing, tending, healing, feeding, mourning, soothing, seeing to the flourishing of intimates and kin, always "helping" rather than "accomplishing." This vitality we partake in through our actively shared existence is what we continue to depend on, what shapes and makes us, and transmits know-hows of living as mutual care and enjoyment, which are part of other, alternative but already present modes of life lived now. It reminds us that, far from a denigrating view of all that is merely life "maintenance"—that category for reproductive labors of necessity and mere reproduction that yield no value—when we carefully tend to our shared being and living, we find more, and then some.

NOTES

CHAPTER ONE. THE WAR TO BE HUMAN

Sections of this chapter were published as "Life-Times of Becoming Human," *Occasion: Interdisciplinary Studies in the Humanities* 3 (2012), http://occasion.stanford.edu/node/75.

1 Stiegler, *Symbolic Misery*, vol. 1; Arendt, *The Human Condition*.
2 Berardi, *The Soul at Work*; Deleuze, "Postscript on the Societies of Control."
3 As Anne Cheng and David Eng and Shinhee Han argue, this melancholia in the US context is predicated on a racist ideal. We might also say that racial melancholia acts as form and content of the subjective dynamics of value. See Cheng, *Racial Melancholia*; Eng and Han, "A Dialogue on Racial Melancholia"; see also my own treatment of the racializing subjective dynamics of value in Tadiar, "Metropolitan Debris," in *Things Fall Away*, 228–47.
4 Césaire, *Discourse on Colonialism*, 36, 36 45.
5 Sartre, preface, xxiv.
6 Tadiar, "The War to Be Human/Becoming Human in a Time of War." This piece was written as the United States began bombing Afghanistan on October 7, 2001. While finishing this book, I did not have the chance to read Zakiyyah Iman Jackson's *Becoming Human: Matter and Meaning in an Antiblack World*, which I believe also grapples with related questions.
7 Tadiar, "The War to Be Human."
8 See, in particular, Wynter, "1492"; Wynter, "The Ceremony Must Be Found"; Wynter, "Unsettling the Coloniality of Being/Power/Truth/Freedom." As is the case in all the modern binary oppositions that accompany and compose it, this global relation is asymmetrical and nonreciprocal, being neither a polarity nor a dualism. The second, degraded term is not simply the negative image of the first. As the ground against which the first is defined (as woman is to man, black is to white, nature is to culture, East is to West, homosexual is to heterosexual), the second exists as a vast unknown, a continent of darkness that by the definition of the first cannot be bound by the universal categories and tools of self-understanding of the first, and therefore ultimately remains unfathomable. This binary opposition repeated in the opposition between value and waste supports the argument that the very form of such binary oppositions is fundamental to capitalist modernity. To this extent, the remainder—that excess of the very surplus being of the secondary term, even as historically more and more of it might be absorbed, assimilated, or claimed by the primary term (just as previous waste can be reclaimed as

value, the once-nonhuman proclaimed as human, the mere object viewed also as subject)—is necessarily an effect of this binary order, its contents changing with political struggles but persisting as a vanishing horizon or threshold so long as a world of value-making (as practical basis and ethos) continues to set the terms of life.

9 Remollino, "Huwag Tayong Bumitaw Sa Ating Pagkatao," 70.
10 Ong, *Neoliberalism as Exception*, 195.
11 Ong, "Experiments with Freedom," 238.
12 Lowe, "The Gender of Sovereignty"; Fregoso, "'We Want Them Alive!'"
13 Wright, *Disposable Women*, 73.
14 Fregoso, "'We Want Them Alive!,'" 114.
15 When it is, as Chandan Reddy writes, actually "freedom with violence." Reddy, *Freedom with Violence*.
16 Talal Asad and Inderpal Grewal, for example, have criticized the work that international legal-juridical agreements and advocacy networks, based on a human rights platform accomplish toward the building of a global hegemony of liberal norms, which underwrites an emerging transnational regime of truth and mode of governmentality. Asad, "Redeeming the 'Human' through Human Rights," in *Formations of the Secular*; Grewal, "Women's Rights as Human Rights." See also Ticktin, *Casualties of Care*.
17 No doubt there is much to be critiqued in MacKinnon's work in terms of the tiresome and aggravating ethnocentric universalism that continues to structure certain prevailing analytical tendencies of Western feminist arguments (e.g., the construction of "women" as a unitary, ahistorical social category or preconstituted social group subject to a transcultural logic of "patriarchy"; the construction of traditional, non-Western "cultures" as bounded social logics of constraint and repression, to be distinguished from invisible norms of freedom and individualism in an unmarked modernity), as Chandra Mohanty, Uma Narayan, and others have exemplarily shown us in other contexts. Mohanty, *Feminism without Borders*; Narayan, *Dislocating Cultures*.
18 See Bernstein, "The Sexual Politics of the 'New Abolitionism'"; and Bernstein, "Militarized Humanitarianism Meets Carceral Feminism."
19 Arendt, *The Origins of Totalitarianism*, 291.
20 See Abu-Lughod, *Do Muslim Women Need Saving?*; and Hammami, "The Politics of Gender in the Flat-Pack 'Peace.'"
21 Higgins, "Review."
22 Marx, "On the Jewish Question."
23 Asad, *Formations of the Secular*, 147, 157.
24 For Marx, political emancipation was not to be confused with human emancipation, by which he meant not freedom, in these seemingly distinct spheres of political and civil society, but rather the liberating transformation of what he and Engels would call the prevailing (capitalist) "mode of production": "a definite form of activity of these individuals, a definite form of expressing their life, a definite mode of life on their part. As individuals express, so they are." Marx and Engels, *The German Ideology*, 37. On this view, the language

of political emancipation expresses the limited mode of being human under capitalism.

25 Dunbar-Ortiz, *An Indigenous Peoples' History of the United States*, 45. Dunbar-Ortiz traces the origins of US covenant society to its history of settler colonialism.

26 Brady, "The Homoerotics of Immigration Control"; Gilmore, *Golden Gulag*; Davis, *Are Prisons Obsolete?*; Sudbury, *Global Lockdown*; Federici, *Revolution at Point Zero*.

27 Brady, "The Homoerotics of Immigration Control," 4. See also Jeff Gammage, "Hundreds of Migrants Die Every Year," *Philadelphia Inquirer*, October 29, 2019, https://www.inquirer.com/news/southwest-border-deaths-desert-heat-20191029.html.

28 Davis, *Are Prisons Obsolete?*; Sudbury, *Global Lockdown*; Bohrman and Murakawa, "Remaking Big Government"; Cacho, *Social Death*.

29 Asad, "Redeeming the 'Human' through Human Rights," 138. For more on the philosophy of human personhood that the rhetoric and rules of US law inscribe and on the forms of dispossession that legal rites materialize, see J. Dayan, "Legal Slaves and Civil Bodies"; and C. Dayan, "Legal Terrors."

30 Sherwin de Vera, presentation on "Archiving Resistance," Alfredo F. Tadiar Library, San Fernando, La Union, Philippines, January 11, 2020. De Vera was noting the use of the law under Duterte to silence critics of human rights violations, agribusiness expansion, destructive dams and mines, and corporate tourism taking place in the Ilocos and Cagayan Valleys of the northern Philippines.

31 Rejali, *Torture and Democracy*.

32 Briggs, *Taking Children*.

33 Barrios, "Ang Pagiging Babae ay Pamumuhay sa Panahon ng Digma," *Ang Pagiging Babae*, 90–91, 90; translation modified.

34 Ticktin, *Casualties of Care*, 126.

35 Arendt, *The Human Condition*; Arendt, *The Origins of Totalitarianism*. Famously, Agamben's notion of "bare life" is based on the notion of *zoē* as the polar opposite of *bios*, or political life. Agamben, *Homo Sacer*. For an indispensable critique of this notion, see Weheliye, *Habeas Viscus*.

36 Arendt, *The Human Condition*, 119–20. Despite her critique of Marx's conception of labor in favor of a concept of "work" that would exemplify such freedom and, furthermore, would produce the "immortality" that distinguished humans from animals and natives, Arendt shares Marx's exaltation of human achievement over the other lower species as the ability to produce their means of subsistence. See Marx, *German Ideology*, 150.

37 Prashad, *The Darker Nations*; Johnson, *The Sorrows of Empire*.

38 McCoy, *In the Shadows of the American Century*; Mamdani, *Good Muslim, Bad Muslim*.

39 Taking up the challenge and model of black studies posed by the work of Sylvia Wynter and Hortense Spillers, Alexander Weheliye articulates this question in the following way: he asks "what it might mean to claim the monstrosity of

the flesh as a site for freedom beyond the world of Man"; "how might the flesh incarnate alternate forms of liberty and humanity that dwell among us in the NOW"? Weheliye, *Habeas Viscus*, 125, 132. My own work strives to heed this powerful question.

CHAPTER TWO. A GLOBAL ENTERPRISE

Sections of this chapter were published as "Life-Times of Becoming Human," *Occasion: Interdisciplinary Studies in the Humanities* 3 (2012), http://occasion.stanford.edu/node/75.

1 The ignominious role we have played—as we partook and continue to partake in wars that targeted us—is as much a part of our consequences for the world as our disposable vitality, which makes for the multifarious serviceability of our peoples' ever-cheapened life-times, and which we ourselves sell to make a living in the contemporary war to be human. Without this part of the story, we will be left with only romantic, idealizing myths about our own noble victimhood, the very myths that the "no longer" and the "yet to be" tell themselves as they rally around their respective decrepit, pernicious states' promises to come to the aid of their redemption.

2 The scholarship and historical evidence supporting this uncontroversial statement is vast. But see Dunbar-Ortiz, *An Indigenous Peoples' History of the United States*; C. Robinson, *Black Marxism*; Morgan, *Laboring Women*; Zinn, *A People's History of the United States*; Grandin, *Empire's Workshop*; and Kiernan, *America*.

3 Cuevas, "Welcome to My Cell."

4 Marx shows how in sixteenth-century England, under Edward VI, enslavement was codified in law as punishment against vagabondage and idleness. "On So-Called Primitive Accumulation" in *Capital, Vol. I*, 897.

5 Davis, *Abolition Democracy*.

6 Gina Dent, Nineteenth Annual Martin Luther King, Jr., Lecture in Social Justice (with Angela Y. Davis), University of Pennsylvania, Philadelphia, January 16, 2020, https://www.youtube.com/watch?v=RiteFqDG758. The phrase "egalitarian punishment" comes from Michel Foucault, quoted in Davis, "Racialized Punishment and Prison Abolition," 97. For the "free world" demarcated by prison as this limit border, see Dent and Davis, "Prison as a Border." See also Cacho, *Social Death*.

7 Singh, "The Whiteness of Police."

8 Ferguson, Missouri, took in $2.5 million in municipal court revenue in 2013, an 80 percent increase from two years prior and a fifth of its total operative revenue. See Mike Maciag, "Skyrocketing Court Fines Are Major Revenue Generator for Ferguson," *Governing: The Future of States and Localities*, August 21, 2014, https://www.governing.com/topics/public-justice-safety/gov-ferguson-missouri-court-fines-budget.html; and Frances Robles, "Mistrust Lingers as Ferguson Takes New Tack on Fines," *New York Times*, September 12, 2014.

9 Joseph Shapiro, "As Court Fees Rise, the Poor Are Paying the Price," NPR, May 19, 2014, https://www.npr.org/2014/05/19/312158516/increasing-court-fees-punish-the-poor/.
10 This economic trend is akin to Luxemburg's analysis of militarism as a province of accumulation, in which taxes, as reductions from people's wages, are a source of already produced surplus value. Luxemburg, "Militarism as a Province of Accumulation."
11 See Marx, "Wage Labour and Capital"; and Marx, *Grundrisse*, 608–10.
12 Gidwani and Reddy, "The Afterlives of 'Waste'"; Pulido, "Geographies of Race and Ethnicity II"; Byrd et al., "Predatory Value."
13 Pulido, "Flint, Environmental Racism, and Racial Capitalism."
14 Gidwani and Maringanti, "The Waste-Value Dialectic." Gidwani and Maringanti also allude to this added layer of productive investment in the contemporary moment: "Capitalist economies produce places like Bholakpur as receptacles of waste, only to cannibalize them at a later moment when land values rise, shifting the imperative to inter waste to other locations" (114). See also Wright, "Gentrification, Assassination and Forgetting in Mexico."
15 With increasing private investment in urban policy and projects through such instruments as social impact bonds—also known as social innovation financing (SIF) and pay-for-success (PFS) contracts—the success of urban programs is determined by the savings they realize, which is then used to repay the investments with interest. Lake, "The Financialization of Urban Policy in the Age of Obama."
16 Gilmore, *Golden Gulag*.
17 Willse, *Value of Homelessness*, 50.
18 It is in the present context of its direct valorization that waste has come to be understood in its dialectical relationship to value. Gidwani and Maringanti, "The Waste-Value Dialectic." This does not deny the profits from financial speculation, which can also be found in the past.
19 In another vocabulary, this would be *formal subsumption*—a throwback and refurbishing of vassalage under early capitalism. See Mamdani, *Saviors and Survivors*; Eviota, *The Political Economy of Gender*.
20 Mann, *Incoherent Empire*; McCoy, *In the Shadows of the American Century*.
21 This is, in fact, what they say. Of the Boers in South Africa, Arendt writes, "Ruling over tribes and living parasitically from their labor, they came to occupy a position very similar to that of the native tribal leaders whose domination they had liquidated. . . . They treated the natives as raw material and lived on them as one might live on the fruits of wild trees. Lazy and unproductive, they agreed to vegetate on essentially the same level as the black tribes had vegetated for thousands of years. . . . The Boers lived on their slaves exactly the way natives had lived on an unprepared and unchanged nature." Arendt, *The Origins of Totalitarianism*, 193–94.
22 Boot, *The Savage Wars of Peace*. In the 1860s and 1870s, the US army adopted small, light, mobile cavalry units in imitation of the defense strategies of the Sioux, the people they aimed to overcome. From the 1890s to the late 1930s,

while the British army learned counterinsurgency lessons from native peoples in Malaysia, Vietnam, India, and South Africa, the US army learned its lessons in the context of its own small wars in Haiti, Chile, Hawaiʻi, Panama, Cuba, the Philippines, Puerto Rico, and Dominican Republic, among many other places. Parenti, *Tropic of Chaos*. See also Grandin, *Empire's Workshop*; McCoy, "Low Intensity Conflict in the Philippines"; and Simbulan, "The CIA's Hidden History in the Philippines."

23 Guha, "The Prose of Counter-Insurgency."
24 In typical colonial reversal, they also adopt the experiential positions of their victims, introjecting the fear and suffering they create as their own besiegement by the same. Ghassan Hage, "Fears of 'White Decline' Show How a Minor Dent to Domination Can Be Catastrophic for Some," *Guardian*, April 14, 2019. See also Hartman, *Scenes of Subjection*.
25 Gidwani and Reddy, "'The Afterlives of Waste,'" 1638.
26 Melinda Cooper argued that this was the turn in the US petrochemical industry, which—facing costly and insurmountable limits posed both by regulations and by the finite resources of the earth—put biological production to work, mobilizing the reproductive capacities of organic life as labor and deliberately curtailing it to ensure "that it no longer reproduces for free." Cooper, *Life as Surplus*, 25.
27 Scott, *Against the Grain*, 253.
28 The "great game" is Hannah Arendt's term for late nineteenth-century imperialism. Arendt, *The Origins of Totalitarianism*. In *Life as Surplus*, Cooper provides a particularly vivid account of this new imperialism in the biotech sector, in which "life itself"—conceived as "a process of continuous autopoiesis, a self-engendering of life from life, without conceivable beginning or end" (38)—is "literally annexed within capitalist processes of accumulation" (19).
29 This is a tendency toward "formal subsumption" that I will argue in the next chapter is internal to and consistent with the "real subsumption" that is purportedly the dominant tendency of capital. This is also in keeping with the widely made observation that capitalist "production" has itself shifted to platform capitalism, whereby "contents" and "forms" are produced not by employed workers but by working nonemployees (e.g., users, content providers, "prosumers," "playborers," etc.) in and through the media platforms owned by capitalists (that is, within protocols that, through aggregated innovations in use, nonemployed content providers also "design" but do not patent).
30 Mies, Bennholdt-Thomsen, and Von Werlhof, *Women*; Mies, *Patriarchy and Accumulation*; Hull, Scott, and Smith, *But Some of Us Are Brave*; Moraga and Anzaldúa, *This Bridge Called My Back*; Federici, *Revolution at Point Zero*; Davis, *Women, Race, Class*; Fortunati, *Arcane of Reproduction*; Nash and Fernández-Kelly, *Women, Men, and the International Division of Labor*.
31 Truong, *Sex, Money and Morality*; Chang, *Disposable Domestics*; Parreñas, *Servants of Globalization*; R. M. Rodriguez, *Migrants for Export*; Choy, *Empire of Care*; Francisco-Menchavez, *Labor of Care*; Guevarra, *Marketing Dreams, Manufacturing Heroes*; Morgan, *Laboring Women*; Glenn, *Forced to Care*; Federici, *Caliban and the Witch*.

32 Federici, *Revolution at Point Zero*, 103.
33 The discussion of militarism as a province of accumulation in the early twentieth century, as in the discussion of "the military-industrial complex" in the late twentieth century, understood this capitalization of war largely in terms of weapons manufacture. "As far as the individual capitalist is concerned . . . there are only commodities and buyers, and it is completely immaterial to him whether he produces instruments of life or instruments of death, corned beef or armour plating." Luxemburg, "Militarism as a Province of Accumulation," 440.
34 Luxemburg, *The Accumulation of Capital* (in *Complete Works*), 258.
35 Luxemburg, *The Accumulation of Capital* (in *Complete Works*), 267.
36 Luxemburg, *The Accumulation of Capital* (in *Complete Works*), 266.
37 Luxemburg, *The Accumulation of Capital* (in *Complete Works*), 262. "Vital necessity" is the Schwarzschild translation of the words translated as "a question of life and death" in the same passage above: "Hence derives the vital necessity for capitalism in its relations with colonial countries to appropriate the most important means of production." Luxemburg, *The Accumulation of Capital* (trans. Schwarzschild), 350.
38 Luxemburg, *The Accumulation of Capital* (in *Complete Works*), 263. In his introduction to Marx's *Capital, Vol. II*, Ernest Mandel, for one, argues that while Luxemburg was able to pose the theoretical problem of the expanded reproduction of capital, her analysis "narrowed down the problem to an excessively monocausal one" (65). He grants, however, that in her analysis of the actual historical conditions of capital accumulation, Luxemburg was fundamentally correct: that "the same value-transferring metabolism" in which capitalism was born in a noncapitalist milieu, enriching itself through plunder, continues in the present (67). As I argue here, however, the notion of plunder (as well as that of extraction), while not incorrect, is itself a reduction of that "value-transforming metabolism" formed between capitalist and noncapitalist modes of production, insofar as it does not take into account the complex permutations and importance for value production of the latter's life-making activities of survival.
39 Luxemburg, *The Accumulation of Capital* (in *Complete Works*), 263. This has been in fact a fundamental insight of feminists since the 1970s who have interpreted Luxemburg's notion of "noncapitalist social formations" in terms of housewives, colonies, older households, and subsistence peasants. See Mies, Von Werlhof, and Bennholdt-Thomsen, *Women*. Davis also remarks on the way Luxemburg's analysis powerfully resonates with the role of the prison in globalization. Dent and Davis, "Prison as a Border."
40 Luxemburg, *The Accumulation of Capital* (in *Complete Works*), 302.
41 Gomez-Barris, *The Extractive Zone*; Estes and Dhillon, *Standing with Standing Rock*.
42 Shiva, *Water Wars*; Roy, *An Ordinary Person's Guide to Empire*; Bello, *The Food Wars*; Shiva, *Earth Democracy*.
43 Simondon, *On the Mode of Existence of Technical Objects*, xiii, 59. Significantly, Simondon's revamped humanism leads him to bemoan the technical object's

state of alienation, encapsulated in its "taking the place of the slave and being treated as such across relations of property and custom" (xiii). The philosophical study of technical objects is an effort of culture to incorporate the human reality contained within them. In this way philosophical thought would fulfill a duty "analogous to the one it fulfilled for the abolition of slavery and the affirmation of the value of the human person" (15).

44 Simondon, *On the Mode of Existence of Technical Objects*, 59.
45 Tsing, *The Mushroom at the End of the World*, 63.
46 "By destroying the non-capitalist milieu on which its expansion is based, capitalism undermines the conditions of its own growth. The disappearance of this non-capitalist (pre-capitalist) environment thus marks the absolute limit of capitalist development." Mandel, introduction, 63. But of course noncapitalist social formations and environments never quite "disappear." They are preserved in internal and external forms (the "native" ineradicable in the becoming-human or in its humanization, segregated and minoritized as Indigenous "tribes" within colonized, Christianized countries). And they are refashioned as modes of survival—to be distinguished from their political conversion into sovereign subjects and territories, as in the "successful" case of Israel, which exemplifies one of the most belligerent cases of the war to be human waged by the yet-to-be-human, a war that has become the permanent condition of its perpetually threatened "existence" (as a settler colonial, capitalist democratic state).
47 This is in fact Luxemburg's critique of Marx. For my own critique of this relation as the basis for the historical gendered and sexualized constitution of the category of labor and for the tendency toward the so-called feminization of labor in the current moment, see Tadiar, "Prostituted Filipinas and the Crisis of Philippine Culture."
48 The collective body of work is formidable. See in particular Barker, "The Corporation and the Tribe"; Simpson, *As We Have Always Done*; Coulthard, *Red Skins, White Masks*; Byrd et al., "Predatory Value"; Byrd, *The Transit of Empire*; and Kauanui, *Paradoxes of Hawaiian Sovereignty*. See also Day, *Alien Capital*; and Park, "Money, Mortgages, and the Conquest of America."
49 Barker, "The Corporation and the Tribe"; Barker, "Territory as Analytic."
50 Barker notes that Fourteenth Amendment rights, analogous to those of "persons," were awarded to corporations in 1886, while concurrent law stripped tribes of legal protections of their rights to governance and land. Barker, "The Corporation and the Tribe."
51 Park, "Money, Mortgages, and the Conquest of America."
52 Barker, "Territory as Analytic," 31.
53 For contemporary ideological practices and legal rulings confirming the personhood of corporations, see Citizens United vs. Federal Election Commission (FEC), the 2010 Supreme Court ruling that political spending by corporations constitutes a form of free speech protected by the First Amendment.
54 Byrd, *The Transit of Empire*.
55 Patterson, *Slavery and Social Death*; Meillassoux, *The Anthropology of Slavery*; Cacho, *Social Death*; Hartman, "The Time of Slavery."

56 Wood, *Empire of Capital*. On the role of recognition in Indigenous dispossession, see also Kauanui, *The Paradoxes of Hawaiian Sovereignty*; Denetdale, "Return to 'The Uprising at Beautiful Mountain in 1913'"; Coulthard, *Red Skin, White Masks*.
57 Barker, "The Specters of Recognition," 52.
58 The building of this modern political structure was the achievement of colonial coercion and tutelage. Such national political independence was itself predicated on US political recognition. Thompson, *Imperial Archipelago*. This reproduced internally the political recognition exemplified in the US granting of political independence to a nation that it colonized in the very moment that it was declaring its own independence from its previous colonizer, Spain.
59 Doyo, *Macli-ing Dulag*; Malayang, "Rights and Exclusion In Tenure"; Delina, "Indigenous Environmental Defenders."
60 Doyo, *Macli-ing Dulag*, 26.
61 "Cordillera: Indigenous People Remember Martyr Macliing Dulag," Unrepresented Nations and People's Organization, April 26, 2010, https://unpo.org/article/11036?id=11036.
62 Sherwin de Vera, "IPRA at 23," *Northern Dispatch*, October 8, 2020, https://nordis.net/2020/10/08/topic/rights-and-welfare/ipra-at-23-respect-and-recognition-of-ips-land-ownership-remains-a-key-challenge/. Beyond its importance to these conventional capitalist industries, the legal and extralegal appropriation of Indigenous lands has been crucial for the latest strategies of capitalist accumulation, including the global reproductive industry (for which many displaced Indigenous peoples have migrated as newly freed service labor [such as the Kankanaey; see McKay, *An Archipelago of Care*]) and a global metropolitan platform economy (a circulation economy for which Indigenous lands have been converted into nodal resource and processing sites).
63 Marx, *Capital, Vol. I*, 885.
64 Quoted in de Vera, "IPRA at 23."
65 For the contentious effects of the Indigenous Peoples' Rights Act (IPRA), and the National Commission on Indigenous Peoples (NCIP), both legacies of the struggle against the Chico River dam project, on contemporary Indigenous dissent against present-day hydropower dam projects, see Delina, "Indigenous Environmental Defenders." According to Jose Mencio Molintas, "Formal registration of land title has become a tool to convert communal ancestral lands into individually titled private lands, especially in town centers and cities in the Cordillera, and has led to the fragmentation of villages in the interior areas." Molintas, "The Philippine Indigenous Peoples' Struggles for Land and Life," 292.
66 The Indigenous Peoples' Rights Act of 1997, Republic Act No. 8371.
67 Marx, *Capital, Vol. I*, 909. Marx is remarking on the conversion of the flax spun by peasants into constant capital, as part of the process of primitive accumulation.
68 This is contrary to notions of the global completion of land enclosure under late capital, and to a widespread indifference to the continuing importance of land in much leftist critique focused on the latest advances in capitalist exploitation.

69 According to Global Witness. Cited in Delina, "Indigenous Environmental Defenders," 2.
70 Combahee River Collective, "Black Feminist Statement."
71 Von Werlhof argues that imperialism is the method of enforcing a continuing original accumulation through so-called extra-economic or direct political violence in the family, against women, outside the family. Direct political violence is thus one of the ways of suspending the rules of free wage labor. Von Werlhof, "Women's Work," 16–17, 19.
72 See, for example, Moore, *The Web of Life*.
73 Morgan's work powerfully demonstrates the foundation role of sex-gender and race codes as "crucial axes around which the organization of enslavement and slave labor in the Americas took place," and concomitantly, as social and cultural norms in the making of the "moral grammar" that arguably continues to shape our contemporary moment, as Hortense Spillers indelibly has shown. Morgan, *Laboring Women*, 69; Spillers, "Mama's Baby, Papa's Maybe."
74 Hall, "Encoding/Decoding."
75 Roediger and Esch, *The Production of Difference*.
76 Lowe, *Intimacies of Four Continents*.
77 Glenn, "From Servitude to Service Work"; Glenn, *Forced to Care*.
78 Choy, *Empire of Care*; Sharma, *Home Work*; Amrith, *Caring for Strangers*.
79 Wright, *Disposable Women*; Ong, *Spirits of Resistance*.
80 Tadiar, *Fantasy-Production*. See also Yuval-Davis, *Gender and Nation*; Parker et al., *Nationalisms and Sexualities*.
81 In "Encoding/Decoding," Stuart Hall argues that before communicative events ("messages") happen, they are first subject to the formal subrules of discourse, a level of coding/signification that organizes the very "form of appearance" of a perceptible "message" (21). We could consider social identities as, similarly, a determinate moment within a larger communicative process, which Hall argues is "homologous to that which forms the skeleton of commodity production offered in Marx's *Grundrisse* and in *Capital*" (20). Similarly, in her famous critique, "Can the Subaltern Speak?," Gayatri Spivak argues that there are two levels of "representational" practice that come to be conflated in the contemporary politics of representation, with the first (that of political representation of subjects) eclipsing the second (that of the making of the very world within which those subjects are made and become legible as such—its "scene of writing"). The latter is the "economic" level of "representation" within which value acts as the "representation/sign of objectified labor." Spivak, "Can the Subaltern Speak?," 278–79.

CHAPTER THREE. BECOMING-HUMAN IN A TIME OF WAR

Sections of this chapter were published as "Life-Times of Becoming Human," *Occasion: Interdisciplinary Studies in the Humanities* 3 (2012), http://occasion.stanford.edu/node/75.
1 Wynter, "Unsettling the Coloniality of Being/Power/Truth/Freedom," 315.

2 Von Werlhof, "On the Concept of Nature."
3 Marx, *Capital, Vol. I*, 144, 143. On whiteness as value and its relation to God in the context of postcolonial redemption, see Tadiar, *Things Fall Away*, 232–47.
4 Beller, *The Message Is Murder*; Foucault, *The Birth of Biopolitics*.
5 The "inner eye" organizing the human is "intricately bound up with that code, so determinant of our collective behaviours, to which we have given the name, *race*." Wynter, "No Humans Involved," 47. This "new master code" functions at all levels of the social order, serving as "the dually status-organizing and integrating principle of U.S. society." Wynter, "Unsettling the Coloniality of Being/Power/Truth/Freedom," 323.
6 Murphy, *The Economization of Life*, 72.
7 McClintock, *Imperial Leather*.
8 Goeman, "Land as Life"; Million, "We Are the Land, and the Land Is Us."
9 Moore identifies this strategy—early capitalism's commodity frontier strategy—as pivotal to the epochal shift in the sixteenth century. "At every turn, land (forests, silver veins, fertile soils) was organized by empires, planters, seigneurs, yeoman farmers, and others as a force of production in servitude to the commodity form—as a mechanism for advancing the productivity of labor. Treating the whole of uncapitalized nature as a force of production, early capitalism was able to remake planetary natures in epochal fashion." Moore, *Capitalism in the Web of Life*, 59.
10 Galeano, *Open Veins of Latin America*, 1; translation modified.
11 Quoted in Galeano, *Open Veins of Latin America*, 79.
12 Galeano, *Open Veins of Latin America*, 40, 54.
13 "'Value as force,' the first appearance of value, is overcome by the latter objectification it sustains. Because 'value as force' is a misdemeanor or atrocity that 'value as form,' as overinvested object or design, will not tolerate, value masquerades both its violence and the revisionary impulses of its belated self-representation by means of the symbolics of a boundary. Presenting a boundary solely as a barrier, solely as a visible and inviolate demarcation (rather than also a site of crossing and exchange), 'value as form' secures itself the site (sight) of value." Barrett, *Blackness and Value*, 20. See also Ferreira da Silva, *Toward a Global Idea of Race*.
14 Puar and Rai, "Monster, Terrorist, Fag."
15 Hannah Arendt's own distinction between labor and work, and between *animal laborans* and *homo faber* rests on this hierarchized distinction between the natural process of life ("the burden, the toil and trouble of life"), common to all species, and the specifically human fabrication of durable, immortal culture; between being "enslaved by necessity" and the transcendence of and freedom from such necessity. *The Human Condition*, 83. These distinctions rehearse in a modern philosophical key the distinctions between reproduction and production, the material separation between which Silvia Federici argues emerges out of the counterrevolutionary response to feudal crisis and rebellion in Europe. Federici, *Caliban and the Witch*. To the ascendance of the ideal of *animal laborans*, and its persistent demand for happiness, Arendt attributes

the turning of the whole economy into a "waste economy, in which things must be almost as quickly devoured and discarded as they have appeared in the world." Arendt, *The Human Condition*, 134.

16 This foregrounding of emasculation was also a characteristic of Marx's critique of labor. See Tadiar, "Prostituted Filipinas and the Crisis of Philippine Culture," *Things Fall Away*, 25–58.

17 Parreñas, *Servants of Globalization*.

18 Harvey, *The New Imperialism*. In contrast, see Byrd et al., "Predatory Value"; and Chakravartty and Silva, "Accumulation, Dispossession, and Debt."

19 Meillassoux, *Maidens, Meal and Money*, 105; emphasis mine.

20 Meillassoux, *Maidens, Meal and Money*, 97.

21 Luxemburg, *The Accumulation of Capital* (in *Complete Works*), 267.

22 Klein, *The Shock Doctrine*.

23 Quoted in Lowenstein, *Disaster Capitalism*, 23.

24 It is also arguable that the revalorization of what is hidden and super-exploited under a recasting of such appropriated activity and being as "labor" or even as "work," in an acknowledgement of the distinction between exploitation and appropriation, reprises the hierarchical distinctions that undergird capitalist operations.

25 Bohrman and Murakami, "Remaking Big Government"; Evans, "Playing Global Cop."

26 Dent and Davis, "Prison as a Border."

27 Katz argues that the dispossession of young people in the United States, particularly African American and Latinx youth, "from viable futures by their exclusion from education through various means," provides conditions for their channeling into industries of detention and imprisonment. Katz, "Accumulation, Excess, Childhood," 53.

28 McCoy, *In the Shadows of the American Century*, 90.

29 USAID, "Mission, Vision and Values," updated February 16, 2018, https://www.usaid.gov/who-we-are/mission-vision-values/.

30 In 2017, the USAID spent almost $20 billion worldwide on these projects. See "Dollars to Results: USAID Investments and Illustrative Results," USAID, accessed November 17, 2021, https://results.usaid.gov/results/.

31 As a service industry, it is closely linked to productive circulation. Mandel argues that where the financing of increased military expenditure at the expense of the working class does not lead to a change in the capacity of workers to accept current norms of social labour, the military could in fact be understood as a third department. Mandel, introduction, 55.

32 Collier and Lakoff, "Vital Systems Security."

33 This is the idea that the most evident features of empire, territorial domination and economic supremacy, are the result, rather than the cause, of an imperial way of life. W. A. Williams, *Empire as a Way of Life*.

34 This Christian Zionist formulation suggests the imperial Christian history out of which capital develops its ideological-philosophical lineaments, expressed and elaborated by its global "bearers"—states, communities, or individuals

that fashion themselves in its image in the quest for legitimated power (or political emancipation).

35 It is not too far-fetched to suggest that this demonstrates that the much-anticipated singularity has already happened, against all the dystopic cultural visions of its coming in the form of the technological "awakening" of artificial intelligence, which is but a denial of it already having occurred. See Beller, *The World Computer*, 86.

36 Negri, "Labor of the Multitude," 17.

37 This is a revision of Marx's humanist formulation in 1844 (in the *Economic and Philosophic Manuscripts*) regarding estranged labor, which makes man's species life the mere means of his physical existence: "It turns for him the life of the species into a means of individual life. . . . Life itself appears only as a means to life." Marx, *The Marx and Engels Reader*, 75, 76.

38 Lorde, "A Litany for Survival," in *The Collected Poems*, 255–56, 255.

39 Marx, "Economic and Philosophic Manuscripts of 1844," 75.

40 Such as the reification of Filipino capacities in the call center industry, as Jan Padios shows. Padios, *A Nation on the Line*.

41 Marx, *Grundrisse*, 105. See also Harootunian, *Marx after Marx*. For Harootunian these "unconquered remnants" are "distinct survivals from different pasts and modes of production" that "still embody untimely temporalities capable of interrupting the environment of a new time" (42).

42 Martin, *Knowledge*, LTD.

43 Raunig, *Dividuum*, 151.

44 This is also what Harry Harootunian argues contemporary interpreters of Marx disclose: "both a contemporary perspective that sees the immediate results of production completed and the conviction that it is capital's aim to complete the process of subsumption in order to set the stage for its ultimate overcoming." Harootunian, *Marx after Marx*, 69. I would only add that there is a masculinist flavor to this particular revolutionary vision of a final showdown, whether or not this is practically or philosophically conceived.

45 Alexander, *Pedagogies of Crossing*; Hartman, "The Time of Slavery"; Spivak, *Critique of Postcolonial Reason*; Muñoz, *Cruising Utopia*.

46 C. Robinson, *Black Marxism*, 67, 64, 122–23. See also Morgan, "Accounting for 'the Most Excruciating Torment.'"

47 Davis, "Unfinished Lecture on Liberation II," in *The Angela Y. Davis Reader*, 54.

48 See Davis, "Women and Capitalism," 171; Davis, "Surrogates and Outcast Mothers," 211; and Davis, "Reflections on the Black Woman's Role in the Community of Slaves," 123.

49 Davis, "Reflections on the Black Woman's Role in the Community of Slaves," 115.

50 In the model of exploitation under industrial capital, labor time that is productive of value is confined to the socially necessary time spent in the production of the commodity. What the condition of domestic labor has shown, however, is that it is not any specific amount or quantity of labor time that is appropriated from the domestic worker–rather, it is her whole bodily being, as a being-for-others, that is appropriated to maintain and enhance the lives of others.

Equated with the naturalized forms of reproductive work she embodies (this gendered labor inseparable from her gendered body), she is appropriated as bodily life, as "life-time" spent in the serving and servicing of others. In the contemporary model of exploitation, "life" itself becomes productive of value, as labor and as resource. For the literal harnessing of "life itself" to capitalist production through the biotech sector, see Cooper, *Life as Surplus*.

51 As Marx explicates in the *Grundrisse*, the worker's living labor is his use value as a specific commodity: "The use value which the worker has to offer to the capitalist, which he has to offer to others in general . . . is his vitality itself, directed toward a specific purpose and hence expressing itself in a specific form" (267). But this vitality, as that capacity of labor he offers up to capital, cannot exist without his "life," "the source in which his own value constantly rekindles itself up to a certain time, when it is worn out, and constantly confronts capital again in order to begin the same exchange anew" (283).

52 Marx, *Grundrisse*, 323.

INTERREGNUM

A previous version of this chapter was published as: ". . . In Reverse," Periscope, *Social Text* Online (2017) https://socialtextjournal.org/tag/requiem-for-m/.

1 The title of the work and exhibition comes from a quotation of the French Jacobin, Saint-Just.
2 Bewes, *Reading with the Grain*, 16.
3 SBTV, "Singapore Biennale 2103: If the World Changed," interview with artist Kiri Dalena, February 3, 2014, https://youtu.be/x1KJY95G4Lg.
4 Debord, *Society of the Spectacle*, 110.
5 Solanas and Getino, "Toward a Third Cinema," 229.
6 R. Ruiz, *Poetics of Cinema*, 26.

CHAPTER FOUR. OF LABOR AND FATE PLAYING

A previous version of this chapter was published as "Life-Times in Fate-Playing," *South Atlantic Quarterly* 111, no. 4 (2012): 783–802.

1 Marazzi, *The Violence of Financial Capitalism*, 48.
2 Marazzi, *The Violence of Financial Capitalism*, 49.
3 Marazzi, *The Violence of Financial Capitalism*, 56.
4 Marazzi, *The Violence of Financial Capitalism*, 57.
5 See Cooper, *Life as Surplus*.
6 Virno, *A Grammar of the Multitude*, 103.
7 Virno, *A Grammar of the Multitude*, 103.
8 Negri, *Marx beyond Marx*; Hardt and Negri, *Labor Of Dionysus*. See also Marx, "Economic Manuscript of 1861–63."
9 Negri, "The Labor of the Multitude," 17.
10 Negri, "The Labor of the Multitude," 18.
11 Negri, *Empire and Beyond*, 4.

12 Negri, *Empire and Beyond*, 230.
13 This argument overlaps with Balibar's critique of Negri. Balibar, "On the Common, Universality, and Communism."
14 Life arguably takes the place of labor as a modern category, an abstraction operating in contemporary society. Abstract human life has become the social unity, the social substance constituting value.
15 Gergen and Vanourek, *Life Entrepreneurs*.
16 Wright, *Disposable Women*, 29–32.
17 Wright, *Disposable Women*, 2.
18 Wright, *Disposable Women*, 83.
19 Benanav, "Misery and Debt."
20 Benanav, "Misery and Debt," 5.
21 Benanav, "Misery and Debt," 6. Marx writes: "The positing of a specific portion of labour capacities as superfluous, i.e., of the labor required for their reproduction as superfluous, is therefore a necessary consequence of the growth of surplus labour relative to necessary. The decrease of relatively necessary labour appears as increase of the relatively superfluous labouring capacities—i.e., as the positing of surplus population." Marx, *Grundrisse*, 609.
22 Benanav, "Misery and Debt," 14.
23 Negri, "The Labor of the Multitude," 20.
24 Luxemburg, "Militarism as a Province of Accumulation."
25 Petit, "¿Y si dejáramos de ser cuidadanos?," 59–67, 60, 59. All translations here and below are mine.
26 Petit, "¿Y si dejáramos de ser cuidadanos?," 62.
27 Petit, "¿Y si dejáramos de ser cuidadanos?," 63.
28 Petit, "¿Y si dejáramos de ser cuidadanos?," 63. See also Martin, *An Empire of Indifference*.
29 Petit, "¿Y si dejáramos de ser cuidadanos?," 59.
30 Birkeland and Jennings, *Internal Displacement*, 8.
31 Nina Bernstein, "Companies Use Immigration Crackdown to Turn a Profit," *New York Times*, September 28, 2011.
32 Tadiar, "If Not Mere Metaphor . . ."
33 Federici, "The Reproduction of Labor-Power in the Global Economy"; Foucault, *The Birth of Biopolitics*, 226.
34 Tadiar, *Things Fall Away*, 60–61.
35 Harding, *Border Vigils*.
36 Federici, "The Reproduction of Labor-Power in the Global Economy"; and Gilmore, *The Golden Gulag*, 178.
37 Conversations with taxi drivers, New York, March 31, 2011, and April 12, 2011.
38 Virno, *A Grammar of the Multitude*, 106.
39 Tadiar, *Things Fall Away*.
40 See Aguilar, "Ritual Passage and the Reconstruction of Selfhood in International Labour Migration." Filipina migrant workers sometimes refer to their sojourn abroad as a form of *pakikipagsapalaran* (adventure), whose root word, *palad*, means fate.

41 Manolo B. Jara, "OFW Remittances Soar to Record High of $20B in 2011," *Oman Tribune*, February 17, 2012, www.omantribune.com/index.php?page=news&id=112366& heading=Business.
42 Neilson, "Provincializing the Italian Effect."
43 Neilson, "Provincializing the Italian Effect," 21. What postcolonial critics emphasize, however, is that capitalism never entirely incorporates nor overwhelms these plural histories. See Spivak, *A Critique of Postcolonial Reason*; Chakrabarty, *Provincializing Europe*; and Harootunian, *Marx after Marx*.
44 As a massive aggregate, the life-times of disposable people serve, like nature, as a free and seemingly infinite resource or fund that underwrites (indeed "securitizes") the profits of speculative financial capital—the very bottom of the Ponzi scheme that allows the first-takers to abscond with the "value" purportedly produced by the market. Marazzi explains how this worked in the financialization of real estate: "The expansion of subprime loans shows that, in order to raise and make profits, finance needs to involve the poor, in addition to the middle class. In order to function, this capitalism must invest in the bare life of people who cannot provide any guarantee, who offer nothing apart from themselves. It is a capitalism that turns bare life into a direct source of profit. It does so on the basis of a probability calculation according to which the lacking debt repayment is considered 'manageable,' i.e., negligible, when considered on the sale of the entire population." Marazzi, *The Violence of Financial Capitalism*, 40.
45 As a French immigration minister said with regard to illegal immigrants in the forest camp of Calais, "The law of the jungle cannot last eternally. A state of law must be re-established in Calais." Quoted in "Calais: French Police Bulldoze Migrant Camp, Detain Hundreds Including Children," *AP/Huffington Post*, September 22, 2009. On the ten thousand immigrants living in the woods in Andalusia, Spain, see Suzanne Daley, "Chasing Riches from Africa to Europe and Only Finding Squalor," *New York Times*, May 25, 2011.
46 Negri quoted in Balibar, "On the Common, Universality, and Communism."
47 Negri, "On the Common," 316.
48 Marx, "Simple Reproduction," 719.
49 Tadiar, "Petty Adventures in the (Nation's) Capital," in *Things Fall Away*, 183–215.
50 Geertz, "Deep Play," 17.
51 Bruce Wallace, "Filipinos Miss the Jackpot," *Los Angeles Times*, August 9, 2005. See also "*Jueteng* Is Embedded in Local Culture," Philippine Center for Investigative Journalism, accessed July 5, 2021, archived at https://web.archive.org/web/20010717173729/http://www.pcij.org/stories/1995/jueteng3.html.
52 "*Jueteng* Is Embedded in Local Culture."
53 See Faier, *Intimate Encounters*.
54 Amin, *Eurocentrism*. Although Samir Amin argues that the tributary mode of production is a more globally encompassing and accurate category for what precedes the capitalist mode of production, it is arguable that modern imperialism, particularly in the US model exemplified in the Philippines, recreates this tributary mode in the relation it establishes between metropolitan and peripheral nations. This has in fact been the radical Philippine left's political un-

derstanding of imperialism. See the chapter, "Revolutionary Imagination and the Masses," in Tadiar, *Things Fall Away*. Following Amin, Gayatri Spivak has also proposed understanding foreign aid and international trade as practice a form of "debt-bondage and tribute system" in the contemporary moment. See Spivak, *A Critique of Postcolonial Reason*.

55 "The underlying pattern appears to have been one of descent groups constantly competing for power in the form of dependents. In this part of the world where land was abundant, buildings impermanent, and property insecure, it was in followers that power and wealth were primarily expressed." Reid, *Southeast Asia in the Age of Commerce*, 120. While this characterization of power and wealth in precolonial Southeast Asia as being constituted primarily by human followers is widely upheld within the scholarship on Southeast Asia, it is also observed by scholars of Africa, expressed as "wealth-in-people." See Guyer, *Marginal Gains*.

56 J. Scott, "Freedom and Freehold."

57 Public discourse and academic scholarship on Philippine kinship systems is broad, extending beyond anthropological studies. Some among many include Roces, *Women, Power, and Kinship Politics*; Hayami et al., *The Family in Flux in Southeast Asia*; McCoy, *An Anarchy of Families*; Nydegger and Nydegger, *Tarong*.

58 J. Scott, "Freedom and Freehold." It is arguable that this relative autonomy also obtained, until the second half of the twentieth century, with respect to capitalist ideological state apparatuses (most prominently, education and media apparatuses). In this context, native vertical relations of obligation have morphed into and engendered political-economic cultures variously termed patronage or patron-client relations, rent capitalism, bossism, and semifeudalism, under postcolonial or "third world" capitalism. The precolonial, colonial, and postcolonial histories of this region would provide a better genealogy and theoretical-political understanding for what I argue are the peculiar social bonding practices comprising both vital platforms and the political-police networks now driving contemporary Philippine transformations.

59 Aguilar, *Clash of Spirits*, 87. "Flight was one of the major problems besetting the friar estates in the Spanish Philippines." Scott, "Freedom and Freehold," 52.

60 Aguilar, *Clash of Spirits*. See also Nydegger and Nydegger, *Tarong*, for a discussion of the "compadre system" as forms of ritual kinship grafted onto Indigenous social bonding relations.

61 Including "jumping ship." Fajardo, *Filipino Crosscurrents*.

62 On kinship as "mutual being," see Sahlins, *What Kinship Is*.

CHAPTER FIVE. OF DISPOSABILITY

A previous version of this chapter was published in "Life-Times of Disposability within Global Neoliberalism," *Social Text* 31, no. 2 (2013): 19–47.

1 See, for example, Martin, *An Empire of Indifference*; Brown, *Edgework*; Guyer, "Cash Economies"; Cooper, "The Living and the Dead"; Foucault, *The Birth of Biopolitics*; and Lazzarato, "Neoliberalism in Action."

2   Debord, *The Society of the Spectacle*, 112.
3   Foucault, *The Birth of Biopolitics*, 226.
4   Foucault, *The Birth of Biopolitics*, 243.
5   Brown, *Edgework*, 40.
6   Martin, *An Empire of Indifference*, 22, 36.
7   Martin, *An Empire of Indifference*, 36.
8   Martin, *An Empire of Indifference*, 37.
9   Lazzarato, "Neoliberalism in Action," 128.
10 As Neil Smith points out, Woodrow Wilson "more than anyone pioneered the transformation of liberalism into a left-leaning immune system against socialism in America." Smith, *The Endgame of Globalization*, 38.
11 Work on race and subprime mortgages is particularly helpful in drawing this out. See especially Cooper and Mitropolous, "In Praise of Usura" (which argues that financial crisis is the effect of usury from below); and also Chakravartty and Ferreira da Silva, "Accumulation, Dispossession, and Debt."
12 Cooper, "The Living and the Dead," 96.
13 Cooper, "The Living and the Dead," 96.
14 Cooper, "The Living and the Dead," 96.
15 Lazzarato, "Neoliberalism in Action,"122.
16 This is in contrast to the commodity that is "labor," the producer of value. It is of course the case that, from the standpoint of capital, "labor power" is also mere medium of value production. As Rosa Luxemburg reminds us, "The sustenance of the working class is merely a necessary evil for total social capital, a mere deviation on the path toward the actual goal of production: the generation and realization of surplus value." Luxemburg, *The Accumulation of Capital* (in *Complete Works*), 336.
17 If life is "a mere means for the valorization of the value advanced; i.e., enrichment as such appears as the inherent purpose of production," as Marx says of the production process, all life is, in many ways, worth expending. But "life worth living" (in the form of life as labor) serves as a means for the valorization of great capital advanced, and therefore serves as an extended production process with the capacity to yield surplus value (to the extent that it uses up "life worth expending," or life-times of considerably lower value, in order to produce more valorizable life-times for itself). Marx, *Capital, Vol. II*, 137.
18 Cooper, "Insecure Times," 520.
19 Cooper, "Insecure Times," 521. On the role of the New World in the constitution of sovereign power and the genealogy of international law, see also the important work of John D. Blanco, "Subjects of Baroque Economy."
20 Cooper, "Insecure Times," 528.
21 Cooper, "Insecure Times," 527, 528. This is exemplified in the discursive deployment of "crisis" during and in the aftermath of financial collapse as part of political maneuvers to restore and even expand the very mechanisms of value extraction and conditions of capitalist accumulation (deregulation, privatization, liberalization) that led to the collapse in the first place.
22 Marx, *Capital, Vol. I*, 787.

23 Walden Bello argues that the most spectacular case of the integration of noncapitalist strata to shore up the fall in the rate of profit is China, "the world's second biggest exporter and the primary destination of foreign investment." It is a primary source not only of goods for US market but also of capital for speculation. Walden Bello, "Capitalism in an Apocalyptic Mood," Transnational Institute, February 20, 2008, https://www.tni.org/en/article/capitalism-in-an-apocalyptic-mood/.

24 Dong, Bowles, and Chang, "Managing Liberalization and Globalization in Rural China," 36.

25 As the European debt crisis made abundantly clear, national debt is the future life of the population (*biopolis*) promised, with its present life as collateral. Hence austerity measures to service this debt entail collecting on this present life—such violence of diminishment that was painfully registered by the unnamed elderly Greek man, a seventy-seven-year old retired pharmacist, who committed suicide in a public square in Athens, yelling, "I don't want to leave my debts to my children!" As the man's protesting remarks underscore, those austerity measures include advancing future life through inherited debts and the discounting of the entire population. Alkman Granitsas, "Man Kills Himself in Athens Square," *Wall Street Journal*, April 4, 2012.

26 Federici, "On Capitalism, Colonialism, Women and Food Politics."

27 Kauanui, *Paradoxes of Hawaiian Sovereignty*; Barker, *Native Acts*; Simpson, *As We Have Always Done*; Goeman, "Land"; Byrd, *The Transit of Empire*; Million, "We Are the Land, and the Land Is Us"; Byrd et al., "Predatory Value."

28 See, for example, the efforts of the Amihan National Federation of Peasant Women (Unyon ng Manggagawa sa Agrikultura [UMA]), accessed November 17, 2021, https://amihanwomen.org.

29 Ngai, Chan, and Chan, "The Role of the State."

30 Ngai, Chan, and Chan, "The Role of the State," 137.

31 Of course, this is also true in the case of regular waged labor, with the house serving as the segregated place of social reproduction where the wage is subsidized by devalued women's domestic work. The difference in the case of floating labor populations is that the entire place of social reproduction is discounted. *Dagong* means "'working for the boss' or 'selling labour.'" "In contrast to *gongren* or urban worker, which carried the highest status under Mao, *dagong* signifies a lesser identity as a hired hand in the market." Ngai, Chan, and Chan, "The Role of the State," 136.

32 Ngai, Chan, and Chan, "The Role of the State," 137.

33 "Cash stands to capitalist money as popular justice to state law: preexisting its incorporation into, and monopoly by, the liberal state but never successfully completely tamed. This analogy and homology is also another reminder of the importance of citizenship in the realization of money's potential. Currency and type and citizenship can be foregrounded or backgrounded as differentiating principles, but the 'legal' component of 'legal tender' is always a constituent of people's capacities to deploy it." Guyer, "Cash Economies."

34 Also see Ho, *Liquidated*.

CHAPTER SIX. OF SURVIVAL

A previous version of this chapter was published in "Life-Times of Disposability within Global Neoliberalism," *Social Text* 31, no. 2 (2013): 19–47.

1 Wang, "Jia Zhangke's World."
2 Zhang, "Poetics of Vanishing," 72.
3 Zhang, "Poetics of Vanishing," 77–78.
4 Zhang, "Poetics of Vanishing," 85.
5 Zhang, "Poetics of Vanishing," 87.
6 Quoted in Mas, "Painting with a Political Camera."
7 "The pseudo-events that vie for attention in the spectacle's dramatizations have not been lived by those who are thus informed about them. In any case they are quickly forgotten, thanks to the precipitation with which the spectacle's pulsing machinery replaces one by the next." Debord, *The Society of the Spectacle*, 114.
8 McGrath, "The Independent Cinema of Jia Zhangke," 89–90. Similarly, Jean Ma argues, "The incommensurabilities plaguing post-socialist China find expression through techniques of temporal distension that insist upon a prolonged gaze at enigmatic ruins of the socialist-industrial past that mingle with signs of the new." Ma, *Melancholy Drift*, 149. Berry cited in McGrath, "The Independent Cinema of Jia Zhangke," 99.
9 Others have remarked on this temporal dilation with respect to *24 City*. Staging the human wasting process intrinsic to the general dynamics of capitalist production, paradigmatically exemplified in the forced lay-off of workers from the permanently shut down factory, *24 City* produces postsocialist time as an epochal change (the transformation of structures of collectivity and their relegation to subsidiary means of production) experienced as an indefinite suspension of the present. Jiwei notes for example how, through his extremely long takes and induced further through the use of poetry and photographic stills, Jia strives "to battle the world in transience: he must act as if his camera could outstrip the fluctuating present by gazing at it hard enough and long enough and by registering its minute-by-minute change, as if reality were always on the cusp of disappearing." Jiwei, "The Quest for Memory."
10 Jia asserts that the images of the nature in *Still Life* (river, mountain, fog) are "taken from fundamental elements in Chinese painting. That is why I use those panning shots, recalling the gesture of unrolling a classical scroll painting, opening it out in space. So, on the one hand, there is that natural beauty and then on the other, there is a certain beauty also in destruction." Quoted in Mas, "Painting with a Political Camera."
11 Karatani, *Origins of Modern Japanese Literature*, 29.
12 Substantification of time and extension in space that is "the undifferentiated mass, floating somewhere outside the passage of time, like an eternal essence." Guillaumin, *Racism, Sexism, Power and Ideology*, 53. As Guy Debord suggests, the expropriation of the time of producers of time-as-commodity is what allows the reign of capitalist progress. It is the resource from which is taken

the "temporal surplus value" enjoyed by the social classes who monopolize the making of history, and therefore the time of the spectacle as the "time appropriate to the consumption of images": "The spectacular restoration of time was only possible on the basis of this initial dispossession of the producers." Debord, *The Society of the Spectacle*, 114.
13 Or what Gayatri Spivak refers to as the regulative psychobiography of the subaltern; and what Hortense Spillers refers to as the experiences of the "one," "a psychic model of layered histories of a multiform past . . . the only riskable certain or grant of a social fiction . . . concrete and specific, even if anonymous." Spivak, "The Political Economy of Women," 227; Spillers, "All the Things," 141.
14 Spillers, "All the Things," 141.
15 Quoted in Mas, "Painting with a Political Camera."
16 McGrath, "The Independent Cinema of Jia Zhangke," 98–99.
17 Beller, *The Cinematic Mode of Production*.
18 "Such individual lived experience of a cut-off everyday life remains bereft of language or concept, and it lacks any critical access to its own antecedents, which are nowhere recorded. It cannot be communicated." Debord, *The Society of the Spectacle*, 114.
19 Scipes, "Global Economic Crisis."
20 Though it is perhaps correct to argue that "the logic of the Marcos regime, like the logic of the earlier Philippine political economy, is much better understood in terms of strategies of accumulation by diversified family conglomerates than in terms of battles among coherent economic strategies or sectors," as de Dios and Hutchcroft argue, it is also true that the extractive strategies deployed by ruling elites changed in accordance with transformations in the regulatory logic of international practice. Crony capitalism as paradigmatically practiced under the Marcos regime as a form of privatization of profits and nationalization of costs and risks (through what would now be called "public-private partnerships") was driven and sustained by foreign loans largely from the IMF and the World Bank, which promoted export-oriented industrialization. De Dios and Hutchcroft, "Political Economy."
21 The labor export industry was built on the US Exchange Visitor Program established at the beginning of the Cold War in 1948, through which the mass migration of Philippine nurses to the United States from the mid-1950s to the late 1960s was facilitated. Choy, *Empire of Care*; R. M. Rodriguez, *Migrants for Export*.
22 Remittances sustain the neoliberal postcolonial state, not only as a source of direct profit through taxation, but also by serving as one of the Philippines' top sources of foreign exchange (US $16 billion in 2008): in July 2009, remittances were the second highest earning export product, after electronic products. R. M. Rodriguez, *Migrants for Export*, xiv. At the same time, remittances subsidize through familial and kinship networks the subsistence of a population permanently excluded from formal employment.
23 In the context of commercial surrogacy in India, Kalindi Vora writes of a similar transfer of "vital energy, rather than value, as the content of what

is produced and transmitted between biological and affective producers and their consumers." Vora, "Limits of 'Labor,'" 684.

24 The aesthetics of both social realism and socialist realism have had a long career of influence in Philippine cinema (exemplified in the work of Lino Brocka and Ishmael Bernal), dominated on the one hand by a commercial tradition of melodrama, fantasy, action, and romance film, and recently challenged on the other hand by a more modern, visually cleaner, and more naturalist version of realism in digital feature films. There is also a strong alternative digital movement, composed of social documentaries and experimental film.

25 Ngai, *Migrant Labor in China*.

26 For Marx, the velocity of the circulation of money reflects "the rapidity with which commodities change their forms, the continued interlacing of one series of metamorphoses with another, the hurried nature of society's metabolic process, the quick disappearance of commodities from the sphere of circulation, and their equally quick replacement by fresh commodities." Marx, *Capital, Vol. I*, 217.

27 In the context of Duterte's war on drugs, Mendoza's film, *Ma Rosa* (2016) exemplifies most explicitly this moral injunction for a deus ex machina intervention, with its complete closure of the social field. The same closure marks Mendoza's *Kinatay* (2009), which, similar to *Ma Rosa*, is about the pervasive and ineradicable vile corruption of the police.

28 Reddy, *Freedom with Violence*.

CHAPTER SEVEN. CITY EVERYWHERE

A previous version of this chapter was published in "City Everywhere," *Theory, Culture and Society* 33, nos. 7–8 (2016): 57–83.

1 Gloria Macapagal Arroyo, "Sixth State of the Nation Address," July 24, 2006, accessed October 10, 2016, http://www.gov.ph/2006/07/24/gloria-macapagal-arroyo-sixth-state-of-the-nation-address-july-24-2006/ (no longer working).

2 Katherine Visconti, "MVP: Telcos Will Be Obsolete; Social Media Is the Future," *Rappler*, June 15, 2012, http://www.rappler.com/business/7018-telcos-are-obsolete,-social-media-is-the-future,-says-mvp/.

3 On the value productivity of circulation, see Marazzi, *The Violence of Financial Capitalism*.

4 Debord, *The Society of the Spectacle*, 113.

5 Simone, *City Life*, 175.

6 Visconti, "MVP."

7 Rappler, "Telcos Will Be Obsolete, Says MVP," YouTube, June 14, 2012, https://www.youtube.com/watch?v=XJWiU39vWGg/.

8 As the rest of this chapter shows, the notion of uber-urbanization signals not simply an intensification of the logics of modernization but a transcendence and overcoming of the limits of older strategies and paradigms of capitalist urban development, precisely a reorganization of its operational principles and political and economic presuppositions (intrinsic to industrial or

manufacturing capital and the international system of sovereign nation-states) through digital mediatization.

9 USAID, "Scaling Innovations in Mobile Money (SIMM) Project," September 21, 2015, https://www.usaid.gov/philippines/partnership-growth-pfg/simm.
10 Tadiar, "Manila's New Metropolitan Form."
11 Mandelbrot and Hudson, *The (Mis)Behavior of Markets*; Batty, *Cities and Complexity*.
12 "Welcome to Rockwell Land," Rockwell Land Corporation, accessed October 10, 2016, http://www.e-rock-well.com/projects/residential-completed.
13 The land development corporations and their patriarchal heads are SM Development Corporation (SMDC) (Henry Sy Sr.), Robinsons Land (John Gokongwei Jr.), Megaworld (Andrew Tan), and Ayala Land (Fernando Zobel de Ayala).
14 See Giedion, *Space, Time, and Architecture*.
15 Caldeira, *City of Walls*.
16 Tadiar, "Metropolitan Life and Uncivil Death"; Galloway, *Protocol*.
17 The International Franchise Association itself traces the origins of commercial franchising to medieval Europe and its development through "early exploration and trading," offering as paradigmatic examples the Dutch East India Company (VOC), founded in 1602 as a franchisee of the Dutch Republic and the means by which the latter came to make sovereign claims over the Hudson Valley in New York and the settler colony of Virginia, as a grant by the English Crown to the London Company in 1607. "The History of Modern Franchising," International Franchise Association, accessed March 27, 2020, https://www.franchise.org/blog/the-history-of-modern-franchising. Not surprisingly, the franchise, as political rights or "the vote," depended on landholding, following English laws premised on the complementarity of interests of individual and state in the settler colony. Smith, "The Franchise."
18 For a demonstration of this suturing of sovereign power and capitalist freedom in the contemporary Philippine context of franchises, see the Supreme Court ruling upholding statutory franchises granted to private corporations for the construction, maintenance and operation of the major tollway systems in Luzon. Supreme Court of the Philippines, G.R. No. 166910, October 19, 2010, https://elibrary.judiciary.gov.ph/thebookshelf/showdocs/1/54585.
19 *Oxford English Dictionary*, s.v. "franchise," accessed December 8, 2021, https://www-oed-com.ezproxy.cul.columbia.edu/view/Entry/74173?rskey=K8lsav&result=1&isAdvanced=false#eid.
20 W. Robinson, "Globalization," 615.
21 Seth Mydans, "Subic Bay, Minus U.S., Becomes Surprise Success," *New York Times*, November 23, 1996.
22 R. Rodriguez, "*Casus belli*," 132.
23 Aarti Nagraj, "Majority of UAE Filipinos Prefer Property Investment in Metro Manila," *Gulf Business*, March 19, 2015, http://gulfbusiness.com/majority-uae-filipinos-prefer-property-investment-metro-manila-survey/.

24 "The Philippine Economy: Coming Up Jasmine," *Economist*, August 23, 2014, https://www.economist.com/finance-and-economics/2014/08/23/coming-up-jasmine.
25 Terranova, *Network Culture*.
26 On the productivity of circulation and cognitive activity, see, respectively Marazzi, *The Violence of Financial Capitalism*; Boutang, *Cognitive Capitalism*; On when circulation can be productive, see also Marx, *Capital, Vol. II*.
27 Carl Thayer, "Analyzing the US-Philippines Enhanced Defense Cooperation Agreement," *Diplomat*, May 2, 2014, http://thediplomat.com/2014/05/analyzing-the-us-philippines-enhanced-defense-cooperation-agreement/.
28 The Philippines, as an exemplary postcolonial nation-state developed under US imperialism, was deliberately made into a franchise of US-style democracy. The 'Filipinization' process under the Commonwealth period of US colonialism provides a model of this political and economic franchising at the level of the nation-state.
29 A. Sundarajan, "A Safety Net Fit for the Sharing Economy," *Financial Times*, June 22, 2015, https://www.ft.com/content/b1d854de-169f-11e5-b07f-00144feabdc0/; Farhad Manjoo, "Uber's Business Model Could Change Your Work," *New York Times*, January 29, 2015.
30 Jodi Kantor, "Working Anything but 9 to 5: Scheduling Technology Leaves Low-Income Parents with Hours of Chaos," *New York Times*, August 13, 2014.
31 Natasha Singer, "In the Sharing Economy, Workers Find Both Freedom and Uncertainty," *New York Times*, August 16, 2014.
32 On Taylorism and media, see Beller, *The Cinematic Mode of Production*; and Beller, *The Message Is Murder*. On legacies of slavery in racial logics in biotechnologies of surveillance, see Roberts, *Fatal Invention*.
33 Marx, "Wage Labour and Capital," 205.
34 Marx, *Grundrisse*, 267, 293, 419. In the *Grundrisse*, Marx argues that the wage worker "only sells a temporary disposition over his labouring capacity," which allows him, as soon as he is able to reproduce the life he has exhausted ("the externalization of his life," or *Lebensäusserung*), to "begin the exchange anew." This selling of a temporary disposition is contrasted to the permanent alienation of one's entire time, which, following Hegel, Marx equates with slavery— "making the substance of my being into another's property" (293n2). Marx argues further that "the wage worker as distinct from the slave is himself an independent centre of circulation, someone who exchanges, posits exchange value, and maintains exchange value through exchange" (419). Legal freedom and formal equality underwrite the capacity to be this "independent centre of circulation," an independent seller of the power of disposition over one's labor power (in today's parlance, an "entrepreneur" of one's self). Even as the worker is thus able to continue to sell this temporary power of disposition over their labor power, after each completed exchange, Marx highlights the fact that, "after constantly repeated labour, he always has *only* his living, direct labour itself to exchange" (293–94). It is a mistake, moreover, to assume that what

takes place, as the worker reproduces their used up life forces and returns to labor anew, is mere repetition. Contrary to the bourgeois economists' enthusiasm for the seemingly infinite capacity of labor (an enthusiasm rehearsed in today's enthusiasm for the infinite reproductive capacity of "life itself"—see Melinda Cooper's work), and worse, their belief in the debt that workers owe to capital for the very fact that they are alive at all, what is consumed by capital in this seemingly endless exchange is a finite amount of vital forces, 'living labor' faced with absolute limits. As Marx emphasizes: *"What he exchanges for capital is his entire labouring capacity, which he spends, say, in twenty years. Instead of paying for it in a lump sum, capital pays him in small doses, as he places it at capital's disposal, say weekly"* (294). Put differently, what appears to be an act of mere reproduction (as repetition) is in fact a protracted process of productive consumption—a spending down of an entire life of "vital force."

35 On effectively forced labor, see Brennan, *Life Interrupted*; The "social organization of unfreedom" comes from Sharma, *Home Economics*, 104–38.

36 Through colonial capitalist sex-gender and race codes that serve to organize divisions of labor in the present, crucial aspects of the relation of domestic chattel slavery can indeed be found to inhere in contemporary legal, social conditions of capitalist servitude. The temporal differences in the legal codification of servitude between transitory, for indentured white women, and permanent, for enslaved black women, which Morgan notes in the historical context of slavery in the United States, might be seen as echoed in the differential legal treatment of citizen and migrant workers in Canada. Sharma, *Home Economics*. While contemporary capitalized servitude, even under conditions of human trafficking, is *not* chattel slavery (see Brennan, *Life Interrupted*) nor a slave mode of production annexed to formal capitalist production (through free, waged labor) as was the case for the plantation, we see here the fractal reproduction of aspects of the status of enslaved Black women within the scattered, private household sites of capitalized reproductive labor (sites of the deterritorialized "social factory"). See Tadiar, *Fantasy-Production*; Glenn, "From Servitude to Service Work." Needless to say, the gendered and racialized treatment of humans as property under the institution of slavery entails particular forms of violence whose history and afterlife is specifically borne by Black women. See Davis, *Women, Race, Class*; Davis, *The Angela Y. Davis Reader*; Spillers, "Mama's Baby, Papa's Maybe"; Hartman, "Belly of the World"; and Hartman, *Scenes of Subjection*.

37 As Nandita Sharma demonstrates, the organized deprivation of social and legal rights of citizens (the denial of protected freedoms) in "receiving" nation-states such as Canada creates "migrant workers" as a social and legal category, which enables the naturalization and depoliticization of what is effectively a system of unfree, indentured labor. Sharma, *Home Economics*.

38 Marx, *Grundrisse*, 389.

39 Marx argued that slaves form part of the means of production. See *Capital, Vol. I*, 874.

40 Simone, "People as Infrastructure," 124, 145.

41 Simone, "People as Infrastructure," 126.
42 Elyachar, "The Political Economy of Movement."
43 Elyachar, "The Political Economy of Movement," 94.
44 Simone, "People as Infrastructure," 410.
45 Adem, *Urban Poverty*.
46 Adem, *Urban Poverty*.
47 Adem, *Urban Poverty*.
48 M. Miller, "The Poor Man's Capitalist," *New York Times*, July 1, 2001.
49 Jocano, *Slum as Way of Life*, 170–72.
50 Jocano, *Slum as Way of Life*, 172; translation modified.
51 Tadiar, *Things Fall Away*, 143–81.
52 S. Jensen, "Stunted Future."
53 Diop, *Atlantiques* (2009).
54 Marx, *Grundrisse*, 398.
55 L. S. Marasigan, "Ten-Year Plan to Ease 'the Worst Traffic on Earth,'" *Business Mirror*, December 21, 2015.
56 Katz, *Growing Up Global*.
57 Cars make up two-thirds of the 2.7 million registered vehicles in metro Manila. Jochebed B. Gonzales, "How Many Vehicles Pass through EDSA Everyday?," *Business World*, July 1, 2018, https://www.bworldonline.com/how-many-vehicles-pass-through-edsa-each-day/. This estimate is also based on the sum of registered cars and SUVs in the National Capital Region, which had a total of 2,405,122 registered vehicles in 2016. CEIC Data, "Philippines No. of Registered Vehicles," accessed February 2, 2018, https://www.ceicdata.com/en/philippines/no-of-registered-motor-vehicles/no-of-motor-vehicles-registered.
58 A driver might have additional skills, skills that are neither recognized nor valued (not valued because not recognized) as skills, or as demands of his job—such as the ability to speak multiple languages: say, Pangasinense, Ilokano, Filipino, and English. He might translate or switch from one to another according to the preferences or limits of those he communicates with, able to detect what those and a whole other host of preferences might be. He might remember people and places and the details of itineraries past, and call any of them up when asked, serving as a memory function that the most advanced automated vehicles of urban life (self-driving cars, smartphones) have incorporated as part of their essential technological functions.
59 Vora, *Life Support*.
60 Tadiar, "Remaindered Life of Citizen-Man."
61 Vital infrastructure is constant capital not paid for by industrial capital, and instead, technically paid for by privatized life as labor (individuals who pay for all the services of social reproduction they require). If the globopolitical lives of citizens, or the sociality capitalized by platform industries, are the "commodities" produced by postindustrial, post-Fordist forms of production, then vital infrastructure constitutes a form of means of production (constant capital) not entirely produced by capital but rather by the harnessed, indepen-

dent activity of its "associated milieus," which continues to be located in the Global South as well as maintained in peripheries internally excluded within core nodes of city everywhere.

62 Barker, "The Human Genome Diversity Project."

EXCURSUS

1 R. M. Rodriguez, *Migrants for Export*.
2 "Record High Remittances to Low- and Middle-Income Countries in 2017," World Bank, press release, April 23, 2018, https://www.worldbank.org/en/news/press-release/2018/04/23/record-high-remittances-to-low-and-middle-income-countries-in-2017. In 2019, Mexico surpassed the Philippines with $36 billion in remittances. Ralf Rivas, "OFW Remittances Hit Record High of $33.5 billion in 2019," *Rappler*, February 17, 2020, https://www.rappler.com/business/overseas-filipino-workers-remittances-2019/.
3 R. M. Rodriguez, *Migrants for Export*; Guevarra, *Marketing Dreams*; Aguilar, *Migration Revolution*.
4 See Prakash, *Bonded Histories*; Salman, *The Embarrassment of Slavery*.
5 Guevarra, *Marketing Dreams*.
6 As exemplarily analyzed in the works of Rodriguez, *Migrants for Export*; Fajardo, *Filipino Cross-Currents*; Guevarra, *Marketing Dreams*; Padios, "Dial C For Culture"; and Padios, *A Nation on the Line*.
7 Pido, *Migrant Returns*; Faier, "Affective Investments in the Manila Region."
8 Pratt, Johnson, and Banta, "Lifetimes of Disposability."
9 The nondistinction enables "human capital theory" to enter into many feminist accounts of affective labor, such that—in these well-meaning attempts to prove the "agency" of the disenfranchised—service economy workers, whether in the domestic, health, care, sex, or customer service industries, can be portrayed as microcapitalists, entrepreneurs of their various forms of affective, cognitive, and cultural "capital," in much the same fashion as neoliberalist discourses.
10 As I argue elsewhere, the category of post-Fordist servility as a category of so-called non-productive labor or unremunerated life is a theoretical subsumption of the figurative properties and concrete activity of Black, third world, and postcolonial domestic servitude. Tadiar, *Things Fall Away*, 130–34.
11 Villarama, *Sunday Beauty Queen* (2016); Bong, *Parasite* (2019).
12 Weheliye, *Habeas Viscus*.
13 Kassamali, *Migrant Worker Lifeworlds of Beirut*.
14 Tadiar, "If Not Mere Metaphor. . . ." See also Tadiar, *Things Fall Away*, 82–93.
15 Fortunati, *The Arcane of Reproduction*, 161.
16 See Tadiar, "Domestic Bodies of the Philippines." On the importance of the "abolitionist" discourse of slavery as part and parcel of the conditions of production of migrant workers, see Tadiar, *Fantasy-Production*, especially 144–49.
17 Arendt, *The Human Condition*, 79–135.
18 C. Robinson, *Black Marxism*.

19 Prakash, *Bonded Histories*.
20 Gibson-Graham, *A Postcapitalist Politics*.
21 Chatterjee, "Decolonizing the History of Slavery."
22 It is on this view that Gyan Prakash considers the colonial construction of debt-bondage an archaeological monument, standing as an example of "archaeological remains of the process by which a bourgeois political economy was installed as the hegemonic discourse." Prakash, *Bonded Histories*, 11.
23 Chatterjee, "Decolonizing the History of Slavery."
24 Bernstein, "The Sexual Politics of the 'New Abolitionism.'"
25 This globalizing view also leads to the celebration or condemnation of such human agency in the form of virtue, merit, or culpability. That is, it leads to a moral judgment couched in a political claim. See also Chatterjee, "When 'Sexuality' Floated Free." The work of Anjali Arondekar is also important in this regard. Arondekar, *For the Record*.
26 The "service" provided by transport of reproductive labor can be consumed productively (as "a stage of production of the commodity that finds itself transported"). Marx, *Capital, Vol. II*, 135.
27 Many well-meaning, redemptive accounts of migrant workers look to find among them the creation of new subjectivities, against the representation of them as "victims." We are constantly taught and reminded by these scholars that migrant workers create their own subjectivities, as proof of their exercise of agency, as if to belabor the point that they too are human (like us). We are regaled with stories of their resilience and flexibility, redemptive stories meant to counter not the structural forces that shape the conditions in which they find themselves, but rather the scholarly, representational forces that serve to "victimize" them. So against anti-imperialist claims of continuity between contemporary global service labor and colonial resource extraction, we are offered more "complex" and more interesting attention to the subjectivities that such service labor forge in this cauldron of global capitalism. And yet when migrant workers and other oppressed groups are portrayed as "actively negotiating" their dire circumstances, are they not in fact merely being portrayed as economic subjects, whose agency is a matter of *bargaining* exchange values, or a matter of particular social practices with distinct use values (pronounced as "culture")? Does this humanizing "ethic" not demonstrate a participation in the soft war of the already human to extend their own privileges to the disenfranchised? Do these humanizing accounts not serve as consolations for those living lives buoyed by the very same misfortunes they wish to redeem through writing?
28 In this way, they function as instruments of labor: "Things through which the impact of labor on its object is mediated, and which therefore, in one way or another serve as *conductors of activity*, all of the objective conditions necessary for the continuation of the labor process. These do not enter directly into the process, but without them it is either impossible for it to take place or possible only to a partial extent. Once again the earth is a universal instrument of this kind, for it provides the worker with the ground beneath his feet, and a 'field of employment' for his own particular process. Instruments of this kind,

29 which have already been mediated through past labour, include workshops, roads, canals, etc." Marx, *Capital, Vol. I*, 286.
29 Home page, BaLinkBayan: Overseas Filipinos' One-Stop Online Portal for Diaspora Engagement, accessed November 17, 2021, https://balinkbayan.gov.ph.
30 Strathern, *The Gender of the Gift*.
31 Drori, *Foreign Workers in Israel*.
32 Sahlins, *What Kinship Is*; McKinnon and Cannell, *Vital Relations*.
33 Villarama, *Sunday Beauty Queen*. Heberer calls these familial, affiliative forms, "migrating intimacies." Heberer, "Migrating Intimacies."
34 As Drori shows, employment agencies take advantage of these informal recruitment systems when searching for workers. Participating in both networks of employment agencies and social networks of their own, migrant workers act as a gateway between capitalist and vital platforms. Drori, *Foreign Workers in Israel*.
35 See Enloe, *The Curious Feminist*; Ehrenreich and Hochschild, *Global Woman*; Chang, *Disposable Domestics*; and Hondagneu-Sotelo, *Doméstica*. The literature on feminized labor, in particular sex work, migrant domestic labor, and manufacturing factory labor, is now vast.
36 On the gendering of contemporary factory organization and labor in Mexico, China, and Malaysia, see Wright, *Disposable Women*; and Ong, *Spirits of Resistance*. For a discussion of the heterosexist constitution of the category of labor, see Tadiar, "Prostituted Filipinas and the Crisis of Philippine Culture."
37 The line between human trafficking and coerced labor is not so clear. Brennan, *Life Interrupted*.
38 Galam, "Utility Manning"; Aurora Almendral, "The Lonely and Dangerous Life of the Filipino Seafarer," *New York Times*, November 30, 2019.
39 Galam, "Utility Manning," 9.
40 Sarah Maslin Nir, "The Price of Nice Nails," *New York Times*, May 7, 2015. The expansion of unremunerated work-time in the form of unpaid internships, compulsory job training, and other forms of free or discounted work while under apprenticeship is now as widespread among higher-value workers and would-be higher-value workers (university and graduate students) in the cognitive and communicative industries as it is among low-value workers in the personal maintenance industry (nail salons, massage parlors) and the shipping industry.
41 Cowen, *The Deadly Life of Logistics*.
42 "Top Reasons Why Pinoys Prefer to Work in the UAE," *Filipino Times*, February 21, 2018, https://filipinotimes.net/top-stories/2018/02/21/top-reasons-pinoys-prefer-work-uae/.
43 Galam, "Utility Manning," 8–11.
44 Galam, "Utility Manning."
45 For dominant representations and contestations of normative Filipino masculinities of seafaring migrants, see Fajardo, *Filipino Crosscurrents*; Margold, "Narratives of Masculinity"; McKay, "Racializing the High Seas."
46 Spillers, "Mama's Baby, Papa's Maybe." For a discussion of the violence of this ungendering in the context of domestic work, see Tadiar, *Fantasy-Production*.

47 Margold, "Narratives of Masculinity," 275.
48 Rubino, *Ilocano Dictionary and Grammar*, 727. It is, important to emphasize, however, that the term *adípen* also bears historical local status hierarchies within and among Philippine communities whose legacies in the present need to be examined further. The verbal conjugation of *adípen* (slave/servant) to *agpaadipen* (to offer oneself as a slave/servant) in an example of contemporary usage suggests both the temporal character of the subordinated status and the conditions of kin obligation under which it might be assumed: "No kasapulan nga agpaadipen tapno makatulong a mangisakad iti pamilia, aramidenna dayta [If it is necessary to offer oneself as a servant/slave (*agpaadipen*, lit. to have oneself made into a servant/slave) to be able to help support the family, he will do that]", 11.
49 As waged labor is generalized to such an extent that it encompasses even kinds of activity that were not waged (e.g., biological reproduction, clinical trials), and as the "right" to become waged is extended to those who had managed to retain forms of livelihood outside formal spheres of employment (through land dispossession, war, and displacement), all of the labor necessary for the bodily (and psychic, affective, and cognitive) maintenance and valorization of the post-Fordist laborer/worker is offshored to other kinds of humans outside the social spheres historically sedimented and naturalized as their "own" (their inheritance of cultural, religious, ethnic identity as a form of private property). Race, sex-gender, and sexuality naturalize divisions of sociality along lines of valued/skilled and devalued/unskilled work, reproductive and productive work, manual/mechanical and creative/intellectual work—all of which inform the distinct life tracks that define food servers and cooks versus chefs, dressers versus designers, traditional third world craftspeople versus artisanal artists, construction workers versus architects, fixers versus presidents.
50 Dan Barry, Miriam Jordan, Annie Correal, and Manny Fernandez, "Cleaning Toilets, Following Rules: A Migrant Child's Days in Detention," *New York Times*, July 14, 2018.
51 As Saidiya Hartman writes of the reproductive labor of enslaved women, Black women's "work of sex and procreation" "not only guaranteed slavery as an institutional process and secured the status of the enslaved, but it inaugurated a regime of racialized sexuality that continues to place black bodies at risk for sexual exploitation and abuse, gratuitous violence, incarceration, poverty, premature death, and state-sanctioned murder." Still, "this brilliant and formidable labor of care" is not exhausted by the "violent structures of slavery, antiblack racism, virulent sexism, and disposability" through which it is produced to be exploited. Hartman, "The Belly of the World," 169, 171.

CHAPTER EIGHT. POWERS OF DEFENDING FREEDOM

1 American Studies Association, "Boycott of Israeli Academic Institutions," December 4, 2013, http://www.theasa.net/american_studies_association_resolution_on_academic_boycott_of_israel/.

2. For an example of both positions, see the 2013 volume of the AAUP's *Journal of Academic Freedom*, available at http://www.aaup.org/reports-publications/journal-academic-freedom/volume-4/.
3. Butler, "Israel/Palestine and the Paradoxes of Academic Freedom"; Butler, "Critique, Dissent, Disciplinarity." Here, "academic freedom" turns out to be the "right" to remain unencumbered by Palestinian suffering, and it serves to protect Israel from criticism—which one can argue amounts to a claim to impunity. Ferguson and Melamed, "Academic Freedom with Violence"; see also "Circuits of Influence: US, Israel, and Palestine," *Social Text Periscope*, June 17, 2014, http://socialtextjournal.org/periscope_article/circuits-of-influence/; and "The Academic Boycott Movement," *Social Text*, November 15, 2016, https://socialtextjournal.org/periscope_topic/the-academic-boycott-movement/.
4. Davis, *Abolition Democracy*, 46.
5. Davis, *Are Prisons Obsolete?* "Criminality" and "illegality" are two designatory categories of unfreedom that serve this ideological/practical function.
6. Hartman, *Scenes of Subjection*, 118.
7. Ritchie, *Invisible No More*; Razzack, "Gendering Disposability."
8. Mahmood, *Politics of Piety*; Abu-Lughod, *Do Muslim Women Need Saving?*; Ong, "Experiments with Freedom."
9. Bernstein, "The Sexual Politics of the 'New Abolitionism.'"
10. Besides those cited above, see Mohanty, *Feminism without Borders*; Grewal, "Women's Rights as Human Rights"; and Reddy, *Freedom with Violence*.
11. W. Robinson, "Globalization"; Grandin, *The Empire's Workshop*; Mamdani, *Bad Muslim, Good Muslim*.
12. We could say that these specific ideas of equality and freedom are thinkable only to the extent that equality and freedom already operate in the field of capitalist exchange. Marx, *Grundrisse*, 245. Equality is what defines the relations of subjects of exchange to each other, while *freedom* is contained in the person, whose juridical moment enters when the subjects of exchange "recognize one another reciprocally as proprietors, as persons whose will penetrates their commodities"—equality and freedom stipulated as attributes of this juridical person who is the individual engaged in exchange. Marx, *Grundrisse*, 244–46.
13. Elsewhere Marx also refers to this as the arena of operation of "*nonpolitical* distinctions," or what he terms "*effective* differences," which, far from being abolished, are *presupposed* and allowed "to *act* after *their* own fashion . . . and to manifest their *particular* nature." Marx, "On the Jewish Question," 33. It is of course true, as antiracist, feminist, and queer critics have abundantly shown, that these differences are not simply allowed to act in their fashion but rather are bolstered by and constitutive of the state as well as dominant institutions of society
14. Ian S. Lustich, "Two-State Illusion," *New York Times*, September 14, 2013.
15. Marx, *Capital, Vol. I*, 916. As Marx shows, the violent forces of primitive accumulation are carried out through "bloody legislation" or the punitive measures of the law, as for example the 1547 Act for the Punishing of Vagabonds in England under Edward VI, whereby the refusal to work (the criminalization of "idling") was made punishable by slavery. The legislation and implementation of Black

Codes in the United States in the aftermath of emancipation served a similar purpose of enforcing "free labor" and the continuity of white supremacy and plantation agriculture. For Marx's contradictory and shifting understanding of primitive accumulation and for an argument for primitive accumulation as an economic force exerted through state violence, see Singh, "On Race, Violence, and So-Called Primitive Accumulation."

16 As Dean Spade demonstrates, the individualist advocacy of trans equality through the expansion antidiscrimination and hate crime laws not only depoliticizes the very structures of racism, sexism, homophobia, transphobia, ableism, and xenophobia that create the conditions of violence face by minoritized subjects (and that are the *basis* of their claims) but also makes these *inadmissible* in a court of law. Spade, *Normal Life*.

17 Reddy, *Freedom with Violence*, 154.

18 Wynter, "No Humans Involved," 60. For Wynter, "The throwaway lives, both at the global socio-human level, of the vast majority of peoples who inhabit the '*favela*/shanty town' of the globe and their jobless archipelagoes, as well at the national level, of Baldwin's 'captive population' in the urban inner cities (and on the Indian Reservations of the United States)" are, as is the case with the discardable environment, *hidden costs* (60).

19 Spade, *Normal Life*.

20 Just as the persecution and degradation of women through witch-hunting, as a deliberate strategy of enclosure, was also instrumental in the rise of the state and in the expansion and development of the modern juridical, legal apparatus in early modern Europe. Federici, *Caliban and the Witch*.

21 Tadiar, *Fantasy-Production*.

22 Said, "Zionism from the Standpoint of Its Victims."

23 Kelley, *Freedom Dreams*; Go, *Patterns of Empire*.

24 A vast body of Philippine studies scholarship has detailed the installation of these institutions. See, for example, Go, *Patterns of Empire*; McCoy, *Policing America's Empire*; Anderson, *Colonial Pathologies*; and Hutchcroft, *Booty Capitalism*.

25 More than half of the total number of OFWs (51.4 percent of 2.3 million, as of April 2019) are in Western Asia. Philippine Statistics Authority, "Total Number of OFWs Estimated at 2.3 Million," April 30, 2019, https://psa.gov.ph/content/total-number-ofws-estimated-23-million-results-2018-survey-overseas-filipinos/.

26 Huw Watkin, "Filipino Seamen, despite Powering Global Trade, Face Growing Threats to Their Livelihoods," *South China Morning Post*, June 6, 2019; "Meet Me in Luneta," *Economist*, February 16, 2019, 34; McKay, "Racializing the High Seas."

27 Nikhil Chadwani, "Philippines' BPO Industry: In 2019 and Beyond," *Entrepreneur*, February 9, 2019, https://www.entrepreneur.com/article/327758/; see also Padios, *A Nation on the Line*.

28 Espiritu, *Body Counts*.

29 Tyner, *The Business of War*, 88–89. As Bobby Tuazon writes, President Gloria Macapagal Arroyo admitted in a news conference that the benefit of the Philippines' enlistment in the "coalition of the willing" was precisely the prospect

of subcontracted work in postwar reconstruction, which would increase OFW remittances to the state. He notes that, as evidenced by the United Kingdom's own benefits—the opening up of a new market for the UK weapons manufacturing industry and the freeing up of state-controlled Iraqi oil for British petroleum firms partnering with US oil companies—this coalition could be rightly dubbed the "coalition of the subcontractors." While Arroyo committed a small contingent of soldiers and police in the early part of the US war against Iraq, popular Philippine protest in response to the kidnapping of a Filipino truck driver working for a Saudi company in partnership with the US military, Angelo de la Cruz, compelled her to withdraw the "troops." Bobby Tuazon, "GMA Boards 'Coalition of the Coerced,'" *Bulatlat*, March 23–29, 2003, https://www.bulatlat.com/news/3-8/3-8-coalition.html.
30 Tyner, *The Business of War*. Together with contract workers from Jamaica, they make up 40 percent of the base population. Li, "Offshoring the Army," 126.
31 Li, "Offshoring the Army," 124.
32 Li, "Offshoring the Army," 173.
33 "Unlike citizen-soldiers whose sacrifices are consecrated by the body politic, military migrant workers toil in war zones in support of a government to whom they are not bound by any social contract. And unlike mercenaries who maximize profits through their specialized military skills, TCNs are locked in deeply coercive contractual relationships that often rise to the level of indenture." Li, "Offshoring the Army," 128.
34 Amar, *The Security Archipelago*.
35 For a brief history of the US information infrastructure, see McCoy, "Imperial Illusions."
36 Alfred McCoy argues that the unprecedented power of the US military's information infrastructure developed out of three moments of imperial engagement or war: the Philippine-American War (1898–1913), the Vietnam War (1964–1974), and the ongoing Global War on Terror beginning in Afghanistan and Iraq (2001–present). McCoy, "Imperial Illusions."
37 Vitug and Gloria, *Under the Crescent Moon*, 8.
38 Richard S. Erlich, "Israel Lends Philippines a Helping Strategic Hand," *Asia Times*, July 4, 2019, https://asiatimes.com/2019/07/israel-lends-philippines-a-helping-strategic-hand/; Alvite Singh Ningthoujam, "The Military-Security Dimension of Israel–Southeast Asia Relations," MEI@75, January 7, 2020, https://www.mei.edu/publications/military-security-dimension-israel-southeast-asia-relations/. The IDF has also been training US law enforcement and security forces in its own well-honed techniques and technologies of mass surveillance, collective punishment, discriminatory and repressive policing, intelligence, deportation and detention, extrajudicial killings, and other forms of militarized violence. Deadly Exchange, "The Dangerous Consequences of American Law Enforcement Trainings in Israel," September 2018, https://deadlyexchange.org/deadly-exchange-research-report/.
39 Pia Ranada, "Duterte Meets Netanyahu: 'We Share Same Passion for Human Beings,'" *Rappler*, September 3, 2018, https://www.rappler.com/nation/211047

-duterte-meets-israel-prime-minister-benjamin-netanyahu-september-3-2018/. In his speech, Netanyahu recalled, "We remember that the Philippines was the only Asian country that voted for the establishment of the State of Israel in the UN resolution in 1947." President Rodrigo Roa Duterte, "Duterte Transcripts: Netanyahu and Duterte. 03 Sept 2018," MindaNews, June 10, 2019, https://www.mindanews.com/duterte-files/2019/06/__trashed-27/.

40 Cherniavsky, "Neocitizenship and Critique." Like many cultural theorists in the Global North, Cherniavsky is drawing on Gilles Deleuze's essay, "Postscript on Societies of Control," and Michel Foucault's writings on disciplinary, normative power in *"Society Must Be Defended."*

41 McCoy, *Policing America's Empire*, 514.

42 Simbulan, *The CIA's Hidden History in the Philippines*; Li, "Offshoring the Army."

43 Collier and Lakoff, "Vital Systems Security."

44 There is more to say here about the role of the separation of people and territory as a technique of settler colonialism that has become central to financialization. In 2005, Ariel Sharon spoke in his address to the UN of "the right of the Jewish people *to* the Land of Israel" while "others" only have rights *"in* the land." Quoted in White, *Palestinians in Israel*, 19. The distinction between citizenship and nationality in the Israeli context is in many ways a model for the emerging distinction between globopolitical humanity and serviceable life.

45 Martin, "After Economy?"

46 As has been explicated by scholars and activists, mandatory, longer sentencing and other racialized "getting tough on crime" policies, "broken windows" policing, and state wars on drugs, poverty, and terrorism have produced, in the US context, gruesome profitable opportunities for state-funded, subcontracted private manufacturing as well as service industries, including communications, food, health care, and more recently, probation and parole. Davis, *Are Prisons Obsolete?*; Sudbury, *Global Lockdown*; Ritchie, *Invisible No More*; Gilmore, *Golden Gulag*. See also note 61 below.

47 "As a value, every commodity is divisible; in its natural existence this is not the case." Marx, *Grundrisse*, 141.

48 Martin, "After Economy?," 100.

49 Dumit, "Prescription Maximization and the Accumulation of Surplus Health." Melinda Cooper and Catherine Waldby write about the labor of clinical trial subjects in the late twentieth-century pharmaceutical industry as consisting in "endurance of risk and exposure to nonpredictable experimental effects." Cooper and Waldby, *Clinical Labor*, 8. The value produced by this voluntary as well as coerced assumption of risk—the "innovation value" of capitalized experimental research—is accrued through the evental time of metabolic exposure (the time of the accident), rather than the measurable socially average time of industrial labor.

50 As Joanne Barker argues, there is an incommensurability between *peoples* and *populations* that is purposefully ignored to the detriment of Indigenous peoples claiming "rights to governance, territorial integrity and cultural autonomy." The latter logic (that of populations as genetic material) is what enables

Indigenous groups to be configured "as mere fodder for genetic research/industry." Barker, "The Human Genome Diversity Project," 594, 584.

51 "The human has become the medium for information; [or] put another way, the medium is human, despite the fact that human potential is foreclosed by its function." Beller, "Paying Attention," 57. Dorothy Roberts shows that the use of DNA phenotyping by law enforcement in the United States and United Kingdom for genetic surveillance has a predictive function with respect to "race" categories, which become increasingly biologized at a molecular, "genetic" level, even as it is accepted to be socially constructed at the level of social identities. Roberts, *Fatal Invention*.

52 Roger Cohen, "Gaza without End," *New York Times*, November 19, 2012; Ethan Bronner, "As Battlefield Changes, Israel Takes Tougher Approach," *New York Times*, November 16, 2012.

53 Li, "The Gaza Strip as Laboratory."

54 "Ministry of Defense v. Gisha 'Food Consumption in the Gaza Strip: Red Lines' Presentation," Ministry of Defense, State of Israel, translated by Gisha Legal Center for Freedom of Movement, September 27, 2012, accessed May 17, 2015, http://www.gisha.org/UserFiles/File/publications/redlines/red-lines-presentation-eng.pdf.

55 The conclusion and recommendations of the report include an emphasis on a "caloric model," a "minimum bar" for meat, agricultural inputs, eggs for reproduction, and nutritional supplements, as part of a "safety margin" intended to avoid the malnutrition of children especially. "Ministry of Defense v. Gisha," slide 9.

56 Weizman, *The Least of All Possible Evils*, 11.

57 Weizman, *The Least of All Possible Evils*, 11.

58 Puar, *The Right to Maim*, 134, 142.

59 Collier and Lakoff, "Vital Systems Security." Indeed, "vital systems" of settler colonial nation-states, such as the United States and Israel, are equated with specific people constructed with the identitarian attribute of colonial settlement (whiteness, Jewishness), which indicates rights *to* land, and distinguished from nationality, which indicates rights *within* territory and therefore rights that are variably accessible.

60 We have only to look at the rise of privatized (offender-funded) probation services and the rise of debtors' prisons in the United States to see how criminalized, poor, mostly Black individuals are subject to cascading tolls of penalties (legal-financial obligations) exacted by courts and probation services—to see how punishment has literally become a mode of value extraction. American Civil Liberties Union, "In for a Penny: The Rise of America's New Debtors' Prisons," October 2010, https://www.aclu.org/report/penny-rise-americas-new-debtors-prisons/; Human Rights Watch, "Profiting from Probation," February 5, 2014, https://www.hrw.org/report/2014/02/05/profiting-probation/americas-offender-funded-probation-industry/.

61 This is the project of Thomas Chadefaux, a sociologist in Zurich who has combed news stories from 1902–2001 using Google's database of newspapers.

Somini Sengupta, "Spreadsheets and Global Mayhem," *New York Times*, March 23, 2014.
62 GDelt Project, accessed April 26, 2014, http://gdeltproject.org.
63 Indeed, what a team assembled by the Holocaust Museum has set out to do—to mine "hate speech" on Twitter and Facebook, or use words as material for the attributive logic of "profiling" for state and parastate policing—is already a model of political engagement and governmentality, as exemplified by the use of Steven Salaita's tweets as the basis of punitive sanctions (bypassing "freedom" altogether, or giving the lie to the notion that "freedom" is at issue in the opposition to the boycott of Israel). Here, communicative acts are considered forms of behavior on which to impose the protocols of "civility," whose logic Salaita asserts is one with the logic of genocide. See Sengupta, "Spreadsheets and Global Mayhem"; and Steven Salaita, "First Peoples, Palestine, and the Crushing of Free Speech," Seriously Free Speech, November 20, 2014, http://seriouslyfreespeech.ca/2014/11/sfsc-event-professor-steven-salaita-first-peoples-palestine-and-the-crushing-of-free-speech/.
64 Tawil-Souri, "Digital Occupation"; Tawil-Souri and Aouragh, "Intifada 3.0?"
65 Tawil-Souri, "Digital Occupation"; Tawil-Souri and Aouragh, "Intifada 3.0?"
66 Magid Shihade, "We Are Fine in Gaza, How Are You?," *Jadaliyya*, November 17, 2012, https://www.jadaliyya.com/Details/27424.
67 The trip took place on January 4–10, 2012, and was organized by US Academic and Cultural Boycott of Israel (USACBI). We listened to gatherings of activists, academics, and community members in Ramallah, Birzeit, Haifa, Jerusalem, Hebron, and Bethlehem.
68 Bamyeh, "Palestine," 827.
69 Hilal, "Imperialism and Settler-Colonialism in West Asia," 59. Birzeit University president Khalil Hindi spoke of this "unholy alliance" in a personal meeting with the delegation on January 5, 2012.
70 Conversation with Robin D. G. Kelley, J. Kēhaulani Kauanui, Bill T. Mullen, Nikhil Singh, Rana Barakat, Magid Shihade, and the author, January 7, 2012, East Jerusalem.
71 Coalition for Defending Palestinian Rights in Jerusalem, "Dispossession and Eviction in Jerusalem: The Cases and Stories of Sheikh Jarrah," 2009, 6, https://www.adalah.org/uploads/oldfiles/newsletter/eng/feb10/docs/Sheikh_Jarrah_Report-Final.pdf. The report also offers historical background and other case histories and personal testimonies of the evictions in Sheikh Jarrah.
72 Shalhoub-Kevorkian, "Palestinian Feminist Critique," 8.
73 Shalhoub-Kevorkian, "Palestinian Feminist Critique," 13.
74 Darwish, *Journal of An Ordinary Grief*, 75.
75 Darwish, *Journal of an Ordinary Grief*, 94.
76 Darwish, *Journal of an Ordinary Grief*, 95.
77 Elia, "Justice Is Indivisible."

CHAPTER NINE. POWERS OF EXPENDING LIFE

1. Augustine, *De diverses quaestionibus in Heptateuchum locationem*, book 6, question 10, quoted in W. H. Scott, *The Discovery of the Igorots*, 26.
2. Scott, *The Discovery of the Igorots*, 26–27.
3. Rengger, "On the Just War Tradition."
4. See J. Williams, "Space, Scale and Just War"; Crawford, "Just War Theory and the US Counterterror War"; and Peach, "An Alternative to Pacificism?"
5. Patricia Evangelista, "This Is Where They Do Not Die," *Rappler*, November 25, 2017, https://r3.rappler.com/newsbreak/investigative/188904-impunity-series-police-killings-quezon-city-ejk.
6. Amnesty International, "If You Are Poor, You Are Killed: Extrajudicial Executions in the Philippines' 'War On Drugs,'" January 31, 2017, https://www.amnesty.org/en/documents/asa35/5517/2017/en/.
7. Emmanuel Tupas, "Drug War Death Toll Now 6,600," *Philippine Star*, June 19, 2019, https://www.philstar.com/headlines/2019/06/19/1927750/drug-war-death-toll-now-6600-pnp/. For the number of unsolved homicides, see Human Rights Watch, "Philippines Events of 2018," accessed August 17, 2021, https://www.hrw.org/world-report/2019/country-chapters/Philippines/.
8. Ronalyn V. Olea, "An Appraisal: Cory Aquino and Human Rights," *Bulatlat*, August 9, 2009, https://www.bulatlat.com/2009/08/09/an-appraisal-cory-aquino-and-human-rights/.
9. McCoy, *Policing America's Empire*. Ramos's successor, Joseph Estrada (1998–2001), declared an "all-out war" against the Moro Islamic Liberation Front, but his presidency would be much more concerned with and defined by gaining national control over the illicit economy, primarily the billion-peso business of jueteng.
10. McCoy locates in the 2002 US military killing of the leader of the Abu Sayyaf militia group—by means of seamless integration of CIA aerial drones with US and local special operations forces—the forging of a new template for the covert assassination campaigns unleashed five years later in Iraq and Afghanistan. McCoy, *Policing America's Empire*, 511.
11. McCoy, "Covert Netherworld."
12. Lara, *Insurgents, Clans and States*, 159.
13. Lara, *Insurgents, Clans and States*, 160. The plan for the massive resettlement of ten thousand Jewish refugees in Mindanao, which was "the only nationally sanctioned Jewish rescue operation in the world," must be viewed against the United States' own initial refusal of sanctuary to Jewish refugees fleeing the European Holocaust. See Harris, "Mindanao: The New Palestine," in *Philippine Sanctuary*, 113–48.
14. Arumpac, *War Is a Tender Thing* (2013).
15. Bauzon, "Ruminations on the Bangsamoro Struggle." The annual average investment influx in Mindanao jumped ten times from a ₱5–6 billion annual average in 2001–2010 to a ₱50–60 billion annual average in 2011–2016, according to an official of the Mindanao Development Authority (Minda). Jennie P.

Arado, "Influx of Investments in Mindanao Increases," *Sun Star Philippines*, March 16, 2017, http://www.sunstar.com.ph/davao/business/2017/03/16/influx-investments-mindanao-increases-531403/.

16 See Curato, *A Duterte Reader*; and Kusaka, *Moral Politics in the Philippines*.

17 See USAID, "Annexes," in "Performance Evaluation of USAID/Philippines Growth with Equity in Mindanao III (Gem-3) Program," March 16, 2014, https://www.usaid.gov/documents/1861/performance-growth-equity-mindanao-iii-gem-iii-program-annexes/.

18 The details of the transformation of policing through the war on drugs, and the formation of its template in Davao (motorcycle-riding assassinations, outsourcing of civilian vigilantes, territorial targeting, salvaging, use of infiltrative-collaborative agents), as developed out of experiences of counterinsurgency in the region, are finely traced in Warburg and Jensen, "Policing the War on Drugs."

19 Many scholars have written on the long history of colonial power and local elites' adaptations of its political and economic bequests to explain the peculiarities of third world, or postcolonial, state formation, including this most stereotypical despotic form that seems immanent among the becoming-human, those populations fated to remain in the shadow state of their continuing unfreedom. While many comparative political studies provide typological categories to explain how these state formations emerged out of their colonial histories in full-fledged political uniform, few situate these formations' peculiar character in a global formation that is itself colonial in its own history and in its continuing, present operation. By this I do not mean to suggest that third world or postcolonial authoritarian states are merely appendages or lackeys to the sovereign powers of imperial nations but instead that they exist and function the way they do not simply because of this past history but because of their present pertinence to a global system, which that seemingly "past" history produced. Against the comparative injunction to treat nation-states as sovereign powers and places, in the way that other social science disciplines treat humans and their psychological and cultural activities as so many kinds and units of sovereign agency (individual and collective subjects), we might see instead the dynamic and enabling, continuing relations that constitute their operational tendencies.

20 McCoy, "Covert Netherworld," 852–56. See also Grandin, *Empire's Workshop*; and Mamdani, *Good Muslim, Bad Muslim*.

21 Certainly, it is in part this international lexicon, upheld by international law prohibiting the drug trade, that connects different nation-states' respective wars on drugs. Koram, *The War on Drugs*.

22 Coronel, "Murder as Enterprise." See also Amnesty International, *"If You Are Poor, You Are Killed."*

23 Coronel, "Murder as Enterprise," 189.

24 See Center for People Empowerment in Governance, *Corruptionary*.

25 See Cooper, *Family Values*; and Martin, "Money after Decolonization."

26 "Power signs . . . express money as capital and the role of money as credit." Lazzarato, *Signs and Machines*, 85.

27 Leila B. Salaverria, "Trade Chief Says Business Booming under Duterte," *Philippine Daily Inquirer*, June 28, 2017.
28 Edu Punay, "Build Build Build Gets P1 Trillion in Duterte's Final Year," *Philippine Star*, August 26, 2021, https://www.philstar.com/headlines/2021/08/26/2122654/build-build-build-gets-p1-trillion-dutertes-final-year.
29 Pia Ranada, "Duterte Signs ₱3.8 Trillion 2018 National Budget into Law," *Rappler*, December 19, 2017; Chrisee Dela Paz, "Duterte Administration Details 'Ambitious' Infra Plan," *Rappler*, April 18, 2017, https://www.rappler.com/business/167256-dutertenomics-build-build-build-infrastructure-plan/.
30 Kusaka, *Moral Politics in the Philippines*.
31 Unlike right-wing populisms in the Global North, Duterte's support was strikingly urbanist. His biggest plurality and margin of victory in the presidential elections, apart from his Mindanao base, came from Metro Manila and its surrounding provinces, urban areas across the country, and overseas absentee voters. Cook and Salazar, "The Differences Duterte Relied Upon to Win." The word *poon* (also, *puón*) is a word in Austronesia-wide usage, meaning trunk or stem, and figuratively meaning origin, source, or cause, and also used to refer to an initiator or leader of a power-gaining journey, which gathers followers. See Fox, "The Discourse and Practice of Precedence."
32 See the brilliant manipulated family photo album zine of Magpies Press, photoshopping Duterte as the father figure in family photographs of the slain: *Para sa alaala ng yumao nating ama*, Daddy Digong Issues 2, November 2017. This to some extent explains the seeming noncontradiction between Duterte's own hypersexist, masculinist persona and the vociferous support of women and transwomen in his campaign (notably by the powerful pro-Duterte media influencers Mocha Uson and Sass Sasot). "Protection" of the nation as clan ensures all is permitted and loved as long as the clan itself is not attacked. Women can be sexual, gender can be fluid, but political correctness will not supersede the nation, "human rights" will not browbeat the hard-working and sacrificing, "feminists" will not harangue those who will actually look after "our" own, and due process, do-nothing critics and protesters, and the liberal media ("presstitutes") will not stand in the way of, or stay, the swift sword of justice. We might also understand this situation as the result of a vigorous disconnection between personal identities (given or chosen) and structural conditions of oppression, poverty, and injustice. Hence the noncontradiction perceived between the transgender rights movement and the death penalty exemplified by the views of Duterte supporter transgender activist Sass Sasot, who understands the transgender movement in terms of the defeat of transphobia, the rise of transgender voices in national politics, and the quest "to have a seat at the table." Sass Sasot, "Solidarity," *Manila Times*, April 16, 2018.
33 We hear in Duterte's repeated threats—to kill and punish addicts, critics, and anyone who defies his injunctions—a similar tone and address as that of the *requerimiento*, the injunction addressed to New World Indians in 1514, demanding fealty and conversion to the order of humanity whose master is Jesus Christ: "But if you do not do this . . . I certify to you that, with the help of God,

we shall forcibly enter into your country and shall make war against you in all ways and manners that we can . . . and we shall do all the harm and damage that we can." Quoted in Todorov, *Conquest of America*, 147.

34 As W. H. Scott writes, because they had neither king nor castle, all their killings, "whether for the purpose of rustling cattle or defending their 'brutish independence,'" are recorded in Spanish accounts as crime. Through just war, "pagan intransigence" and the "uninhibited exercise of this independence" become redefined as criminality. W. H. Scott, *Discovery of the Igorots*, 3, 20.

35 Condemned for impeding the "innocent passage" of colonizing forces, for violating the freedom of movement, trade, and speech, deemed the prerogative of the imperial gospel. For Francisco de Vitoria, one of the pinnacles of Spanish humanism in the sixteenth century who criticized the conquistadores, "just war" was nevertheless possible in the case of violations of "the natural right to society and communication" on the side of the Christian Gospel. The rights of guardianship can be licitly exercised when citizens "are not, or are no longer, capable of governing themselves any more than madmen or even wild beasts and animals." Quoted in Todorov, *Conquest of America*, 150.

36 Drugs bear a long colonial history as the dark commodity, imbued with a denigrating power to transform people into subhumans, but the notion of their capacity to pose "an existential threat to humanity" can be traced to the nineteenth century. Koram, *The War on Drugs*.

37 RESBAK (Respond and Break the Silence against the Killings), *Dalawampu't Siyam Na Libo*, collectively published zine.

38 See Lasco, "Pampagilas"; and Lasco, "Call Boys."

39 Mora, *The Nightcrawlers* (2019).

40 Von Werlhof, "On the Concept of Nature."

41 Carlo Pacolor Garcia, "Mula Sa Vocábulario ng Casaláulaan," RESBAK (Respond and Break the Silence against the Killings), *12000*: 7/1/2016–6/12/2017*, collectively published zine.

42 This practice is directly traceable to the counterinsurgency methods deployed by the US military in its colonial war against the Philippines in the early twentieth century, when the US military conducted and legitimized the burning of houses of "noncombatants" as *punishment*. See Graff, *American Imperialism and the Philippine Insurrection*. Psy-ops were formally developed during the Hukbalahap struggles as symbolic-cultural state terror that was part of its low-intensity warfare strategy. McCoy argues that the origins of the US military doctrine of low-intensity warfare came out of the context of counterinsurgency against the Hukbalahap. McCoy, "Low Intensity Conflict in the Philippines."

43 Lazzarato, *Signs and Machines*, 85.

44 Yean, *Tulong*; see also Kusaka, *Moral Politics in the Philippines*. While there is an ontological distance between help as unpayable "lending" and help as exchange-value, the fusion of both is precisely what structures relations of patronage.

45 Glenda Gloria, panel presentation at the Watching the Philippines, Reporting Duterte conference, Columbia University, October 18, 2017; Don Kevin Hapal, "Oplan Cyber Tokhang on Facebook: 'Extrajudicial Reporting,'" *Rappler*,

December 1, 2016, https://www.rappler.com/newsbreak/investigative/154099-oplan-cyber-tokhang-facebook-security/.

46 See Maria A. Ressa, "Propaganda War: Weaponizing the Internet," *Rappler*, October 3, 2016, https://www.rappler.com/nation/148007-propaganda-war-weaponizing-internet/; and Ong and Cabañes, *Architects of Networked Disinformation*.

47 Davey Alba, "How Duterte Used Facebook to Fuel the Philippine Drug War," *BuzzFeed News*, September 4, 2018, https://www.buzzfeednews.com/article/daveyalba/facebook-philippines-dutertes-drug-war/; Shibani Mahtani and Regine Cabato, "Why Crafty Internet Trolls in the Philippines May Be Coming to a Website near You," *Washington Post*, July 25, 2019, https://www.washingtonpost.com/world/asia_pacific/why-crafty-internet-trolls-in-the-philippines-may-be-coming-to-a-website-near-you/2019/07/25/c5d42ee2-5c53-11e9-98d4-844088d135f2_story.html.

48 "Maria Ressa, the CEO of the news website *Rappler*, told *BuzzFeed News* that during an April 2017 meeting with Facebook, she mentioned to Mark Zuckerberg that 97 percent of Filipinos who had access to the internet also had Facebook accounts (which was true at the time). Zuckerberg frowned, Ressa recalled. Then he asked: 'What about the other 3 perncet?'" Alba, "How Duterte Used Facebook." The complicity of Facebook with the Duterte platform includes Zuckerberg's partnership in the building of an undersea cable to improve internet service, as well as the allowance of hate speech, slander, and other forms of attack on sponsored accounts.

49 Alba, "How Duterte Used Facebook"; Mahtani and Cabato, "Why Crafty Internet Trolls."

50 See also the Alyx Arumpac's documentary, *Aswang*. In the film *Ma Rosa*, which naturalistically depicts the capture and ransom extortion of a petty drug dealer by a narcotics team, which is itself on the take, Mendoza puts us through the paces of the daily struggles of illicit everyday life, showing that the paces are the same across a range of small-time to medium-time dealers, paces shared by the police machine. All are engaged in networks of "help" that they call on to activate extended being and to summon flows of obligation, calling in debts and obligations across kin/affines (ritual compadres/brods). Even in exchanges for money, there is the summoning of "help" out of affective debts that exceed the price expressions of equivalence and commensurability. The police rely on and induce betrayal along the vertical chain to protect their own, and the vital platforms of people's kin and social affiliative communities are effectively mobilized to source petty cash in the aggregate—a coerced subcontracting of vital platforms. Although Mendoza's keen realism portrays the convoluted entwinement and replication of these platforms with great insight, the film ideologically separates out the innocent and the guilty, holding out an idealized image of "family" as the lost or fallen possibility, or as what is destroyed and what must be redeemed. In this way, the film also renders the dominant ideological solution to the social problems it presents, which would lead to an external, outside supraforce capable of

surmounting this closed system binding the poor and the police, which finds embodiment in Duterte.

51 Unlike its usage in much contemporary literature, which borders on making "dividuality" a new or old universal form of personhood (whether precapitalist or as the effect of "societies of control," in which the individuals molded by disciplinary societies have become "dividuals," as Deleuze famously asserted), Sahlins clarifies that the "dividual" is not merely the negation of the individual but "has a content that precisely involves the participatory sense of kinship relations." Dividuality is not simply partibility or divisibility but also importantly "*co-presence*," involving "the transpersonal distribution of the self among multiple others" and "transpersonal practices of coexistence." Sahlins, *What Kinship Is*, 26, 25, 28.

52 Byaie Balagtas See, "Gunmen Hunting Drug Suspect Kill 7," *Philippine Daily Inquirer*, December 30, 2016.

53 Bianca Ysabelle Franco, "Women in the Shadows of Duterte's Drug War," *Rappler*, June 30, 2018, https://www.rappler.com/voices/imho/205871-stories-women-duterte-war-on-drugs/.

54 Weiner, *Inalienable Possessions*, 4.

55 "I kept asking the police why they killed my son without investigating him first. They told me my son died because I was a *kunsintidor* (enabler), when I know for a fact that my son was a good son." Krixia Subingsubing, "Lola, 85, Is Single Parent to Seven Kids in EJK Case," *Philippine Daily Inquirer*, October 29, 2017, https://newsinfo.inquirer.net/941286/war-on-drugs-drug-killings-extrajudicial-killings-lola-trining-baigani-kristina-gaerlan#ixzz6kfg4uvfU/.

56 Sahlins, *What Kinship Is*, 28.

57 Subingsubing, "Lola, 85, Is Single Parent to Seven Kids in EJK Case."

58 Against scholarship that sees the "freeing" of workers from ties of personal dependence as part of the process of primitive accumulation, anthropological scholarship has reevaluated the role of kinship relations in capitalism. See, for example, McKinnon and Cannel, *Vital Relations*. Much of this work, however, focuses on kinship and family within capitalist firms. Other scholarship focuses on kinship and family in postcolonial institutions of political power. For the "foundational" values of family reinscribed under neoliberalism, see Cooper, *Family Values*. Kinship is of course what populations subjected to chattel slavery were denied, as a matter of their continuous depersonalization and desocialization.

In the postcolony, the preservation of kinship relations and their role in an extant domestic economy in which goods and care (objectified and "immaterial" services) are shared and allocated, as well as exacted, is crucial to the double extraction of labor-rent and surplus value characteristic of imperialist capitalism. Capitalists do not so much block the extension of capitalism into these spheres of domestic economy as much as they affirm, through morality, the "exemption" of these spheres from ostensible capitalization through notions of the private, the family, religion, the human, "customary" laws, and the like—making the domestic sphere akin to the "reserves" where populations were confined in apartheid settler colonies (such as South Africa), as "natural" reserves of labor maintained through restrictions on social reproduction which kept it at the level of subsistence. Kinship to some extent might be considered a persisting means of survival that becomes a resource of capital.

59 Jensen and Hapal, "Police Violence and Corruption."
60 I write about fixers among the urban poor as a form of "petty adventurism" in "Petty Adventures in (the Nation's) Capital," in Tadiar, *Things Fall Away*, 183–216.
61 Jensen and Hapal, "Police Violence and Corruption."
62 "When it's my turn to settle down, / Promise me that you will sing about me." Kendrick Lamar, "Sing about Me, I'm Dying of Thirst," on *Good Kid, m.A.A.d city*. See also the album *Kolateral* (2019), by Sandata.

CHAPTER TEN. LIVE BORROWINGS, LIVING CONNECTIONS

1 Bauman, *Wasted Lives*, 6.
2 Is not the notion of imperial ruination as environmental power, i.e., as a power on the scale of "nature," itself the ultimate conceit of imperial subjects (even as critics): to contemplate this sublime image of power, an image projected by capital itself (this encompassing of all of nature, of *being* nature) before which it can shudder and from which it can pull back and regain its cognitive power, reassured and safe once again in its being, as the ethical human subject of the Global North. While they are its critics, they are still its benefactors (and its patronymic beneficiaries).

Colonial studies scholars, now scholars of empire, may be all too thrilled to have such an all-powerful, all-pervasive, iniquitous doppelgänger before them to provide an infinite challenge with indefinite duration—permanent war. Renewed, zealous energy in arguing that imperial power continues is almost laughable in its belatedness and banality. As for the predictable question of the sense-making, life-making practices of those descendants of the colonized who live not simply *with* the consequences of such imperial orders, but also *in spite* of them—as for them and for the work not merely of thinking *about* those practices but also of *heeding* them in one's own theoretical work, that, it seems, is for "others" to do.

3 "Solution or Utopia: Design for Refugees," exhibition, Stedelijk Museum, May 20–August 26, 2017, Amsterdam, Netherlands. See https://www.stedelijk.nl/en/exhibitions/solution-or-utopia-design-for-refugees/.
4 The competition and other projects of the UNHCR are examples of its "humanitarian innovation," an entrepreneurial approach to its mission to protect and assist refugees. Created in 1950 to help Europeans made homeless in the aftermath of World War II, it outlasted its three-year mandate to become a permanent global institution, now celebrating its sixty-ninth anniversary and seeking to continue its work as a life-regenerator in an era of permanent war. See "History of UNHCR," accessed November 18, 2021, https://www.unhcr.org/en-us/history-of-unhcr.html.
5 Nicolas Bourriaud argues, "Contemporary art does not deny the existence of waste as such: now, nothing and no one can be deemed non-integrable. The

vigour of the work of art stems from participating in both categories, circulating freely between the universe of products and the world of waste, simultaneously constituting a remainder and a value; it exploits its sociocultural utility and its dysfunctional quality by turns. Art's social function involves reconciling these two worlds by giving them meaning." Bourriaud, *The Ex-Form*, 95–96.

6   Baudrillard, *For a Critique of the Political Economy of the Sign*, 115. One might argue that this opposition merely reflects the separation of production and consumption, of materiality and semiotics. Baudrillard is here concerned with consumerism, as part of a history of cultural critique in advanced capitalist societies, seeing in consumerism the logic of sumptuary values, devolved from aristocratic excess and debauchery: "The great dinosaurs of 'wasteful expenditure' are changed into innumerable individuals pledged to a parody of sacrificial consumption, mobilized as consumers by the order of production. Expenditure has thus radically changed its meaning. The fact remains that it is because the collective phantom of lost (sumptuary) values is reactivated in expenditure and in mass-mediatized consumption, that this practice can be lived individually as gratification—as fulfillment—and so act as ideology" (119).

In the postcolony, as now in the new global economy, life currency expenditures are the transubstantiation of signs into monetary exchange values. We see here modes of living off of consumption, producing out of acts of self-expenditure to produce sign values for exchange. Such productive consumption might be considered the fusion of older modes of social reproduction of domestic communities and colonial, capitalist modes of production (the consumption of the vitality of others and its transubstantiation into wealth, moral value, and political power).

7   Baudrillard, *For a Critique of the Political Economy of the Sign*, 107.
8   Ezra Acayan, personal communication, October 19, 2017.
9   Spivak, "Can the Subaltern Speak?," 279. Spivak is referring to "representation in the economic context," the representation/objectification of labor power as value, or what we might understand as the logic of abstraction and reification that undergirds the dominant realities of a society of spectacle.
10 McKittrick, "Mathematics Black Life," 18.
11 In RESBAK (Respond and Break the Silence against the Killings), *7025: (7/1/2016–1/22/2017)*, collectively published zine.
12 Garcia, "Mula Sa Vocábulario ng Casaláulaan."
13 See the work of Alwin Reamillo in RESBAK (Respond and Break the Silence against the Killings), *7025: (7/1/2016–1/22/2017)*; and the work of Max Santiago and M. C. Joecyl S. Bril in RESBAK (Respond and Break the Silence against the Killings), *12,000*: (7/1/2016–6/12/2017)*.
14 Kiri Dalena, personal communication, July 2, 2017.
15 Faye Cura, "Ang Pagsagip kay Prinsesa Laoanen," *Laoanen: Kababaihan/Digmaan/Kapayapaan*, 2017, 5–11, 6; my translation.
16 For Baudrillard, the logic of sumptuary values is continuous between high art and consumerist culture, converting economic exchange values into sign

exchange values, and by this means, assuring and perpetuating dominant classes through its monopoly of the code.

17 In other words, for art to continue to exist as an autonomous zone, its institutions must be defined by the very same protocols of capitalist production and consumption that individual works might critically reflect upon, attempt to intervene in, or ameliorate.
18 Katz, "Accumulation, Excess, Childhood," 56.
19 See Manalansan, *Global Divas*; See, *The Decolonized Eye*; and Burns, *Puro Arte*. See also Beller-Tadiar, "Punny Company."
20 Kiri Dalena, personal communication, July 2, 2017.
21 Quintos, "Lamentations," *Kill List Chronicles*, Medium.com, July 24, 2016, https://medium.com/@kill.list.lit/lamentations-16ffeb42756a.
22 Sissako, *Timbuktu* (2014).
23 These are concepts found in Mandelbrot and Hudson, *The (Mis)Behavior of Markets*; and Batty, *Cities and Complexity*.
24 Quoted in Pratt and Johnson, *Migration in Performance*, 113. Luis's recollections are among the life stories of overseas Filipino workers that Johnston and Pratt carefully gather in the course of their remarkable, experimental research project, propelled by community participatory performances of their traveling play, *Nanay*.
25 For the story of the ASA resolution and the broader US academic and cultural boycott as an organized movement, see Maira, *Boycott!* It is no accident that at the American Studies Association, those who found themselves responding to the Palestinian political call for solidarity with the Boycott, Divestment, and Sanctions movement were themselves involved in the social struggles and striving of communities of the dispossessed, those whose peoples were the direct targets and victims of US empire. See "Palestine," *Social Text* Online, https://socialtextjournal.org/periscope_topic/palestine/; and "The Academic Boycott Movement," *Social Text* Online, https://socialtextjournal.org/periscope_topic/the-academic-boycott-movement/. See also Tadiar, "Why the Question of Palestine Is a Feminist Concern," January 27, 2012, https://thefeministwire.com/2012/01/why-the-question-of-palestine-is-a-feminist-concern/.
26 Simone, *Improvised Lives*, 4.
27 Heymann, *Paper Dolls* (2006). I saw the play *Care Givers* produced by PETA in Manila in 2012. For an analysis of the play, see Serquiña, "Out and About."

THRESHOLDS

A previous version of this chapter was published in "Thresholds," *Environment and Planning D: Society and Space* (October 2021): 1–18, https://doi.org/10.1177/02637758211046959.

1 "The appellations deem these places uninhabitable, not fit for human habitation, environments full of toxicity and violence, fast and slow." Simone, *Improvised Lives*, 9, 11.

2. Erik de Castro, "Manila's Slums an Endless Battle for Firefighters," *Reuters*, June 21, 2018, https://widerimage.reuters.com/story/manilas-slums-an-endless-battle-for-firefighters/.
3. Adem, *Urban Poverty*, 127.
4. Jocano, *Slum as Way of Life*, 6.
5. Igal Jada San Andres and Patricia Lourdes Viray, "Demolition by Fire: Burning Urban Poor Communities A Government Tactic?," *Bulatlat*, April 27, 2012, https://www.bulatlat.com/2012/04/27/demolition-by-fire-burning-urban-poor-communities-a-government-tactic/.
6. Berner, "Globalization, Fragmentation and Local Struggles," 138.
7. Cited in Dizon, "Philippine Housing Takeover," 112.
8. Shatkin, "The City and the Bottom Line," 395.
9. Figures drawn and collated from Princess A. Esponilla, *Eviction Monitor 2017, Urban Poor Associates Annual Report* (Quezon City: Associates of the Urban Poor, 2017); and Salome B. Quijano, *Eviction Monitor 2012, Urban Poor Associates Annual Report* (Quezon City: Associates of the Urban Poor, 2012), http://urbanpoorassociates.org/whatwedo.php#.
10. A phrase from Henri Lefebvre, "right to the city" has become the clarion call of policy-oriented social welfare activists working toward the inclusion of the urban poor in civic and government programs and services as well as economic planning. Mary Racelis, "Demanding a Place in the City: From Squatter to Informal Settler to Homeowner," magisterial lecture, Ateneo de Manila University, 2021, accessed August 3, 2021, https://www.youtube.com/watch?v=QP6z3dfJivs. Mary Racelis, "Change the Paradigm!" *Philippine Daily Inquirer*, May 28, 2015, https://opinion.inquirer.net/85263/change-the-paradigm.
11. Ortega, "Manila's Metropolitan Landscape of Gentrification."
12. Said, *Culture and Imperialism*.
13. KM64, "Isang Libo, Isang Buwan," Facebook, January 16, 2017, https://www.facebook.com/KM64.Web/posts/isang-libo-isang-buwan-bryan-costaisang-libo-isang-buwanhindi-ito-ang-halaga-ng-/1892253241005884/.
14. *Oxford English Dictionary*, s.v. "limen," https://www-oed-com.ezproxy.cul.columbia.edu/view/Entry/108451?rskey=u3MC62&result=2#eid.
15. Tadiar, "Metropolitan Dreams," in *Fantasy-Production*, 92–97.
16. I write about this bulimic behavior as the state's gendered expression of a contradiction between ideal images of national sovereignty and illegitimate desires of global capitalism in its relation to the urban excess (displaced or refugee "surplus" populations from the countryside). See Tadiar, "Metropolitan Dreams," in *Fantasy-Production*, 92–97.
17. "Bypass-implant urbanism," Gavin Shatkin calls it, whereby large-scale property developers have obtained government franchise (so-called public-private partnerships) to envision and implement urban planning and policy, installing entire urban systems or environments in sites that bypass overcongested and high-density areas. Shatkin, "The City and the Bottom Line," 389.
18. For memories of this urban settlement during World War II, see Arumpac, *Nanay Mameng* (2012).

19 Jensen and Hapal, "Police Violence and Corruption in the Philippines."
20 Pia Ranada, "Duterte Trust, Approval Ratings Unchanged after Recto Bank Incident," *Rappler*, July 17, 2019, https://www.rappler.com/nation/235600-duterte-trust-approval-ratings-pulse-asia-survey-june-2019/.
21 Byaie Balagtas See, "Gunmen Hunting Drug Suspect Kill 7," *Philippine Daily Inquirer*, December 30, 2016.
22 Quoted in Patricia Evangelista, "Impunity: Welcome to the End of the War," *Rappler*, February 7, 2017, https://r3.rappler.com/newsbreak/in-depth/158886-impunity-end-drug-war/.
23 The evolution of technical objects as "the individualization of technical beings . . . is made possible by the recurrence of causality within a milieu that the technical object creates around itself and that conditions it, just as it is conditioned by it." Simondon, *On the Mode of Existence of Technical Objects*, 59.
24 Luxemburg, *The Accumulation of Capital* (in *The Complete Works*), 263.
25 This logic of platform capitalism can perhaps be seen as superseding what Simondon views as characteristic of the "dialogue between labor and capital," that is, the prioritization of the end result over means under manufacturing production. Here, where what is produced for consumption is not the result of a production process apart from the means—in other words, the use that the user brings to the platform—but rather is the very condition or state of self-regulated functioning of the machine or platform, where "all causality has a sense of finality, and all finality a sense of causality." Simondon, *On the Mode of Existence of Technical Objects*, 135.
26 "The singular person, then, regarded as a derivative of multiple identities, may be transformed into the dividual composed of distinct male and female elements." The multiple person is described as "partible, an entity that can dispose of parts in relation to others." Strathern, *The Gender of the Gift*, 15, 185.
27 Cannell, *Power and Intimacy*, 248.
28 There is another global (time) fantasy that complements the drive to uber-urbanization in the global (space) fantasy of city everywhere. This fantasy is a history that traces the evolutionary shift away from the liberal humanist subject, constructed on the basis of homeostasis and equilibrium as a self-possessing, self-regulating being with an agency, desire, or will of its own, to the cybernetic posthuman, constructed on the basis of privileging information over embodiment, pattern over presence, as a form of "distributed cognition located in disparate parts that may be in only tenuous communication with one another." Hayles, *How We Became Posthuman*, 3–4. I want to suggest that there are genealogies that are bypassed in this provincial Euro-American account of how information lost its body and how "we" became posthuman, genealogies already implicit in that global history of colonialism and slavery to which I alluded earlier. In the analytical descriptions of some of the anthropological work I cite here, I read the very conditions of virtuality understood to have emerged as the cultural effect of the information age. Such conditions are to be gleaned in the analytical attention of these scholars to the way that persons are imagined and behave as dividuals, and as derivatives of plural

social relations, as fractal entities—terms that have also been used to characterize the posthuman world. See also Wagner, "The Fractal Person." Cannell's and Hayles's books were published the same year. One was writing within the conceptual category of "culture," the other within that of "cultural production," both in effect looking for what Gayatri Spivak calls the chains of value coding underwriting differentiated sites within a broader imperial formation, with the anthropologist seeking the value coding of a particular (i.e., national, regional area) cultural formation, and the literary-theoretical critic seeking the value coding of a "general" (i.e., global) cultural formation. Spivak, *The Critique of Postcolonial Reason*, 103.

29 Sahlins, *What Kinship Is*; Carsten, *After Kinship*.
30 Aurora Almendra, "Why 10 Million Filipinos Endure Hardship Abroad as Overseas Workers," *National Geographic*, December 2018, https://www.nationalgeographic.com/magazine/2018/12/filipino-workers-return-from-overseas-philippines-celebrates/.
31 Yean, *Tulong*, 70.
32 S. L. Jensen, "Philippine Prison Marriages."
33 Simone, *Improvised Lives*.
34 Adem, *Urban Poverty*, 106, 107.
35 Dizon, "Philippine Housing Takeover."
36 Cunanan describes this spatial practicality in terms of a range of practices of "creative modification and cooperative endeavor." Cunanan, "Slum-Fit?," 51. See also the films on the lives and struggles of the urban poor: Gonzales, Carreon, Quizon, and Lugtu, *Sentro* (2019); Sacay, *Pira-pirasong Pangarap* (2019); Quijano, *Puso ng Lungsod* (2012); and Delvo and Sulicipan, *Bukid, Gulod, Libis* (2017).
37 Davey Alba, "How Duterte Used Facebook to Fuel the Philippine Drug War," *BuzzFeed News*, September 4, 2018, https://www.buzzfeednews.com/article/daveyalba/facebook-philippines-dutertes-drug-war/; Mahtani and Cabato, "Why Crafty Internet Trolls in the Philippines May Be Coming to a Website near You."
38 Pratt, *Families Apart*; Francisco-Menchavez, *The Labor of Care*.
39 Simondon talks about "non-noble technics" as "a technics related to living beings," one equated with slaves, utility artisans, children, and primitive societies. This is a technical subconsciousness acquired by children growing up in a community fully saturated with schemes of know-how (work and knowledge, inseparable from each other), acquired through participation, which requires "vital conditions" of communitarian life. Simondon, *On the Mode of Existence of Technical Objects*, 104, 107, 108.
40 Evangelista, "Impunity."
41 Evangelista, "Impunity," modified translation. She also says, "When you are a rich person, you're treated like a VIP. But when you are a poor person, the treatment is RIP."
42 Barrios, *Ang Pagiging Babae*.

43 Berger, *Hold Everything Dear*. Drawing on the work of Stephen Pyne, Nigel Clark argues that biopolitics is first and foremost a "pyropolitics," "centered on the regulation, manipulation and enhancement of fire." As he writes, "Much of the management of human populations, of energy, of life itself in which the modern West has engaged itself, both at home and abroad, I argue has been premised on the drive to contain or channel fire." Clark, *Inhuman Nature*, 165. In the modern, metropolitan European worldview, fire come to be "an expression of social unrest or breakdown, a mark of excess and disorder," "a squandering of resources," inaugurating "the era of proscribed burning"—the suppression of rural traditions of burning fallow, free ranging fire, and indigenous fire practices (177, 178).

44 Cochrane, *Tropical Fire Ecology*.

45 Marx, *Grundrisse*, 361.

46 Wright, "Gentrification, Assassination and Forgetting"; Fregoso, "We Want Them Alive!"

CHAPTER ELEVEN. BYPASS AND SPLENDOR

A previous version of this chapter was published as "By the Waysides, or, Bypass and Splendor," *Modernism/Modernity* 2, no. 4 (2018), https://doi.org/10.26597/mod.0036/.

1 Lyra Garcellano, *Sweep*, mixed media installation, Final Art File Gallery, December 9, 2014–January, 3, 2015, Makati City, Philippines. See http://www.finaleartfile.com/sweep-lyra-garcellano/.

2 Video from Garcellano, *Sweep*.

3 "An art aware of itself is an analysed art. There is a convergence between the analytical process and the compositional process." Adorno and Paddison, "On the Problem of Musical Analysis," 176. Adorno did not understand description as interpretation, as I practice it here, insofar as he opposed description to the kind of immanent critical analysis he upheld as a valuable political method. However, the kind of description I have in mind is much closer to his own understanding of analysis as a form in its own right, which serves as a medium through which the work unfolds, an organ of the historical momentum of the work itself, but that also pushes beyond that individual work.

4 Adorno and Paddison, "On the Problem of Musical Analysis," 176.

5 Adorno, "Cultural Criticism and Society."

6 For Franco Berardi, the new form of alienation under post-Fordism is constituted by the loss of self and life through the exploitation of one's cognitive and mental life as labor—or, "putting the soul to work." Berardi, *The Soul at Work*, 11.

7 Tang, *Unsettled*.

8 Including a comic strip where she pokes fun at artists' ironic, banal, subjective experiences of the tacit demands of the global art world within the broader attention economy of social media (the art world's extension and avatar).

9 See Raymundo and Tolentino, *Kontra-Gahum*.

10 Kelley, "Mike Brown's Body."
11 J. T. Ruiz, "Old Pain."
12 S. Jensen, "Stunted Future," 46.
13 S. Jensen, "Stunted Future," 54.
14 S. Jensen, "Stunted Future," 53.
15 The soft, meandering, yet intimate and attentive focus on life adjacent to a world-stage event—a court hearing of the case brought against the World Bank and the IMF by the people of Africa—in Abderrahmane Sissako's *Bamako* (2006) is one of the most vivid demonstrations of the heuristic of remaindered life.
16 R. Williams, *Marxism and Literature*.
17 This is both like and unlike the spatial notion of "margins," which was a political concept for the diminished and disempowered in a field of static centers and spheres representing power in the geopolitical image of territorialized polities. Where it departs from this still absolutely important modern political concept—and what social media and new technologies allow a better view of (insofar as they also make it possible and normal)—is the condition of dynamism and virtuality, such that the "road" might be better conceived as the (financial, cultural, technological, and social) means or media of *fluency*. The bypassed must therefore be understood also in the sense of what might slow down or impede this fluency of circulation, and therefore what might corrode the codes of information that allow the circulation of any content whatsoever—that is to say, other codes.
18 One could argue that the lack of concern about or indifference to originality or newness in these contemporary works is specific to our times of digital technological reproduction. But it is also the case that the history of the colonized is the history of a long habituation to reproduction. For the colonized, copying or "borrowing" has always functioned as a way to matter, to be heard, to be seen, to be noted, as well as a way to make fun, to play, to make surplus out of the gap—a form of survival, as well as a form of elaboration of being. The legacy of derivatives as what the colonized are, as well as make, is the legacy of Global South artists: emptying things of their original referents and infusing them with different contents, different connections. See chapter 10.
19 Adorno, *Minima Moralia*, 151.
20 Solanas and Getino, "Toward a Third Cinema," 231.
21 Toscano, "The World Is Already without Us."
22 De León, *The Land of Open Graves*.
23 Tadiar, *Things Fall Away*.
24 Next to the 1912 eruption of Mount Novarupta in Alaska. See Chris Newhall, James W. Hendley II, and Peter H. Stauffer, "The Cataclysmic 1991 Eruption of Mount Pinatubo, Philippines," US Geological Survey Fact Sheet 113–97, February 28, 2005, https://pubs.usgs.gov/fs/1997/fs113-97/.
25 See Bautista and Tadem, "Brimstone and Ash," 14; Mercado, Lacsamana, and Pineda, "Socioeconomic Impacts of the Mount Pinatubo Eruption"; and Bautista, "The Mount Pinatubo Disaster and the People of Central Luzon."

26 The team included Maria Cynthia Rose Benzon Bautista, Leonora C. Angeles, Carolyn Medel Añonuevo, Maria Luisa T. Camagay, Teresa S. Encarnacion, Maria Carmen C. Jimenez, Maria Cecilia T. Medina, Dolly G. L. Mibolos, and Doracie Zoleta Nantes. Eduardo C. Tadem was part of the early discussions but was out of the country while the team lived in the municipality of Concepcion, Tarlac, in the aftermath of the eruption, from October to December 1991. Bautista, *In the Shadow of the Lingering Mt. Pinatubo Disaster.*

27 Bautista and Tadem, "Brimstone and Ash," 10.

28 Rodolfo, *Pinatubo and the Politics of Lahar*, 73–74. Rodolfo writes that while the earthquake alone did not cause the eruption, it is possible that the shaking may have caused the magma to begin rising.

29 Tsing, *The Mushroom at the End of the World.*

30 Moore, "Cheap Food and Bad Climate."

31 See "Environmental Assessment" appendix, in "The Study on Sabo and Flood Control for Western River Basins of Mount Pinatubo in the Republic of the Philippines: Final Report," Japan International Cooperation Agency, 2003, https://openjicareport.jica.go.jp/617/617/617_118_11734589.html.

32 Watanabe et al., "Vegetation Succession and Land Recovery Process"

33 "Like the sturdy talahib strands of San Simon that struggled on to sprout forth and grow stronger amidst barrenness, anyone can rise above the ashes to inspire others to set the pace, even set the standard in nation-building." San Simon has become a site of steel factories and other manufacturing businesses, and it produces 60 percent of the national production of steel billets. "Town's Future Looks Bright," *Manila Standard*, January 8, 2018, https://www.manilastandard.net/lifestyle/travel-and-leisure/255803/town-s-future-looks-bright.html.

34 Its very taxonomic title, *Saccharum spontaneum*, or wild sugar, alludes to its relations to and differences from *Saccharum officinarum*, the cultivated sugarcane first domesticated in New Guinea and island Southeast Asia and spread through movements of Austronesian peoples and the primary sugar cane species for modern capitalist sugar production. Genomic studies show that, as a result of "nobilization" of *S. officinarum* with its wild relative, *S. spontaneum* (a process of "interspecific hybridization with backcrossing to noble cultivars"), *Saccharum spontaneum* has "contributed to the development of modern cultivars by conferring resistance to most major diseases, providing vigor and hardiness for increased abiotic stress tolerance (such as cold and drought), increased tillering and improved ratoonability." Paterson, Moore, and Tew, "The Gene Pool of *Saccharum* Species," 56, 49.

35 Mazoyer and Roudart, *A History of World Agriculture*, 101–42.

36 The legend suggests that the Aetna had made their homes around Mount Pinatubo before the Buag eruption, which scientists date to 0.8–0.5 Ka BP, or eight hundred to five hundred years before the present. Rodolfo and Umbal, "A Prehistoric Lahar-Dammed Lake."

37 De Rose et al., "Land Cover Change on Mt. Pinatubo"; Watanabe et al., "Vegetation Succession and Land Recovery Process."

38 Raymundo, "Folk Beliefs as Source of Resource Management."
39 "To summon a history of abundance is not to be restored to value, but rather to be set adrift upon more intrepid economies of meaning—sometimes harmonious, sometimes dissonant—that come together to upend genealogies of historical recuperation and representation." Anjali Arondekar, "Memory Histories: I Am Not Your Data," *Agitate!*, accessed November 19, 2021, https://agitatejournal.org/memory-histories-i-am-not-your-data/.

CHAPTER TWELVE. AND THEN SOME

1 Haley, *No Mercy Here*, 230.
2 Wynter, "No Humans Involved."

BIBLIOGRAPHY

Abu-Lughod, Lila. *Do Muslim Women Need Saving?* Cambridge, MA: Harvard University Press, 2013.

Adem, Elisa S. *Urban Poverty: The Case of the Railway Squatters*. Manila: University of Santo Tomas Social Research Center, 1992.

Adorno, Theodor W. "Cultural Criticism and Society." In *Prisms*, translated by Samuel and Shierry Weber, 17–34. Cambridge, MA: MIT Press, 1997.

Adorno, Theodor W. *Minima Moralia*. Translated by E. F. N. Jephcott. London: Verso, 2005.

Adorno, Theodor W., and Max Paddison. "On the Problem of Musical Analysis." *Music Analysis* 1, no. 2 (1982): 169–87.

Agamben, Giorgio. *Homo Sacer: Sovereign Power and Bare Life*. Translated by Daniel Heller-Roazen. Stanford, CA: Stanford University Press, 1998.

Aguilar, Filomeno V., Jr. *Clash of Spirits: The History of Power and Sugar Planter Hegemony on a Visayan Island*. Honolulu: University of Hawai'i Press, 1998.

Aguilar, Filomeno V., Jr. *Migration Revolution: Philippine Nationhood and Class Relations in a Globalized Age*. Singapore: NUS Press; Kyoto: Kyoto University Press, 2014.

Aguilar, Filomeno V., Jr. "Ritual Passage and the Reconstruction of Selfhood in International Labour Migration." *Sojourn: Journal of Social Issues in Southeast Asia* 14, no. 1 (1999): 98–139.

Alexander, M. Jacqui. *Pedagogies of Crossing: Meditations on Feminism, Sexual Politics, Memory, and the Sacred*. Durham, NC: Duke University Press, 2006.

Althusser, Louis. *On the Reproduction of Capitalism: Ideology and Ideological State Apparatuses*. Translated by G. M. Goshgarian. Brooklyn: Verso, 2014.

Amar, Paul. *The Security Archipelago: Human-Security States, Sexuality Politics, and the End of Neoliberalism*. Durham, NC: Duke University Press, 2013.

Amin, Samir. *Eurocentrism: Modernity, Religion, and Democracy: A Critique of Eurocentrism and Culturalism*. New York: Monthly Review Press, 2010.

Amnesty International. *"If You Are Poor, You Are Killed": Extrajudicial Executions in the Philippines' "War on Drugs."* London: Amnesty International, 2017.

Amrith, Megha. *Caring for Strangers: Filipino Medical Workers in Asia*. Copenhagen: NIAS Press, 2017.

Anderson, Warwick. *Colonial Pathologies: American Tropical Medicine, Race, and Hygiene in the Philippines*. Durham, NC: Duke University Press, 2006.

Arendt, Hannah. *The Human Condition*. 2nd ed. Chicago: University of Chicago Press, 1998.

Arendt, Hannah. *The Origins of Totalitarianism*. New York: Harcourt, Brace, Jovanovich, 1973.

Arondekar, Anjali. *For the Record: On Sexuality and the Colonial Archive in India*. Durham, NC: Duke University Press, 2009.

Arumpac, Adjani, dir. *Nanay Mameng*. Philippines: Kodao Productions, 2012.

Arumpac, Adjani, dir. *War Is a Tender Thing*. Philippines: Saltwater Cinema, 2013.

Arumpac, Alyx Ayn G., dir. *Aswang*. Philippines: Cinematografica Films, 2019.

Asad, Talal. *Formations of the Secular: Christianity, Islam, Modernity*. Stanford, CA: Stanford University Press, 2003.

Balibar, Étienne. "On the Common, Universality, and Communism: A Conversation between Étienne Balibar and Antonio Negri." *Rethinking Marxism* 22, no. 3 (2010): 312–28.

Bamyeh, Mohammed A. "Palestine: Listening to the Inaudible." *South Atlantic Quarterly* 102, no. 4 (2003): 825–49.

Barker, Joanne. "The Corporation and the Tribe." *American Indian Quarterly* 39, no. 3 (2015): 243–70.

Barker, Joanne. "The Human Genome Diversity Project: 'Peoples,' 'Populations,' and the Cultural Politics of Identification." *Cultural Studies* 18 (2004): 571–606.

Barker, Joanne. *Native Acts: Law, Recognition, and Cultural Authenticity*. Durham, NC: Duke University Press, 2011.

Barker, Joanne. "The Specters of Recognition." In *Formations of United States Colonialism*, edited by Alyosha Goldstein, 33–56. Durham, NC: Duke University Press, 2014.

Barker, Joanne. "Territory as Analytic: The Dispossession of Lenapehoking and the Subprime Crisis." *Social Text* 36, no. 2 (2018): 19–39.

Barrett, Lindon. *Blackness and Value: Seeing Double*. Cambridge: Cambridge University Press, 1999.

Barrios, Joi. *Ang Pagiging Babae ay Pamumuhay sa Panahon ng Digma / To Be a Woman Is to Live at a Time of War*. Manila: Institute of Women's Studies, St. Scholastica's College, 1990.

Batty, Michael. *Cities and Complexity: Understanding Cities with Cellular Automata, Agent-Based Models, and Fractals*. Cambridge, MA: MIT Press, 2007.

Baudrillard, Jean. *For a Critique of the Political Economy of the Sign*. Translated by Charles Levin. St. Louis, MO: Telos Press, 1981.

Bauman, Zygmunt. *Wasted Lives: Modernity and Its Outcasts*. Cambridge: Polity, 2004.

Bautista, Maria Cynthia Rose Benzon, ed. *In the Shadow of the Lingering Mt. Pinatubo Disaster*. Quezon City, Philippines: CSSP Publications, University of the Philippines, and Center for Asian Studies, University of Amsterdam, 1993.

Bautista, Maria Cynthia Rose Benzon. "The Mount Pinatubo Disaster and the People of Central Luzon." In *Fire and Mud: Eruptions and Lahars of Mount Pinatubo, Philippines*, edited by Christopher G. Newhall and Raymundo S. Punongbayan, 151–64. Quezon City, Philippines: Philippine Institute of Volcanology and Seismology; and Seattle: University of Washington Press, 1996.

Bautista, Maria Cynthia Rose Benzon, and Eduardo C. Tadem. "Brimstone and Ash: The 1991 Mt. Pinatubo Eruption." In *In the Shadow of the Lingering Mt. Pinatubo Disaster*. Quezon City, Philippines: CSSP Publications, University of the Philippines and Center for Asian Studies, Amsterdam, 1993.

Bauzon, Kenneth E. "Ruminations on the Bangsamoro Struggle and Neoliberal Globalization." In *The Moro Reader: History and Contemporary Struggles of the Bangsamoro People*, edited by Bobby M. Tuazon, 59–71. Quezon City, Philippines: CenPEG, 2008.

Beller, Jonathan L. *The Cinematic Mode of Production: Attention Economy and the Society of the Spectacle*. Lebanon, NH: University Press of New England, 2006.

Beller, Jonathan L. *The Message Is Murder: Substrates of Computational Capital*. London: Pluto Press, 2018.

Beller, Jonathan L. "Paying Attention." *Cabinet Magazine*, no. 24 (Winter 2006–7): 53–58.

Beller, Jonathan. *The World Computer: Derivative Conditions of Racial Capitalism*. Durham, NC: Duke University Press, 2021.

Beller-Tadiar, Luna. "Punny Company: Western Linguists Meet Mga Bakla and the Fil-Ams." Unpublished seminar paper, Yale University, December 16, 2016.

Bello, Walden. *The Food Wars*. London: Verso, 2009.

Benanav, Aaron. "Misery and Debt: On the Logic and History of Surplus Populations and Surplus Capital." *Endnotes* 2 (2010): http://endnotes.org.uk/articles/1/.

Berardi, Franco. *The Soul at Work: From Alienation to Autonomy*. Translated by Francesca Cadel and Giuseppina Mecchia. Los Angeles: Semiotext(e), 2009.

Berger, John. *Hold Everything Dear: Dispatches on Survival and Resistance*. New York: Vintage Books, 2007.

Berner, Erhard. "Globalization, Fragmentation and Local Struggles: Squatter Organizations in Metro Manila." *Philippine Sociological Review* 46, nos. 3–4 (1998): 121–42.

Bernstein, Elizabeth. "Militarized Humanitarianism Meets Carceral Feminism: The Politics of Sex, Rights, and Freedom in Contemporary Anti-trafficking Campaigns." *Signs: Journal of Women in Culture and Society* 36, no. 1 (2009): 45–71.

Bernstein, Elizabeth. "The Sexual Politics of the 'New Abolitionism.'" *differences: A Journal of Feminist Cultural Studies* 18, no. 3 (2007): 128–51.

Bewes, Timothy. "Reading with the Grain: A New World in Literary Criticism." *differences: A Journal of Feminist Cultural Studies* 21, no. 3 (2010): 1–33.

Birkeland, Nina M., and Edmund Jennings, eds. *Internal Displacement: Global Overview of Trends and Developments in 2010*. Geneva: IDMC, 2011. http://www.internal-displacement.org/publications/global-overview-2010/.

Blanco, John D. "Subjects of Baroque Economy: Creole and Pirate Epistemologies of Mercantilism in the Seventeenth-Century Spanish and Dutch East Indies." *Encounters* 1 (2009): 27–62.

Bohrman, Rebecca, and Naomi Murakawa. "Remaking Big Government: Immigration and Crime Control in the United States." In Sudbury, *Global Lockdown: Race, Gender, and the Prison-Industrial Complex*, 109–26.

Bong Joon-Ho, dir. *Parasite*. Republic of Korea: Barunson E and A, 2019.

Boot, Max. *The Savage Wars of Peace: Small Wars and the Rise of American Power*. New York: Basic, 2014.

Bourriaud, Nicolas. *The Ex-Form*. London: Verso, 2016.

Boutang, Yann Moulier. *Cognitive Capitalism*. Translated by Ed Emery. Cambridge: Polity, 2011.

Brady, Mary Pat. "The Homoerotics of Immigration Control." *Scholar and Feminist Online* 6, no. 3 (2008). http://sfonline.barnard.edu/immigration/print_brady.htm.

Brennan, Denise. *Life Interrupted: Trafficking into Forced Labor in the United States*. Durham, NC: Duke University Press, 2014.

Briggs, Laura. *Reproducing Empire: Race, Sex, Science, and U.S. Imperialism in Puerto Rico*. Oakland: University of California Press, 2003.

Briggs, Laura. *Taking Children: A History of American Terror*. Oakland: University of California Press, 2020.

Brown, Wendy. *Edgework: Critical Essays on Knowledge and Politics*. Princeton, NJ: Princeton University Press, 2005.

Burns, Lucy. *Puro Arte: Filipinos on the Stages of Empire*. New York: New York University Press, 2012.

Busby, Cecilia. "Permeable and Partible Persons: A Comparative Analysis of Gender and Body in South India and Melanesia." *Journal of the Royal Anthropological Institute* 3, no. 2 (1997): 261–78.

Butler, Judith. "Critique, Dissent, Disciplinarity." *Critical Inquiry* 35, no. 4 (2009): 773–95.

Butler, Judith. "Israel/Palestine and the Paradoxes of Academic Freedom." *Radical Philosophy* 135 (2006): 8–17.

Byrd, Jodi A. *The Transit of Empire: Indigenous Critiques of Colonialism*. Minneapolis: University of Minnesota Press, 2011.

Byrd, Jodi A., Alyosha Goldstein, Jodi Melamed, and Chandan Reddy. "Predatory Value: Economies of Dispossession and Disturbed Relationalities." *Social Text* 36, no. 2 (2018): 1–18.

Cacho, Lisa Marie. *Social Death: Racialized Rightlessness and the Criminalization of the Unprotected*. New York: New York University Press, 2012.

Caldeira, Teresa P. R. *City of Walls: Crime, Segregation, and Citizenship in São Paulo*. Berkeley: University of California Press, 2001.

Cannell, Fenella. *Power and Intimacy in the Christian Philippines*. Cambridge: Cambridge University Press, 1999.

Carreon, Kristen Lindley, Kim Louise Gonzales, Noreen Claire Quizon, and Jean Louise Lugtu, dir. *Sentro*. Quezon City, 2019.

Carsten, Janet. *After Kinship*. Cambridge: Cambridge University Press, 2003.

Center for People Empowerment in Governance. *Corruptionary: A Dictionary of Filipino Corruption Words*. Manila: Anvil, 2010.

Césaire, Aimé. *Discourse on Colonialism*. Translated by Joan Pinkham. New York: Monthly Review Press, 2000.

Chakrabarty, Dipesh. *Provincializing Europe: Postcolonial Thought and Historical Difference*. Princeton, NJ: Princeton University Press, 2000.

Chakravartty, Paula, and Denise Ferreira da Silva. "Accumulation, Dispossession, and Debt: The Racial Logic of Global Capitalism—An Introduction." *American Quarterly* 64, no. 3 (2012): 361–85.

Chang, Grace. *Disposable Domestics: Immigrant Women Workers in the Global Economy*. Chicago: Haymarket Books, 2016.

Chatterjee, Indrani. "Decolonizing the History of Slavery." Lecture, University of California, Santa Cruz, December 3, 2013. https://vimeo.com/91461685/.

Chatterjee, Indrani. "When 'Sexuality' Floated Free of Histories in South Asia." *Journal of Asian Studies* 71, no. 4 (2012): 945–62.

Cheng, Anne. *The Melancholy of Race: Psychoanalysis, Assimilation and Hidden Grief*. Oxford: Oxford University Press, 2001.

Cherniavsky, Eva. "Neocitizenship and Critique." *Social Text* 27, no. 2 (2009): 1–23.

Choy, Catherine Ceniza. *Empire of Care: Nursing and Migration in Filipino American History*. Quezon City, Philippines: Ateneo de Manila University Press, 2003.

Clark, Nigel. *Inhuman Nature: Sociable Life on a Dynamic Planet*. London: Sage Publications, 2011.

Cochrane, Mark A. *Tropical Fire Ecology: Climate Change, Land Use, and Ecosystem Dynamics*. Chichester, UK: Praxis, 2009.

Collier, Stephen J., and Andrew Lakoff. "Vital Systems Security: Reflexive Biopolitics and the Government of Emergency." *Theory, Culture and Society* 32, no. 2 (2015): 19–51.

Combahee River Collective. "A Black Feminist Statement." In Moraga and Anzaldúa, *This Bridge Called My Back: Writings by Radical Women of Color*, 210–18.

Cook, Malcom, and Lorraine Salazar. "The Differences Duterte Relied Upon to Win." *ISEAS Perspective*, no. 34 (2016): 1–12.

Cooper, Melinda. "Insecure Times, Tough Decisions: The Nomos of Neoliberalism." *Alternatives* 29 (2004): 515–33.

Cooper, Melinda. *Life as Surplus: Biotechnology and Capitalism in the Neoliberal Era*. Seattle: University of Washington Press, 2008.

Cooper, Melinda. "The Living and the Dead: Variations on De Anima." *Angelaki: Journal of the Theoretical Humanities* 7, no. 3 (2002): 81–104.

Cooper, Melinda, and Angela Mitropolous. "In Praise of Usura." *Mute* 2, no. 13 (2009). https://www.metamute.org/editorial/articles/praise-usura/.

Cooper, Melinda, and Catherine Waldby. *Clinical Labor: Tissue Donors and Research Subjects in the Global Bioeconomy*. Durham, NC: Duke University Press, 2014.

Coronel, Sheila. "Murder as Enterprise: Police Profiteering in Duterte's War against Drugs." In Curato, *A Duterte Reader: Critical Essays on Rodrigo Duterte's Early Presidency*, 167–98.

Coulthard, Glen. *Red Skin, White Masks: Rejecting the Colonial Politics of Recognition*. Minneapolis: University of Minnesota Press, 2014.

Cowen, Deborah. *The Deadly Life of Logistics: Mapping Violence in Global Trade*. Minneapolis: University of Minnesota Press, 2014.

Crawford, Neta C. "Just War Theory and the U.S. Counterterror War." *Perspective on Politics* 1, no. 1 (2003): 5–25.
Cuevas, Ofelia O. "Welcome to My Cell: Housing and Race in the Mirror of American Democracy." *American Quarterly* 4, no. 63 (2012): 605–24.
Cunanan, Kaloy M. "Slum-Fit? Or, Where Is the Place of the Filipinx Urban Poor in the Philippine City?" ACME: *An International Journal for Critical Geographies* 19, no. 1, (2020): 35–69.
Curato, Nicole, ed. *A Duterte Reader: Critical Essays on Rodrigo Duterte's Early Presidency*. Manila: Ateneo de Manila University Press, 2017.
Dalena, Kiri Lluch, dir. *Requiem for M*. Philippines, 2010.
Dalla Costa, Mariarosa, and Selma James. *The Power of Women and the Subversion of the Community*. Bristol, UK: Falling Wall Press, 1972.
Danticat, Edwidge. *Brother, I Am Dying*. New York: Vintage, 2008.
Davis, Angela Y. *Abolition Democracy: Beyond Empire, Prisons, and Torture*. New York: Seven Stories Press, 2005.
Davis, Angela Y. *The Angela Y. Davis Reader*. Edited by Joy James. Malden, MA: Blackwell, 1998.
Davis, Angela Y. *Are Prisons Obsolete?* New York: Seven Stories Press, 2003.
Davis, Angela Y. "Racialized Punishment and Prison Abolition." In *The Angela Y. Davis Reader*, 96–110.
Davis, Angela Y. "Reflections on the Black Woman's Role in the Community of Slaves." In *The Angela Y. Davis Reader*, 11–128.
Davis, Angela Y. "Surrogates and Outcast Mothers: Racism and Reproductive Politics in the Nineties." In *The Angela Y. Davis Reader*, 210–21.
Davis, Angela Y. "Women and Capitalism: Dialectics of Oppression and Liberation." In *The Angela Y. Davis Reader*, 161–92.
Davis, Angela Y. *Women, Race, Class*. New York: Random House, 1981.
Day, Iyko. *Alien Capital: Asian Racialization and the Logic of Settler Colonial Capitalism*. Durham, NC: Duke University Press, 2016.
Dayan, Colin. "Legal Terrors." *Representations* 92 (2005): 42–80.
Dayan, Joan. "Legal Slaves and Civil Bodies." *Nepantla: View from South* 2, no. 1 (2001): 3–39.
Debord, Guy. *The Society of the Spectacle*. Translated by Donald Nicholson-Smith. New York: Zone Books, 1994.
de Dios, Emmanuel S., and Paul D. Hutchcroft. "Political Economy." In *The Philippine Economy: Development, Policies, and Challenges*, edited by Arsenio Balisacan and Hall Hill, 46–70. Quezon City, Philippines: Ateneo de Manila University Press, 2003.
de León, Jason. *The Land of Open Graves: Living and Dying on the Migrant Trail*. Oakland: University of California Press, 2015.
De Rose, Ronald Charles, Takashi Oguchi, Wataru Morishima, and Mario Collado. "Land Cover Change on Mt. Pinatubo, the Philippines, Monitored using ASTER VNIR." *International Journal of Remote Sensing* 32, no. 24 (2011): 9279–305. https://doi.org/10.1080/01431161.2011.554452.

Deleuze, Gilles. "Postscript on the Societies of Control." *October*, no. 59 (1992): 3–7.
Delina, Laurence L. "Indigenous Environmental Defenders and the Legacy of Macli-ing Dulag: Anti-dam Dissent, Assassinations, and Protests in the Making of Philippine Energyscape." *Energy Research and Social Science* 65 (2020): 1–13.
Delvo, Christelle, and Brian Sulicipan, dir. *Bukid, Gulod, Libis*. Philippines, 2017.
Denetdale, Jennifer Nez. "Return to 'The Uprising at Beautiful Mountain in 1913': Marriage and Sexuality in the Making of the Modern Navajo Nation." In *Critically Sovereign: Indigenous Gender, Sexuality, and Feminist Studies*, edited by Joanne Barker, 69–98. Durham, NC: Duke University Press, 2017.
Dent, Gina, and Angela Davis. "Prison as a Border: A Conversation on Gender, Globalization, and Punishment." *Signs: Journal of Women in Culture and Society* 26, no. 4 (2001): 1235–41.
de Vera, Sherwin. Presentation on "Archiving Resistance" panel, BLTX Small Press Forum, January 11, 2020, Alfredo F. Tadiar Library, San Fernando, La Union, Philippines.
Diaz, Lav. "The Decade of Living Dangerously: A Chronicle from Lav Diaz." Interview with Brandon Wee. *Senses of Cinema*, February 2005. https://www.sensesofcinema.com/2005/filipino-cinema/lav_diaz/.
Diop, Mati, dir. *Atlantiques*. France: Anna Sanders Films, 2009.
Dizon, Hazel M. "Philippine Housing Takeover: How the Urban Poor Claimed Their Right to Shelter." *Radical Housing Journal* 1, no. 1 (2019): 105–29.
Dong, Xiao-Yuan, Paul Bowles, and Hongqin Chang. "Managing Liberalization and Globalization in Rural China: Trends in Rural Labour Allocation, Income and Inequality." *Global Labour Journal* 1, no. 1 (2010): 32–55.
Doyo, Ma. Ceres P. *Macli-ing Dulag: Kalinga Chief Defender of the Cordillera*. Quezon City, Philippines: University of the Philippines Press, 2015.
Drori, Israel. *Foreign Workers in Israel: Global Perspectives*. Albany: State University of New York Press, 2009.
Dumit, Joseph. "Prescription Maximization and the Accumulation of Surplus Health in the Pharmaceutical Industry." In *Lively Capital: Biotechnologies, Ethics, and Governance in Global Markets*, edited by Kaushik Sunder Rajan, 45–92. Durham, NC: Duke University Press, 2012.
Dunbar-Ortiz, Roxanne. *An Indigenous Peoples' History of the United States*. Boston: Beacon Press, 2014.
Ehrenreich, Barbara, and Arlie Russell Hochschild, eds. *Global Woman: Nannies, Maids, and Sex Workers in the New Economy*. New York: Metropolitan/Owl Books, 2004.
Elyachar, Julia. "The Political Economy of Movement and Gesture in Cairo." *Journal of the Royal Anthropological Institute* 17 (2011): 82–99.
Eng, David L., and Shinhee Han. "A Dialogue on Racial Melancholia." In *Loss: The Politics of Mourning and Melancholia*, edited by David L. Eng and David Kazanjian, 343–71. Berkeley: University of California Press, 2003.

Enloe, Cynthia. *Bananas, Beaches and Bases: Making Feminist Sense of International Politics*. London: Pandora, 1989.
Enloe, Cynthia. *The Curious Feminist: Searching for Women in a New Age of Empire*. Berkeley: University of California Press, 2004.
Espiritu, Yen Le. *Body Counts: The Vietnam War and Militarized Refugees*. Berkeley: University of California Press, 2014.
Estes, Nick, and Jaskiran Dhillon. *Standing with Standing Rock: Voices from the #NoDAPL Movement*. Minneapolis: University of Minnesota Press, 2019.
Evans, Linda. "Playing Global Cop: U.S. Militarism and the Prison-Industrial Complex." In Sudbury, *Global Lockdown: Race, Gender, and the Prison-Industrial Complex*, 215–30.
Eviota, Elizabeth Uy. *The Political Economy of Gender: Women and the Sexual Division of Labour in the Philippines*. London: Zed, 1992.
Faier, Lieba. "Affective Investments in the Manila Region: Filipina Migrants in Rural Japan and Transnational Urban Development in the Philippines." *Transactions: Institute of British Geographers* 38, no. 3 (2013): 376–90.
Faier, Lieba. *Intimate Encounters: Filipina Women and the Remaking of Rural Japan*. Berkeley: University of California Press, 2009.
Fajardo, Kale Bantigue. *Filipino Crosscurrents: Oceanographies of Seafaring, Masculinities, and Globalization*. Minneapolis: University of Minnesota Press, 2011.
Federici, Silvia. *Caliban and the Witch: Women, the Body and Primitive Accumulation*. New York: Autonomedia, 2004.
Federici, Silvia. "On Capitalism, Colonialism, Women and Food Politics: An Interview with Silvia Federici by Max Haiven." *Politics and Culture*, November 3, 2009. http://www.politicsandculture.org/2009/11/03/silvia-federici-on-capitalism-colonialism-women-and-food-politics/.
Federici, Silvia. "The Reproduction of Labor-Power in the Global Economy: Marxist Theory and the Unfinished Feminist Revolution." Lecture, January 26, 2009, University of California, Santa Cruz. http://culturalstudies.ucsc.edu/EVENTS/Winter09/Federici.html.
Federici, Silvia. *Revolution at Point Zero: Housework, Reproduction, and Feminist Struggle*. Oakland, CA: PM Press, 2012.
Ferguson, Charles, dir. *Inside Job*. Hollywood: Sony Pictures Classics, 2016.
Ferguson, Roderick A., and Jodi Melamed. "Academic Freedom with Violence: A Response to the AAUP Journal of Academic Freedom, Volume 4." *Journal of Academic Freedom* 4 (2013). https://www.aaup.org/JAF4/academic-freedom-violence-response#.YWxwIi2ZPOR.
Ferreira da Silva, Denise. *Toward a Global Idea of Race*. Minneapolis: University of Minnesota Press, 2007.
Fortunati, Leopoldina. *Arcane of Reproduction: Housework, Prostitution, Labor, and Capital*. Translated by Hilary Creek. New York: Autonomedia, 1995.
Foucault, Michel. *The Birth of Biopolitics: Lectures at the Collège de France, 1978–1979*. Translated by Graham Burchell. New York: Palgrave-Macmillan, 2008.
Foucault, Michel. *"Society Must Be Defended": Lectures at the Collège de France, 1975–1976*. Translated by David Macey. New York: Picador, 2002.

Fox, James J. "The Discourse and Practice of Precedence." In *Precedence: Social Differentiation in the Austronesian World*, edited by Michael P. Vischer, 91–110. Canberrra: ANU E Press, 2009.

Francisco-Menchavez, Valerie. *Labor of Care: Filipina Migrants and Transnational Families in the Digital Age*. Urbana: University of Illinois Press, 2018.

Fregoso, Rosa Linda. "'We Want Them Alive!': The Politics and Culture of Human Rights." *Social Identities* 12, no. 2 (2006): 109–38.

Galam, Roderick G. "Utility Manning: Young Filipino Men, Servitude and the Moral Economy of Becoming a Seafarer and Attaining Adulthood." *Work, Employment and Society* 33, no. 4 (2018): 580–95.

Galeano, Eduardo. *Open Veins of Latin America: Five Centuries of the Pillage of a Continent*. Translated by Cedric Belfrage. New York: Monthly Review Press, 1997.

Galeano, Eduardo. *Las venas abiertas de América Latina*. Madrid: Siglo Veintiuno, 1971.

Galloway, Alexander R. *Protocol: How Control Exists after Decentralization*. Cambridge, MA: MIT Press, 2004.

Geertz, Clifford. "Deep Play: Notes on the Balinese Cockfight." *Daedalus* 101, no. 1 (1972): 1–37.

Gergen, Christopher, and Gregg Vanourek. *Life Entrepreneurs: Ordinary People Creating Extraordinary Lives*. San Francisco: Jossey-Bass, 2008.

Gibson-Graham, J. K. *The End of Capitalism (As We Knew It): A Feminist Critique of Political Economy*. Minneapolis: University of Minnesota Press, 2006.

Gibson-Graham, J. K. *A Postcapitalist Politics*. Minneapolis: University of Minnesota Press, 2006.

Gidwani, Vinay, and Anant Maringanti. "The Waste-Value Dialectic: Lumpen Urbanization in Contemporary India." *Comparative Studies of South Asia, Africa and the Middle East* 36, no. 1 (2016): 112–33.

Gidwani, Vinay, and Rajyashri N. Reddy. "The Afterlives of 'Waste': Notes from India on a Minor History of Capitalist Surplus." *Antipode* 43, no. 5 (2011): 1625–58.

Giedion, Sigfried. *Space, Time and Architecture: The Growth of a New Tradition*. 5th ed. Cambridge, MA: Harvard University Press, 2008.

Gilmore, Ruth Wilson. *Golden Gulag: Prisons, Surplus, Crisis, and Opposition in Globalizing California*. Berkeley: University of California Press, 2007.

Glenn, Evelyn Nakano. *Forced to Care: Coercion and Caregiving in America*. Cambridge, MA: Harvard University Press, 2010.

Glenn, Evelyn Nakano. "From Servitude to Service Work: Historical Continuities in the Racial Division of Paid Reproductive Labor." *Signs: Journal of Women in Culture and Society* 18, no. 1 (1992): 1–43.

Go, Julian. *Patterns of Empire: The British and American Empires, 1688 to the Present*. New York: Cambridge University Press, 2011.

Goeman, Mishua. "Land as Life: Unsettling the Logics of Containment." In *Native Studies Keywords*, edited by Stephanie Nohelani Teves, Michelle Raheja, and Andrea Smith, 71–89. Tucson: University of Arizona Press, 2015.

Gomez-Barris, Macarena. *The Extractive Zone: Social Ecologies and Decolonial Perspectives*. Durham, NC: Duke University Press, 2017.

Graff, Henry T., ed. *American Imperialism and the Philippine Insurrection: Testimony Taken from Hearings on Affairs in the Philippine Islands before the Senate Committee on the Philippines, 1902*. Boston: Little, Brown, 1969.

Grandin, Greg. *Empire's Workshop: Latin America, the United States, and the New Imperialism*. New York: Metropolitan/Owl Books, 2006.

Grewal, Inderpal. "Women's Rights as Human Rights." In *Transnational America: Feminisms, Diasporas, Neoliberalisms*, 121–57. Durham, NC: Duke University Press, 2005.

Guevarra, Anna Romina. *Marketing Dreams, Manufacturing Heroes: The Transnational Labor Brokering of Filipino Workers*. New Brunswick, NJ: Rutgers University Press, 2010.

Guha, Ranajit. "The Prose of Counter-Insurgency." In *Selected Subaltern Studies*, edited by Ranajit Guha and Gayatri Chakravorty Spivak, 45–88. New York: Oxford University Press, 1988.

Guillaumin, Colette. *Racism, Sexism, Power and Ideology*. New York: Routledge, 1995.

Guyer, Jane I. "Cash Economies." Unpublished paper presented at the Rethinking Economic Anthropology: A Human-Centered Approach conference, January 11–12, 2008, London School of Economics.

Guyer, Jane I. *Marginal Gains: Monetary Transactions in Atlantic Africa*. Chicago: University of Chicago Press, 2004.

Haley, Sarah. *No Mercy Here: Gender, Punishment, and the Making of Jim Crow Modernity*. Chapel Hill: University of North Carolina Press, 2016.

Hall, Stuart. "Encoding/Decoding." In *The Unfinished Conversation: Encoding/Decoding*, edited by Gaëtane Verna and Mark Sealy, 1–29. London: Power Plant, 2016.

Hall, Stuart, Chas Critcher, Tony Jefferson, John Clark, and Brian Roberts. *Policing the Crisis: Mugging, the State, and Law and Order*. Basingstoke, UK: Palgrave Macmillan, 2013.

Hammami, Rema. "The Politics of Gender in the Flat-Pack 'Peace': GBV (Gender-Based Violence) Programming and Global Governmentality in Occupied Palestine." Lecture, Columbia University, October 29, 2014.

Harding, Jeremy. *Border Vigils: Keeping Migrants out of the Rich World*. London: Verso, 2012.

Hardt, Michael, and Antonio Negri. *Empire*. Cambridge, MA: Harvard University Press, 2001.

Hardt, Michael, and Antonio Negri. *Labor of Dionysus: A Critique of the State-Form*. Minneapolis: University of Minnesota Press, 1994.

Harootunian, Harry. *Marx after Marx: History and Time in the Expansion of Capitalism*. New York: Columbia University Press, 2015.

Harris, Bonnie. *Philippine Sanctuary: A Holocaust Odyssey*. Madison: University of Wisconsin Press, 2020.

Hartman, Saidiya. "The Belly of the World: A Note on Black Women's Labors." *Souls* 13 (2016): 166–73.

Hartman, Saidiya. *Scenes of Subjection: Terror, Slavery, and Self-Making in Nineteenth-Century America*. New York: Oxford University Press, 1997.

Hartman, Saidiya. "The Time of Slavery." *South Atlantic Quarterly* 101, no. 4 (2002): 757–77.

Harvey, David. *The New Imperialism*. New York: Oxford University Press, 2005.

Hayami, Yoko, Junko Koizumi, Chalidaporn Sngsamphan, and Ratana Tosakul, eds. *The Family in Flux in Southeast Asia: Institution, Ideology, Practice*. Kyoto: Kyoto University Press, 2012.

Hayles, N. Katherine. *How We Became Posthuman: Virtual Bodies in Cybernetics, Literature, and Informatics*. Chicago: University of Chicago Press, 1999.

Heberer, Feng-Mei. "Migrating Intimacies: Media Representations of Same-Sex Love among Migrant Women in East Asia." *Sexualities* 20, no. 4 (2017): 428–45.

Heymann, Tomer, dir. *Paper Dolls*. Culver City, CA: Strand Releasing, 2006.

Higgins, Tracy E. Review of *Are Women Human? and Other International Dialogues* by Catharine A. MacKinnon. *Yale Journal of Law and Feminism* 18, no. 2 (2006): 101–22.

Hilal, Jamil. "Imperialism and Settler-Colonialism in West Asia: Israel and the Arab Palestinian Struggle." *Utafiti* 1, no. 1 (1976): 51–70.

Ho, Karen. *Liquidated: An Ethnography of Wall Street*. Durham, NC: Duke University Press, 2009.

Hoffman, Cecilia. "Prostitution as Choice." Feminist Archives, Isis International. Accessed July 5, 2021. http://feministarchives.isiswomen.org/36-feminist-archives/women-in-action/women-in-action-1995-1/525-prostitution-as-choice/.

Hondagneu-Sotelo, Pierrette. *Doméstican: Immigrant Workers Cleaning and Caring in the Shadows of Affluence*. Berkeley: University of California Press, 2001.

Hutchcroft, Paul D. *Booty Capitalism: The Politics of Banking in the Philippines*. Ithaca, NY: Cornell University Press, 1998.

Jensen, Sif Lehman. "Philippine Prison Marriages: The Politics of Kinship and Women's Composite Agency." *Conflict and Society* 6 (2020): 18–33.

Jensen, Steffen. "Stunted Future: Buryong among Young Men in Manila." In *Ethnographies of Youth and Temporality: Time Objectified*, edited by Anne Line Dalsgård, Martin Demant Frederiksen, Susanne Højlund, and Lotte Meinert, 41–56. Philadelphia: Temple University Press, 2014.

Jensen, Steffen, and Karl Hapal. "Police Violence and Corruption in the Philippines: Violent Exchange and the War on Drugs." *Journal of Current Southeast Asian Affairs* 2 (2018): 39–62.

Jia Zhangke, dir. *Platform*. China, 2000.

Jia Zhangke, dir. *Still Life*. Beijing: Xstream Pictures, 2006.

Jia Zhangke, dir. *24 City*. China, 2008.

Jiwei Xiao. "The Quest for Memory: Documentary and Fiction in Jia Zhangke's Films." *Senses of Cinema* 59 (2011). http://www.sensesofcinema.com/2011

/feature-articles/the-quest-for-memory-documentary-and-fiction-in-jia-zhang
ke-%E2%80%99s-films/.
Jocano, F. Landa. *Slum as a Way of Life*. Quezon City, Philippines: New Day Publishers, 1975.
Johnson, Chalmers. *The Sorrows of Empire: Militarism, Secrecy, and the End of the Republic*. New York: Metropolitan Books, 2004.
Karatani, Kojin. *Origins of Modern Japanese Literature*. Translated by Brett de Bary. Durham, NC: Duke University Press, 1993.
Kassamali, Sumayya. "Migrant Worker Lifeworlds of Beirut." PhD dissertation, Columbia University, 2017.
Katz, Cindi. "Accumulation, Excess, Childhood: Toward a Countertopography of Risk and Waste." *Documents d'Anàlisi Geogràfica* 57, no. 1 (2011): 47–60.
Katz, Cindi. *Growing Up Global: Economic Restructuring and Children's Everyday Lives*. Minneapolis: University of Minnesota Press, 2004.
Kauanui, J. Kēhaulani. *Hawaiian Blood: Colonialism and the Politics of Sovereignty and Indigeneity*. Durham, NC: Duke University Press, 2008.
Kauanui, J. Kēhaulani. *Paradoxes of Hawaiian Sovereignty: Land, Sex, and the Colonial Politics of State Nationalism*. Durham, NC: Duke University Press, 2018.
Kelley, Robin D. G. *Freedom Dreams: The Black Radical Imagination*. Boston: Beacon, 2002.
Kelley, Robin D. G. "Mike Brown's Body: Meditations on War, Race and Democracy." 2015 Toni Morrison Lectures, Princeton University, Princeton, NJ. http://aas.princeton.edu/publication/mike-browns-body-meditations-on-war-race-and-democracy/.
Kiernan, V. G. *America, the New Imperialism: From White Settlement to World Hegemony*. London: Verso, 2005.
Klein, Naomi. *The Shock Doctrine: The Rise of Disaster Capitalism*. New York: Picador, 2008.
Koram, Kojo, ed. *The War on Drugs and the Global Colour Line*. London: Pluto Press, 2019.
Kusaka, Wataru. *Moral Politics in the Philippines: Inequality, Democracy, and the Urban Poor*. Singapore: NUS Press and Kyoto University Press, 2017.
Lake, Robert W. "The Financialization of Urban Policy in the Age of Obama." *Journal of Urban Affairs* 37, no. 1 (2015): 75–78.
Lamar, Kendrick. *Good Kid, m.A.A.d city*. Carson, CA: TDE, 2012.
Lara, Francisco J., Jr. *Insurgents, Clans and States: Political Legitimacy and Resurgent Conflict in Muslim Mindanao, Philippines*. Quezon City, Philippines: Ateneo de Manila University Press, 2014.
Lasco, Gideon. "Call Boys: Drug Use and Sex Work among Marginalized Young Men in a Philippine Port Community." *Contemporary Drug Problems* 45, no. 1. (2018): 33–46.
Lasco, Gideon. "Pampagilas: Methamphetamine in the Everyday Economic Lives of Underclass Male Youths in a Philippine Port." *International Journal of Drug Policy* 25 (2014): 783–88.

Lazzarato, Maurizio. "Neoliberalism in Action: Inequality, Insecurity and the Reconstitution of the Social." *Theory, Culture and Society* 26, no. 6 (2009): 109–33.

Lazzarato, Maurizio. *Signs and Machines: Capitalism and the Production of Subjectivity*. Translated by Joshua David Jordan. Los Angeles: Semiotext(e), 2014.

Li, Darryl. "The Gaza Strip as Laboratory: Notes in the Wake of Disengagement." *Journal of Palestine Studies* 35, no. 2 (2006): 38–55.

Li, Darryl. "Offshoring the Army: Migrant Workers and the U.S. Military." *UCLA Law Review* 62, no. 1 (2015): 124–74.

Lorde, Audre. *The Collected Poems of Audre Lorde*. New York: Norton, 1997.

Lowe, Lisa. "The Gender of Sovereignty." *Scholar and Feminist Online* 6, no. 3 (2008). http://sfonline.barnard.edu/immigration/print_lowe.htm.

Lowe, Lisa. *The Intimacies of Four Continents*. Durham, NC: Duke University Press, 2015.

Lowenstein, Antony. *Disaster Capitalism: Making a Killing out of Catastrophe*. London: Verso, 2016.

Luxemburg, Rosa. *The Accumulation of Capital*. 2nd ed. Translated by Agnes Schwarzschild. New York: Routledge, 2003.

Luxemburg, Rosa. *The Accumulation of Capital: A Contribution to the Economic Theory of Imperialism*. In *The Complete Works of Rosa Luxemburg: II, Economic Writings 2*, edited by Peter Hudis and Paul Le Blanc, 6–342. London: Verso, 2016.

Luxemburg, Rosa. "Militarism as a Province of Accumulation." In *The Accumulation of Capital*, 434–47.

Ma, Jean. *Melancholy Drift: Marking Time in Chinese Cinema*. Hong Kong: Hong Kong University Press, 2010.

MacKinnon, Catharine A. *Are Women Human? and Other International Dialogues*. Cambridge, MA: Harvard University Press, 2006.

Mahmood, Saba. *Politics of Piety: The Islamic Revival and the Feminist Subject*. Princeton, NJ: Princeton University Press, 2005.

Maira, Sunaina. *Boycott! The Academy and Justice for Palestine*. Oakland: University of California Press, 2017.

Malayang, Ben, III. "Rights and Exclusion in Tenure: Implications to Tenure Policies in the Philippines." Paper presented at the Second Annual Meeting of the International Association for the Study of Common Property (IASCP), September 26–October 2, 1991, University of Manitoba, Winnipeg, Canada.

Mamdani, Mahmood. *Good Muslim, Bad Muslim: America, the Cold War, and the Roots of Terror*. New York: Pantheon, 2004.

Mamdani, Mahmood. *Saviors and Survivors: Darfur, Politics, and the War on Terror*. New York: Pantheon, 2009.

Manalansan, Martin. *Global Divas: Filipino Gay Men in the Diaspora*. Durham, NC: Duke University Press, 2003.

Mandel, Ernest. Introduction to Karl Marx, *Capital: A Critique of Political Economy, Vol. II*, 11–79. London: Penguin Classics, 1993.

Mandelbrot, B., and R. L. Hudson. *The (Mis)Behavior of Markets: A Fractal View of Risk, Ruin and Reward*. New York: Basic, 2004.

Mann, Michael. *Incoherent Empire*. London: Verso, 2005.

Marazzi, Christian. *The Violence of Financial Capitalism*. Translated by Kristina Lebedeva. Los Angeles: Semiotext(e), 2010.

Margold, Jane A. "Narratives of Masculinity and Transnational Migration: Filipino Workers in the Middle East." In *Bewitching Women, Pious Men: Gender and Body Politics in Southeast Asia*, edited by Aihwa Ong and Michael G. Peletz, 274–94. Berkeley: University of California Press, 1995.

Martin, Randy. "After Economy? Social Logics of the Derivative." *Social Text* 31, no. 1 (2013): 83–106.

Martin, Randy. *An Empire of Indifference: American War and the Financial Logic of Risk Management*. Durham, NC: Duke University Press, 2007.

Martin, Randy. *Knowledge LTD: Toward a Social Logic of the Derivative*. Philadelphia: Temple University Press, 2015.

Martin, Randy. "Money after Decolonization." *South Atlantic Quarterly* 114, no. 2 (2015): 377–93.

Marx, Karl. *Capital: A Critique of Political Economy, Vol. I*. London: Penguin, 1976.

Marx, Karl. *Capital: A Critique of Political Economy, Vol. II*. London: Penguin Classics, 1978.

Marx, Karl. "Economic and Philosophic Manuscripts of 1844." In Marx and Engels, *The Marx-Engels Reader*, 66–125.

Marx, Karl. "Economic Manuscript of 1861–63." In Marx and Engels, *Collected Works*, vol. 34, *Marx: 1861–1864*.

Marx, Karl. *Grundrisse: Foundations of the Critique of Political Economy*. London: Penguin Classics, 1993.

Marx, Karl. "On the Jewish Question." In Marx and Engels, *The Marx-Engels Reader*, 26–52.

Marx, Karl. "Simple Reproduction." In *Capital, Vol. I*, 711–72.

Marx, Karl. "Wage Labour and Capital." In Marx and Engels, *The Marx-Engels Reader*, 203–17.

Marx, Karl, and Friedrich Engels. *Collected Works*. Vol. 34, *Marx: 1861–1864*. Edited by Ben Fowkes. New York: International, 1994.

Marx, Karl, and Friedrich Engels. *The German Ideology*. New York: Prometheus Books, 1998.

Marx, Karl, and Friedrich Engels. *The Marx-Engels Reader*. Edited by Robert C. Tucker. New York: Norton, 1978.

Mas, Stéphane. "Painting with a Political Camera: An Interview with Jia Zhangke." Translated by Paul Willemen. Accessed February 21, 2013. https://peauneuve.net/article.php3?id_article=171.

Mazoyer, Marcel, and Laurence Roudart. *A History of World Agriculture: From the Neolithic Age to the Current Crisis*. Translated by James H. Membrez. New York: Monthly Review Press, 2006.

McClintock, Anne. *Imperial Leather: Race, Gender, and Sexuality in the Colonial Contest*. New York: Routledge, 1995.

McCoy, Alfred W., ed. *An Anarchy of Families: State and Family in the Philippines.* Madison: University of Wisconsin, Center for Southeast Asian Studies, 1993.

McCoy, Alfred W. "Covert Netherworld: An Invisible Interstice in the Modern World System." *Comparative Studies in Society and History* 58, no. 4 (2016): 847–79.

McCoy, Alfred W. "Imperial Illusions: Information Infrastructure and the Future of U.S. Global Power." In *Endless Empire: Spain's Retreat, Europe's Eclipse, America's Decline*, edited by Alfred W. McCoy, Josep M. Fradera, and Stephen Jacobson, 360–88. Madison: University of Wisconsin Press, 2012.

McCoy, Alfred W. *In the Shadows of the American Century: The Rise and Decline of U.S. Global Power.* Chicago: Haymarket Books, 2017.

McCoy, Alfred W. "Low Intensity Conflict in the Philippines." In *Low Intensity Conflict: Theory and Practice in Central America and South-East Asia*, edited by Barry Carr and Elaine McKay, 51–64. Melbourne: La Trobe University, Institute of Latin American Studies; Clayton: Monash University, Center of Southeast Asian Studies, 1988.

McCoy, Alfred W. *Policing America's Empire: The United States, the Philippines, and the Rise of the Surveillance State.* Madison: University of Wisconsin Press, 2009.

McGrath, Jason. "The Independent Cinema of Jia Zhangke: From Post-socialist Realism to a Transnational Aesthetic." In *The Urban Generation: Chinese Cinema and Society at the Turn of the Twenty-First Century*, edited by Zhen Zhang, 81–114. Durham, NC: Duke University Press, 2007.

McKay, Deirdre. *An Archipelago of Care: Filipino Migrants and Global Networks.* Bloomington: Indiana University Press, 2016.

McKay, Steven. "Racializing the High Seas: Filipino Migrants and Global Shipping." In *The Nation and Its People: Citizens, Denizens, Migrants*, edited by John Park, 155–76. New York: Routledge, 2014.

McKinnon, Susan, and Fenella Cannell, eds. *Vital Relations: Modernity and the Persistent Life of Kinship.* Santa Fe, NM: School for Advanced Research Press, 2013.

McKittrick, Katherine. "Mathematics Black Life." *The Black Scholar: Journal of Black Studies and Research* 44, no. 2 (2014): 16–28.

Meillassoux, Claude. *The Anthropology of Slavery: The Womb of Iron and Gold.* London: Athlone, 1991.

Meillassoux, Claude. *Maidens, Meal and Money: Capitalism and the Domestic Community.* Cambridge: Cambridge University Press, 1981.

Mendoza, Brillante, dir. *Kinatay.* Philippines: Centerstage Productions, 2007.

Mendoza, Brillante, dir. *Lola.* Philippines: Swift Productions, 2009.

Mendoza, Brillante, dir. *Ma' Rosa.* Philippines: Centerstage Productions, 2016.

Mendoza, Brillante, dir. *Tirador.* Philippines: Centerstage Productions, 2007.

Mercado, Remigio A., Jay Bertram T. Lacsamana, and Greg L. Pineda, "Socioeconomic Impacts of the Mt. Pinatubo Eruption." In *Fire and Mud: Eruptions and Lahars of Mount Pinatubo, Philippines*, edited by Christopher G. Newhall and Raymundo S. Punongbayan, 1063–69. Quezon City, Philippines: Philippine

Institute of Volcanology and Seismology; Seattle: University of Washington Press, 1996.

Mies, Maria. *Patriarchy and Accumulation on a World Scale: Women in the International Division of Labour.* London: Zed Books, 1986.

Mies, Maria, Veronica Bennholdt-Thomsen, and Claudia Von Werlhof, eds. *Women: The Last Colony.* Atlantic Highlands, NJ: Zed Books, 1988.

Million, Dian. "We Are the Land, and the Land Is Us: Indigenous Land, Lives, and Embodied Ecologies in the Twentieth Century." In *Racial Ecologies*, edited by Leilani Nishime and Kim D. Hester Williams, 19–33. Seattle: University of Washington Press, 2018.

Mohanty, Chandra. *Feminism without Borders: Decolonizing Theory, Practicing Solidarity.* Durham, NC: Duke University Press, 2003.

Molintas, Jose Mencio. "The Philippine Indigenous People's Struggles for Land and Life: Challenging Legal Texts." *Arizona Journal of International and Comparative Law* 21, no. 1 (2004): 269–306.

Moore, Jason W. *Capitalism in the Web of Life: Ecology and the Accumulation of Capital.* New York: Verso, 2015.

Moore, Jason W. "Cheap Food and Bad Climate: From Surplus Value to Negative Value in the Capitalist World-Ecology." *Critical Historical Studies* 2, no. 1 (2015): 1–43.

Mora, Alexander A., dir. *The Nightcrawlers.* London: Genius Loki and Violet Films, 2019.

Moraga, Cherríe, and Gloria Anzaldúa, eds. *This Bridge Called My Back: Writings by Radical Women of Color.* New York: Kitchen Table: Women of Color Press, 1983.

Morgan, Jennifer. "Accounting for 'the Most Excruciating Torment': Gender, Slavery, and Trans-Atlantic Passages." *History of the Present* 6, no. 2 (Fall 2016): 184–207.

Morgan, Jennifer. "Archives and Histories of Racial Capitalism: An Afterword." *Social Text* 33, no. 4 (2015): 153–61.

Morgan, Jennifer. *Laboring Women: Reproduction and Gender in New World Slavery.* Philadelphia: University of Pennsylvania Press, 2004.

Muñoz, José Esteban. *Cruising Utopia: The Then and There of Queer Futurity.* New York: New York University Press, 2009.

Murphy, Michelle. *The Economization of Life.* Durham, NC: Duke University Press, 2017.

Narayan, Uma. *Dislocating Cultures: Identities, Traditions, and Third World Feminism.* New York: Routledge, 1997.

Nash, June, and María Patricia Fernández-Kelly. *Women, Men, and the International Division of Labor.* Albany: State University of New York Press, 1983.

Negri, Antonio. *Marx beyond Marx: Lessons on the Grundrisse.* Translated by Harry Cleaver, Michael Ryan, and Maurizio Viano. Edited by Jim Fleming. New York: Autonomedia, 1991.

Negri, Antonio. *Empire and Beyond.* Translated by Ed Emery. Cambridge: Polity, 2008.

Negri, Antonio. "The Labor of the Multitude and the Fabric of Biopolitics." Translated by Sara Mayo and Peter Graefe with Mark Coté. *Mediations* 23, no. 2 (2008): 8–25.

Neilson, Brett. "Provincializing the Italian Effect." *Cultural Studies Review* 11, no. 2 (2005): 11–25.

Ngai, Pun. *Migrant Labor in China: Post-Socialist Transformations*. Cambridge: Polity, 2016.

Ngai, Pun, Chris King Chi Chan, and Jenny Chan. "The Role of the State, Labour Policy and Migrant Workers' Struggles in Globalized China." *Global Labour Journal* 1, no. 1 (2010): 132–51.

Nydegger, William F., and Corinne Nydegger. *Tarong: An Ilocos Barrio in the Philippines*. New York: Wiley, 1966.

Ong, Aihwa. "Experiments with Freedom: Milieus of the Human." *American Literary History* 18, no. 2 (2006): 229–44.

Ong, Aihwa. *Neoliberalism as Exception: Mutations in Citizenship and Sovereignty*. Durham, NC: Duke University Press, 2006.

Ong, Aihwa. *Spirits of Resistance and Capitalist Discipline: Factory Women in Malaysia*. 2nd ed. Albany: State University of New York Press, 2010.

Ong, Jonathan Corpus, and Jason Vincent A. Cabañes. *Architects of Networked Disinformation: Behind the Scenes of Troll Accounts and Fake News Production in the Philippines*. Leicester: Newton Tech4Deve Network, 2018. http://newtontechfordev.com/wp-content/uploads/2018/02/ARCHITECTS-OF-NETWORKED-DISINFORMATION-FULL-REPORT.pdf.

Ortega, Arnisson Andre. "Manila's Metropolitan Landscape of Gentrification: Global Urban Development, Accumulation by Dispossession and Neoliberal Warfare against Informality." *Geoforum* 70 (2016): 35–50.

Padios, Jan Maghinay. "Dial C for Culture: Telecommunications, Gender, and the Filipino Transnational Migrant Market." In *Circuits of Visibility: Gender and Transnational Media Cultures*, edited by Radha Hegde, 212–28. New York: NYU Press, 2011.

Padios, Jan. *A Nation on the Line: Call Centers as Postcolonial Predicaments in the Philippines*. Durham, NC: Duke University Press, 2018.

Parenti, Christian. *Tropic of Chaos: Climate Change and the New Geography of Violence*. New York: Nation Books, 2011.

Park, K-Sue. "Money, Mortgages, and the Conquest of America." *Law and Social Inquiry* 41, no. 4 (2016): 1006–35.

Parker, Andrew, Mary Russo, Doris Sommer, and Patricia Yaeger. *Nationalisms and Sexualities*. New York: Routledge, 1992.

Parreñas, Rhacel. *Servants of Globalization: Women, Migration, and Domestic Work*. Stanford, CA: Stanford University Press, 2001.

Paterson, Andrew H., Paul H. Moore, and Tom L. Tew. "The Gene Pool of *Saccharum* Species and Their Improvement." In *Genomics of the Saccharinae*, edited by Andrew H. Paterson, 43–71. New York: Springer, 2013.

Patterson, Orlando. *Slavery and Social Death: A Comparative Study*. Cambridge, MA: Harvard University Press, 1982.

Peach, Lucinda J. "An Alternative to Pacifism? Feminism and Just-War Theory." *Hypatia* 9, no. 2 (1994): 152–72.

Petit, Santiago López. "¿Y si dejáramos de ser cuidadanos? Manifiesto por la desocupación del orden" (What if we desist being citizens? A manifesto for the disoccupation of the order). *El viejo topo*, no. 272 (2010): 59–67.

Pido, Eric. *Migrant Returns: Manila, Development, and Transnational Connectivity*. Durham, NC: Duke University Press, 2017.

Prakash, Gyan. *Bonded Histories: Genealogies of Labor Servitude in India*. Cambridge: Cambridge University Press, 1990.

Prashad, Vijay. *The Darker Nations: A People's History of the Third World*. New York: New Press, 2007.

Pratt, Geraldine. *Families Apart: Migrant Mothers and the Conflicts of Labor and Love*. Minneapolis: University of Minnesota Press, 2012.

Pratt, Geraldine, and Caleb Johnson. *Migration in Performance: Crossing the Colonial Present*. New York: Routledge, 2019.

Pratt, Geraldine, Caleb Johnson, and Vanessa Banta. "Lifetimes of Disposability and Surplus Entrepreneurs in Bagong Barrio, Manila." *Antipode* 49, no. 1 (2016): 1–24.

Puar, Jasbir K. *The Right to Maim: Debility, Capacity, Disability*. Durham, NC: Duke University Press, 2017.

Puar, Jasbir K., and Amit S. Rai. "Monster, Terrorist, Fag: The War on Terrorism and the Production of Docile Patriots." *Social Text* 20, no. 3 (2002): 117–48.

Pulido, Laura. "Flint, Environmental Racism, and Racial Capitalism." *Capitalism Nature Socialism* 27, no. 3 (2016): 1–16.

Pulido, Laura. "Geographies of Race and Ethnicity II: Environmental Racism, Racial Capitalism, and State-Sanctioned Violence." *Progress in Human Geography* 41, no. 4 (2017): 524–33.

Quijano, Ilang-Ilang, dir. *Puso ng Lungsod*. Philippines, 2012.

Quintos, Floy. "Lamentations." Medium, July 24, 2016. https://medium.com/@kill.list.lit/lamentations-16ffeb42756a.

Raunig, Gerald. *Dividuum: Machinic Capitalism and Molecular Revolution*. Translated by Aileen Derieg. South Pasadena, CA: Semiotext(e), 2016.

Raymundo, Sarah. "Folk Beliefs as Source of Resource Management and Motor of Indigenous Struggle." Paper presented at the Crossroads Conference of Cultural Studies, August 12–15, 2018, Shanghai.

Raymundo, Sarah, and Roland Tolentino, eds. *Kontra-Gahum: Academics against Political Killings*. Manila: IBON Publishing, 2006.

Razzack, Sherene H. "Gendering Disposability." *Canadian Journal of Women and the Law* 28, no. 2 (2016): 285–307.

Reddy, Chandan. *Freedom with Violence: Race, Sexuality, and the U.S. State*. Durham, NC: Duke University Press, 2011.

Reid, Anthony. *Southeast Asia in the Age of Commerce, 1450–1680*. Vol. 1, *The Lands below the Winds*. New Haven, CT: Yale University Press, 1988.

Rejali, Darius. *Torture and Democracy*. Princeton, NJ: Princeton University Press, 2007.

Remollino, Alexander Martin. "Huwag Tayong Bumitaw Sa Ating Pagkatao." In *Subverso: Mga Tula at Kuwento Laban sa Pulitikal na Pandarahas*, edited by Mykel Andrada, Joi Barrios, and Rolando B. Tolentino, 70. Quezon City, Philippines: ACT- CONTEND, 2006.

Rengger, Nicholas. "On the Just War Tradition in the Twenty-First Century." *International Affairs* 78, no. 2 (2002): 353–63.

Ritchie, Andrea. *Invisible No More: Police Violence against Black Women and Women of Color*. Boston: Beacon, 2017.

Roberts, Dorothy E. *Fatal Invention: How Science, Politics, and Big Business Recreate Race in the Twenty-First Century*. New York: New Press, 2012.

Robinson, Cedric. *Black Marxism: The Making of the Black Radical Tradition*. Chapel Hill: University of North Carolina Press, 2000.

Robinson, William. "Globalization, the World System, and 'Democracy Promotion' in U.S. Foreign Policy." *Theory and Society* 25, no. 5 (1996): 615–65.

Roces, Mina. *Women, Power, and Kinship Politics: Female Power in Post-war Philippines*. Westport, CT: Praeger, 1998.

Rodolfo, Kelvin S. *Pinatubo and the Politics of Lahar: Eruption and Aftermath, 1991*. Quezon City, Philippines: University of the Philippines Press and the Pinatubo Studies Program, Center for Integrative and Development Studies, 1995.

Rodolfo, Kelvin S., and Jesse V. Umbal. "A Prehistoric Lahar-Dammed Lake and Eruption of Mount Pinatubo Described in a Philippine Aborigine Legend." *Journal of Volcanology and Geothermal Research* 176 (2008): 432–37.

Rodriguez, Robyn Magalit. *Migrants for Export: How the Philippine State Brokers Labor to the World*. Minneapolis: University of Minnesota Press, 2010.

Rodriguez, Rommel. "*Casus belli*." In *Kontra-Gahum: Academics against Political Killings*, edited by Rolando B. Tolentino and Sarah S. Raymundo, 127–34. Quezon City, Philippines: IBON Foundation, 2006.

Roediger, David R. *Wages of Whiteness: Race and the Making of the American Working Class*. London: Verso, 1993.

Roediger, David R., and Elizabeth Esch. *The Production of Difference: Race and the Management of Labor in U.S. History*. New York: Oxford University Press, 2012.

Roy, Arundhati. *An Ordinary Person's Guide to Empire*. Cambridge, MA: South End Press, 2004.

Rubino, Carl R. Galvez. *Ilocano Dictionary and Grammar: Ilocano-English, English-Ilocano*. Honolulu: University of Hawai'i Press, 2000.

Ruiz, Jose Tence. "Old Pain." In *Lyra Garcellano: Old Pain*, exhibition catalog, 2–4. Manila: Finale Art File, 2009.

Ruiz, Raúl. *Poetics of Cinema*. Paris: Dis Voir, 1995.

Sacay, M. C., dir. *Pira-pirasong Pangarap*. Philippines, 2019. Accessed December 8, 2021, https://www.youtube.com/watch?v=ckH-B69y718.

Sahlins, Marshall. *What Kinship Is—and Is Not*. Chicago: University of Chicago Press, 2013.

Said, Edward. *Culture and Imperialism*. New York: Vintage, 1994.

Said, Edward. "Zionism from the Standpoint of Its Victims." *Social Text*, no. 1 (1979): 1–79.

Salman, Michael. *The Embarrassment of Slavery: Controversies over Bondage and Nationalism in the American Colonial Philippines*. Berkeley: University of California Press, 2001.

Sandata. *Kolateral*. Calgary: NoFace Records, 2019.

Sartre, Jean-Paul. Preface to *The Wretched of the Earth*, by Frantz Fanon, translated by Richard Philcox, xliii–lxii. New York: Grove Press, 1961.

Scipes, Kim. "Global Economic Crisis, Neoliberal Solutions, and the Philippines." *Monthly Review* 51, no. 7 (1999): 1–14.

Scott, James C. *Against the Grain: A Deep History of the Earliest States*. New Haven, CT: Yale University Press, 2017.

Scott, James C. "Freedom and Freehold: Space, People and State Simplification in Southeast Asia." In *Asian Freedoms: The Idea of Freedom in East and Southeast Asia*, edited by David Kelly and Anthony Reid, 37–64. Cambridge: Cambridge University Press, 1988.

Scott, W. H. *The Discovery of the Igorots: Spanish Contacts with the Pagans of North Luzon*. Quezon City, Philippines: New Day Publishers, 1974.

See, Sarita. *The Decolonized Eye: Filipino American Art and Performance*. Minneapolis: University of Minnesota Press, 2009.

Serquiña, Oscar Tantoc, Jr. "Out and About: Migrant *Bakla*, Perverse Intimacies, and the Musical of Migration in Liza Magtoto's *Care Divas*." *Kritika Kultura* 27 (2016): 199–248.

Shalhoub-Kevorkian, Nadera. "Palestinian Feminist Critique and the Physics of Power: Feminists between Thought and Practice." *feminists@law: An Open Access Journal of Feminist Legal Scholarship* 4, no. 1 (2014): 1–18. https://doi.org/10.22024/UniKent/03/fal.108.

Sharma, Nandita. *Home Economics: Nationalism and the Making of 'Migrant Workers' in Canada*. Toronto: University of Toronto Press, 2006.

Shatkin, Gavin. "The City and the Bottom Line: Urban Megaprojects and the Privatization of Planning in Southeast Asia." *Environment and Planning A* 40 (2008): 383–401.

Shiva, Vandana. *Earth Democracy: Justice, Sustainability and Peace*. Cambridge, MA: South End Press, 2005.

Shiva, Vandana. *Water Wars: Privatization, Pollution, and Profit*. Cambridge, MA: South End Press, 2002.

Simbulan, Roland G. "The CIA's Hidden History in the Philippines." Lecture, August 18, 2000, University of the Philippines, Manila.

Simondon, Gilbert. *On the Mode of Existence of Technical Objects*. Translated by Cecile Malaspina and John Rogove. Minneapolis: Univocal Publishing, 2017.

Simone, AbdouMaliq. *City Life from Jakarta to Dakar: Movements at the Crossroads*. London: Routledge, 2010.

Simone, AbdouMaliq. *Improvised Lives: Rhythms of Endurance in an Urban South*. Cambridge: Polity, 2018.

Simone AbdouMaliq. "People as Infrastructure: Intersecting Fragments in Johannesburg." *Public Culture* 16, no. 3 (2004): 407–29.

Simpson, Leanne Betasamosake. *As We Have Always Done: Indigenous Freedom through Radical Resistance*. Minneapolis: University of Minnesota Press, 2017.
Singh, Nikhil Pal. "On Race, Violence, and So-Called Primitive Accumulation." *Social Text* 34, no. 3 (2016): 27–50.
Singh, Nikhil Pal. "The Whiteness of Police." *American Quarterly* 66, no. 4 (2014): 1091–99.
Sissako, Abderrahmane, dir. *Bamako*. London: Artificial Eye, 2006.
Smith, Neil. *The Endgame of Globalization*. New York: Routledge, 2005.
Smith, Samuel C. "The Franchise." In *American Eras*, vol. 2, *The Colonial Era, 1600–1754*, edited by Gretchen D. Starr-Lebeau, 219–21. Detroit: Gale, 1997.
Solanas, Fernando, and Octavio Getino. "Toward a Third Cinema." In *Film Manifestos and Global Cinema Cultures: A Critical Anthology*, edited by Scott Mackenzie, 230–50. Berkeley: University of California Press, 2014.
Spade, Dean. *Normal Life: Administrative Violence, Critical Trans Politics, and the Limits of Law*. Durham, NC: Duke University Press, 2015.
Spillers, Hortense J. "All the Things You Could Be by Now if Sigmund Freud's Wife Was Your Mother." In *Female Subjects in Black and White*, edited by Elizabeth Abel, Barbara Christian, and Helene Moglen, 135–58. Berkeley: University of California Press, 1997.
Spillers, Hortense J. "Mama's Baby, Papa's Maybe." In *Black, White, and in Color: Essays on American Literature and Culture*, 203–29. Chicago: University of Chicago Press, 2003.
Spivak, Gayatri Chakravorty. "Can the Subaltern Speak?" In *Marxism and the Interpretation of Culture*, edited by Cary Nelson and Lawrence Grossberg, 271–313. Basingstoke, UK: MacMillan Education, 1988.
Spivak, Gayatri Chakravorty. *A Critique of Postcolonial Reason: Toward a History of the Vanishing Present*. Cambridge, MA: Harvard University Press, 1999.
Spivak, Gayatri Chakravorty. *In Other Worlds: Essays in Cultural Politics*. New York: Routledge, 1988.
Spivak, Gayatri Chakravorty. "The Political Economy of Women as Seen by a Literary Critic." In *Coming to Terms: Feminism, Theory, Politics*, edited by Elizabeth Weed. London: Routledge, 2012.
Stiegler, Bernard. *Symbolic Misery*. Vol 1. Cambridge: Polity, 2014.
Strathern, Marilyn. *The Gender of the Gift*. Berkeley: University of California Press, 1988.
Sudbury, Julia, ed. *Global Lockdown: Race, Gender, and the Prison-Industrial Complex*. New York: Routledge, 2005.
Tadiar, Neferti X. M. "Domestic Bodies of the Philippines." *Sojourn: Journal of Social Issues in Southeast Asia* 12, no. 2 (1997): 153–91.
Tadiar, Neferti X. M. *Fantasy-Production: Sexual Economies and Other Philippine Consequences for the New World Order*. Hong Kong: Hong Kong University Press, 2004.
Tadiar, Neferti X. M. "If Not Mere Metaphor . . . Sexual Economies Revisited." *Scholar and Feminist Online* 7, no. 3 (2009). http://barnard.edu/sfonline/sexecon/tadiar_01.htm.

Tadiar, Neferti X. M. "Manila's New Metropolitan Form." *differences: A Journal of Feminist Cultural Studies* 5, no. 3 (1993): 154–78.

Tadiar, Neferti X. M. "Metropolitan Life and Uncivil Death." *PMLA* 122, no. 1 (2007): 316–20.

Tadiar Neferti X. M. "Remaindered Life of Citizen-Man, Medium of Democracy." *Southeast Asian Studies* 49, no. 3 (2011): 118–48.

Tadiar, Neferti X. M. *Things Fall Away: Philippine Historical Experience and the Makings of Globalization*. Durham, NC: Duke University Press, 2009.

Tadiar, Neferti X. M. "The War to Be Human/Becoming Human in a Time of War." In *The Color of Violence: The Incite Anthology*, edited by Incite! Women of Color against Violence, 92–96. Cambridge, MA: South End Press, 2006.

Tang, Eric. *Unsettled: Cambodian Refugees in the New York City Hyperghetto*. Philadelphia: Temple University Press, 2015.

Tawil-Souri, Helga. "Digital Occupation: Gaza's High-Tech Enclosure." *Journal of Palestine Studies* 41, no. 2 (2012): 27–43.

Tawil-Souri, Helga, and Miriyam Aouragh. "Intifada 3.0? Cyber Colonialism and Palestinian Resistance." *Arab Studies Journal* 22, no. 1 (2014): 102–33.

Taylor, Keeanga-Yamahtta. *From #BlackLivesMatter to Black Liberation*. Chicago: Haymarket Books, 2016.

Terranova, Tiziana. *Network Culture: Politics for the Information Age*. London: Pluto Press, 2004.

Thompson, Lanny. *Imperial Archipelago: Representation and Rule in the Insular Territories under U.S. Dominion after 1898*. Honolulu: University of Hawai'i Press, 2010.

Ticktin, Miriam. *Casualties of Care: Immigration and the Politics of Humanitarianism in France*. Berkeley: University of California Press, 2011.

Todorov, Tzvetan. *The Conquest of America: The Question of the Other*. New York: Harper and Row, 1984.

Toscano, Alberto. "The World Is Already without Us." *Social Text* 34, no. 2 (2016): 109–24.

Truong, Thanh-Dam. *Sex, Money and Morality: Prostitution and Tourism in Southeast Asia*. London: Zed, 1990.

Tsing, Anna Lowenhaupt. *The Mushroom at the End of the World: Life in Capitalist Ruins*. Princeton, NJ: Princeton University Press, 2015.

Tyner, James A. *The Business of War: Workers, Warriors and Hostages in Occupied Iraq*. London: Taylor and Francis, 2017.

Villarama, Baby Ruth, dir. *Sunday Beauty Queen*. Mandaluyong City, Philippines: Voyage Studios, 2016.

Virno, Paulo. *A Grammar of the Multitude: For an Analysis of Contemporary Forms of Life*. Translated by Isabella Bertoletti, James Casciato, and Andrea Casson. Los Angeles: Semiotext(e), 2004.

Vitug, Marites Dañguilan, and Glenda M. Gloria. *Under the Crescent Moon: Rebellion in Mindanao*. Quezon City, Philippines: Ateneo Center for Social Policy and Public Affairs and Institute for Popular Democracy, 2000.

Von Werlhof, Claudia. "On the Concept of Nature and Society in Capitalism." In Mies, Bennholdt-Thomsen, and Von Werlhof, *Women: The Last Colony*, 96–112.

Von Werlhof, Claudia. "Women's Work: The Blind Spot in the Critique of Political Economy." In Mies, Bennholdt-Thomsen, and Von Werlhof, *Women: The Last Colony*, 13–26.

Vora, Kalindi. *Life Support: Biocapital and the New History of Outsourced Labor*. Minneapolis: University of Minnesota Press, 2015.

Vora, Kalindi. "Limits of 'Labor': Accounting for Affect and the Biological in Transnational Surrogacy and Service Work." *South Atlantic Quarterly* 111, no. 4 (2012): 681–700.

Wagner, Roy. "The Fractal Person." In *Big Men and Great Men: Personifications of Power in Melanesia*, edited by Maurice Godelier and Marilyn Strathern, 159–73. Cambridge: Cambridge University Press, 1991.

Wang Hui. "Jia Zhangke's World and China's Great Transformations: A Revised Version of a Speech Given at 'The *Still Life* Symposium' at Fenyang High School." *positions* 19, no. 1 (2009): 217–28.

Warburg, Anna Braemer, and Steffen Jensen. "Policing the War on Drugs and the Transformation of Urban Space in Manila." *Environment and Planning D: Society and Space* 38, no. 3 (2020): 399–416.

Watanabe, Makiko, Sadao Takaoka, Wataru Morishima, Nobuo Sakagami, Mario Collado, and Takashi Oguchi. "Vegetation Succession and Land Recovery Process Based on Soil Properties in the Upper Mt. Pinatubo, the Philippines." *Chigaku Zasshi Journal of Geography* 120, no. 4 (2011): 631–45.

Weerasethakul, Apichatpong, dir. *Cemetery of Splendour*. Bangkok: Kick the Machine Films, 2015.

Weheliye, Alexander G. *Habeas Viscus: Racializing Assemblages, Biopolitics, and Black Feminist Theories of the Human*. Durham, NC: Duke University Press, 2014.

Weiner, Annette B. *Inalienable Possessions: The Paradox of Keeping-While-Giving*. Berkeley: University of California Press, 1992.

Weizman, Eyal. *The Least of All Possible Evils: Humanitarian Violence from Arendt to Gaza*. New York: Verso, 2011.

White, Ben. *Palestinians in Israel: Segregation, Discrimination, and Democracy*. London: Pluto , 2012.

Williams, John. "Space, Scale and Just War: Meeting the Challenge of Humanitarian Intervention and Trans-national Terrorism." *Review of International Studies* 34 (2008): 581–600.

Williams, Raymond. "Culture." In Williams, *Marxism and Literature*, 11–20.

Williams, Raymond. *Marxism and Literature*. New York: Oxford University Press, 2009.

Williams, William Apple. *Empire as a Way of Life: An Essay on the Causes and Character of America's Present Predicament, along with a Few Thoughts about an Alternative*. New York: Oxford University Press, 1980.

Willse, Craig. *The Value of Homelessness: Managing Surplus Life*. Minneapolis: University of Minnesota Press, 2015.

Wolfe, Patrick. "Settler Colonialism and the Elimination of the Native." *Journal of Genocide Research* 8, no. 4 (2006): 387–409.

Wood, Ellen Meiksins. *Empire of Capital*. London: Verso, 2005.

Wright, Melissa W. *Disposable Women and Other Myths of Global Capitalism*. New York: Routledge, 2006.

Wright, Melissa W. "Gentrification, Assassination and Forgetting in Mexico: A Feminist Marxist Tale." *Gender, Place and Culture* 21, no. 1 (2014): 1–16.

Wynter, Sylvia. "No Humans Involved: An Open Letter to My Colleagues." *Forum NHI: Knowledge for the Twenty-First Century* 1, no. 1 (1994): 42–71.

Wynter, Sylvia. "Unsettling the Coloniality of Being/Power/Truth/Freedom: Towards the Human, after Man, Its Overrepresentation—An Argument." *CR: The New Centennial Review* 3, no. 4 (2003): 257–337.

Yean, Soon Chuan. *Tulong: An Articulation of Politics in the Christian Philippines*. Manila: University of Santo Tomas Publishing House, 2015.

Yuval-Davis, Nira. *Gender and Nation*. London: Sage, 1997.

Zhang Xudong. "Poetics of Vanishing: The Films of Jia Zhangke." *New Left Review*, no. 63 (2010): 71–88.

Zinn, Howard. *A People's History of the United States: 1492–Present*. London: Taylor and Francis, 2013.

INDEX

abidance, 77, 135–36
abolition: Angela Davis on, 68–69; prison, 7, 15, 200; and technical objects, 341n43; of slavery, 46, 206
abolitionism: colonial logic of, 8, 181–82; and migrant domestic workers, 174, 361n16
abstraction: artistic, 79; as desocialization, 255; labor and, 91, 349n14, 378n9; quantitative, 282, 286; of time, 110, 120; value and, 44, 221, 216
academic freedom, 199–200, 365n3, 370n63
Acayan, Ezra, 262, 270, 298
addiction. *See* drug users
Adem, Elisea, 290
Adorno, Theodor, 304, 309, 314–15, 383n3
adulthood, 191
aesthetics: cinematic, 110, 115, 123–24, 128–31, 134–35, 356n24; of circulation, 177, 305, 313; of Duterte regime, 264–65; of remaindered life, 274–75, 313–14; of separation of server and served, 176–77; of social reproduction, 70, 89, 99; of splendor, 275. *See also* art; realism
Aeta people, 320, 322, 325–26
Afghanistan, 5, 58
after economy, 215
agency: eurocentric views of, 181–82, 258, 275–76, 362n25; "help" and, 249; law as, 15; of nonhuman nature, 317; posthumanism and, 381n28; servitude and, 184–85, 361n9, 362n27; of postcolonial nation-states, 372n19; of urban poor, 293
Aguilar, Miko, 239, 242–43
algorithms: humanism as, 14; colonialism as, 47; racism as, 308–9; social media, 219–20; and state violence, 26, 217–19, 227, 255–56, 282
Amar, Paul, 210
Ampatuan, Andal, 74, 80–81

antitrafficking campaigns, 174, 182
Aquino, Corazon, 153, 231
arbitrageur, 111, 216, 232
archipelago: imperial, 343n50; security, 210, 233; of slums, 366n18; urban, 26, 141, 148–52, 167, 284, 316
Arendt, Hannah, 12, 17–18, 180, 308, 339n21, 340n28
Arroyo, Gloria Macapagal, 8–9, 74, 143, 154, 165, 232, 307, 311, 366n29
arson, 280–81
art: modern, 304, 314, 378n16, 379n17, 383n3; waste as, 258–60, 315, 377n5; world, 79, 271, 309, 383n8. *See also* Dalena, Kiri; Dy, Jason; Garcellano, Lyra; RESBAK
Arumpac, Adjani: *Nanay Mameng*, 276–78; *War Is a Tender Thing*, 318
Asad, Talal, 13, 15, 336n16
Asia-Pacific region: capitalist development in, 60, 130, 206; Philippines as US platform in, 208, 210–11; sexual economies of, 46
associated milieu, 37, 287, 360n61. *See also* milieus
Atlantiques (Diop), 167
"at-risk" populations, 96, 112–13, 115
attention economy, 50, 79, 135, 137, 262, 330, 383n8
Augustine, Saint, 230
authoritarian modernization, 17–18, 147, 281

bailouts, 39, 118
bakla, 163, 272–74, 278, 294
Balinkbayan, 185
bare life, 77, 102, 115, 137, 247, 337n35, 350n44
Barker, Joanne, 38–40, 342n50, 368n50
Barrett, Lindon, 53, 345n13
Barrios, Joi, 16–17
Bataille, Georges, 259
Baudrillard, Jean, 259, 378n6, 378n16

Bauman, Zygmunt, 257
Bazin, André, 128
beauty pageants, 272–73
becoming-human, 5–7, 15–17; agency of, 184; after decolonization, 21, 331, 372n19; attaining status of already human, 177; geopolitical claims of, 212; Indigeneity and, 326, 342n46; killings and, 9; and liberal democracy, 20, 204, 222; milieu of capitalism provided by, 55–57; and neoliberal temporality, 137–38; remaindered life-making practices of, 14, 68–70, 274, 278, 331; as vital infrastructure, 63–64; and vital platforms, 65, 291
Beller, Jonathan, 217, 248, 369n51
Benanav, Aaron, 92–93
biopolitics, 43, 45, 68, 105, 130; of development aid, 60; disposable life beyond, 101–2; geopolitics and, 116; humanity and, 17; labor and, 90–95; of national debt, 353n25; and remaindered life, 102–3, 115
Black radical tradition, 67, 200
bodies: as infrastructure, 160; versus life-times, 215; in Marcos's counterinsurgency, 247; as power signs, 247–49; racialization and sexualization of, 177, 180, 364n51; representation of, 81, 260, 262–63, 311; value extracted from, 252, 254, 285; in the war on drugs, 222, 231, 238, 245, 264; work and, 64, 163–64, 286
borders, 27, 54, 58, 61, 93, 96, 183; in art, 302–5, 315; in cities, 167, 279–80; of citizen humanity, 26, 98–99; of Israel, 224, 227; US-Mexico, 10–11, 15, 97, 100, 297, 317
Brown, Wendy, 111
"Build, Build, Build," 41, 240, 322
Burns, Lucy, 274
buryong, 166, 313
Bush, George W., 8, 31, 209
business process outsourcing (BPO), 207
bypass, 167–69, 171, 305, 307, 311–12, 384n17; franchised rights to, 156; in transportation infrastructure, 143, 150, 380n17

Cajipe-Endaya, Imelda, 9
capitalism: as addiction, 247; binary oppositions and, 335n8; bourgeois humanism of, 49–52; crony, 105, 251, 253, 351n58, 355n20; culture and, 304–306, 313; and dead bodies, 248; disaster, 58; end of, 108; equality and freedom under, 202–4, 221; financial, 87–89, 104, 113–14, 238, 350n44; formal subsumption under, 101, 103; imperialism and, 32–36, 43–44, 60–61; innovation valorized under, 275–76; kinship and, 253, 376n58; land appropriation under, 115–16, 345n9; life and, 6–8, 10–11, 14, 138, 179, 295–96, 324–25; Marx on, 13, 336n24; Luxemburg on, 35–37, 44, 57, 287, 341n33, 341nn37–39, 342n47, 352n16; noncapitalist milieus of, 51, 55–57, 65, 181, 184, 342n46, 353n23; platform, 340n29, 381n25; post-Fordist, 89–91; postindustrial, 24, 29, 360n61; sex-gender and race codes of, 45–48, 180, 187, 244, 307; and social media, 250; social reproduction under, 62–63, 70–71, 185–86, 297; and vital platforms, 65–66; and violent dispossession, 24–27; waste exploited by, 27–33, 263
capital punishment, 26, 196, 237, 291, 307; border policing as, 15; demolition as, 281; under Duterte, 33, 231, 237, 247
Care Divas, 278
Casimiro, Linda, 133, 136
Cemetery of Splendor (Weerasethakul), 311
Central Intelligence Agency (CIA), 247, 371n10
Césaire, Aimé, 5, 225, 307
Chatterjee, Indrani, 181–82
Cherniavsky, Eva, 213
Chico River dam project, 40–42, 343n65
China: cinema of, 110, 121, 123–26, 364n8; and the Philippines, 41, 119, 130–31, 208; as rising global power, 24, 131, 353n23; rural workers in, 119; "unskilled" labor in, 91; urbanization in, 117
Christianity, 5, 8, 45, 50, 55, 181–82, 374n35; artistic allusions to, 263; Duterte and, 242; and financialized subjectivity, 111; justice in, 230, 326; and migrant workers, 264; transphobia in, 292–93; Zionism and, 224, 346n34
cinema: of China and the Philippines, 110, 115, 356n24; of Kiri Dalena, 73–74, 80–83; as financial speculation, 137; Global South cities as, 145; of Jia Zhangke, 123–29, 134–35, 354nn8–10; landscapes in, 315–18; of Brillante Mendoza, 129, 131–36, 356n27, 375n50; of remaindered life, 313; and surplus populations, 121; surplus value, 82, 316; of urban poverty, 382n36; violence and, 262

circulation: as aesthetic, 177, 313; congestion blocking, 167; of dead bodies, 248, 264; derivatives and, 238; of disposable life, 118, 183, 291; fines and, 26, 244; highways and, 143, 145, 154, 384n17; Marx on, 356n26, 358n34; military and, 346n31; of money, 113–14, 133; and service work, 184, 187, 189, 193, 207; temporality of, 311; and urban stratification, 162, 177, 246, 260, 286–87; as value productive, 63, 71, 88–89, 144, 155–56, 159, 305, 358n26; and vital infrastructures, 160–61, 169, 195

citizenship: capital life and, 94, 113, 204, 217, 287; decolonization and, 206; gender and, 12–13, 16; globopolitical, 6, 17, 62, 66, 164–65, 217, 279; exchange rates and, 178, 189; and the "free world," 212; Israeli, 368n44, 369n59; migration and, 95–99, 119, 158, 167, 174, 291, 359n37; money and, 353n33; neoliberalism and, 10, 65, 111, 136–37, 213; and racial subjection, 25–27, 200–201; security promised to, 233, 235, 237; and servitude, 176, 309; traffickers and, 183; and US military, 156–56, 367n33

city emulants, 148–52; foreign investment in, 155; as franchises, 156; and slum demolition, 284; US military bases redeveloped as, 153–54

Ciudad Juárez, 10, 297–98

civility, 370n63

coding, 42–47, 51, 344n81, 381n28; humanism and, 11; of value, 344n81, 381n28. *See also* algorithms; sex-gender and race codes

coin, 53, 99, 147, 164–65; drug users as socially dead, 255; exchanged for life, 133–34. *See also* currency

Cold War: counterinsurgency and, 8, 31–32, 201–2, 232, 234, 247, 287; closure of China during, 130; decolonization and, 18, 30; development and, 60, 233; and US-Philippines "special relationship," 206–11, 355n21; and war on drugs, 236

collateral: and Indigenous dispossession, 39; land as, 316; migrant workers' lives as, 98, 171; national population as, 353n25; surplus populations as, 99–100, 118, 154

collateral damage, 154, 218–19

colonialism: agents of, 30–31; art and, 265, 384n18; as coding operation, 44–47, 51–52, 90–91, 381n28; drugs and, 374n36; franchises and, 152, 357n17; Galeano on, 52–53; humanitarianism as, 19, 174; humanity and, 5–8, 13–14, 50; Indigenous dispossession under, 38–40, 106–7, 234, 322–23; Israeli, 203, 217–18, 221, 278, 342n46, 368n44, 369n59; "just wars" of, 229–30, 236–37, 374n35; Luxemburg on, 35–37, 287, 341n37, 341n39; and non-Western social reproduction, 34–35, 181, 297; and postcolonial states, 343n58, 351n58, 358n28, 372n19; punitive logic of, 25, 230, 245, 374n42; racism and, 54, 177, 307–309, 340n24; servitude and, 157–58, 180, 183, 296, 359n36, 362n27; temporalities of, 66–67, 275–76; and urban fires, 295; waste and, 257–59. *See also* counterinsurgency; decolonization; imperialism

commodity: art as, 79, 304; cinema as, 82, 110, 135, 354n12; discourse and, 344; fetishism of, 180; financialization and, 215, 217; and gift economy, 251; identity as, 101; land as, 316, 345n9; life as, 51–53, 71, 93, 115, 158, 244, 281, 347n50, 348n51; reproduction and, 11, 46, 57, 352n16, 362n26; time as, 166; versus human, 49–50

communism, 60, 130–31, 208, 212, 214, 245, 247, 255

consumerism, 378n6

Cooper, Melinda, 113, 115–16, 340n26, 340n28, 368n49

Cordillera Range, 40–43, 229–30, 343n65

Coronel, Sheila, 237

corporations, 39–40, 58, 62, 114, 146, 149; as franchises, 152–53, 156, 357n18; kinship and, 253; as juridical subjects, 212, 342n53

Costa, Bryan, 283

counterinsurgency: under Arroyo, 73, 154, 232; capitalist exploitation of, 30–35, 58, 222; colonial history of, 8, 339n22, 374n42; and "democracy promotion," 201–2, 211; developmentalism and, 17–18, 33, 60, 234–35, 247–48; and informal economy, 18–19; legality and, 15; neoliberalism and, 213; Philippines as US base for, 207, 213, 232; policing and, 26, 244, 255, 309, 372n18; representation of, 262, 287; slavery and, 68; and war on drugs, 236

Index • 413

criminality: of drug users, 236, 247, 255, 264, 285; and hate crimes, 366n16; of human traffickers, 182–83; of idleness, 365n15; in informal economy, 59, 164, 171, 287; legality and, 15, 205, 212, 355n5; in Brillante Mendoza's films, 133; slavery and, 180, 182, 365n15; under Spanish colonialism, 230, 245, 374nn34–35; of state actors, 19, 80, 231–32, 253–54; and "tough-on-crime" policies, 233, 246, 368n46; urban, 279, 282; value extraction from, 26–27, 47, 54, 100, 215–16, 369n60. *See also* policing; prisons; punishment

crowdsourcing, 89, 233

culture: capitalism and 304–5, 313; as cultivation, 314; humanization and, 362n27; *jueteng* as, 103; liberal ideal of, 151; national, 190; posthumanism and, 381n28; serial, 213; subaltern life-making as 69–70; versus nature, 180, 275, 335n8, 345n15

Cura, Faye, 271

currency: crypto-, 147; detainees as, 95; devaluations of, 118, 120, 129, 194, 260; drug users as desocialized, 255; exchanges between, 32, 97, 170–71, 178, 164, 189; hard versus soft, 53, 121, 165, 185, 188–89, 306; human social capacities as, 106; in informal economy, 288; law and, 353n33; life, 183, 378n6; petty, 99–100, 103, 133, 375n50; as power sign, 239

Daddy Digong (*Tatay Digong*), 242

Dalena, Kiri, 75–76, 256, 298, 314, 318; activism in work of, 78–79, 267–69; radical bereavement in work of, 74, 77; in Southern Tagalog Exposure, 73–74; *Requiem for M*, 80–83; *Tungkung Langit*, 309, 311

Darwish, Mahmoud, 227

Davao, 233–35, 249, 372n18

Davis, Angela, 25, 59, 68, 200, 341n39

dead exchanges, 203, 221–22, 249, 256, 265, 278

Debord, Guy, 110, 145, 354n7, 354n12, 355n18

debt: bondage, 105–106, 350n54, 362n22, 369n60; growth fueled by, 43, 117, 129, 154, 211; kinship and, 375; of migrant workers, 98–99, 171, 187–99, 293; national, 54–55, 353n25; in postcolonies, 66; and surplus life, 92–93, 118, 252, 350n44; as time of others, 120

de Chavez, Heart, 292–95

decolonization, 18–19; becoming-human and, 20–21; capitalism shaped by, 23, 29–30, 62–63, 116, 222, 290; derivatives and, 216; humanism and, 5–6, 338n1; as insurgency, 203; as ongoing struggle, 108, 276; and remaindered life, 331

dehumanization, 9–14; Arendt on, 17–18; and European bourgeois humanism, 5, 49–50, 181; of Palestinians, 217–18; punishment and, 244–45; under slavery, 68–69, 177, 339n21; versus subaltern life-making, 296; in war on drugs, 196, 255, 263–64, 285–86, 293–94, 373n3; of war to be human, 8

de Leon, Jason, 317

democracy: and academic freedom, 199; citizenship and, 94, 98, 213; and colonial codes, 47; versus demographics, 217, 368n50; Duterte and, 232–33, 248, 251, 264; finance and, 88, 105, 215, 241; humanity and, 3–5, 47; imperialism and, 13, 19–20, 31, 66, 153, 202, 214; and Indigenous dispossession, 40; and "just wars," 230; and life worth living, 62; and national subjectification, 212; and Palestinian dispossession, 203, 223–24, 342n46; Philippines as symbol of, 104, 206, 209–11, 358n28; prisons and, 25–26, 200–201, 212; rejection of, 3, 222; and remaindered life, 103; as stratified social order, 9, 16, 150; surplus populations of, 99, 204; terrorism and, 231

demographics, 217–20, 222, 227, 248, 282

demolition: in Chinese development, 124–25; of Indigenous monuments, 43; of Manila during World War II, 321; of Palestinian homes, 219, 224, 227; of slums, 247, 280–84, 290, 295

Dent, Gina, 25–26

dependency theory, 54

derivatives, 215, 220, 254; in art, 267, 313, 384n18; *diskarte* as practice of, 104; as "money after decolonization," 216; persons as, 288, 381n26, 381n28; policing and, 26, 222, 227, 237–39, 251, 254, 293; social logics of, 65–66; of war, 61; waste and, 28–29, 32, 217, 260, 263

De Soto Polar, Hernando, 165

detention centers, 27, 208, 215, 225, 306, 346n27; labor versus waste in, 58–59, 61, 95–96; modernity and, 257; servitude in, 196; slums as, 166. *See also* prison

Deunida, Carmen, 276–77

development: agrarian reform and, 118; in China, 124; and Cold War, 19, 60, 210–11; counterinsurgency and, 17–18, 33, 60–61, 234–35, 247–48; in dependency theory, 54; export-oriented, 117, 129, 207, 355n20; and Indigenous dispossession, 40–42; in Operaismo, 101; and sexual economies, 46, 55; urban, 143–44, 147–49, 284, 321, 356n8; and US military bases, 153–54, 322

Diop, Mati, 167

disappearance: in Ciudad Juárez, 10; and disposable life, 7, 127; liquidity and, 134, 171, 356n26; of Indigenous peoples, 39–40, 118, 227; in Maguindanao massacre, 81; in Philippine history, 154, 231–32, 247, 262; of noncapitalist social formations, 38, 43–44, 342n46; poetics of, 124; racism and 309; representation of, 73–74, 79–80, 306–7, 314; of slum communities, 290; survival against, 67

disenfranchisement, 158; agency and, 361n9, 362n27; drug users embody, 245; gendered and racialized, 12, 16; and informal economy, 216; legal, 204–5; liquidity and, 165, 183; predation and, 183, 251; in prisons, 26, 56, 200–201; servitude and, 193, 196; urban, 166, 289–90; weakens social connections, 254

diskarte (resourcefulness), 103–4, 135, 290, 313

disposable life: in art, 260, 268, 271, 274; "at-risk" populations as, 96; as biogenetic material, 27, 101, 217, 368n50–369n51; versus capital life, 62, 91, 114–15, 156; in cinema, 82, 124–27, 129, 135–36; in cities, 141, 161, 164–65, 167, 171, 246, 281; as culture, 70–71; financialization of, 118–21, 215, 239–40, 260, 350n44; gendered and racialized, 10–11, 26, 28–29, 47–48, 52–53, 244, 308, 364n51; humanitarianism and, 258; humanity and, 4, 21, 51, 196, 286–87, 313; land and, 316, 326; in media, 262, 293; Palestinians as, 224; versus remaindered life, 14, 69, 71, 97, 105, 330; and rule of law, 16, 205; serviceable labor produced by, 194; servitude as, 55, 176; and social reproduction, 65, 67, 102–3, 130, 179, 184–85, 211; surplus populations as, 92–93, 119; temporality of, 100, 137–38, 338n1; value and, 6–7, 94; war and, 33, 61, 222, 233–34, 237, 290

dividuality, 64–66, 252, 288, 376n51, 381n26; posthumanism and, 381n28; in vital platforms, 250, 270, 297

Doctor, Bam, 265–66

domestic labor: anti-eurocentric genealogy of, 181–82; gendered and racialized, 10–11, 46–47, 54–55, 96, 180, 190–91, 359n36; humanity and, 9, 16, 287; imperialism and, 56, 61–62; intimacy of, 278; itinerancy of, 289; kinship and, 186, 193, 251, 253, 376n58; as life-time rather than labor-time, 114, 98–99, 347n50; as machinery, 10, 158–59, 170, 286; as Philippine export, 173–75, 207; versus servile labor, 176, 361n10; social enjoyment among, 178–79; "utility men" performing, 187; wage labor subsidized by, 353n31

drivers, 98, 163, 168, 246

drones, 211, 213, 220, 371n10

drug users: in cinema, 133; dead bodies of, 231, 236, 248, 263; excluded from humanity, 244–45, 255, 263–65, 285, 373n33; *kunsintidor* (enabler) of, 252, 376n55; liberated from freedom, 247; as participants in drug war, 239; service workers as, 246

Dulag, Macli-ing, 41, 43

Dunbar-Ortiz, Roxanne, 15, 24

Duterte, Rodrigo: aesthetics of, 264, 273, 374n33; artists' resistance to, 242–43, 260, 263, 265–71, 283; as Davao mayor, 233–34; and Indigenous peoples, 40, 326; "just war" waged by, 229–30; law under, 19, 248–49, 337n30; media coverage of, 231; Netanyahu's relationship with, 211–12, 222; as product of international politics, 232–33, 236–37; support for, 135, 196, 240–42, 249–50, 284–85, 373n31, 375n50; on transwomen, 373n32. *See also* war on drugs

Dy, Jason, 242–43, 263

earthquakes, 319–20, 385n28

East Jerusalem, 223–26

ecology. *See* environment; nature

Elyachar, Julia, 160–61

Index • 415

enclosures, 18, 33, 147, 274, 295, 343n68, 366n20; cultural, 70, 77, 309; of rights, 99; urban 161, 282. *See also* primitive accumulation

encoding. *See* algorithms; coding systems

encomienda system, 46, 55, 152

energy: fire as, 383n43; infrastructure, 40–42, 61, 145–46, 162, 219, 280; vital, 246, 250, 355n23; waste as, 32, 259–60

enfranchised, 26, 69, 95, 99, 162, 170, 177, 204, 221, 223, 246, 286. *See also* disenfranchisement; franchise

entrepreneurship: and affective labor, 361n9; cities and, 155–56; and financial inclusion, 165; in humanitarianism, 377n4; of life, 91, 94, 98; Marx and, 358n34; of migrant workers, 171, 185; as neoliberal subjectivity, 50, 96, 110–12, 115, 120, 130, 217; and state violence, 19, 237; of urban poor, 216

environment: as agent, 317; in art, 318; capitalism and, 37; defenders of, 43–44; devastation of, 28, 32, 34, 280, 283; disposable life-times etched in, 316; of dispossessed, 205; foreign investment in, 60–61; Pinatubo's eruption impacts, 318–20; sustainability and, 258–59; talahib and, 323–25. *See also* land; landscape; nature

Estrada, Joseph, 104, 165, 371n9

Evangelista, Patricia, 248, 292–93, 382n41

evictions: in Cairo, 160–61; in Palestine, 223–26, 370n71; in Philippines, 150, 281–82, 290

exchange rates, 170–71, 178, 189; of labor reproduction, 119; of life-times, 97, 100, 120–21, 133–34, 164, 182–83, 185, 188, 255

expanded reproduction of capital: and globopolitical life, 62, 281; and land appropriation, 116; late imperialism as, 24, 32–36, 214; and noncapitalist social formations, 57–58, 63–65, 287, 341n38; servitude as condition of, 189, 193, 196; surplus populations required for, 92; and urban demolition, 281

expendable life. *See* disposable life

export-oriented industrialization, 117, 129, 207, 355n20

expressways, 143–45, 153

extrajudicial killings, 231–32; under Arroyo, 8, 77, 154, 306–7, 311; artists' resistance to, 260–63, 265–69, 272–74, 307; and devaluation of urban poor, 254–55; under Duterte, 33, 54, 222, 233, 235–40, 249, 376n55; in Israel, 367n38; in Maguindanao massacre, 80–83; under Marcos, 247; transphobia and, 292–93; in the United States, 201

Facebook: Duterte and, 249–50, 375n48; Filipino users of, 291; moderation of "hate speech" on, 370n63; political resistance on, 267, 272

family. *See* kinship

fascism, 47, 221, 241, 264

fate playing, 97, 100–101, 105, 107–8, 171; with atmosphere and environment, 317–18; and remaindered life, 103, 298, 331

Federici, Silvia, 43, 98, 118–19, 345n15, 366n20

feminism: in anthropology, 288; of artists, 271; Duterte campaign on, 373n32; on femicide in Ciudad Juárez, 297; history and, 66–67; and human rights, 11–13; imperialism and, 44, 57, 182, 201, 244, 336n17; labor and, 9–10, 34, 187, 297, 341n39, 361n9, 363n35

feminization, 10, 34, 187, 284, 342n47; of industrial labor, 46, 363n36; as racializing process, 180; servitude as, 54–55, 96, 190, 244–45, 264

Ferguson, Missouri, 26, 338n8

film. *See* cinema

financialization, 87–89, 115–17; cinema and, 110, 126; discursive, 221; "inclusion" and, 147, 164–65; of life, 51, 91, 120–21, 137, 350n44; punishment and, 237–39, 248, 254; and security wars, 196, 227; servitude and, 185; and social media, 220; and social reproduction, 6; waste and, 260 and urban policy, 28–29, 154–55, 161, 241, 339n15. *See also* derivatives

fines, 26, 225, 338n8

fires, 295, 383n43; agricultural use of, 325; in Manila, 280–81, 283

fixers, 97–98, 103, 165, 182, 238, 324, 364n49; police as, 253–54

flight, 102–3, 105–7, 196, 241, 351n59

Flint, Michigan, 28–29

flyovers, 143, 147–48, 248, 284, 380n17

416 • Index

force of production: culture as, 304; nature as, 52, 345n9; punishment as, 27; subaltern, 294
Fordism, 88–89. *See also* post-Fordism
foreign aid, 54–55, 60, 234, 350n54
foreign direct investment, 155, 240
Foucault, Michel, 96, 110–11, 113; Melinda Cooper on, 115–16
fractal, 5, 28, 359n56; persons as, 381n28; expansion of state violence, 255–56; urban expansion as, 146, 148, 150–52, 305
franchise, 152, 357nn17–18; city emulants as, 156, 380n17; disenfranchisement and, 165; in encomienda system, 55; freedom as, 20; Philippines as, 358n28; prisons as, 59; security state as, 306; servitude and, 193; of state violence, 33
Francisco-Menchavez, Valerie, 291
freedom: academic, 199–200, 365n3, 370n63; addiction and, 247; Arendt on, 17–18, 337n36, 345n15; as *casus belli*, 19; as dead exchange, 203, 221–22; as eurocentric ideal, 181; executed by law, 204–5; flesh as site of, 337n39; franchises and, 20, 152, 156, 357n18; and globopolitical humanity, 3, 11, 14, 233, 240; as ideological-practical code, 209; imperialism and, 8, 116, 200–202, 210–12, 374n35; innovation as, 275; in liberal feminism, 12, 336n17; Marx on, 13, 158, 202–203, 336n24, 358n33, 365n12; and migrant labor, 119, 359n37; Palestine and, 218–19, 223, 226; and Philippine democracy-making, 206–207; prisons and, 25–26; of remaindered life as practice of, 78, 105; slavery and, 68–69, 174
freeport zones, 153–54, 209, 233, 322
funerals, 79–80, 82, 270, 285, 298; extortion and, 238, 252; transphobia in, 292–93

Galam, Roderick, 187–88, 190–91
Galeano, Eduardo, 52–54
Garcellano, Lyra, 304, 308–9, 315, 318; *Short Stories*, 306–307; *Sleepwalk*, 310–11; *Sweep*, 301–3, 305–7, 314
Gaza, 54, 58, 215, 217–18
gender. *See* sex-gender and race codes
general intellect, 90, 99
Gidwani, Vinay, 27–28, 32, 54, 339n14, 339n18

gift, 41, 127, 254, 256, 294; economy, 64, 251, 288; gendered and racialized, 244; remaindered life as, 331; servitude and, 191, 193; words and images as, 270–71, 278
Gilmore, Ruth Wilson, 29, 98
Global Database of Events, Language, and Tone (GDELT), 220
globalization, 23–24, 109; cities and, 143, 164, 233, 281, 290; citizenship and, 94; gender and, 284, 380n16; maquiladoras and, 297; and migrant workers, 11, 180; plural histories of, 101; prisons and, 341n39; representations of, 306; of reproductive labor, 16, 55, 194; smugglers and, 182; and US hegemony, 15, 201, 232. *See also* globopolis
Global South, 18; artists and filmmakers of, 314, 316–17, 384n18; cities in, 145, 160, 162, 164–65; destruction of life in, 34, 44, 262; kinship in, 253; life-making and, 31, 61–62, 114, 313; migration from, 7, 189; neoliberalism and, 117, 136–37; numerical representation of, 282
globopolis, 99; citizenship in, 6, 17, 62, 66, 165, 183, 217, 368n44; culture and, 313; development and, 141; disenfranchisement in, 158; Duterte and, 233, 240, 291; Filipinos in, 241; franchises of, 156; as "free world," 212; future of, 329; servility versus servitude in, 176; slums beyond, 279, 281; vital infrastructure and, 287, 360n61; war and, 209, 222, 224; and war on drugs, 246
governmentality, 109, 112, 115, 213, 232, 307, 336n16, 370n63
Guantánamo Bay, 208
Guyer, Jane, 111, 351n55, 353n33

Hartman, Saidiya, 200, 364n51
"help" (*tulong*), 191–93, 249, 294, 296, 332–33, 374n44; exploited by police, 251, 375n50; as unpaid labor, 187–88; words and images as, 270–71
highways, 142–48, 153, 318, 321–22; facilitating state violence, 154
homelessness, 29, 259, 307, 315, 377n4; in Palestine, 224; and urban demolition, 282
Hong Kong, 130, 146, 153, 177–78, 186
hukou system, 119
human capital, 110–14, 287, 361n9

humanity, 11–14; abolitionism and, 174, 181–82; as capitalist, 44, 298; citizenship and, 25, 98–99, 183; colonialism and, 5–6, 35, 40, 47, 275, 342n46, 374n35; culture and, 313; defined against drug users, 245–46, 255, 285, 374n36; as freedom from servitude, 240; gendered and racialized, 244; and "humanizing" stories, 286–87, 294; and images of death, 262–63; Jia Zhangke on, 128; legal recognition of, 42–43; as life-form of value, 49–52; of migrant reproductive workers, 174, 291; nationality and, 196, 212; and numerical representation, 282–83; and Palestinian dispossession, 224–25; queerness and, 274; and remaindered life, 67–72; Simondon on, 341n43; and stateless people, 308; urban, 141, 161, 165; waning belief in, 3–4; waste as abjected part of, 258; and work/labor distinction, 180, 345n15. *See also* dehumanization; human media; posthumanism

humanitarianism, 7, 11–12; in the arts, 258–59; becoming-human and, 17; and human trafficking, 174, 182; imperialism and, 19, 60, 201, 210, 214, 230; in Palestine, 218; as vital systems projects, 61; UNHCR and, 377n4

human media, 157–58, 168, 176, 184–85, 296

human rights, 11–13, 337n29; Duterte's condemnation of, 373n32; emergence of, 9; versus security, 218; temporality of, 3–4, 101; violations of, 73–74, 233, 337n30, 369n60; and US imperialism, 18, 206, 335n16

human trafficking, 24, 93, 183, 187, 202, 359n36, 363n37; humanitarian campaigns against, 174, 182

identity: capitalism and, 185; and expendable urban life, 246; national, 212; of migrant workers, 119; and settler colonialism, 217–18; value and, 46, 113, 193, 353n31, 364n49; versus vital platforms, 288–89, 291–92, 294, 296–97

idling, 32, 167, 315; criminalization of, 365n15

Ilarde, Nilo, 78–79

Ilokano language, 64, 191, 193, 360n58, 364n48

immaterial labor, 61, 63, 66, 88–91, 376n58; versus disposable life, 98, 330; platforms and, 144, 170; vitality and, 71–72

immigration. *See* migration; migrant workers

imperialism: in biotech, 340n26; demographics and, 217; as environmental power, 377n2; gender and, 344n71; geopolitics of, 116, 151, 208, 210, 213–14, 343n58, 367n36, 372n19; legality and, 13–14, 19, 39, 43–44; and liberal democracy, 201–2, 205–6, 209–12, 221–24, 358n28; and noncapitalist production, 56–57, 106, 108, 287, 350n54; and reproduction of capital, 33–36, 61–62, 92, 102, 376n58; resistance to, 18, 234; wars of, 24, 58, 63, 374n42; as war to be human, 7–8, 40; waste and, 30–33, 257–58. *See also* colonialism; primitive accumulation

indentured servitude, 34, 61, 54–55, 61, 100, 106, 191; migration and, 189, 359n37, 367n33; slavery and, 200, 359n36

Indigenous peoples: as coin, 53; colonial wars against, 8, 229–30, 244, 339n22; as disposable life, 10–11, 52; dispossession of, 36, 38–43, 55, 57, 234, 343n62; Duterte's targeting of, 326; Eurocentric accounts of, 181; feminist scholarship of, 67; versus Indigenous populations, 368n50; land use practices of, 325, 383n43; legal status of, 201, 230, 245, 322, 343n65; nature and, 49–50, 180, 275, 337n36, 339n21; Pinatubo's impact on, 320; resisting subjugation, 64, 106–7; as "tribes," 342n46

Indigenous Peoples' Rights Act of 1997, 41–42, 322, 343n65

informal economy: as congestion, 171–72; counterinsurgency and, 18–19, 236; drug use in, 246; and exclusion from employment, 131; and extrajudicial killings, 237–39; fixing in, 97–98; flyovers and, 147–48, 284; human smugglers in, 93, 97, 182–83; "human" stories eclipse, 287–88; jueteng and, 103–104; as liquidity, 162–64, 290; in Brillante Mendoza's films, 133–35; policing and, 59, 251, 235–54; value extraction from, 33–34, 107, 114, 164–65. *See also* slums

infrastructure: dispossession and, 56; Duterte's investment in, 240, 322; financial, 147; foreign investment in, 60, 155, 235; freedom as, 221; of imperialism,

205–206, 209, 211, 237; internet, 250; in Manila, 145–50, 321; noncapitalist milieu as, 38, 57, 65; poverty and neglect of, 28, 162; private control of, 146, 156; transportation, 142–45, 150; and US military, 153–54, 367n386; and vital systems security, 219. *See also* vital infrastructure
Inside Job, 88
Insurance, 25, 97, 232. *See also* protection
insurgency, 32, 68, 105, 220; Duterte's regime as, 235. *See also* counterinsurgency
international community, 212, 224
International Monetary Fund (IMF), 147, 282, 355n20, 384n15
internet trolls, 170, 184, 249–50, 291
interpretation, 303–4, 314, 383n3
In the Shadow of the Lingering Mount Pinatubo Disaster, 319–20
Iraq, 58, 201, 208, 211, 320, 366n29, 367n36, 371n10
Islam: in Palestine, 226; in the Philippines, 211, 234, 245, 255, 289, 318, 371n9; in social movements, 271; as US enemy, 31, 208–9, 224, 212
Israel, 93, 342n46; boycott of, 199–200, 278, 365n3, 370n63, 370n67, 379n25; citizenship versus nationality in, 368n44, 369n59; military and police operations of, 217–19, 223–24, 227, 367n38; Philippines' relation with, 195, 207, 211–12, 234, 256, 367n39; as putative liberal democracy, 201, 203, 206, 210, 221, 224–25; settler violence in, 225–26

Jia Zhangke, 134–35, 354nn8; *24 City*, 354n9; *Still Life*, 110, 123–29, 315, 354n10
Jocando, F. Landa, 166
jueteng, 103–105, 165, 251, 371n9
justice: Christian versus indigenous, 326; of counterinsurgent war, 255; criminal, 26, 200, 254; among disposable people, 133–34; formal versus substantive, 12; for Palestine, 224, 227; law and, 15, 353n33; social, 18; and state violence, 77, 80–81, 232, 262, 285, 298, 373n32. *See also* "just war"
just-in-time production, 32, 157, 167, 193
"just war," 8, 374nn34–35; Augustine on, 230; as central to capitalism, 24–25, 62; and global security architecture, 236–37; and representation of death, 263; war on drugs as, 19, 243–44

KADAMAY (Kalipunan ng Damayang Mahihirap; National Alliance for Filipino Urban Poor), 270
Kalinga people, 41–43
Kassamali, Sumayya, 178
Katz, Cindi, 274, 346n27
kinship, 252–56, 332; dividuality and, 64, 376n51; drug users lacking, 245; as infrastructure, 160; itinerancy and, 289–90; with land, 326; masculinity and, 191; personhood and, 130, 288, 294, 296, 376n58; as political order, 105–7, 242, 251, 351n55; remittances and, 355n22; serviceable labor produced by, 194; transnational, 241, 293; as vital platform, 65, 169–70, 186, 250–51, 291, 375n50
Kippenberger, Martin, 78–79
Komikero, Andoyman, 261–62
kunsintidor (enabler), 252, 376n55

labor: as gendered and racialized category, 187, 284, 364n49; as human capital, 112; as inadequate category, 58–59, 87–90, 94, 175, 185; versus life-time, 70–72, 96, 98–99, 102–3, 114, 347n50; and racial violence, 180; slavery and, 358n24; socially necessary labor time, 49; versus vitality, 295–96; versus waste, 95; versus work, 345n15. *See also* domestic labor; immaterial labor; migrant workers; reproductive labor; servitude
lahar (volcanic mudflows), 318–24
land: as animate, 51–52, 55, 318; appropriation of, 115–18, 123, 343n68; development of, 148–49, 154; inaccessible to slum dwellers, 290; and Indigenous peoples, 38–43, 106, 322, 325–26, 342n50, 343n62, 343n65; as means of production, 45–46, 64, 118, 345n9; reclamation of, 282, 284; as scroll, 316–17; and settler colonialism, 203, 218, 224–27, 234, 275–76, 368n44, 369n59; and surplus populations, 119
landscapes, 42, 321–23; in art, 74, 78, 80, 302–6, 311, 314–15; in cinema, 123–27, 315–19; numbers as, 283; shaped by *lahar* flows, 321; of talahib, 323–25

Index • 419

Lasco, Gideon, 246
law: cash and, 353n33; death and, 77; under Duterte, 19, 248–49, 337n30; equality and freedom in, 200, 202–5; franchise, 357n17; humanity and, 11, 99, 337n29; immigration and, 350n45; and Indigenous peoples, 39–43, 201, 230, 245, 322, 342n50, 343n65; international, 116, 236, 352n19; of Israeli apartheid, 225; martial, 40, 232, 271; nondiscrimination, 366n16; policing and, 54, 254; and primitive accumulation, 365n15; rule of, 13, 15–17, 43–44
Lazzarato, Maurizio, 112, 248
Lebanon, 178, 207, 211
Lerma, Raffy, 268–70; "Pietà," 231, 263, 275, 284
liberalism: citizenship and, 17, 98; derivatives as challenge to, 215; and human rights, 11–14, 18, 336n16; imperialism and, 47, 116, 201–2, 205–6, 221–22; and Indigenous peoples, 40; innovation valorized by, 275; labor and, 112; versus neoliberalism 109; as normative ideal, 104; and racial domination, 200–201; rejection of, 3–4, 18–20, 222, 230, 373n32; and urban space, 151, 235; violence occluded by, 25; vital platforms exceed, 65. *See also* democracy; freedom; neoliberalism
Li, Darryl, 208–9, 214, 367n33
life: addiction defined against, 247, 263; Arendt on, 17–18; bare, 77, 137, 337n35, 350n44; Franco Berardi on, 383n6; as capital, 62, 156, 193, 209, 239, 246, 279, 284; as commodity, 51–53, 71, 115, 133; financialization of, 120–21, 215, 220, 350n44; and "human" stories, 286–87; Indigenous, 42–44, 181; as labor, 6, 51, 72, 89, 99, 108, 114, 158–59, 179, 184, 340n26, 347n50, 360n61; land and, 115–16, 118; Marx on, 13, 296, 347n37, 348n51, 352n17; as natural resource, 55; Antonio Negri on, 90–91, 102; neoliberalism and, 111, 113–14, 120, 130; new political economy of, 92, 94, 187, 245, 248, 276, 286, 309; security and, 60, 218–19, 233–34, 237; shared, 107, 170, 186, 195, 291, 297; under slavery, 68; subsumption of, 13–14, 34, 47, 64, 89, 101, 158, 214; and urban demolition, 281, 283, 295; value and, 49–50, 67, 130, 176, 240, 244, 256, 348n51, 349n14, 352nn16–17, 356n23, 378n6; as waste, 30, 33, 51, 93, 95, 156, 217. *See also* disposable life; life-times; life worth living; serviceable life; remaindered life
life-times, 93; in arrears, 98, 188; in cinema, 128–29; exceeding capitalist subsumption, 101; expenditure of, 215, 260, 352n17; versus labor time, 70–72, 96–99, 102–3, 114, 347n50; landscapes and, 316; liquid, 100, 134, 170, 217, 290; of surplus populations, 99–100, 120–21; and transnational exchange, 177–78, 189. *See also* disposable life; life; life worth living; remaindered life; serviceable life
life worth living, 61–62; "freedom" and, 222; versus life worth expending, 93–94, 112, 177–78, 241, 256, 260, 281, 295, 352n11; versus remaindered life, 71; threshold of, 296
liminality, 9, 44, 112, 193, 283–286, 294, 296; of servitude, 191
liquidity: of disposable life, 100, 119, 121, 126, 134, 287–88, 290–91; enabled by drug use, 246; and identity, 289–90; as itinerancy, 289–90; of migrant workers, 171, 185; and racialized punishment, 26–27; of service workers, 287–88; of urban poor, 131, 141, 148, 161–64, 251; waste and, 29, 157, 165, 217
Lola (Mendoza), 110, 131–33, 136
López Petit, Santiago, 94
Los Angeles revolts of 1992, 332
Luna, Juan, 265
Luxemburg, Rosa, 35–37, 44, 57, 287, 339n10, 341n33, 341nn37–39, 342n47, 352n16
Luzon, 40, 142–44, 153, 357n18

Mabanglo, Elynia, 77
MacArthur Highway, 142–43
machinery: capitalist platforms as, 170, 291, 381n25; entrepreneurial subject as, 110; versus human labor, 51; Israeli state violence as, 218; land as, 52; migrant domestic workers as, 10, 158–59, 286; noncapitalist milieus as, 55, 57; of policing, 236, 248, 251, 375n50; social reproduction as, 45, 57, 65, 179, 185, 193, 250
MacKinnon, Catherine, 12–13, 336n17
Magpies Press, 242, 373n32
Maguindanao massacre, 74, 80–83

Manalansan, Martin, 274, 294
Mangudadatu, Esmael, 80
Manila: cars in, 360n57; congestion in 167–68, 172; development in, 149, 282, 321–22; Duterte and, 233, 373n31; fires in, 280–81, 283; flyovers in, 147–48; highways to, 142–44, 153, 318, 321; as metropolitan archipelago, 150; migrant workers invest in, 175; migration to, 129, 289–90; peripheries of, 166. *See also* slums
maquiladoras, 10, 91, 297
Marazzi, Christian, 88–89, 350n44
Marcos, Ferdinand: in art, 265; development strategies of, 129–30, 147, 150, 233, 281, 355n20; extrajudicial killings under, 231–32, 247, 262; Indigenous expropriation under, 40–42
masculinity: and capitalist subsumption, 347n44; of Duterte, 373n32; labor coded by, 70, 190–91, 297; humanity and, 51; in Manila slums, 313; sovereignty as, 51, 180, 275
Martin, Randy, 65–66, 96, 111–12, 215–16
Marx, Karl: Arendt on, 337n36; on circulation, 356n26; and dead exchanges, 221; on equality and freedom, 13, 202–3, 336n24, 365nn12–13; Harootunian on, 347n44; on imperialism, 102; on instruments of labor, 362n28; on life, 296, 347n37, 348n51, 352n17; Luxemburg and, 341n38; on machinery, 159; on noncapitalist modes of production, 65; on primitive accumulation, 343n67, 365n15; on punishment, 26, 338n4; on slavery, 158, 358n34, 359n39; on surplus population, 92, 349n21
McCoy, Alfred, 59, 232–33, 236, 367n36, 371n10, 374n42
McGrath, Jason, 126, 128
means of production: disposable life as, 27; land as, 45–46, 118; from noncapitalist milieus, 35–36, 57, 253, 360n61; service workers as, 184, 362n28; slaves as, 359n39; versus valorized labor, 51, 71, 170. *See also* force of production.
Meillassoux, Claude, 56
melancholia, 4, 335n3
memes, 220, 248, 264, 268
Mendoza, Brillante, 129, 135; *Lola*, 110, 131–34, 136; *Ma Rosa*, 356n27, 375n50
mercantilization, 62, 90, 93–94

metabolism, 187, 356n26; between capitalism and noncapitalist milieu, 36–38, 44, 287, 341n38; servitude and, 51–54
Mexico: colonial extraction in, 52; femicide in, 297; manufacturing in, 91, 363n36; remittances to, 361n2; US border with, 10–11, 15, 54, 97, 100, 317
migrant workers: in cinema, 125, 127; citizenship and, 94–95, 99, 158; contemporary capitalism and, 63; in Davao, 234; versus drug users, 264; and exchange rates, 97, 177–78, 188–89; gendered, 10–11, 96, 180, 190, 363n45; humanizing narratives of, 196, 362n27; Indigenous, 343n62; as investors, 175, 184–85; itinerancy of, 289–90; kinship and, 130, 194, 186, 291, 293, 363n34; legal treatment of, 359nn36–37; Philippines as exporter of, 9, 101, 173–75, 291, 355nn21–22; rural, 118–19, 129; sadness among, 277; smugglers and, 97–98, 183; speculative risk-taking of, 100, 103, 105, 171, 349n40; temporality of, 178–79; unpaid labor of, 187–88; US military supported by, 208–209, 367n33; as vital infrastructure, 159, 170; in West Asia, 195, 366n25
migration: citizenship and, 94–95, 158, 308; as flight, 106–7; humanity and, 8, 17, 101–2, 167; of Indigenous peoples, 343n62; kinship and, 171, 186; into Mindanao, 234; political opposition to, 31, 236; punishment of, 15–16, 58, 196, 317; rural-urban, 119, 121, 129; slums and, 290, 350n45; and waste-value dialectic, 54, 98–100. *See also* borders; migrant workers
milieus: of art, 271; becoming-human as, 63, 184, 331; of covert operations, 232–33; environment as, 318, 326; legal coding of, 42, 204–5; noncapitalist social formations as, 36–38, 44–45, 51–52, 65, 253, 341n38, 342n46; Philippines as, 206–7; of the prison industry, 59; as subsumed social capacities, 55–57, 184, 210, 216, 287, 318, 360n61; vital platforms exceed, 186–87
military bases. *See* US military bases.
Mindanao, 60, 233–36, 289; in documentaries, 312, 218; Duterte's popularity in, 240; investment in, 371n15; Jewish resettlement in, 234, 371n13; war on terror in, 232, 326

Index • 421

minimum subsistence basket, 218, 369n55
mobility: flyovers and, 143–44, 148; versus liquidity, 162, 165, 246, 306; and slums, 166–67; and vital infrastructure, 286–87
money: as capital versus medium of exchange, 53, 113–15, 120–21, 133, 185; cinema and, 82; derivatives as, 216; and disposable life, 83, 118, 134, 252; as gift, 294; Jane Guyer on, 353n33; humanity and, 50; in informal economy, 288, 375n50; Marx on, 356n26; mobile, 60, 147; as power sign, 239, 242–43, 245, 248–49, 254, 372n26; in precapitalist societies, 29. *See also* liquidity
monoculture, 45, 52
Morgan, Jennifer, 46, 344n73, 369n36
Moro Islamic Liberation Front, 371n9
Moro National Liberation Front, 289
motherhood, 68–69, 294–95
mourning, 77, 80–81, 83, 227, 267, 332
Muslims. *See* Islam

nail salons, 188, 363n40
Nanay Mameng (Arumpac), 276–77
national debt, 54–55, 353n25
nation-state: capital and, 62, 117, 136–37, 215, 306–7; gendered and racialized, 45–47, 54–55, 180, 212, 369n59; geopolitics and, 53, 116, 120, 178, 206, 209, 236, 356n8; Israel as, 224–25; law and, 12, 204–5. *See also* postcolonial states
native, 49–50, 180, 275, 326, 337n36, 339n21
Native peoples. *See* Indigenous peoples
nature: appropriation of, 33–37, 42, 345n9; and gender and race, 190, 244, 339n21; in financial imagination, 276; versus humanity, 49–50, 326; imperialism and, 44–45, 377n2; Jia Zhangke on, 354n10; as remainder, 276, 335n8; social formations as, 64; state of, 17; talahib and, 324–25
necropolitics, 10, 68, 286. *See also* biopolitics
Negri, Antonio, 90–91, 102
Neilson, Brett, 101
neoliberalism, 23–24; in China, 123; citizenship under, 10, 65, 136–37, 213; and cost-benefit analysis, 13; in feminist accounts of affective labor, 361n9; kinship and, 376n58; land and, 115–19; neocolonialism and, 5; in the Philippines, 129, 235; subjectivity under, 50, 96, 112–15, 131, 185; temporality of, 109–11, 120–21, 126–27, 130, 137–38. *See also* liberalism
Netanyahu, Benjamin, 211, 222, 367n39
Nightcrawlers, 262, 270
Nixon, Richard, 236
numbers, 282–83, 286; of extrajudicial killings, 262; and Pinatubo's eruption, 319–20

Obama, Barack, 19, 28, 31
Occupy movement, 87
on-demand labor, 32, 157, 193, 286
on-demand mobile services (ODMS), 157, 164
Ong, Aihwa, 10
Operation Enduring Freedom, 201, 209
Oplan Bantay Laya (Operation Freedom Watch), 8, 73, 232
Oplan Tokhang (Operation Knock and Plead) 236, 249, 272–73
original accumulation. *See* primitive accumulation
Overseas Filipinos Act of 1995, 174
Overseas Filipino Workers (OFWs), 174, 191, 240, 264, 277, 289, 291; in Western Asia, 366n25. *See also* migrant workers

painting, 78–79, 265; classical scroll, 127, 354n10; Lyra Garcellano's practice of, 302–12, 315
Palestine: acts of survival in, 226–27; and boycott of Israel, 199–200, 365n3, 370n63, 370n67, 379n35; care workers and, 195, 278; dead exchanges in debates about, 203; evictions in, 223–26, 370n71; and Israeli nationality, 368n44; military operations against, 217–219; Mindanao and, 234, 371n13
palit-ulo ("head exchange"), 255
Pampanga, 318, 321
PANAMIN, 40–41
Pangilinan, Manuel V. (MVP), 144–46, 148–49
Paper Dolls (documentary), 278
paramilitary groups, 8, 15, 18, 234–35, 247. *See also* extrajudicial killings; proxy wars
patronage, 104–5, 241, 251, 253–54, 351n58, 374n44; drug users dispossessed of, 245; in Duterte regime, 235, 248–49

peripheries, 63, 115, 138, 222, 253, 350n54; in dependency theory, 54; feminized, 52–53; landscapes and, 316; newly created, 34; urban, 165–66

Philippines: as exporter of reproductive workers, 9, 100–101, 173–75, 241, 291; foreign investment in, 155, 239–40; Indigenous peoples in, 40–43, 230; Israel and, 195, 211–12, 234, 256, 367n39; labor policies in, 289; liberal democracy rejected in, 222; natural disasters in, 318–320; "special relationship" with United States, 206–10; war on terror in, 8, 19; women in, 17. *See also* Duterte, Rodrigo; uber-urbanization

"Pietà" (Lerma), 231, 263, 275, 284

Pinatubo, Mount, 318–20, 324–26, 385n28, 385n36

platform: capitalism, 57, 287, 340n29, 360n61, 381n25; city emulants as, 148, 152–55, 284; corporations as, 62; flyovers and, 147; metropolitan/urban, 144–45, 164, 167–68, 233, 279, 343n62; military, 206–9, 213, 322; within "social factory," 184; social media, 151, 219–20, 242, 250–51, 260, 267, 272, 375n48; software-as-business, 32. *See also* vital platforms

Platform (Jia), 125

play: in art, 263, 272–75, 312, 315, 384n18; children's, 226, 306, 309; deep, 103; as labor, 135, 274, 340n29. *See also* fate playing

plunder, 44, 55, 341n38. *See also* primitive accumulation

poetry, 9, 16–17, 21, 74, 77, 283

policing, 15–16; in art and cinema, 74, 132–34, 262, 268, 272, 284, 356n27; of borders, 97–99, 183, 317; "broken windows," 368n46; counterinsurgency and, 309, 366n29; kinship and, 106, 252–54, 351n58, 375n50; and labor discipline, 187; and liberal democracy, 200–201; in Maguindanao massacre, 80; neoliberalism and, 213; in Palestine, 223, 225, 227; in the Philippine war on drugs, 19, 222, 231–32, 235–38, 247, 255, 292–95, 372n18, 376n55; power signs and, 248–49; as revenue extraction, 25–26, 237–39, 243–44, 285, 375n50; of surplus populations, 93, 120; of urban movement, 150. *See also* prison

political emancipation, 12–18, 200, 336n24

pollution, 28

populism, 18, 240, 246, 373n31

postcolonial states, 18, 206–8, 351n58, 355n22, 358n28, 372n19; exceeding capitalist command, 57, 181; feminized, 54–55; Indigenous populations in, 40; informal economies in, 164; and international finance, 66, 116–17, 156; remittances to, 175, 355n22; social bonding in, 106–7; as US proxies, 30, 358n28; "world class" cities in, 145

post-Fordism, 6, 89–91, 94, 101, 360n61, 364n49, 383n6; and migrant workers, 96, 99, 101, 130, 159; racialized punishment under, 26; and servility/servitude distinction, 158, 176, 361n10

posthumanism, 4, 7, 288, 381n28; racism and, 309

post-Marxism, 88–91, 94

power signs, 239, 245, 247–49, 256, 372n26

Pratt, Geraldine, 175, 291, 379n24

primitive accumulation, 24, 32, 44, 101, 116–18; as coding operation, 51; as expenditure, 259; kinship and, 344n71, 376n58; law as instrument of, 40–42; Luxemburg on, 35–37, 341nn37–39; Marx on, 204, 338n4, 343n67, 365n15; Meillassoux on, 56; settler colonialism as, 38–40

prison: for debtors, 369n60; democracy and, 25–26, 200–201, 205, 212, 338n6; Gaza as, 215; as incapacitation, 15; versus informal justice, 134; migrant workplace as, 277; and security architecture, 209, 219, 236–37; and surplus populations, 29, 69, 93, 166; value extracted from, 27, 58–59, 95; youth and, 346n27. *See also* detention centers; policing

private military companies (PMCs), 58–59

proletariat, 58, 90, 92, 103, 117, 119, 182

protection: corporate, 39, 61; Duterte promises, 20, 241–42, 373n32; and expendable life, 245, 254, 281; of freedom, 200; humanitarian, 13, 17, 174; rackets, 25, 235, 238; state as agency of, 232; traffickers provide, 183; wars of, 8, 93

protocols, 151, 206

proxy wars, 8, 18–19, 30, 153, 201–2, 209, 213

psy-ops, 32, 247, 374n42

Index • 423

Puar, Jasbir, 218–19
public-private partnerships, 149, 156, 185, 306, 355n20, 380n17
Pulido, Laura, 28
punishment: capital, 33, 237, 247, 281, 291, 307; cities and, 156, 166; as force of production, 27; inadequacy of, 81; and juridical rights, 204–5; as labor discipline, 180, 189–90, 338n4, 365n15; racialized morality of, 230–31, 373n33; in US military campaigns, 374n42; as value extraction, 24–26, 59, 196, 219, 235, 243–45, 369n60. *See also* criminality; policing
pyropolitics, 295, 282n43

queer: art, 272–73; "living labor" as, 90; scholars, 66, 365n13; socialities, 69, 70, 186, 274; survival, 294
Quintos, Floy, 275

Rabara, Mikael, 264
racism: abolitionism and, 182; algorithmic, 309; citizenship and, 99, 137; of contemporary global capitalism, 10, 180, 307–8; environmental, 28–29; and expendable life, 215, 246; histories of, 67; humanism and, 5, 50; law and, 204, 366n16; and liberal democracy, 25–27, 200–201, 203, 221; melancholia and, 335n3; nation and 212; punishment and, 219, 244–45, 368n46; risk and, 112–13; servitude and, 158, 176, 179–80, 190, 359n36; sexuality and, 364n51; and subaltern life-making, 69–70; value and, 53–54. *See also* sex-gender and race codes.
radical bereavement, 74, 77, 285
Ramos, Fidel, 231–32, 281
Ramos, Patricia, 265–66
ransom, 25, 93, 243, 251–52, 254, 289; in war on drugs, 237–38, 255, 284, 294, 375n50
rape, 68, 173, 233, 255, 285
Raymundo, Sarah, 326
"real economy," 88, 117
realism, 126–27, 131, 137, 375n50; in documentary, 263, 270; neo-Bazinian, 128; socialist, 123, 356n24; *See also* aesthetics
Reddy, Chandan, 32, 136–37, 204
refugees, 7, 58, 73, 95, 222, 308, 380n16; displaced by US security wars, 208; and humanitarian art, 258–59; Jewish, 234; 371n13, 377n4; as outcasts of modernity, 257–58; Palestinian, 225–26
remaindered life, 14, 67–72, 102–103, 105; aesthetics of, 77–78, 274–76; and binary oppositions, 335n8; in cinema, 110, 121, 129, 136, 313–14, 278, 384n15; versus labor time, 114; neoliberalism and, 112–13, 115, 138; versus resistance, 330–32; talahib as, 294–95, 324; temporality of, 107–8, 298
remittances, 160, 171, 361n2; and financial inclusion, 147; and the Philippine state, 100–101, 130, 173–75, 264, 355n22, 366n29
Remollino, Alexander, 9
rent extraction, 245, 338n8, 351n58, 376n58; in cities, 146, 154–55; jueteng and, 104–5; from migrant labor, 98–99; policing as, 26, 237–38, 244, 248, 251, 253–54
representation: democratic, 88, 151, 217; Duterte and, 241, 264; as form of action, 249–50, 270; of humanity, 286–87; of migrant workers, 362n27, 363n45; numerical, 282; politics of, 79, 81, 215; versus power signs, 247–48; realist, 127; of remaindered life, 129; Spivak on, 262, 344n81, 378n9
reproductive labor: Arendt on, 17–18; capitalization of, 114, 175; versus drug addict, 244–45, 264; informal, 131; international division of, 34, 55, 130, 207; life-times and, 70, 96, 101–3, 348n50; as machinery, 184–85; and remaindered life, 333; slavery and, 174, 359n36, 364n51; transportation of, 182, 362n26; as vital infrastructure, 63–64, 159; and vital platforms, 291; waste and, 30, 62–63, 179. *See also* social reproduction
Requiem for M (Dalena), 80–83
RESBAK, 260–63, 265–74
Right of Way Act, 156
right to the city, 282, 380n10
risk: and "at-risk" populations, 96–97, 112–13, 115; in clinical trials, 368n49; derivatives and, 65–66, 216; disposable life absorbs, 118, 120–21; and drug use, 246; geopolitics of, 116–17; in Global South cities, 165, 168; in informal economy, 103–105, 107, 251; under Marcos, 355n20; and migrant workers, 170–71, 209; in military strategy, 213–14, 218–19; neoliberalism and, 109, 111; taken by smugglers, 183

ritual, 103–104; kinship, 65, 106, 251, 253, 351n60, 375n50; speech, 270
Rockwell Center, 149
Rodolfo, Kevin, 320, 385n28

sadness, 276–77
Sahlins, Marshall, 252, 376n51
salot (pestilence, rot), 247, 263–65, 285
San Fernando, Philippines, 142–43, 153, 318
Sartre, Jean-Paul, 5, 68
Sasot, Sass, 373n32
Saudi Arabia, 178, 207, 277, 289
Scaling Innovations in Mobile Money (SIMM), 147
Schmitt, Carl, 116
Scott, W. H., 230, 374n34
security: architecture, 210, 236–37; border, 27, 97, 99; capitalism and, 35, 93, 222; citizenship and, 137, 204; as Cold War strategy, 130; and covert operations, 232–33; expenditure of life as basis for, 215, 218, 233, 256, 260; finance and, 113, 214, 239, 241, 243–44, 298; IDF trains US police in, 367n38; imperialist wars of, 8, 31, 60, 201–2, 211, 214, 241; and migrant workers, 208–209; as neoliberal governmentality, 109, 213; privatization of, 58–59, 95–96, 214; sex-gender and race central to, 47; and social media, 250; in urban space, 151, 154, 208, 235; vital systems, 219, 369n59
See, Sarita, 274
semiotic commons, 160–61
Señorita extraviada, 297–98
Serbis (Mendoza), 131–32
Serco, 58, 95
serial culture, 213
serviceable life: as becoming-human, 17; citizenship and, 368n44; and expendable life, 72, 195–96, 214–15, 222; "human" stories eclipse, 287–88; as infrastructure, 51, 246; migration and, 178; versus remaindered life, 71; versus servile life, 176; social reproduction of, 186, 194, 291. *See also* servitude
servility: gendered, 190; versus servitude, 158, 176, 361n10
servitude: colonial history of, 52–55; exemption from, 152–53, 240–41; gendered and racialized, 190–91, 263–64, 309; and life worth expending, 214, 244–45, 256; lineages of, 179–83; as means of labor, 184–86, 345n9; naturalized as liminal state, 191–93; versus servility, 158, 176, 361n10; and slavery, 174, 179–80, 187, 359n36; uber-urbanization and 156; unpaid, 187–89, 363n40; and unserviceable lives, 166; vital infrastructure as, 170; and vital platforms, 195; waste and, 157, 159, 189–90, 196
sex-gender and race codes, 44–47; humanity and, 50–51; intrinsic to capitalism, 44, 180, 187, 242, 244; juridical recognition of, 204; of kinship, 186; servitude and, 190–91, 359n36; slavery and, 344n73; and urban grade separation, 177; wage labor and, 364n49, 365n15
Sheikh Jarrah, 223–26
Short Stories (Garcellano), 306
Simondon, Gilbert, 37, 287, 341n43, 381n23, 381n25, 382n39
Simone, AbdouMaliq, 160–61, 278, 290
slavery: capitalism and, 183, 358n34, 359n36; coin and, 52–53; contemporary, 174, 187, 191, 364n48; Angela Davis on, 68–69; democracy and, 200, 204, 206; humanity and, 8, 17, 45, 50, 67, 177, 244, 296, 339n21, 341n43; and Indigenous disappearance, 40; Meillassoux on, 56; punishment and, 24–26, 338n4, 366n15; and reproductive labor, 46, 179–80, 190, 364n51; and social media, 157–58; in South and Southeast Asia, 181–82; waste and, 31. *See also* servitude
Sleepwalk (Garcellano), 310–311
slums, 131, 279–80, 293; in Brillante Mendoza's films, 132–33, 135; demolition of, 281–84; fires in, 280–81, 83; informal economy in, 164–65, 284, 287; itinerancy in, 289–90; planet of, 115; temporality in, 166, 313; support for Duterte in, 240; thresholds and, 283; temporality in, 313; and war on drugs, 231, 235, 239, 245, 255, 264, 267, 272, 284–85
smugglers, 97, 182–83
social bonding, 106–7, 351n58, 351n60
social death, 40, 64, 115, 245, 255, 264
social factory, 63, 90, 159, 176, 184, 193, 359n36

Index • 425

social media, 260, 383n8, 384n17; Duterte's use of, 242, 249–50, 264, 375n48; as fractal enterprise, 148, 151; "hate speech" on, 370n63; humanity shaped by, 157, 262, 313; migrant workers and, 193; Philippines as hub for, 291; predictive analytics of, 219–220; resistance to extrajudicial killings on, 267–68, 270, 272; as vital platform, 65, 170, 186, 250–51

socially necessary labor time, 49, 347n50. *See also* labor

social reproduction: assaults on, 13–16, 68, 102, 183; activism and, 271; Arendt on, 17–18, 345n15; and contemporary capitalism, 6, 24–25, 30, 62–64, 155; diskarte and, 313; and disposable life, 101–3, 114; environment produced by, 317–18; eurocentric view of, 181–82; as human capital formation, 110–11; imperialism and, 34, 45, 61–63, 210–11, 214; kinship and, 376n58; labor as inadequate category for, 175–76; as machinery, 57, 179, 185, 193, 250; and migrant workers, 9–10, 96, 98–99, 130, 159, 174–75, 188–89, 291; neoliberalism and, 120, 137; policing and, 27, 251, 253; post-Fordism and, 89; productive consumption as, 378n6; and remaindered life, 67–72, 332–33; and rural-urban migration, 118–19; servitude and, 55, 194; under slavery, 364n51; as vital infrastructure, 170, 360n61; as vital platform, 65, 185–86, 195, 297; wage labor subsidized by, 353n31, 358n34; words and images as means of, 268. *See also* domestic labor; expanded reproduction of capital

software-as-a-service (SAAS), 156–58, 170

Southern Tagalog Exposure, 73–74

sovereignty: of finance, 114, 116–17, 212; franchises and, 152, 156, 357nn17–18; gendered and racialized, 54, 180, 204, 275, 380n16; of God, 50; and human rights, 11–13; Indigeneity and, 39–40, 245, 342n46; legality and, 15, 352n19; life and, 98, 103, 256; money and, 120–21; mourning and, 77; as possessive individualism, 100; postcolonial, 372n19; and state terror, 236–37, 247–48, 262–63, 291; territorial, 43, 119, 215, 224, 276, 317

Spanish Empire, 55, 106, 201, 206, 245, 343n58; 374nn34–35; artists' resistance to, 265; and "just war" doctrine, 8, 25, 229–30

special economic zones, 153–54, 209, 297, 322

spectacle, 82–83, 127–29, 135–36, 229, 316, 378n9; dead bodies as, 81, 248, 262; Debord on, 110, 145, 354n7, 354n12, 355n18

Spillers, Hortense, 128, 190, 337n39, 344n73, 355n13

Spivak, Gayatri, 262, 344n81, 350n43, 350n54, 355n13, 378n9, 382n28

splendor, 311, 313–15, 318, 325, 331

Spolarium (Luna), 265

squatters, 133, 219, 247, 279–81, 283, 289–90. *See also* slums

statelessness, 12, 17, 106, 308

Still Life (Jia), 110, 123–29, 315, 354n10

Strathern, Marilyn, 186, 381n26

Stray Dogs (Tsai), 316

structural adjustment, 34, 110, 116. *See also* neoliberalism

subaltern, 53; cinema, 124; drivers of capitalism, 57, 140–41, 164, 186; life-making, 56, 69, 78, 106, 191, 296; Spivak on, 344n81, 355n13; urban, 164–67; vital platforms, 169–72, 250, 256, 288, 294

subprime mortgages, 29, 39, 97, 118, 350n44,

subsumption: derivatives and, 216; formal versus real, 63, 101, 179, 339n19, 340n29; and "human" stories, 286; labor and, 175; law and, 42–43; of life, 30, 47, 68, 89, 158; of life worth expending, 62; Antonio Negri on, 90; of noncapitalist formations, 51, 57, 64–65, 210; of the Philippines, 207; and political machines, 251, 253; and primitive accumulation, 35; remainders beyond, 14, 103, 105, 110, 136, 276, 331; in reverse, 66; and social media, 250; and surplus populations, 92–93; as teleology, 347n44; theoretical, 91, 94, 361n10; uber-urbanization and, 146–47

Suleiman, Eliah, 278

Sunday Beauty Queen, 178–79

super regions, 143–44

surplus populations, 33, 92–93; as cash, 120–21, 162, 185; in cinema, 126; financialized, 117–18, 154, 164, 215, 238; Marx on, 349n21; migrants as, 95–99, 119;

and Philippine neoliberalism, 130–31; punishment of, 27, 156; refugees as, 58; unbanked, 147
surrogacy, 68, 93, 355n23
Sweep (Garcellano), 301–3, 305–7, 314
swidden agriculture, 322, 325

Taiwan, 130, 186; cinema of, 128, 315–16
talahib (*Saccharum spontaneum*), 321, 323–26, 385nn33–34
taxi drivers, 98, 149, 163, 246
Taylorism, 157, 193
technical objects, 37, 287, 291, 341n43, 381n23, 381n25, 382n39
telecommunications, 144–45
temporality: in cinema, 82, 110, 124–28, 131–34, 313–14, 354nn8–9; Debord on, 355n12; colonial, 275–76; detention and, 95–96, 196; of disposable life, 98, 100, 121, 217, 316; of environmental restoration, 324–25; of expectation, 108, 298, 326–37; financialized, 111–13, 116–17, 120; in Lyra Garcellano's work, 311–13, 315, 318; of globalization, 23–24, 101; of history, 66–67, 81, 125, 329, 372n19; of humanism, 3–4; life-times and, 70–71, 97, 214, 296; of migrant workers, 177–179; of neoliberalism, 109, 130, 137; noncapitalist, 347n41; posthumanism and, 381n28; of remaindered life, 115, 298; servitude and, 191–93, 364n48; in slums, 166, 313
Three Gorges Dam, 123, 125, 315
thresholds, 283: of human life, 115–16, 137, 177, 282, 296, 335n8; between labor and non-labor, 89; of neoliberalism, 112, 114, 131; of political meaning 226; urban, 280–81, 284–85
time. *See* temporality
Time That Remains, The (Suleiman), 278
Tirador (Mendoza), 110, 131–33
Tokhanginamo Unabes!, 272–74
tolls, 144, 146, 244, 357n18, 369n60; of traffickers, 183
Torrado, Ea, 270
totalitarianism: Antonio Negri on, 90–91; platform, 240–43, 250
totality, 66, 89, 91
transgender people, 292–95; as care workers, 278; devaluation of, 16, 69, 204;

Duterte on, 373n32; law and, 366n16; remaindered life-making of, 70, 294
transportation: grade separations in, 150, 177, 380n16; highway, 142–48, 153–54, 318, 321–22; imperialism and, 61, 210, 219, 227; as industry of circulation, 291; migrant workers and, 175; public, 149, 151; by private drivers, 156, 168–69, 360n58; of reproductive labor, 362n26; shipping, 207; traffic impeding, 167; of undocumented immigrants, 95, 182–83; value extraction from, 26, 244
tribes, 31, 39–40, 342n46, 342n50. *See also* Indigenous peoples
tributary mode of production, 105–106, 191, 251, 350n54, 351n58
trolls, 170, 184, 249–50, 291
Tsai Ming-liang, 128, 314; *Stray Dogs*, 316
Tsing, Anna, 38, 324
24 City (Jia), 110, 129, 354n9
Tungkung Langit (Dalena), 309, 311

Uber, 156–57, 183
uber-urbanization, 141, 146–47, 152, 156–57, 306, 356n8, 381n28; as counterinsurgency, 154; congestion and, 167
undocumented immigrants, 11, 17, 27, 94–99
United Nations Human Rights Council (UNHCR), 258, 377n4,
urbanization: archipelagic, 149–50, 55; as dispossession, 43, 117, 161, 186, 282, 322; disposable peoples as driver of, 171; as divestment in semiotic commons, 160–61; Duterte and, 233, 235, 237, 241; highways and, 144, 321, 380n17; migrant workers invest in, 175; "re-peasantization" and, 119; of servitude, 193; slums and, 279, 284; sustainable, 60. *See also* uber-urbanization
US Agency for International Development (USAID), 60, 147, 234–35
US military bases, 153–56, 207–8, 213, 243; destroyed by volcano, 322; migrant workers maintaining, 208–9, 367n30
utility men, 187–91, 363n45

value: Baudrillard on, 259, 378n6, 378n16; circulation of, 155, 305, 358n34; cities and, 156, 171; of culture, 313; and dead exchanges, 221; and exchange rates,

Index • 427

value *(continued)*
188–89; finance and, 65–66, 88–89, 113, 118–21, 254, 350n44, 368n49; gendered and racialized, 10, 34, 44–48, 53–54, 190, 309, 335n3, 345n3, 345n13, 364n49; land and, 316–17, 322; life and, 6, 13–14, 49–52, 62, 67, 72, 91–94, 115, 130, 240, 348n51, 349n14, 352nn16–17, 356n23, 378n6; migration and, 97–99, 362n27; and noncapitalist milieus, 36–38, 56, 341n38; punishment and, 26–27, 239, 244–45, 251; remaindered life unabsorbed by, 71, 330–31; and social reproduction, 63–64, 89–90, 99–100, 159, 176, 184–85, 347n50, 353n31; Spivak on, 344n81, 378n9, 381n28; and vital infrastructure, 170; war and, 61; versus waste, 28–29, 40, 95, 179, 335n8, 339n14, 339n18

Virno, Paolo, 89, 158

Visiting Forces Agreement of 1999, 155, 213, 322

vital infrastructure, 159–61; becoming-human as, 63–64; drivers as, 168–69; global service work as, 185–86, 194–95; as means of production, 360n61; migrant workers as, 159, 208–9, 286–87; posthumanism and, 288; smugglers as, 183; versus vital platforms, 169–70

vitalism, 36, 71–72

vitality, 71–72, 194–95, 290, 294–97, 348n51

vital platforms, 65, 170, 195–196, 270, 363n34; of the city, 142; versus individual personhood, 288, 294, 296–97; kin networks as, 186, 242, 250, 291; versus laboring subject, 185; and political-police machines, 251, 293, 351n58, 375n50; versus vital infrastructure, 169–70; words and images as part of, 268

volcanoes, 318–20, 322, 325

war, 24, 31, 83; derivative enterprises of, 58–61, 208, 237, 341n33; dispossession and, 222; neoliberalism and, 213; and new political economy of life, 214; for resources, 37, 366n28; as waste-making, 33. *See also* "just war"; proxy wars; war on drugs; war on terror; war to be human.

War Is a Tender Thing (Arumpac), 318

warm-body export industry, 9, 174, 180, 291

war on drugs: artists' resistance to, 260–63, 269, 272–74, 283; counterinsurgency and, 372n18; as derivative enterprise, 237–40; development and, 235; drug users racialized by, 245–46, 374n36; Heart de Chavez murdered in, 292–95; and international law, 372n21; as "just war," 19, 230; media coverage of, 231; on social media, 249; as war to become human, 196, 222, 229; and US influence on Philippines, 236; in slums, 284–85; and waste-value dialectic, 54; value extracted from, 251, 368n46

war on terror, 5–8, 30–31, 54, 93, 367n36; and liberal democracy, 25, 201; Palestine and, 224; profits from, 368n46; in the Philippines, 8, 19, 74, 207–11, 232, 236, 326

war to be human, 4–9, 11, 54, 87, 338n1; of capital itself, 62; counterinsurgency and, 31–32, 211, 222; decolonization and, 18–19, 22; humanitarianism as, 182; as enterprise, 25–26, 60; Israel's, 226, 342n46; as punishment, 25; rights and, 65; refugees from, 163, war on drugs as, 196, 222, 229

Washington consensus, 24, 116

waste, 6, 14, 24, 335n8; in *24 City*, 354n9; as art, 258–60, 315, 377n5; converted to on-demand labor, 157; imperialism and, 30–33, 182, 257–58; land as, 40, 153; of noncapitalist reproduction, 65; and quantified life, 217; prisoners as, 59; profiting from, 29–30; and remaindered life, 69, 71, 115, 136, 274–75, 332; reproductive labor as, 159; servitude and, 189–90, 196; social enjoyment as, 179; talahib as, 323–24; value and, 27–28, 91–94, 156, 263, 339n14, 339n18

Web 2.0, 89, 99, 219

Weerasethakul, Apichatpong, 311–14

Weheliye, Alexander, 337n39

Weizman, Eyal, 218

welfare state, 34, 59, 137

witch-hunts, 366n20

World Bank, 40–41, 60, 118, 147, 235, 355n20, 384n15

World War II, 5, 44, 321

Wright, Melissa, 10, 91–92

Wynter, Sylvia, 6, 49, 51, 332, 335n8

Zhang Xudong, 123–24

Zionism, 206, 221, 224, 346n34